D0447887

Out of the Class Closet:

Lesbians Speak

Edited by Julia Penelope

✳ The Crossing Press • Freedom, CA 95019

My thanks to the following authors for granting me permission to reprint their work in this anthology. Copyrights for all works published in this anthology belong to the authors and cannot be copied, reprinted, or excerpted without their written consent.

Chrystos, "Headaches and Ruminations," *Gay Communinty News* 17, #29 (February 4–10).

Elliott, "Funeral Food," *Sinnister Wisdom* 45 (Winter 1991/1992).

Elliott, "Whenever I Tell You the Language We Use is a Class Issue, You Nod Your Head in Agreement—And Then You Open Your Mouth," *Lesbian Ethics* 4, 2 (Spring 1991).

Lee Evans, "Dykes of Poverty: Coming Home," *Lesbian Ethics* 4, 2 (Spring 1991).

Fox, "Why Women Are a Class," *Lesbian Ethics* 1,1 (Fall 1984) (published in that issue as "Why Men Oppress Women" under the name Jeanette Silveira).

Juana Maria Gonzalez Paz, "From Battered Wife to Community Volunteer: Testimony of a Welfare Mother," *Sin Fronteras, A Gay Latino Journal* 1, 1 (Summer 1984).

J.P. , "Nowhere at Home," *Bridges* 2, 2 (Fall 1991/5752).

"Journal Notes: Exploring the Possibility of an Essay on Class, Poverty, etc.," *Bridges* 3, 1 (Spring/Summer 1992/5752).

Felice Yeskel, "Coming Out about Money: Cost Sharing across Class Lines," *Bridges* 3, 1 (Spring/Summer 1992/5752).

zana, "Mixed-Class Confusion," *Lesbian Ethics* 4, 2 (Spring 1991).

Photo Credits

Jamie Lee Evans by Jean Weisinger © 1993
Nett Hart by Ana Hid Sarkissian
Pam McMichael by Bill Svendsen
Bonnie Morris by Debbie Rich © 1991
Alien Nation by Liss Spencer & Alien Nation
Julia Penelope by Ann DelaVerne

Library of Congress Cataloging-in-Publication Data

Out of the class closet: lesbians speak/edited by Julia Penelope.
    p. cm.
  ISBN 0-89594-704-8 (paper)
    1. Lesbians—United States—Social conditions. 2. Lesbians—United States—Economic conditions. 3. Minority women—United States. 4. Social classes—United States. I. Penelope, Julia, 1941-
HQ75.6.U5C65 1994
305.48'9664'0973—dc20   94-17401
                                      CIP

CONTENTS

Pauline B. Bart
Introduction   1

Julia Penelope
Class and Consciousness   13

Catherine Odette
Potato Skins   99

Alien Nation
A Very Moving Story   105

Helen Elaine Lee
Goodbye to the House   125

Paula Gerber
Journal Notes:
Exploring the Possibility of an Essay on Class, Poverty, etc.   149

Merril Mushroom
the camaraderie of the toothless, or the story of an ordinary, nice
well-educated, middle-class, white, ashkenazi jewish girl   155

Lee Evans
Dykes of Poverty: Coming Home   161

Karen Chaney
Shifting Horizons: Navigating a Life   173

J.P.
Nowhere at Home   181

Joan Schuman
Lay All That Mess Down and Talk   185

Terri de la Peña
Chicana, Workingclass and Proud:
The Case of the Lopsided Tortilla   195

Jessica Robbins
We Didn't Even Have Words   207

Christian McEwen
Growing Up Upper Class   241

Elliott
Whenever I Tell You the Language We Use is a Class Issue,
You Nod Your Head in Agreement—and Then You Open
Your Mouth   277

Susan J. Wolfe
Getting Class   285

Jamie Lee Evans
What It Means to be the Daughter of My Mother   293

Marilyn Murphy
One of the Murphy Girls   299

Debbie Alicen
WANTED: An Organization for Debutante Dykes Anonymous   315

Anna Livia
Back to the Bare Bones...and the Broken Teeth   325

Elliott
Funeral Food   333

Pam McMichael
Toothpaste, Socks and Contradictions   339

zana
mixed-class confusion   349

Juana Maria Gonzalez Paz
From Battered Wife to Community Volunteer:
Testimony of a Welfare Mother   355

Fox
Why Women are a (Set of) Class(es)   361

Nett Hart
The NEW! IMPROVED! Classless Society   385

Bonnie J. Morris
Class Beyond Classroom   391

Jackie Anderson
Personal Revelations Concerning Class   397

Pat Dean
Class-ification by Intelligence: Some Questions   403

Linnea Johnson
"Just Who Do You Think You Are?"
A Sockdolager on Social Class vis-à-vis Women, in Catechetics,
Poem, Story, and Cha Cha Cha, and featuring The Lettermen,
me and my mom and dad, John Wayne as Elvis, and Spam   405

Chrystos
Headaches and Ruminations   419

Donna Allegra
Comparing Class Notes   427

Bọ (rita d. brown)
Just the Facts Ma'm   435

Joanna Kadi
(Un)Common Justice   441

Felice Yeskel
Coming Out About Money: Cost Sharing Across Class Lines   451

Contributors' Notes   473

Introduction

The Policy of Containment or, Can A Nice Jewish Girl from Brooklyn Find Happiness with an Upper Upper Class WASP?

Pauline B. Bart

In your world
The personal is not the political
It is guarded by the Fourth Amendment
And privileged communication.
Privacy is inviolate
Silences become high principles.
Nothing is presented in its original state
Naked
Glistening with amniotic fluid and blood
All is birthed virgin
Or from the head
And served in containers.

Poor WASP children
Never to know where their milk was bottled
That sugar is the second most important component of almost everything
That Special K has the following vital amino acids
And how many calories granola has
With skim milk
And with regular
For food is always transferred from its original to another container
Before being served
For life is always transferred from its original to another container
Before being lived
Form more important than content
Ritual more important than faith
BHA added
To preserve freshness.

I
A New York Jew
Uncivilized
Unsocialized
Talking with my mouth full, the urgency of the ideas compelling the speech
Food clinging to my magnetic hair
I
Must contain
My rage
My fears
My terror
My tears
My female hysteria
And set myself at your place
On the ironed linen napkin
To the right of the white Surrey cup in the deep saucer
And hope
You will take me
With your coffee.

When I was about eleven I used to read *Calling All Girls* and I remember being puzzled by a letter that appeared. The girls said that they were no longer allowed to play with certain friends because they were from a different class. I thought they meant from a different grade, and so it made no sense to me. I didn't associate it with my grandmother's referring disdainfully to one of my friends as "The butcher's daughter." When I was even younger I thought the world was divided into the Irish and Jews — ethnicity was the important factor. Even in Hunter College (one of the free New York City Colleges which I attended for two years) traveling back and forth on the subways and trolley, ethnicity remained the most salient differentiating factor. I knew there were poor people and felt that socialism would some day solve their problems. I knew we weren't poor because my mother wouldn't let me babysit, saying the available jobs should go to poor girls. (Unlike Protestants, Jews didn't believe that children should work to build character.) Like most Americans, I had only a vague sense of class. I took it for granted that my teeth would be fixed, and my aunt, our doctor, would take care of any illness. My mother taught me how to shop for bargains - "Look to see if the label is cut out" she would say when we went to Klein's and Orbach's. I wouldn't buy a dress until it was marked down. I'm still a world class shopper.

Then I studied sociology and learned that I wasn't just Jewish, or the child of immigrants, or smart. I was also middle class. We didn't spend money we didn't have. We dressed in "good taste." We had nutritious meals with salad and vegetables. My mother took nutrition courses so we never ate white bread. Our family always voted Democrat, idolizing the Roosevelts, especially Eleanor. My aunts had worked in sweatshops when they arrived from Russia. I learned about the Triangle Shirtwaist fire caused by the greed of the Bosses, and my mother told me never to cross a picket line.

In Marxist terms, which defines class in terms of relation to the mode of production, we were capitalist-bourgeois, because my father owned a small business. In psychological terms, we were not capitalists since we didn't identify with big business—they voted Republican. I met my first Republican (who was from St. Louis) when I was fourteen. When my parents moved to Santa Barbara, California, there were neighborhoods with covenants restricting from living there Jews and people of color, no matter how much money they had.

The writers in this book range from what Marx would have called the "lumpen proletariat" (the undeserving poor) through the upper upper class, although many who were working class in origin became upwardly mobile. A psychiatric study *Mobility and Mental Illness* (Myers and Roberts), found that upwardly mobile women had a higher rate of mental illness than upwardly mobile men, because the women became estranged from their families and felt guilty about abandoning them; they received less help from them than did their brothers, and they didn't receive the rewards they expected. They were, after all, still women and, as Fox says in this book, as such born a class by themselves. Another author says "Class mobility is different worlds living in you with different values, different wants, different demands. I felt increasingly split, confused, and compromised, and that I had no personal integrity".

An example of how the American dream of upward mobility doesn't work for women the way it does for men is the life of my friend, one of the first of the second wave of feminists, Marlene Dixon, who was of lower lower class background. Because of her high IQ, she was sent to "good" schools and bought "good" (but still not like her classmates') clothes by social workers. When she had to go out on the academic job market, I went shopping with her to make sure she would dress "appropriately" for job interviews. I remember being absolutely furious when she bought a green purse to match her green dress when my back was turned. As a proper bourgeois I knew that one buys accessories only in neutral colors if one has very little money to spend. I don't know how I knew that. Clearly she didn't. Her class origins and particularly her husband's (he wasn't upwardly mobile—he hadn't gone to graduate school) gave her problems at the University of Chicago where she landed a job. She was not rehired after three years, went to McGill, and then dropped out to found a revolutionary organization. Many of her interpersonal and ideological problems were class related. I understand she is now a street person in Florida.

Class is multidimensional. It's not just about money—it's about power and Prestige and self-concept and self-image and "life style," and whether you can get your teeth straightened or your nose straightened (my sister had both done), and whether you want to do so.

One of this book's strengths is that it deals with the dilemma of Jews and class. One of the articles points out that the model of working class behavior is non-Jewish, so that second generation working class Jews didn't know they were working class. Lesbian culture (at least that of the seventies) further complicated matters with the mechanical competence we were expected to exhibit. In the seventies and part of the eighties, working class skills were valued, especially by those lesbians living on the land. I was impressed with the confidence the working class lesbians in this book felt in their ability to make mechanical things work. I feel utterly helpless, although, because of my middle class verbal skills, I can call someone with those skills and she can tell me what words to use so the TV repairman or auto mechanic will not think I am ignorant and try to cheat me. For a while I lived with a voluntarily downwardly mobile auto mechanic, now a lawyer. She had lived in a radical lesbian collective in Ann Arbor where everyone was downwardly mobile and practiced acting rude, resocializing themselves, so they wouldn't be nice girls. She was criticized there for being too articulate.

As part of my nice middle class girl socialization I didn't learn to lie, an extremely useful skill. I had to start from scratch in my late twenties and still do it badly. I always say, somewhat ironically, that I was culturally deprived. I certainly did not learn the survival skills many of the women in the book, of necessity, learned.

I was asked to write this introduction because I am a sociologist and class is one of our variables, although we use terms like status and power from Max Weber's reformulation, as well as class. We learn from Marx about class conflict, and that one's class stems from one's relation to the mode of production. Thus there are the owners, or capitalists, and the proletariat or workers, who are exploited by the former. When workers come together they become not simply a class in itself but a class for itself, ready to make the revolution. We can compare this process to women's consciousness raising groups when we learned that we were not suffering from private problems, but public issues, and that there were no individual solutions. For an all too brief period we became a class by contradicting ourselves. With the decline in consciousness raising groups and the increased emphasis on coalition politics and diversity it became unfashionable to speak of women as a class for itself. Many women would have said it was inaccurate and even racist to do so. Some socialist feminists said it made class solidarity between working class women and working class men impossible. It is no accident that such women de-emphasized the problems of violence against women and focused on strictly economic issues as well as emphasizing women's agency and desire rather than our victimization, as if women cannot use agency to react to the victimization, as did the women in my study who avoided rape when attacked. Many radical feminists/lesbian feminists still conceptualize women as a class, a particularly useful stance when discussing violence against women. Fox discusses this in more detail.

From Marx we learn about ideological analysis, a major feminist method used to understand patriarchal hegemony. Marx says it is the ideas of the ruling class that are the ruling ideas. We say it is the ideas of ruling class men that are the ruling ideas. MacKinnon's *Signs* articles (1982; 1983) brilliantly demonstrate patriarchy's epistimological perfection in constructing our world. Whatever class, or status group we examine, women are subordinate to men although the extent of subordination can vary. Being a subordinate upper class woman is different from being a subordinate working class woman and being subordinate in the Middle Ages is different from being subordinate in post-industrial society, needless to say, but women of all classes and ethnic groups are vulnerable to male violence and to medical misogyny. They are also fair game on the street, although the streets may be in different parts of the city. Women going to clinics are more likely to be experimented on and do not have the opportunity to choose their doctors. At Planned Parenthood where I went for birth control precisely *because* I was educated and would remember to bring in the urine specimens and take my temperature every day, I was told when I ovulated and wanted to finalize my Ph.D.(???). "You're not like the other women who come here. You can have a baby." I hadn't told them I wasn't married.

Max Weber's approach to stratification greatly influenced American sociology. Sociologists have conducted innumerable occupational prestige surveys which show Supreme Court judges at the top and day-care workers near the bottom. Female occupations for the most part have lower status and lower pay than male occupations, and men in traditionally female occupations are more occupationally upwardly mobile. They are likely to be head nurses and principals of elementary schools. When occupation changes from male to female (????) it loses prestige and money, and vice versa. Women in male occupations are in the lower rungs. Thus they tend to be pediatricians rather than surgeons.

Sociologists also speak of status crystallization—do all your statuses match. If you are a white Anglo Saxon, able bodied male surgeon you have high status crystallization. If you are an African American, lesbian surgeon you have low status crystallization. Gay men who are professionals have higher status crystallization than do lesbian professionals because they are male and therefore supposed to be dominant. Since low status crystallization is associated with political liberalism, that may be why gay men are more conservative than lesbians, except on issues directly effecting them, such as AIDS.

Frequently sociologists use combinations of factors to construct indices of class or status—income, occupation, education, life style (when measurable). What to do with women has been a problem. Traditionally a woman's class was dependent on that of her father and then her husband. Lesbians of course rarely have husbands. Do you use their father's class? Do you use their occupation? Do you combine their income and their partner's? I like to use a woman's mother's education to label her class. In fact this was the only social class variable that differentiated women who were attacked and were raped from women who were attacked and avoided being raped. Women with mothers with graduate school education were almost never raped when attacked, and no African American woman or Jewish woman who had a college graduate mother was raped when attacked (1985).

Sociologists also knew that people make finer distinctions about the social status of people near them and broader distinctions about those below or above. The rich distinguish between new money which one *makes* and old money which one *has*. In my research, African Americans distinguish among "pill hill" (where the Black bourgeoisie lived), public housing and private low rent housing. Whites call it all "the ghetto" or the South or West Side, all areas grouped as being dangerous. Middle and upper class whites distinguish between the deserving and undeserving poor. Being on welfare and having more than two children is currently considered almost criminal and there are several plans to punish those women and their children (but not their sperm donors). If the women use drugs they are even more undeserving.

In this book the working class whites tended not to make distinctions between middle and upper class whites, or between ethnic groups, lumping Jews and immigrants together with other folks. But out-groups of whatever kind don't know the rules of behavior since they are not spelled out. I finally learned most of the rules from my upper and upper upper class friends, but I still haven't learned the exceptions. I was told I could pass at a Lutheran Church supper but not an Episcopalian one.

I haven't found it true, as one woman writing in the book claims, that middle class people think the world is fair. Only my WASP friends thought that the world was fair and that Affirmative Action would work and they would get tenure. My WASP friends also believed that letting their sons be arrested when driving without a license or smoking marijuana would teach them a lesson. Jews got defense lawyers for their kids. The working class mother of one of my WASP friends told the FBI her daughter's address when they asked for it. I can't imagine a Jew or an immigrant or a person of color doing so. I learned quickly that the University like the rest of society consisted od Cossacks (a generic term used by Eastern European Jews to refer to the Russian Czar's horsemen who would sweep down upon villages killing and beating and raping any Jews around. (Phyllis Chesler's grandmother was cut in four by a Cossack. My great grandfather and great granduncle were whipped in the public square.)

This week Jacqueline Kennedy Onassis died. Every report mentioned how superbly she controlled herself when John Kennedy was shot and how dignified she was. Earlier, invidious comparisons were made between her composure at her husband's funeral and the wife of a policeman weeping at her murdered husband's funeral. The reports also focused on "Jackie's exquisite redecorating of the White House" and her important role in showcasing "high culture" there: Her penchant for privacy was also praised. In short, she was admired for exhibiting the hallmarks of upper upper class women who would no more exhibit emotion in public than they would urinate in public. We are implicitly told that she is the standard against which we are to judge ourselves. It is not only the ideas of the ruling class, as Marx said, that rules society. It is their slender forms, their pronunciation, their clothes, their well modulated voices, their entire way of being in the world, or at least in public, that is considered correct for all of us. Yet it is very difficult to learn that behavior after childhood. And not all women want to. One law professor who grew up Catholic working class was told not to trust rich people—that they would only hurt her (and they did). She is most comfortable around people whose parents worked in factories as hers did, but who are upwardly mobile. She says she is an overachiever because she always feels insecure. Another professor, this one lesbian, who teaches at an upper class school but whose mother worked in a factory, needs to buy very expensive clothes so she will dress better than or at least different but equal to her students. She is constantly aware of class difference isolating her.

As this book demonstrates, lesbians come in all classes. The Paris lesbians of the twenties were upper class, certainly different from the bar dykes of the fifties. Natalie Barney and her friends had class privilege and didn't worry about being arrested by the police. But I have observed that class privilege kicks in higher up the ladder for women than for men, since most women depend on men (some lesbians on their fathers or other relatives) for their money and their status. Only the upper upper class women I know have a male sense of entitlement, a self-presentation that shows as their aura of competence. My father was willing to give an upper upper class lover of mine 70,000 dollars after meeting her briefly if she would set up a law practice with my son. A lawyer she met at a party offered to take her into her firm (and she hadn't even passed the California bar). As soon as she passed the bar in another state, she went from being a change-girl in a casino to being head of Consumer Affairs and then Chief Civil Prosecutor—and she was a Democrat and a dyke in a state with a Mormon Republican governor. She quit because she didn't like to take orders from anyone. She had no money but she was to the manor born, boarding schools and all that. When the police raided the women's bars she was never arrested. She told me "They never arrest WASP women. Just because you wear men's clothes doesn't mean you have to wear working class men's clothes." Women less than upper upper class are, well, just women—i.e., people who say "excuse me" when they bump into fire hydrants and trees, who never feel good enough or thin enough, and are vulnerable to battery and rape although when raped it is usually in different neighborhoods, depending on class. We should remember that upper upper class Virginia Woolf was incested, however, so even upper upper class privilege only goes so far for women.

A hallmark of class is knowledge about higher education. When I taught at U.C. Berkeley, every sociology graduate student had either gone to a prep school or to a rich suburban high school with most of the advantages or a prep school, such as Beverley Hills High School. But one of the women with whom I lived went to an inadequate local school and state university while her brothers were sent to prep schools and ivy league colleges. They had equal class origins but were given different class opportunities because of sex. My ex mother-in-law forced my ex sister-in-law to take a secretarial rather than an academic course in high school, unlike her brothers, so she wouldn't be too educated to get married, like her aunts with masters' degrees who were "old maids." A working class friend of mine had a scholarship to Northwestern, but her parents didn't know the difference between Northwestern and Chicago Circle Campus of the University of Illinois so she attended the latter, a working class college. I didn't know that I was "supposed" to take my children to different colleges to see which ones they liked, even though I was a faculty member at Berkeley at the time, because my parents were immigrants and no one in the neighborhood I grew up in had parents who took them to different colleges. I didn't learn about college tours until my friends, all of whom were younger than I was, had children of college age. When I myself was ready for college I looked up the list of colleges in the back of Webster's Collegiate Dictionary and applied to the ones that sounded interesting. When I wasn't accepted at Ohio State where my cousin went, or Barnard, where my mother wanted me to go, I went to Hunter College, a free New York city college. I knew I was supposed to go to college but didn't know concepts such as "the public ivies" or which were the best small colleges, even though by then my parents could afford to send me any place. The college tour is a sure sign of at least upper middle class status. One exception: sometimes it isn't necessary to survey the possibilities: one goes to one's parent's college, another sure sign of class.

I have taught upper class, middle class and working class students both as a substitute teacher in high school and junior high, and as a college professor. The working class students at Chicago Circle have much better work habits than the middle upper class students at Berkeley who need less structure, were more creative, but were frozen by existential angst and writers' block. Working class students couldn't afford writers' block—they worked forty hours a week and went to school. I liked all my students but for different reasons.

The concept of "choice," dear to the hearts of conservative and liberal ideologues, is not relevant for the working class, whether it be the choice to have a baby or abort (some poor women want the baby but have to abort for financial reasons or because the sperm donor forces them to), to select one's doctor or dentist, or, as one writer said, to choose to get one's teeth fixed or pay one's tuition. As one author said:

> "They don't have to kill us, they just constrict our lives to the point where suicide is the easiest way. Some of us die right away, some of us have shortened life spans, and some of us have a time-bomb that ticks away until some unknown source sets it off."

A major constricting force in women's lives, especially single mothers (and many lesbians are single mothers) is children, although they may also be a source of pleasure. Mothers are underrepresented in this book, probably because they didn't have time to write down their experiences. Buying milk for the house, signing notes for the teacher, and getting laundry done take up all the discretionary time. It's the hardest thing I ever did.

I will close with my mother's life which demonstrates the paradoxes of class for women. She is 92, can barely see or hear, and is in a good nursing home. A good nursing home is of course an oxymoron, but compared with other homes it is good. She has individual care by loving caretakers. This is her class privilege. But her life and particularly her pathway to the nursing home after my father's death shows the complexity of class for women and points up the lack of material on mobility, geographic and social, and aging in this book. My mother was born to a middle class family in a small town in what is now Byelorusse. She was sent away to a fancy boarding school (called gymnasia) where she felt out of place because she didn't know urban table manners and my grandmother visited her wearing a shawl, not a coat. My grandfather was sent to the U.S. in disgrace because he went bankrupt and my aunts and one uncle went with him. When World War I broke out my mother and grandmother were refugees, traveling on the roads, boiling acorns to make coffee. After the war her family in the U.S. sent money to travel storage class to the U.S.; my mother tells of her terror that she wouldn't pass the health test at Ellis Island and be sent back (non-storage passengers didn't have to undergo those tests). When she arrived in the United States her sisters sent her to bookkeeping school, because they didn't want her to work in the sweatshops (garment factories) as they had.

When she married my father she had an illegal abortion because she didn't think they had enough money to have a baby. My father started his business in the basement of our house and later did well enough so that my grandparents could move out of our apartment to the "finished" basement and he could move his business to a rented factory loft. My father wanted to divorce my mother and marry one of the many other women in his life but she refused. When I interviewed her and I asked if women had to allow their husbands to have sex whenever and with whomever they wanted she said "I'm ashamed to say 'yes'." After World War II he insisted that we move to Santa Barbara, California where my mother, in fact all of us, felt out of place. I got married and my sister had her nose "fixed." My mother had her first psychotic depression there. Gradually she adjusted to Santa Barbara. When my father died he left quite a bit of money but put my sister in charge. She moved my mother to San Francisco where my mother knew no one and became depressed again. Had my mother been a male with those resources she would have refused to move and demanded full-time help in her home, since her eyes were failing. But as a woman she had no sense of achievement and didn't want to make "trouble". She left all her possessions and all her friends in Santa Barbara. When she became depressed again in the San Francisco Board-and-Care home my sister put her in, my sister had her declared incompetent. Fortunately I was able to go to court to obtain a professional conservator of person rather than my sister. When my mother was hospitalized again, every night she would come to the desk with a bag of her belongings and ask when they were going to take her to the park, because she thought she was going to be one of the homeless women. And in fact she was homeless, in spite of her money. After numerous unnecessary medical treatments which only made her worse, she went to a nursing home. I maintain that had there not been so much money involved my sister would not have been so eager to gain control over the situation (she also attempted to have me considered incompetent but a letter from my lawyer friends threatening libel stopped that strategy).

My mother's class, status and power fluctuated throughout her life from being bourgeois, an impoverished refugee, a "greenhorn" (immigrant), a middle class wife subordinated by my father who made the money, and now one of "the frail elderly" totally dependent on the kindness of paid strangers. Now you tell me why women aren't a class and about my mother's fortunate location in the social structure and her privileges.

Julia Penelope with her mother and father, circa 1943.

Class and Consciousness

One of the pleasures of working on an anthology is the anticipation of opening each envelope when it arrives in the mail.Editors may choose topics—coming out, mothers and daughters, fat politics—but it's the contributors who determine the contents of the anthology, the final material realization of what began as a very general idea. Each author has her own story to tell, her unique approach to the subject, a voice that is hers alone, and a style that evokes her voice, transcribing her tones and stresses to our minds as we read her words on the page. In this way, anthologies create a kind of magic in our lives, allowing us to savor a diverse range of voices and styles and stories within the pages of a single book. Out of two endeavors that are essentially cognitive, writing and reading, and often widely disparate in time and space, the printed page joins the minds of writer and reader in a collaboration of understanding. This anthology is like any other anthology in its purpose: to bring the minds of different writers together with the minds of many readers.

But this is no ordinary anthology. Its subject is class and how class has affected our lives. When Elaine Gill called and asked me if I were interested in taking on a project on women and class that Christian McEwen had begun, I knew immediately it was something I wanted to do. I'm still walking the corridors of my mind trying to piece together all the ways in which my own class background, and its connections to other aspects of my life—my femaleness, my pink skin, my intelligence, my aspirations, my politics, my lesbian self—have influenced the choices I've made in my life and how I've perceived what my choices were at given times. Editing this collection of stories, theories, conceptual ramblings, and the practical essay by Felice Yeskel ("Coming Out about Money: Cost Sharing across Class Lines,")[1] has helped me in ways I didn't anticipate at first, but then began to look for. Each author, as she told her story, brought to my mind memories, connections, realizations about my experience that continue to expand and accumulate as more and more of my early life becomes available to me in memory.

Perhaps readers who have always had a more or less complete chronology of their childhood and adolescent years will not immediately understand why I am so excited by the ways these authors have awakened memories that have lain hidden and inaccessible to my conscious mind for fifty years. Perhaps they will not quickly apprehend what I mean when I say that almost all of my life, from its beginning until I was in my forties, was lost to me. I knew that I had to have memories somewhere, but there was little I could recall. My memories, the few that I could call to my conscious mind, were similar to movie previews: I had only the highlights, events here and there that I remembered—some happy, some not—but between those events was a gray fog stretching across the landscape of my life, broken here and there by a person or an event that stood out clearly in the otherwise close mist that hid my life from me. These authors have, in a literal sense, given me back the memories I might otherwise have never regained. (The italicized portions in this text are parts of my own story of class, unless explicitly attributed to another author in this anthology.)

CLASS

"It gets complex" (Pam McMichael) "

...it would be accurate to say amerikans have never understood class."(see Nett Hart's essay)

Class. What is it? What is it to me? What "class" do I "belong to"? What does "class" mean in my life? Women like myself, my friends, are familiar with the feelings of lostness and confusion we experience when we try to talk about class. To say that the issue of class In the U.S. is complicated is to say something familiar. I've been in many a conversation about class that has foundered on complexity. Nothing about class in our lives seems simple and clear-cut.

The trappings of poverty. My mother's flat had no bath. We heated water on the stove and poured it into a tin tub. There we bathed my little sister while my mother and I showered at the college where she worked and I was a student. This is as true, as vivid and as significant as the summers we spent back in Ireland swimming in my grandparents' private pool, playing tennis on their courts, while the gardener picked the best of the raspberries and brought them to us in a little basket.

It is not hard for me to know both these things, to be the person of whom both these things are true. What is hard is representing myself to the world which likes its truths to be simple, single-celled creatures. (see Anna Livia's essay)

Similarly, saying those of us born and raised in the U.S. don't understand class as a concept or as an actuality is to point out the obvious. Though both assertions are true, they block attempts at initiating discussions about class stratification in the U.S. rather than encourage it. Only a few of my friends grew up, as Nett Hart and Marilyn Murphy did, in families where class and its effects were common topics. And Marx's framework and his resulting analysis don't accurately describe how we experience class and its effects in this country. (For a heap of reasons why Marxism is inadequate to the class system in the U.S., see the essays by Fox, Nett Hart, Chrystos, and Linnea Johnson.)

> ...I have found that in the United States class consciousness is so low that many people cannot identify their class background or their present class status. This is the result partly of class mobility (which is greater in the U. S. than in most places), but largely it is due to the myth that 'we are all middle class.' This myth equates the 'middle class' with the status quo. (see Felice Yeskel's essay)

Some of us did believe we were "middle class" when we were children. That is, we thought we were "just like everyone else," having no other information that might contradict our assumptions. But there are other reasons why we don't talk about class as adults. We may not be sure what class *is*, but we are *very* sure that talking about class is more often than not a painful and dangerous subject, especially if we don't know each other before we start to talk about it. In fact, "talk" is a relatively harmless word when the topic is class. That's not how class becomes the topic in a roomful of women. Words we are more likely to hear when class is the subject are *confront, challenge, call [someone] on her privilege.* These aren't friendly words, and they warn many women away from participating in arenas where such descriptions are heard. We are afraid that other women will attack us if we reveal that we were born into one of the owning classes.[2] We are afraid that, if we expose ourselves as born into one of the underclasses, we'll be looked down on, patronized, scorned, rejected, or, worse, *pitied.*

Many of us cannot articulate how U.S. society is stratified by class boundaries or describe where we "fit" or "belong" in a class structure we find fuzzy and confusing. As children, we may know that some people have and some don't, but we lack the perspective provided by accumulated experience, and so may perceive as individual instances what we will later recognize as systematic class differences.

> ...the discrepancy between the way my classmate Jane, the pharmacist's daughter, lived, and the way my neighbors' kids lived, was not about *class*. It was about specific people, living under specific conditions. I didn't 'get it.'(see Susan J. Wolfe's essay)

By comparing ourselves to others, we may become aware that some people have more than we do and some have less.

> I always thought we were rich, and assuredly, by comparison to poverty, we were;...(see Merril Mushroom's essay)

Or, we may assume that other people live in circumstances similar to those of our family. Catherine Odette describes how her evaluation of her childhood experience of poverty changed when she moved away from home.

> In my house there was almost no food. Ever. I didn't really know how bad it was until I lived away from home for the first time and saw how some people ate—every day—three times a day. (see Catherine Odette's essay)

As children, we may know there are quantitative differences between our experience and that of others, but our accounts of those differences don't approach theory until some event later in life startles us into a search for patterns and connections in our past that will help us to understand the present.

> If our thinking about class lacks scope and comprehension, it is at least partially due to the fact that we lack a way of naming our experiences of class. There's not much language for recognizing class issues because we're taught that America is a class-less society with equal opportunity, and that anyone can make it rich. While most of us are fluent about racism, sexism, homophobia and able-bodied-ism, money and the classes it creates are not spoken of or easily identified with any openness or sophistication. (see Donna Allegra's essay)

In Jessica Robbins' interview, Helen speaks eloquently about how important having a vocabulary with which to name her perceptions was to her in developing a class consciousness and feeling that her anger was "justified":

> HELEN: 'We had stopped that heavy drug scene and we both got really serious about politics. And that's when I learned about class consciousness. For the first time both of us could identify who we were and have a name to our experience and to who we were in the world. It was the absolute first time that I had any fucking understanding about our past and about our history. It was like this fucking door opening…I mean it was the very first time in my life that I had any inkling that I was who I was not because I just wasn't smart enough or brilliant enough or white enough or whatever the fuck you're supposed to be, that I didn't feel like I was a stupid person, you know. That I actually belonged to a class.'
>
> JESSICA: 'Yeah, you were totally convinced that you were stupid up until this time?'
>
> HELEN: '…And it was the first time I think we felt like we had a right to be angry,…'[3] (see Jessica Robbin's interview)

We are confused by class as an abstraction because, in spite of the fact that the life of each of us has been defined by the class into which we were born, the culture, and the institutions that support class stratification, do not provide us with a vocabulary for talking about class. Several contributors to this anthology write about their own inability to *know* about class as a factor that imposed limitations on their dreams *or* opened doors to opportunity for them. In some ways, the class we're born into is invisible to us when we're young; like our internal organs, class is so much a part of our daily lives that it isn't readily accessible to us as an object we can explore and describe. Terri de la Peña describes her humiliation when she read in a newspaper that a hospital Christmas party she went to every year was actually held for children categorized as "underprivileged":

> I remember being stunned at that description, but nevertheless scurrying for my mother's dog-eared dictionary.. . .I recall being too embarrassed later on to admit having attended those parties.

Class is not a topic for discussion in the U.S., and the silence about it is institutionally approved of and perpetuated. Our parents may try to shield us from realizations like Terri de la Peña's, and teachers may try to foster in us the idea that we're "just like everyone else" and that we all have the same opportunities to "succeed" (as it is defined in the U.S.).

There are all the stories about the founding of this country and the accompanying rhetoric about "government of the people, by the people, for the people," a litany of democratic pap that we are force-fed as we grow up. Teachers and parents tell us that all we have to do to be successful is to study and work hard, and take pride in doing a good job.

> he [my father] takes pride in the hard work, hard saving, and intelligence that allowed him to escape poverty. (see zana's essay)

But the truth is that hard work and intelligence are simply not sufficient qualifications to guarantee a majority of us the "good" life.

> I never bought in to the American myth about working hard and making it. I knew no one could work any harder than my parents, and making it meant survival. There are others who work hard and don't survive. My mom has health insurance. Many do not. (see Pam McMichael's essay)

In spite of the evidence that surrounds us, the media and teachers continue to urge children to study and work hard. With those urgings goes the standard description of this country as a "melting pot" that we learn in history classes, a myth buttressed by story after story of immigrants and assimilation.

> In my elementary school social studies classes, I was taught that America is a class-less society. This was learned in the same breath as my ABCs and arithmetic—basic concepts never challenged....It

is no more true than the notion that this is the land of the free, home of the brave; that America welcomes 'tired masses yearning to be free.' (see Donna Allegra's essay)

· But I *did* buy the line—ALL of it. I sincerely believed that if I
. worked hard, and studied hard, and behaved "well," that I, too,
· would "succeed," which I understood to mean that I would be able
. to move out of my class of origin and "up" into the middle class. To
· some extent, I did manage this by earning a Ph.D. and teaching at
. the university level. Certainly, I have been *perceived* by other women
· as having gained some measure of "privilege" because I had a Ph.D.
. For example, other lesbians have asserted more than once that,
. because I have a Ph.D., I can "publish anywhere I want to." This
· would be laughable if the accusation didn't also imply that my work
· is published only *because* the Ph.D. is believed to have, somehow,
. magically conferred privilege on me and not for whatever inher-
. ent value my ideas may have. What I've only recently grasped is
. the fact that I did not "leave behind" my class of origin and all its
. characteristics, including my "street style" of walking and talking
. and engaging others. Of course, I took with me my entire history,
. all of my experiences—behaviors and attitudes that had not worked
· well for me as well as those that had—into my career as a univer-
. sity teacher, and those behaviors and ways of moving eventually
· meant that I didn't "fit" in academia because I simply did not know
. how to act in ways that my colleagues thought I "ought to" act. I
· didn't find this out until years after I'd left my tenured job at the
. University of Nebraska (UNL). I'll give only one example here: I
· found out that, after I'd interviewed for the job at UNL, one of my
. colleagues-to-be commented that I "looked like [I] bought my
· clothes at a thrift store." Ironically, I had bought my clothes for
. job interviews in a thrift store. (But how did they know?)

Second, for the generations after mine, there's the stupifying effect of television programming and newscasting that feeds everyone with a TV set, which is most of us, a steady diet of carefully edited and presented "information." Because television is, mostly, a commercial medium, our access to information is thoroughly controlled by the government and the corporations and businesses whose advertising dollars determine what we will and won't see. The "entertainment" provided to us by corporate advertising is merely a vehicle for increasing our desire for more and more material goods: toys, brighter teeth, faster cars, and beer, beer, beer—lite, dry, cold-brewed, draft in a bottle. And everything presented to us is bathed in the flattering glow of PROGRESS. We are bombarded with the message that the only obstacles to success—in love, at work, in life—are our own inadequacies, and that the way to rid ourselves of our inadequacies is to *buy, buy, buy* so that we'll have fresher breath, bodies that don't sweat, tighter buns, longer lashes, faster cars, more dates. We are bombarded with messages about *class*, messages about who has it and who doesn't.

In America everyone wants to be what they are not. Advertisers engender self-doubt, promote the notion that what we are is not good enough and sell 'classiness.' The idea is that if you buy the image that the product advertised represents, you can change the person. We buy goods and services to signal a certain class identity. (see Donna Allegra's essay)

We are sold Grey's Poupon mustard by two old men in limousines. A sign in Bruegger's Bagel Bakery in Amherst, Massachusetts (whose inhabitants pride themselves on their political correctness!), advertises "Coffee beans so rich they grow up on estates." A billboard in Connecticut, advertising bread from the J. J. Nissen company, says, in big letters: DEFINITELY UPPER CRUST!

Television advertising and the programming it supports have raised the expectations of two or three generations, expectations about what they will be able to buy, what they "ought" to own, and how they "should" live to be "with it," to be "cool," to be *"better" than someone else.*

When I was growing up,...[n]o identification of our class systems and subcultures came up in anyone's conversation; in fact, there was much denial about it. Yet everyone in America wants to be better than someone else. (see Donna Allegra's essay)

"Better" is a word that surfaces over and over in these narratives. My parents wanted me to have a "better" life than they did. Christian McEwen, growing up upper class in Britain, remembers its implication in jokes about her family's Catholicism, "Must you go on about it?":

Behind these questions (never stated) lurked another two, basis of all mistrust from childhood on. 'Don't you think I'm good enough for you? Do you think you're better than I am?'

Because the subject of class doesn't "come up" on television,[4] by design, because all the families populating our screens are usually white and middle-class, with no warning that *maybe* not everyone has the money to *pay* for the sanitized, deodorized, white, middle-class existence presented to us as "taken-for-granted," we are now reaping the harvest of generations of disappointed expectations: violence, in all its forms, and despair.

When "underclass" (Chrystos' term) children raised on television images of the world find out that they cannot get the jobs that would earn them the money to buy the goods that television has promoted to them as their "right," they despair. They drop out of school; they join gangs; they sell drugs; they become addicted to drugs; they imitate the violence they've seen on television. If some of them move "up" in the world of the streets, they can afford those fast cars, expensive clothes, and lots of gold jewelry. Eventually, they pay the price exacted by the social lies underwritten by corporations and perpetuated by institutions: they end up in prison, or homeless, or dead.

Have I said that virtually all the programming, all the advertising, is directed to men? We were taught that we live in a democracy, not just any democracy; the U.S. is touted as the "leader of the free world." We were taught that our "democracy" is modeled on the democratic state of ancient Greece. No one told us that the only "citizens" of ancient Greece were *men*. No one told us that women and children were the legal property of Greek men, nor did they explain that women and children in the U.S. were, until very recently, also merely the chattel of husbands and fathers. We were taught that we are "all equal under the law."

As a female, it was a rude shock when I found out that I was not considered the equal of the most stupid, incompetent men. A lesbian raised by a working mother from the time I was six until she remarried, when I was eleven, I hadn't gotten the "message" at all.

> At 24, I'm standing in the hall of the building at The City College of New York (CCNY) that houses the Department of English (and Classics and a tiny linguistics program taught by a single faculty member), shortly before my graduation, and I'm talking with that teacher of linguistics. He is my mentor, and he's warning me to be prepared to be discriminated against in graduate school (and academia in general) because I'm a woman. I'm incredulous; I don't believe him. Why would anyone discriminate against me because I'm a *woman?*

Oh yes! You see, I'd been raised to believe that I was "special" because I was very bright. I believed that my intelligence was an attribute valued in U.S. society. I didn't know that smart women were perceived by the maleocracy as though we were dancing dogs, and just as significant. (I'll return to the subject of intelligence later in this introduction.)

It might be convenient to say that only those born and raised in the middle class can be ignorant about how class shapes our lives, our values, even the way we talk. Jackie Anderson, an African American raised middle-class, attributes the attitudes about class she learned to her family's focus on solidarity among African Americans. Differences in class were not to be acknowledged.

I now see that I was raised to ignore class....I was taught that class divisions were betrayals.

Lack of awareness in Jackie's upbringing wasn't fostered by arrogance but by her parents' focus on what it means to be an African American in a racist society. They were concentrating on the survival of their race, not survival as individuals. It is also true that some of us raised in an underclass spend some portion of our childhoods unaware that we don't have as much money, or clothes, or whatever as other children. For some of us, it was our mothers who carefully managed the deception. Juana Maria Gonzalez Paz speaks as one of those clever mothers:

...I've done such a good job of living within my income that she [her daughter] doesn't seem to know that we're poor people and she regularly tells people that we 'have a lot of money.'

I remember the years of my childhood in Miami, those before my father died and after my mother and I were allowed (by the courts)[5] to reoccupy our home, as happy.

I don't remember consciously comparing what I had as a child to what other children had. It's likely that the kids I played with in my neighborhood didn't have much more than I did. But there were four of them and only one of me. I was an only child. I do know that I didn't think of my mother and me as "poor." We had what we had because she made $45. a week working six days a week as a switchboard operator at a nearby jalousie company. "Extras," like my bicycle and my bookcases, were bought used by men hoping to win my mother by courting me. Other cherished possessions, like my basketball, I bought and paid for myself by saving nickels and dimes I earned by doing chores.

But when I recently asked my mother which class she thought best characterized our family, she staunchly maintained that we were middle-class. "Why? " I asked. "Well, honey," she responded, "our house was paid for by an insurance policy your father had taken out."

Because our experiences of class as children may be inchoate, even deeply buried in our subconscious, our efforts to begin discussions about class and our experiences of it are frustrated by the intense emotions—anger, resentment, defensiveness, envy, fear, shame, rage, guilt—that well up inside us, frighteningly beyond our control. Many of us aren't sure whether our emotions are aroused by experiences that are related to class or other factors, or a combination of several factors. Yet, the intensity of these emotions tells us that we are touching on something integral and vital to our sense of who we are in the world, something so basic, so taken-for-granted that we become inarticulate. Possibly, as Fox suggests, we have to begin to think through the class system in the U.S. and find ways to talk about it, because women and men do not experience the effects of class in the same ways:

> The woman we call a 'working class woman' and the man we call a 'working class man' do not in fact belong to the same class.. . .We need to find new terms for women and men; every time we use the old terms we erase awareness of male supremacy.

Nett Hart argues that, within the women's movement, where a lot of discussions about class have taken place, we have treated class as an identity that individuals "have" and have failed to produce an analysis of the class system in the U.S. Without a thorough-going analysis of class and the many ways it affects our lives, we continue to approach the topic haphazardly and rarely accomplish any-thing worthy of the label "adequate."

> Because the examination of class takes place as an oppression within, though not caused by the movement, the discussion goes only so far as to analyze and check attitudes and behaviors of individuals with respect to their would-be peers, which is to say feminism takes on class as an identity politic but does not take on class....To take on class within the women's movement would be to develop an analysis of how class defines and shapes expectations and opportunities and then level the playing field.

If we flounder and flail in our efforts to talk about class, it is because we are trying to understand a social structure that is rarely visible. Unlike citizens of most nations, few of us born and raised in the U.S. have a class identity that tells us exactly what our "place" is in terms of class.

> In the u.s., class has none of the clear boundaries of accent & historical control that it has in europe. (see Chrystos' essay)

We may have an unclear sense of our "class identity," but each of us surely learns our "place" and that of others. These lessons are taught to us by our parents, guardians, whoever takes on the job of raising us. And they tell us explicitly, almost every day of our lives, "who we are" with respect to the family next door, the family upstairs, the family down the street. We are taught to compare, contrast, and gauge our differences. Oh yes——we have some ideas about where we stand socially and economically with respect to other people we come in contact with. But the word *class* is rarely uttered in our presence and, when we do hear it, the word is used to describe some person, some action, some object,"Aren't you the classy bitch!" "She's a class act." "You got no class," and the word *class* is always used as though the whole of its reference assumed the "goodness" of owning class characteristics conventional in a capitalist society. The possibility that people who have very little or nothing at all is invisible in the capitalist vocabulary; their lives are never included in the meaning of *class*. "Having no class" is the same as "having nothing" and, therefore, "being nothing," "being nobody" in English.

In English, *up* vs. *down* and *high* vs. *low* are the central opposites that structure our vocabulary about class and organize the hierarchical relationships among classes. George Lakoff and Mark Johnson, in *Metaphors We Live By* (Chicago: U of Chicago Press, 1980), name metaphors based on space and time *orientational metaphors* because they label emotions, states, conditions, and other abstract experiences in terms of our bodies and our orientation with respect to a horizon (actual or figurative) (pp. 14-19). Orientational metaphors organize "a whole system of concepts with respect to each other" (p. 14) as though the concepts occupied space as our bodies do and are perceptible within the usual scope of our visual abilities.

The orientational metaphors derive from the very general evaluative metaphors UP/HIGH is GOOD and DOWN/LOW is BAD. (Lakoff and Johnson represent these metaphors as GOOD IS UP and BAD IS DOWN, and include them along with other orientational metaphors rather than as *source* metaphors for the others.) Whatever we perceive as "good" in our lives—happiness, blue skies, health, sunny days, life, pleasure—is "up" or "high": "She's on *top* of the world," "We were *high* after dancing all night," "Graduating from college was a *high point* in my life." Conversely, whatever we perceive to be "bad" and undesirable—disappointment, sunless days, sickness, death, pain—is "down": "Don't be so *down* in the mouth," "She's feeling *low* these days," "Don't bring me *down*," "Stocks hit a new *low* yesterday."

The suggestion that such metaphorical concepts originate in our sensory experiences of the world may account for the coherence of the entire system of descriptive metaphors, but it fails to explain why we equate *up* and *high* with good and *down* and *low* with bad. That is, there seems no inherent motivation to value the relative spatial positions differently, and there are examples from various contexts in which *down* is good and *up* is bad. When we're exhausted, we say, "I need to get *horizontal*." If we feel that someone hasn't given us all the information we need, we say, "Don't leave me *up* in the air." In spite of such apparently contradictory usages, and whatever the perceptual bases of such metaphors, directional metaphors are our primary means for describing class relationships, with the result that we conceive of class in terms of relative spatial *positions*. Class, then, is inherently relational: we "look up to" some people, and "look down on" others. "Equals" are those we perceive as occupying a *place* or *position* similar to ours.

Our vocabulary for talking about class is derived exclusively from the orientational metaphors having to do with vertical direction in an imagined space. What is added to the oppositional adjectives *high/low* and *up/down* is the pair *rich/poor*: RICH is UP (or HIGH), POOR is DOWN (or LOW). These concepts turn up all the time in the expressions we use to talk about class:

high- /low-class	upward/downward mobility
upscale/downscale	highborn/lowborn
highbred/lowbred	highbrow/middlebrow/lowbrow
high comedy/low comedy	highlife/lowlife

In the U.S., no one wants to be called a "lowlife" or described as "low-minded." We'd rather live the "highlife" or be thought of as "highpowered," without being "highfalutin." The "lowly" (read: humble) are always thought of as "looking up" to those in "high places" from their position on the "bottom" of what zana calls the "class ladder". If we do occupy a "bottom rung" on that ladder, then we want to be "moving' on up." Status, literally, *standing* in one's community, defines our relationship to others. We are taught to strive to be "pillars in our communities" rather than "the dregs of society."

The metaphor, "pillar of the community," suggests other adjectives related to the pairs *up/down*, *high/low*, and *rich/poor* which does account for the values we assign to those positions: *hard/soft*, *strong/weak*, *active/passive*, *stiff/limp*, and *firm/flaccid*. In each pair, as with the orientational adjectives, the first term is what linguists call "privileged": the term that is frequently used as a *basis of comparison* is the *privileged* term. In the contrastive adjectives *tall* and *short*, *tall* is the privileged adjective, because we ask "How *tall* is so-and-so?," not "How *short* is so-and-so?," although there's no logical reason for preferring *tall* to *short* in our query. Similarly, if we were asking a question about the height of a bridge or building, we'd more likely ask, "How *high* is it?" rather than "How *low* is it?" Just as *male* and *man*, rather than *female* and *woman*, are privileged terms in English, so *hard*, *strong*, *active*, and *stiff* are privileged terms with respect to their opposites, *soft*, *weak*, *passive*, *limp*, and *flaccid*. "Pillars" of the community are *upright* and *upstanding*. They are *erect*. They are *potent*. They have power, and they are "in control." They keep a "stiff upper lip." More to the point, they aren't "limp dicks." They can "get it up" and "keep it up." They have "hard-ons"; they are men.

It's no accident that the nonprivileged adjectives *soft*, *weak*, and *passive* are just those commonly used to describe "feminine" qualities. What male culture posits as "good" qualities in women are, in fact, those perceived to be "bad" qualities in "people," that is, *men*. No man wants to be described as "*soft* in the head," yet that is the stereotyped quality perceived as "good" in a woman. "Hard-headed," or "hardhearted," or "hard-nosed" women aren't properly "feminine."

Neither is it accidental that English speakers also rely on orientational metaphors to contrast "reason," "logic," and "sanity" with "irrationality," "illogic," and "insanity,"[6] nor that the first set of these contrasting terms is applied to men, and the second set to women. Women are said to be emotional, irrational, and illogical, but men are credited with being intellectual, rational, and logical. In the patriarchal paradigm, men (naturally) control women. Lakoff and Johnson represent the underlying conceptual metaphors for these adjectives as RATIONAL IS UP and EMOTIONAL IS DOWN. What they go on to say, and the connection they draw between control, rationality, and men is telling; it's exactly the sort of male "reasoning" that I can speak of only within scare quotes.

> ...In our culture people view themselves as being in control over animals, plants, and their physical environment, and it is their unique ability to reason that places human beings above other animals and gives them this control. CONTROL IS UP thus provides a basis for MAN IS UP and therefore for RATIONAL IS UP.

It's no wonder that Lakoff and Johnson were unable to explain why "up is good" and "down is bad" in English. They begin by speaking of "our" culture, as though all speakers of English were homogeneous and shared their attachment to white male culture. Their use of the word *people* is pseudo-generic. It refers only to white males, for they do, indeed, conceive of themselves as having control over everything in the world, including (other) animals, plants, and their physical environment. Their belief in their unrestrained, unlimited, and totally "natural" control of the world is one of their most important defining delusions. And it is this delusion that underlies men's unequivocal faith in the metaphor CONTROL IS UP, and which accounts for Lakoff and Johnson's leap to "MAN IS UP and *therefore* (my emphasis) RATIONAL IS UP." (Why is it, I wonder, that men seem unable [or unwilling?] to control themselves and their penises, when they perceive control *over* everything else as "good"?)

Because the English vocabulary for talking about class is binary, distinguishing the "haves" from the "have nots" and then excluding the "have nots" from the reference of the word *class*, I will use only two terms: *underclass*, (which doesn't avoid the orientational metaphors), from Chrystos' essay, "Headaches & Ruminations," which includes people usually referred to as the poor, the workingclass, and the lower middle class, and *owning class*, which includes people from the middle middle class through the most wealthy. I think there are obvious reasons why people perceive being poor as a bad thing and, until we make a world in which no one is poor, I see no reason for avoiding the negative descriptions of poverty.

I realize that using only two terms with such broad reference fails to note important distinctions in economic and social experiences, but it also avoids some of the errors created by the labels we're familiar with. As Chrystos notes, the label *working class* makes it sound as if no one else but members of the "workingclass" work, which is not true. And, although common usage of the familiar class labels opposes the middle class to the "working class," marxist analysis includes the middle class within the reference of the term *proletariat*. Using only two labels will enable me to attend to the most important distinguishing factor, whether or not we are born into an underclass, one in which our parents do not (a) own property, (b) work at a job or jobs with income above (these days) $18,000., or are transitory, and (c) have so many children that they cannot adequately care for their needs.

Being born into an underclass means living without the certainty that one will be fed, have a roof over one's head the next day, or be warm during the winter. Being born into an *owning class*, in contrast, means being able to go from one day into the next with the assurance that one will (a) have enough food to eat, (b) have a roof over one's head, and (c) be warm when it's cold outside. Belonging to one of the owning classes means that one's parents could afford (a) to own property if they wanted to (even though they may rent),[7] (b) to ensure that all of their children's needs were met (even if, in fact, they were negligent), and (c) worked at a job or jobs that weren't day-to-day labor and paid more than $18,000. While there's no system of recognizing class distinctions to which there aren't going to be exceptions, using only two labels seemed the most accurate way of talking about class stratification in the U.S., if we bear in mind that there is some flux and mobility along what are really class continua.[8]

In my own experience, in that of others in this collection, *class* was never used to describe or hint at something that might be systematic, that might be something institutionalized that we have no control over. To be poor, or to remain poor, was to fail, *personally*. Joanna Kadi's mother passed on her estimation of "how the world is" to her and set Joanna's expectations by repeating, "Life isn't fair," thereby teaching Joanna that she could not expect justice in her life. Certainly, no one would have suggested that our failure could be explained as *institutionalized injustice*.

If the messages we get about class in the U.S. are downright lies, class in other countries is often an essential element in one's sense of self. Anna Livia, for example, contrasts "working class identity" in Britain with "getting rich" in the U.S.

> Whereas in Britain there seems still to be strong working class iden-
> tity, in the States communities are more likely to form on the basis

of ethnic identity than class ties. Getting rich in the States involves no break from a sense of class belonging, thus there is nothing to lose but poverty.

While Chrystos is right when she says that the U.S. lacks "the historical control" of the class systems in Europe and India and other nations, we do have some clear boundaries of accent and regional boundaries that serve very well as class markers. Just as Christian McEwen's way of speaking marks her as upper class in Britain, so specific dialects, such as those of the Bronx and Brooklyn and Southern states, are ridiculed and equated with ignorance in the U.S., as are the areas where the stigmatized dialects are spoken. And, while an observer like Anna Livia may think that we bond more readily along lines of ethnic identity than class, we don't always know how to distinguish between our ethnic and class identities because our race, ethnicity, and sex are entwined with class, one's race or ethnic background, as with African Americans or Native Americans, or sex, in the case of women, being used to "justify" the discrimination that keeps people marginalized and in poverty.

At either extreme of the class system in the U.S., one's "place" in that system is very clear.

I knew a lot about class before the summer of 1975, when I went to Sagaris, a feminist 'think tank,' and learned about class as a concept. When I was growing up, poverty lived with us, quietly wreaking havoc within a family that lacked the emotional strength to survive with cooperation and love. Poverty allows no privacy for disagreements, no time for reasoned debates.. . .I knew, from my earliest years, that my mother blamed my father for our poverty, and my father, guilt-ridden over our poverty, tried, unsuccessfully, to blame Mother for her 'inability' to make the money 'stretch.' The motif of their litany of blame was, 'If you were a real man, you would be making more money, etc.,' and 'If you were a good wife, you would know how to economize, etc.' (see Marilyn Murphy's essay)

For women, however, class has been something we are said to derive from the men, our fathers to begin with, who may or may not have inherited it from their fathers, and so on. "Class membership perpetuates itself" (Helen Elaine Lee, "Goodbye to the House"). Women who want to "better" themselves, if they're beautiful (in a conventional way) and know how to use their attractiveness, can marry into a higher class than the one they were born into. "Marrying up" it's called, and women who do so are called "gold diggers." (There is no parallel term for men who marry for money.) It's a trite Hollywood plot. Most often, though, women marry men who are available to them——the men of their fathers' class. Prior to the middle of this century, women, without careers, without access to education beyond high school, without a way of living financially independent of men, of *some* man, had very limited "choices," if one could call them that. In fact, a woman's "choices" remained pretty much what they'd been since the Middle Ages: marriage, a nunnery, prostitution. With World War I, women of Europe and North America added a fourth possibility, joining the military.

Lurking somewhere beyond or at a subterranean level, there's been that unspeakable "fifth" choice, the lesbian. Sometimes lesbians marry men, seeing nothing more promising in their lives or because they believe that being married to a man will provide them with a cover for their lesbianism. (Lesbians in the military, lesbian teachers, and those who work in the steel mills marry men so that they won't be identified and lose their jobs.) Sometimes lesbians become nuns, sometimes prostitutes. In this century, many lesbians have joined a branch of the military. In the past, some Lesbians became cross-dressers and lived as men. Some were successful—probably the ones we'll never learn about—others weren't. Lesbians are women. Our choices, by and large, are no better or worse than those other women have. Like I said, we don't have many.

There is a significant way in which lifelong lesbians differ from our heterosexual sisters: those of us who have always been lesbians, who have never lived as heterosexuals, grew up knowing that we were going to have to earn a living for ourselves because we refused to live as dependents of a man. We knew we were going to have to support ourselves. Until very recently, a majority of heterosexual women looked forward to marriage, not to a career; the only heterosexual woman who had to think about how she was going to feed herself as an adult was the one who was "unmarriageable." The stranglehold that men have on the economy, on education, on jobs that pay a decent wage, all these factors keep many women in marriages where they are battered, abused, and raped. Lesbians who have been married know how binding economic dependence is, and they know how their perspective changed when they realized that they had to get out of a marriage in order to live as themselves, as lesbians. A lesbian living as a lesbian must work for a living, unless she gets lucky and finds a woman with enough money to support both of them, and there aren't that many wealthy lesbians. There are some, not many.

> When I was a teenage lesbian, I analyzed my options. I had three. I could go on to college, IF my grades were good enough that I could get into one, IF I got a scholarship. Lots of IFs. Whether or not my grades were "good enough," or even if they were, I might still end up working in one of the factories in Hialeah or driving a wagon or diaper truck, some job that didn't pay much but that I could make a "living" at. You see, one of my conditions for a job

was that I didn't have to wear a skirt or dress. (Femmes had other
job possibilities, telephone operator, saleswoman, waitress, but they
weren't paid much more for wearing skirts.)

As women and as lesbians, class is something we didn't grow up thinking much about unless our father was active in a union.

> Until this year, I never subjected my adult life to any sort of class
> analysis. I wrote of coming out as a Lesbian in a small Midwestern
> university town, of being Jewish, but I did not write about my
> working-class origins. As I said, I didn't feel oppressed about 'hav-
> ing been' working-class...I felt fortunate to have 'gotten as far as I
> did.' (see Susan J. Wolfe's essay)

Like Susan, whatever class awareness I have is a late, and still only partial,
acquisition. Like Pam McMichael,

> I have often told people that I grew up poor but not hungry.
> That means I grew up poor but didn't really know how poor
> until I was older and able to see things with adult eyes and ac-
> tivist understanding.

Because a woman's "class" (even the possessive feels strange) in the U.S. is
most often derived from that of the men with whom she is identified, we
don't usually think of ourselves as "belonging" to a class in any analytical
sense. When asked to *which* class we "belong," we fumble for an intelligible
answer. There may be none.

> There is much written about class; class alliances; class conflict;
> where women fit into men's class divisions; if we do; how class and
> race and gender interact. It seems to me often to have little rel-
> evance to my life, or the lives of women I know. The divisions are
> so clearcut, unchanging....I have tried to...outline some of the
> contradictions and conflicts which are my daily life. (see Anna
> Livia's essay)

But if we feel unable to make a response that is both meaningful and true to
our experience, perhaps what we perceive to be our own inadequacy has
more profound origins. Linnea Johnson cautions us against relying on male
definitions and classifications that have nothing to do with our lives *as*
women.

> Patriarchal constructs like social class have women asking the wrong
> questions—like 'my goodness, into which social class do I fall,
> lodge, wedge, cower?'

If we continue to try and understand our experiences in terms of the categories and social strata as men have described and formulated them, we
may never develop an analysis that clarifies our lives.

Patriarchal constructs like 'social class' are like the Busy Box a beleaguered parent straps to the bars of a curious-fidgety child's crib—it's
all levers and flaps, mirrors, wheels, and buttons designed solely to
buy time for the parent by keeping the kid's hands occupied—...(see
Linnea Johnson's essay)

If we remain fixated by men's descriptions, we might never get around to
asking who benefits from *any* social stratification, whose interests are served
by any difference offered as a reason why some people, and only a few, at
that, should have so much while so many make do with so little.

We recognize that something isn't fair in wealth's distribution and
poverty's none-too-distant threat, yet we've also been brainwashed
to believe that we all have a fair shot at achieving riches, if we just
work hard enough. (see Donna Allegra's essay)

We need to remember that women are at the bottom of every social system created by men.

When the Women's Liberation Movement said, 'the personal is
political,' we meant that what the maleocracy *calls* personal is *in
fact* a **political system**. This meaning is seldom understood now,
the phrase usually being interpreted to mean that even if we are
focused on what is *in fact* personal we can still *call* ourselves political. This turnaround is evidence of the power of the lie the phrase
was originally intended to confront. The personal is political. The
personal is also economic. Women are outside an analysis of the
economy, but we are inside the economy. On the bottom. (see
Fox's essay)

We need to remember that women and children all over the world, including the U.S., eat dirt to fill their bellies after they serve men the best of
what's available.

Poverty and abuse and dead women. . .the story is as old as dirt.
(see Lee Evans' essay)

We need to remember that:

Women do between two-thirds and three-quarters of the work in the world;
Women produce 45 percent of the world's food;
Women receive only 10 percent of the world's income;
Women own only 1 percent of the world's property.[9]

As often as we may have heard and read those percentages, we must do
more than remember: We should carry the truth made plain by those statistics on the tips of our tongues. We must remember that class is not an
individual eccentricity. We ALL "got class": whatever class we grew up in
plus whatever overlays and facades we've acquired as strategies for social
and economic survival in situations outside our childhood home(s). It isn't

something we created, and it isn't something we can dismantle unless we work together.

Class stratification is a social institution. As such, it serves interrelated functions that maintain the male social order: it limits women's social mobility and perpetuates our dependence on male "benevolence"; it insures that only men have access to economic and political power; it insures that only men have access to resources and that women are only *one* of many resources available for male exploitation; it maintains a class—women—who do all the crucial maintenance work of daily life and who, in addition, also serve as breeders to maintain population levels as they are determined by the men who rule. Fox makes an important point in her analysis of the advantages union men gained by making deals with capitalists. In addition to keeping women out of the labor market,

[t]he least advantage a privileged male worker gets out of the family wage is more free time than women. If he has a housewife. . .he can extract even more surplus. She is on call and working for him 24 hours a day. In addition, a housewife's labor can substitute for commodities, if she grows vegetables or cans food for instance. *The more housework she does, the more of his wage the man keeps. The man can use his surplus time and money for leisure and hobbies.* (Editor's emphasis)

The economic and social differences in power between women and men created and maintained by sexual politics may mean that, although the earning power of a father/husband is assumed to "trickle down" to his "dependents," and traditional class analyses assume that women and children "belong" to the same class as the men who control them, the fact that men often reserve to themselves the "right" to keep and use "their" money as they see fit—to buy expensive fishing equipment, boats, and women, to spend getting drunk with "the boys" down at the local tavern, to wager in weekly poker games, or on the horses, or in casinos—and dole some portion of it out to women as "household allowances," often means that men's "dependents" live poorer than men's earned wages indicate they should. The discrepancy between what men earn and what they are willing to share with wives and children results later in confusion when we try to figure out exactly which class pigeonhole we belong in. The contrast between the probability of "must have" and the flat certainty of "would not" in the following description by Anna Livia captures the puzzlement we feel when a parent's income suggests an affluence greater than our specific and painful memories of childhood deprivation.

We had moved to England when I was fourteen and my father was making television programs about Africa. He must have had a good salary, but he would not spend it on his children.

Regardless of the actual amount of money our parents may have earned or inherited, children still may not get enough food to eat, or have adequate medical care when they need it, or wear shoes that fit. Alcoholic parents may spend all their money on booze and none of it on the needs of their children. Abusive parents may refuse to get children what they need. Parents who are selfish may earn sufficient money but their decisions about how to spend it will be determined by what they *want*, not what their children *need*. Whatever the actual situation of our childhoods, the personalities, faults, and idiosyncrasies of our parents create differences among us that make generalizations about class based solely on money impossible.

Lacking a theoretical framework that might help us comprehend our individual experiences of class and, at the same time, provide a conceptual structure for discerning the patterns among those experiences, lesbians and other women must begin with ourselves, with our lives, with our understandings, with our attempts to grasp the significance of our experiences.

I wanted to make sense of things, to tell the truth of what I knew. Talking about class was part of that: an attempt to face the tangles, to draw the pain and awkwardness out into the open. (see Christian McEwen's essay)

Most importantly, we have to stop holding other women responsible for our pain, our fears, the secret doubts we don't even admit to ourselves.

Women, who most often bear the burden of performing unpaid labor, housework and child care (when there is a husband who's the primary bread-winner), are frequently forced into the role of being the one who must somehow "make ends meet" when "the ends," paychecks, home gardens, food stamps, just don't "meet." Christian McEwen describes how she colluded with her father to blame her mother for their lifestyle; Marilyn Murphy admits her own bitterness when her mother went out and bought some expensive furniture to please herself; Debbie Alicen guesses that her mother, not her father, was the one who had to find ways to bridge the gap between what he earned and the way he expected her to entertain his business acquaintances.

That women, and especially single mothers, must struggle to support themselves and their child (or children) is the primary reason why many women are imprisoned. Shut out of the labor force by different kinds of discrimination, allowed only to work at the most menial jobs, those that don't provide a living wage for one person, much less several, denied the day care facilities that would allow them to work, unable to get the education that would qualify them for jobs that pay a decent wage, women must find other, extra-legal ways to piece together a bare "living." BǪ (rita d. brown) names our "crimes":

women's crimes are economic: forgery, bad checks, fraud, stealing, prostitution.

As Fox demonstrates in her essay, regardless of how we approach the class system in the U.S., women, whatever our class, whatever our race or ethnic background, whatever our sexuality, simply cannot be categorized with the economic classes that describe men's relations to the means of production. The same social system that decrees that the "place" of women is interior, within the dwelling, also has determined that this interior, this "private sphere," is to be controlled and ruled over by men. Because the "house" (apartment, tenement, condo) has been "off limits" to legal oversight, the violent acts men commit within those walls—marital rape, wife-beating, child rape—have only recently, and reluctantly, been recognized as (maybe!) crimes. Likewise, the labors women perform as services for men and children aren't recognized by the male social order as "real work." The fulltime occupations of many women, still, are housework and child care, labors that male economic systems and analyses refuse to recognize. Even in households in which women do work outside the home, their income is perceived and described as "secondary" or "supplemental" income to some male's "primary" (read: more significant) earnings.

This past year I learned how many women really make very little money. We don't have great economic strength. (a participant quoted by Felice Yeskel)

Lesbians, most of whom refuse to service men's needs (prostitutes are an exception), many of whom are single mothers, must compete with other women for the few occupations open to us. If we aren't willing to wear femme drag to work, our options are drastically reduced.

Isolated from each other culturally, socially, and financially, women continue to accept men's valuation of our labor. There is no economic analysis that places women's economic situations at its center. We will have to do this for ourselves. As long as we perceive our labor as inconsequential and our financial problems as individual "failures," we won't perceive our economic oppression as systematic and, therefore, feel no compelling reason to organize to win for ourselves some measure of justice. Finally, we must recognize that the word *class* is a euphemism for the economic violence that kills women every hour of every day, and persist in making the connection between women's economic dependence on men and the male violence directed at women and children. Lack of money and the skills necessary to secure jobs that pay adequate wages are the reasons most frequently given by women living in situations where their lives (and their children's) are endangered by male presence. By continuing to live as dependent on men's whims, women place their lives in jeopardy and give men access to themselves and their children. It is within the walls that define the male "private sphere" that men abuse, batter, and rape anyone they have unlimited access to, making the "home" the most dangerous environment for women in the U.S. We must continue to insist on gaining financial autonomy for women and the social programs that will make such autonomy possible—free day care, affordable public transportation, on-the-job training, and access to education—if we are serious about creating a society in which women have *real* choices.

We can learn from each other, we can help each other, and our differences can strengthen rather than divide us. The alternatives to understanding, analysis, and change are hopelessness, conformity, and the escalating despair that is becoming all too familiar. We cannot change what we don't understand.

We can start by sharing our stories.

OUR STORIES

At the end of "Growing Up Upper Class," Christian McEwen describes a vision she has when she writes, in which hundreds of thousands of people are gathered around the ruins of the Tower of Babel: "...there are never any problems with translation."

> We sit together, and we tell our stories. And in that conversation, everything gets said.

Whatever our individual stories may be, their significance cannot be overstated. Our stories both betray and reveal us. It is the stories we share with each other, over kitchen tables, on barstools, during late-night gabfests at music festivals, that enable friends and acquaintances to profile us in their minds. The stories we tell, and how we tell them, define us.

> ...we use our stories to check each other out. Our reactions will answer important questions we must ask of each other at this stage. Are you so sheltered that you think this unusual? Does my life make you squeamish? Do you use humor and laughter to talk about hard things? Are you smart enough not to poke around in feelings that are so carefully contained? Do you have the caring and the attention span and the strength to bear witness? I've used this test many times, a familiar dance between Dykes of scarcity. It is often not conscious, and rarely talked about. (see Lee Evans' essay)

A part of this process is realizing that not everyone we talk to can listen to us; not every person can attend to the details of our stories because they are hearing something we don't know we're telling. Sometimes, our audiences are listening to what we say from their own class perspective, not ours. Susan Wolfe describes just such a situation and her own dismay:

I remarked that we [Susan and her brother] hadn't seen much of each other in the past twenty years. . .which made me remember how much fun we'd had together as kids. So I told them [the people gathered at her father's funeral] we'd had fun, and then reminisced a bit about the things we used to do. I don't remember everything I told them, but the highlight of my account was our subway adventures, and, suddenly caught up in nostalgia, I guess I forgot to pay attention to my audience.

When I stopped, I realized the room was completely, awkwardly silent, and the guests were staring at me.. . .I stood for a moment, shocked by the realization that I'd *embarrassed* these people. They were sorry for me for having had to play on subway trains, or perhaps surprised that the children of one of their friends did such things, or something. *But they had not heard my story.* (see Susan J. Wolfe's essay)

It is precisely moments like that reported by Susan that often impel us to introspection, small surprises at our own assumptions and those of other people that open doors of insight and widen the scope of our self-awareness.

Women are far from the effortlessness of McEwen's vision. Now, as we try to engage each other in conversations about our differences, one or more of us must constantly strive to make our experiences intelligible to others because we have no languages about class that would enable us to translate our meanings. First, we must have words and phrases in our different vocabularies that make translation and understanding among us possible. Before we can imagine vocabularies that will enable us to translate passages between our realities, we have to know something about what it is we want to describe. This anthology, with authors from different classes, a range of ages and abilities, and a variety of ethnic and racial heritages, can be one beginning of our conversations about class.

It is only one beginning. If class is something we'll have to learn how to talk about, it's also about aspects of our lives that we are often reluctant to offer up to the scrutiny of others.

Of all the things I'd love not to write about, this tops the list. (see Debbie Alicen's essay)

Susan Wolfe points to the intimate nature of our class experiences, something that makes it hard for us to be articulate about them:

I'm beginning to sense that class may have been the central, driving force shaping my thinking, my feelings, my relationships. In fact, the influence of class has been at once so pervasive, and so woven into my sensibilities and reactions, that I've never been able to isolate or analyze it before.

What we have learned to take for granted in our lives may be at once so obvious and so much a part of us that we cannot step back from it and treat it as the impelling force in our lives that it is. It is also true, as Lee Evans says, that, for some of us, our pasts were so painful that we have believed, at some points in our lives, that our class origins are irrelevant to who we are at the moment, regardless of what class we may identify with.

   ...we are so willing to put the past behind us.

As our lives develop out of the stir of hopes, perceived opportunities, choices and the decisions they require, and the happenstance and randomness of life over which we have no control, we discover that, no matter how much we change or try to change, there are truths about our past, patterns and assumptions about ourselves and our place in the world, that inhabit the very cells and neural paths in our bodies and brains,[10] and fundamental elements of our character that continue, continuities we cannot deny, ways of being we cannot suppress (for very long). Not only women of the underclasses try to leave our pasts somewhere "behind" us. Women of the owning classes can be just as eager to try to forget their pasts.

> I used to think I could drop my background, and start again from the beginning, unhampered by old patterns and allegiances. What does seem possible is to name the patterns, claim the allegiances, and with a little luck and kindness, to move on. (see Christian McEwen's essay)

For some percentage of us, especially those who were physically and/ or sexually abused in our biological families, loss of memory may have been a useful survival strategy for us. Having suppressed large portions of our pasts, memories of our early, formative years are lost to us until we undertake the reclamation of memory that will return our lives to us. For years, I have lived almost exclusively in the present. Each day slid past me to join the accumulated years of days and weeks and months piled up behind doors in my mind I did not open. Every day, I thought, was a new beginning and so I kept repeating old, failed patterns because I had no way of identifying and abandoning them.

> As I grow older, more and more memories come back to me, but it is a piecemeal, gradual reclaiming of old territory. Much of it surprises me. Its lateness in coming to me: I didn't mourn the loss of my father until I was thirty-four. My ability to forget, for years at a stretch, a woman I loved. When I do remember her, finally, my body is contracted by a pain and a grief so searing that I wonder how I carried it inside me, unacknowledged, for so long.

A delusion about the extent of our autonomy, which once seemed possible and desirable, becomes instead a realization that we can never really leave behind any aspect of our selves.

In order to bring some perspective to our analysis of class and its effects in our lives, we must first remember and then claim our histories, whatever they are, in order "to move on." An important part of our individual processes is listening to other women's stories.

> I need the things I'm trying to explain to myself here, and I believe that other people need them too.(see Christian McEwen's essay)

And we must initiate this process of identification and description by being as honest about our lives as we dare to be, with ourselves and with other women.

> I suspect all of us of lying to each other. (see Anna Livia's essay)

Nett Hart thinks that, if we are lying to each other, at least part of our reason for not talking about our resources fully is a consequence of treating class within an identity politic:

> ...at worse it [treating class as an identity politic] causes dishonesty and incomplete information about one's true resources and ability to be supportive of women's institutions and other women.

Joan Schuman, a middle-class Jewish lesbian, wonders if she will be able to be honest as long as she accepts financial support from her parents:

> *As I confront class issues in my life, I wonder if my arguments will be honest as I continue to take money from the safety net.*

Honesty is not an attribute we can take for granted, even in ourselves. Memory isn't always trustworthy. There are distortions, inaccuracies, misperceptions, gaps, and combinations of events that don't actually belong to the same period in our lives.

> For example: I thought my father had died in the hurricane of 1947 until I talked to my mother in 1977 about my father's death (for the first time!). I don't know where I'd picked up that idea or why I'd believed it, but apparently, for lack of better information, I'd made up a story that "made sense" to my child's mind.

I don't think my "false" memory harmed anyone, but sometimes what we believe to be "memories" can cause harm to others.[11] We'll also have to be scrupulous and self-conscious about our feelings and perceptions and where, in our lives, they come from, especially if we've been lucky enough to enjoy some form of privilege.

it seems to me thât the first step in combating classism is being honest about the facts of our lives. it's hard to talk about money. hard to admit to privilege. (see zana's essay)

How We Grow Up

"for years i've tried to make order out of something that doesn't want to be orderly" (zana)

Class, our experiences of it, our understanding of it, like ethnicity and racial heritages, are bequeathed to us, in most cases, by our families of origin. Other factors, the death of one parent or both, being placed in an orphanage or being adopted (or not), being moved into and out of a succession of foster homes, having felt that we were or were not loved, become interwoven to make up our childhood memories.

When I was eight, my mother placed me in an orphanage for the summer before we moved back to Miami. I think she did it because I got on my grandparents' nerves and was "too much" for them to handle while she was at work. Whatever the reason, living in that orphanage for only a few months left indelible memories of terror and the potential for danger in my life. I remember being suddenly and painfully awakened from my sleep one night when several of the older girls decided it'd be "fun" to travel the length of the dormitory by jumping from one occupied bed to the next. In quick succession, one girl after the other landed on my abdomen. After that experience in that place, restful sleep was inaccessible to me.

At that time, I also had a thick head of hair that had grown down to below my waistline, and the women who worked at the orphanage refused to wash my hair once a week because "it took too much time." I was humiliated by their treatment. My mother was furious about my filthy hair when she came to visit me.

There are other memories of that place, but the one emotion I associate with it is *terror*.

Although I was not an adopted or foster child, I have some experience of what orphanages are like to the children for whom they're "home," and consider myself lucky that I didn't have to live in one any longer than I did. There is, in fact, at least one book that ought to exist on adoption and class, one in which adopted children talk about what it's like to be adopted into a class they weren't born into, about what it's like to be constantly reminded of how they were "saved" and "how lucky they are" by members of their adoptive households, and what it feels like to carry inside a fury mixed with the humiliation of gratitude and the helplessness of dependence that have no useful means of expression. Furthermore, we need to acknowledge how social and economic class are used to qualify only *some* people to adopt children—those who belong to the owning classes—and expose the imperialism of buying babies from destitute women in urban ghettos and Third World countries, a practice common among lesbians these days. We need to understand the economic and cultural displacement that become significant elements in the lives of children who've been bought.

Whatever the particular circumstances of our early childhoods, it is the people who accept the responsibility of raising us that impress us with what they think is important. From them, we learn our first values, and we are utterly dependent upon them for how we value ourselves.

> It is my belief that poverty, in and of itself, is not the cause of our lack of self-esteem but, rather, how we were valued by our families. (see Chrystos' essay)

I think Chrystos is right: The idiosyncratic nature of many of the behaviors we attribute to class are more readily understood as habits we acquired during our childhood. Helen Elaine Lee (U.S.) and Christian McEwen (Scotland), both upper-class, write movingly of their parents, other relatives, ancestors, and describe their homes with the eloquence of love. We can't underestimate the many ways our families imprinted on us their struggles, their successes, their despairs, and their joys, whether, in the end, we love them or not. Whoever served as "parents" in our lives—guardians, foster parents, grandparents, single parents—the ways and habits of living they practiced are the way we think everyone lives, including ourselves, even though we may adopt very different ways of doing things later in life. Take something small, like whether or not we brush our teeth once or twice or a day or not at all. If we grew up with books, if reading was highly valued, chances are books and the acquisition of knowledge will remain important in our lives. Or think about the kinds of food we serve for an everyday meal versus a "fancy" meal, like when company's coming to dinner. So much of what we "take for granted" comes from those who raise us and the stories they tell us.

> *Translation sometimes makes it difficult to clearly understand what class one belongs to: the knowing is filtered through nostalgia, exalted stories and hazy memories. The messages are generationally transcribed.* (see Joan Schuman's essay)

Some, even much, of our inheritance from those days may be good and, undoubtedly, some of it is bad. However we think of it, we learn our most useful lessons in the first years of our life, but their control, often indirect, extends throughout our futures. In more ways than we know, those early "stories," learned before we knew we needed our independence, form the bedrock on which we construct our identities.

Families also try to control us by telling us who we can associate with. Usually, this kind of control comes in the form of orders to stay away from someone who's "not good enough." Contributors to this anthology report growing up with frequent admonitions not to act in ways thought to be "inappropriate" to their class. When I'd get to be "too big for my britches," my grandmother would tell me not to "get on my high horse" or "put on airs." Other people were "trash" or "riff-raff." Of course, these descriptions applied only to other people, "them," not us. Not us, not our families, none of our friends. Marilyn Murphy recalls one of her mother's sayings, "I don't want you associating with riff-raff". Christian McEwen describes her puzzlement at not being allowed to play with the local children who lived near her family home of Marchmont:

'You can't play with the local kids. Your friends must be imported. You're better. They're not good enough for you.'

Debbie Alicen, a white Southerner, says that, in her own liberal family, class was treated as a more significant feature than race.

I was never discouraged from having black friends, of course, but my parents did actively discourage me from having working-class white friends.

Although some of us may imitate our parents in many ways, and although some may adopt parents' values and attitudes largely without question, others of us rebel against aspects of our parents' lives. Karen Chaney, for example, talks about feeling that she was betraying her rural Missouri upbringing and her class origins when she was a graduate student at Harvard, and her struggle to find ways to unify different elements of herself. Her intelligence had given her access to a privileged education in an environment that caused conflict with other elements of her identity, such as her rural background.

While graduate education was moving my friends and lover back into solid places within their home communities, it was moving me further and further from my own. I felt I was betraying my community and family in my increasing worldliness.

After she moved to San Francisco, and, shortly after that, took up country-western dancing, she fell in love with a woman from Missouri for the first time, and began to understand herself in new ways:

It was a time of recovery of lost parts of myself, parts that had never been allowed to live fully before. I felt very country, very female, and very free.

I, in contrast, was raised in the South in an urban environment, Miami, Florida. I yearned to leave the South to live in Greenwich Village and rebelled against everything Southern. Fancying myself superior and an intellectual because I was being groomed for college, I pretended to enjoy classical music, sneered at "hillbilly" music, toted books by Kierkegaard and Sartre around with me, and cultivated my own brand of bizarreness. Although I was ambivalent about "being different," and although a part of me longed for the conformity that would gain me acceptance by my peers, I chose to reject the values and culture of my class and region and to exaggerate my differentness. Karen Chaney decided to embrace her origins; others of us rejected them.

However imperfect and unclear our earliest memories are, whether we adopt or reject our cultural heritages, our feelings about life as our parents, grandparents, even great-grandparents presented it to us, about the limitations and possibilities of their lives, become the foundation of who we will be as adults, an integral part of our understanding of ourselves and how we move through the world. For years, we may not know *why* we act and react as we do.

It takes years to understand the meaning of these attitudes and behaviors. We never really unlearn those early behaviors, assumptions, expectations, and ways of moving in the world. (see Felice Yeskel's essay)

Class, and our knowledge of how it functions in our lives, are ingrained in the cells of our bodies and brains, so deeply intuitive that we are unable to identify experiences as *class* experiences until we consciously begin to look for them. Usually, some incident compels us to undertake the process of discovery.

> I am puzzled. I am enraged. For the second time in as many years, I've stormed out of the home of another lesbian because she attacked me for teaching in a university, an occupation that she has left behind. My attempts to explain that I believe that I am doing something positive for lesbian students by teaching in the academic environment only further anger her. She yells and rants at me, belittling and demeaning both my intentions and accomplishments in a patriarchal institution. She screams her scorn for what I am doing.
>
> Months later, I am still puzzled, still fuming about her treatment of me, when a lesbian from another city comes to visit me. She wants to know why I'm not speaking to this other lesbian. We're walking down the front steps of my house as I describe the event. I am furious, not about her challenging my politics, but because she screamed at me. My visitor says, "She treats you that way because she's upper class and you're workingclass. Haven't you ever wondered how she manages to live without working? Haven't you

ever asked her where her money comes from? She inherited a lot
of land and that's what enabled her to leave university teaching.
Whenever she needs money she sells another piece of land." This
information brings me to a standstill. It is a revelation. "No," I say,
"It never occurred to me to wonder how she lives without having
to work."

I turn this information over and over in my mind for years, but I
don't know what to do with it. For one thing, I'd never thought of
myself as workingclass. I'd never identified my experiences as having anything to do with class, and that information placed many
things about my life in a new and unfamiliar perspective.

The events and objects that initiate our explorations of class and its
effects in our lives need not be large or important. It may be something
that others regard as insignificant: toothpaste, toilet paper, the kind of
plates we eat on, whether our last meal of the day, if we have one, is called
dinner or *supper*, if our family can afford to "stock up.".

I'm house/farm sitting for …[a] good friend…and one of the things
I love about her and her home is that this place is always full. By
that I mean, you don't run out of things. There is always toilet
paper, coffee filters, the right medicines or herbs in the cabinet.
(see Pam McMichael's essay)

To those of us raised poor or workingclass, these seemingly "ordinary" objects of daily life represent plenty and fullness, the sense of "entitlement"
so taken for granted by those who haven't had to wonder where the next
meal or tube of toothpaste was coming from. Often, however, we didn't
realize that we had less than other children, and it is a "small" thing that
causes us to realize that objects and experiences we learned to think of as
"normal" were actually indications of our family's lack of economic resources.

Several contributors to this anthology report experiences similar to
Susan Wolfe's moment of realization during her father's funeral. Small, routine activities and events, suddenly perceived from a new perspective, compel us to reanalyze and recontextualize what we have long believed to be
"facts," surprising us with startling reinterpretations of our childhoods. Pam
McMichael describes a conversation with a friend who'd borrowed Pam's
baking soda toothpaste on a camping trip. Her friend didn't like the toothpaste; Pam explained to her that it was a "comfort" item for her because,
when she was a child, her family used salt and baking soda to brush their
teeth when they ran out of toothpaste. Several months later, while Pam
was house-sitting for the same friend, she was brushing her teeth with
baking soda and remembered the conversation they had had on the camping trip:

...and a new realization took my knees out from under me a bit. My family ran out of toothpaste, not because we lived on a small farm and couldn't get to the store. We ran out of toothpaste and used salt and baking soda because we couldn't afford to buy more toothpaste until the next payday.

While I was working on this essay, I called my mother to check dates, names, and chains of events. When I asked her which class she thought we (her, my father, and me) belonged to, she said we were middle-class. *I'm* sure we were workingclass. Seeking some logic for this difference in our perceptions, I asked for more information. My mother said, in her classical southern dialect, "Oh, honey, we're descended from aristocrats." I stifled a laugh and replied, in as even a tone as I could manage, *"Fallen* aristocrats, mother. *That* never put any food in our mouths."

My mother and I are both right. At the beginning of "mixed-class confusion," zana sounds a warning for those who want to hurry to generalizations that distort and falsify our experience:

> many people's backgrounds are mixed—their parents were from different classes, and they (or their parents) have moved up or down on the class ladder.

We cannot assume that class membership is static from one generation to the next, even though some of the behaviors stay with us. Even within a single family, as several contributors say, individuals may identify with or belong to different social or economic classes than their parents and siblings. My family has been up and down the class continuum in our native countries and in the U.S., and, as an individual, I've been up and down, too, because, after my stepfather kicked me out when I was eighteen, I managed to get a B.A. and a Ph.D. by (literally) "begging, borrowing, and stealing." When I was finished, in 1971, I was $35,000. in debt to the federal government and the Rockefellers (Chase Manhattan Bank). I was shocked when women meeting me in the '70s and '80s assumed I was born into the middle class, unaware that my "educated" behaviors were a facade patched onto my earlier experience. Now, away from academia and having not much use for middle-class ways, I believe that we may change classes, but only if we restrict our definition of class to economic factors. Even some behaviors—gestures, ways of talking, favorite expressions, ways of writing—may be retained, but we also acquire new habits by imitating people we admire.

And money, as the contributors to this anthology illustrate over and over, is only one factor among many. What we believe we know about "class," once we have the word in our vocabularies, is often an overlay of stereotypes (of ourselves and others), misinformation, exaggeration, and memories of pieces of conversations and arguments we witnessed or over-heard as children. It isn't until we leave our childhood dwellings that we begin to realize how much of what we were told at home was only one version of "how it is." Like Donna Allegra, I didn't realize my mother and I were poor until much later in my life; she thought her family was middle-class until she went to Bennington.

> I never felt poor or realized that we weren't financially middle-class until I went to college and read some sociology.. . .I never heard my parents worry aloud or complain with any ferocity about money. It was a given, somehow by osmosis, that we children should not ask for too much.

Merril Mushroom, once "out in the world," discovered that gentiles assumed she was rich and well-educated because she's a Jew.

> When I left the sanctuary of my home community, I learned that, as a Jew, I was automatically assumed to be (1) rich, (2) highly educated, and (3) different. I thought of other Jews I had known when I was a kid who were neither rich nor well-educated, like the old folks on South Beach who ate out of the garbage....

Carried into adulthood without critical examination, the stereotypes we have of ourselves may set us up for disappointment and disillusion-ment; the stereotypes of other people we hold onto may lead us into mean-ness and destructiveness. As a Southerner who finally finished my bachelor's degree in New York City, I know how inferior to yankees I felt because I believed that my education *had* to've been inferior (because it was segre-gated), and how scornful of Southerners people are in the North.

> On both coasts, the midwest and the south are considered vast cultural wastelands, and those in urban coastal communities have a difficult time believing that there is life—or intelligence—be-yond their parameters, particularly in the south. (see Karen Chaney's essay)

Racist stereotypes of African Americans in the U.S. characterize them as "lazy" and/or "stupid." Jackie Anderson describes how her parents brought her up with "middle-class values" because African Americans live "under the gaze of white eyes."

> One reason that it was possible to ignore class was that most Afri-can Americans of my generation were raised with what might be characterized as middle-class values. We were not allowed to speak other than standard english at home; our table manners had to be 'right'; and education was understood to be of unquestioned im-portance. We lived very much under the gaze of white eyes ready to judge us as unworthy at any moment. There could be no oppor-

tunity for 'them' to confirm any of their stereotypes of 'us' through any behaviors of ours.

To say now that I have been able to ignore class is something that I recognize as an expression of privilege, similar to white people saying that they can ignore race when people of color cannot. But that is new knowledge—...

Donna Allegra's terse statement says it all: "Hierarchy is the name of the game". By one device or another, whoever's got the power and the money decides who's going to be underneath them; the rest of us are left to scrabble among ourselves about who's going to be on the bottom of the bottom. In the U.S., Caucasians think African Americans, Native Americans, most people of color *except* Asians, are inferior, and that Jews and Asians are *really* smart, but, nonetheless, despicable. Easterners and Westerners, with their coastal chauvinism, think people who live in the Midwest are lazy and stupid; Northerners think Southerners and Midwesterners are stupid and lazy (the ordering doesn't matter).

The stereotypes we learn as children damage everyone, those who profit from them as well as those who suffer the damage they cause. The ugly difference is that those who perpetuate stereotypes, those who choose to go on believing them long after they already know their falsity, get something for their ignorance: money, privilege, the "best seats in the house," whatever the "show" is. Christian McEwen knows the plot from the inside.

From across the Atlantic, the British upper classes seem harmless enough. Faded gentry, honorable civil servants, at best they're brilliant figures from the past, there to entertain whenever Brideshead is revisited....As a child and adolescent, I tried to balance my growing knowledge of such stereotypes (and their occasional truth) against the human fact of my family, whom I loved. This wasn't easy. For a long time I thought the stereotypes were actually 'right,' and took them in, internalizing a tremendous amount of self-hatred and confusion. Then, because I was afraid, I didn't talk about my life at home. The oddities and confusions went unnamed and unconfirmed....Despite the flood of upper class memoirs, journals, anecdotes and collected letters, very little has appeared which tries to question such an upbringing from inside, either in its own terms or in relation to the rest of society. Meanwhile, life in Britain continues to be dominated by the class system, to a degree perhaps unimaginable in other countries. People do not talk easily or honestly across class barriers, and the stereotypes remain extremely powerful.

Privilege, whatever its supposed "basis," enables someone to "look down" on someone else. The trick is not to end up at the very bottom, something that "happens" to others, not, we hope, to us. So we dog-paddle as hard as we can. Sinking "down" is ever so much easier than struggling "up" to break the surface. Kate Moran has pointed out to me that what we euphemistically call "downward mobility" is what the privileged call "slumming." Those who have the luxury of choices can *pretend* to lead an impoverished life, sometimes going so far as to live without electricity, running water, or indoor plumbing, without having to sell any of their stocks.

If we are serious about dismantling the class system in the U.S., we have to begin by ridding our minds of the stereotypes we refuse to relinquish:

People who are rich are: cold, snobs, quiet, hypocritical, etc.

People who belong to the middle class are: also quiet, and conventional, unimaginative, boring, etc.

People who are working-class are: dirty, sweaty, crass, loud, ignorant, and wave their hands around when they talk, etc.

Poor people are: not only dirty and loud but smelly, lazy, stupid, and, besides, "deserve it."

I've previously quoted Christian McEwen about the importance of naming the "old patterns" of class behaviors and attitudes we learned as children. In order to name those patterns, however, we first have to know what we're looking for. The contributors to this anthology repeatedly mention specific external and internal ways that class manifests itself in our lives. Although I can't unfailingly identify the points at which we internalize "external" factors of class so that they become attitudes and values, I can identify some the things that seem the most likely to be entwined with class: money, resources, access/privilege and skills, food, manners, the way we feel about our bodies, our health, and our ability to take care of ourselves, clothes and appearance, our senses of humor and the kind of music we like. We take all of these accessible factors as indicators of class membership. What we've learned about them underlies the values and attitudes we take with us into adulthood, and they're entwined with other differences, race and ethnicity, that are used to set us apart from others.

Money

Readers who've engaged class issues in their own lives and the lives of other women will already know how difficult it is to talk about money. Too often, in my own experience, one or more of us terminates the discussion, begun with good will and the "best intentions," by walking out. These apparently abrupt endings start with thoughtless statements, emotional outbursts, or angry denunciations that few of us know how to deal with once our own wounds are reopened. I've already said that discussions of class are "dangerous," and money seems to be one of the unsafest topics to broach (although language has to be a close second).

Because we deny there is a class system even as we speak of 'high class' and 'low class,' we also deny that there is enormous wealth and poverty. The main, but not the only, factor to class is wealth. (see Donna Allegra's essay)

It's no accident that the women willing to bring up class and money are members of the underclasses. It's no accident that women of the owning classes are reluctant to talk about money and resources, but the reasons for their reticence are often more complicated because the U.S. isn't a homogeneous society. Not everyone in the owning classes is Caucasian; not everyone in the underclasses is a person of color, although racism accounts for the numbers of First Nations peoples and African Americans who are poor or workingclass. One of the recurring, successful lies of anti-Jewish propagandists has been, and continues to be, the assertion that a "conspiracy" of "Jewish bankers" is responsible for the economic woes of the world. This lie has been repeated for at least a millennium, and millions of Jews have been made scapegoats, harassed, ostracized, and murdered wherever their enemies have stirred the embers of hatred. The Holocaust of Hitler's Nazi Germany is only the most recent example of how virulent this lie is. With the resurfacing of anti-Jewish hatred in the U.S., Jewish women are rightly wary of talking about money among gentiles.

I was...pushed up against the realities of anti-Semitism (both internalized and otherwise), as I feared talking about money issues with a predominantly non-Jewish group. I feared being misunderstood and my particular money patterns being associated with the fact that I am Jewish. (see Felice Yeskel's essay)

This self-protectiveness is also operative in any contexts in which women interact with those who belong to a more privileged group:

It is difficult for me, as a white, middle-class woman, a Jew, to talk about money with those I perceive have power over me: men, members of the upper class, the corporate world, the elite, white Anglo-Saxon Protestants, my parents. (see Joan Schuman's essay)

Even if we believe that money—the having of money, the ability to get money, the ability to insulate oneself economically—is *the* determining factor of class membership, we'll quickly find more complexity rather than less. In the U.S., there is *some* upward class mobility, perhaps more previously than in these years following Reaganomics. Felice Yeskel, in her essay about the cost sharing process at a Jewish feminist retreat, acknowledges such flux, for example describing one participant "raised working-class" who "now has upper class resources." (Her "Cheat Sheet on Class Background," admittedly simplified, nevertheless provides specific descriptors for points on a class continuum.)

· What class *am* I? I was born in 1941, in Miami, Florida. My parents were both half German and half English/Irish/Scottish. My father was named Frederick William Stanley, Jr., after Kaiser Wilhelm II, king of Prussia and emperor of Germany (1888-1918). Parts of both families were descended from Prussian aristocracy. My mother was a Manston on her mother's side (the anglicized form of the Prussian surname von Mannstein), and a Cartledge on her father's. My father was from Yemassee, North Carolina and my mother was from Atlanta, Georgia. My father was raised poor or workingclass. According to my mother, he was a "brain," and was going to college on a football scholarship until he broke both his ankles. They met in Miami at a restaurant where she was a waitress, near the grocery store where he was a butcher.

My great-grandmother, Lora Manston, and her husband were upper class and had servants. My mother says that my grandmother, Nell Manston, was "spoiled." While she was still fairly young, her father died suddenly and the family lost everything, including the rights to the process for developing color film that he'd invented, stolen by the *Atlanta Constitution*, because he left no will. After that, my grandmother worked at various jobs to make a living, including baking cakes.

When I was a very young child, my great-grandmother often visited us, and I remember sitting cuddled up to her while she told me stories about the family I "came from." I don't remember all the stories or the details of any single one, but my favorite was about my great-great-grandmother Julia Penelope, for whom I'm named. She was married to a Colonel in the Confederate Army (Victor Manston) and they lived in Corinth, Mississippi. When General Sherman was marching toward Atlanta, he stopped in Corinth and broke into the house where my great-great-grandmother lived because he knew she had a map that showed where her husband was hiding with his troops. Instead of handing over that map, she chewed it up, swallowed it, and dared him to go after the pieces. I was very proud that I'd been named after her, but I was already teaching at the University of Georgia before I felt comfortable using my full name, Julia Penelope Stanley.

Still, these are "stories" to me, and believing them is something I don't find easy. Recently, though, my mother gave me a print of a photograph of my grandmother that her father published in the *Atlanta Constitution* around Easter one year, so I figure my great-grandfather Manston at least worked for the newspaper.

I've briefly described how my mother and I lived after my father was killed, but there's more. When I was around eleven, my mother married a man who became my stepfather, Eddie Smith. He was working-class, from Bloomington, Indiana, and I hated him (he tried to rape me one night while my mother was in the hospital for a hysterectomy). Eddie, as I called him,had come down to Miami to open a drugstore with a man named Russ. Eddie ran the luncheonette and Russ ran the pharmacy. When I was thirteen, my stepfather sold the little cinder block house I'd spent all but two years of my childhood in and moved my mother and me to a small house in the more affluent suburb of Miami Springs, where the luncheonette was located.

Eddie was the short-order cook; my mother, in spite of his insistence, before they married, that my mother was to be a housewife, became the cashier, and I was the drudge during the summers: I waitressed, I mopped and waxed the floor, I cleaned the public toilet, and I scrubbed the wooden slats behind the counter (there for sanitary reasons) and all the large, metal garbage cans that stood out in back of the luncheonette with bleach and a pine cleaner.

It was 1954, and I was entering the ninth grade in a brand-new school, Hialeah High. My "difference," and my awareness of it, steadily widened the chasm between me and my classmates. Now, I was not only distinguished from my peers by intelligence and my lesbianism, but also by my class background. The teenagers I rode the school bus with were mostly middle and upper middle-class. Not only were they giggly around the boys but they were also able to spend Saturdays together looking for the clothes and cosmetics that would attract the boys to them. I tried vainly to mimic their behaviors, to share their interests, but it wasn't "in" me. Instead, I longed to be invited to spend the night with this girl or that girl, to be invited to slumber parties. I was never invited to a slumber party, but, occasionally, one girl or another did invite me to spend the night, and, sometimes, the invitation was clearly loaded with sexual innuendo. I turned those invitations down because I was equally terrified that I was misinterpreting the sexual message I perceived behind the invitation or that my interpretation was correct, that the attraction was, indeed, mutual, and that I'd have to do...*what???* I had no idea.

My high school years remain a turbulent mix of pain, adolescent sexual yearnings, and ostracism by the groups of girls, especially those who were also athletic, whose companionship I craved. But I was also beginning to understand that my wit and intelligence could, to some extent, get me, not only retaliation against those who snubbed and ridiculed me, but also privileges not meted out to those who were "merely" average intellectually, and so I began to hone both my wit and my brains, making of both an efficient and deadly

49

weapon with which I could cut my way through the social jungle in
which I was at an disadvantage. I was beginning to understand that
my brain was something that could not only protect me and advance me, but that it was also something irrevocably mine. No one
could take it away from me. My grades in the ninth grade were
barely average. By my senior year I was channeled into the "college
prep" courses, I was a member of National Honor Society, and I was
selected to take the *National Merit Scholarship test.*

A "Busy Box," indeed! Where do I "fall, lodge, wedge, cower" in a class system in which I am marginalized (as a woman, as a lesbian), and which, still,
remains undescribed and unanalyzed? According to traditional class analyses, by the time I was sixteen, I'd been in and out of two or three different
classes, if one defines class only in terms of money: workingclass or lower
middle-class for the first five years of my life, when my father was alive; poor
or working-class when my mother was raising me by herself; middle- or
upper-middle-class during the years I lived under my stepfather's roof.

In women's communities, we often approach each other assuming
that the person we are dealing with in the present is who we perceive her
to be, and that who she is *now* is who she's *always* been, where she lives *now*
is where she's *always* lived. While I was working at the University of Nebraska, for example, women I met assumed that I was *from* Nebraska, apparently unaware that, in academia, we go where there's a job. Because I had a
Ph.D., they also assumed that I (at least) had middle-class privilege.

The fact that individuals may move back and forth among classes
means that attempts within the women's movement to address class issues
as money issues are inadequate. As Felice Yeskel points out,

> All of the. . .methods of attempting to address our class differences
> only take into account people's current financial situation, and usu-
> ally only people's yearly income.

One of the false equations we have to confront is the one which
posits that class and money "go together." If there is one myth that virtually every contributor addresses it is the one that derives one's class membership from the amount of money one has access to. Christian McEwen,
born into the British upper class, describes wearing hand-me-downs and
how her father made money by organizing hunting trips for wealthy men
from the U.S. Anna Livia wonders if her class accounts for her own achievements and the well-intentioned acts of others:

> How many of my achievements have I imputed to my own intelli-
> gence, wit or charm which would more honestly be explained by
> class position? Did my headmistress pay my train fares because

she liked me and valued my intelligence or because it seemed wrong that a nice middle class girl like me should be down on her luck?

"Down on her luck." A telling phrase, one that suggests the assumed immutability of one's class background, in Anna Livia's case, middle-class. A decline in one's fortunes is treated as though it were temporary, a decline that can be reversed by the appropriate action or another "change in fortune." It's a phrase that insists that our failures are haphazard, random, individual, one that denies that class stratification and our opportunities or lack thereof are systematic and predictable; a phrase that encourages us to believe that we might succeed if only we're in the "right place" at the "right time."

Failure is a matter of "luck." Success is attributed either to "luck" or "hard work," as though members of the underclasses haven't worked "hard enough." "Down on one's luck" implicitly asserts a distinction between (apparent) social class and (apparent) economic class. It also implies that, while economic class may be temporary (one's financial situation may improve or decline), social class is somehow an indelible characteristic of our lives. Debbie Alicen posits a distinction between social class and economic class that has to be incorporated into any analysis of the class system in the U.S.

> All during my adolescence my family was on the outskirts of wealthier society—what I would now term lower upper class—a position conferred by my father's fame as a newspaper columnist. His credibility and visibility as a public figure bestowed a level of social rank that was several notches beyond my family's economic position. The pay my father received did not put us in an economic class commensurate with the social class status conferred by the job.. . .For all that we had food and shelter and never really risked not having it, my mother was frequently frantic about money. Growing up in the Depression certainly had something to do with it, but a lot of it was also status-related, involving pressure to achieve congruence between our social status and our economic status, and her feelings about it all being connected to middle-class shame.[12]

Debbie's mother was "frantic about money" because she lived through the Great Depression, but also because her husband's income placed them in the middle class while the status of his job required them to socialize with and entertain people of similar social status who enjoyed a wealthier lifestyle.

Money and class often don't go together in the U.S. One can make a lot of money yet still be perceived and treated as belonging to an underclass. A familiar stereotype of this situation is the "nouveau riche," people who have earned their way into the owning classes by making a lot of money but whose "manners" and behaviors belong to their underclass origins. Conversely, one can earn not very much money but, if the work is perceived as conferring social status, be treated as belonging to an owning class. Once upon a time, teaching was a profession that conferred social status without equivalent economic benefits.

> When I was a student at Florida State University, my history teacher came into class one day and ranted about how little money he made. He was angry because garbage men made more money than he did. After teaching in state universities for eighteen years, I knew exactly how he felt.

In 1958, teaching was still a respected profession even though it didn't pay wages commensurate with the years of education required to do it. Now, however, teaching may offer some financial rewards in some states, but it has also lost social status. Culturally, a lot of lip service has been paid to the possession of above-average intelligence, but intelligent people have never earned a lot of money because of their brains, especially in the liberal arts. Money has been used as the "carrot" to lure intelligent people into those jobs deemed "important" by politicians. When this society thinks it needs more engineers or physicists or accountants, it offers financial rewards to attract people into those fields of study. During the Viet Nam war we called it "channeling." Specific areas were given preferred status, and students in those fields were exempted from the draft. But intelligence *per se* is not culturally valued.

The trade union movement of this century accounts for some of the disjunction between social and economic class, especially for men. Those trades in which the workers are usually men, such as truck driving, plumbing, carpentry, and construction, pay very well. Jobs usually performed by women, such as teaching, nursing, and secretarial, don't pay well. It has generally been the case that men are channeled into specific occupations while women are discouraged from working outside the home by a combination of social pressures and the fact that the salaries in jobs open to us are so low that the salary, in and of itself, isn't the reason women "choose" the kind of work we do. That is, men are "attracted" or "recruited" into one field or another; women are actively discouraged from entering the labor force, and these processes are controlled by men. The best-known example of this kind of male control occurred during World War II. When the U.S. entered WW II, huge numbers of men were needed in the military, and women were recruited to perform the jobs that men had been doing and the new jobs created by war industries. When the war ended, however, women were pushed out of the work force to make room for the men returning from the European and Pacific theaters.

I can't go into all of the social, political, and economic forces that drive the class system in this country, but I can mention a few. In the mid-1990s, we are still suffering the combined effects of Reaganomics and the numerous financial scandals his social and economic policies fostered in the 1980s, and which created what seems to be an ever-widening chasm between the "haves" and the "have nots." For example, we have more homeless people, both urban and rural, in the U.S. than we've had since the Great Depression of the 1920s and '30s, most of them made poor by Ronald Reagan's presidency. A war won't improve their economic chances. Technology and its effects are changing the labor requirements of U.S. society, and many workers, women as well as men, are unemployed or retraining themselves so that they can work in a much-changed world of work. The economic upheavals in the U.S. that started in the early 1970s made it possible for married women to enter the work force, especially in part-time jobs, to supplement their husbands' earnings. Finally, the politicians and bureaucrats have barely begun to address the havoc wrought by the "tax-payers' revolt" which drastically cut the funds available for education, maintenance of roads, bridges, and highways, and other crucial social programs. The U.S. is a country in deep financial trouble, but that is only part of the problem. Political expedience and corruption have done extensive damage to our educational system, our economic system, and our morale. Adolescents have good reasons for their nihilism: no matter how much education they get, no one can guarantee that there'll be a job for them in the future. Those who do manage to get jobs will be poorly educated. A high school education, something prized by my mother's generation, is worthless these days, and a college education isn't worth any more. Our populace is increasingly illiterate and the percentage is growing. What we have now is a huge underclass, a majority of us, and a very small owning class, and changing the situation becomes increasingly difficult as privilege for the few reduces the rest of us to competing for scraps at the bottom of the heap.

Privilege

Social and economic class may not be easily equated in the U.S., but *privilege* still determines what any of us may aspire to. *Privilege* consists of one's access to resources, social, economic, educational, and the resources available to us limit the future we can imagine for ourselves.

> Differences in clothes, manners, the way you speak and carry your body are external dimensions of class, but internal differences in life expectations, aspirations, horizons—considerations I am again facing. (see Karen Chaney's essay)

Privilege may be inherited, along with class; some privileges can be acquired through upward mobility. But privilege earned is not the same as privilege inherited. Inherited privilege, and the assumption of it, is something one carries in one's very bones. It is something one is raised to.

> ...I know that the attitudes that come with an inheritance of privilege must be challenged, if I am to look at the way class works in this society, and fight against the messages received. (see Helen Elaine Lee's essay)

Privilege makes access to skills and resources easier, and the assumptions of what privilege makes possible in one's life are manifested in how we move through the world and among other people. Among the kinds of privilege operative in the U.S. are skin privilege and class privilege, and these intersect in our lives in complex ways. Helen Elaine Lee has class privilege but not skin privilege because she is African American, and she describes how irrelevant her class privilege is in a racist society. I have skin privilege but not class privilege. Jackie Anderson explains that social and economic class remain distinct for African Americans and how class differences were handled in her middle-class family.

> I was taught that we were a people and that there was 'them' and 'us' and that 'they' [white people] made no distinctions, so we should not make distinctions. I was also taught that those of us who could had a responsibility to those of us who could not, and that the only 'bad' Negroes were those who did not understand their responsibility to the 'less fortunate.'. . . .I always knew that I was more fortunate than many of my friends, but I saw that as a function of material wealth and not social class. In our family discussions, differences in economic class were attributed to the effects of racism.

The skin privilege Caucasians enjoy in a society that despises people of color is real; we whites (or "pinks," as Chrystos describes us) can and do use our skin privilege to open doors ordinarily closed to people of color, whether or not we recognize the fact. Pam McMichael relates an example of how her skin privilege got "better service" for an African American friend when she took her to the emergency room one night.

> Her nose was bleeding and it would not stop. With head tilted back in the examining room chair, my friend joked, 'I think that nurse has a crush on you. I'm getting a lot better service than when I was here last week.' (Her daughter and son-in-law had brought her then.) But we both knew the reason behind 'better service.' I had no money in the bank, but in that situation my white skin still had bought my friend better care.

Skin privilege, because it can gain one *access* to things that money often buys, like better medical care, must be weighed as a factor in class privilege, which is primarily about what money can buy. For an underclass child, going to college is an aspiration, a dream of what *might* be; for an owning class child, it is a given, especially if the child is not female. If the underclass child manages somehow to get a college degree and then is able to get a decent job because of the college degree, that individual may acquire some kinds of privilege because of her enhanced "earning ability." That is, she may be able to travel for recreational purposes, or invest a portion of her income to pass on to her children or use for her retirement, or insure that she will always have access to good medical care. But no matter what she achieves, she will never enjoy the assumptions of inherited *privilege*.

As the stories in this anthology attest, privilege is an attitude one is raised with. Anna Livia describes an instance when she was able to get back into England without a passport because she's Caucasian and middleclass. "One time," she says, "my accent and attitude, borrowed from a generation ago, did smooth away all obstacles." When she concludes the story, she imagines that, if she were workingclass or Black British, she "would have been turned back and possibly arrested" by the British customs official. Or, more likely, she doubts that she'd have even tried to get into England without a passport. Looking back on the incident, Anna Livia's evaluation of her statement is blunt:

> I look back at that statement, 'One time my accent and attitude did smooth away all obstacles. . .' One time? I ask myself. Only once? What a wealth of class privilege rests in that simple statement. What I mean is there was one time when I had to notice where my privilege got me.

Privilege is attitude; it's about how we walk, how we talk, where we go to school, what kinds of jobs we can get, how much of our income goes to survival and how much goes to "extras." Privilege is about whether or not we believe we'll be able to eat again and when. (Do we know where our next meal is coming from?) It's about what we eat, how much we eat, how often we eat, and where we eat it. Privilege is about survival.

> Stopping class oppression isn't about needing a better philosophical understanding of privilege. It's not about being anti-oppressive or being a more effective ally, because class isn't about theory. Class is about survival, about which of us will and won't make it. (see Elliott's essay "Funeral Food")

Being malnourished by choice, whatever the reasons (anorexia, bulimia, fear of fat, being a model or a ballerina, dieting to wear a bikini), cannot be confused with the experience of starving because you or your family don't have choices. Privilege is about the clothes we wear: Are they store-bought or homemade? Can we afford to dress according to current fashions?[13] (Do we care?)

Choices

Somehow, we have to develop ways of handling our class differences that recognize the complexities of our individual lives without glossing over the significant ways in which we are different. As several contributors point out, there's a qualitative difference between being, for example, a single mother living on welfare, and a middle-class woman who describes herself as "broke this month" because she bought a new stereo system. Having cash flow "problems" is not the same as being poor. Women and lesbians of the owning classes may sometimes not have cash in their pockets, because their financial assets aren't liquid. That is, they have stocks, bonds, real estate, parents willing to bail them out or give them money when they need it; the truly wealthy often have trust funds that dole out a specific sum of money to them each month. Having such resources is described as living with a "safety net," some form of financial backup one can count on when she has "cash flow" problems. Becoming aware of this difference and how it affects our choices, expectations, and goals is an important first step of clarification that women of the owning classes must take.

> There is a vast difference between being oppressed by not having choices, not having enough, not having a sense of entitlement that allows any expectation of having your needs met and being oppressed by class because you are of a class that is owned by its capital, that makes life choices valuing the maintenance and development of one's possessions over self development. (see Nett Hart's essay)

Joan Schuman first became aware of her class position when she was a college student by paying attention to how her situation differed from the options other students did or didn't have.

> *By the end of the semester I am keenly aware that I did not need a scholarship to go to this school but I did not get an allowance from Daddy or use of the extra car with the vanity plates that sat waiting for me in a suburban garage. It is the first time that I notice my middle class status between those that have money to throw away and those that have to count every cent.*

Christian McEwen, whose immediate family wasn't as well-off as other relatives, describes how crucial owning Marchmont was to her sense of self:

> Being the Marchmont ones [branch of the McEwen family] gave us status, both in the immediate family and beyond it. Papa might be poorer than his brothers. Our clothes might come to us sec-

ond-hand, in big soft cardboard boxes sent by Mama's friend,. . ..
But always there was Marchmont to return to.

Yes, money is an important factor in how we understand class and our place(s), but it isn't the only factor, or necessarily even the most important one. The significance of "coming from money" or not lies in knowing what is or is not possible for us. In a fundamental way, our awareness of class is grounded in the kinds of choices we thought we had. Some of us believed that we had *no* choices.

. . .poverty is about having no choices... (see Lee Evans' essay)

When we are children, "having" or "not having" determines how we imagine our future, as well as whether or not we get medical care when we need it. What Lee Evans has described is the *sense* that we have "no choices," but in my own experience what I've perceived as having no choices, as having only one option open to me, were situations in which I may have had several different choices, but none of them were what I thought were **good** choices. Oh yeah, children raised in poverty may have choices, but they differ qualitatively and quantitatively from the options open to children of the owning classes. From the time we're old enough to realize that other children have choices unavailable to us, *we may think of ourselves as having* **no** *choices.* This can be dangerous for us, because we do have choices. It's just that we don't like the ones we have. We want different, *better* choices. We want the opportunities open to people of the owning classes. Isn't that, after all, what equality is supposed to be about in the U.S.? Having "equal opportunities"? What can it mean to a teenager to tell her that she has crucial choices to make when what are offered to her are the bad choices, the leftovers, when other students her age are going off expecting to become lawyers, doctors, and politicians? How do her choices between having an abortion and staying in school with only the *hope* of graduating stack up against being able to choose between one Ivy League college and the other, or even choosing between the publicly-supported universities in two different states? There are choices, those that expose to us the poverty of our lives, and then there are CHOICES, the kind others have, that seem to unfold into days of bounty and the richness of promise.

There is a tremendous difference between choices of *need* and choices of *want*. Some choices are just plain ugly. These are the choices people of the underclasses must often make between one need and another and another and another. It's painful to know one must choose between paying the rent OR putting food on the table OR replacing shoes that have holes in them. Choosing between one want and another may feel hard, it may not feel "easy," but it's a pleasure compared to the desperate choices among needs, choices made knowing that some or all will suffer deprivation regardless. Lee Evans describes the distance she felt between her and a friend when Lee tried to explain the difference between "need and want":

> This feeling must be the cold steel bars that drop down between my friend and me when I try to explain the difference between need and want, and her not seeing any difference, and me realizing that I had trusted her.

When Juana Maria Gonzalez Paz says, "...I believe the answer for all of us lies in the ability to increase our own and each other's choices", I think she means that we must not only *increase* the choices women have, we must all have *better* choices available to us. Increasing the number of bad options we have, which is what happens in real life, won't change the class system.

The conflicts we experience as women when we try to deal with "class issues" often originate in the ways our horizons have been foreshortened by having always to choose among competing needs and never having the luxury of choosing among wants. With mild sarcasm, Christian McEwen describes how her father illustrated his insistence that "the best things in life are *cheap*" by citing kippers and eggs. Men of the owning classes have often been given to romanticizing the "cheap," the "simple," the "rural"; it's easy for them to praise and elevate to virtues what, for the underclasses, is "making do" with the "bare necessities." The higher one lives in the class hierarchy, the more *possibilities* one has to choose from. Members of the owning classes can choose the "cheap" or the "simple" but, unlike the underclasses, their range includes the expensive, the luxurious, and the sophisticated as well.

Other women who wrote for this anthology discuss how they experience the difference between needs and wants, but Nett Hart states it most simply: "Downward social mobility is only fashionable for those who can go down". It's one thing to extol the virtues of living without excessive wants (eating kippers and eggs), but quite another to be so poor that kippers and eggs are a rare and welcome "treat." "Downward mobility" is not a "choice" for those never offered the opportunity to move *up*, and it's not an honorable "choice" when the person making it knows she'll receive a specific sum of money every month of every year from a trust fund, unless she's decided, out of political integrity, to live simply and economically in order to use her money to improve the choices available to others.

And there *are* choices people make that are firmly grounded in a politics of integrity. Joan Schuman describes her feelings about such a choice that her parents had to make and how she feels now about similar choices she makes.

> *I think a lot about what it meant for my parents not to have income for three months* [while they were on strike] *and about the choices people make, the*

> options people have when it comes to money for their beliefs.. . .I feel lazy when I
> indulge my politics—a powerful message—because often I do not make enough
> money to live on.. . .if it weren't for the yearly (sometimes twice yearly) middle
> class safety net of my parents, I would not be able to pay my rent.

She understands that the choice of acting on one's political beliefs is, in some ways, a luxury she cannot afford, and she's ambivalent about a time when her parents did choose to live without paychecks because of their political beliefs. The safety net provided by Joan Schuman's parents makes it possible for her to act on her own beliefs, and she accepts their help but feels guilty about not being able to pay for all of her needs.

Like Pam McMichael, I try to be appreciative of women who conscientiously weigh their own choices and who, aware of their financial privilege, find ways to use their privilege/money to improve other women's lives. zana, talking about how being a disabled woman affects her decisions about how much money she can afford to share from her income, describes her choices as generosity:

> i recognize the point at which i still hold power and control: i
> choose which wimin i will be generous with and in what situa-
> tions: i decide how much of my income i can spare.

Unfortunately, I think politically conscious women, like zana, are harder on themselves than they should be, and I think other women take advantage of them. I think it's entirely fair that zana has control of her money, but I don't understand how that can be misidentified as having power *over* other women. Because zana is a woman with a disability, she has to retain whatever control and power she can in her own life to make decisions that enable her to take the best care of herself she can. No one else has the right to ask a woman for more than she can afford to give or to give what she doesn't have. At some point we have to trust that each of us makes our choices with political integrity and conscience. If we don't, well, then, we're certainly no worse than other people in this world.

I think that it's time, has been time for a long time, for women to stop monitoring other's women's choices, especially when we don't know them or have any knowledge of what they have to do to get through a day, and start challenging *men's* choices on a full-time basis. Of the two sexes, women earn less, inherit less, and own less than men; it is men's choices which will condemn us all to a quick or a slow death, depending on which mode of death they think will make them more money. It's time for women to sit down together and talk openly about what we do own, what our resources are, if we have resources, do we ever hope to have resources, and, if so, how we go about acquiring them, without taking all of our stored-up anger and pain out on each other. Sitting down together is the best way for us to identify which angers spring from deep in our histories, which are responses to something in the immediate context, and then figure out how we differ from one another and *learn* to incorporate that knowledge in our living.

> . . .cost sharing helped women clarify their own class backgrounds and the impact of their backgrounds on their feelings, attitudes, values and choices. (see Felice Yeskel's essay)

Money is the tangible symbol of two more important aspects of our early class experience: access to resources and access to skills. Having access to resources—safety nets, land, goods that make one's life easier or more comfortable, winning a million dollars from Publishers Clearinghouse—determines how hard and how long we must work.

> My partner, who identifies as a daughter of upperclass parents, tells me, "Class isn't about money." I say, "Yes, it is." She says, "No, it's not." I know she's partially right, in spite of my own focus on money. We are very different in our handling of money, saving money, spending money. I fritter away money in small purchases, but I feel uncomfortable when I spend more than $25. She doesn't often spend money, but when she does, large dollar amounts don't faze her. For years I've been the one who clips coupons and scours grocery store circulars for sales so that I can simultaneously take advantage of sales and double coupons; I'm proud that I hardly ever pay the retail price for anything. In the past, she has refused to take coupons when she went shopping. But lately I've noticed that she checks for coupons in bags of dogfood and is disappointed when the piece of paper she finds is just an advertisement, and, when she does find a coupon, she leaves it where she knows I'll find it and file it in my coupon box.

We continue to learn from each other. Our differing approaches to handling money enable us to do OK on her salary. Coupons. Double coupons. Sales. The necessary buying strategy of those who have some but not "a lot." An apparently petty difference between us, but one that symbolizes a great difference in how we perceive money, how we spend or don't spend it, what we feel we must do to survive. I tell her I figured out that one has to have enough "surplus" money to save by stocking up when stores have sales, and how angry I was because I didn't have "extra" money I could tie up buying things I didn't immediately need. I couldn't invest $4.99 in twelve rolls of toilet paper when I could only afford to buy one roll at a time. Knowing how to take the best advantage of sales is a skill it's taken me years to acquire. Having access to skills, and the specific skills we bring with us into adulthood, these, too, are determined by our class membership.

Access to Resources and Skills

> ". . .I know full well that I do not want to be poor, financially vulnerable, without resources. That's death to a Black person. It means lesser health care, lesser life expectancy, greater stress, greater exposure to crime, increased disrespect from everyone around you, etc."(see Donna Allegra's essay)

Money is very important because of what it can buy: decent health care, a place to live, ways to unwind from a stressful day, and respect, however grudging, from people we have to interact with. Lesbian communities aren't very different from other marginalized groups and adopt similar survival strategies: bartering skills and time, passing on things one no longer needs (clothes, furniture, cars), personal loans, and generosity. It's not unusual to find a chair once owned by one friend in the home of another, or a friend wearing jeans or a sweater that you'd passed along to someone else. In this way, lesbians, often from different class backgrounds, form extended "families" in which everyone looks out for the other. The crowd of lesbian friends I hung out with in Miami had developed an entire genealogy, with "fathers" who had brought out "sons," all of whom who had other butch friends, called "brothers." (Gaymen friends were "sisters.") Bo briefly mentions how "family" groups of women form around butches and their "wives" in prisons:

> These extended families are a key factor in survival—they watch each other's back, help obtain food and cigarettes and spread the news about who is in the hole, up for parole, etc. (see bo's essay)

Because so many of us know what it's like to be cut off from our biological families, to be barely able to get from one day to the next, to live on the dexterity of the "five-fingered discount," we look to each other for help along the way. Pam McMichael, describing a friend of hers who gladly shares whatever she has, points out that she has identified two responses among those who've watched the struggles of relatives to survive: "One says, 'I'm never going to live like that,'. . .The other says, 'I don't want to live that way, and I don't want anyone else to have to, either.'" Observing that her friend is one who has made the second response to others' struggles for survival, Pam McMichael concludes, ". . .I call it generosity that comes from class survival, a giving that knows what it's like to be without, and doesn't want anyone else to be there".

Money isn't the only useful thing we have to offer each other, nor do we even have to be friends. Sometimes, it's the "kindness of strangers," unasked for generosity, that helps us through a difficult or painful experience.

In 1960, I was driving from Miami to visit my grandparents in Atlanta. Just north of Valdosta, a tire on my 1952 Ford blew, and I had no spare. I'd barely stuck my thumb out to hitch a ride back to a gas station when two women went by, stopped about a quarter of a mile past me, then backed up to where I stood and offered me a ride. On the way into Valdosta, they told me they were gay and were on their way to Miami for their vacation. They were from Dayton, Ohio, and they'd stopped for me because I was obviously gay, too. They hung around while I got my tire patched, drove me back to my car, and helped me put the tire back on. Before they drove off, I gave them my phone number and offered to show them around the gay bars of Miami and Miami Beach. They took me up on my offer.

I have skills and access to information that you want and need. (see Joan Schuman's essay)

We have much to give each other. We have much to learn from each other. Our economic class determines whether we'll have access to specific resources, our social class and our biological sex determine which skills we'll be allowed to learn. Children of the owning classes aren't allowed to learn to work with their hands; it is assumed that they will always have someone else to do "menial"[14] work *for* them. Children of the underclasses are raised to work with their hands, to perform "menial" labor. In all classes, the kinds of skills children are taught are determined by sex. Boys learn to fish, play team sports, fix cars, climb trees, hunt; what boys learn are *outside* skills. Outside skills are valued because they're owned by men; things men do are more highly rewarded than the things girls are *allowed* to do. Girls learn to cook, arrange flowers, do their hair, do their nails, apply cosmetics, clean house, buy clothes, choose furniture, wallpaper, colors of paint, change diapers; girls learn *indoor* skills. Indoor skills, *women's* skills, are not valued. That's why housewives aren't paid for their multiple labors. Regardless of our class, the skills we are allowed to acquire are just those we are expected to need for a conventional, heterosexual marriage.

Long before I knew anything about class propaganda, I was not the eldest boy, I was a girl. Boys could be clever and brave and independent and as naughty as they wanted. Girls had fewer choices.. . .Boys were the important ones, the ones whose choices were taken seriously. (see Christian McEwen's essay)

Women learn how to take care of *other* people's needs. If, in the process, we learn to do for ourselves, okay, but it's not the **purpose** of what we're taught.

The specific skills may differ from one class to another, but taking care of men and babies is really what women's lessons are all about.

Once we're adults, we begin to realize how many things can go wrong, can break, can stop working in a single day. We learn how many things we don't know how to do—mow a lawn, shingle a roof, clean a gutter—and how many things we don't know how to fix——a flat tire, a leaking toilet, a broken pipe. If we were born into an underclass family, we may approach such commonplace nuisances with an attitude like Alien Nation's, which she describes because of a fight she and her nephew got into with her then-girlfriend while they were all trying to move Alien Nation's house:

> She just couldn't believe we were moving my house without having a step-by-step plan, backed up by knowledge and experience. Shoot, my nephew and I grew up around people who were all the time doin' stuff they didn't know how to do. Ya jus' jump right in and figure it out as ya go along. You can't break it if it's already broke.

Alien Nation attributes her then-girlfriend's frustration to a "communication problem," but the fight, as she reported it, was really about very different assumptions about what one can or can't do, how much knowledge or experience is *needed* to undertake a specific project, and I'd wager that the girlfriend's assumptions about a "plan" for moving the house were connected to her class or to her family's.

The attitude, "You can't break it if it's already broke," stands in stark contrast to Christian McEwen's increased feelings of competence and her joy in her accomplishment when she learned, after moving to the U.S., that she could, indeed, take care of herself.

> I was looking after myself, paying my own way. Living in a communal house with five other people, I learned to cook and clean, to fix the washing-machine when it broke down. To my housemates, these achievements were entirely mundane. To me, they were extraordinary: opportunity for pride and celebration.

To some extent, what we do or don't know how to do marks our class as surely as what we do or do not own.

> How much control do you have over whether or not you make rent, bills and food next month? How refined are your money management skills? (see Elliott's essay, "Funeral Food")

Joan Schuman, writing of the conflicts in a relationship with another woman that she traces to class and race differences, wonders why feminists don't address issues about differences among women connected to our access to specific kinds of skills and the ability to get the information we need.

> *Why is there seldom a discussion in feminist arenas about the extent to which 'skill' privilege, in the form of access to knowledge and information, plays a part in class and race differences as well as in other power differences...? I am now aware of this once-silent privilege in my life and its power over my relationships.*

But I remember a time when there *were* such discussions among feminists about "skill privilege." In the early 1970s in the U.S., women tried to spread around different skills within the women's movement, to share knowledge, to encourage each other to try new skills, and there was a willingness to learn how to do things we'd previously been told we couldn't or didn't need to know. In those days, when the "personal was political," we were learning that what we'd believed were our own inadequacies and ignorance were, in fact, systematic features of our oppression as women, and class was integral to our analysis of oppression. Then we didn't do those things anymore. Felice Yeskel, talking about why feminists abandoned efforts to "level the playing field," speculates that "many of us grew tired of having every decision scrutinized," with the result that "the '80s seemed to swing towards a 'there's no one right way, so do your own thing' type of isolated individualism".

We needn't even sit around and talk in groups if we don't want to. We can learn new skills by observation, by trial and error, by paying attention to the situations in which the skills we have work and when they don't. Certainly, there's no reason for holding on to behaviors that don't work, and we become more adept at maneuvering in the world if we know which behaviors work in some situations but not in others. Self-consciousness is often a good way to figure out what works and what doesn't. Diversifying the breadth of our repertoire of behaviors by learning from each other will expand the range of our choices. Christian McEwen, discussing her own lack of skills, reveals her fear:

> For a long time I had only the negative versions of choice. 'No, I don't want that—'. . .I had very little money ('bourgeois ambition'), nor did I know how to acquire it (upper class ignorance and lack of practical skills). Underneath it all, I was enormously afraid.

Along with fear, we may also feel tremendous frustration when our ways of dealing with other people aren't "working," i.e., we aren't getting what we want.

> In 1986, my partner and I were living in St. Louis. I was having a hard time dealing with the white men who seemed to own every service I needed: mechanics, car dealers, movers, plumbers. She came home one day to find me crying wildly, hysterical because I had had it with the car dealer I'd paid to repair damage to my truck. After four visits to this particular dealer, having made do without a vehicle for four different stretches of days at a time, the

paint job on my truck was terrible. It looked like they'd buffed it with steel wool. I'd been on the phone complaining to the body shop manager, and he was absolutely unwilling to take responsibility for the shitty job his men had done. I'd ended up screaming "Fuck you!" into his ear and hanging up. Maybe I'd said "Fuck you" more than once. Whatever, my street ways of "getting the job done'" were clearly *not* getting anything done, at least not to my satisfaction.

She calmly said, "I'll deal with it."

And she did. She picked up the phone and called the manager I'd been trying to deal with, and she said to him, after describing the problem with the paint job on my truck, just as calmly, "This is not satisfactory." She said it quietly but with great emphasis. She didn't need to raise her voice or cuss. Whatever he said, she just kept repeating, "This is not satisfactory." And, to my amazement, it worked! She got the dealership to redo the paint job at their expense, which was what they should've done in the first place.

Our different class upbringings and the strategies we learned from our families differ in their effectiveness depending on the context. I learned from my partner that, sometimes, simply saying "This is not satisfactory" gets results in situations where all the yelling and cussing in the world won't get someone to budge once they get dug in to a position. She, in her turn, has learned street ways of dealing from me, ways of getting things done that work just as effectively in other contexts. In the course of our relationship, each of us has, by watching the other in action, acquired a wider range of approaches to getting what we want. She's learning skills related to squeezing as much as she can out of every single dollar. I'm learning a little finesse in my efforts to get what I want from everyday encounters.

Our differences *can* be our strengths when we share the information and skills we have with each other, and when we understand that the success of different approaches to a problem isn't an absolute value. No approach is "bad," and no approach is "good." Some ways of dealing work better in some situations than in others, and having a variety of strategies available to call upon in differing situations is better than having only one or two ways. Each of us has learned specific skills, ways of getting around in the world, ways of getting around the law, ways of getting what we need *or* want, and the skills and knowledge we have depend on our class experiences. Debbie Alicen talks about how she has learned to use middle-class behaviors and attire, with purpose, to help other women.

My middle-class background has given me the skills—demeanor, style of speech—to challenge and advocate effectively. Middle-class ways of conducting myself are no longer who I am, but things I can do to accomplish the purpose at hand.

Even with all the debt and uncertainty about future money, I like my life very much the way it is, realizing as fully as I can that one reason that may be so is that my life is as it is largely by choice. Unlike many others, I have the option of being better off financially. I have the knowledge and the life history that would permit it.

Elliott writes eloquently about the importance of making sure that our theories grow out of our experiences as women and as lesbians and that they address our real issues and needs.

We need theories and communities that are serious about understanding and meeting the needs of lesbians and all wimmin.

I don't think that meeting needs instead of throwing tea socials is a new idea. But as I sit here, wearing used clothes and typing on a used typewriter, I know that my world isn't about new; it's about available, useful, comfortable, and long-lasting. And that's exactly how this redneck dyke wants her families and communities and the theories growing from them—available, useful, comfortable, and long-lasting. (see Elliott's essay, "Whenever I Tell You...")

Food

Food, the eating of it, the getting of it, the preparing of it, are very much class issues, but hardly any well-known writer on the subject of class has devoted attention to the ways food and class are connected. Although I can scarcely do justice to how our perceptions of food derive from childhood experiences, and are, therefore, somewhat hard to generalize about, I think it's important and so do several contributors. Elliott, to name only one, devotes an essay about class, "Funeral Food," to exploring the interconnections among her rural, poor childhood, money, aspirations, and control over one's life.

As adults, eating among friends, sharing jokes over potluck offerings, surprising a loved one with breakfast in bed—meals remain central in our daily lives, whether our memories of family meals are happy ones or our stomachs go into spasms of anxiety at the thought of eating with relatives. And we must have shelter and food in order to survive; that we can lose either or both of those necessities makes "class anxiety" a very real fear. The food we grew up eating, whether we liked it or not, is a point at which our class, biological sex, religious, ethnic and racial origins intersect. Whether or not we have food to eat, if we do, how much and what kind of food we're allowed to eat, whether a parent or someone who didn't sit down to eat with us served us our food, as well as the family rituals around food that we learn, all these things are determined by our family's class, racial and ethnic background, and whether we're female or male. Pam McMichael describes her discomfort when she discovered that the "hired help" of a friend's grandparents had sectioned her grapefruit before bringing it to her.

Class and privilege inhere in every aspect of our mealtimes and are even embedded in the names we use for foods, especially meats, since the successful Norman invasion of England in 1066. The French nobility, at the top of the English food chain, dined on venison, mutton, beef, pork, and veal, while the peasants ate deer, sheep, oxen, swine, and lamb. At some point, the "classiness" of Norman French must have persuaded upwardly mobile English speakers to abandon their native vocabulary. Only *lamb* continues to compete with *veal*. Do we eat with silverware, tableware, dinnerware, or utensils? How many forks are placed next to our plates? Do we know the order of their placement? Do we care? (Karen Chaney relates how, as she became "increasingly bitter," she found herself noticing "who reset the silverware 'correctly' on the table" after she left the room). How were we expected to dress when we came to our family's supper table? Where did we eat? In the kitchen, in a dining room, or on TV tables in the living room? Do we eat on plastic, melmac, stoneware, or china? More importantly, what kind of food is on those plates? And, equally important, is there enough food there to satisfy our hunger? If there's not enough, can we have seconds, even thirds?

Catherine Odette, rummaging around for reasons why she hadn't wanted to eat in public until twelve years ago, after coming up with several plausible reasons, finally says that she never liked eating in public because of the "food things" she learned in her family. Those "food things" form a complex matrix of poverty and charity, Catholic anti-Semitism (from the woman who brought them bread ends from a nunnery every Saturday), her father's memories of a Nazi concentration camp, and gratitude for having anything at all to eat and the bitter resentment for feeling gratitude.

> Everybody learns about food in the family they grow up in. We learn our attitudes about food. How food is dealt with, how eating is valued or devalued. How much strain it is to feed people in that house. Is there enough money for food? Was there a decision to buy food instead of oil for the heater? Is food wasted? Thrown away? Served by people who don't sit down to eat with you?

Sometimes, not knowing much as a child is a blessing, but the pain, whenever it comes, lacks none of its power to hurt.

zana, describing how the Great Depression had had a permanent effect on her parents, says she "felt like a freak" when she found out that other children didn't have to save scraps of everything imaginable. Although she identifies as middle-class, not poor or working-class, her family lived by the proverb, "Waste not, want not."

> i used to feel that in our house the depression had never ended. i first saw a piece of moldy food at the age of 11 in someone else's house. food waste in our house was more than a crime—it was unthinkable. we saved string, bags, rags, rubber bands, gift wrap, you name it. to this day i have rarely bought any of those things which are gotten for free. back then i felt like a freak when i found out other kids didn't save those things.

It isn't just the scarcity of food that frightens us.

> In my mind's eye, I can still see my grandfather bending down to salvage a rusty screw, a nail, a bolt, or a paper clip from the sidewalk. It never occurred to me to be embarrassed. I still have all of those screws, nails, and bolts, and they're still where he put them, according to type and size, in the small Sanka jars that my grandmother faithfully washed and saved. I've moved them now from Georgia, to Tennessee, to Nebraska, to Missouri, to Massachusetts. (After moving such things so many times, is saving them no longer "economical"?)

zana still feels strange when another dyke notices things she's saved:

> ...still today I feel [like a freak] when one of my dyke land-sisters opens my sewing basket and exclaims, 'wow, look at all those safety pins!' yeah, and a lot of them are over 34 years old: the little brass ones that came on doll clothes i shoplifted. i've had the basket that long, too. you don't buy new things when the old suffice.

Food, and our feelings around food, the mortal contrast between scarcity and plenty and how we understand those abstractions, are the least understood differences among the classes. We carry the information about where we grew up in the class system in our (literal) guts. Lee Evans talks about the monotony of poor food, and how, when her mother died, she became her family's cook.

> Poor food varies from home to home. We ate monotonous dinners: rice and tomato sauce, hamburger, Spam, canned vegetables, and always water to drink.. . .When I was thirteen my mother died, and I became the cook in the family. Cereal and cookies for breakfast, peanut butter for lunch, and pancakes for dinner.

Years later, at a time when she believed she'd put the memory of hunger where it could no longer surprise her, she *is* surprised by the strength of her reaction when her boss suggested missing a meal.

Yet just last week my boss suggested that because of an unusually heavy workload, I might not be able to go to lunch. I stared at him in disbelief, and then felt a very old and familiar panic welling up from that place I thought was left behind. I've come so far, yet a missed lunch can still grab me by the throat and drop-kick me twenty-five years into the past, to a time when food meant survival, and my hunger was never satiated.

I, too, know how strong are those old memories of not having enough food, of wanting more to eat than my mother could afford to feed me, and how they rise up from my bowels when I think they've lost their power to control me.

In 1986, my partner and I rented a small house in Maplewood, Missouri, after we'd been evicted from an apartment owned by a closeted lesbian couple. The house didn't have a refrigerator when we moved in, but the guy we were renting from swore he'd get one in for us immediately. We waited. Three weeks went by, and we realized that our idea of "immediately" and his didn't match. And I became increasingly anxious about not having a refrigerator. I knew that my anxiety wasn't caused by the money we were having to spend on eating out, although it was certainly a concern. No. I was feeling anxious because we didn't have a refrigerator. Finally, I realized that, for me, the kitchen is the most important room wherever I live, the refrigerator is the center of my kitchen, and the refrigerator must be full of edible food. A refrigerator with bare shelves, or shelves filled with old leftovers, causes me to panic.

Knowing that I have food to eat, and that I can choose what to eat, makes me happy. Because food represents security to me, I have little sympathy for girls and women who go to great lengths to void or avoid food. What are now lumped together as "food issues," anorexia, bulimia, and fat, have their origins in very different environments, largely, but not entirely, determined by class. Anorexia and bulimia are responses that are possible only when there is enough food that one can eat to satiety if she wishes. They are diseases of choice, tactics chosen in order to ward off the specter of "obesity," a "disease" created in the twentieth century by the U.S. medical profession. No one (I think) would label the people starving to death in Third World countries anorexic or bulimic because their starvation is caused by factors over which they have no control: imperialism and colonialism, the earth's weather cycles, and war. The peoples of Biafra don't choose to starve. (Neither have the homeless and other poor people of this country, but many people with jobs and homes persist in believing that the poverty of others is "chosen.") Anorexia and bulimia are, if anything, the individual's exercise of control over her life in a context in which she feels "out of control." Fatness is now generally recognized as an inherited trait. Sometimes, as in my own case, it's also a response to being sexually molested by relatives, the theory being that the rape will cease if one is fat and, according to conventional values, "unattractive."

> As a young child, I was very sickly. In addition to having all the usual childhood diseases—whooping cough, chicken pox, measles (five times)—I developed severe sinusitis when my mother and I lived in Georgia with my grandparents. I spent so much of my time at home, sick, that I barely remember the second grade. What I do remember are the sulfa drugs and the long metal tube used to get them up into my sinuses. Then, between fourth and fifth grades, I began to develop athletic skills and "bulk up." I became very strong and agile.
>
> Between my sixth and seventh grades, my mother married my stepfather, and he tried to rape me while she was in the hospital for a hysterectomy. His betrayal affected me in many ways: I withdrew and became a loner, I lived in my bedroom with the door always locked, and I began to gain a lot of weight. Although the strategy was not conscious on my part—I didn't say to myself "I'll gain a lot of weight to make my body repulsive to him"—looking back, I understand that my need to repel him made growing larger a useful way to exist under the same roof with him.

I'm not the only fat incest survivor I know who gained weight in order to repel a rapist she had to live with as a child, but children use whatever they think will work in their efforts to protect themselves.

"Food issues," including fatness, are very much tied in with class issues. Someone denied sufficient food as a child may, if she can afford it as an adult, make up for the hunger of her childhood. In "Funeral Food," Elliott describes the complexities of our feelings about food and what it represents for us by comparing the similarities and differences between her and two other lesbians.

> Mari is lower-middle class, grew up one generation away from farming in a Midwest city, went to state universities, is culturally x-tian. Otter is upper-middle-class, grew up in a ritzy suburb of a big east coast city, went to private colleges, is Jewish....But Mari and I share a background of good, commonsense Midwestern food and a tradition of 'supper on the table when Dad comes through the door,' while Otter and I have a similarly twisted mass of cultures in which food is love and comfort and family ritual, and, as fat girls and wimmin, the control and denial of food as 'love.'

For me, a full refrigerator symbolizes security. For others, like Pam McMichael, the availability of meat, being able to afford to eat meat, may represent plenty.

> ...my reluctance in finally becoming a vegetarian is because meat was so connected to my working class family survival.

Meat and dairy products figured prominently in Juana Maria Gonzalez Paz's strategy for feeding herself and her daughter on her food stamp allotment.

> ...by eliminating expensive meat and dairy products from our diet and cooking from scratch a lot, I could feed both of us on my food stamp allotment.

Generalizations about the ways class and food are connected for us may be impossible at this time, in this book, but we need to recognize that some of our emotions about food and eating originate in our childhoods and our families. A further complication is introduced when we realize that mealtimes were also perpetual battlegrounds on which the war called "manners" was fought.

Manners

"I hate nice." (Elliott)

> "it is obvious to me now that both niceness and betterness are maintained on a firm foundation of unasked questions.....Across classes, its [the pattern of exchange] function becomes altogether more sinister."(see Christian McEwen's essay)

In our relationships with other people and our expectations about the kinds of behavior that we will meet with, what is called "manners" is one of the most obvious differences we recognize, if only because it refers to the system of customs and habits which govern our interactions with other people. The word *manner* isn't Germanic in origin; it was borrowed into Middle English from Anglo-French (after the Norman Invasion), and is thus intimately connected with the court customs of the Norman French elite. Ultimately, the word can be traced back to the Vulgar Latin term *manuarius* ('handy', 'convenient') from the Latin word for 'hand', *manus*, which suggests behaviors relating to the treatment or handling of people.

> Upper class betterness is built on centuries of other people's work. It is built on land and industry maintained by other people, income and profits got at their expense. Most of those involved are well aware of this, and the feelings (understandably) are strong. Guilt and fear and ignorance on the part of those in power, anger and resentment on the part of the workers, threaten to burst forth at any minute. Under the circumstances, niceness is a very useful tool. It gives the upper classes some sort of camouflage to operate

> behind, at the same time as it aims to distract everyone else from
> what is actually going on. (see Christian McEwen's essay)

No wonder "niceness" makes Elliott want to spit. Who among us, knowing
that we are being "treated (or handled) with kid gloves," would willingly
cooperate in such an interaction? Yet, we often do just that, backing away
from interactions in which we sense some danger to our integrity.

Because "manners," understood as customs of treatment among people,
differ greatly from one culture to the next, the subject remains one of the
most difficult to talk about without getting angry, if only because the word
refers to a complex of behaviors, attitudes, and ways of speaking that are
freighted with social meanings and judgments. The related concept, *polite*
(and the abstract noun *politeness*), reveal other reasons for mistrusting the
systems of rules we learn for social behavior, speech, and other modes of
interaction. The adjective *polite* has two distinct, but interrelated, senses.
First, it denotes considerate and self-aware behavior toward others, *I mus-
tered my composure to make a* polite *response.* Second, the word can refer to the
entire code of behaviors common to the ruling class, understood to be
synonymous with words like *refined, polished,* and *elegant: She moved easily in*
polite *society.* This second sense, and the assumptions about customs of
behavior that it recognizes as "good," reflect the ethnocentricity of judgments about the customs of cultures different from one's own in which
words like *civilized, cultured, advanced,* and *enlightened* figure prominently and
contrast with negative terms like *uncivilized, barbaric, heathen. primitive, savage,*
and *unenlightened.* (Not too long ago, the word *unchristian* would have been
in the latter list, and served to justify religious and cultural imperialism in
Third World countries; currently, *undeveloped* and *underdeveloped* serve the same
purpose, without specifying the male agents who arrogantly assume it is
their "duty" to "develop," "civilize," and "enlighten" other cultures.) The
ethnocentricity of the ideas behind such words becomes obvious when we
notice that all of them require an implicit *standard* of behaviors to which
other people and cultures are unfavorably compared, and that *standard of
comparison* is the cultural mores of the speaker's society. There simply is no
way to define any of the words that reflect the speaker's ethnocentricity
without incorporating all his assumptions of superiority and "right" (often
labeled *duty* or *obligation,* i.e., the "white man's burden") to subjugate and
coerce those he deems his "inferiors." Without these assumptions, not a
one of these words would exist; they serve no honorable purpose.

Also derived from elitist assumptions of superiority is an entire set of
adjective pairs (and their related adverbs) that refer to social judgments
about "right" and "wrong" ways of behaving, and the use of any one of
them can make me froth at the mouth: *proper/improper, appropriate/inappropri-*

ate, acceptable/unacceptable, fitting/unfitting, becoming/unbecoming, seemly/unseemly, refined/unrefined, polished/unpolished, polite/impolite (not to mention *coarse, crude, and rude*). Raised in the South, and a tomboy, I was constantly admonished to "act like a lady," to "behave in ways appropriate to a young lady," or being informed that the things I liked to do and the ways I wanted to act were "unseemly in" or "unbecoming to" a young lady. I was told, "Be polite," "Don't be rude," "Say 'thank you' to the nice lady (or man)," and "Mind your manners, young lady!" "Show respect for your betters!" Whatever the particular social infraction of which I was judged guilty, the warning always ended with "young lady." I knew from the frequent repetition of such cautions that I was being groomed to become a "proper woman." It was a role to which I did not aspire.

Nevertheless, some of the training did penetrate my thick skull, or maybe I perceived *some* reasons for having and using "manners" in specific contexts. I was taught, for example, to treat anyone I interacted with with respect, to treat each person as I hoped she would treat me. I was taught not to call other people disparaging names like *nigger, kike, shrimp, chicken legs, mick, redskin, fatty, cracker, pimple face*, and *spic*, although I heard them on the playground daily. The one time I did experiment by using the word *nigger* in my mother's presence, she promptly washed my mouth out with soap. I was taught not to stare at other people, not to point at anyone else, and not to run in the house. All these ways of behaving I still practice, because I was also taught to "put myself in the other person's shoes." I don't like being called "fatty," "lezzie," or "cuntlapper." The respectful behaviors my mother taught me were grounded in a (hopefully) mutual agreement among people not to hurt each other. This has seemed a decent way to behave.

Manners labels many different kinds of behavior, some of which, like not calling other people insulting names, seem useful, and others that serve only to distinguish the owning classes and set them apart from those they perceive to be their "inferiors." Some behaviors, and the social judgments made of them, have more insidious uses and degrading outcomes, especially those involving how one eats and how one looks, which can cover everything from what one wears to how one's hair looks. What are called "table manners," those customs connected to eating rituals, include not slurping one's soup, not using the "wrong" fork, not eating "too fast," not talking with a mouthful of food or reaching across the table instead of asking someone to hand you what you want. Karen Chaney observes that "Table manners seem to evoke some of the ugliest class righteousness", yet eating habits vary widely between one culture and another and from region to region in the U.S. I was taught not to belch at the table (or anywhere else), but in some cultures belching demonstrates appreciation for the meal.

Elliott, addressing women of the owning classes as though they are the only ones who have "manners," describes their use in much the same way as Christian McEwen does, as ways to manipulate and control others:

> Manners are just the way you learned to identify each other and to brand outsiders. If, through your social skills and politeness, you have the ability to make any of us feel comfortable, realize that we know you also have the skills and tools to make us feel *uncomfortable* and that we've seen you use them in this way even if you don't think you ever have....

"Manners" are among the most variable and, therefore, volatile aspects of our behaviors that express class membership, but they are also part of our ethnic, racial, and regional heritages, and attributable to different standards of what is defined as "appropriate" for the two sexes. The stereotypes we learned represent the display of emotions as a behavior women can and do indulge in freely, whereas men are supposed to be impassive, stoic, and expressionless: women can cry, men aren't supposed to. Crying is a "sign of weakness," a feminine attribute, but men *do* cry; they're extremely "emotional." It's just that the kinds of things that make them cry for joy or despair are different from things that make women cry. Watch any televised sport. When the camera pans around the sidelines at the end of a game, you'll see the male players weeping openly if they've lost or waving their arms and jumping all over each other if they've won.

Because the ways we show our feelings are a complex of behaviors, deciding that only one factor, such as class, molded us, is erroneous. All of us learned "manners" as children; all of us have "manners." We differ in what we understand to be "good" or "bad" manners. Women raised in the underclasses, for example, often claim that the voice level they use for addressing others is a class trait, and that it's "middle-class" to perceive a raised voice as "hostile," "angry," or "threatening." J.P., speaking of her own way of using her vocal and gestural habits, says that she learned them from her family, but still perceives different expressive habits as originating in class:

> I come from a family that screams and uses broad hand movements when talking. I struggle every day to control my voice and my gestures in 'middle-class style' so I can be 'acceptable at work.'

Stereotypes that connect how we express ourselves to our class backgrounds are misleading. I doubt that the ways we express emotion are simply class-inherited, or that our "misunderstandings" about vocal expressiveness are "class differences." I think we learn how to express our emotions by watching how people around us express their emotions, and I think our expressive styles are conditioned by our race, ethnic group, the area of the U.S. we grew up in, and our sex. By observation, I learned from my mother not to yell or scream when I'm angry, even though we were underclass economically. I knew when my mother was very mad at me because she spoke to me in a very low, steely voice. When she lowered her voice, I knew I was going to get a spanking. Even as an adult, when someone says to me, in a low voice, "I want to talk to you," my intestines contract and my mouth gets dry because the delivery says, "You're in deep trouble." (Bosses use exactly the same style to terrorize employees.) What I learned from my mother about voice level and emotion in general was quiet and silence, not high volume. In that early home, we weren't demonstrative about emotions at all. I grew up in silence about my father's death, and so had no idea how to grieve my losses as an adult. I'm still unsure about expressing emotions, and I don't think I want to most of the time.

Language

The way we speak, our idiolect,[15] like our "manners," is a combination of several factors, of which class is but one, and most people subscribe to one or more of the stereotypes about differing dialects of English. There are two kinds of dialect, *social dialect* and *regional dialect*. "Regional" dialects include those identified with a specific region of the U.S., but also those of Britain, Australia, and Canada. "Social" dialects are those directly related to our class, but are also influenced by whether we grew up in a rural or urban environment. One of the pleasant surprises for me about putting together this anthology was how many contributors discussed language as a factor in their experiences of class, how attuned they were to how people reacted to their dialect, and critical of the common associations among dialect, education, and intelligence.

Each of us speaks a unique version of English (our idiolect) made up of linguistic elements learned, first, from family members, and then, second, overlaid by what we were taught about "proper English" during our schooling. In school, some effort is usually made to eradicate our native dialects,[16] but, however compliant we may be, many of us retain some elements of our "first" dialect. Some dialects are held in high esteem, others are interpreted as a sign of "ignorance," or, worse, "bigotry."[17] Our race, ethnic group, region, whether we were raised urban, suburban, or rural, in the South, Midwest, or North (within each region there are also numerous dialects; southern "accents" from the Louisiana bayous, south Georgia, and Tidewater Virginia differ quite distinctly), and our sex all contribute to our idiolects. The men who control the media in the U.S. continue to maintain that their audiences "prefer" to hear men's voices rather than women's because women speak with a "higher" pitch than men, but sociolinguists are still debating whether the pitch of our voices is a secondary sex characteristic or the result of social conditioning. To speak with any of the Southern dialects, whether one is African American or Caucasian, is to be dismissed as intellectually inferior, in spite of the fact that linguists demonstrated more than two decades ago that (what was then called) Black English has a grammar[18] of its own. Donna Allegra, discussing how often people told her that she didn't "sound African American," wryly comments:

> It was better to sound white. My dialect raised me a notch on the class rating scale. Consider the fact that I had no trouble identifying with Stephen Gordon when I read Radclyffe Hall's *The Well of Loneliness*... Didn't these people know that I was spiritually an upperclass British noblewoman who could fence, ride a horse and play tennis?

White Southerners, in contrast, aware that we speak what is called a "stigmatized" dialect, often perversely exaggerate it when we speak, because we think the way yankees react to our speech is funny. Elliott renders her mother's rural speech in a written approximation of her pronunciation and the rhythm of her delivery.

> Ya see, the pride in my mom's voice, the laughter of whoever was hearing the story, wasn't about defeating or upholding racism. Not that she didn't enjoy perpetuating hate with the openness learned from being herself very poor and not quite white enough—no middle class pretensions in her speech.

Our prejudices and responses to differences of idiolect and dialect are every bit as much prejudiced as our perceptions of others' behaviors. A British "accent" continues to represent to many U.S. citizens the prestige dialect, a dialect that bespeaks the privilege and power of the owning classes. Britons who've also lived in the U.S. become acutely aware of their dialect and its social meanings.

> Because we spoke with the 'right' accent, we were special, more than special, we were better, we were best....When I first came back to Britain for my brother's funeral, I was bombarded with information about class. I doubt, now, that it would strike me quite so forcibly. But returning, easy and anonymous, from the United States, I saw it plain in everyone I met: class, and the nervous knowledge of their place on the social scale, where they belonged, or were thought to belong. Accent in particular assumed extraordinary importance. My own, university-educated, upper class, made me immediately acceptable in some circles, while in others it set me on a razor edge of disapproval. It was no longer just a 'pretty

English accent.' It had a power and an identity of its own. (see Christian McEwen's essay)

As Christian McEwen says, our dialect may gain us immediate entry into places otherwise "off limits" to us or, in a different group, instantly arouse hostility and disapproval. Speaking a prestige dialect is interpreted in politically "radical" circles in the U.S. as affected and pretentious, as Anna Livia reports:

> At Berkeley my English accent gets there first and imposes the interpretation: English therefore wealthy and well-read....It never matters what I have said; the point is that I said it in an English accent and that is against all the downwardly-mobile ethics of the radical community.

Similarly, those of us who grew up speaking (what we were told was) a "substandard" dialect are distrustful of those who speak "standard" English.

> it was painful to be told that wimin didn't trust me because i spoke in a precise way, with school-perfect grammar. (see zana's essay)

We are equally as sensitive to (well-meaning) efforts to "correct" either our speech or our writing. In fact, those of us who speak or write in any of the alleged "substandard" dialects can become downright huffy if someone is ignorant and presumptuous enough to "correct" us.

> Since I came out I've written about all kinds of wonderful and horrible things, but almost nothing about my birth culture and even less about the moments of shock, confusion, embarrassment and shame that too often surround me in my now mainly middle class world. The stories I have to tell don't fit on a page because the language isn't right, forced into Standard spelling and constructions or mangled by the apostrophes and quotation marks that scream, 'Warning! Substandard dialect ahead!' and if I leave these little marks of deviance out, some well-meaning editor—lover, friend or stranger—is bound to put them in, assuming, I spose, that I don't know what I meant to do, and even if this doesn't happen the written form is still only an approximation of real talk, anyhow. (see Elliott's essay, Funeral Food)

In fact, what is presented to us as "standard" English in the public schools was originally intended to create a uniform dialect for *writing*, especially to promote one way of spelling words, something that seemed necessary after the invention of the printing press. In the U.S., where feelings of cultural inferiority seem entrenched and we are known throughout the English-speaking world as the most *conservative* speakers of English, retaining speech characteristics dropped centuries ago by the British, we continue to *believe* that speaking "standard" English makes one "better" than someone else *and* that ways of speaking indicate one's intelligence.

To top it off, they [members of the lower classes] are looked down upon and blamed for being 'stupid,' 'ignorant,' and 'low-life.' The poor person who can acquire the mainstream fashions of knowledge and demonstrate intelligence in a manner that the privileged can recognize as their own has an advantage over those who use 'bad grammar' and 'non-standard' English, i. e., the manner of the ruling class being the standard.(see Donna Allegra's essay)

After almost a century of linguistics as a scholarly discipline, and efforts by linguists to convince English teachers that all dialects of English should be valued equally, English teachers persist in teaching that there is one "true and good" dialect and all others are sub- or nonstandard, with the result that people in the U.S. don't know much about language in general and English, in particular. The intellectually pretentious will quickly rally around any John Simon, William Safire, or Edwin Newman[19] who raises the cry that "English is dying" and it's the "unwashed masses" who're "killing" it, and people who speak dialects of the underclasses still apologize for "not talking right." The irony here is that most of us who speak nonstandard dialects often make more of an effort to talk "correctly" because we believe our language use is "nonstandard," while all those persnickety folks sit mesmerized in front of their TVs listening to everyone standing in front of a camera gabble on in nonsentences and nonsense. (If anything, English, in all its varieties, is alive and well; it has become, through imperialism and colonialism, a "world language," because it's used all over the world to conduct business.)

How we interpret the social significance of the ways we speak, like our social behaviors, is something we have to renegotiate. We must put aside much of what our teachers told us about "standard" and "nonstandard" varieties of English, abandon the stereotypes of ourselves and others that we learned, including the demeaning stereotypes and judgments passed on our dialects, and claim the features of our speech habits that make up the diverse and unique range of dialects in the language. English is, indeed, a "various language."

Intelligence

"Who is the agent in the statement 'A mind is a terrible thing to waste'?" (Pat Dean)

If grading contributions to this anthology were an appropriate thing to do—and it's not, and I didn't—then Pat Dean, a woman who possesses the contrary, brilliant sort of mind not given to conformity, would have flunked, because she ended up sending me what amounted to two manuscript pages of questions about the relationship(s) we assume to hold among class, mobility, education, and intelligence . Worse (or better, depending on your point of view), she didn't suggest any answers to her questions, but asking the questions is the first step to finding answers. I recommend thoughtful consideration of the difficulties her questions raise, because, although we use the word *intelligence* every day as though we know what it means to "be" intelligent or "have" intelligence, the object(s) to which the word is assumed to refer are still not understood, and the definitions we have of the phenomenon are culturally loaded.

We have known for years that the IQ tests we took as children were culturally biased. That is, implicit in the kinds of "intelligence" the tests were constructed to identify was middle-class, Caucasian cultural information. Because what was defined as "intelligence" was narrowly construed, the tests failed to measure the intelligence of underclass people and of oppressed racial and ethnic groups. Combined with language barriers—for many children in the U.S., English is *not* the language spoken in their homes—this limited concept of "intelligence" is has done untold damage to the capacity to aspire in children who belong to marginalized groups.

In the public schools, teachers and students alike labor under the assumption that talking about intelligence, *as it is conventionally understood*, is acceptable, and help to perpetuate the myth that "intelligence," coupled with diligence, will be rewarded by the elite of U.S. society. When we're in elementary school, we're actually taught that being "smart" is a "good thing." At least this was true for me, and for Donna Allegra.

> Intelligence is universally admired in and of itself. We somehow believe that intelligence is an attribute of the upper classes, 'our betters.'

Because of the assumed connection between succeeding, wealth, and intelligence, those of us born into an underclass believe that our "intelligence," whatever that is, will gain us entry into the owning classes.

> I expected to be an American-dream success. I was smart, i.e., I got good grades in school and I was well-behaved. In my family, we took pride in our intelligence. We saw this as something that made us better than the rest of the class. Points *up* on the scale....I can now admit that I consciously wanted to be in a higher class than I lived. I aspired to be able to claim superiority on the basis of my intelligence, by being smarter than other people. (see Donna Allegra's essay)

We were both in for a rude shock, and, as Pat Dean's questions imply, one important factor in the social valuing of our intelligences was the fact that we were born girls. Because we were female, we just weren't supposed to be able to think. Yet, Donna and I were fortunate to have relatives and teachers who encouraged us to develop our minds.

Early in the first grade, a good teacher guessed that I could read well beyond my age level and took the time one day to have me read through all the "Dick and Jane" books for that grade, while my bored classmates sat idle. When I'd successfully completed all the books, she made arrangements for me to spend reading time in the school's library.

Unlike Donna, though, I didn't find that intelligence was "universally admired." I don't know whether being of different races or born in different times, or both, accounts for our contrasting experiences. In fact, what I discovered was that my chronological peers, up through high school, disdained intelligence. Back in the '40s and '50s we didn't have names like *nerd* and *geek*, but I was called an "egghead" frequently, and it was intended as an insult. (Perhaps the proliferation of disparaging names for intelligent people is connected to the times in which we live.)

The "special" treatment I received in the first grade greatly increased the harassment and violence I got from my male classmates and ensured my exclusion from the companionship of other girls. I can remember being stoned on the playground during the first grade because of the special shoes I had to wear. The more I tried to "blend in," to be and act "just like" other kids, the more aware I became of my difference. My intelligence, at least what my teacher identified as my intelligence, became a hazard, and I grew to fear recess. What for other children was an anticipated time for playing and developing friendships became, for me, a time of violence and dread. I hid in the bushes hoping that no one would find me.

As I grew up, it became clearer and clearer to me how different I was from other children, I became more and more of a loner, and I spent my Saturdays at the huge public library in Miami's Biscayne Park. This haven became increasingly more difficult to enjoy as I grew older and my stepfather accused me of going to the park to pick up men! Well, I wasn't "just" going there to read. He was right about that. I roamed the library and the park hoping some woman would notice and befriend me. Although I'd known the mechanics of heterosexual intercourse since I was nine, I still had only very vague ideas about how women might be sexually intimate with each other. But I daydreamed about holding hands and snuggling with women. Even the sensuality of kissing was unimaginable to me; I'd only kissed my great-grandmother, my grandmother, and my mother. I was smart, maybe, but I was also very naive in social ways.

Like Donna Allegra, I was identified (in the sixth grade) as being exceptionally bright, and I quickly learned that this gave me not only an improved status among the teachers but also earned increased "privileges" for me, in spite of the hostility of my classmates. My IQ score and a propensity for being disruptive when I was bored finally got me skipped a grade.

> I've been told that I am being moved from seventh to eighth grade. In the principal's office, a woman has given me my student file and I am told to take it to my new eighth-grade teacher. But I detour and go out to one of the portables[20] where I quickly read it, and discover that one of my teachers has written: 'Mother allows child to run the streets.' When I tell my mother about this, she becomes furious and goes down to the school to "set them right." I don't understand why she's so angry, but I'm excited that she's going to go down to the school and give 'em hell. The principal is furious with the woman who gave me my file in the first place. No students were supposed to find out what had been written about them by teachers and administrators. I am smug: I not only got to read what the adults at the school thought about me and my mother, I also know what my IQ is.

Looking back at this event, I am ambivalent. I am glad I got to skip a grade because it got me out of the public schools a year early, but I'm not sure it was an entirely "good" thing because it thrust me into association with children who were already entering adolescence. Although I had begun to menstruate, trying to befriend girls who were becoming "boy crazy" heightened my awareness that I was "different." I had no interest in boys, and *lots* of interest in the girls. I didn't understand my mother's fury about what teachers had written in my file until just a few months ago.

As long as I've pondered intelligence and the issues it's raised in my own life, I still have only some partial answers to the questions Pat Dean asks. I believe, for example, that women's intelligence has nothing to do with the class into which we're born, but I know for certain that the values about education held by the family that rears us profoundly affect the development of our native intelligence and whether or not we get opportunities to exercise it. If someone took the time to read to us when we were children, we're likely to talk earlier than other children and to have linguistic skills beyond our chronological age. If we're raised with books around us, we're likely to read for pleasure. Our first environments establish our values and whether or not we'll dare to dream beyond our immediate horizons.

Money, too, determines our intelligence. Adequate nutrition, for example, is crucial to the child's developing brain; poor nutrition damages our capacity to think. If our mothers smoked, drank, or took drugs (prescription or otherwise) while they were carrying us, we may be born with portions of our brains destroyed or malformed. I've been convinced for years that all of us born in modern hospitals with medical doctors delivering us suffer varying degrees of brain damage caused by the doctor's inept use of the metal clamps they use to pull our heads out of the birth canal. By holding the clamps too tightly against our temples, they mash our still soft skulls and, probably, some proportion of our growing brain cells are killed as a result. Diseases of childhood can also result in brain damage, and adequate medical care when we need it is often critical. Finally, of course, money is often the deciding factor in whether or not we can finish high school, or hope to attend college, and it certainly determines which colleges and universities we are able to attend.

In another world, in some different time, Pat Dean's questions might be meaningless. Because we live in a patriarchal society, thinking about her questions and trying to answer them in nonpatriarchal ways is one method of reconceiving women's intelligence and what it means to each of us. There is no direct correlation between, for example, being a "powerful woman" and an "intelligent woman." Class plays a large part in whether an intelligent woman becomes powerful. Women who are powerful in patriarchal terms, like men, are often not the most intelligent of their generation. Here, too, class determines one's access to power, and so the few women who do manage to grab some power from men aren't necessarily the brightest or the best of a generation, but they may be very cunning and adept at playing patriarchal power games and so succeed (in terms they understand). However we frame our questions about our intelligence, whether or not we are able to educate ourselves and whether we manage to attend "prestigious," i.e., expensive, schools determines the ways we'll be able to use our intelligence. A single mother living on welfare who dropped out of school will use her intelligence to figure out how she can survive while trying to raise her child or children without any of the skills she needs to earn a livable wage. How we use our brains is limited to the realms in which we can exercise it.

Education

Many, but not all, of the contributors to this anthology have bachelor's degrees, and several, like myself, have graduate degrees. Others are still working on advanced degrees.

> For years, my mother carefully saved the money she received from my father's social security in what she called my "college fund." I was to be the first person in my family to go to college. My

mother has told me that she married my stepfather so that she could be sure there was money for me to get a university education. But my stepfather helped himself to a chunk of my money so he could buy a fishing boat. In the fall of 1958 I went off to college, not to Middlebury to study languages, or Barnard (to study lesbians in Greenwich Village), as I'd hoped, but to Florida State University[21] (FSU) in Tallahassee, where I supplemented what my mother could send me by working as an "assistant" in the Department of Modern Languages. For the $400. a year that I earned typing up exams and class handouts, I had to promise to teach a specific period of time in the Florida public school system.

Then, my identity as a "known" lesbian brought my days at FSU to an abrupt end.

The work, and my promise, ended abruptly in the spring of 1959 when I and my gay friends returned to Tallahassee after Spring vacation. While we'd frolicked and partied in Miami, Charlie Johns and his investigating committee on Communism and homosexuality had set up shop in the town of Tallahassee because the administrators at FSU had refused to give him access to student and faculty files. To make a long story short, the Dean of Women offered to let me continue my studies at FSU with certain conditions: I was to see a school psychiatrist once a week; she would choose my roommates for me to make sure that none of my roommates were "susceptible" to my "disease." Or, she suggested, I could transfer to another school for a year, like the University of Miami, where she knew the Dean of Women, giving her an opportunity to erase the word homosexual from my student file. Then I could return to FSU and begin anew, as though nothing had happened.

In the fall of 1959, I was supposed to be living with my mother and stepfather. That had been the agreement with the Dean of Women at the University of Miami that got me admitted. As a known, and now "officially" recognized lesbian, I couldn't (after all!) expect to live in the women's dorms, where I might "corrupt" other girls. After eight weeks at the University of Miami, I was kicked out for living off-campus (I wasn't twenty-one and so was too young to live in my own apartment.) Ironically, my illegal housing situation was brought to the attention of the University by a woman who lived across the hall from me. She reported me to them because I had "men sleeping in my apartment."[22] The Dean of Women called me in to find out why I wasn't living at home. I explained that my stepfather had kicked me out of "his" house and I couldn't go back, so she called my mother in to make sure that what I'd told her was true. Having ascertained for herself that I was telling the truth, she took my case to the board of regents to try and convince them to make an exception so that I could remain at the University. They refused. When she called me in to tell me about their decision, she took the opportunity to inform me that I had a "good mind," and that it was my "duty" to use it for the "good of society." I responded to her assertion by asking if I had any "duty" to use my mind for the improvement of the very society that denied me the right to be who I was. She said "yes." And I then told her that it was my mind, and if I decided to use it for anyone's "good," it would be on my terms, not theirs.

After that, I tried to enroll in UCLA and Georgia State (in Atlanta) but was denied admission because I still didn't believe that I had to lie about being a lesbian. Eventually, I ended up moving to New York City so I could attend The City College of New York (where I did, finally, have the sense to lie).[23]

The City University of New York has graduated several well-known lesbian writers, and other contributors to this anthology earned bachelor's degrees because of New York's city colleges.

Because I did well in school, it was always assumed by my parents, my teachers and myself that I would go to college. When the time came, there was no discussion as to which university I would go to. When I graduated from high school the City University of New York charged no tuition. I went to Queens College,...(see J. P.'s essay)

I believe that, for several contributors, our self-confidence and our belief that we are intelligent, competent, and deserving of being heard is connected to whether or not we have gone beyond a high school education. Chrystos, for example, expresses her fears about being listened to, about whether others will pay attention to her words.

I carry the scars of an under class child: fear that I'm not smart enough to write this; that I won't 'talk right' & thus be judged negatively; that nothing I have to say will mean anything to anyone or is important in a general sense. This is despite the fact that I am better read than many college professors I meet. Immediately, I realize that the 'correct' phrase is 'more well read.' The very structures of language have a class system and I am acutely aware that I use 'big words' to convey the inadequacy I feel because I do not have a good education.. . .In becoming an intellectual, in order to be taken seriously as a writer, I feel I have betrayed my originating class, as well as my ethnic group of First Nations people, who also do not speak in this way. Writing is a constant class struggle of translation. This lack of self-esteem and confidence to 'take space' is the most clear class division I sense in my relationships with over class Lesbians, even though I am seen as a very confident woman.

Somehow, knowing that she is smart, self-educated, and a poet doesn't begin to erase the negative messages she gets from others or contradict her sense that she's betrayed her class and First Nations origins. As she says, Chrystos carries "scars."

Not only are our values and attitudes toward books and education learned in our first environments, but we also carry within us the stereotypes that we learned there about which ethnic and racial groups prioritize education for their offpsring. Jewish families are often held up as people who treasure books and education, but they aren't the only ones for whom education is important, nor is the stereotype necessarily accurate. Joan Schuman and Felice Yeskel have very different perspectives on the stereotype and its affects.

> *My understanding for a long time included other ideas about Jews: that they were educated and determined to send their kids to college; that learning was an important part of life; that books lined every Jew's house. These were stereotypes that lived within me as much as the ones about the non-existence of working-class Jews.* (see Joan Schuman's essay)

> Some Jewish values, such as the emphasis on education, are similar to middle-class values. This can make things quite confusing for poor and working-class Jews who may share values with middle-class folks, while having vastly different access. (see Felice Yeskel's essay)

Both Helen Elaine Lee and Jackie Anderson recall the importance of being raised in families in which books and knowledge were highly valued. Their experiences contradict the racist stereotypes of African Americans as disinterested in education. Terri de la Pena describes how her own aspirations differed from her parents' expectations, "college was a foreign concept," and also separated her from her Chicanita friends:

> As one of the 'St. Anne's brains,' I wound up in college prep, though my parents insisted I take business courses, too; neither of my parents had finished high school, and they expected their children to find jobs, not attend college. I had never even known a college graduate; to me, college was a foreign concept. Yet, having spent so much time reading on my own, I became excited about being in classes with other 'smart' kids, but I also felt cut off from my long-time Chicanita friends.

Public and private schools, colleges and universities, primary sites of socialization, instill sexist and racist values in children, thereby fostering the internalized self-hatred through which we perceive the behaviors of women around us, and we often express our devalued selves by judging them as we know we have been judged. J.P., a Jewish contributor, describes her own feelings of "distaste" for her middle-class Jewish classmates:

...I had a particularly great distaste for the middle-class Jewish women students at Queens. They did not take their studies seriously, chased boys and used their daddy's charge cards. They appeared lazy and pampered... While I realize now that the term JAP (Jewish American Princess) is a racist, sexist and anti-Semitic term, I cannot accurately recount my college years without recalling that I used this term to describe these women....I did not understand that the material avarice of these students was an expression of their parents' deprived childhood.

I can guess how the thinking that stereotypes the owning classes as "intelligent" and the underclasses as "stupid" came to seem so plausible. Also associated with the owning classes is the ability, the resources, to finish high school (because they don't need to quit school to go to work to help support their families), and go to college, because going to college often requires the financial support of one's family. But the rich aren't the only ones who go to college; often, the financial cost of "getting an education" depends on the school. The wealthy may attend expensive private schools like Harvard or Yale, Smith or Wellesley, but many people from the underclasses find ways to get an education. Several of the contributors to this anthology worked their way through college or obtained full scholarships. And it hasn't always been true that people had to go to high school or college to be "educated." What happened to the phrase "self-educated"? Many people continue to read and learn, to acquire new knowledge, without feeling the necessity to pass a grade, or a test, or have someone hand them a piece of paper.

> My grandfather worked for Railway Mail and was quite literate. He was also quite vocal. Every Wednesday night he wrote letters to newspapers letting them know what he thought about world events, political machinations, and goings-on in the sports world. My mother and father were very proud that they'd finished high school, and were what is now (disparagingly) called "upwardly mobile." My father taught me to read. On Sunday afternoons he'd get down on the floor with me, spread out the funny papers, and tell me to go and get the huge Webster's dictionary. Then he'd point to a word, ask me what it meant, and tell me to pronounce it. By the time I was four, he'd also taught me to count, tell time, and write my name.
>
> I don't remember a time growing up when it was not assumed that I would go to college. Even after the death of my father, I was told that I was going to college.

Equating one's degrees and the language one speaks with social class or access to wealth is to mindlessly accept the assumptions of prevalent stereotypes, but I cannot ignore the role that early environment plays in our capacity to envision a life for ourselves that's better than that of the people who raise us. Often what is required is the encouragement of a teacher or a minister who perceives our potential, plants within our minds the desire to learn, and explains to us how we can realize our dreams. Whatever our achievements, those of us from the underclasses who did manage to get university papers are often ambivalent about the meaning of our accomplishment.

> I have come to feel undergraduate education in the United States primarily serves a socialization function, where those of us from non-formally educated backgrounds learn what to say and what not to say, what to keep quiet about our lives and desires, how to pass as educated, as someone not shameful. (see Karen Chaney's essay)

How deeply enmeshed in our senses of self we feel this intertwining of our worth, the way we speak and write, our intelligence and, hence, our "significance" in the world, and education is frequently mentioned by contributors. Elliott, for example, points out how often women and lesbians use the field we're studying, our degrees, or the getting of them as a means of identifying ourselves.

> At a Young Separatist/Young Radical Feminist Lesbian conference in 1990, we went around the room introducing ourselves. One of the first dykes talked about where she was in college and what she was doing there and everyone after her did the same. Partway around one dyke spoke out about how identifying ourselves by our educations was really elitist and made her uncomfortable and sad.

Yet, for underclass women to take pride in our achievements is not a categorically "bad thing," and it isn't inherently elitist to be proud of having worked hard for something, whether it's a college degree or owning a business.

At least one aspect of our ambivalent attitude toward "higher" education is its association with the owning classes and, specifically, the middle classes. "Having" an education is often described as if it were the sole possession of the middle classes. Helen, interviewed by Jessica Robbins, makes this equation unambiguously, at the same time acknowledging that colleges and universities are about the only institutions where we find any kind of teaching that goes beyond the social programming that characterizes most of what's called "education" in the U.S.:

> When you have middle class life, you have academia. In that setting, you have the liberty that you don't have anywhere else to be very challenging with thinking and ideas, and from that there's always generated tremendously liberating ideas. Always... .in the academic setting you have the generation of challenging, radical ideas that come from every fucking university community across

the world and across history. So yeah—valuable shit comes out of that class. But when you put it all together, it's still real messy.

Any discussion of class is going to be "messy" because the stereotypes we accept of social and economic class membership and our own feelings, which originate in our own experiences, become so confused that gaining any sort of perspective is difficult, if not impossible. The fact remains that women of the owning *and* underclasses succeed in graduating from colleges and universities. What separates us are two things: Whether we were encouraged, even pushed, to continue our education as far as we were able, and how good the schools were we could go to. The elite colleges and universities, such as the Ivy League schools and small liberal arts colleges, are usually (but not always) open only to the owning classes, because of their cost, if nothing else. Underclass students seeking degrees beyond high school most often end up at state universities or junior colleges. The places where we get our college degrees brand us as surely as our clothes. Like automobiles, the most prestigious degrees are, generally, those that cost the most, so students who can't attend a 'good'(read: expensive) school are still perceived to be "inferior," no matter how hard we worked to attain our goal or how good the school is. (Many state universities provide excellent educations, but only a few are rated among the best)

Many factors, such as the post-World War II "baby boom" and grade inflation, have recently made a college education a "waste of time" (if one perceives it as only a means to get a certain kind of job), and college graduates are finding that there are no white-collar or professional jobs waiting for them and end up working as cashiers, clerks, and at other blue-collar jobs. Still, many of us from the underclasses have earned college degrees, whether they enabled us to "move on up" or not, and it seems not only wrong, but needlessly cruel, to assume that a woman or lesbian who has one or more degrees is, by definition, of the owning classes and then to punish her for that accomplishment. At what point in and about which aspects of our lives are we "allowed" to feel good about who we are and what we've done? Must we always apologize to someone for our dreams?

> I too am middle class, by education and aspiration though not by wealth, access to wealth or expectation of inherited wealth. (see Anna Livia's essay)

When are our pain and scars "enough" to qualify us as persons worthy of respect? When will we be able to stop apologizing to anyone for the choices we've made?

GEOGRAPHIES

There are other aspects of our lives that reveal (expose?) our class, some of them, I think, more clear-cut than those I've chosen to talk about. The kinds of things we laugh at, the kind of healthcare we've had during our lives, the music that makes us feel good and the music that "irritates" us, even how we feel about our bodies, whether or not we listen to National Public Radio, all these "personal tastes" can be related to our class origins. For some reason, our teeth seem to be one part of our bodies that we associate closely with class, financial resources, and access to healthcare when we need it.

> So I keep my mouth shut, for my mouth is of one the places I carry evidence of my poverty.(see Lee Evans' essay)

> Over the years, I realized that attitudes and behavior were important associations with regard to class, and so, as I suspected, was education; but the most important factor of all was having money! Also, this having or not having of money, I discovered, was very much associated with having or not having teeth....Teeth are expensive to maintain, cheaper to lose, expensive to replace....Somehow, as I lost my teeth, I felt as though my Jewish ethnicity as well as my middle-classness was being threatened. (see Merril Mushroom's essay)

Even our ability to withstand physical pain may be connected to our class, as zana suggests:

> one of the hardest realizations for me has been that many wimin from poor or working class backgrounds push beyond pain and fatigue in ways i don't. i grew up getting medical care for physical problems.

Our appearance, especially the clothing we wear, can be interpreted as external evidence of class membership, and Joan Schuman, Debbie Alicen, and Pam McMichael discuss the social significance of the clothes one does (or doesn't) wear. But at least some of our differences in the way we dress and value clothing may be attributable to racial, ethnic, and age differences as well as economic resources.

> ...[among African American lesbians] I do find that dressing fashionably and acting 'correctly' are highly valued. (see Jackie Anderson's essay)

What I am calling "geographies" is a complicated mix of experiences, and our interpretations of them—our cultural and racial origins, the language we speak and our fluency, how we speak and how often, the topography of the country, region, place, address where we were born, how we experience, understand, and use space and time and money, our aspirations and disappointments, the things we have believed and found to be lies or misrepresentations—all the things that make us who we are and make up what some would call our "mind," and others would call our "personality" or "character."

From time to time, there have been literary critics who have made the connection between a writer's work and the country or region where she (or he) lived, and feminist theoreticians are talking about a "politics of location" as one way of accommodating women's diversities. I mean something less abstract, more (literally) *grounded* when I use the term *geographies*. To the best of my knowledge, the scholar whose work comes closest to what I'm getting at is Annette Kolodny, who wrote two books analyzing how North America was experienced and described by early Caucasian settlers. In the first book, called *The Lay of the Land: Metaphor as Experience and History in American Life and Letters* (1975), Kolodny used metaphorical descriptions from men's writings to show that they viewed and treated the land as if it were female, what she calls the "land-as-woman" metaphor. That metaphor, translated as experience for those men, left no perceptual place for women in the myth of westward "expansion." In her second book, *The Land Before Her: Fantasy and Experience of the American Frontiers, 1630-1860* (1984), she used three centuries of women's writings to show how they perceived themselves *in relation to* the unfamiliar geographies of the west, imagining them to be "gardens to be cultivated."

But I mean something even less abstract, a point (or range of points) located both in space and time, the intersection of those points at which we imagine ourselves to stand and the place from which we imagine ourselves to speak. These "geographies" (or "topographies") include how we experience wind or windlessness, how we perceive the horizon or are unaware of it, how we conceive of space, of being "crowded" or "isolated," and those points in time we use as references. In our minds, do we stand in relation to the past, the present, or the future or some combination of them? One can describe herself as "isolated" living in the hills of Tennessee or the Castro District of San Francisco. Likewise, one can feel herself to be part of a network of relationships wherever she presently dwells.

Space

In the U.S., we are born north or south of the Mason-Dixon Line; we live east or west of the Rockies or the Mississippi River; maybe we've never seen an ocean or mountains or the Great Salt Lake or White Sands. These continental features and our consciousness of them become features of who we are. Some readers may be familiar with a joke map of the way people living in New York City perceive the rest of the United States: The five boroughs are oversize with respect to the rest of the country, and everything west of the Hudson River becomes smaller and smaller, and more and more squished together, the further west one goes from New York City.

The "locations" of which I speak construct our perspectives and the "directions" in which we gaze. Many, on first visiting the Midwest, report how the sheer breadth of the horizon terrifies them because they are accustomed to the "cozy" landscape created by the forested, eroded Eastern mountains in which one can only see beyond the trees from the top of a mountain. Others, like myself, are initially conscious of the constant, driving wind that comes off the eastern slopes of the Rockies, sweeps across the Great Plains, but then is interrupted, muted, by the palisades that form the eastern shore of the Mississippi River. It is a wind that stops only before a violent storm breaks. It is a region perceived by "coastal chauvinists" as a cultural "wasteland."

The "urban experience" differs radically from rural experiences, from one coast to the other, and on either side of the Mason-Dixon Line. I recall walking along Broadway with a New York City friend one night: She looked up past the tall buildings into the starry sky and said, "Isn't the ceiling beautiful tonight?" For those raised in an urban environment, those who may never have been outside of a city, the sky itself, rarely seen without obstruction, is another "ceiling," a roof. Susan Wolfe recalls her realization that sharing an urban background determined the kinds of speakers in books she could or could not identify with:

> One day, in the middle of class, I suddenly realized that I was able to identify with many stories because they were set in urban poverty, and realized, too, that my inability to identify with characters in my elementary-school readers was due to their setting— middle-class suburbia—...

We aren't always conscious of location, its relativity to other locations, or the ways it structures others' perceptions of us:

> I was 27 and in grad school before it clearly dawned on me that where I grew up is what is called "rural." After all, I was clearly a townie in the city kid/country kid split in school, and Waverly is the second largest town in Morgan County, with more than 1,500 people. I don't find my shock of realization charming or quaint.(see Elliott's essay, Funeral Food)

Terri de la Peña provides a detailed map of the streets of Santa Monica where she grew up and describes the social and economic *meaning* of specific locations. In doing so, she tells us how we can "locate" the place from which she speaks.

> [Santa Monica's] wealthier inhabitants lived north of Wilshire Boulevard, its middle-to-working class occupied the area roughly between Wilshire and Olympic Boulevards, and its poorer neighborhoods were south of Olympic Boulevard. Through a Depression foreclosure sale, my thrifty parents and maternal grandmother jointly purchased a lot with a two-bedroom home on the corner of 15th Street and Broadway, a couple of blocks north of Olympic, a few blocks south of Wilshire. Owning property was a major accomplishment for my immigrant mother and grandmother, and for my father whose familial roots were sunk deep within Santa Monica soil. I grew up in a neighborhood away from most of my Mexican-American classmates.

We occupy another kind of physical space in our minds—home—a figurative one based on whatever dwellings we've identified that way. For Christian McEwen, the family home that figures so prominently in her narrative is an integral part of her identity. For J.P., her class identities conflict, creating in her a sense of "homelessness":

> My class position remains fragile and this position gives me the sense of being nowhere at home.

Time

Time, and the ways we think of it, is the other significant structural element of our life maps. Time, like space, is often spoken of as though it were a "resource," or a space containing relationships and boundaries in the metaphors we use to place ourselves in time. Some of us "waste our time" or "invest time"; we "spend time" at the beach, at work, reading, exercising; we think of time as "coming," "going," "passing by," or "arriving," as though we stand at a point *in* time which moves toward or away from us. "Having time" is directly related to our class identification, as though it were quantifiable. Christian McEwen recalls how upperclass privilege provided her and her siblings with ample space and time for exploration:

> …there's no doubt that we were privileged. We grew up with space around us, both physical and mental. Arriving home for the holidays, our time was marvelously our own. Everything was done for us:…There was time…to investigate new things, to make experiments, and encouragement to do so.

Pam McMichael describes her difficulty imagining a life in which each day was a span of uncommitted time she could decide how to "use." She wonders how it "feels."

> ...I sometimes resent her [a friend] control of her time and free-
> dom. I cannot imagine the ability to choose exactly what she
> wants to do with her day, every day. I can't fathom 'not having to
> work.' I would love to know how it feels.

And Juana Maria Gonzalez Paz discusses how she resented the assumption that, because she lived on welfare, she had lots of "free time."

> One of the biggest obstacles to achieving my full potential is
> people's continued presumption that I am not working and my
> time is available,...

All of these geographical elements—continent, country, region, city,
town, or farm, neighborhood, street, and dwelling—along with how we
think of time, combine to create our individual maps, to make us as we
know ourselves and show ourselves to be. They define where we imagine
ourselves to *stand*, both in relation to the earth beneath our feet, in a
terrestrial time/space, and to the sky above us, the universe in which our
planet travels. The constellations we know and can see at night are determined by where we happen to be on earth. In a 1992 issue of *Bridges*,
Aurora Levins Morales described a quilt made by an African American
woman that was displayed at the Oakland Museum. The woman "had
embroidered the constellations as seen from her front porch, then quilted
in each field of the plantation with the lines of plowing to show the
contours of the hills." For Aurora Levins Morales, the quilt was that African American woman's "view, a map of the place where she had lived her
life."[24] Each of our minds is, I believe, just such a map, one with coordi-
nates and latitudes, temporal dimensions, and constellations, which identifies the "place from which we speak," and, when we say we've "found"
our voice, we mean that we are aware of our location in space/time and
how it structures our "meaning" with respect to the worlds of other people.
Our internal worlds map differences as much as similarities. Karen Chaney
contrasts the pace of her implicit world with the competitive worlds she
rejected:

> ...the thought of moving back into these worlds [professional or
> intellectual], where the dominant mode of interaction is compe-
> tition, the primary value achievement, the pace quicker, and the
> people mostly from privileged backgrounds, feels usually beyond
> my capacity—or interest—to sustain.

Terri de la Peña describes how anglos are unaware of the worlds of
others, assuming that theirs is the only "world," and her ability to "world"-
travel (as María Lugones has described it)[25]:

They [Caucasians] do not realize that, unlike them, I have the ability by virtue of my background to move back and forth between the workingclass ethnic world and not only the everyday working world of the university, but beyond it to the literary community.

I think each of us has a map, more or less distorted, of the world beyond our own "boundaries," which describes the space and the time we imagine other people to occupy. It is the elaboration and detail of our individual maps that increases as we grow in awareness of how the maps of other people differ from our own, and I'm suggesting that our sense of our own "boundaries" gradually becomes an internalized, taken-for-granted, universe in which we imagine ourselves to move.

Class, then, is more than economic status; it is also about the special boundaries we keep. (see Bonnie J. Morris' essay)

Our map, and the boundaries it assumes, is the central metaphor that structures our consciousness; it underlies our sense of being "marginalized," that is, pushed out to the blank, unattended spaces of *someone else's* page. Anna Livia describes this awareness:

Because I grew up along the margins of what was then white-dominated society, it is my experience that people who are assumed to have money are treated with more interest, consideration and respect than those who are known to have none. One learns these things, one never mentions them, but one acts on them just the same. (see Anna Livia's essay)

When we try to talk to each other about "class," our "worlds collide," and, in the resulting confusion of speech and preconception, we split and fragment. We may never reach anything like Christian McEwen's vision of a place and time in which translation is never necessary. But we can develop our awareness of the worlds occupied by others and compile atlases of our geographies. Our first attempts to chart our worlds has been, and will continue to be, as crude as the efforts of the first mapmakers, but we can add details as we perceive them more clearly. As we map the limits and scope of the worlds we inhabit, class is an axis of orientation we must explore in great detail in the course of this collaboration of understanding.

Julia Penelope
July 1994

FOOTNOTES

[1] Readers need to know that the feminist group Felice Yeskel describes is a mixed group of lesbians and nonlesbians. Regardless of individual sexualities, I think the observations of participants in the cost sharing group, quoted throughout Felice Yeskel's article, are relevant to the class experiences of other women.

[2] Several contributors to this anthology say that we need a new vocabulary, new terms, if we are to describe women's experiences of class. In her essay, Chrystos suggests using the terms *overclass* and *under class*; Nett Hart suggests that we create a new vocabulary for talking about class, and Fox and Linnea Johnson discuss at length why terms borrowed from Marxism don't apply to women's experiences of class in the U.S. For the purposes of my introduction, I've chosen to refer to the "owning classes," which includes the more familiar middle, upper middle, and upper classes, and I use "underclasses" to refer to the homeless, the poor, and the working class.

[3] I spent decades of my life in silence about my feelings of anger (and other feelings, too), always trying to decide when, and if, my feelings were "justified." I think many women never decide that their anger is justified.

[4] Susan Wolfe reminded me of *The Honeymooners*, a popular sitcom of the 1950s, in which Jackie Gleason played a bus driver (Ralph Cramden) and Art Carney a worker in the sewers (Norton), and pointed out that Norton's job was treated as *inherently* funny. That is, the substance of a white-collar job or "professional," with the exception (maybe) of lawyers or proctologists, is not funny in and of itself. Similarly, a sitcom of the 1980s, *Sanford & Son*, treated Sanford's (played by Red Foxx) occupation—owner of a junkyard— as inherently funny even though he owned the business, because he was an African American.

[5] At that time, according to Florida law, my mother was a nonperson. Her husband (my father) was "missing," not legally dead, and the courts refused to declare him dead until he'd been missing for seven years. So she moved us to Atlanta, where we lived with my grandparents for two years while she fought to get our house back.

[6] I've put scare quotes around these words because I'm not sure exactly what they refer to. What men call "logic" and "reason" usually seems to me to be irrational and illogical, so I cannot use these words as though they name something I take seriously.

[7] "Renting" isn't a sure indicator of one's class membership, especially in urban areas, where the neighborhood, even the street, one lives in (or on) is more significant. In New York City, for example, wealthy people may rent apartments on Central Park West, while only a couple of blocks west poor people rent apartments on Amsterdam or Columbus Avenue. Both the rich and the poor may live in midtown Manhattan, but their addresses symbolize very different classes.

[8] I use the plural *continua* here because, as the contributors to this anthology make very clear, our class membership is determined by factors other than financial assets, for example, by sex, race, and able-bodiedness. An African American, Native American, Asian American or Caucasian woman's salary is most likely to be less than that of a man who belongs to the same racial group. Biological sex, in effect, creates two separate and *un*equal class continua, as Fox argues. Along the continua created by sex, one's racial or ethnic background affects the kinds of jobs one can get and the salary one will be paid. Caucasian women often make more money than women of color even though they're

working at the same job. If a woman is disabled, her options are further limited. To be a disabled Latina is to have fewer options than a similarly disabled Caucasian woman. To be a disabled Caucasian lesbian means having fewer options than a disabled Caucasian heterosexual woman. Opportunities are the critical factors across all continua and their sub-strata.

[9] These statistics were presented at the 1980 United Nations Conference on Women in Copenhagen, and are cited from *The War Against Women* by Marilyn French (New York: Summit Books, 1992), p. 30. As she observes, these statistics "remain true today."

[10] Susan Wolfe, discussing recent research on the human brain and the phenomenon we call "mind," cites William Calvin, a neurobiologist and author of *The Cerebral Symphony: Seashore Reflections on the Structure of Consciousness* (New York: Bantam Books, 1990), "who notes that up to half of the interconnections in our cerebral cortex are lost by maturity; the pruning of synapses, he theorizes, may serve both analysis and storage functions, or, to put it differently, may channel how we think and determine what we remember" (unpublished paper, 1994:24). She goes on to suggest what she calls a "more counter-intuitive approach," namely, that "we learn not by making connections, but by losing them—. . .by narrowing the range of neurological paths along which electrochemical impulses can travel" (*loc. cit.*). In a very literal sense, what we may call our "consciousness" or "sense of self," that matrix of memory and experience that underlies our identities and interconnects them, is the result of gradual pruning and cerebral reorganization which eliminates neurological pathways. We are what we have not learned.

[11] By mentioning my own "false" memories, I am not indicating that I condone or support the efforts of the rightwing and xtian fundamentalists to discredit women's reports of rape by family members or ritual abuse by labeling them "false memory syndrome." This is a tactic for trying to silence us when we finally find our voices.

[12] *Shame.* It's a word, along with *ashamed* and *shameful*, that several contributors, from different classes, repeat. There's another book in that single word, a book about all the ways every single one of us has been made to feel shame: shame about where we were born; shame about who our parents were or were not; shame about the clothes we wear, the way we eat, what we eat (or don't), who we know (or don't). There seems no end to the things in our lives we're expected to feel shame about. [13] If we're fat, it doesn't matter whether we can afford to dress "fashionably." We have to wear what we can find in our size, and, too often, the manufacturers who supply clothes for fat people and the buyers who purchase them and the stores that sell them don't care if the clothes they sell us are "in fashion." We're supposed to be "grateful" to find *any* clothes in our sizes.

[14] Middle English speakers borrowed the word *menial*, as you might have already guessed, like *manners* and *polite*, from (yup) a Norman French word that meant "a group or suite [sic] of attendants, followers, dependents, etc.; household." In English, the archaic word *meiny* is also related through Norman French to *manse*, *mansion*, and *remain* from Latin *manere*, 'to remain'. Ain't etymology a stitch!

[15] One's idiolect consists of her individual speech patterns. No two people speak in exactly the same way.

[16] Most people think of a dialect as an "accent," a distinctive way people from the same region or side of town have of pronouncing certain sounds or words, but our dialects include distinctive features of vocabulary and sentence structure as well.

[17] "I Want My Accent Back," a poem by Susan Leigh Star, is one of the few things about class and dialect ever published in the lesbian (or feminist) media. In the poem, she relates discovering that she "had an accent" during her first week at Radcliffe College "sitting on the floor / with Andover and Exeter and Taft,/ stoned,. . .." After the "good natured / hearty chuckle" of Andover, with which "the others join[ed] in," Star reports, "by 9:00 the next morning my accent disappeared. except / when I talk too fast, or to you / my soft r's my dull t's my idears / are invisible I clip / my speech / . . .I have sat / in my room / nights trying to get it back. . ." (*Sinister Wisdom* 16 [Spring 1981]:20-23).

[18] I'm using the word *grammar* here as linguists use it, to refer to the system of language rules each of us learns as children. What most people in the U.S. call "grammar" is really a restrictive, prescriptive version of English used to discourage us from speaking our native, and often, "substandard," dialects. Prescriptive "grammars" aren't grammars at all; they're linguistic books of "etiquette." [19] All three of these men are linguistic reactionaries (political, as well) who regard attempts by women or people of color to change English or to valorize their own dialects as "insurgency." John Simon published a monthly column on how radicals were "destroying" English in *Esquire* magazine during the 1970s, and William Safire continues to rant in the pages of the *New York Times Magazine.*

[20] "Portables" were temporary, one-room buildings, set on cement blocks, in which classes were placed that couldn't fit in the crowded school building. My fourth-grade year was spent in a portable.

[21] Florida State had a reputation then as a "gay" school because, up until only two years earlier (I think), it had been an all-women's teachers' college, what they used to call a "normal school." I learned this from two lesbians I met (at the apartment house we gay kids called Sex Manor) who were graduate students at FSU in sociology. Yes, FSU had lots of lesbian and gay students and faculty, but everyone (almost) was deep in their 1950s closets. Only the gay men were willing to be seen with me, and so we provided each other with a spurious sort of cover that gave us some respite from the inquiring and gossipy tongues of roommates and other students.

[22] Yes, I did have men sleeping in my apartment, and they were *sleeping.* They were two gaymen friends who lived north of Miami, in Hollywood, and it was too long a trip to make after our late rehearsals for *Lysistrata.* They needed a place to stay close to the University so that they could get to their early morning classes on time, so I let them sleep on my floor.

[23] The colleges that make up what is, today, called The City University of New York—City College, Hunter College, Brooklyn College, Queens College, and Baruch College—were once tuition-free. Many people whose parents were immigrants or underclass were able to get an almost free college education. When I started night school at City College in 1962, I paid only a $12. student fee each semester.

[24] "Tsu Got Vel Ikh Veynen," *Bridges* 3, 1 (Spring/Summer 1992/5752):74-7.

[25] "Playfulness, 'World'-Travelling, and Loving Perception," *Hypatia* 2, 2 (Summer 1987):3-19.

REFERENCES

Calvin, William. 1990. *The Cerebral Symphony: Seashore Reflections on the Structure of Consciousness.* New York: Bantam.

French, Marilyn. 1992. *The War Against Women*. New York: Summit.

Kolodny, Annette. 1975. *The Lay of the Land: Metaphor as Experience and History in American Life and Letters*. Chapel Hill: University of North Carolina Press.

———. 1984. *The Land Before Her: Fantasy and Experience of the American Frontiers, 1630—1860*. Chapel Hill: University of North Carolina Press.

Lakoff, George, and Mark Johnson. 1980. *The Metaphors We Live By*. Chicago: University of Chicago Press.

Morales, Aurora Levins. 1992/5752. "Tsu Got Vel Ikh Veynen," *Bridges* 3, 1 (Spring/Summer):74-7.

Wolfe, Susan J. 1994. "*Victor/Victoria* at *The Well of Loneliness*: Gender, Sexuality, and the Subjective Observer." Unpublished paper.

Potato Skins

Catherine Odette

The first time I saw potato skins on the menu, I was at the S & S restaurant, a well-known eatery in Cambridge, Massachusetts. It was known as a popular place for dykes to eat after the many events the Boston-Cambridge area had to offer. It was close to Harvard Square, and a short drive from downtown Boston where the lesbian bar was. The seating was OK for big dykes, the access was OK for wheelchair-using dykes, the portions good for the money spent, the food Jewish-style enough to satisfy. The range of food satisfied a variety of palates from hearty to delicate. I went elsewhere with vegetarian friends.

I loved being there on some Thursday nights when the volleyball team arrived after practice. I loved watching the line of oh, twenty or more strong women's faces pass by, as I listened to my internal dykeo'meter nearly screech in resonance and recognition.

I loved being there on Sunday mornings when a huge variety of dykes came for breakfast or brunch. Mostly these were women I didn't see too often because they were in their own social circles and we didn't overlap much. Some came with the Sunday paper under their arm, some came with their babies, some with a group. I loved the variety of women I saw. I imagined their lives, making a game of guessing their work. "She's a teacher, and she's a doctor, and she's a printer and she's a secretary who wishes she was a farmer and she's. . ." It was a good time to get together with others because the energy of the restaurant on Sunday mornings was almost festive, jolly even (if you don't mind the word).

Informal meetings were planned at the S & S around tea and toast or bagels. The price was OK, and Wednesday mornings meant pretty leisurely meetings without the guilt of sitting overlong. I could go there any time of the day or evening and see dykes. I mostly imagined they could see me too.

Since I'd been in the Boston area for about 40 years, and the restaurant had been in business that long and longer, friends were surprised that I'd only started going there in the last 12 or so years. "Well," I explained, "there's a little 'thing' I've got about eating in public. It's about spending money for having other people wait on me. Well, maybe it's more about buying food when I've got perfectly good food waiting for me to cook. Uh, actually, it's got to do with me being fat and eating in public because I often get trashed about my size. Or, maybe it has more to do with looking lesbian and not liking how I got treated by the hets."

Awright. Awright. ALRIGHT. It's about food, OK!? I learned food "things" in my family. No surprise there, right? Right. Everybody learns about food in the family they grow up in. We learn our attitudes about food. How food is dealt with, how eating is valued or devalued. How much strain it is to feed people in that house. Is there enough money for food? Was there a decision to buy food instead of oil for the heater? Is food wasted? Thrown away? Served by people who don't sit down to eat with you?

In my house there was almost no food. Ever. I didn't really know how bad it was until I lived away from home for the first time and saw how some people ate—every day—three times a day.

We loved—and hated—Saturdays, because Mae, our next door neighbor who worked at the convent, brought us the big bag of bread ends on Saturdays. The nuns, for some reason, didn't eat bread ends and these had been collecting all week, so those Jews, the poor Jews, the only Jews in the neighborhood, got to eat them. It was Mae's act of Christian charity. She told us so every time, as she stood in the entryway of our door. I know this is "Sunday" for you, she would say, but she wanted to bring this by while it was still fresh. Yes, she said, she felt blessed to be able to help us out. About once every other month, Mae would bring us the bread ends, buttered, made into sandwiches. Two bread ends, the crust turned to the inside, with butter in-between. I think she thought it would be a treat for us, and mostly it was. But it did cut down the amount of food overall by doubling the individual portions.

My family had little gratitude toward her charity. My father hated the white bread, so unlike the heavy, chewy dark rye he wished for. My mother complained about it being soft, mushy bread, good for the babies, but not enough for the rest of us. My father resented Mae and her plumber husband. They talk about us, he said. Listen! Listen right here, right here at the wall, he'd rant. Our shared wall gave us too much information about Mae's life and her opinion of us. My mother wished the bread arrived in paper instead of the plastic she washed so carefully and returned to Mae, and she rarely failed to ask if there was, perhaps, a cabbage with the ends this time. She never quite understood that it was only bread ends that we were going to get. We were not supposed to understand that the crusts were (wrongfully!) thought to be inferior bread, even though the nuns had rejected it. This charity, given and received, would have individual meaning and impact gradually revealed over time, to those who would work to understand. I could have learned bread values, bread etiquette from someone who thought my family was trash. I, as the best English speaker in the house, had to accept the bag from Mae and give my parents the message that came with it. "G-d will help," she told me. "Pray to g-d to make you better." That meant I was already not good. I understood she wanted to cure us of being Jews, Christ killers, babies' blood drinkers. That's what was needing to be made better. I smiled at her as I took the bag. It was required.

In my house, mealtimes were really a reenactment of the War. Until I was a teenager, hunger was a shared, daily, family experience. Spilled milk or dropped food was a reminder that millions of people had starved to death in Europe for want of the few ounces of milk that were dripping onto the floor. That led to stories about the camps where people were delighted when they got a bowl of maybe warm, mostly water soup and sometimes a small crust of bread for a whole day's ration. All of which reminded my parents that many days there was nothing at all given to eat. That reminded my parents that we would have leftovers for our next meal.

"Leftovers" was the euphemism for trash food. My mother prided herself on never throwing out ANYTHING, foodwise. Scrape off as little as possible and eat around the fuzz. A bruise is nothing to worry about. Shriveled food, a celery that flopped over like a short length of rope, a potato whose "eyes" could grow long, leafy, interesting. Any food, in any condition, could be made into soup. No scrap of food was ever thrown out. I never saw an egg in a whole shell until I lived away from home. We bought the "cracks," the broken eggs willingly bought by us after the eggseller had been around to everyone else in the neighborhood, and in his clumsiness had broken half a dozen or maybe a whole dozen, egg white oozing into the carton. We put the "cracks" into a jar, precious and rare good food. On those Saturdays when we got the buttered ends, butter, scooched off the bread, would be put into a pan to grease it, and then eggs could be cooked in the fat. Sometimes during a bounty, my mother would scoop solid white potato out of the skin to make soup or mashed potato. The potato rind, left thick for a second use, was combined with onion and some of the bread-sandwich butter, and then all tossed together in one of her cast-iron frypans. The coffee bean residue, imprinted into the metal of the pan, added **oomph** to the flavors. Mae was often mentioned during this fragrant, pungent, filling meal. Potato skins! Ummm, heaven! Anger and cruel humor sizzled in my parents' remarks as gratitude was abandoned during this, our most recent moment of plenty.

The vegetable seller parked at the end of our street on the weekends. I can still hear his unintelligible call, a kind of worker's music, all the names of all the fruits and vegetables fused into one, becoming a song, the words impossible to decipher but the song melody always the same. The women ran to his truck when he sang. Our street was the last stop, and the produce, to my mother, was a bounty. Vegetables and fruit that had been in the summer heat for a day was the offering and the women from my street, husbands off at the meat-packing plant, swarmed around the truck—appraising, tweaking, touching and buying. Our bag was always ready when we got there. All I had to do was hand over the two quarters and get the bag or sometimes two bags. It was all the garbage this guy was going to throw out. Why not get half a buck for it? It's better than nothing at all, and my mother was "delighted" to have it. There was almost always a soft green pepper; some black onions; some black potatoes; pale, limp string beans; squishy tomatoes; flexible carrots and stalks of bending celery. Sometimes, some brown bananas would peak out, sometimes apples, pears or other fruit. I didn't ever feel shame at buying that food; I shared my mother's feelings. When I could manage both bags without help, I thought I was really something. Me, carrying the bags, one balanced on each hip, down the four cement stairs into our kitchen area.

Food was an agony at my house. In the present, it was tangible proof of our poverty. My mother roasted coffee beans daily and overnight, huge cast-iron frypans full, for a local restaurant. It was our income. My father sat, mostly in one spot for the day, in the house. Unable to work, unable to enjoy, unable to parent. He told the camp stories. He wanted us to know what they did to the Jews. Food was part of every story. Food was one form of savior, food was one form of torture. He told about being walked by the food preparation area, where good food was being made into meals to give comfort and strength to the nazis, so that they could murder and torture more Jews. Spotting a cluster of scrap food, onion skins, potato skins, carrot tops—a banquet!—he yielded, bending quickly to grab some of the scraps. As the story continues, he now speaks in his native German, sometimes tearing at himself for his stupidity to bend and try to collect the scraps which led to another beating. His sorrow, his rage, his torture invested and invaded every morsel of our food.

Now, having lived to my middle-40s, I was eating my first serving of potato skins since I was a kid; since the time when my mother fried potato scraps in the butter scraped off crusty bread-end sandwiches; since the time when eating potato and other food scraps was just how we ate at home. Maybe a survivor of the nazi concentration camps invented and marketed the idea of potato skins. It feels possible that she or he would think to add melted cheese and sometimes (gadzooks!) bacon bits. Waste not, we are reminded.

Some forty years after watching my mother cook food in the butter that was mortar for the bread sandwiches from the convent, I sat with my partner, Sara, and our friends at the S & S restaurant. Seeing potato skins on the menu transported me back to my mother's kitchen. I could smell the roasting coffee beans, a smell so deep and thorough and thick I believed I could write on the cloud of that scent. I saw the rooms I shared with my parents, two sisters and three brothers and remembered oh, how we fought! I felt the sting of those Saturdays and my encounters with Mae. I remembered all of her lessons: bread ends are bad; Jews are bad; dirty little girls are bad; fathers at home all day are bad; mothers who speak foreign languages are bad; we dressed oddly, spoke funny, behaved like heathens; we needed a bath, some manners, and English lessons; we should go to work, get a loan, go on relief; we should sleep later and get out of the house earlier; we needed more than she was going to provide and we weren't grateful for her charity. . .and our house always reeked of frying and oleo.

I ordered potato skins—without bacon. I ordered them in some skewed form of honoring victims and survivors of the nazi war against Jewish people. I ordered them honoring my survival. I ordered them honoring my mother's work and her cooking that fed us when she could, in the best way she could. I ordered them for lessons learned and for lessons rejected.

Alien and her house leaving Adobe's Land, October 1991.

Alien's house before the move.

A Very Moving Story

Alien Nation

How to move a house...

First you must have one to move, second you must have a place to move it to. Third, you must be a lot desperate, and a little crazy to boot, and I fit that bill. I had a house—actually, according to the county it is a three-room structure that did not meet housing codes. According to my mom, it's just a shack and she can't understand for the life of her why I insist on living like this.

Flashback: My big brother Bobby an' I are standin' in the bathroom in front a the sink. It's dark, the only light is from the winda on the back porch. The water runnin' fast, splashin' us as it hits the white porcelain, whirlin' away down the drain. We are gigglin' together in amazement that we are gonna have runnin' water in our new house in town! I am four, he is twelve. It's 1964 in rural Missouri.

Only part two was missing...

We were being evicted, illegally, unethically, and immorally from Adobeland, the wimmin's land outside of Tucson. The whats and why-fors are a whole 'nother story. Two dykes and their two kids had already moved into a one-bedroom apartment in town. They were scared to fight it, with welfare breathing down their necks and all. Couldn't risk it. They'd got out a few months ago, early in the struggle. That left five of us to go. In the summer, one of us, a wommin of fifty, had moved onto some land she was buying about one hundred miles away. She was living out of her car until she got a lean-to or something banged together, before the winter cold arrived. Another of us, a thirty-ish disabled wommin, got a funky RV and moved to an illegal trailer court about twenty miles away to live in un-wanted isolation. That left three of us "troublemakers" on Adobe's Land...another disabled wommin who had been renting a trailer from Adobe for over seven years, and me and my twelve-year-old daughter. I'm a single disabled mom; my daughter, a pre-teen.

Flashback: I'm standin' on the back porch of Janna's house waitin' for her ta come out ta play. She's three years younger than me an' lives next door. She's the only girl in the neighborhood who will play with me, an' she won't play with me if any a the other kids are around. We got in trouble yesterday for pickin' apricots. We were jus' tryin' ta help, but it turns out that they weren't ripe yet. Her mom comes out onta the back porch an' tells me that Janna can't play with me any more, an' then turns around an' heads back inta the house. Without even thinkin' I spring forward an' grab ahold the edge of the door an' ask "How come?" Mrs. Rhodes turns around an' by the look on her face I know I'm really in trouble now. She acts like my hand has dog poop on it the way she pushes it off her door. With that mean snotty voice I've heard from other kids' moms, she says ta me "Cause ya ain't nothin' but a white trash troublemaker an' my little girl don't have to play with the likes a you. Now git on home where ya belong an' don't be comin' 'round here no more, ya hear!"

Being evicted...

We all had gotten evicted or were being evicted from Adobeland. None of us really had a good place to go, and some of us didn't have *any* place to go. We were all living on welfare, SSI or Social Security Disability, which means none of us had enough money to solve our problem. So we acted like a bunch of pinko-commie-dykes and formed a land trust. A land trust is a legal framework for a nonprofit corporation to own land. This removes the land from the power of one owner and puts the power in the hands of a board of directors. It also keeps any individual from making money off the land, or off of the resources of the land trust. The land trust that we formed gets rid of landlord dynamics by the way we set it up which is as follows: A group of wimmin who are interested in living together get together and form a land group. They decide how they want to live, what type of agreements they want to have, etc. Then they do fund-raising and figure out ways to buy the land that they want. The land is then purchased by the land trust with this money. There are lots of reasons to have the land purchased by the land trust, some of which are that it takes the power out of the control of individuals who might change their minds later on, or who don't get along any more and want to sell; it's not-for-profit which means it's eligible to be tax-exempt from local property taxes, state and federal income taxes, which means less money for the boys and their toys, and more for us and our dreams. Theoretically, once the land is paid for it can remain forever for wimmin (the exception would be some unusual circumstance like the government deciding to build a highway through the middle of it). Even if for some reason the land was sold, all the money from the property would remain part of the land trust, which means different land could be bought. This removes land from the real estate/speculation market, and makes it available to wimmin who usually wouldn't have access.

Flashback: It's hot already even tho' the sun is still on the other side a the house yet. I'm sittin' on the porch swing where mom told me ta sit. She's carryin' Grandma's bag out ta Aunt Opal's car for her. Now it's Aunt Opal's turn for Grandma ta live with her for a while. Grandma will live up in the attic. It's dark an' scary an' I don't like ta go up there. Grandma will come back an' live with us when school starts jus' like she always does. Grandma use-ta have an apartment a long time ago, but when my mom an' daddy got married she didn't have any money ta pay the rent, 'cause my mom was the one who made all the money workin' down at the shoe factory. So Grandma started livin' with her kids. She stays with each one a them for a while an' then packs up her bag an' moves ta the next one's house. I miss her when she's gone but her an' my daddy fight a lot an' that's scary. I jump when Aunt Opal honks her horn ta hurry Grandma up. Grandma gets in the back seat an' my mom hands her the bag ta put on her lap. I wave bye to Grandma, but she doesn't see me 'cause she's lookin' down in her lap like she always does when she's around Aunt Opal.

Next was a land community...

After we formed the land trust we formed our land community. The two wimmin with two kids decided to stay in town for a while. The rest of us decided that since we had already lived together we still could. We knew each other, had a basis for trust, and shared similar values. We started fundraising and looking for land. We found a tiny two-acre lot that we felt good about, and could collectively manage to pay the land payment. The fund-raising was difficult at first, and the five-thousand-dollar down-payment came mostly from loans and gifts from our families & friends. All this wasn't as easy as I'm making it sound, but it also wasn't as hard as I thought it would be.

Flashback: I'm on the floor huggin' the toilet in a run-down efficiency apartment. I've got mornin' sickness. The smells of hot grease an' onions from the other apartments, the July humid heat of Missouri, an' the stale beer breath from my husband all make me sick. A baby is cryin' upstairs, doors are slammin' down the hall. Some asshole out back is cussin' out his girlfriend. One of our biker friends is on his Harley out front. I can feel the motor vibrations in my teeth. The landlady is poundin' on the door across the hall ta collect the late rent. I know she'll be here next, an' that passed-out prick on the bed spent our rent money on last night's drunk. I put my head down on the edge of the cool rim. Swallowin' my vomit an' tears, I reach up an' flush the toilet ta drown out the noises of my life.

So now we have a place to move the house to...

When moving a house there are about thirty-seven things that have to be done first. Since I'd never moved a house before, I'm sure I did some things in the wrong order, but don't ask me what. The week of the big move my twenty-five-year-old nephew hitchhiked down from Sacramento to help me. Weird how my white trash family always comes through. He was on unemployment, and knew I have a "bad" back, so it just made sense to both of us that he'd come help out for a while...especially since lesbians weren't exactly lining up to help me with this project. That's not to say none helped. Some did, but only my girlfriend-at-the-time committed herself to actually hang in there until the house was moved. So my nephew came down the first week in October. Although officially fall, this year it was still over a hundred in the afternoon on the Sonoran Desert.

Anyway back to the first things to be done. We had to clear the new house site which meant moving a fence, and digging up bushes and cactus. It was a good day's worth of work. A new cement foundation for the house had to be built, involving about twenty-five holes, sixteen inches deep and square, which had to be dug with a pickax in the adobe dirt. Now these holes couldn't be just anywhere. They had to be exactly in the same places and positions as the ones were under the house when it was originally built. This involved measuring and remeasuring the original foundation and doing the same with the new holes. In each hole a sixteen-inch square slab, twelve inches thick, had to be poured. This was the bottom of the foundation, which all together was twenty-five cement block pillars. Each pillar was a stack of three cement blocks, on top of the slab of cement, with a piece of rebar sticking down through the whole mess. Mortar was smeared between each block, and then the whole stack was filled up with cement. We are talking about seventy eighty-pound bags of cement mix, fifteen bags of mortar mix and seventy-five cement blocks. While we were digging holes, we miraculously remembered that because of the "L" shape of the house we could only get the foundation ready for two of the rooms. After these two rooms were moved and in place on the foundation, we would build the foundation for the last room. Another thing to do even before all this was to figure out how to pay for the supplies, which was about five hundred dollars. Once that problem was solved, I had to figure out how to get all this stuff the thirty miles from the hardware store on the other side of the mountain, when alls I have is a Toyota. Luckily I also have a generous friend with a pickup.

Flashback: Trompin' through the snow up the path in-ta the farmhands' house where I'd lived on an' off with my husband for the past five months. I was holdin' on-ta the metal railin' on the back steps ta make sure I didn't slip on the ice an' bust my nine-month pregnant ass. The back door

108

was hangin' open an' I could tell that that son-of-a-bitch had already been there. It was all gone. I'd only left him two days ago, after he beat me up again. Only this time real bad, an' then he'd went out on a drunk. All my clothes, all my furniture, all my art work from high school art class. Even the goddamn gas heater my mom had got for me. Gone. The house was empty. Nothin' but dust an' snow blowin' across the floor.

All at the same time…

While pouring the foundation was important, so was locating the right type of equipment to beg, borrow, or steal. I ended up renting a three-quarter-ton pickup with a hitch, a ton flatbed trailer (which is about as long and wide as a pickup truck), and a five-ton flatbed trailer (this was a BIG mama…the kind they haul bulldozers and stuff around on). I also rented about a hundred feet of log chains, and two come-alongs (which are winches that have hooks on the ends of the cables and you crank it by hand). I had to locate a "major credit card" to rent most of the equipment. This is kinda tricky when you get food stamps. Luckily, someone in my blood family had one, and with lots of promises to pay for any charges, I was able to use it for the rental stuff…not to *pay* for the rental stuff, just to be able to rent it. The rental charges were over five hundred dollars for three days.

Flashback: Walkin' down the dusty aisle a the grocery store, holdin' on-ta my mom's dress. She didn't take nothin' off the wood shelves. She'd jus' walked right up ta the dark wooden counter that Mr. Mister stood behind in his dirty white apron, lookin' down on us through his wire glasses an' tiny beady dark eyes. His shiny pink head stuck up outta a ring of fuzzy straight hair that looked like it went across his forehead, but part of it is really his eyebrows. Mr. Mister isn't his name but that's how I always think of 'im. "Good mornin', Mrs. Scott," he says through his yellow smile, chewin' on a toothpick. My mom smiles her nervous smile an' answers "Mornin'. Fine day ain't it? I'll jus' be gettin' a few things ta'day…a bag a flour, let's say twenty-five pounds, a ten-pound bag a sugar, a big can a coffee, an' a carton a Camels please. That oughta do us for a while." Mr. Mister's yellow smile disappears into a frown as my mom is talkin'. "Now Ruth, you know that we gotta settle up 'fore I can do any more biz-nes with ya," he says, slowly shakin' his chewed-on toothpick at my mom. She's a-lookin' down at her tennis shoes as he continues ta tell her how long he's been waitin' for us to settle up, that food ain't free, that we gotta pay our bill 'fore he's gonna let us get anything else on credit. She's lookin' so hard at her shoes that I lean around out from behind her ta see what she's lookin' at but they ain't nothin' but her dirty white tennis shoes that she always wears. She has ta cut a hole in her shoes where her big toenail can stick out 'cause it's all ugly lookin' an' hurts her if she don't. When Mr. Mister shuts up, mom looks up an' starts talkin' real quiet like, in that voice she uses when daddy's been down ta the tavern and he comes home mad in the middle of the night an' gets us all up outta bed an' is yellin' at us. In that kinda voice she says ta Mr. Mister, "We'll settle up as soon as we get the crops out an' we get our share, ya know we will. Now don't we always?" Mr. Mister puts his chewed on toothpick back in the corner of his mouth an' says in his mean voice, "Well now Ruth, by what I heard, you already got the crops out an' your husband's already settled his tab down the street." He was meanin' at the tavern. "Oh, no," my mom says, "that wasn't our crop money, that was just a little 'xtra he got from sellin' coons ta the legion for their coon supper. Ya know I would be in here first thing, as soon as we get our crops out. I wouldn't be puttin' *you* off, now ya know that." Mr. Mister slowly turns around an' picks up a sack a flour off the floor an' sets it up on the counter sayin', "Well ya jus' better be sure ya do now Ruth. Ya jus' better be sure ya do."

Before the equipment arrives...

The house has to be emptied, which turns out to be worse than moving the regular way. At the new place, we had to clean up the barn and a little metal storage shed to make room for all my stuff to go in while the house was being moved and put back together. It all had to be sorted and packed in shifts. The stuff that I don't use much, and would stay in storage, had already got packed up and was ready to go. But the stuff we used all the time had to get packed up at the last minute, and taken over to the other house on the land where we'd be staying for two weeks while we put my house back together. Cleaning out the storage spaces and moving my stuff turned into a three-day ordeal.

When my nephew isn't helping with the moving he's over at my house starting on the job of separating the three rooms. When I get done carrying carloads of boxes to their special places, I go and help him. We take out the windows and the big sliding glass doors and they get driven over to the barn in my car so they won't get broke. Next the plumbing and electricity get disconnected. The pipes to and under the house are cut, and the outside wires are cut and pulled out of the conduit. Miscellaneous pipes of both kinds get gathered up and all this makes up a couple more car loads to the barn. The phone has been turned off by the company, but we have to disconnect it from the house. The little phone box on the side of the house is locked with some type of special screw, so in frustration and rebellion, I just say "Fuck it" and cut the wire. So much for disconnecting the phone.

Messing with the phone reminds me that I gotta call the electric company and have them come out and move the "guy wires" that are across the road 'cause we'll never get this house *under* them. That takes about a half a day to arrange...with the usual runaround. Some wommin tells me, "I'm sorry I can't help you with that. You'll have to talk to Mr. So-and-So," who turns out to be on a perpetual coffee break. When I finally do get to talk to Mr. So-and-So (who I always think of as Mr. Mister), he acts like there is absolutely no way for them to move the wires without charging me hundreds of dollars. I tell him, "Listen Mr., I don't *have* hundreds of dollars. If I did I might consider paying you to do it, but I don't. I'm gonna be moving my house in three or four days, and if those wires are in my way, they are gonna get pulled down. Then you will hafta send an emergency crew out, plus have a whole bunch of unhappy customers. And on top of all that, *if* I get hurt by your wires that you are refusing to move, I won't hesitate to try to sue your ass off." Mr. So-and-So puts me on hold for about three minutes then comes back to tell me that the supervisor has decided to waive the charges since this is such an unusual circumstance. Now that we got that settled it takes about forty-five seconds to make the rest of the arrangements.

Flashback...It's the beginning week of my junior year of college. I'm setting outside the office of the director of financial aid waiting for my "when-we-can-work-you-in" appointment. Yesterday, after waiting in line for about 3-and-1/2 hours with my pre-schooler, I was told my financial aid had been canceled. No one could say exactly why, just that it had been. I would have to reapply and *maybe* it might come through for winter semester. It's not that I woulda minded having the semester off, but I was counting on that money to take care of a few things the next few months...you know, things like rent. And now, when I shoulda been in class, and my daughter shoulda been at day care, here we were sitting in this ugly office waiting for some man to tell me where my money was. The longer I waited the madder I got. Shit like this was always happening. I sat there thinking about last winter when my welfare got canceled 'cause they said I was working when all the time I was in the hospital. When they cancel your welfare they also cancel your insurance. Now, there I was in the hospital, no money coming in, and no insurance either...all 'cause of some screwup on their part. Then, when they finally figured out *they* had screwed up they didn't want to go back and reinstate it from the time they started screwing up. No, they just wanted to go back to the time that they had *figured out* they had screwed it up. I had to get a lawyer from legal aid before they would go back and fix it like it shoulda been, so my hospital bills were covered and to get my back checks for all that time they were screwing around. Suddenly, the receptionist called my name and the director would see me now. I gotta admit I went in there mad as hell. I told him what happened, he looked over my file, and repeated the same story about reapplying. No, he didn't know why it had been canceled, but I was gonna just have to wait and see what happened when the money for the winter semester came through. Sorry, there just wasn't a thing he could do about it. Didn't seem to matter much that we were talking about my life here. I listened to all his crap, then I stood up and walked over to his door. With my hand on the knob, I motioned for him to come over to me. He looked puzzled. I said, "C'mon over here. I wanna show you sum-thing." He got up from behind his big desk and came over by me...not too close, just close enough to see what I was talking about. I opened his door, an' out on the couch was my little baby girl, sitting quietly, just like I'd told her, colorin' in her colorin' book. I asked Mr. Director, "See that beautiful little girl sitting out there on your sofa?" He nodded and I continued, "Well, that pretty little thing is my daughter and if you don't straighten this mess out, right here an' now, I'm gonna go out there an' get her all gathered up. Then me an' her are gonna go over to the bookstore an' buy us a couple of bike chains an' padlocks. Then I'm gonna call the downtown newspaper an' tell 'em how this university is treating welfare mothers. An' I'm gonna suggest to them they might wanna come over to the campus an' take a picture of me an' my baby girl, 'cause I'm gonna take those chains an' chain her an' me to the banister out in front of this here financial aid building. I can just see the headlines now...'University Denies Financial Aid to Struggling Welfare Mom.' Whatcha think, Mr. Director? Think they'll come?" He stood there staring at me for a few moments with a kinda strange expression on his face, a mix of rage, disgust, and fear. The fear musta won out 'cause he asked me to sit back down for a few minutes while he made a few inquiries. When he left the room I was scared to death that he was gonna go call the cops or something. I thought I was gonna puke by the time he came back in the room. He didn't have no cops along, just that familiar pink voucher form for me to take up to the cashiers so I could get my money.

Almost ready to move it...

The last thing to be done to my house was to separate the rooms. When I designed the house, I did it so it could be moved—just in case. Now I was glad I did. The house consisted of three rooms, a tiny bathroom we added on last winter, and a small uncovered porch, or deck. Of the three rooms there was my room, which was the largest and doubled as our living room, the kitchen, and my daughter's bedroom. My room was the main part of the house. It had four solid walls. The bathroom was kinda just tacked on to the back. The kitchen and other bedroom were joined onto my room, one on the west, and one on the south so that the house formed an odd-shaped "L". These two rooms only had three walls; they used the walls where they joined my room to form their four-walls-box-shape. They were attached with nails where they joined the big room. To get to these nails, part of the roofing, and part of the drywall on the walls and ceiling had to be removed. Each of about one hundred nails had to be cut with a handle-type hacksaw. A handle-type hacksaw is basically a plastic handle, sorta like a knife handle, that has a foot-long flat 1/2-inch-wide blade that slides down through the handle. The good thing about this saw is you can saw in tiny places like in the cracks between rooms. The not-so-great thing is that it's a lot of hard work and really frustrating because the blades break a lot. While my nephew had this fun job, I was underneath the house taking the nails out of the anchor plates. The anchor plates are two-inch-wide, foot-long, strong, flat, metal strips that have about six holes on one end. The other end is buried in concrete in each one of the cement block pillars that make up the foundation. Each strip is attached with nails to the bottom of the house, usually on floor beams, but sometimes to the floor joists (which are like beams but not as big). When I designed the house, I'd also thought of this and specified that double-headed nails were to be used. A double-headed nail is a weird-looking nail that looks like a regular nail but has two flat heads on the end. First there's the head like a regular nail. Then, attached to that is a short section of what looks like more nail, then another head. You hit the top head, and pound it in. The bottom head keeps the nail from going in all the way, which leaves it sticking out just a little bit. This little bit is enough to get the claw of a hammer or rip tool under and pull the nail out. The whole idea behind these nails is that you use them in places where you might need to get the nails out again later (as long as there's room for them to stick out a little on whatever you are building). They would have worked perfect for this but for some reason they weren't used like I'd specified. A local trade school had provided free labor so their students could get practice. This arrangement was what had enabled me to get my house built in the first place, and I am grateful. But when I was under my house in the dirt and dust, I sure cussed those students for using regular nails on the anchor plates! I spent hours prying the plates loose with a screwdriver, then working the hammer or prying tool claw under the head of the nail and finally pulling it out. The anchor plates are designed to be strong and not bend, or wiggle, or do anything which would make getting them loose easy. About a day-and-a-half later I got the last of the hundred or so nails out. I was very relieved to get out from under the dirty, tiny crawlspace under the house.

Flashback: I'm down in the basement. Mom sent me down ta get some potatoes out a the potato bin, an' a quart of green beans. I hate comin' down here. It's cold an' moldy. There's spider webs (an' spiders) all over everything. The walls an' floor is just dirt so it's always wet an' sorta muddy. Ta turn the light on I gotta reach up in the corner a the doorway an' I'm always afraid I'm gonna reach in a spider web an' get bit. I'm jus' *sure* if a spider ever gets on me, or if one bites me, I'll die for sure! Ta get ta the potatoes an' jars a stuff, I gotta go through the first room…the weird room. In the weird room, there's some shackles that are in the wall, kinda up high. My daddy says that's where they use-ta put bad slaves a long time ago. My mom wants him ta pull 'em outta the wall, but he says no, they're gonna stay an' remind us. I don't know what they's suppose ta remind us of. I jus' think they's creepy. Then there's the big green barrel that my daddy keeps snappin' turtles in. He catches 'em down outta the river and then brings 'em home an' puts 'em in the barrel full a water till he sells 'em ta somebody ta make soup outta. They can bite your finger clean off. My daddy showed me once. He took a stick an' stuck it down on the edge a that barrel an' that mean ole turtle jus' came right outta that water an' bit the end a that stick clear off! It scared me for sure, I tell you. I know when he's got turtles in the barrel 'cause I can hear 'em scrapin' their claws on the insides a that metal barrel, tryin' ta get out I guess. I ain't spose ta go over there in that part a the basement anyway, even when there ain't no turtles around, 'cause that's where the floor's broke. Not the basement floor, the kitchen floor, which is really the basement ceilin'. Daddy put this funny lookin' thing, which he says is a jack, under the kitchen floor. He says if I get over there an' mess around with it I could make the whole darn house fall in on me an' that'd kill me for sure. So I don't mess around in this room at all. I jus' walk right through real fast till I get ta the doorway a the other room. I gotta turn on 'nother light but this one's not so bad 'cause I can see from the light behind me if there's spiders on the switch or not. Then, quick as I can, I go get some potatoes an' put 'em in the IGA bag an' grab a jar a beans off the shelf. Sometimes I gotta find somethin' ta get the spider webs off the jars, or off the potato bin. I get really scared if I gotta reach back in a dark corner ta get anything. There's always spider webs back in the corners. I turn 'round, an' I'm real careful not to run 'cause I might drop sumpin' an' cut my foot off. I always remember ta shut off both lights, 'cause if I forget, then I gotta go back down a second time an' that's always worse. Then I'm real careful on the steps 'cause they are slick an' once I slipped an' fell all the way down 'em. I screamed an' screamed an' my mom came arunning, but there wasn't nuthin' wrong but a bump on my head an' a few spider webs in my hair. All that night though, I kept feelin' spiders crawling 'round on my head an' down my neck, even though my mom said there weren't none there. When I get ta the top a the stairs I put everythin' down an' I close the basement door. It shuts down flat an' it's part of the floor. It's real heavy, an' I gotta be careful not ta drop it on my toes. When the door is shut, then I can take a big-big breath 'cause I feel like I didn't breathe the whole time I was down there in that horrible ole basement.

Now we're ready to do it…

Everything is detached, disconnected, and we're determined. About now, my-girlfriend-at-the-time starts asking, "What's the plan?" My nephew and I look at each other and simultaneously answer, "To move the house." This was one area where we had some difficulties. She thought we were just being smart-asses, which we weren't. We didn't realize that she thought we knew how to move a house, which we didn't. After about the third or fourth time she asked the same question, and we always gave her the same answer, it turned into a bit of a fight. That's when we all realized it was a communication problem. She just couldn't believe we were moving my house without having a step-by-step plan, backed up by knowledge and experience. Shoot, my nephew and I grew up around people who were all the time doin' stuff they didn't know how to do. Ya jus' jump right in and figure it out as ya go along. You can't break it if it's already broke. And besides what choice did I have? I either needed to move it or lose it, so what the hell. Couldn't be much worse off moving it, than if I was to lose it. At least I'd have a house, even if I had to do a bunch of fixin' up on it after we got it moved. My big concern was that nobody got hurt in the process.

Because of the "L" shape of the house, we had to move my daughter's room over onto the land, but not put it on the foundation yet. We backed the trailer up to the edge of her room and positioned it to drag the room onto it. Then we put a couple of hydraulic jacks under the edge of her room, and very SLOWLY jacked it up about eight inches, on the end farthest away from the trailer, which was the end that had been attached to my room. We did this to get the room to slide away from my room a little so we would have space to slide the chains through. To keep the chains from tearing up the wood, we used a heavy-duty nylon towing strap and hooked the chains to each end. We formed a big "U" around the room and connected the open end of the "U" to a couple of come-alongs (remember, those are big winches), then we connected the come-alongs to the middle of the front of the trailer. We let down the jacks and moved them to the other end of the room and jacked it up about three inches. We'd SLOWLY start to crank the come-alongs, trying to crank together in a rhythm. We had to stop every three or four cranks to either adjust the come-alongs or to move the jacks. We'd also have to stop and jack up the room each time the bottom of the floor got stuck on the trailer or foundation. While it was still up on jacks we'd give the come-alongs a couple of cranks until the room moved enough for the jacks to fall over. We are talking moving the room an inch, or an inch-and-a-half at a time. This took us almost all day.

After we got it on the trailer, the room was sticking out over both sides. My nephew got in the truck and drove it, about 5 mph, over to the new land. I followed in my car with my flashers on, just in case someone came around the corner. Luckily, we only had to drive about a block on a rural dirt road. I asked him to drive the truck 'cause he's driven pickups all his life, and I can count the times on one hand that I have. I didn't figure that this was the time to go experimenting.

We backed the trailer into an empty out-of-the-way space on the land and jacked one end of the room up at a time. We put concrete blocks under each corner while it was jacked up. We just pulled the trailer straight out from under it, and left it sitting on those stacks of blocks until it was time to put it on the foundation. It was getting dark by the time we all staggered into the other house for supper and showers. We were really excited about how well it had went, but were still a bit worried about moving the BIG room tomorrow.

Flashback: I was layin' down, feelin' all nervous an' excited about tomorrow. We were gonna go ta Six Flags in St. Louis! My daddy had promised that if I did good in school we would go. An' sure enough, when I brought my report card home and the teacher had said I was gonna go to the third grade next year, my daddy said "Well, I guess that settles it. We're gonna be goin' ta St. Louie on Wednesday mornin'. Bright an' early. Mom, ya hear that? Ya better make sure this kiddo gets ta bed early on Tuesday night, ya hear?" Well, I'd done jus' like he said. It wasn't even dark outside an' here I was in bed. I'd even taken a bath even though it was the middle of the week. Daddy wasn't home yet. He was still downtown but I jus' knew he'd be home soon. He'd promised this a long time ago, 'bout christmas time I guess. I wasn't doin' so good in second grade, even tho' I tried real hard. But after he promised ta take me ta Six Flags if I did good, I started tryin' even harder. And then my mom went ta talk to my teacher an' I got ta change classes. They was a real nice teacher in my new class. I didn't care if the kids in my old class said I was in the class for dummies now, I liked my new teacher a whole lot. So I jus' knew my daddy'd be home anytime now. I laid there thinkin' about all the fun we was gonna have ridin' all those rides an' seein' all that stuff. I wasn't real sure what all was at Six Flags 'cause we ain't never been there 'fore this. But I knew it was jus' like a big carnival 'cept you could ride the rides as many times as you wanted 'cause they didn't cost nuthin'. I was jus' 'bout ta go ta sleep when my mom came in an' sat down. She looked at me kinda funny for a minute or so, then started talkin' in her sad voice that she uses when my daddy's done sumpin' bad after bein' down at the tavern. "Now maybe ya shouldn't be aplannin' on goin' ta Six Flags tomorrow. Your daddy's not home yet, and ya know how he is after he's been downtown. Ya best not be thinking too much about Six Flags. Maybe we'll go some other time." "Nu-huh," I said, real quick like. "My daddy promised. He PROMISED." I almost yelled at her. She made that small sound she makes when she's givin' up, an' got up an' walked back inta the kitchen. I musta fallen asleep 'cause next thing I knew it was mornin'. I knew right away sumpin' wasn't right. Daddy was sposta wake me up real early but he hadn't. I went out inta the kitchen, but nobody was in there. I could see out through the screen door that mom was out workin' in the garden. I got that sick feelin' in my stomach. She wasn't sposeta be workin' in the garden. She was sposeta be fixin' us a picnic lunch to take along with us to Six Flags. "Maybe daddy's in his bedroom still gettin' dressed," I thought, even though I knew that wasn't it. Daddy's always the first one awake unless he's been downtown the night before. I ran through the house ta their bedroom. When I got ta the door, I stopped an' whispered "Please Jesus, please make my daddy take me ta Six Flags today like he promised. I won't never do nuthin' bad again, ever." Then, real careful-like, I opened their bedroom door. There daddy was, on his bed. He was layin' there, on his back, with his mouth hangin' open. I walked over and stood next to his bed. "Daddy?" I whispered. "Wake up. Ya sposeta take me to St. Louis today. We gonna go ta Six Flags." He mumbled sumpin' an' rolled over on his side towards me. He was still asleep an' I could smell 'im. He smelled real bad, like he always does after he's been downtown. I knew we weren't gonna go nowhere, specially not to St. Louis, but I just couldn't give up. Not yet. "Daddy," I said in my regular voice, shakin' his shoulder a little. "Daddy, wake up!" He reached out, quick as a flash, an' even tho he was sleepin', smacked me up side the head, all at the same time tellin' me "God-Damn-It, I told ya ta git the hell outta here." I hurried up an' got outta there, bein' careful not to make any more noise when I shut his door. I went out onta the front porch an' sat down on the cement step. My face was stingin' where he'd smacked me one. The cement edge on the step scratched the back a my legs but I didn't pay no 'tention to it. I just sat there, lookin' out at the street thinkin' how I wasn't never gonna get excited or want nuthin' again 'cause this always happens. Ya get all excited and let 'em know how much ya want sumpin' and ya never get it then. It's better jus' not ta care 'bout it at all, that way ya might accidentally get sumpin' every once in a while. Maybe.

Two more rooms to go...

The next morning we were up at dawn. We basically repeated the same process to load the big room onto the trailer. First we had to tear out the cement pillars that the little bedroom had been setting on and drag them outta our way. We put the big room on the big trailer, which was scary. We weren't even sure if the pickup would be able to pull the trailer with the big room on it or not, 'cause it could hardly pull the big trailer just by itself. You are supposed to use a big truck, like a dump truck, to pull those kind of trailers, but I didn't have the money to rent one of those. So we started out real slow, with the truck pulling that big trailer, with that big room sitting up there on it like it had been built up there. On our way out of the driveway we had to cross a ditch where the wash ran, and of course it got stuck. This is what we'd been worried about. The truck was on one side of the ditch, the trailer on the other, and the hitch & tongue were forming a deep "v" in the middle where we were stuck. About then, one of the wimmin who lived on the land came up to me all upset. "I have to leave for work in a half hour. You ARE going to have that moved by then, AREN'T you?" Here I was, with part of my house sitting on a rented trailer that was costing me about $175 a day, stuck in a ditch, and this wommin wants me to stop and worry about her getting to work on time. Why hadn't she moved her vehicle over to the other drive? It wasn't like she hadn't known that I was gonna be moving my house today! I felt like telling her to go fuck herself. And that her getting to work on time was the least of my problems. But instead of getting all caught up in it, I looked right at her and said real evenly, "I'll do the best I can," before I walked off to get some shovels. She was gone when I got back. Much to our surprise and relief we just had to shovel a little bit from around the place where the tongue was digging into the dirt and it drove right out on our first try, and away we went. It was quite a sight, this huge room sitting on this gigantic trailer, being pulled down the road by this small looking pickup.

Flashback: Movin' day. I'm goin' off ta college which is a two-hour drive away. I'm terrified. I've never even driven in a city before, let alone lived in one. I know I'm gonna get murdered or sumpin' awful. The whole family is here ta see us off. None of us has ever went ta college before. My big brother works for a farmer, and the farmer loaned us a trailer ta move my stuff on. It's all stacked out in the front yard waitin' for my brother ta arrive. Pretty soon I see his beat-up truck comin' down the street. I can't believe my eyes. He's pullin' the biggest trailer I ever did see! It looks bigger than a semi! He pulls up an' jumps outta his truck an' comes over with a big grin on his face. He says, "Well, watcha think? Think it'll be big enough?" I'm laughin' an' I tell 'im that trailer is so big we could move the whole damn house! The rest a the family has already started loadin' my junk on it. I don't have much, jus' the baby bed, a dresser, a big color t.v. that don't work but I'm takin' it along jus' in case I meet somebody who knows how ta fix it. There's a little kitchen table an' a couple a chairs an' that's about it. I gotta couple a garbage bags a clothes an' stuff in the car, an' a box of dishes. Mom sticks a box a groceries in the back seat while I'm puttin' the baby in her car seat. My friend from next door runs across the drive an' hugs me goodbye. I can tell she's been acryin' 'cause her eyes are all red an' puffy. We've lived next door to each other since we moved ta town when I was four, an' she was still a baby. She's jus' a junior so she's gonna be here for a while. I'm gonna miss her. One a my sisters comes up an' gives me a quick hug an' slips a five-dollar bill in my pocket, saying' "Jus' in case ya have car trouble or sumpin'." My other sister is sittin' on the porch swing, holdin' one a the babies that she babysits for so she jus' waves from there. My dad, standin' by the screen door, tosses his cigarette down on the porch an' goes in without even lookin' at me. He's pissed off 'cause I'm movin' away an' takin' my baby with me insteada leaving her there with them. Mom shuts my door for me an' spends a few minutes warnin' me about all the horrible things that's gonna happen ta me up in the city. My brother an' his wife are in the truck waitin' for me. He honks his horn ta hurry me up. A bunch a my nieces an' nephews come tearin' 'round the corner a the house an' stand at the edge a the road wavin' an' yellin' goodbye as we pull out. I have ta laugh at the sight a that big ole trailer...it's gotta be at least twenty feet long an' all my stuff is piled up in a little pile on the front takin' up not more'n six feet a space.

We got it here...

Now what? We take the big room and back up as close to the foundation as we can get. Basically, we just reverse the procedure to get it off the truck. We wrap the chains and strap 'em in a big "U" around the house, and attach the come-alongs to a telephone-pole fence post. We are worried that the post won't hold, but it does. We have a few problems when the bottom of the house catches on one of the pillars and pushes the pillar right over before we even notice. We make a make-shift pillar outta a stack of concrete blocks. After we get the house on the foundation, we have to straighten it out so that the anchor supports will all be in the right place. To do that, we spend hours jacking it up, cranking the come-alongs and twisting the room. Once, while we had it jacked up, my nephew yelled something from the other side of the house. I thought he said to let the jack down, so I did. Turns out that's not what he said at all and when I let my jack down, it caused the corner of the room to come crashing down off the pillars and everything. "She's falling!" he screamed, but by then my-girlfriend-at-the-time and I had grabbed each other and took off. He came racing around the house to see if we were alright. He and I took one look at the mess and we both busted out laughing. My girlfriend-at-the-time was still shaking and got really pissed about us laughing. She thought we were both "sick and crazy," especially when he and I calmly started to jack the house back up again. She went and took a break, while we figured out just what to do next.

By evening we had got it back on its foundation and had fixed the gaping hole that we busted in the floor when we dropped it. My nephew and I had started a new saying...instead of "Don't drop the ball" we were saying "Don't drop the house." Since we were so calm about the whole thing, my girlfriend-at-the-time was thoroughly convinced that we didn't have the good sense to come in outta the rain. My nephew and I had a hard time realizing that she was really upset, 'cause for us it was all over. We decided it all had to do with our families!

Even though we were dog-tired and it was gettin' dark we weren't finished for the day. After supper we had to go back out and build the foundation for the other bedroom. (Remember, we couldn't do it earlier 'cause of the shape of the house.) Now that the big room was in position, we could go ahead and move the little bedroom as soon as the foundation had set up enough. We figured the cement would need about twenty-four hours to set up good. Since we only had the rental equipment for one more day, that meant we had to build the foundation that evening so it would be hard by the next evening. Dark caught us out there diggin' holes and pour-ing cement. We strung a couple hundred feet of extension cords and kept on working by lamplight. We didn't have those big fancy lamps that con-struction workers use, so we just used my regular table lamps. We took the shades off and held 'em up high like big torches! By the time we dropped into bed that night we were bone tired after working sixteen hours.

Flashback: It's hot an' muggy but jus' won't rain. There's a drought on an' the crops are failin'. Our garden didn't do much this year an' what did come up has already turned brown an' died. My daddy an' I are out at the stupid lake, the one on my uncle's stupid farm. The darn mosquitoes are eatin' me up. I didn't wanna come, but my daddy said he needed my help...that he couldn't carry his cane, the bag, an' the flashlight. Well that may be true, but I still didn't wanna come. I feel guilty an' mad. I know it's not my daddy's fault that he's disabled an' can't hardly walk. But damn it, how come I always gotta be the one lookin' out for him? So what if there ain't anybody else. I know I should be more understandin', so I'm feelin' guilty 'cause I ain't. I still think what we're doin' out here is gross. We are walkin', as quiet as we can, along the edge a the lake, in the mud an' cow shit. I keep gettin' stuck, an' my boots make a loud sloshin' noise. Half the time they come right off my feet when I try ta pull 'em outta the muck. Daddy's in front with the flashlight. He's tied one a his blue handkerchiefs over the end so the light ain't so bright an' is walkin' along in his slow way, leanin' on his walkin' sticks. He's usin' them kinda like crutches. He decided he'd better not chance it, jus' usin' his cane, 'cause what if he fell down an' got hurt out here in the middle a nowhere. I ain't old enough to drive yet. Knowin' daddy, he'll never let me learn even when I am old enough. He don't believe girls should be out runnin' all over tarnation by themselves. If either one a my brothers still lived at home, he wouldn't even have let me come along tonite, even if I'd wanted, 'cause frog catchin' ain't for girls. Daddy stops an' holds real still for a minute. I can see the eyes of a big bullfrog shinin' in the light. The frog is quiet now, tryin' ta figure out what's wrong. Daddy's watchin' an' waitin' for that frog ta relax. Sure enough, a big bubble a skin under his chin starts ta swell up. Jus' when it looks like his throat is gonna pop, that frog opens his mouth an' out comes a croak so loud it's hard ta believe that it came from sumpin' so small. Even standin' there watchin' it, it's hard ta believe. Course this ain't the first time I saw a bullfrog, but I'm always the same way about the sounds they make. It's puffin' up again an' suddenly Daddy reaches out an' grabs him quick as a wink. I open up the top a the gunny sack an' he drops him in with the others. I don't care if we ain't got nothin' else to eat, I still think it's gross. I ain't gonna eat no frog legs. Well, maybe I will, but I ain't gonna like 'em.

We're in the home stretch...

Almost done. Our last day with the equipment. We all wake up tired and are feeling the pressure of the time limit on the equipment. I ain't got enough money to rent it an extra day so we gotta finish today. We go over and load the kitchen on the trailer without much problem. By now we have our system down and are feeling like pros. Even then, it still takes about four hours just to get it on the trailer, and another three to get it off and in place on the foundation. We go get the little bedroom, which is easy 'cause it's just setting up high on those blocks waiting for us. Putting it on its foundation is a little tricky because we want to be real careful since the foundation was just poured yesterday. We've got it in place before sunset. Only the tiny bathroom left to move and that shouldn't be nothing after what we've done. We go back to get it, but we can't agree how to do it, and end up in a big argument. Our first since the "What's the plan?" fight. Since it's my house, the other two throw up their hands and say, "OK, we'll do it your way." My way turns out not to be such a great idea, and we end up pulling the bathroom off its foundation, but not *onto* the trailer. After a bout of hysterical laughing, I decide, "Screw it! I'll tear it apart and move it in pieces." We go home and fall into our beds.

Tidying up...

That's all that's left to do. A few days later we wrap the chains and strap around two rooms at a time and use the come-alongs to pull the rooms tight together. While they are strapped together, we replace the nails we cut earlier, and when we take the straps off the rooms stay! We use the jacks and a bunch of wooden wedges to level up the whole house. Last of the essential items is to crawl underneath and nail the anchor straps to the bottom of the floor. We're finished in a day. The house is now officially moved!

Nine months later...

Our lives still don't even remotely resemble our usual routine. I got some do-it-yourself books from the library and wired the whole house for electricity and put up a meter on the electric pole. That took us weeks, both the actual wiring and the trench digging. It didn't pass the first electrical inspection from the county, but much to my surprise the inspector was real helpful and gave me some tips. The second inspection went without a hitch. Pretty impressive since I'd never even wired a lamp before!

Then came time for the final building inspection, which was required in order for it to be legal for us to live in the house. I wouldn't have bothered except we knew that our neighbors were already calling and making complaints to the county authorities about us. That's what happens when dykes move into the neighborhood. So we jumped through all the county's bureaucratic hoops. My house passed its final inspection with flying colors, and the neighbors can just go blow it out their ass!

We still aren't all the way settled in. My daughter just finished repainting her bedroom. We had to replace the drywall on the ceiling and walls that we'd torn out to get to those nails we cut when we moved the house. I'm in the process of painting my bedroom and kitchen, repairing drywall, etc. I figured, "What the hell. Now's as good a time as any to redecorate!"

We don't have our bathroom back on yet. We'll have to install a septic system first. I have hooked up cold water to the kitchen sink. The drain runs out onto my flowers, which I think is great, but is very much frowned upon by the county. I'm not real sure how to do the septic and plumbing stuff yet, but I'm sure not knowing how isn't gonna stop me!

We are also settling into our community and its changes. There's four of us who live here full-time and a couple of part-time wimmin. We've fenced the entire two acres with six-foot-tall wooden privacy fence. It felt strange at first, but at least now we can run around naked without the neighbors having a conniption fit. We've also added a set of trailer hook-ups and moved a large RV onto the land. The thirty-ish wommin is no longer living in unwanted isolation. The wommin who used to rent a trailer from Adobe now lives in the other house on our land. Hopefully we've got her leaky roof fixed...we'll know when the summer monsoon rains arrive. The wommin who had moved to her land spent most of the winter with us. She lived in our "Casita," a little house, which the rest of the country would call a shed. We continued to organize with the land trust, put out a news-letter, do fund-raising, and try to take care of the legal stuff like taxes, not-for-profit exemption certification, and leases. We need more help. We need more money. We get lots of inquiries from wimmin wanting to know about wimmin's land, or who want to come and live with us. We'd like to tell 'em all, "Sure come on ahead and join us," but we simply don't have the space for all those wimmin. Instead we tell 'em our story and encourage them to do the same. We'll try to help out any way we can, but we can't do it for 'em. I always encourage wimmin to go ahead and take the risks, even if they don't know how to. Not knowing how ain't no reason to stop us. Wimmin are amongst the most brilliant creatures on this planet and learning is a beautiful part of living!

Helen Elaine Lee with her brother and parents.

The family's house in Fullerton in the early 1960's.

Goodbye to the House

Helen Elaine Lee

Three years ago this autumn, as the turning of the leaves began, my parents moved from the house where I grew up. Their big old Detroit house that was in constant need of fixing had become too much for the two of them, with my father's escalating illness and need for constant care. When they were burglarized, their leaving became a matter of urgency.

When my mother decided to move to an apartment downtown, I went to help, and the process of sorting through a collection of possessions, amassed over generations, began.

As my father lay in the hospital fighting to live, my mother, my brother, George, and I sat on the attic floor and sorted through letters and pictures, books and clothes and toys. Sifting through the surviving symbols of our lives, we decided which pieces of the past to take along to our new homes, and which to examine and leave behind. The flood of memories triggered by these objects, yellowed and wrinkled with age, became too much at times, and we paused. The richness of our years in the house passed before us, passed through us. The difficulty and the pain. The survival, the laughter, the joy.

From other generations, there were testimonies. Greeting cards and scrapbooks. Dog tags from World War I. A leather and china doll who was missing her hair. Sepia-toned photos and embroidered dresser scarves. Fragments hinting at my ancestral past.

We found documentations of my father's life: articles on professional achievements, business cards and briefcases. There were photos of his segregated WWII army unit and an article about his top Harvard Law School honor of best oralist in the 1949 Ames Competition. And alongside it, scores of rejection letters stretching from 1949 into 1950, as he tried for a year to get a job.

We came across clippings from the local "colored" newspaper. There were pictures of my mother as a young girl at social affairs, and articles on the scholarships she won, which praised her "beauty and brains." There were report cards and a Delta Sigma Theta pin, graduate school papers and the icing-encrusted bell from my parents' wedding cake. And articles published as she gritted her teeth and did enough scholarly writing to get university tenure and do the teaching that she truly loved.

There were pictures of family gatherings at Oak Bluffs on Martha's Vineyard, and echoes of the more recent past. Evaluations from the unconventional school my brother and I attended that didn't believe in report cards. The finger paintings and school essays that parents save with such pride. Polaroids of neighborhood kids with the graduated tear-off edges still attached, and painful images of the shy, chubby, pre-pubescent girl with thick glasses I have tried to forget.

What happened in the house, where I grew from infancy to adulthood? Who am I and how have race and class shaped me and my family? What of me is rooted in this place, I asked myself, at this time of taking leave?

I returned to Detroit a month after the move for Thanksgiving, and helped my brother bring my father home from the hospital. The move had happened over the several months of his hospitalization, while he was transferred from intensive care to a regular floor, and then to a rehabilitation center. Confused about where he was and where he was going, he asked me, "Where is home? I have so many homes." We decided to take him by the house, so that he would better understand the move.

"We're going to Fullerton, Dad," I said, "to the old house. So that you can say goodbye." He nodded and said, "Okay." When we pulled up he said, "Yeah. That's the house," and asked my brother and me about the tenant's car that was parked in the driveway. We explained that someone else was living there now, and that we were going to the new place. We sat out front looking at it for a while. And then we said goodbye to the house.

"Goodbye house," I said, and he did the same, understanding finally that we were going to our new home. "Goodbye house," he said, waving, and we drove away.

When I began to think about writing a piece on growing up different, I thought, "different from whom?" Everyone grows up different from everyone else. As I thought over the forces of race, class, gender and sexuality on my past, I realized that I have usually felt like a stranger, different from just about everyone.

In the private attic where my memories are stored, there is a lifetime of hateful racist looks, and faces filled with surprise and rage at my competence. Looks of desperation for a category to fit me in. There are those days, long ago, when the neighborhood kids teased and excluded me for the way I talked and the way I looked, for going to a "fancy" private school. And the "bourgie" blacks, kin and acquaintance, for whose elitism I have felt such shame.

There are the threatened men I chose as lovers, who sought something so different from what I was looking for that we might as well have spoken different languages. And stored there also is the time I told a colleague I wasn't interested in a date with an athlete she knew because there was this woman I was in love with, and she looked at me across a chasm of fear and insecurity, puzzled by my "feminine" and seemingly normal exterior, and asked me had I always been "like that."

These memories of exile are with me always, and with my brother, too, who is artistic, offbeat, and sensitive, and says it has been hard to find a sense of belonging. I fight against their crippling force, struggling to use the greater awareness they provide, and to connect, now and then, in some fundamental way that transcends category. My identity must be forged by drawing something from each world that I inhabit, for if I allow myself to be pressed into choosing a single aspect of my identity, I must deny crucial parts of myself, and reduce the complexity of my political and artistic vision.

As the writer, Elizabeth Alexander, says in her work on African-American literature,[1] the medium of collage is a useful way to discuss black female identity. Rather than a monolithic way of looking at things and feeling comfortable in the world, collage expresses the simultaneous habitation of the different elements of ourselves. She expands the motif of "twoness," used by W.E.B. DuBois and other African-American scholars, as a way to talk about the bifurcation of being African-American and American, because this model has presumed the male sex, and has failed to address the implications of sexuality and class.

Alexander uses the example of artist Romare Bearden's use of a brown paper bag in the creation of collage. She points out that this piece of the work is identifiable as coming from somewhere else; it is both the brown paper bag that it was in its other life, and also a part of the new whole. The parts of myself are distinct, and give me membership in several recognizable communities, but I am more than any of these categorical identities, and more, too, than their assemblage.

It only makes sense to examine and discuss my identity as multiple and dynamic, and the challenge, then, is to integrate the coexisting and often warring aspects of myself, and in doing so, to open the way towards building coalitions with people of disparate experience and common values.

Although it is more difficult to view the world simultaneously through several lenses, it is also a gift which has prepared me for the solo flight of writing fiction. As I pull from my experience and piece together the various parts of my identity, making of my life a collage, I am sure that there will never be a smooth fit for me. But if it means I am challenged to turn the comfortable presumptions that come with easy group members on end, that instead of accepting prescribed roles I define and redefine myself, then this not fitting in has got its blessing side.

This differentness is a painful, yet liberating thing. In it there is the power to invent myself.

The Family Attic: Role Models of Differentness

"I never really fit in anywhere." I have heard my mother say this countless times. The only child of parents who moved a lot, she never stayed anywhere long enough to make friends. Her parents came to Detroit in the 1920s, when she was only a few years old. When we unearthed the scrapbook put together by her father, Victor, from the attic, his life became three-dimensional for me.

He was born in 1896, and raised in Columbia, Missouri, where, in the black community, his family was known as "The Rich Hickses" because they owned a farm, some land, and a general store in town. Victor barely looked black, and much was made of this fact, in his family and in the communities where he lived. It is clear from his letters and his scrapbooks that he identified as a black man, and it was said of him that he could talk to and relate to absolutely anyone. Once when boarding the "colored" section of a train, he was stopped by a porter and asked, "Are you a nigger?", to which he answered, with pride and self-mockery, "You're damned right, I'm a nigger. I'm a BIG nigger." His experiences must have brought with them confusion and a twisted sense of skin color caste instilled by the climate in which he grew up and in which, to a great extent, we still live.

Victor's commission as a Second Lieutenant of Infantry in an all-"colored" unit in World War I is affixed to the pages of his scrapbook, along with photos from his college years at the University of Illinois, where he was a member of the Beta chapter of the black fraternity, Kappa Alpha Psi. His induction certificate, dated 1916, is pasted prominently in his book, and for the rest of his life he was an active Kappa, serving on the National Board of Directors and in other positions. It was, for him, a true brotherhood. Underneath a 1917 portrait of this group, he wrote in his scrapbook in the 1950s, "Each of these men has remained true to one another through the years. Most of them have been more than just successful, none have failed, all are representative citizens of the communities in which they now live."

Pasted on the crumbling pages of Victor's memory book are scraps of his family life in Columbia, Missouri: letters from his grandfather, seeking pensions for himself and other Civil War veterans; his mother's high school spelling exam (in which *sycophant* is misspelled); and a photograph of the woodshed and smokehouse on his grandfather's farm. He wrote, "I remember the hams and bacon in the smokehouse and the hickory chips and green apple wood stacked up in the fall preparatory to smoking the winter kill. The small sheds were filled with cord wood in the fall for winter heating." Fond memories of his small town growing-up.

There was a magical quality about Victor. A picture now sits in my study, of Victor and my grandmother, Helen, near the end of his life. The two of them are standing in a garden, laughing, and she is encircled by a flock of doves. His arm is raised as if, with an incantation, he has made them appear.

Helen, who my brother and I called Nanny, was born in 1898 in Boston, to a family that was prosperous for blacks. Her mother died when she was only ten, from cancer, which she knew she had for years. She chose not to risk surgery while her children were young, hoping to see them into their teens.

Helen's father, John, was a railroad conductor, an elite job for blacks of his generation. The elementary school photographs of Nanny and her sister, Dot, show only a handful of black faces. Membership in their social world was determined largely by skin color. I have heard stories of how they resisted the exclusion of their best friend, Mamie, who was dark-skinned. Nanny always lived in the shadow of Dot, whom everyone said was the smart one, the pretty one. In most of their girlhood photographs, Nanny is looking down, while Dot's chin tilts up defiantly.

Nanny went to Posse Normal school, a teachers college which was later absorbed into Emerson College, and then ventured out on her own to teach physical education at Virginia State College. She must have found her first experience of an all-black community intoxicating, as she told my mother that during her year in Petersburg she had the most fun of her life. After that year, she moved to St. Louis, where Dot lived, and taught high school.

It was there that she met Victor, who was working at a series of office jobs. Once they were married, in 1923, and had a child, he went behind her back and quit her job for her because he didn't want his wife to work. Although she went along with this, she was deeply resentful. Another aspect of their lives which caused raging fights was his habitual infidelity. Nanny, who lived twenty-five years beyond Victor, until I was fifteen, and stayed in our house for several years, is in many ways a mystery to me. She was extremely close to my mother, whose every thought she shared, living vicariously in order to round out her own experience. She sublimated her will and desires to those of her family, with her sharp tongue and her passion emerging unchecked periodically, as evidence of a toughness of spirit.

Among the things uncovered in an attic box is a dusty leather-bound copy of Tennyson's poems, containing her favorite, "Ulysses," which she was fond of reciting, fist raised and perched atop a chair: "To strive, to seek, to find, and not to yield..." Whenever my mother hears this poem, she chokes back tears. Nanny never really had a chance to define herself, but I think she had an iron will, and after Victor died she made an interesting life for herself, investing profitably in an apartment building and taking trips all over the world.

In the early 1930s, when Dot was suffering from an illness, Nanny had turned for spiritual help to Christian Science. My mother was raised in this church, of which they were the only black members, compounding her sense of differentness. My mother says she will never forget walking up as a girl from her church said to another child, "Here comes the little nigger girl." And the memory lives also of that day in school when the little white girl backed her into a corner and said, passionately, her eyes brimming with tears, "You CAN'T be colored, YOU CAN'T, YOU CAN'T!" because she had liked my mother and thought her smart. A lonely, only child, she found her greatest comfort in reading. Holed up in her room alone, she could visit any place she wanted by way of her imagination.

The Hickses never had much extra money, but Victor had a lot of ingenuity in getting by. He was a storyteller and a passionate reader, mostly of history and politics. He was also something of a schemer, an unconventional risk-taker, and although he died at the age of fifty-two, before I was born, he is the inspiration for one of my hero characters in my novel-in-progress.

After relocating from Missouri to Detroit in the late twenties, Victor and Helen moved a lot, and Victor worked at a variety of office jobs. During the Depression, he worked as a chauffeur for affluent white people, and as a swami who advertised the ability to divine the number. He spent his later years as the first black clerk for the Wayne County Circuit Court. In the 1940s Victor was a Democratic Party worker, and he ran for Congress in 1946 and lost the Democratic primary, but not by much.

Victor had a strong sense of community, and was a founder of the "Seminar Society," a group of black men who took turns writing and presenting research papers. The papers had to be on topics outside their fields of employment or profession. He also put in his scrapbook the Constitution and By-Laws of a Detroit organization, "The Pioneers," which he helped start, and whose stated purpose was to study the problems and issues affecting "the total life of the Negro community," and to foster and encourage programs in Detroit which would contribute to the community's well-being.

My father's paternal grandfather was a hard-driving, unforgiving man. He was the president of Florida A&M University, wrote a math textbook, and helped Booker T. Washington develop the academic program at Tuskegee Institute. Each of his many children was pushed mercilessly to upraise the race, and was expected to do something distinguished. His entire family was intimidated by him, including his wife, who is seldom mentioned in family stories. As a measure of her general demureness and fear, she died of colon cancer that grew completely unchecked, rather than submit to a physical examination. My father's father, whom we called Pop, was born in 1888, and never seemed to be able to do enough to please his father. Although he was chided for being less capable than his siblings, he went to Howard University and became a pharmacist.

My father's mother, Mama Ring, was born in 1896 to a family that lived in the Cumberland Mountains of West Virginia. I have heard that her mostly white father was quite color-conscious, and objected to her marriage to Pop, who was brown-skinned. Mama Ring's mother was part Native American, of the Susquehannock tribe, and, according to family stories, she identified strongly as Native American. Mama Ring went to Minor Teachers College in Washington, D.C., where she met Pop, who was then in pharmacy school. She and Pop began their life together in Newark, where Pop had his own drugstore. Like Nanny, Mama Ring was a housewife, except for during the Depression years, when she worked as a social worker. After Pop lost his store in the Depression, they moved to Baltimore, a segregated city, where Pop worked an office job in the daytime, came home for dinner, and then went to his second job as a pharmacist, which he loved. One of the pictures that surfaced in the attic shows Pop standing proudly in his drugstore, filled with medicines, jars and jars of penny candy, and an old-fashioned marble-topped soda fountain and wrought-iron cafe chairs.

We saw Mama Ring and Pop on summer trips to Baltimore, and I remember these gatherings as lively, filled with jokes and stories, poker games and lots of drinking. I can't say I knew who Mama Ring really was, but Pop, who lived longer and visited us in Detroit, seemed to be a jovial, loving man. My father had childhood memories of parental conflict and periods of heavy drinking by Pop, and says that only in adulthood did they become friends.

My father, who was brown-skinned, went to segregated schools growing up, and told the story often of how he stood day after day and watched the construction of a miniature golf course not far from where he lived. When it was finally completed, he and his fair-skinned friend ran home to get the admission fee from their mothers, never imagining that when they got to the entrance gate, one would be admitted and one denied.

He went from Talladega College, a black institution in Alabama, to Harvard, where he began in a graduate Psychology and Social Relations program on a Rosenwald fellowship. He always had a couple of jobs and a couple of hustles, among them a summer gig waiting tables at a "restricted" country club. When he was applying to graduate programs, the University of Maryland, unable to deny him entrance on the basis of his qualifications, offered to pay him not to enroll. He served in the army in World War II, and although he had been trained in Boston for the Signal Corps, he could not be assigned to a unit where his skills could be used, because the army was segregated.

During the war, he made himself indispensable at the base, heading up every possible athletic team and organization. He had no zeal to fight for freedom and democracy as a member of a segregated army. Among the many things he did was write comedy scripts for the shows that traveled to other bases to entertain the enlisted men. As his unit travelled through the South in preparation for shipping out, they stopped at a segregated train depot where they could not be served. He sat with his unit outside the depot restaurant, eating a sandwich out of a brown paper bag. Through the glass, he watched a group of German prisoners of war being served in the restaurant on china and linen tablecloths.

When my father returned from the army, he was able to do what he had had in mind all along, and become a criminal defense lawyer. While he was at Harvard Law School, he met my mother. She was in graduate school, and was to be the first woman, and the first black person, to get a Ph.D. in comparative literature from Harvard. Theirs was a strange and isolated experience. When I recently met a couple who went to Harvard in the 1950s, I was struck by how eager they were to connect with people who understood their story. "Did your parents tell you about this...?" they asked, "and what about this...?" I was struck by how isolated this small group of folks must have felt in such an alien white world of money and privilege. The duality of their experience must have been overwhelming. The pressure. The pride. The self-doubt.

My mother had come to Cambridge from Detroit's Wayne State University, which was the school her parents had been able to afford. She was either discouraged from academic achievement by the teachers at Wayne, or treated as the "exception" to racial stereotypes. Although she was told not to bother studying French because a black woman could never be a professor in that field, she got her bachelor's and master's degrees in

French, and was accepted at Harvard to study comparative literature, a relatively new field at the time, with a focus on French, Spanish and English.

My mother's background was distinct from those of the other graduate students, and her life was different, also, from the black folks in Detroit with whom she grew up. She was the one and only black woman in graduate school at Harvard, and her university-based friends were the white women with whom she roomed, and those studying Romance languages. Because the pursuit of a Ph.D. by women was uncommon in the Forties, there was a certain female bond of otherness between them. Of the nine women my mother lived and studied with, only three finished their doctorates, and only two used them professionally. But despite the academic link between these women, their social worlds were entirely separate. The handful of black students spread among the colleges in the Boston area comprised a community. These students went to parties together and dated amongst themselves.

My mother was one of the two women in her group to finish and use her doctorate, teaching literature at the University of Michigan-Dearborn. She says she chose the field of comparative literature because it spoke to her about transcending boundaries. It is an interdisciplinary way of examining literature for a person who resists categorization. The blessing side of being different.

She is the rare kind of teacher who makes students feel that the books they are reading are about them. She connects with them and they love her, saying often that she has given them a new window through which to view the world, and the possibility of communion through art. I know that the things she teaches were lifelines for her, and she has instilled in me the understanding of the power of words, and of beauty, to change people's lives.

Her study has always seemed a kind of sacred place. I enter it still with wonder at the walls lined with books, not because we weren't welcome there or because it was formal, but because doing so seemed a chance to travel. Her books, her "friends," she says, are arranged by genre and period. When we began to pack them up in preparation for the move to the apartment, I pulled some volumes from the poetry shelf, and found to my amazement that along with Dante, Emily Dickinson and Robert Hayden, there was a small familiar one. My mother had saved the book of my poems, bound in blue flocked contact paper and with sheets of faded construction paper, that I had given her for her birthday when I was nine.

It was hard to make an even living at criminal defense work in the days when I was growing up, and the money was seasonal. But my father was passionate and gifted, and became legendary in Detroit. He was determined to be the best courtroom lawyer he could be. As with all performers, the zeal of his advocacy was part ego, encompassing the high of competition and the joy of winning, but it stemmed also from a belief in the right of the disenfranchised to excellent representation. Because the stakes were high, he lived and died emotionally with every case.

In his professional life, he was difficult to get along with, disinterested in administration, and terrible at politics, but as a lawyer he was an ingenious risk-taker, who lived just this side of contempt of court. There was the time he put a transcript on the witness stand and cross-examined it, because the witness on whose testimony the case depended could not be called. And the time he told a racist judge in open court, "Your honor is merely displeased that the Ace of Spades speaks the King's English."

My image of him during childhood is double-edged. He was an energetic and full person, interested in politics and current events, athletic and charming. On weekends he worked, also maniacally, in the yard and around the house, and hit the tennis ball against the backboard he built, or rode an exercise bike to keep fit. He loved words and, for a while, it was a game for us to come up with a new one each day. Once, when he was hospitalized, he read the dictionary to pick up new words. He joined the Seminar Society, and worked conscientiously at his papers. We had challenging family discussions, and raucous poker games. And he was always telling jokes and stories. But he had an angry, tormented side as well. Life on Fullerton was, at times, an emotional and economic roller coaster.

His alienation and rage was sometimes focused inward, and with my mother, he was often withdrawn. Ingrown and misshapen, his anger was expressed in episodes of alcoholic stupor, and sometimes it was turned on his family.

Perhaps my parents' marriage lasted through times of turmoil because in a world where they never belonged fully to a group, they had each other. Their life together was textured and, I think, passionate. I recall them saying that when they got to the parties that my mother periodically pushed him to attend, wanting now and then to belong, they ended up talking to each other, and realized how deeply they felt linked.

My family, it seems, saved everything. We found an old tan leather suitcase with navy stripes down the middle and Dot's monogram in the attic. It had fifty years of letters inside, through which, in part, I have come to know Victor and his stories, which took liberties with the truth. He is an original (I think of him in the present tense) and his "lying" was right in the African-American storytelling tradition.

In one letter, he regales Dot with an account of how "routinely charming" he was at a Kappa dinner, self-mockingly entertaining her with tales of his "sartorial splendor," and then he tells a whopping tale about a fellow named "Tennessee Coal and Iron Company Jones."

Victor was the quintessential entertainer, with an understated presentation that pulled folks in, and a wild imagination that held you once you were there. "Now you KNOW you're lying!" people cried, but he never admitted it was so. He was a maverick in a world of restricted choices.

Black folks have always been expert at making something out of nothing, surviving with creativity and style. Whether sneaking pies out under his chauffeur's cap and adopting the persona of swami, or sneaking his new pair of shoes past Nanny into the house, Victor was hustling to get by, and blurring the lines between lie and truth. He was inquisitive, and passed down to my mother his thirst for knowing about things, through reading and living fully. He used to say to my mother when she was a child that, "the love life of a bullfrog is interesting, if you know enough about it." My brother and I both received his messages, and he reflects it in his work as a graphic designer. I like to think Victor speaks through my writing.

"The feeling in this picture is clear," I thought as I picked it up, "to anyone who's paying attention." Two women sitting side by side, just touching, in the long cotton bathing bloomers of the Twenties. They both smile, a little abashedly, and the warmth and intimacy is unmistakable. These women are in love.

My great aunt, Dot, and her female lover, Vee, are my role models for loving in exile. Together for close to fifty years, they had a long and rich marriage. Although the sexual nature of their relationship was never discussed openly, they were "Dot and Vee," both family, who came to visit regularly, and lived together in a house of their own, in St. Louis.

Through the pictures I uncovered in their scrapbooks documenting their years together, and their community of gay black folk, I have been able to claim a part of my cultural heritage that had been hidden. I have shown friends snapshots of the gatherings of their community taken in the 1940s and 1950s which look so contemporary: haircuts, clothing and timeless camping. The self-recognition is redemptive. Visibly moved, friends have exclaimed, "My god, this is our history!"

Vee was a high school teacher and Dot was a seamstress. Dot had been crippled since she was thirty by something never discussed, which I only found out in college was an illegal abortion. She struggled to make something rich out of the misfortune she was dealt. She sewed for both rich white folks to make her living and for her family, and the clothes she made were beautiful. Although Vee got a Master's from Radcliffe in the

1920s, Dot had no formal education beyond high school, but she was the most widely read person I have ever known. Vee was a demanding and talented English teacher, and had an acerbic wit. They were indomitable spirits. They loved music, and sports, and reading. They had cutthroat Scrabble games, and played cards, told stories, and followed politics. And boy, did they love to talk. They have helped me to define the hero journey, and inspired two of the principal characters in my novel.

They are role models in multiple ways. As strong, talented women who made their own way creatively. As full-living, spirited sisters who said "Yes!" to life. And as women liberated enough to love each other as openly as possible as far back as the 1920s.

They were in touch with their power, which they lend to me, and they invented, and reinvented themselves.

Captured again in a 1960s photo, they sit in the living room where they have aged together, in chairs that wear slipcovers made by Dot. Vee holds their adored cat, Muffin, in her lap. Her hair is closely cropped and she wears pleated trousers and a loose buttondown shirt. Dot leans on the arm of her chair, wearing a print dress that she made. Their years together show on their faces in a kind of weathered intimacy. They are worn into each other, not seamlessly, but with the living they have done together.

The Stranger in the Picture: Race and Class

Several years ago, when I was working on a social policy analysis project in Savannah, Georgia, a place of scarce opportunity and rigid class and race stratification, I began to stay regularly in an elegant Victorian inn. Each time I crossed the threshold, opening the large carved oak doors with beveled glass, I entered through my multiple identities. I was a woman travelling on business on her own, with many parts of my life hidden, in a deeply homophobic place. Most importantly, I was black. I never forgot that the owners of this inn doubtless once owned slaves, and that not so long ago my entry would have been barred. Even in 1990, my patronage was, indeed, a novelty that threw the other guests off balance.

This was a place where the elderly black worker who lived on the grounds was referred to as the "houseboy." And more than once, there had been hesitation, and then a question that revealed the assumption that I was staff. Despite even after a year of monthly visits, the manager had called my companion, who aside from being black, couldn't look more different from me, by my name.

The black staff members enjoyed seeing me come to stay there, and one of them invited me to her home. With another, I chatted about Savannah and D.C. politics, and sat up into the night waiting for Hurricane Hugo to hit. There was a special unspoken kind of community between us, as we shared smiles of secret amusement at the ways of white folks. And yet, I felt uncomfortable. What acceptable things explain the gap between my privileges and the wants of others? Who was I within this world, and where did I fit into the picture of genteel Victoriana? I felt an almost physical discomfort when I tipped the "maids" for my breakfast tray, as I read a mixture of expressions on their faces: puzzlement, pride, resentment. All at the same time.

In the photograph stamped "1970" along the bottom, the chubby girl looks out tentatively from behind thick glasses, her hair in long braids, her head lowered. This child has survived within me, too much, I find. These days, she is in combat with the self-assured, driven part of me who predominates and is presented to the world. I have been unable to escape her, and I can hardly bear to look at her picture. Why does this child look like such a stranger? What made her feel this way?

My parents say I was a happy, busy child, given the name "Captain Jolly" because I laughed so much, and pictures of me as a little girl reveal a jovial spirit. When did my sense of differentness begin?

I bury the picture of the chubby girl among the later ones I find, the ones reflecting that she has shed a little of her shell of insecurity, exchanging her plump body for one that she starved a few years later to be pathetically thin, eventually replacing her glasses with contacts and finding her own style in clothes.

Mine has been an experience of belonging and not belonging. And of viewing the world and my place in it through the lenses given me by race and class.

In terms of the microcosm, we were privileged, and in terms of the macrocosm, oppressed. It only makes sense to talk about these two forces together, because my privilege is what separates me from the experience of most black people. There is the shared thing, the depth of which cannot be articulated. And yet there is the gulf that class creates.

My experience was different from the neighborhood kids, all black, who went to the local public school. Different from folks who have grappled with basic questions of survival, and suffer a crisis of meaning so many of my people feel. Except for a few seasons of big cases and fees for my father, we never had a lot of money, but we rarely wanted for things either. The advantages we had were those of education and exposure, of self-confidence and choice. Although the doubts of others have been a primary motivator in my life, and have inevitably instilled insecurity as well, I have never had to struggle with a sense of alienation from the world of school and of books. Given the fact that knowledge is the thing that can't be taken away, this has been quite a gift.

In an effort to enhance our academic opportunities and encourage our individuality and creativity, my parents sent us to Roeper, an offbeat private school in a suburb of Detroit. Before that decision was made, my brother had sat, bored and stifled in a first-grade public school class, breaking crayons one by one while the teacher tried merely to maintain order and get the students to follow school rules. Started by a Jewish couple who had barely escaped the Holocaust, Roeper was called "City and Country School," with the idea that the students would come from all kinds of backgrounds. It was a place where individuality was celebrated, and this was liberating at the same time that it was limiting.

The school was situated in a former mansion on a richly wooded lot with treehouses, playing fields, and even a creek. Although it lacked traditional facilities like a gymnasium, and was always struggling to get by financially, the classrooms were small and the teachers committed. Admission was based on an IQ test, which nobody seemed to realize was culturally biased.

My mother used to say that when she visited the school, it was a scene of organized chaos, one kid swinging from a banister, one playing a flute in the hallway, a class being held outside on the grass. The classrooms for the youngest kids, "The Domes," were round, and made of styrofoam. There was a recognition that each child learns in a different way, at a different pace. In keeping with this philosophy, we were not evaluated by grades, but by reports which discussed what we seemed to be interested in and excited about, or vice-versa. There was great creative freedom to learn through projects. It was a place that felt open. At weekly assemblies of the entire school and staff, everyone raised a hand to speak, even the Headmaster.

Roeper's student body was a collection of bonded oddballs, which included a handful of blacks, and I felt different from the white kids at the school, whose homes I visited. Of course, when my parents were growing up, this extracurricular intersection would never have happened. A law school friend told my father, casually, that although he would like to invite him home, such a thing would be unacceptable. When we came across a class high school picture of my mother's she said she hadn't even known where the white girls she went to school with had lived.

In my Roeper days, I slept over at homes in affluent areas where no blacks lived, and I have a distinct recollection of being dressed up in stiff lavender, around the age of eleven, to go to dinner with a classmate and her father at the Detroit Athletic Club, which until quite recently excluded blacks. I recall the strange complex of feelings that flooded me when the elderly black waiter came to serve us. And after visits and sleepovers in the suburbs, we went back to our part of town. Back from the suburbs to small city plots and avenues lined with used car lots, liquor stores, and beauty shops.

At the same time that I felt estranged from the white kids at school, I felt separate from the kids in the neighborhood. They all went to the school four blocks away. From them, I heard how I thought I was better because I went to the suburbs to school, because where they went wasn't good enough. I heard how I talked funny and looked funny, and had "good hair." How I must be like those white girls I went to school with.

As puberty began I was teased, also, for being overweight, and for my thick glasses, which I had worn since the second grade. Afraid to dance because I might not do it well, I shied away from heightening my differentness, and hesitated to call attention to my body. I sat on the sidelines and watched the other kids who seemed to participate with such ease, feeling like an alien. The arena where I knew I could function was school. Even today, the times I have felt least alone have been with literature. But because of this, I was excluded for being a bookworm.

As we grew up, I became even closer to the other black students at Roeper, and remained tight with a Japanese girl, who seemed as different as I felt. Our community of black teenagers listened to the same music, made up dance routines, and fantasized about the Jackson Five and our soon-to-be-blossoming social lives. We lived in Detroit and rode to school together, while the white kids lived in the suburbs, and were on the whole more affluent than we were. We were misfits together.

When we became interested in boys, the white and black worlds diverged even more. The boy I chose to like, even at thirteen, was one of two black males in my class. And my first real boyfriend and sexual partner was another of the black males at the school. Perhaps I was so desperate to keep him, no matter how he treated me, because he lived in similar country. We inhabited the same divided world, and there was a kind of safety in that.

As my mother and I went through the things in the attic, I came across class pictures and evaluations from Roeper, and my graduation program and tassel from high school. Even at predominantly black Cass Tech High School, the public school where I insisted on spending the ninth through twelfth grades so that I could "see the real world," as I told my parents, and maybe make a more comfortable place for myself, I was one of a few black students in the honors curriculum. This sense of differentness would continue at Harvard College, where I lived, partially, in the world of my white roommates and classmates. And later, in law school at Harvard, at the law firms where I have worked, and at Yaddo.* It continues.

I have so often been the only black, and there are always the little reminders, important really, lest one become too comfortable. The liberals who let slip the judgments they are fighting to hide. The writers and scholars who are completely uninformed about black and African literature. The well-appointed lady at the Yaddo garden party function who rushes up to me and calls me by the name of the black woman writer who was there the previous year. The law firm where I recently worked that only in the last few years got its first black attorneys, most of whom seemed afraid to identify with me enough to speak.

Much of what went on at Harvard, the altogether different scale of privilege, the boarding schools, the Finals Clubs, had nothing to do with me. But the fact that my parents had gone there made it less foreign than for many of my friends, and it helped me to feel that I had as much business being there as anyone else. I was very absorbed in the academic part of school, and much of my self-esteem lay in getting A's. When I got a B on a Freshman expository writing paper, I was highly upset, and I made sure it didn't happen again.

My freshman year, I inhabited the white world at Harvard, and another one, separate and cherished. On Friday afternoons, my roommates and I made plans, dressed, and primped for the coming evening, and then went our separate ways. The two worlds intersected, but there was an untouchable part of my life in which they couldn't share. Once among the black students, I had to fight feelings of insecurity, afraid that no one might ask me to dance, or that people could tell how isolated I felt. Because it seemed like everyone else fit in so well and interacted with such ease, these times were agonizing, perhaps also because I wanted to be accepted by men. I went to those parties and took part in black student activities because it was so important to me to be a part of this community, but I was always a little afraid of not being welcomed.

Later in my college experience, I found black friends who didn't fit in so smoothly either, and the man I became involved with felt different, too. He was West Indian, and came from a distinct cultural world of immigrants. He truly had to juggle membership in different worlds. After settling in the U. S., he had lived in Harlem, one of six children abandoned by their father. Then he was "discovered" by the "A Better Chance" program and sent to boarding school at Phillips Andover on a scholarship. I admired his fighting spirit, and he knew what not belonging was.

*Yaddo is a prestigious (read: elite and mostly white) artists' colony in Saratoga Springs, New York.–ED.

Roeper's idealistic approach to things was not an adequate framework, by itself, for functioning in the larger world. We were taught to give people the benefit of the doubt, and that sensitivity and individuality are valued. We got the message that the world is a fair and loving place. These are important parts of who I am, but they are accompanied by other consciousness. Many of the students who went to Roeper have had a hard time functioning with their naivete outside of the bubbled environment created in that house in the woods. My brother has expressed anger at the myths he learned there. I believe in people's possibilities, but I deal in what I see.

Fitting things together in the context of discrimination has not been easy. My approach now is to bring to my interactions a knowledge, ever-expanding in its complexity, about what attitudes are culturally inherited by colonizer groups, the groups with the resources, and are reinforced. This is the given. What I look for, then, is a spirit of vigilance, in turning on end the comfortable, white and male supremacist attitudes, behaviors and assumptions that are reinforced by our media, our legal system, America's materialistic system of values and beliefs. And I look for indices of energy directed at overcoming them.

In this white supremacist society, whose messages filter in from everywhere, where racism works not just on the personal level, but with the systematic dehumanization and povertization that perpetuates a history of disenfranchisement, there is no escaping how much of what happens turns on race. My blackness is a bond, because it determines a great deal of what happens to me, and also because of a shared, rich cultural heritage. I have felt this bond, on the streets of the cities where I have lived, in the workplace, and even when my mother and I were in Venice and we saw a group of black folk sitting at a cafe. We rushed up to them and practically embraced. Complete strangers in a literal sense, theirs were faces from home. And when I walked along the main drag of Saratoga Springs while at Yaddo, and came upon a black man, we paused, said hello, and smiled, showing each other that we were relieved, comforted, to see one of ours.

While growing up, the backdrop of racial tension and hatred, the macrocosm, was very real. In my memory space there is the time of rioting, in 1967, when we were returning from a vacation on Martha's Vineyard, where we had lost track of the news. While stopping at a filling station somewhere between Massachusetts and Detroit, an attendant noticed our license plate and mentioned the riots. We rode into town through nighttime streets, fires blazing and sirens screaming, my brother, my mother and I on the floor of the car. That summer, sleep was broken as my parents rushed into our rooms and pushed us to the floor, when the sirens and the shooting grew too close. Rage erupted in Detroit that summer of curfews, when I was eight, and we were in the middle of it all.

There was the climate of the sixties and seventies, and my father's cases, reflections of the turbulent times. There were the newspaper articles, the hate mail and death threats, the students withdrawing from my mother's classes when she was the first black to teach in avowedly racist Dearborn, a city adjacent to Detroit.

Among the things unearthed in our attic excavations are the pictures that make up my "ancestor wall." In a corner of my study I have hung them: pictures of my great aunt and her lover, my parents, the oldest traced ancestor on my father's side, who was a slave. There is a shot of Pop in his drugstore, and my maternal great-grandfather standing next to the Flying Yankee, the train out of Boston on which he was a conductor.

It's a hard thing to reconcile the pride I feel in my family's accomplishments, because I have a sense of what they cost. As role models they have given me a sense that I can do anything. But it is important to me to be vigilant, in the way that I look for in white people, about class. Just as white people must struggle to transcend the attitudes and assumptions they are dealt by virtue of their racial membership (more comfortable to retain than to shed) I know that the attitudes that come with an inheritance of privilege must be challenged, if I am to look at the way class works in this society, and fight against the messages received.

Part of the picture is that the elitism of those blacks with advantages has also been shaped by racism. The privileges and opportunities enjoyed by my family, which have moved me to a place of choices and opportunity, were conferred, at least in part, for despicable reasons. Class membership perpetuates itself. I know that I have travelled to places like Harvard not because of my achievement alone, but due to a series of events put in motion when a woman who is my ancestor lay writhing in pain beneath the man who owned her, her limbs pressed down and her cries swallowed. She bore a fair-skinned child with wavy hair, on whom the advantage of house, rather than field, work was conferred, due to the "humanization" rendered by her caucasian blood. Class division among black people began there, and it continues. On my application to Harvard, I was able to list that my parents went there, and that helped pave my way. And my parents went there, in part, because they were fortunate enough to be exposed to a broader set of opportunities, and encouraged in a way that was not open to most black people.

These are not things I had anything to do with, and they should, therefore, instill neither pride nor shame. But here's where the shame comes in. I know the kinds of attitudes that many of the black bourgeoisie hold, and I am aware that they feel little class consciousness, or responsibility, or identification. Many believe they are where they sit because they are special, better than others, and there is an ever-widening gulf between them and the black underclass. Growing up, I felt profoundly different from Detroit's black elite, too.

I carry shame for my own family attitudes, for how Dot railed against the transition from "Negro" to "black," arguing, "I am not black. It's just not accurate to call me so." For the aesthetic that equates beauty with light skin and straight hair. For the description of straight hair as "good."

My grandparents' generation of privileged blacks had little or no social interaction with white people. But they didn't want to identify with "common folk" either. Similarly, many of the black elite of today consider themselves black-identified. They belong to black, not white, clubs and sororities. Most would be upset if their kids married white. Theirs is a veiled self-hatred, which expresses itself in mimicry of the white upper class, and horror at things considered "too" black. My own family felt fear of the militancy of the sixties, and my brother and I did not get a black nationalist message at home, as my parents struggled with the concepts of armed struggle and pride in their blackness.

We work at loving and believing in ourselves, against the messages we receive about our competence from every source. "Mmmm," we are wont to say when we mess up, "My people." We find out from a survey reported in *The Washington Post* (January 9, 1991) that 62% of non-blacks think we are more likely to be lazy than they are and 53% think we're less intelligent than they are. Of those who don't say so, how many think it? How many of us suspect it, underneath, as well, and work at our achievements to prove it isn't so? We try desperately to free ourselves from the judgments of white society and the warping of their racism, aiming at self-definition. In my father, in so many of us, angry as we are at white folks, contempt for our own sometimes surfaces.

Countless times I have seen and dreamt the look, in condemning, patronizing blue eyes, the cancelling look that says, "As I suspected, you are not quite good enough." I have nightmares about the typographical error in a letter I wrote when I worked as an attorney at a corporate firm, and how later, when I told the partner I was leaving, she nodded and said, "Yes...that's probably a good idea. You probably don't have the right attitude for a future here." I rage against the editor of a fiction journal, who wrote me that in my story inspired by Dot and Vee, words like "direct confrontation," used by a third person narrator, were "above and beyond the scope of the world they describe." I try not to take it to heart, and to know that here the limitation of vision is the editor's. I try not to lose my voice. Not to see myself through his lens. In all that I do, I strive to perform, to prove what white folks think about us isn't so.

The black bourgeoisie of Detroit shop at Saks and drive Lincoln Continentals or Mercedes Benzes and are never seen in the same outfit twice. And there is a club of black professional men whose sole purpose it is to give black Detroit's most lavish annual party. People come from other states for this affair, and they don't even hire a black caterer to do the work. They give their functions at the best restaurants and hotels, buy lavish homes, and cherish their minks. They try to do, separately, just what the monied white population is doing, and there is really nothing African-identified at all about their activities or concerns. They are, in fact, embarrassed by the segments of the black population who are not playing the game as they are. They fear that identification with the underclass will cost them the legitimacy they have worked for from white society. I know a member of Detroit's black bourgeoisie who declares proudly that no one in her family has ever been a slave.

My generation's counterpart of these people, I am told, still talks about the importance of marrying a light-skinned man with hair that isn't nappy: "Just think of your children, girl. Your mother thought of you."

The Detroit Study Club, a black women's association in which papers and speakers are presented, is a testimony both to an interest in the arts worthy of pride, and also to majority group molding of our perspectives. It was started in 1898 as a Browning society, at a time when it was fashionable for upper-class ladies to gather and study the poetry of Robert Browning. Membership in the Study Club was a matter of caste, since you had to be invited to join, and most invitees were the daughters of members. One might think the founders would have been interested, instead, in Paul Laurence Dunbar. But they were busy doing what white ladies did.

Seeking to facilitate our friendships with children from similar experiences, my parents joined "Jack and Jill," a club for the children of the black elite, which has a stated civic purpose, but is predominantly for socializing. My experiences with this group were painful. Their snobbery and flaunting of material things—clothes, houses in the Detroit gold coast black neighborhoods, Palmer Woods and Sherwood Forest, and later, new cars as gifts—made me squirm with discomfort when I was around them. We didn't live in one of those neighborhoods, and my parents generally didn't believe in giving expensive clothes and new cars to teenagers.

When we became teenagers, discussions about which light-skinned straight-haired anglo-featured girls were the most desirable made me feel excluded. I didn't feel like I was the kind of girl any of them would find attractive. As far as I was concerned, my clothes weren't chic enough, I wasn't pretty, I wore glasses, and I wasn't thin. I didn't know the in-group, and I was a bookworm. I was just wrong. I found out recently that at my first parties, my brother, unable to bear seeing me excluded, went to the boys he knew and asked them to dance with me. Because it was clear that this could never really be a community for us, my brother and I seldom attended these events.

Isolated among the white students, my peers in the neighborhood, and the Jack and Jill crowd, where could I find a place? For years I felt like a stranger. But I have learned to feel more comfortable with myself, and there have been moments of deep connection, unexpected and unannounced. Meeting places, rare but possible, across region, class, age, and even race.

There is my former lover, who grew up quite different from me in South Central Los Angeles, and continues to be my sister. We felt, sometimes, like a community of two. There is a white college roommate with whom I have stayed close, and the white poet from Yaddo who grew up working-class, with whom I feel an uncommon connection. And the political prisoner at the D.C. Jail who has dedicated her life to fighting for the rights of disenfranchised peoples. I read a piece of my novel to this white woman who is my sister, too, across a scarred metal table in a glassed-in cubicle where inmates have legal visits, to the sound of iron bars in the background. They happen, these bridges.

On one of my trips to Savannah, I found a bond with a black woman in her eighties who couldn't read, and had spent a good portion of her life cleaning bathrooms at the local paper bag plant. We revealed ourselves to each other, I clumsily and she with much grace. She took my hands and opened her home and her past to me, weeping as she told me of black blood spilt by white men long ago. I shared a meal with her, and we told each other, across region, class and age, about our lives. For an afternoon, we were joined by a delicate and fleeting bond, and I felt, in some unspeakable way, that there was something we both knew. That we had been somewhere together.

Compounded Differentness

In my mother, I had a role model of a woman who was self-determined in terms of career. And Nanny, who as a married woman rarely satisfied her own needs or desires, later made a way for herself and was working her way around the world. And I have had family heroines who have inspired my fiction in Dot and Vee.

But my mother, at the same time that she is unconventional, is traditional. An inveterate pleaser, she subordinates her own needs and is ultimately other-oriented. I am struggling to free myself from this same mentality, and from the most insidious messages of sexism that are transmitted in subtle expectations, the cultural messages that get communicated in every part of our daily lives and shape our sense of ourselves and our possibilities.

I was not really afraid to be an outsider in the way that loving women makes me, and the embracing of my family and true friends has helped to make this so.

When I stood along the edges of high school and college parties where the women waited to be chosen or passed over, I felt a deep discomfort, and I fumbled for emotional connections with the men who were my lovers. The first time I went to a lesbian bar, in college, years before I had any real consciousness of myself as belonging there, I was struck by how varied the women were. They seemed freed up, somehow, dancing with each other, and alone. They were dressed all kinds of ways, and they were making up their roles for themselves. It felt free, and daunting, too. There seemed to be fewer rules about how to be.

Although I have been able to look back on my growing up and recognize my infatuations and deep love for women in my life, it was not until the age of twenty-five that I became interested in and open to exploring this part of myself. I met a remarkable woman and said "Yes" to her love. Partly because of her strength and uncompromising conviction in following her heart, I did not have severe doubts about this path. The lesbian community felt like a place where community was defined differently, and it didn't expect me to be like anyone else in background or experience in order to belong. The myriad of voices were celebrated.

We come to the experience of loving women in so many ways. Among my friends I see a woman who has had her most important relationships with women and is now involved with a man. There is one who had three children with her husband before she realized her lesbianism. And another who has never dealt with a man. We all have a place here because we are unified by this common experience. We have known about this thing and it will forever be part of who we are.

There have been those who, like my colleague, have asked me had I always been "like that." And there have been a few who distanced themselves from me, some noticeably and some subtly. And although I am able to structure my life so that I don't deal with homophobic people in a close setting too frequently, it is painful when I realize the virulence, the depth of the sickness of people's feelings about same-sex love.

Once I became involved with a woman, the presumptions our society makes about heterosexuality were glaring, overwhelming to me. I heard them everywhere, as people talked about weekend plans, and in more offensive ways, with ridicule. And I have also lately heard gay and lesbian intolerance at my honesty about loving both women and men. This part of my life, where I cannot be easily categorized, has provided me with multiple lenses, with other ways to turn group attitudes, vigilantly, on end.

There is simply not room for all the things we have discovered in the attic. We have chosen what to leave behind: pictures where we can't identify the faces, and greeting cards and keepsakes that can't be placed, and tried to save what is important to us. We have picked the dearest of the things, and stored most of them away, the lace, the books and the dolls, the quilts. Everything we found has been a part of our lives, tied up in the house on Fullerton.

I am working on knowing that it is all right to be a stranger. The world, after all, is not a place of absolutes, and the challenge is to balance between and embrace the duality of all experience.

Of the scraps in my internal storage space, I can create a collage, as many people in my family did, with the ingenuity and instinct for survival that are the ways of black folks.

These days, I serve time in the white male world of a corporate law firm to pay the rent, working not as an associate attorney, for which I was trained at the paradigmatic Harvard, but as a consultant. There is no accurate category or title to describe me in the firm roster; I am paid less than the attorneys; and I sit with the paralegals and am required to jump the hoops reserved for staff, rather than professionals. People treat me quite differently when they find out I am a lawyer, Harvard trained, and then they are puzzled by what would make me give that up. This place where I go each day, in which I have nothing emotional or ideological invested, is a study in social stratification. I remind myself that this job is about income, and try to use the insights it provides in my writing. But it is so difficult to integrate it with the rest of my life. And I am different, again, from everyone around me.

This is partly where I draw my power as an artist, and indeed, writing must be grappled with alone. In my fiction I am interested in examining the function of community: its redemptive power, and its limiting tendencies. After all, an examination of membership is also, in part, about what it means not to belong. The most interesting question for me as a fiction writer is what kind of individuals make hero journeys, who are the risk-takers, and how and why. The hero must rise beyond the limitations of convention and group prescriptions to find answers in more thoughtful and more expansive definitions of community and family.

The solitary risk of being a writer both frightens and frees me. Fighting to create amidst the practical demands of living, there is no order that is not self-imposed and few immediate rewards from the outside. It is just me and the words I try to shape into something that approaches art.

Fitting nowhere smoothly is helping me to love with complexity: to look back at my father, who died a year after the move from the house, and recognize his flaws while seeing his courage and tenacity. To perceive the love with which he struggled, and the ways he was misshapen by racism, classism, and limited cultural concepts of gender. To look past the exterior of things. To see the isn't and the is.

As I packed up the things I had put aside for saving in a box, preparing to return to my home in D.C., the picture of that shy chubby girl slid from a pile of snapshots and floated to the floor. I stared down at it, fighting the urge to hide or destroy it. Instead, I bent and gently lifted it, adding it to my box. This girl is a stranger and she isn't. She is for keeping.

Goodbye house.

FOOTNOTES
[1] *Collage: An Approach to Reading African-American Women's Literature and Culture*, Unpublished Ph.D. Dissertation, University of Pennsylvania, 1992.

Journal Notes: Exploring the Possibility of an Essay on Class, Poverty, etc.

Paula Gerber

A letter from *Bridges* came in the mail today, inviting comments on my experiences as a working-class or poor woman. I wonder, what do these classifications mean? Where does "poor" end and "Jewish immigrant" begin? Raised by my Jewish immigrant grandmother (after my mother's death when I was seventeen months old), I have, like her, come to think of myself as an outsider, a foreigner, someone who does not belong here. Is this an issue of class or an issue of immigrant sensibility?

Friends (whether gentile or Jewish) seem to have entry to a world which continues to mystify and evade me. They travel on roads not accessible to me. Their houses are bigger, cleaner, better furnished, less messy. They know what to fix for lunch. They know the appropriate thing to serve and whom to serve and when and how. As much as possible I avoid these events but find that I'm almost always nervous in certain situations, ill at ease, wondering what I'm not doing that's expected of me.

Peers publish books, appear in prestigious magazines, are awarded grants, editorial positions, stride through a world that seems their own, a world they are at home in. I share at least a little of their world. Like them, college was expected, assumed of me. But I lay awake in my adolescence, worrying that without parents (by then my father had disappeared), how could I enroll in college? Didn't one have to have parents to attend? And wasn't the same true for a wedding? Although marriage was secondary to education in my grandmother's value system, still, wouldn't parents arrange these things? I never asked. Somehow it had already been communicated to me that I did not have the right to ask.

And where did that begin? The trauma of being an orphan (with its built-in message of no rights), living on tentative status with my neurotically unhappy grandmother (her own ambitions and dreams buried in the sweatshop), and abandoned by my father, and other relatives? Our Jewishness or our poverty? Poverty of the pocketbook or poverty of the heart?

Bridges—no small irony, this name. Inviting me to create a bridge into my pain, to step out of isolation, to experience my process in community. Yet here is one more irony: the invitation to share intensifies the reality of my aloneness. I am approached to submit not on the basis of my years of training and skill as a writer and teacher (of some reputation, I cautiously add) but to write of my poverty. I will be accepted, through the back door, if I am willing to humiliate myself. I sit here, crying as I write, ashamed to admit how alien I feel. One small chapbook and that practically against my will, my poems almost absconded by a friend who had access to a press. Poets of lesser talent publish book after book, hustling, confident, knowing how to play the game of literary politics (dare I add, often on the backs of other women). Is it a game created by the middle class?

Or is there another way to perceive this? Perhaps that *Bridges* approached me on the basis of poverty instead of skill is a good sign. At least someone is listening now. Are they being "politically correct"—or attempting to move beyond traditionally literary politicking? I can only conjecture, but no matter what motivates them, this provides me with an opportunity to break out of a space of immense loneliness and isolation. If they romanticize or condescend, I cannot control that. But I can speak. And perhaps some will listen. And that is a beginning.

And this is the battle I must engage in to arrive at the place of beginning:

So what constitutes poverty? Growing up in Brooklyn in a one-bedroom apartment with ants and bedbugs and rats? I slept on a couch in the living room, for years thought it was a "lunch"; now I realize my grandmother was trying to say "lounge." The living room was crammed with a dresser, my bike, a rickety table with wobbly rows of books, an ancient typewriter, cardboard boxes stuffed with comic books, clothes, *shmates*,* maybe old letters; between the shade-drawn windows, a desk, an "easy" chair where I sat, drinking glasses of hot tea and reading books (*Jane Eyre, Pavlova, Nancy Drew*) while the November wind roared outside the window. Some gentile working-class women deride the value I place on education. Can I be of the working class and still love reading, writing, learning? Can I have grown up in an environment where that was fostered? In fact *programmed*.

Here is where it gets confusing—the gentile model for working class that has been presented to me simply does not hold in a Jewish environment. At least not in mine. All three of my grandmother's sons grew to be lawyers, married college-educated women, one a teacher. Working class? Lawyers, teachers, dreams of college, you call this working class? But *she* worked in a sweatshop.

"Oh, you can't be working class," a gentile once said. "You went to the Catskills or the beach three or four times" (to escape—briefly—New York heat waves and polio epidemics). This, from a woman who lived in a

*shmates: Yiddish, *rags*

middle-class neighborhood in a small Midwest town with swimming ponds and shaded tress and country lanes. Later, when I spoke of this to another gentile woman, she asked where my grandmother worked. "In a sweatshop." "Oh, then you *are* working class," she assured me, as if I had gained entry to a club. Somehow I felt entry or its lack had little to do with me.

Discussions of class never engaged me. Now I understand why: a gentile model had been used. A model which did not reflect her face in the *shabbes** candleglow, encouraging me to go on, urging me to consider ancestors, the thousands of Jews who had never known the opportunity that awaited me here in America. No, the streets were not paved with gold as she'd been told; still, this was *America* where "Jews can be anything."

Years later, after running away, after a teenage marriage to a working-class gentile, five children, a divorce, single-parenting on welfare, I entered college, lugging a shopping bag full of books to the bus, looked skyward and said, "Okay, Mama. I'm doing it, at last." And cried. With joy.

Savored each moment in college (even biology class!). Knew each moment was a privilege. My ex-husband had run out on support. Our home was foreclosed. We moved every two to three years. We lived on welfare. I had a car (granted during the divorce) but couldn't afford gas to drive to school. Got rides with students. Got scholarships, from Mt. Hood Community College, Portland State University and Reed College, used college loan money to buy clothes for my children. Broken windows were padded with cardboard. We made a game of wrapping ourselves in blankets when the utility company turned off the heat. Buying a calendar to tear out the pictures, one by one, to cover the cracked walls, to brighten the small house with hope.

Bending and ducking and swerving to move from one overcrowded room to the next. Sitting up late at night, writing term papers on *Madame Bovary*, the Wife of Bath, Ibsen's Nora. Drunk on the ecstasy of learning. Savoring, smiling, *kvelling.***

Later, downwardly mobile women would talk to me about college as middle class privilege, or how easy it was, especially for Jews, to articulate. Again, their categories seemed miles from my life. Often I overheard students deriding welfare bums. I flinched as I do with anti-Semitism. A new stigma.

One day a favorite instructor sidestepped his lecture to talk about a student on welfare. I cringed: here it comes, here it comes. Instead, he spoke of how she had articulated abuses to which welfare mothers and children are subjected. How he valued and admired her. No slurs about

*shabbes: Yiddish, *Sabbath*
**kvelling: Yiddish, *feeling joyful and wonderful; the human equivalent of a cat purring*

welfare bums that day. I went to the rest room, locked myself into one of the metal stalls and sobbed. *Someone understood. Someone did not point the finger and blame. One voice in all those years. One golden voice.*

Medical coupons. But I could not find a dentist who would accept them and treat my children until the Black Panthers came along and opened a dental clinic.

My children stealing from stores. From each other. Police. Detention officials. Social Workers. Neighbors reporting us. Emergency rooms in County hospitals. Later, abortions and drugs. And wondering, always wondering how much could be alleviated with money. Not all, but how much. One bright light: college. An immigrant's dream, a legacy of streets of gold, shining now in the college corridors I walked each day.

Going onward. Getting the degree. Working class? What class are you when you're on welfare? The welfare bum, America's scapegoat, condemned across all races and ethnic groups and classes. Three percent of the nation's economy and often blamed for all the economic ills of this country. Sound familiar?

Welfare. With how many do I share this part of my life, even now? It is my secret. For I am bad, I am wrong. I am the ultimate failure to be this thing.

Later my friend, Dympha, said, "People will write about you, about women like you. You'll be recognized as heroes because you survived such economic abuse." This comment was made in reference to an event that occurred when I was in graduate school. Laws enacted during the Nixon administration resulted in many women being imprisoned for going to college (another "best-kept-secret" since the abuses of the disenfranchised are rarely media events). Rule: welfare mothers may only attend five hours of classes. However, to qualify for a loan, you must take ten hours. Do so, as many did, self included, and you risk imprisonment. Perhaps the law was only intended to intimidate? Surely they won't implement it, I asked someone at Purdy's Women's Prison. "After all, it would cost the government so much more to place children in foster homes, etc." The response: "They will—and have—and are!"

Clearly, I was dedicated to getting an education but this pushed even my limits. Hence, to avoid the possibility of prison, I married a Vietnam Vet (on a pension) who earned more for two years of non-combat service than I had for sixteen years of mothering. He had promised to kill and I had promised to nurture and the country's values were reflected in how we were rewarded...or not.

"You're the same person, except that now you're Mrs. H—and they're off your back," he observed incredulously. We married on Halloween. I was dressed as a witch. After the wedding, he went to his apartment with the best man and I went home with the matron of honor. A contract marriage in which we agreed to live separately. As it turned out, he had a hidden agenda, harassed me for more than what we'd agreed on. Divorce #2. Now the Nixon-Ford housing crunch. A squelching of funding for low-rent housing. Divorced, I could no longer afford the home we were in. Three minor children at home. My graduate thesis rejected because it included poems that celebrate women, love between women, though no one came out and said so, openly. I dropped out.

I faced the streets or separation from my children. After all these years of struggle, how could it come to this? Also, how could I not complete my graduate work? Yet under these circumstances, how could I continue? A friend told me of someone selling a small house for no profit; she was looking, in fact, for a poor woman with children, someone who would benefit. With my friend's help, we negotiated. I moved in with my children. Reentered school. Wrote another thesis, in neutral gear. (Read: went into the closet. Stayed there.)

Continued writing. Began teaching. Continuing Education classes. Independent classes.

Also, I began to develop a grassroots writing community for women (workshops, readings, etc.), and ongoing work which continues to nourish us. In this environment where women can "reexperience" the healing power of sitting in a supportive circle and creating, many find their "long-silenced" voices and begin to write and share their stories. Some go on to publish for the first time and beyond.

Meanwhile, I continue my inner work on childhood trauma. I dare to look more deeply into my poverty, class, and ask how it fits into the larger story. Where does being Jewish end and poverty begin?

And if we speak of poverty of the pocket, must we not also speak of poverty of the spirit? And if I speak of the hunger of my children, must I not also speak of the hunger of the woman who raised me, from whom I inherited the clumsiness of the outsider and the light of the dreamer?

Now teaching independent and continuing education classes. Still tentative, dancing on the edge. Still earning less than the declared poverty level. Tentative with my teaching (avoiding a full career, though I now teach ongoing accredited classes, too), tentative with my writing (holding back my responses to opportunities, uncertain, fearful), yet confident or joyous in my teaching, in my inner world, confident in the classroom, confident at my desk writing. And more than confident. At one with the universe when I write. And bringing that sensibility to the classroom. Living well when I allow myself to *have* this.

Ahh…having. Is that it? Poverty precludes having. Or letting go of the old to move into the new. So the old ragged Beggarwoman invades my inner world, cackles: *No no not too much joy now or they'll take it away,* and when I turn to the outer world she is really fierce; she stands with arms outstretched, blocking me: *No,* she shouts. *It is not safe out there. A* goyishe* *world. Not yours. A world for* yentes *with parents and living rooms and real beds.*

And I believe her, I believe her. But look! Mama (my grandmother) on that distant hilltop, smiling waving me on, saying in fact, "Come, *sheyna meydele,*"** daring me to reach for the sky. Don't let those *gonifs*† take this away from you too. They've taken too much away from too many of us already," she says. "Yes, it's a *goyishe* world, but I'm out here now in it. And I'm bigger than all of them."

And she is! I look overhead where her face now fills half the sky. And I say "yes" to her and decide to respond to the letter from *Bridges*.

*goyishe: Yiddish, *non-Jewish*
**sheyna meydele: Yiddish, *pretty little girl*
†gonifs: Yiddish, *thieves*

the camaraderie of the toothless, or
the story of an ordinary, nice, well-educated,
middle-class, white, ashkenazi jewish girl

Merril Mushroom

I grew up Jewish in South Florida in the '40s and '50s, in a middle-class, secure family. I always thought we were rich, and assuredly, by comparison to poverty, we were; but by comparison to real wealth, we were not. However, we certainly were comfortable. I had all I needed of the basic material things in life like food, clothing, and shelter, but I was not especially indulged—I didn't have my own car or stylish clothes or other fashionable, popular accoutrements of living.

My folks were not concerned with appearances or following trends and fads. However, they WERE concerned with what they considered manners and breeding, and we were taught to be polite and well-kempt. My upbringing included basic health and hygiene, which involved regular medical and dental care, and until I went out into the world, I don't recall ever seeing a person beyond the tooth-losing years of childhood who was missing teeth.

I attended the same schools in the same neighborhood from kindergarten until I graduated. Dental health was part of the curriculum. The students were all white and primarily Jewish with a few Hispanics, also primarily Jewish. I was not included in the rich, popular crowd, because I was not rich and did not have any particular physical attributes or social skills that would make me especially attractive. My best friends through school were all middle-class, working class, or poor. We were mediocre to excellent students. We had all our permanent teen teeth, and some of us wore braces on them to straighten them out. We participated to some degree in school and community events and tended to be a little wilder than the classy set but not as wild as the trampy set—the sluts, bikers, and kids from the South end of The Beach, the "white crackers" and kids from broken homes. These teenagers were tough. They often had crooked teeth and cavities in front. They never wore braces. I was attracted to these South Beach kids. I thought they were different, interesting, and somewhat glamorous and enticing.

155

In ninth grade, a girl I had a crush on spoke to me. Her name was Sue, and she was from the North part of Miami Beach where a lot of the very rich kids lived. She had perfect teeth. Sue asked me how many hotels my father owned. Unfortunately, he didn't own any, and I told her so. Sue had nothing more to say to me, and she and her friends snubbed me, and my crush on her soon disappeared. One fine day she wore an expensive purple blouse to school, and I was glad to see deep, dark sweat stains develop under the arms and that she was embarrassed by this.

I was not especially drawn to the comradeship of the rich kids—I thought their lifestyle attractive but phony. I aspired to be wild, but my upbringing was much too strict. I was too compliant a child to rebel more than halfheartedly, and I never would dare to be openly defiant; but I surely gravitated toward the company of those who smoked, rode motorcycles, and sported tattoos (boys and girls both). Some of these teenagers were actually missing permanent teeth where it showed, which was strange for me to see. I pretended not to notice.

My dad came from an urban working class Jewish family. He had been a boxer and a sign painter and now was in show business, a profession that was not anywhere near as acceptable to the kids I wasn't friends with as hotel-owning or banking or restauranteering or politics or gambling or gangstering or any other form of empire-building, but neither was it as unacceptable to them as blue-collar work or public service or trades and labor.

My dad's income enabled my mom to work as a full-time homemaker for our family, which gave me an extra point on the class scale as compared to girls whose moms had to work outside the home for a salary, or worse, whose moms were single parents or, in the case of one of my friends, whose mom was a barmaid. My mom was an "intellectual." She was not a member of the social elite and did not go in for joining clubs or keeping up with the Joneses. She did educational and cultural events and volunteer work. She and my aunts went to operas and symphony concerts, and for a long time, to me, listening to classical music was a significant mark of class distinction.

When I left the sanctuary of my home community, I learned that, as a Jew, I was automatically assumed to be (1) rich, (2) highly educated, and (3) different. I thought of other Jews I had known when I was a kid who were neither rich nor well-educated, like the old folks on South Beach who ate out of the garbage and who occasionally bought a can of dog food or cat food for a special treat. I thought of the Holocaust survivors, short-sleeved in the South Florida heat, with numbers tattooed on their forearms. I remembered Jewish kids I knew whose parents both worked (if there were two parents) long hours just to make ends meet and who immediately entered the labor force as soon as they reached the legal working age of sixteen. I even remembered Jewish kids I knew who were lowlifes and sleazeballs. No, we were not all rich or highly educated, but we all were, regardless of our class standing within our own culture, most certainly different from the gentiles in our society. This difference often was the focus of relating with Jews by many of these gentiles. I was constantly reminded of the fact that there was a certain mythology about Jews held by many gentiles, and that a person might be feared, venerated, or tolerated simply because of the fact of being a Jew.

The realization that other people often viewed me in terms of stereotypes was a profound experience which enabled me to understand that I also did the same to others. I became increasingly sensitive to the fact that some people considered other people to be inferior or unworthy because of their race, age, income, level of ability, socio-cultural affiliation, or physical appearance. I also began to perceive how issues of class permeated all other forms of oppressive behavior, overlapping and infiltrating race/age/gender/culture issues.

Although I became a "white collar professional," enjoyed my job, and never considered giving up the financial security, I was drawn to the street life. As a young adult, I often frequented places where less affluent folks and folks who were involved in professions that were outside the law hung out. I dearly loved the friends I made in the bars and on the streets. I didn't consider the "issue of class" in my relationships, and I was ignorant of the possibility that this MAY have been an important consideration of others.

During this time I discovered that one of the most distinctive features of class divisions is not education or language or behavior or moral standards or leisure pursuits or even musical preference, but the absence or non-absence of teeth. During this time and in these places, I became familiar with the culture of another social class of folks and made the acquaintance of many people who had obvious spaces in their mouths—places where teeth were missing, dark spots in the whites of their smiles. Seeing this startled me at first, and I couldn't help staring. After all, these were actual adults, not children or teenagers. I was fascinated by the almost perverse differentness of these gappy mouths, but after a while I got used to it, even began to find it attractive in some people.

Over the years, I realized that attitudes and behavior were important associations with regard to class, and so, as I suspected, was education; but the most important factor of all was having money! Also, this having or not having of money, I discovered, was very much associated with having or not having teeth. This fact made a great deal of sense to me. Teeth are expensive to maintain, cheaper to lose, expensive to replace.

My parents had all their teeth. My grandparents had most of their natural teeth and filled in the rest with bridgework. Even through all my consciousness-raising and developing awareness of unfairness and oppression and classism, even through my own changing attitudes and new acceptances and understandings, I still, deep in my belief system, somehow equated missing teeth with the more unacceptable manifestations of low-class-ness.

I learned that there was a difference between class and culture, but that the two were inextricably interrelated. In general, class hierarchy seemed to me to be defined through the socioeconomic value judgments of the people in power who perceive all reality through their own experiences of life. As far as I could determine, these financially privileged folks truly had no idea that other people could actually have different experiences and opportunities from their own. These privileged folks were recognizable to me by their overwhelming egocentrism and narrow-mindedness and their tendency to blame the victim. I became more and more aware of oppression on many levels.

Then I moved to the Very Rural South, and suddenly, many many folks, even the rich and the high-class, were missing teeth, had obvious spaces in their mouths where enamel should have been. I considered that these folks probably had different attitudes around teeth from what I was used to; however, I found that, by and large, they had the same old attitudes around class and money that I'd encountered in other places. In the South, the primary indicators of class distinction were money and ancestry, and missing teeth seemed to have more to do with culture than with class. Anti-Semitism was also firmly ingrained in the Southern Culture, and, like racism, was largely considered to be more of a fact than an attitude.

There were few, if any, Jews where I lived, and there was a great deal of ignorance and misunderstanding among many Southern Christians who viewed Jews in terms of all the stereotypes of wealth, education, difference, and even malevolence (some Fundamentalist sects equated the Jew with Satan). I retreated into the closet as a Jew, fearful for my safety at times.

Meanwhile, in secret even from myself, periodontal disease was beginning to take place in my mouth, preparing to wreak havoc on my own full set of pearlie off-whites.

Soon I had my first tooth extracted. After months of trying to save it and many expensive, painful treatments, I finally made my peace with the situation and decided to give it up. I immediately had a permanent bridge affixed in its place, but somehow I still felt damaged, sullied, blemished. I was ashamed of the space, even though no one except me knew it was there.

In order to earn money to live on in the Very Rural South, I got a job doing construction work on a large building project. There were thousands of employees in the labor and trades force. I knew of one other Jew. However, on this project I worked very closely and sometimes with a great deal of trust with many people who had poor teeth, few teeth, or no teeth at all. After a while, it was a full set of teeth that began to look strange to me.

During the years I did construction work, I learned that another defining factor of class was the presence or absence of sweat and dirt. I encountered a great deal of coldness, rudeness and superiority from people I had to deal with in the non-construction world while I was sweaty and dirty after a day's work. Saleswomen placed my change on the counter to avoid touching my hand. But I also learned that money could overcome dirt in people's attitudes. One of my women friends on the job was a machinist. Machinists made excellent wages. My friend was new in the community and had opened up an account at the bank near her home. The teller who took her first week's check was rude to her, deliberately avoiding touching her work-stained hands and picking up her check gingerly. The second week was the same. When my friend deposited her third week's check, the teller asked, "Is this your *weekly* paycheck?" My friend smiled and nodded her head. That teller had a decidedly different and very respectful attitude from that day forth.

I worked other jobs after that, and did not make much money, and when my gums finally started to lose their grip to the point that I HAD to do something, I heard in the nick of time about the dental college in Nashville where I could get my teeth taken care of practically for free.

Sitting in that great waiting area brought me back to the old days of my youth when I used to hang out at bus stations and bowling alleys with the gay kids, the rednecks and scuzzies, the folks I loved so dearly, the folks with whom I had touched souls so many times. Here at the dental college, we were bound by the camaraderie of low-income folks who had dental needs and would see to them, of working-class and unemployed folks, students, homemakers. There was very little privacy. We all sat in rows of dental chairs in classrooms to have our teeth worked on by the students. It reminded me of the rows of folks in recliners at the plasma banks across the country from New York to New Mexico where I had sold my blood. But the greatest camaraderie was yet to come.

The first round of teeth I lost was in the back, so the spaces didn't show very much, and I was easily able to deal with this. But several years later, the disease had spread to all but the three middle teeth on top. The extractions were painful, the recovery slow, but worst of all was the fact that now I had very obvious spaces which even showed my gums when I smiled, and there was nothing I could do about this until my gums healed and I could get false teeth.

I was extremely self-conscious at first. Somehow, as I lost my teeth, I felt as though my Jewish ethnicity as well as my middle-classness was being threatened. It was not so bad in my very rural home territory, but when I went to "professional" meetings in the city, I felt extremely obvious. My professional acquaintances were among the few Southerners who did not sport spaces in their mouths. These folks thought I was pretty weird anyhow, and I wasn't sure if my missing teeth made me seem even stranger or, possibly, somehow more acceptable.

But back in my home hills and hollows, I felt as though I belonged. Here were Eva, Bonnie, Jim, Mike, and others who had space-filled smiles, snaggly teeth, or no teeth at all. We smiled wide at each other, exhibiting our gums. Any self-consciousness I had fled when I was with my toothless acquaintances. I'd smile proudly, at every opportunity, as if to say, "See? I do fit in. In spite of all our differences, in spite of class, ethnicity, education, lifestyle, we all can get along. We can always find some point of commonality, some place of shared experience," and I'd smile widely, easy with the state of my mouth, there in the camaraderie of the toothless.

Dykes of Poverty: Coming Home*

Lee Evans

Dear Jeanette,

I can't do it.

A while back you asked JMax, Shoney and me to edit the next issue of Lesbian Ethics *which was to be on class. I was excited because it offered me an opportunity to work with two Dykes who I really liked, working on an issue we felt was important.*

Months after making that commitment, JMax killed herself, and that changed everything. Discussions of 'lack of resources' and 'class privilege' gave way to the concrete results of classism...loss, violence, death. At times like this, words like 'oppression' and 'classism' seem as dry and empty as old cicada shells, outlining only the barest contours of our stories.

I can't edit this issue. With JMax's death, memories of poverty and abuse have come home to roost in my own backyard. My thoughts drag me to the door of my childhood, to glimpses of the shameful taste of a school lunch I begged a friend to buy for me, to the guilt I felt for not cursing my mother's family when they called my father poor Mexican trash, to the crust that forms on little girls' feelings from getting too little, too late and being subject to too much, too soon. Poverty and abuse, violence and death; words like 'classism' do little to capture the reality.

I can't edit this issue. I have no interest in balance right now, in looking at the big picture. My attention is riveted on Dykes of Scarcity, on the price we pay for our silence. I have heard so few Poor Dykes talk about their lives...we are so willing to put the past behind us. Who benefits from our silences, what is the cost of passing? What keeps us from talking to each other about poverty? How will our communities change when we speak the truth?

I can't edit this issue, Jeanette. I'm very sorry, but I hope you understand...for JMax and myself, I need to talk to other Poor Dykes. It's time to head home.

Lee

Thanks to my friends for their encouragement during the early drafts of this story, to Ellen Catlin for helping me get to the point, and especially to Kim for going home with me.

No Escape

One night last spring I had a dream, or rather, I was visited. My two grandmothers, long dead, came to me. "You can choose not to have children, but you cannot choose not to be a part of this family." Then they were gone. I thought about it the next morning, and then put it out of my mind. That night male ancestors appeared in my dreams, but I have no idea what they were saying. The message never got through. (I'm a Separatist.) My dreams have always evidenced my deepest emotions and passions, so I taught myself to remember them, to be attentive to their messages. But this message was very disturbing. Since I left home at the age of seventeen, I have not looked back. Two nights of dead relatives was alarming, so I went to a close friend who I think knows about such things. "Girl," she said, getting very serious, "You'd better listen when the ancestors talk. Because they gonna keep tellin you till you get it."

The third night my grandmothers came again. Hovering above me, wrapped in their importance, they once again deliver their message. My Mexican grandmother does the talking, my Welsh-German grandmother nodding in agreement. Two formidable women united in their purpose, they once again say, "You can choose not to have children, but you cannot choose not to be a part of this family."

For many months I pondered that message, thinking hard about its meaning. But their message was not understood through reason, through logic. It came to me when I heard the news about JMax, that awful moment when all the air rushed out of my lungs, and I wasn't sure if there would be enough air in the room to ever fill my lungs full enough so as not to feel this drowning sensation. At that moment, and in that space, where everything predictable and automatic stops, it was then I understood. "Stop. Stop breathing, stop thinking, stop running. You can't escape your past. It's time to go home."

Litany of My Childhood

Harry, we need groceries…no money, no money…Kay, did you pay the electric bill?…no money, no money…Mom, can I have thirty-five cents for the school field trip tomorrow?…no money, no money…Mommy, why don't you go outside with us? Because I don't have a winter coat, honey. Why not, mommy?…no money, no money…Mom, there's a bill collector at the door…no money, no money…I'm pregnant again, dear…no money, no money…Can I have a glass of milk?…no money, no money…Mom, is there any way we could get a telephone?…no money, no money…Don't ask Mom for anything this week. She and Dad were fighting again last night over…no money, no money…The washing machine is broken, and the baby needs clean diapers…no money, no money…Mom, can I have…no money, no money…no money, no money…

You Shall Know Us By Our Teeth*

As a poor Dyke, I think about my teeth a lot. I have a memory of a day spent swimming at a lesbian-owned retreat when the subject of dentists came up. One Dyke, a dental student, asked, "What kind of parents wouldn't provide their children with something as important as dental care?" shaking her head in what I think must be disapproval. No one says anything. My friends, a group of ten Dykes from upper-middle-class, middle-class and working-class backgrounds, change the subject.

I grow quiet as I think of my childhood, of not having gone to the dentist until I was in my mid-teens (and only then because I was visiting relatives who felt obligated to take me), of having teeth pulled because they were too decayed to fill, of knowing that what stood between the pain of an infected tooth and the relief of novocaine was something as simple and elusive as a couple of twenty-dollar bills. Shame washes over me as I realize that I am the type of person the dental student is talking about, shame that my parents couldn't manage money better, shame that there wasn't more money to manage. Yet, I am more ashamed of myself for whining about it. We believed we didn't have it all that bad. Other people had it far worse.

I have the urge to stop this playful group, this group of friends that have gone on to other topics, and tell them, "The answer to that question is my kind of parents, my parents couldn't provide their kids with dental care." But as I watch my friends playfully splashing each other, gossiping about friends and lovers on a sunny summer afternoon, there is no context to talk about poverty, about scarcity. So I keep my mouth shut, for my mouth is one of the places I carry evidence of my poverty.

My younger sister was the only kid in my family to have braces. When I knocked out one of her permanent front teeth in a wrestling match, a third one grew in sideways, and between her bottom two eye-teeth where four teeth should have been, five pushed their way in all raggedy and crooked. A poor kid's mouth if there ever was one, much like a poor kid's life, too much crowded in too small a space. Braces were in order, and once again my mom's family intervened by paying for my sister's dental care.

*With acknowledgment to Elana Dykewomon. They Will Know Me By My Teeth (Northampton: Megaera Press, 1976). Poems.

My aunt and grandmother knew the value of a dollar. They talked to a country-club friend of theirs who was a dentist, and he agreed to straighten my sister's teeth. His role was to do the work as fast and as cheaply as possible, my aunt's and grandmother's roles were to provide the charity, and our roles were to be grateful for their help.

My sister's braces caused her a lot of pain. My dad yelled at her for crying. She didn't smile much that year.

Fifteen years later, my sister woke up with one of her front teeth lying on her pillow. She was referred to a specialist. "How long were your braces on for? It looks as if the dentist who did your braces did the work too quickly, in too short a period of time. There was too much pressure put on your bone, so your upper jaw bone has been severely traumatized and is beginning to crumble. If you ever get hit in the face, your bones will fall apart like old plaster. You can expect to lose more teeth. The good news is that we can do a bone graft from your hipbone, and then fit you with false teeth. It will cost several thousand dollars. What kind of dental insurance do you have?" "None."

Two more teeth on her pillow a week later, another while eating dinner a few weeks after that. Teeth dropping from her mouth, no longer a surprise. The dentist, my aunt and my grandmother have all been dead for many years now. There's not even anyone left to get mad at.

With poverty nothing much ever changes. My sister still doesn't smile much.

Hunger Pains

Poor food varies from home to home. We ate monotonous dinners: rice and tomato sauce, hamburger, Spam, canned vegetables, and always water to drink. Milk for six kids cost too much. Bologna or peanut butter sandwiches for school lunches. Ketchup and mustard sandwiches for snacks. Food of the rural poor, food that kept us alive, food for which we should be grateful. We were told kids in India had far less. It was many years later that I realized much of the food we ate was an act of charity on the part of the man who ran our small neighborhood grocery store. He let my mother buy food on credit, knowing the bill wouldn't get paid, knowing that when all is said and done, hungry children still need to eat.

When my father was laid off, we were offered free milk in the school cafeteria. The school nurse came to our house and told my mother and me of this generous offer. My mother taught us kids to be polite and gracious, and she awaited my well-mannered response. In a moment of irritation, I refused the offer unless the school nurse would up the ante and make it chocolate milk. Many children had far less, but I was eleven and already tired of being grateful.

When I was thirteen my mother died, and I became the cook in the family. We would eat pancakes for what seemed like weeks on end. Cereal and cookies for breakfast, peanut butter for lunch, and pancakes for dinner. Cheap food, and all on credit, of course. Many people ate far worse and had much less. Me, I ate as much as I could, often fighting with my older brother over food. Fights that erupted into screaming matches, with us punching and hitting to make the other let go of the last bowl of ice cream. When my grandmother would visit, she would often chide me for trying to take as much food as my brother. She would dish out the food, giving me half what she gave him. "This is how it should be done," she explained. "Boys need more food."

Lois, the next door neighbor lady, would invite me over every afternoon after school, and she would feed me. She loved to watch me eat, laughing and shaking her head, but always giving me more. She was big and loud and defiant and laughed at my father's rages, encouraging me to be mouthy and tough. She communicated to me through cursing, food, and laughter.

"You little shit, if I ever catch you skipping school again, I'll beat your ass good. Have some more rabbit." ... "So, you and your father are fighting again, get a piece of that chocolate cream pie and tell me about it, but first quit your goddam crying and be sure and wash that plate when you're done." She taught me lessons: how to fight back, how to turn fear and sorrow into anger, how responsibilities don't stop just because you have more than you could ever handle in two lifetimes, how to spit back at adversity, and how to take care of myself and my sisters and brother the best I could.

Lois also knew that at the age of fourteen, I needed something to sustain me, something I could hold on to, and this she provided in abundance. Afternoons of laughing at problems, of turning bad times into comedy routines, all the while feeding me: food and laughter, laughter and food. These were the tools of survival, Pennsylvania style.

Food became a place to focus my attention when things got bad at home. The summer I was fifteen I developed late night food cravings. I would wake up some time in the night, my mind racing with problems. Cooking and cleaning and keeping house and raising my three younger siblings, staying out of my father's way, lying to bill collectors, putting up with my older brother's alcoholic tantrums, trying to find a way to take the younger kids and run away on a Greyhound bus...to where? That summer my middle-of-the-night hungers were so immediate, so intense, that I would bully my younger sister into going outside to the plum tree at 3 a.m. to pick the not-yet-ripe plums, and I would eat away my night terrors.

This anxiety about food developed into food rituals that I have only in the last few years come to understand. I would get panicky waiting in lines for food, sure that they would run out just before it got to my turn. My friends remarked that I would always leave a little food on my plate. I would take more than I could possibly eat, and always throw some out. Wasteful, my friends called me. True. But the other truth is that not having enough food created a terrible anxiety in me. If I could leave food on my plate after a meal, enough to throw away, surely that was a sign of plenty. Surely it was a sign that life wasn't all that hard. I was in my thirties before I could eat a plate of food, only taking what I needed, finishing it all, and not feel anxious. Yet just last week my boss suggested that because of an unusually heavy workload, I might not be able to go to lunch. I stared at him in disbelief, and then felt a very old and familiar panic welling up from the place I thought was left behind. I've come so far, yet a missed lunch can still grab me by the throat and drop-kick me twenty-five years into the past, to a time when food meant survival, and my hunger was never satiated.

Fear of Falling

I was seventeen, and my father had kicked me out six months earlier. I had a toothache that hurt so bad I was up for two days and a night, the pain enough to make me hysterical. I chose a dentist out of the phone book and called for an appointment. I had no money to pay him right away, but he told me to come in and we would work something out. I was so relieved. He examined me and decided my tooth could be filled. After drilling my tooth part way, and hitting the nerve one too many times, he suggested that hypnotism might help if the novocaine was wearing off. "Just listen to my voice, you're getting sleepy, it's very hot in here, pretend you're on a beach, it's getting hotter and you're getting uncomfortable. Take off your blouse and bra." I stared straight ahead, not believing...only vaguely aware of his hand, like a large hairy spider, crawling up and down my thigh. I pretended not to hear his instructions. My tongue searched out the half-drilled tooth, as I sat frozen not daring to move. When he finished filling my tooth, he said that if I didn't have the money to pay my bill, he was sure we could work something out.

Special financial arrangements are often available to poor females. Not reading the fine print can be costly.

JMax and I talked about teeth the first time we met. I told her about the molester dentist, and about my sister's teeth. She told me that the nuns of her high school and their dentist had conspired to have her teeth pulled at the age of 17. "Poor people can't afford to take care of their teeth, you might as well have them pulled and you'll be fitted with false teeth," they explained to her. I've had teeth pulled before, and I remember the incredible pressure and the sound of crunching. I think of this Dyke I like so much, this Dyke who is strong and competent, and I imagine her having her teeth pulled because some prick dentist thought that poor people didn't take care of their teeth anyway. I respected her strength too much to be emotional when she told me. I know she understood, because she was raised poor too, and knew that it was too soon for emotion. Instead, we use our stories to check each other out. Our reactions will answer important questions we must ask of each other at this stage. Are you so sheltered that you think this is unusual? Does my life make you squeamish? Do you use humor and laughter to talk about hard things? Are you smart enough not to poke around in feelings that are so carefully contained? Do you have the caring and the attention span and the strength to bear witness?

I've used this test many times, a familiar dance between Dykes of scarcity. It is often not conscious, and rarely talked about.

JMax and I look at each other and nod our heads, our eyes acknowledging that we have passed this first important test. "Yeah, they're real fuckers out there, alright. They'll get you every time they can." A thin strand of trust is cast between us, as tentative as spider silk, and just as strong. I hope this is the beginning of a web of trust, a safety net for when the next strong wind blows.

A friend once told me that she had to take Valium before going to the dentist. "Why?" I asked. "Because I'm afraid of going to the dentist," she explained. "Did something happen?" I wanted to know. "Oh, no, I'm just afraid of the pain." What a luxury, I thought. To know that you're afraid and to be able to pinpoint your fear so specifically, and then to leave your fear at the dentist's office when you walk out the door.

I begin to understand that I rarely feel fear, and yet I have often been in frightening situations. My jobs have been dangerous for many years now. Working with abused teen-age girls who respond with fists and teeth, going into crack houses to talk to drug dealers and strawberries* about sexually transmitted diseases, helping a battered woman get her kids and belongings out of the house before her abusive biker-husband comes back from the bar. And I wonder what fear feels like, except that surely it must be that feeling of anxiety when my car breaks down, and there is no money to repair it. It must feel like having no way to get to work, and with no

* Strawberries are crack cocaine prostitutes, young women who sell themselves so they can obtain crack. Young men who prostitute themselves so they can buy crack are called raspberries.—ED.

167

work comes no money to repair the car. Is it like the time I had no money, and had to steal toilet paper from restaurants, and sold a battery for food money? It must be that feeling of needing money, and having no one to ask, because they're broke too, or because it's just too hard to ask middle-class friends for money to pay the loan that's three months behind. This feeling must be the cold steel bars that drop down between my friend and me when I try to explain the difference between need and want, and her not seeing any difference, and me realizing that I had trusted her. It must be coming home to find the electricity shut off; it is the bill collector on the phone; it is the phone being shut off; it is a letter saying I'm being sued for unpaid bills. It feels like the worry of knowing my younger sister has a kidney infection, and she has no money to pay a doctor. It is the day my mother died and they came to repossess the furniture. It is being fifteen, and coming home to an empty house with my eight-year-old brother's blood splattered on floor and walls, a shotgun in the bedroom, and knowing that I shouldn't have let my guard down for a minute because something bad always happened. It is living with a father who was a sadist, and who nailed baby birds into their birdhouse, with their mama frantically trying to get in to feed them, until a few days later their peepings finally weakened and stopped. It is knowing that if my father poisoned the neighbor's dog to stop it from barking, then what did he do to us kids to keep us quiet? It's knowing that my mother, who married into poverty at the age of 21, died at the age of 44 from hard work and too many babies, and her mother, who had a middle-class standard of living all her life, lived to be 92. It's being fifteen and having my father ask me to make the decision whether my younger sisters and brother and I should be put into foster homes, or if he should hire a housekeeper to supervise us kids better, and then telling me to remember that he has...no money, no money. It's knowing if I begin to feel fear, I will end up on the floor, croaking out my terror, unrecognizable to my friends and to myself. And knowing that this will never happen because strength is its own curse, and no matter how many times I feel I've hit my limit, I realize that for some of us, there are no time outs. Limits are a luxury when life doesn't stop to acknowledge them. Surviving has made me strong; it means always being ready for the next crisis, for the next time I lose my footing. Yet, for people with no safety net, the fall is sometimes deadly.

"You feel afraid?" I ask my Valium-taking friend, but I think she was raised with many cushions, and doesn't know what I am asking.

In the Cellar

A friend called one Sunday in late November and told me JMax had killed herself. JMax and I were not close friends, but our backgrounds gave us some common bonds. We met at a Separatist conference a few years ago, and immediately liked each other. She was one of the first Dykes I knew who talked openly about being raised poor, who wasn't trying to pass. We talked about classism, about our childhoods, gossiped about people we knew, made each other laugh, liked each other's politics. Eventually we committed to co-editing the *Lesbian Ethics* issue on class.

The safety net we had so carefully begun to weave when we first met never really developed any further…her in New Mexico, me in Ohio, time and distance hindering our developing anything more sustaining than occasional phone calls. A few weeks earlier, I had had a conversation with JMax that left me alarmed and worried. She told me she wanted to kill herself, that she was tormented with prolonged and torturous incest flashbacks. We talked some about them, and I had hoped she could hang on, this tough Dyke who had already survived so much.

And now, I was on the phone hearing the news of her suicide, the image of JMax with a gun burned into my mind, my grief sliced clean with the rhythm of Audre Lorde's words, "They never meant for us to survive."

After years of expecting the worst, of being on constant guard, I still wasn't ready. Poverty and abuse and dead women…the story is as old as dirt.

Lack of access to medical care and food, unpredictable everyday violence, threats and harassment, watching those you love suffer, these are the things that leave body and soul stunned and weary. Do we know what this does to little girls? The result is that the struggle to maintain day-to-day functioning becomes too overwhelming, and people begin to lose their will to live. Death often comes from stress-related diseases, avoidable accidents, and suicide. When it happens in Nicaragua we call it "low-intensity warfare." It doesn't have the Rambo-like glory of full-fledged warfare, but it is much more cost-effective. They don't have to kill us, they just constrict our lives to the point where suicide is the easiest way. Some of us die right away, some of us have shortened life spans, and some of us have a time-bomb that ticks away until some unknown source sets it off.

There is a dream I've had for most of my life. I am standing outside the Pennsylvania home I grew up in, and it is a late summer afternoon. I watch the sky turn a sickly yellow, and know something is happening. The sky begins to darken and the wind picks up. Soon leaves are ripped from the trees, and whirl about my head. On the horizon I see a twister begin to form. A tornado is headed our way. I scramble around, gathering cats and kids, taking them to the cellar. They climb back out. I cannot be heard above the roaring as I scream that we are in danger. Garbage cans, and people, and animals fly by the basement window as the foundation of the old house shakes and groans. I gather the kids and cats again, and again, and again. Every time they climb out of the cellar, I drag them back. They don't realize the danger. They are too young to know of such things. A mighty storm rages outside, and the only safety is in the cellar. This I know to be true.

I have been told this dream is about abuse. "Yes," I reply, "didn't you know poverty is one form of abuse?"

I talked to my sister last spring, and asked her if she was saving money for her dental work. I was suspicious because she had been sending me money for tuition as I was making a final push to finish up my bachelor's degree at the age of 38. "I'd rather you take the money and try to get your teeth fixed," I said, trying to convince her. "Your health is affected by not having teeth." She shot me a look that told me she knew the choice she was making, and wanted me to understand. "You have to get a degree, you're smart, and Mom would have wanted that. This way you'll always have something to fall back on," she explained. I was stunned as a realization resonated through me; my sister loved me enough to pay for my reservation in the cellar. She knew the bottom line was survival.*

Creating a Home

My Radical Lesbian Separatist politics are rooted in my life experiences. While I now have enough money to live on, I believe it is only a matter of luck that keeps me from being poor again.** Poverty, abuse, and strong women have been some of my strongest influences. I can have money, but I can never erase the experience of poverty.

Lesbians often fail to address the fact that in any given group of Dykes there are those who are on the thin edge of survival, who may be struggling to get adequate medical care, enough food, money for essentials, or maybe just the time and space and support to crawl out from under their load. In a movement that is designed to help us distinguish between choices that are liberating and choices that are false, why do so few Lesbians understand that poverty is about having no choices? If we are not actively

---

*As Irene Weiss pointed out in conversation, poor and working-class Dykes often think of a college degree as a kind of union card. We think it means that we will always be able to find work (above minimum wage) and therefore it is our ticket out of poverty.

**On reading this, Jeanette reminded me that it has only been a few months since I had been unemployed for over a year, was out of money, was living at a friend's house, and had a car that didn't work.

addressing the survival of Lesbians, then can we say we're serious about designing real alternatives? Are we playing house without creating home?

Creating alternatives to patriarchy means that we have to shit or get off the pot. We all have a responsibility to make our communities truly diverse, and a place where all Dykes can feel at home. I leave it to upper-class, middle-class, and working-class Dykes to figure out what their responsibilities are. As for Poor Dykes, I can only speak for myself. It is time for me to come home. It is time to stop passing and start talking with other Poor Dykes about the truth of our lives. I have had to be strong in order to survive. I thought that was enough. It was only in the quiet moments after JMax's death that I began to realize how much this strength costs me and other Poor Dykes. I grieve for us, and especially for the ones who didn't make it.

Karen Chaney with her brothers.

Shifting Horizons: Navigating a Life

Karen Chaney

Crossing the mississippi at 18
i didn't know what i'd find
but i never looked back
lived ten years in a daze
filled with here and now
and other people's passions
learning the hurts and joys of other lives
oblivious to my own

oblivious to the damage done over years
of living without maple trees   hot humid summers
  thunderstorms cracking the skies
escaping the pain   losing my strength
  as i swam to freedom on the other side.

One of the consequences of living in an out-of-body state for much of your life is that you can find yourself living two (or more) distinct lives. One of the consequences of cultural dislocation is never becoming ethically whole.

Casting Out

I was raised in rural Missouri. My body, my spirit, my slow pace and skeptical manner all reveal this about me. But while growing in rural Missouri I did not live in my body, I lived in my mind—a safe haven into which I retreated in a sometimes difficult and at times abusive family situation. I left home at eighteen on scholarship to a midwestern university, knowing quite a lot intellectually and very little socially, having lived in a very isolated world of books. While in college, I maintained in effect two lives in two worlds: My friends were for the most part first-generation college students from working- and middle-class Catholic families in the area; my intellectual peers in classes, however, were primarily from educated, professional families back east. My encounters with these students were usually mixed: They usually liked my mind and liked me as long as I fit with the rules and norms of their communities, as long as I was not too country, too hick. I have come to feel undergraduate education in the United States primarily serves a socialization function, where those of us from non-formally educated backgrounds learn what to say and what not to say, what to keep quiet about our lives and desires, how to pass as educated, as someone not shameful.

My experiences of explicit class hostility during college included having a fellow student (male, rich, gay) announce in the cafeteria in front of other students that he would not eat at the same table as me until I learned to eat properly. (Table manners seem to evoke some of the ugliest class righteousness.) Another called my family "pigs" because he knew I was from a hog farm. I was told when visiting a friend's family that I could not play tennis with them because I did not have the right clothes. I would show pictures of my family to friends from more privileged backgrounds and have them look away, unable to accept my obviously rural/working roots (one said my family looked very "casual"): I was only acceptable *apart* from my family, my roots. I was left from these experiences with much unnamed (and unconscious) rage and shame. In retrospect, I see a quite vulnerable 18-year-old who had not been prepared for the level of contempt that would come her way in the larger world.

The academic world, paradoxically, also provided a relatively safe haven for me in my twenties in which I could succeed without much effort and basically learn and live in a world demanding little emotionally or interpersonally. After moving first to New York then to Boston after college, I began graduate school at Harvard in 1983, and found my social circles increasingly rarified over time. I found myself in my late twenties with a lover from a professional suburban family, and friends and peers who had never had to work for money (one friend excitedly told me of her first job at age twenty-seven). Although intellectually I fit in the circles in which I was living, socially I did not. Different things were sacred, humors did not mesh. I found NPR* annoying. They made insulting remarks about working-class culture. I was rude to rich people. They were rude to working people. I didn't understand their ties to propriety and liberal intellectual status symbols (e.g., NPR). They didn't understand my ambivalent relationship to authority. They joined political affinity groups. I felt empathy with the working-class police officers having to drag their bodies into

* *National Public Radio—Ed.*

police vans. They did "meaningful" work in low-paying jobs and still had money to buy VCRs, cars, and travel to Nicaragua to observe the revolution. I worked in non-PC business settings to pay my bills.

Over time I found myself becoming increasingly bitter and resentful of the differences in resources between myself and my friends and peers and noticing each difference: Who was living on trust funds as I worked three jobs; who reset the silverware "correctly" on the table after I left the room; who offered to give me their hand-me-downs; who wouldn't eat my food; who found discussing our differences in money embarrassing as if I were discussing something shameful or dirty. I also began to recognize my cultural invisibility in the world in which I was living, including my invisibility to myself. I would watch *Norma Rae, Country, Silkwood, In the Heat of the Night* and find myself crying with a deep loss. I encountered a religious sect in Amish-like clothes one day in Harvard Square and burst into tears, feeling a strong sense that I had betrayed my people by leaving home. I had two sets of friends: one set from rural, Southern, or working backgrounds, the other from upper-middle-class, educated suburban families, both of whom were content within the boundaries of their own worlds.

Class mobility is living in different worlds with different languages. Class mobility is different worlds living in you with different values, different wants, different demands. I felt increasingly split, confused, and compromised, and that I had no personal integrity. At times, I was ashamed of my family and community; at times, ashamed of the values of the people with whom I now socialized. While graduate education was moving my friends and lover back into solid places within their home communities, it was moving me further and further from my own. I felt I was betraying my community and family in my increasing worldliness. As my woman friends were moving into positions of authority, I felt at once admiration (because they were women), hostility (because they were from backgrounds where everyone believes they *deserve* to be on top—and miraculously end up there by their thirties), and resentment (because I couldn't assume such authority without betraying core loyalties to my own people). My sense of identity, my sense of community, my sense of place in the larger world would all need to change significantly for me to "move to the top" where my peers were heading, which, as well as not being ethically clean, would not be painless and definitely not unconditionally rewarding. I increasingly felt the loss of my home, but was not able to embrace (or fit into) the world in which I was now living. I could no longer speak in public easily as in the past, as I was unclear any longer who was speaking. I suppose had I retained my lifelong mind/body split, I could have continued to manage this dual-system life, suppressing whatever side of me I was called upon at the time to suppress. Instead, I was unable to cope any longer and I crashed out.

I moved through a deep depression in my late twenties, resurfacing slowly into a more conscious, less conflicted living. I began to realize that Cambridge was not my home, and that my heart would never rest there. Attending the March on Washington for Gay and Lesbian Rights in 1987 reaffirmed this feeling in finding the Missouri contingent filled with people who were both very gay and very country. It was around this time that *Desert Hearts* and k. d. lang also appeared on the cultural horizon, and this integration of lesbianism and country-western life awakened a desire I had never felt before, having come of age as a lesbian in eastern academic settings. It pointed to the possibility of a different type of life centered way to the west of Cambridge. I visited San Francisco for the first time that year and found myself engaged with its relaxed atmosphere, comfortability with sexuality, and openness towards life. Responding to an offer by a chorus in the Lesbian and Gay Freedom Day Parade to "Consider yourself at home," I decided to do so, and moved west to California the next year. No one had ever welcomed me whole, welcomed me home, so unconditionally as San Francisco.

Homecoming

San Francisco, like a good friend, provided me with room to breathe and to begin to sort out the terms of my life. As a city of many expatriates and immigrants, it felt very welcoming to one who was unclear any longer on social identity. It also provided a very diverse gay community in which to live, which has helped me sort out who I am and who I am not in a way that did not feel possible in Cambridge, where the lesbian culture is much more monolithic, primarily political, and primarily upper-middle-class. I began country-western dancing, which might sound insignificant except to those who know the power of moving your body, your heart to the music of your own people for the first time. I began working out at the Y as well as attending Quaker services, which resonated with the values and depths of my own traditions in rural protestantism in their simplicity and quietness. I also fell in love with a woman from my home state for the first time, feeling a depth of passion I had never experienced and coming home to parts of myself that had never been expressed. I understood myself as a woman in new ways, in deeper, more congruous ways. I felt attractive for the first time in my life. It was a time of recovery of lost parts of myself, parts that had never been allowed to live fully before. I felt very country, very female, and very free.

In reflection, I see this cultural reclamation of my early thirties involving a similar process as my integration of feminism in my twenties: a near total separation from a world that was damaging to me (in this case, east coast professional and intellectual cultures; in my twenties, patriarchy); a personal integration of a new way of seeing the world sliced along the lines of class and culture (before, gender); and an awareness of underlying rage towards people from educated, privileged backgrounds (before, men). When encountering people from these backgrounds, I found myself often feeling furious at their questions, their assumptions, their arrogance and easy authority, and would give them as little information as possible about my world, sometimes withholding my name. "*Rich kids*" was my ultimate indictment, whether the "kids" were 20 or 50. I would not say what I did for a living, as "What do you *do?*" is the question used to place you in the pecking order, determining whether you are worthy of further conversation. At times, I have felt there is no such thing as an innocent question among the privileged—that all conversation is directed at maintaining, securing, or reinforcing dominance. Social settings sometimes have felt like seas of sharks, and I have found it tiring, exhausting to have to be so on guard, having to defend my life and choices or prove myself worthy at all times. This period was one of laying low with friends from these backgrounds in the way that my male friends were kept more peripheral before, knowing on some level that they should not bear the burden of the rage I was feeling and knowing that any slight would spark much deep feeling.

I turned down possible Ph.D. work during this time, feeling a gut-level resistance to returning to what felt like a hostile environment in its values and orientation, where verbal abuse commonly occurs under the guise of "academic criticism," and in which my people and my passions would again be invisible and/or contemptible. In some ways, the academic world had been a protective cocoon for me emotionally that I was ready to shed; returning felt like a step back into an unhealthy situation rather than a move forward into a more open living. I decided at this time I would rather be an emotionally well-rounded secretary than a neurotic professor, that I didn't want to fight anymore, but rather to attend to my continued emotional and spiritual growth, wherever that would lead. I continued my temping work in the face of the bewilderment of family and friends, and faced my own anxiety in stepping out of what had been the stable and predictable (and upwardly mobile) academic path of my life into a void. I felt alone and for the first time without a context for my life—that I had just burned the final plank on the bridge that I had begun disassembling with my move west. My mind was saying this might not have been wise, but I was beginning to feel that who I was was enough, that in my new world I was fine. I was finding a joy and self-acceptance in my life for the first time, and I was not willing to let this go.

Venturing Forth Once More

It was three years before I felt safe and solid enough in my own life, content and centered in my own life, to begin considering questions of vocation again, this time from a more solid ground: What role do I want to have in the world? What is the role of work in my life? If I want to assume more responsibility, in what sphere? Within what horizons can I live? Differences in clothes, manners, the way you speak and carry your body are external dimensions of class, but internal differences are in life expectations, aspirations, horizons—considerations I am again facing. In a way, I have felt like Dorothy in Oz, exposed to the truth lying behind the wizard's curtain—the human face of the creation of culture and social power—but unclear of what to do with this knowledge or of my role in this drama. Unlike Dorothy, I know I can't return to Kansas, as it would be dishonest innocence. Yet I continue to work as a word processor, which I have done for most of my adult life, in part due to the safety and comfort of working with middle- and working-class people, with whom I can be more myself than with people from more privileged backgrounds. I find the scope of middle-class living comforting in some ways and have found my work satisfying in its development of a certain set of skills and competencies, and having these skills recognized within a particular community of people. However, I miss the active intellectual engagement with the world that I had before and am aware of the larger cultural world in which I am no longer participating. With friends from more professional backgrounds, I am sometimes embarrassed by my life currently lived within middle-class horizons, having once been a part of a world of professional, highly educated people—a telling fact given I doubt if any of them feel embarrassed by only socializing and working with others from their own backgrounds. Although my mind and spirit push me towards more professional or intellectual worlds, the thought of moving back into these worlds, where the dominant mode of interaction is competition, the primary value achievement, the pace quicker, and the people mostly from privileged backgrounds, feels usually beyond my capacity—or interest—to sustain. Perhaps as a function of my thirties, I am increasingly aware of the question of horizons: How far can I stretch, emotionally and intellectually? How far do I *want* to stretch? What battles do I want to fight? What are my limits? How can I live within these limits with integrity? At this point, I am unsure of the answers.

I have realized that I will never be completely accepted or welcomed by many in more educated, professional circles regardless of my education, given my less refined, more rural ways and unwillingness to "transform" into someone living by the values of those worlds. To find intellectual companionship, I must usually encounter intense class insecurity and class hatred or contempt on the part of peers and live in a world which uses words and language for battle, which feels to me an unnecessary pain and an unnecessary loss. I wish for more class consciousness in this country, for more of a "common language" about class. Like women confronting patriarchy without language, tools, or peer support, I know that my encounters with these larger forces will continue to be damaging as long as I do it alone. It has been very helpful and heartening to me to speak with other women I have met in San Francisco who have experienced crossing class barriers—in relationships and in education/work—as it has moved many of my personal experiences from the private to the public, common realm where they can begin to heal and a new consciousness can begin to grow.

In the past years I have also faced some of my own personal prejudices and doubts: How can one be intellectually creative from a working-class background? How can one be a truly sophisticated thinker from Missouri? How could I ever consider myself to be an artist? Honoring my own creativity and thoughts has been a major struggle for me, as little in my background rewards either, and much of our larger culture makes it very difficult as well: On both coasts, the midwest and the south are considered vast cultural wastelands, and those in urban coastal communities have a difficult time believing that there is life—or intelligence—beyond their parameters, particularly in the south. Working-class, or even middle-class, authority is usually presented in the media as reactionary, e.g., the Jerry Falwells and other right-wing leaders, and usually as laughable. Rural America is depicted either anachronistically and/or nostalgically as in *The Waltons*, or as the subject of camp, e.g., *Green Acres*, *Hee Haw*, or *The Beverly Hillbillies*—none of which has contributed to my ease of assuming authority in the larger culture. I have also found few role models from rural or southern backgrounds within the intellectual culture of our country. Several generations ago it was more common, and I have turned to writers such as Mark Twain and artists such as Thomas Hart Benton to understand what it means to be a Missourian and an artist, rural and creative, grounded and intellectual.

The question of voice has continued to be a major one for me—as a woman, as a lesbian, as a Missourian: What voice is legitimately mine? When I speak, who is talking? A smart-assed, cynical Missourian à la Mark Twain? A rational, detached Harvard graduate? A country woman?

Integrating my mind and my life continues to be a slow, painstaking process in order not to recklessly sacrifice either all I know or all I feel. I read the diaries of Joe Orton, the writings of Dorothy Allison, Judy Grahn and others, to find company and guidance in this journey. I find myself drawn to artists from backgrounds that have not encouraged their expression, from worlds that have not been held up or honored in the mainstream intellectual culture. Since I had left home until moving to California, my center of culture had continually been the east coast (specifically New York and Cambridge), and I have realized how damaging that assumption has been for me in rendering my own culture and values invisible or contemptible. The voices in which I have learned to think and to work, to read and to write—academic voices, culturally critical voices—had all been based in cultures that were not my own. I realized I had to hear my own voice, had to develop my own voice. I have grown weary of seeing and interpreting life through a lens that will never allow me to appear whole and which intellectually I find increasingly stale. California's quasi-frontier nature seems to allow more room for new voices, visions and self-expression, for an "intellectual" world that does not need to hold "popular" culture in contempt. Living on the Pacific Rim beyond the cultural hegemony of New York or Cambridge has been for me a very freeing experience, and I greatly enjoy the Bay Area cultural scene for this reason.

Through this journey I have realized my sustaining community is people who have lived in more than one world, in particular more than one class, and who have experienced in some way being cultural outsiders. I am inspired by the work of people who honor their own communities through their work, such as Toni Morrison, and who combine a knowledge and appreciation of the subtleties of their own communities with a wider intellectual perspective. I seek more peers who value tolerance, who have a genuine openness to life and love for people, and who maintain a personal engagement within the larger world. With my friends and lovers, I am working towards mutual respect and appreciation, trying to be more honest about my own strengths, limits and values, and working towards a life of greater integrity and stronger character. I see a community where I will accept being held accountable, work where I can honestly live my life with challenges *and* support, and friends who understand and appreciate my journey. Throughout my life, I hope to sustain my love for people and my love for intellectual life, my sense of compassion and fondness for humanity.

Nowhere At Home

J.P.

I am a thirty-six-year-old Jewish lesbian. I grew up working class in Woodside, Queens, which is literally Archie Bunker territory. Archie Bunker's bar on *Archie's Place* was located on Steinway Street, the main shopping drag of the neighborhood. My father worked as a "distributive worker" in the garment district in Manhattan. Distributive worker is a euphemism for a schlepper. My father was one of the guys who pushed hang trucks full of material and clothing between factories along city streets. My mom was "just a housewife" throughout most of my childhood. The main activity I remember mom doing is shopping. She looked long and hard to try to stretch the dollar to feed and clothe us.

I was one of the few Jewish kids in my grade school class. The neighborhood, at this time, was very Catholic. Most of the kids were of Irish or Italian descent. As a girl, I was the local "kootie bug," the kid everyone picked on and teased. I was selected to be tormented because I was Jewish. I was subjected to anti-Semitic attacks as a kid, especially when Easter and Christmas came. I was told I personally killed Jesus and would rot in hell because I did not go to Sunday mass. This was all very confusing to me because my parents were unobservant. My dad, however, kept telling me Jews had been scapegoated throughout history as a diversion.

I always felt I never quite belonged. I was certainly different from most of the kids in my class. During "release time" I was one of only three or four students who did not go to the local Catholic school. During release time, every Wednesday afternoon from 1:30 p.m. to 3:00 p.m., Catholic students were discharged from public school so they could go for religious instruction.

As a child, I was teased because my height and weight were different from most of the other girls in my class. Janis Ian's song "At Seventeen" rang true for me, except I learned I was "the other" by age seven and not as a teenager.

My parents taught me I was somehow better than all the kids around me because I was Jewish. I remember one of my few friends was an Ulster Protestant girl. I was always jealous of her at Christmas time because her house was decorated and she was given the best presents. I remember one year being particularly envious because she was given a very soft and life-like "Thumbelina" doll. Mom tried to soothe my pain by telling me I should be glad I was not my friend because my friend's father drank, unlike my father. The tone of my mom's voice implied that she thought Jews would not waste hard-earned money on drinking like the *goyim*.

Working-class economics shaped my life in subtle and not so subtle ways. I wore hand-me-downs from my cousin who was five years older. Even my new clothing was shabby and out of style. Anything new was purchased in bargain basements, or Klein's or May's or other stores cater-ing to poor and working-class people. My parents were always fighting about money. There was much tension in our house as my parents struggled to pay the bills and meet living expenses.

Because I did well in school, it was always assumed by my parents, my teachers and myself that I would go to college. When the time came, there was no discussion as to which university I would go to. When I gradu-ated from high school the City University of New York (CUNY) charged no tuition. I went to Queens College, one of the CUNY schools. Queens College was a "commuter college," without dorms. All students traveled each day from home to campus. To save money, I continued living in my parents' apartment.

It was at Queens College that I first came in contact with middle-class kids from such well-to-do areas as Fresh Meadows, Forest Hills and Jamaica Estates. Although not out to myself as a lesbian while going to college, I gave very little thought to the middle-class Jewish men attend-ing Queens College. However, I had a particularly great distaste for the middle-class Jewish women students at Queens. They did not take their studies seriously, chased boys and used their daddy's charge cards. They appeared lazy and pampered.

While I realize now that the term JAP (Jewish American Princess) is a racist, sexist and anti-Semitic term, I cannot accurately recount my college years without recalling that I used this term to describe these women. My life felt so different, almost opposite, from these privileged middle-class Jewish women. My mental energy went into my school work, my job and the women that I encountered in my classes, while their greatest expressed interest was finding a nice, middle-class, Jewish boy to marry.

I did not stop to think that these women were second-generation middle class. They were the daughters of a parent who made the transition from working class to middle class during the parent's lifetime. I did not understand that the material avarice of these students was an expression of the internalized insecurity of their parents' deprived childhood.

In order to pay for books and activity fees I worked my way through school. My first job in college was marking clothing in a department store basement. Most of the other markers were Black or Hispanic. For these people this was their full-time job. They had little hope of finding a better life. They resented me because I was an upwardly mobile, white, college student. These workers knew that working in a demeaning environment doing degrading work was only temporary for me.

As a working-class student, I felt guilty because I was taking steps to become middle class. This job was a transitory stop in my life, a means to a greater end. I felt totally alienated from my coworkers who were stuck in dead-end low-paying jobs. I felt totally alienated at school from the middle-class people who had material goodies and a comfortable existence. I was nowhere at home.

After I graduated from college I went on to law school. I financed my law school education with state and federal loans. I wrote the check for the final payment on those student loans in May 1991, eleven years after graduation. I have been a lawyer for the past ten years.

My experience of feeling nowhere at home continues to date. When involved in feminist organizations, I feel cut off from the fashionably "downwardly mobile" middle-class women who seem to dominate. These hip, politically correct people grew up middle class but now live in genteel semipoverty. A lot of them continue to be supported by their parents. These women look down their noses at me because they think I am a "sell-out" attorney. This attitude plays on my own doubts because my job does not involve social change advocacy. Many of these feminists don't really know what it means to have to pay bills because they have a safety net. For them, mom and dad will come to the rescue if things get really rough. For me, my family could not come to my rescue, even if they would want to do so.

Growing up working class makes me different from most professionals. I come from a family that screams and uses broad hand movements when talking. I struggle every day to control my voice and my gestures in "middle-class style" so I can be "acceptable at work." Part of this difference was illustrated when I experienced emotional and visual flashbacks of my childhood when I had to use the bathroom in a working-class department store. I broke out into a cold sweat as memories of the shame I felt when I shopped in that store with my mother flooded over me.

I feel estranged from the big-egoed middle-class lawyers at work. I am treated with suspicion because of my working-class background. The pompous male lawyers treat their women secretaries like dirt. This bad attitude toward their secretaries is shown by male attorneys in tones of voice, temper tantrums and contempt. I experience this shabby treatment myself when I go to different law offices to conduct depositions, being often mistaken for a stenotype operator, because I don't usually wear a suit. When I identify myself as an attorney I carefully watch the male attorney's shift in voice tone and body language.

Most of the women lawyers I meet in my field are completely male-identified, and act like clones of men. In order to be taken seriously they become as abrasive and as pushy as their male colleagues. I find it hard to resist the pressure to act in this manner.

There is also a wall between myself and the "girls at the office." The secretaries and clerks gossip with each other, watch soap operas during their lunch breaks, and complain about their husbands behind their backs. This barrier comes from the fact that the office workers correctly perceive me as being one of their bosses. I find it very difficult to accept myself as management, not labor. In my heart of hearts I see myself as a worker and identify with the women who type my briefs. However, I know there is a big gulf between us in terms of the salary we receive and the respect accorded our work.

Part of the wall between myself and the people I work with comes from the fact that I never discuss my private life, except in the most general terms. While I don't talk about a boyfriend and my lover calls me at the office at least twice a week, I have never told anyone at work that I'm a lesbian. At times, I think they have to know, but then, the secretaries will start ogling a picture of a man modeling a swimsuit in a mail order catalog and ask me if I think he is cute.

It is a thin line I walk, not working class, but not fully a member of the middle class. My working-class background makes it hard for me to act middle class, to be acceptable in the corporate environment. This consciousness makes me realize that what is required of workers is fundamentally oppressive. As a woman I earn less than most male attorneys and as a lesbian, my income is smaller than most middle-class heterosexual women who can share their male partner's larger income.

As an attorney, I am no longer a member of the working class. I direct my own work and enjoy economic benefits not available to most workers. My class position remains fragile and this position gives me the sense of still being nowhere at home.

Lay All That Mess Down and Talk

Joan Schuman

When we hold hands or make love, the contrast of our skin mesmerizes me. Our physical connection is so powerful these first few months, it's as if we don't need to talk.

Goyim, Schvartze. Nigger-lover. Whitey. Jew. Shiksa. Kike. JAP. She think she so cute. Lezzie. Lower class. Dyke. Bulldagger.
Some words from my childhood, not heard in my parents' home.

People stare as we stroll down the street, grinning, arms interlocked, the autumn sun splashing over us. Are they uncomfortable because we are women or because one of us is Black and the other is white?

Oh, sometimes how I wish you were different. And then I love your difference. How much of what I feel has to do with race? Am I being a snob or making stereotypes? Your soft, full brown lips combine with your smell, your voice, to draw me in. But along with this attraction is the lack of other important connections—critical thinking, especially about politics of difference. As in other relationships, I have questions about our differences, our compatibility, but because you are Black and I am white, I'm afraid that my judgments and criticism of you might be racist.

In the beginning, I do not know how to talk about class or cultural polarities. It must be a racial thing, really.

1964. I was three years old when we moved to a big old stone house in a mostly Jewish, mostly white urban neighborhood where we fit in, more than the place we left that was Jewish, but different, somehow, insular or...hmm...racist, maybe. Four or five years after we moved in, a family bought the house next door. The kids were louder than the others on the block. Their house was dirtier and smelled different from mine or anyone else's I'd ever been in before. I felt strangely afraid when I'd run inside to use the bathroom that reeked faintly of piss—like somehow I wasn't supposed to be in that house. There was no father, just a tired mother, who wasn't very attentive or nice, and an older, stern brother with the biggest afro I'd ever seen, bigger than the guy on "Mod

Squad." I had never been in a Black family's house before. Or a poor family's house either. The only Black people I spent time with were our cleaning woman (that's how we referred to her), who took two buses and a subway to get to our house three days a week, and a few kids in my school classes who were smart and wore the same kind of clothes as I did and didn't really seem any different from me or my white friends.

You grew up in the projects. I used to look at those buildings from a locked car, windows shut tight, and wonder what little girls' lives were like in there. You said, "There was pride back then, not like now." Your grandmother and grandfather made a good family for you. Safe.

I was embarrassed sometimes to go shopping with my father. Not because of him, but because of where he took me. Places with names like "House of Bargains" and "ShopRite" and the "Amazing Store" with bulging cartoon-like green dollar signs on the store marquee, often neon or blinking, shouting, "Shop here! It's cheap!" He loved to bargain hunt— to "birddog" as he called it—to rummage through piles of clothes, finding the best deal. There were never any dressing rooms in these stores. He'd point me towards the back, behind an overflowing counter, where I'd slip on a skirt over my pants—first check for rips, holes, number of buttons, dye irregularities, and matching length of sleeves or legs, where appropriate. By 13, I was mortified. I wanted real dressing rooms and nicely hung perfect clothes on racks. I didn't want pimply 16-year-old store clerks in Catholic girls' school uniforms to stare at me. I didn't want the older Jewish women, who invariably managed these stores, to embarrass me with their loud, nasal voices. Why did they work here? Why weren't they doing something more meaningful with their lives? These jobs were for lower class people, for uneducated people, not Jews.

You and I didn't talk about the young Black woman who worked in my mother's family, who cleaned Jews' houses and took care of their children. She came up from the south at the age of 16 in 1943, she couldn't read or write and my grandmother called her the "girl." You and I didn't talk about how this woman came to work in my family when my mother started having babies in the late '50s. We didn't talk about the language I learned at an early age and how I understood the power that my relatives wielded when they talked about the "goyim" and the "schvartze." And how I understood exactly what to do when this woman told me to stop being so "sassy."

Being a Jew meant being middle class or richer although I didn't know any Jews who had more money than we did, but I knew there were rich Jews because the world said there were. My understanding for a long time included other ideas about Jews: that they were educated and determined to send their kids to college; that learning was an important part of life; that books lined every Jew's house. These were stereotypes that lived within me as much as the ones about the nonexistence of working-class Jews.

Reality: my grandparents' lives were a mixture of working- and middle-class values and financial situations, depending on when you measured (pre- or post-Depression catastrophes). They didn't go to college. Their children, my parents, have master's degrees and were the first in their families to attend a university.

Translation sometimes makes it difficult to clearly understand what class one belongs to: the knowing is filtered through nostalgia, exalted stories and hazy memories. The messages are generationally transcribed.

You are difficult to argue with because you never disagree with me. Instead, you sheepishly change yourself to fit what I want. You do not talk to me about your ideas or your feelings unless I ask. You say you are done with your old life, the one where you were beaten and abandoned. Although I have not pounded my fist into your face, I have been unfair with my thoughts, my words; I have left you behind in the dust of my fear.

I went to the neighborhood public elementary school. There were two classes per grade: the smart class (mostly white kids) and the slow class (Black and poor white kids). Out of 33 students in my second-grade class, four were Black, the rest were white. In excited anticipation, on the last day of school, we got our assignments. The white kids looked at each other, puzzled: were they putting us in the slow class or were the Black kids catching up? No one said anything, but it was scary for a minute, for my 8-year-old self to deal with, to possibly lose my safety, my comfort. Things were changing. It was the same year my older sister and brother went to the big neighboring junior high. They were part of a group of white kids sent by well-meaning liberal parents to integrate the all-Black school. My brother came home with bicycle chain imprints on his neck. My sister was called names and had things stolen from her. White parents kept their kids home on the still-raw anniversary of Malcolm X's assassination. Just in case.

"Is this because I'm Black?" you ask over and over when we fight about whether to continue with our rocky relationship. There is so much more to us than Black and white, yet we don't look at all the pieces. As you heap the Black/white weight on me, blaming yourself and staying in your victim status, and as we both fail to look at class and culture and just plain personal differences, I wonder, "Can we ever talk?"

You tell me you want to follow your girlhood dreams and open a feminist bookstore and quit your job as a social worker so you can stop answering to other people. Despite the relationship problems, I decide to follow your dreams. I set my limits and then quickly smash through my own boundaries: I agree to coordinate the weekly writers series and order the journals for the store; soon I find I am organizing the bills, doing the publicity, buying the books, dealing with creditors and collectors, and staffing the store while you work your day job. I am putting all my energy into your dreams while squeaking by on part-time paid work. You do not confront the growing mountain of bills. When we discover that two women involved in the store have stolen a total of $3,000 in the first few months after we opened, you laugh nervously on one side of your face while tears run down the other side.

If you cannot cope with the fact that this dream business of yours is real, then I will have to step in and take over. I imagine there are reasons to ignore reality when that could mean the end to dreams fought so hard for.

My Jewish education consisted of five years (ages 9-13) of secular folk shul where I learned a lot about history and culture and politics and much less about synagogue rituals and restrictions. Although I complained every Sunday about getting up for class, in retrospect, being part of this environment was like being home: no translation, no explanation.

You asked, at the onset of the war, whether I had any "people" over there. As bombs rained over Israel, I wanted to scream, "It's not just Jews who are being terrorized in the middle of the night!" If anything, you should have been asking me about my people in Eastern Europe where I have more of a cultural connection. You couldn't do anything right, then.

I never had the sense that we were anything but comfortable, financially. My parents owned their own house, their own car, and had money in the bank. And then, when I was just beginning sixth grade, things changed. My parents, both public school teachers, both active in union politics, went on strike and were out of work for three months. We stopped eating steak for dinner, we didn't get any new clothes or books or toys, and our Hanukkah and birthday gifts were limited to $10 each that year. I learned a lot about sticking to political beliefs as I watched my sixth-grade teacher bust past the picket line I was in with my mother, who also taught at this school. I grumbled "scab" under my breath and glared at her. I felt righteous in my bones that I was on the other side of that line, getting a different kind of education that year. It was the only year I was allowed to curse the evil mayor who seemed to cause our financial situation.

In the summer, I was invited to go to Italy to visit my best friend who had moved there that year. My mother insisted I was too young to fly alone. Years later, she told me they didn't have the money to send me abroad. Why did she wait so long to tell me that truth?

I think a lot about what it meant for my parents not to have income for three months and about the choices people make, the options people have when it comes to money and their beliefs. My parents could live their politics and not become homeless, lose their jobs or children, or compromise their values. As I question my own life and choices—working often on projects that pay me little or nothing but allow me to further my beliefs in working to change the world or redirect my goals and energy—I realize I'm doing what my parents did, twenty years ago. I feel lazy when I indulge my politics—a powerful message—because often I do not make enough money to live on. My belief that the administrative work I do to support myself is so often a waste of my time and doesn't really change the system that oppresses women, lesbians, working-class people, people of color is hard to reconcile when, if it weren't for the yearly (sometimes twice yearly) middle-class safety net of my parents, I would not be able to pay my rent.

The most money I have ever taken from my parents since graduating from college ten years ago (which they paid for entirely) was $4,000 to buy a used car. I also "borrowed" $3,000 to bail me out of a bad business deal and several installments of $500-$1,000 over the years to pay for taxes and bills and health insurance. Last year I made about $15,000. I have not been able to pay for my own car insurance for the last 2 years ($800/year). My parents had to co-sign my credit card application. Unless I get a job paying at least $20,000 with benefits (which I had once and still couldn't pay my bills), I will need to take money from them.

To talk about this stirs the jumble of feelings that surround the arguments I have with myself about what it means to be financially independent. As I confront class issues in my life, I wonder if my arguments will be honest as I continue to take money from the safety net.

I want agreements about money and time worked in writing. You want it verbally. For two months before the store opens, you pay me a salary from the loan you got to open the store plus money you saved over the years. You joke with me about our agreement, and it seems like a cover for your discomfort with the amount. I hear through the grapevine that you thought my salary those two months, and any request for money at all from me, was ripping you off.

It is difficult for me, as a white middle-class woman, a Jew, to talk about money with those I perceive have power over me: men, members of the upper class, the corporate world, the elite, white Anglo-Saxon Protestants, my parents. I wonder about your jokes, your need to avoid talking about money with me and with creditors and the power dynamics at play between us. You make more money than I do at your social work day job; I have access to parents' money. You have kids—two nieces and a nephew—

to support with government money; I am the only person I worry about financially. You are Black; I am white. You were raised Baptist and now do not talk about identifying spiritually; I am clearly Jewish-identified. You own this business; I have called myself employee, the owner's lover, co-owner. I have skills and access to information that you want and need.

Are we both owners of this business if you contribute money and I contribute time, organization and access to skills? What about contribution of dreams, where does that fit in to defining who is and is not the owner?

High school, 1975. I begin 9th grade in the all-girls, academic public school, making new friends, having new feelings at 14. I sleep over at her house, lie next to her on the hard floor in a sleeping bag; she has no furniture other than her bed, next to the empty living room and kitchen. It doesn't look like a family lives here. We giggle all night. I wish I could lie next to her, in the bed, smell her warmth, touch her skin. Her skin. Her skin is darker than mine, a milky coffee mixture from her white mother and mysteriously absent Black father. I'm nervous about inviting her to my house. I explain to my diary that it'll be OK to invite her over… "she's mostly white, anyway."

It was your choice, not your Baptist, bible-thumping grandmother's, to go to a Catholic girls' parochial school. You were one of only a handful of Black girls there, in your navy blue winter uniforms and pale yellow spring jumpers.

You tell me now that it has been years since you dated a Black woman.

1979. I pack up my clothes, my new stereo bought with graduation money, a few record albums and my confusion (no diary, I'm too old for that, now) and drive the two hours up the East Coast with my parents to a private liberal arts university, not quite Ivy League, less expensive, less prestigious, but not a state school. My roommate is Black and so are most of the women on this dorm floor, most of them from Queens, Jersey City and Newark, on scholarship. Panic, like the kind I felt at the end of second grade, surges. The panic is quieter, deeper this time. By second semester I have chosen a new roommate (white, Jewish, suburban middle-class) in another (entirely white) dorm building. It is not that I do not want to live with Black women—I reason that I want to live with my friends. My friends are all white.

By the end of the semester I am keenly aware that I did not need a scholarship to go to this school but I did not get an allowance from Daddy or use of the extra car with the vanity plates that sat waiting for me in a suburban garage. It is the first time that I notice my middle-class status between those that have money to throw away and those that have to count every cent.

1981. I return to school. Not the private country club one in New Jersey, but the big-city university back in Philadelphia—the one I scorned and vowed I'd never go to when I was in high school here. Only people who couldn't get in anywhere else or those who had no money went to this school.

I often compared this university with the Ivy League school in the same city, the one I should have been enrolled in, the one my parents would only let me go to if I moved back home. I thought it was their scheme to get me away from the older boyfriend I was living with; in reality, it was three times as expensive as the city school and they were paying my way. The only difference to me, after the first semester at Temple, was that everyone there wore Converse high tops while Penn students dressed up in their Adidas tennis shoes. Class was about fashion and affordability.

You went to a community college for the first two years and then were excited to be going to the "real" university, the same one I scorned and attended. Later, you got your master's degree, at the same school, something no one ever expected you to do.

1981. English Lit class. She's interesting and different, somehow, and I want to know her. It's hard to make friends here at this commuter school. This woman talks about her attractions for women in a way that is smooth and rich, open; I cannot touch those thoughts that creep in and then, quickly, out of my reach. We spend hours on the phone. She lives in her own apartment, has a car, is on her own, is a year older than me. She lives on an unexpected inheritance from her parents who died suddenly the year before. Does this mean she's rich? She talks about growing up in the country, about her father's self-made money she didn't have access to until he died. I snap my jaw shut as questions worm their way out: don't ask her about the money, it's not polite, it came from her dead parents.

Years later, she tells me exactly how much money. It is an amount I cannot fathom, like winning the lottery.

Class distinctions for me came in the form of materiality and ownership. Paying for college, getting hand-me-down clothing with cousins' names sewn in the back which meant they went to overnight camp, having one car, owning a home, shopping at cut-rate stores, always buying things on sale, always looking at the right-hand side of the menu first.

Some questions from the community at large: Is the bookstore really going to be in *that* neighborhood, down the street from the men's shelter, next door to the abandoned building—one of many on this quickly changing block—but not swift enough for some white women? Was there really going to be a bookstore just for women with a focus on oppressed communities (lesbians, feminists, women of color, working-class women)? Was it really owned by an African-American lesbian with a white Jewish dyke behind her instead of the other way around? What does the big, established, popular lesbian and gay bookstore think about us?

The media had lots of assumptions, too: Why were we doing this? How would this store be different from others in the area, and were we sure it would succeed? One newspaper headlined a story about the bookstore, making a pun of its name, Girlfriends Bookstore, and questioning our relationship by asking in bold type, "More Than Just Girlfriends?" This same newspaper made some slippery moves. The author of the article interviewed both of us, took down our names, got the correct spelling, took our picture in the shining sun outside the soon-to-be-opened bookstore, hardly quoted the clearly acknowledged owner of the store and then printed a picture where the darker of the two of us was a blotchy ink blot, hardly recognizable. But I, the white woman and obviously the assumed owner, showed up clearly.

The questions and assumptions continued through our own transitions, from my being a lover's sidekick to our calling me a co-owner. And then, later, women clucked, "Oh my, you two broke up...what will happen to the store now?"

We were excited by some things in this store: our working together as Jew and African American in lesbian and feminist communities; building bridges through words, language, writing. Some of our dreams came true, despite our differences and problems. Women—of all sexual orientations and cultures and stages of awareness—told us how important this store was to them. Women showed up consistently to buy books at Girlfriends— or at least to browse—and to support our benefits and weekly writers series. In deciding which writers to bring to the store, I wanted to forge connections between communities. So when Essex Hemphill came to read about the experience of Black gay men, a bridge was built with earlier visiting writers—with poet Irena Klepfisz, a lesbian Holocaust survivor, with poet Colleen McElroy, a heterosexual Black writer, with Chrystos, a Native American working-class lesbian poet, with Joyce Warshow, a writer of old lesbians' experiences, with Loraine Hutchins, a bisexual activist and writer.

Our differences, our shared experiences of oppression, our alliances, our jokes, our combined efforts were successful. To a point.

I will not tie up any discussion about difference—race, class, culture—with a nice, pretty, definitive ribbon. It's too messy a subject to compartmentalize each issue and use it as a reason for why a relationship fails or thrives. I will acknowledge that in the year since I left the bookstore, in the year-and-a-half since my lover and I split up, I have begun to look at the ways in which class, more than any of our other differences, impacted our relationship, both in our business and personal life.

Why is there seldom a discussion in feminist arenas about the extent to which "skill" privilege, in the form of access to knowledge and information, plays a part in class and race differences as well as in other power differences including gender, sexuality, age, ability, and culture? I am now aware of this once-silent privilege in my life and its power over my relationships. Just because I am a Jew, a woman and a lesbian, doesn't mean I can intimately feel the oppression of others. Nor does it mean I can ignore the ways in which I am privileged and what I do with that power.

It's over now and we don't talk anymore. It's time to work through our differences alone. There were nights when we lounged in bed and read Toni Morrison quotes to each other because her work was something we shared well. I thought this one was for you but now I think it is meant for me, to stop fighting, to follow the wise words of someone I admire and can learn from.

"Lay em down," Sethe heard the voice of her dead grandmother, Baby Suggs. "Lay all the mess down. Sword and shield. Both of em down. Down by the riverside."

I have laid down my own heavy knives of defense, as Sethe was advised, and placed them one by one on a bank where clear water can rush over them.

Terri de la Peña in 1951.

Chicana, Workingclass and Proud: The Case of the Lopsided Tortilla

Terri de la Peña

In March, 1992, the month *Margins* was published, I opened a letter from Julia Penelope and read in part: "...I am looking for personal narratives...which I hope will allow for many women's voices to be heard. For this purpose, short stories, fictionalized accounts, won't work. Also, although analysis of one's personal experience is welcome, I don't want theoretical or analytical essays, either."

Since she did not want fiction, I first thought I would not submit a manuscript; writing nonfiction brings on anxiety attacks. But I was curious about what Julia had in mind. In the months that followed, I had many distractions, and even managed to forget her deadline until she sent a reminder letter toward the end of summer. I had trouble ignoring Julia after that, but I still procrastinated until time began to run out.

After work each evening, I wrote a few pages here, a few there, inserting sections of personal recollections and notes from previous panel discussions on gender, race and class. Several days later, I wound up with this somewhat unwieldy product, reminiscent of the lopsided flour tortillas I made as a child. But that is fitting, I think, because my formative years in a working-class home molded me into the Chicana lesbian I have become: a somewhat malleable mixture of family tradition, a touch of humor, spiced with feminist ideals, my own brand of creativity, and the constant bittersweet twinge of never quite belonging.

I grew up where the mountains meet the sea, in a southern California beach town, a descendant of the Marquez-Reyes families who came from Nueva España to Alta California in the late 18th century. The Mexican government officially granted the two families El Rancho Boca de Santa Mónica in 1828. After the U.S. wrested control of northern Mexico in 1848, the Treaty of Guadalupe Hidalgo offered the Mexican people in what is now the U.S. Southwest full citizenship, protection, and the right to bilingual education. My paternal grandmother, Amelia Enriquez, born twenty-one years after the signing of the Treaty, was a U.S. citizen by birth, but she spoke Spanish as did most of her contemporaries; she never became fluent in the English language.

In 1873 when Amelia was four years old, Colonel Robert Baker bought 2,112 acres of El Rancho, of which he later sold a three-quarter interest to Senator John P. Jones. The senator then laid out the Township of Santa Monica, and in 1875 began development of his railroad and wharf. My grandfather Esteban de la Peña, whom Amelia married, joined local crews, mostly Mexicans and Mexican-Americans, unloading the sailing ships docked in Santa Monica Bay. During my late father's childhood, Santa Monica lost the "harbor war" to San Pedro. The long, curving wharf became a tourist attraction which the city eventually dismantled in 1921.

With the statehood of California, the subsequent influx of white settlers and the declining fortunes of the land-grant families, the Mexican-American population became the working class and the poor. Their numbers increased with the advent of Mexican immigrants fleeing the Revolution of 1910, with hundreds journeying northward to the barrios of East Los Angeles. My maternal grandmother, Hijinia Alarcón de Escobedo, and my mother, Juanita Escobedo, were among these, first settling on the Eastside, then opting for the seaside community of Santa Monica.

When I was born, ninety-nine years after the Treaty of Guadalupe Hidalgo, twenty-six years after the dismantling of the long wharf, two years after the end of World War II, Santa Monica remained a small town. Its wealthier inhabitants lived north of Wilshire Boulevard, its middle-to-working class occupied the area roughly between Wilshire and Olympic Boulevards, and its poorer neighborhoods were south of Olympic Boulevard. Through a Depression foreclosure sale, my thrifty parents and maternal grandmother jointly purchased a lot with a two-bedroom home on the corner of 15th Street and Broadway, a couple of blocks north of Olympic, a few blocks south of Wilshire. Owning property was a major accomplishment for my immigrant mother and grandmother, and for my father whose familial roots were sunk deep within Santa Monica soil. I grew up in a neighborhood away from most of my Mexican-American classmates, though cousins lived down the street, another lived two blocks distant, and some African-American families were less than a block away.

Prior to my birth, Juanita, my mother, had owned a beauty shop, a thriving enterprise which definitely added to the family income. My father, Joaquín, too young for World War I, too old for World War II, had spent the Depression and War years as a chauffeur for affluent Westsiders, and later became a vulcanizer and foreman for an auto supply and tire company located across the street from his childhood home. Hijinia, my maternal grandmother, lived with my parents and contributed to their income by being a housekeeper in well-to-do homes, later working in food service at St. John's Hospital. By the time I came along, my mother had given up her business, due to neuralgia and the complications of a miscarriage. Although I cannot recall hearing it discussed, I suspect the family's income changed drastically when my mother ceased being a full-time beautician. Her doctor had advised her not to have any more children, but being a devout Catholic, she gave birth to me and two younger sisters before having a hysterectomy in the mid-1950s.

During my childhood in St. Anne's, a parochial school located in an industrial area of the city, with a mostly Mexican-American student body and a sprinkling of Anglos and African-Americans, I had no clue St. Anne's was any different from St. Monica's, the large Catholic parish north of Wilshire. My parents had once belonged to St. Monica's, and my older brother and sister had gone to school there; although they rarely spoke of it, they were among the few children of color attending. Shortly before I entered first grade, the Archdiocese of Los Angeles designated St. Anne's Chapel a parish, and our home fell within its boundaries. Never the type to protest, my parents dutifully changed parishes. Whether they realized it or not, their decision had a profound effect on how I began to perceive myself, on my educational prospects, and on who I am today.

Unlike my older siblings schooled with Anglo classmates, I spent my childhood mostly with brown children like me. Neither my brother nor sister has as strong a connection to Chicano issues as I do; neither feels as strongly about racism and classism as I do. Years apart, but in the same family, we came of age under differing circumstances. Their classmates were the children of doctors, lawyers, teachers and engineers; mine were the children of immigrants, small grocery owners, factory laborers, seamstresses, and custodians. My siblings, respectively eleven and seven years my senior, grew up with ambitious aspirations; eventually, they bought and owned a successful business together. I grew up wondering who and what I could be.

Even so, I considered myself more fortunate than Mexican immigrant classmates who spoke no English. There were times when I envied those fair-skinned children from Jalisco who could have passed for white if only they had been able to speak English without an accent; I thought it unfair that I, a native Californian, looked more "Mexican" than they did. Somehow I did not equate the immigrant children with my beloved Grandma who often told me stories about those early years in Chihuahua. I existed in the narrow confines of my strict Catholic family and the parish, and had no concept that the town's white majority would see no difference between my brown skin and that of the kids I called "those wetbacks." Ironically, my Nanita Amelia had expressed similar sentiments during my parents' courtship; she had objected to her son's dating a Mexican girl. Even Grandma Hijinia, who had worked for wealthy families in Mexico, Texas, and California, perceived herself as superior to those recently arrived from Mexico; she saw them as superstitious and ignorant, "rancheros," the equivalent of country bumpkins.

But weren't we Mexican-Americans superior to the Mexican immigrants? After all, we were U.S. citizens, spoke fluent English, had our own home, a car, a television set, a playhouse and swings in the back yard. During the summers, our whole family would pile into the Chevrolet and go to Disneyland, or drive to Sequoia National Park for a few days, or visit my mother's friends in El Paso. In retrospect, I realize we fell into that stratification trap: objectifying the Mexican immigrants as "others," refusing to recognize our similarities, denying our common ethnic and cultural bonds, just as many U.S.-born Latinos behave toward Central American immigrants today.

Every year Grandma's employer, St. John's Hospital, hosted an elaborate Christmas party for St. Anne's students. En masse, the entire student body would walk two blocks to the hospital and up the stairs to the seventh floor auditorium. There musicians and singers, cartoonists and ventriloquists would entertain us. Imagine my surprise one December at reading in the local newspaper that the hospital had held its annual Christmas event for "underprivileged children." I remember being stunned at that description, suspecting its definition, but nevertheless scurrying for my mother's dog-eared dictionary. I read: "Underprivileged: deprived through social or economic condition of some of the fundamental rights of all members of a civilized society: poor." How could that describe my classmates and me? We all lived in private homes, not tenements; we all attended private school. My mother's response was, "Well, we're not rich, not poor either. But some of the kids at your school *are* poor." That answer temporarily satisfied me, but I recall being too embarrassed later on to admit having attended those parties.

Not long afterwards, when I was an eleven-year-old seventh grader, both my grandmothers died, a month apart. Unlike Nanita Amelia, Grandma Hijinia had lived with us, helped raise us, and offered the affection my "super parish volunteer" mother was often too busy to give. Grandma's death plunged me into depression, the first one I can recall experiencing. I remember feeling detached from everyone in my family and from my friends.

While I was mourning Grandma, my female classmates were discovering boys. Often, I wonder if my encompassing depression and its accompanying isolation further obscured my lesbianism. After losing Grandma, I was too miserable to deal with reality, much less with my own puberty and lack of interest in the opposite sex. A scrawny adolescent with buckteeth and acne, I withdrew, becoming woefully self-conscious, scrupulously religious, and proceeded to read every book in sight. In fact at my St. Anne's graduation, I won an award for reading eighty-three books that academic year. No one suspected I read to escape my grief—and myself.

Though aware of the "underprivileged" label, I was unprepared for the culture shock of attending St. Monica's, the only Catholic high school in the city. Raised with brown and black children, I found myself suddenly surrounded by Anglos, some from wealthy backgrounds, others from show-business families. Those white girls seemed to have no inkling of events occurring across town where "progress" by the name of the Santa Monica Freeway encroached into Mexican-American neighborhoods, destroying what once had been the barrio: urban renewal meant Chicano removal. Secure in their homes north of Wilshire, the white girls were concerned with being blonde and popular, knowing the latest surfer slang and music. For the first time in our young lives, we St. Anne's kids whose parents could afford St. Monica's tuition were outnumbered by whites. To further emphasize our "otherness," we became separated into "college prep" and "business" classes.

As one of the "St. Anne's brains," I wound up in college prep, though my parents insisted I take business courses, too; neither of my parents had finished high school, and they expected their children to find jobs, not attend college. I had never even known a college graduate; to me, college was a foreign concept. Yet having spent so much time reading on my own, I became excited about being in classes with other "smart" kids, but I also felt cut off from my longtime Chicanita friends. To add to my confusion, the Anglo kids and even the nuns made comments like: "I can't believe you came from St. Anne's," implying that I was unlike those "Mexican girls." Meanwhile, the St. Anne's kids, who had teased me about being a book-worm, felt betrayed by my hobnobbing with "snotty gringas."

The "brainy" kids were not "boy-crazy," so seemed likeliest to be my friends; at least, we had books in common. Trying to find my niche, I decided not only to continue reading, but also to try writing fiction. After all, I knew I was different from my classmates; I had nothing to lose by hiding behind creativity and trying to be a writer.

With few women writers as role models—certainly no Chicanas—I began to write what appealed to me most: westerns! My stories were set in the Southwest and most of my characters were white males; few women and no people of color populated those early attempts at fiction. Self-conscious and shy, I had already absorbed a sense of invisibility, of being insignificant in comparison to the white girls at the school. Without hearing it actually said, I sensed that people like me could only be working class, unrepresented in education, politics, and in all phases of the media, including fiction. Brown girls, even brown boys, did not matter to the white people around us. Recalling the family history, I knew we had been land rich, money poor, and had lost some of the most valuable real estate in southern California. That proved we were failures and would never amount to anything. Somehow I did not remember the strength and courage of my parents and grandparents, struggling to make our lives better than theirs. Is it any wonder then that I wrote from a white point of view, denying my own reality and the richness of my cultural heritage?

Those early stories illustrated my worst adolescent fears—being orphaned, being betrayed, being victimized. And after I graduated from St. Monica's near the top of my class, yet without any college or scholarship counseling, I began to realize that writing was personal, a way of doing something for myself alone, without needing to explain or justify it to anyone. I dreamed about writing a novel someday, though I never expected that to become a reality; I could not even imagine someone like me being a fictional character, much less a published writer. Yet through my characters, I could forget my shyness, my gawkiness, my acne-scarred face, my sense of being different from everyone else; I could even forget about being "underprivileged." My characters often were wiseguys—my direct opposites. Too naive to name my lesbianism, I considered myself an eccentric late bloomer, too involved with reading and writing to actually live my life. Lacking role models, initiative, and encouragement, I had no motivation to try getting published and certainly none to be the first college graduate in the family.

I lived with my parents, worked at clerical and secretarial jobs at UCLA, and kept on writing. When I was twenty-four, I survived what could have been a fatal hit-and-run accident; the emergency room doctor considered it miraculous that, despite my broken bones, I had not even sustained head injuries. I recalled the erstwhile "brainy" label and figured my still intact brain was probably my biggest asset. Was that why I had been spared? Was I supposed to put my brain to better use? With no easy answers about my potential, I drifted into the Chicano movement, feminism, and in and out of depression.

In 1979, I finally decided to attend evening classes at Santa Monica College. Through one of my psychology instructors, I found a feminist therapist and, with her guidance, began to accept myself as a lesbian and as a writer. I remained unpublished, but by then my fictional characters were exclusively Chicanas, and writing continued to keep me alive. It sustained me as nothing else could, through good times and bad, and I transformed myself through the evolving personalities of my characters. When I came out as a lesbian in 1983, I realized I could no longer hide my writer's identity either.

After working off-campus for some years, I returned to UCLA employment in 1982, and continued to confront the changes within the university and within myself.

November 1988

I pause in the doorway. The office once crowded with desks and filing cabinets is now a remodeled conference room. Against the compelling East Los Angeles mural, next to where I used to sit and type manuscripts, stand a sofa and a long table. Huichol yarn paintings break the monotony of the university walls. Slightly disoriented, I stare at this transformed environment. More than anything else, shyness has prevented me from returning—but not today. I enter quietly.

In 1972-73, I held a staff position in the Chicano Studies Research Center by day and wrote fiction by night. Surrounded by Chicanos who celebrated our Mexican heritage, I regained the pride I had once felt in being a descendant of a land-grant family, even though some considered my Westside upbringing less legitimate than their own Eastside backgrounds. I had to deal with openly sexist Chicano authors and editors while working there, but their attitudes and comments did not prevent me from being a secret writer. Fearing ridicule because I lacked a college degree, I did not dare admit my own creativity to those men who prided themselves on their ethnic solidarity. In those days, I wrote only for myself, too intimidated to share my work, much less submit it for publication. Staff women in Aztlán were to be seen and not heard—certainly not expected to be creative, of all things.

Years later, the one-time office is filled with Chicana students and staff, campus feminists, brown women like me. They mill about, platicando con amigas; there are hardly any male students around. Among las Chicanas, I recognize no one, but somehow do not feel alienated; I feel as if I am among my former classmates, among people I have known all my life. The reality is: these are the "brains" of the younger generation and I am a forty-one-year-old office worker, not exactly one of their peers. I am relieved no one seems to notice me.

Neat rows of chairs await Sandra Cisneros' reading. For a moment, I forget my self-consciousness and ponder the best vantage point. Finally selecting a seat, I turn when someone calls and suddenly find the smiling face of Helena Viramontes. We met in UC Irvine in 1986, when I was awarded one of the Chicano Literary Prizes for fiction. I move closer.

Helena and I talk about writing. Como siempre, she encourages me, and we commiserate over the long-term task of writing novels. Helena reveals Cisneros is her houseguest, and invites me to join them for dinner after the reading. I am honored.

Helena considers me her peer even though I have published only one story. In the 1970s, I never would have been invited to join a visiting writer for dinner. But then, in the 1970s and long before, there had been no one like Sandra Cisneros and Helena Viramontes. Glancing around, I marvel again at the many compañeras gathered to listen to una hermana read and discuss her work. I am amazed at the advances the years have made possible.

With irony, I realize that a bold Chicana—una mujer unafraid of telling her stories in poetry and fiction—has lured me back to this Center. Sandra Cisneros, Helena Viramontes, y sus compañeras Cherríe Moraga and Gloria Anzaldúa, are Chicana writers who have inspired many of us to dare to be heard. And sitting with Helena, waiting to listen to Sandra, I know that I have changed even more than this room has.

I am proud to be the Chicana daughter of a fourth-generation Californian father and a Mexican immigrant mother. It has taken me so many years, so much reading and introspection, to realize my cultural heritage and working-class background give me a unique bicultural perspective—one I am to continue exploring through fiction. For being Chicana is the world I know, the internal one I live in, the one I choose to write about. And, these days, I call myself a writer, and I will be silent no more.

August 1992

Four years later, I attend another campus-related event, and again come to terms with the changes of the past decade.

The morning is sunny, promising to become sweltering. Narrow rays of sunlight streak through the overhead windows of the Venice Family Clinic's meeting room. Incoming staff, about fifty in all, begin to fill the spacious room. I feel some apprehension while they enter with coffee cups and sweet rolls, taking seats at the rectangular tables arranged in the room's center. I study their faces—noting their varying shades of brown and black, like the faces of my long-ago classmates. The staff is mostly Latina, with some Latinos, African-Americans and Asian-Americans; the majority of their supervisors are white. A few staff nod towards us while others stare straight ahead as if we are invisible; most are non-committal, their faces masking their discomfort.

They are in this room to attend a mandatory homophobia workshop organized by the university's staff affirmative action office; the mandatory nature of the workshop no doubt accounts for the unfriendly attitudes. The clinic is a community branch of the university's medical center and, under its administration, subject to the same antidiscrimination policies against racism, sexism and homophobia as on-campus schools and departments. There have been complaints about homophobia in this workplace, and the affirmative action staff is here to respond.

Because I am an "out" Chicana lesbian, as well as a member of the Lesbian and Gay Staff and Faculty Network and the Latino Staff and Faculty Association, I am a logical choice to participate in the workshop. My co-participant is Peter, a Japanese-American gay man, a campus activist, and a veteran of many such workshops. I am a neophyte at this, more accustomed to being invited to speak to women's studies classes or to read my fiction in local bookstores. I am learning that being a published Chicana writer and a lesbian as well brings a variety of invitations, some more anxiety-producing than others.

And I am not exaggerating about my anxiety level; despite my cool seersucker outfit, I am steaming from a combination of fear and PMS. Coming out in public is less stressful when I am in my writer persona, with a story to read to an audience that wants to listen. Today the usually chatty writer is a nervous university staff worker, not unlike the people of color seated resentfully before me.

Peter and I make quick introductions before showing "Pride and Prejudice," a video documentary on homophobia produced by Dorothy Engleman for Santa Monica City Cable TV. I am one of the lesbians in the video, and hope that will make my coming out story a bit easier to tell. The staff seems attentive during the screening, especially when they recognize me. Some snicker when the title of my coming out story flashes on the screen: "Good-bye Ricky Ricardo, Hello Lesbianism." Desi Arnaz is a Latino icon; I wonder if esta gente thinks I have desecrated his memory. I feel their curious stares and my face glows hot. Then I remember how, after unexpectedly viewing the documentary on local cable TV, my next-door neighbors, a Mexican immigrant family steeped in tradition, quit speaking to me. And I wonder if this predominantly Latina staff will do likewise, becoming even more resistant to what Peter and I have to say.

When the video ends and the whispered conversations cease, I begin to tell my story. I feel as gawky as a teenager; I even hear my voice shake. I know I break many cultural taboos: I have no man, I have no children, I wear no makeup, and not only am I a Chicana lesbian, but I also am willing to talk and write about being one. To people unaccustomed to hearing such candor, I talk about my adolescent confusion in a strict Chicano Catholic family that never spoke of sexual matters.

I look at the many brown faces before me, some haciendo caras (making faces), repulsed, others stoic, their visages like chiseled bronze, and I feel as if I am revealing myself to my family all over again. And I am: these working-class people of color *are* mi familia. Many in this room could be my relatives; we look alike, grew up alike, yet we are so different. Those childhood feelings of difference well up again, but this time I am not teased for being the shy bookworm; this time I proclaim myself a Chicana lesbian, a tortillera, a maricona. To these Latinas who otherwise could be my sisters, I am the "other."

To ease my churning mind, I remember another time, another room, when that evanescent sense of difference began to fade, when I felt at home, momentarily safe.

April 1992

I read a section of my recently published novel to a campus audience brought together by the Chicana-Latina Collective of the Chicano Studies Research Center. A self-taught writer and former employee of the Center, I am euphoric, experiencing a sense of validation from the assembled faculty, staff and students of color present; even my brother and sister have shown up. Writing *Margins* has been a lonely but empowering period of my life; I wrote it to save myself after losing my father to pancreatic cancer, a younger sister to homophobia, a friend to AIDS, a lover to apathy. I wrote it because I needed to read it myself, and I rejoice in being able to share its words and ideas with people who mean so much to me.

While I read, I notice a few Latino students congregated at the rear of the room. They do not seem to be enjoying themselves, and for a brief moment, I wonder if I am about to be confronted with sexist and/or homophobic comments. Distracted, I stumble over some words, but quickly decide to ignore those students in the back. Soon I begin to answer questions from the audience, and while I sign copies of my book, I learn the reason why those students had whispered together: they had just heard that the police officers charged with brutalizing Rodney King were acquitted.

The climate of the room changes immediately. The festive air becomes charged with anger and pained bewilderment. My euphoria melts into the heat of frustration; I feel dizzy with conflicting emotions. Why is there no justice for people of color, for the poor, for women, for anyone who is considered "different" in this so-called "land of the free, home of the brave"? We verbalize this to each other before the students leave. We all sense trouble, and the students are worried about heading to their families in Pico-Union, in South Central, on the Eastside. And I leave, too, with my family. We wonder what the evening will bring.

Everyone knows that evening and the subsequent fiery days and nights brought the unleashed sentiments of the disenfranchised, the disadvantaged, the "underprivileged" to the point of explosion. Living on the Westside, working on the campus, I am surrounded daily by white people, co-workers and acquaintances, many of whom consider me "different" from the furious people of color in the inner city. They have known me for years, enjoy my sense of humor, seem to value my opinions, but their comments are reminiscent of those long-ago Anglo classmates who could not equate me with "those Mexican girls." These white people are uncomfortable when I remind them I am the daughter of a Mexican immigrant mother, that I have experienced racism all my life, that I am fully aware that living in my hometown, working on the campus, writing fiction in solitude, shelters me much as parochial school shielded me during my childhood. They and many other white people do not recognize that off-campus and in other parts of the city I am just another brown woman, subject to racist, sexist and homophobic comments. They do not understand that I face this schizoid reality daily, and since the Los Angeles uprising, I am even more aware of it. They do not realize that, unlike them, I have the ability by virtue of my background to move back and forth between the workingclass ethnic world and not only the everyday working world of the university, but beyond it to the literary community.

At a very young age, I learned how to balance myself between the realities of being a Chicana and, by necessity, surviving among white people. Because I grew up along the margins of what was then white-dominated society, steeped in its culture and propaganda, I had to know more about "them" than they will ever know about me; this may explain why I put myself "on hold" for so many years, to figure out how to exist without obliterating myself. Yet the emotional and psychological scars of feeling like a perpetual outsider remain; they have not faded with time.

Whenever I face a majority white audience in a bookstore, class or auditorium, I cannot shake the feeling of being an "imposter," as Chicano artist David Avalos describes himself. Like him, I am self-taught in my craft, which enhances my feelings of "otherness." Sometimes I joke about "beating the system," being a published novelist without a B.A. or M.F.A.; at other times, I feel like a cheater, a phony soon to be found out, especially when asked about writing techniques and authors who have inspired me. How do I explain that I do not meditate or do yoga before starting a creative project? I spend forty hours a week at my campus job and write during the evenings. My warm-up technique consists of answering the piles of correspondence on my desk. I simply dig in, and my inspiration lies in adding Chicana and Chicano characters to the world of fiction. I write to keep sane, to convince myself that I can be creative because of, not despite, my workingclass background. But nowadays, there is also that nagging sense of being a "politically correct" resource person, of being available for whoever needs a multi-hyphenated type (read Chicana-lesbian-feminist-writer).

A friend describes me as a "cross-over person," and I have no quarrel with that. Raised where Chicanos were the minority, I coped with feeling "different" and learned to blend into the majority community, even though I never really fit. This resilient coping mechanism serves me daily, though it does prevent me from observing life through actual inner-city eyes. Some Chicanas have called me "too white," while some whites say I do not "act like a Mexican." While these comments sting, I prefer to think my ability to cross over—whether over borders of class, race, gender or sexual orientation—improves my chances of listening to and working with others, breaking stereotypes, expressing viewpoints, often by letting my fictional characters speak for me.

And so with that conclusion, I wrap up this asymmetrical tortilla of sorts, noticing that bits of carne, lechuga, queso y salsa dribble out here and there, but I hope the combination of memories and observations gives others a taste of how my working-class experience has both sensitized and strengthened me.

We Didn't Even Have Words

by Jessica Robbins

This interview was taped on June 27, 1992, in Madison, Wisconsin. The two women interviewed, Helen Pytz (H) and Gin Lee Myers (G), are both 39-year-old, white, working class lesbians. Helen now works as a registered nurse; Gin does data entry work, but is currently unemployed. They are ex-lovers and lifelong friends. The interviewer, Jessica Robbins (J), has known them both for a long time.

J: We want to talk about class. What was it like coming up as little working class dykes on the West Side of Chicago? How did Gin bring you out?

H: She threw me in the bushes. We were in sixth grade and she threw me in the bushes cause I wouldn't talk. Right?

G: I threw you in the bushes cause I liked you. But that's right, you wouldn't talk. You were such a good girl. Boy, I don't know how we ended up together. It was a miracle.

H: I wasn't 'a good girl,' that was the problem. The problem was I was pathologically withdrawn and really fucked up. That's why we ended up together. [Laughter]

J: So what happened after you threw her in the bushes?

H: I fell in love with her. I was thrilled to death. I'd walk home from school every day hoping she'd follow me home.

G: And did I?

H: Yeah, a lot of the time. And then eventually you stopped throwing me in the bushes. You didn't throw me in the bushes for long, it was only a few months and then we started being friends.

J: How often did she throw you in the bushes?

H: I don't know, man. A couple times a week, maybe, for a while.

G: The more I liked her, the more I pushed her in the bushes.

H: I mean, I wasn't always thrilled to death. There was a part of it that was a little bit intimidating.

J: And then?

G: I only remember throwing you in the bushes, and you being real quiet and good in school, real quiet all the time, and me being real loud and being in trouble all the time, and then it's like the next thing I know…we were together already.

H: The next thing you remember we were sleeping together?

G: Yeah, and out, man, at least I was out.

H: Yeah, but there was this little period of time in between when we were doing these little boy things.

G: Like what?

H: Jim.

G: Oh, man…[Laughter] Don't be telling me that shit.

H: You played 'Breaking Up Is Hard To Do' a thousand fucking times…

G: I did not. Fuck you.

H: And you'd sit there and cry and cry and cry and cry over Jim.

G: I never fucking cried over no boy in my life. See, you can't be telling that shit.

H: Okay. Strike that. Gin never cried about Jim.

J: But in between, at some point, you had words, besides her just throwing you in the bushes.

H: No, man. I didn't talk. We didn't have no words.

G: Well, I talked.

H: We started hanging out together. We became friends. And I think our lives changed when we started hanging out together.

G: Well, we didn't just hang out together. I mean we just like…[pause]

H: Glommed on to each other. We glommed on to each other. It was real obsessive.

G: It was like we were always together.

H: Yeah, it went from she threw me in the bushes, we were kind of friends, for a while there was this little period of time when we were just friends, we weren't real close, and then all of a sudden we were like this [holds up two fingers pressed together].

G: Always together.

H: Always together. And that was every day at school…Well, was it every day at school, you think? All summer. Every day in the summer. It was real obsessive stuff. We clung on to each other really tough. But I think for me, it was…like, you know, she saved my motherfucking life, man. I was just…going nowhere. I was totally terrified…

G: Yeah, like being with me was going somewhere, right? [Laughter]

H: Yeah, somewhere, I don't know where, somewhere. So I was pathologically fucking withdrawn, man, and then Gin made me not be so scared. Cause I lived with terror, constant, fucking terror. And then, I don't know what it meant for you. Why did you do that with me? Why did you glom on to me?

G: Cause I was in love with you, man. I fell in love with you. I don't know, I know it sounds real weird but there was something that seemed stable about you. I know that sounds really funny but my life was real crazy and there was something that felt stable about being around you.

H: Yeah, because I was a forever kind of person.

J: What were your families like? What did your parents do?

G: My dad was real crazy. He's German—he was born in Chicago but my grandparents or great-grandparents were German—and he was fucking in love with Hitler and the Nazi Party. He drove a truck for a living—he drove a cement truck. My ma did some kind of office work—I think she was a bookkeeper or something. And I know that they were real young when they had me. They were maybe nineteen. And I got two brothers and one sister.

H: My parents worked in factories. My father was alcoholic. He was violent. They were European immigrants. And they were definitely not into assimilating—my father wasn't. There was nothing about this country he wanted to take in. So anyway, both our lives were real crazy at home, real fucking crazy, and we were like two fucking lifesavers hanging on, I think. Right? Real fucking crazy. And so we just left the houses and hung on to each other outside, on the streets a lot, or in my home when my parents worked, cause they were gone, so we'd be at my house a lot. Then Gin started spending the night, because we weren't together enough, being at school and outside and being on the streets together, we had to sleep in the same bed.

G: We were together from early in the morning until fucking late at night and that wasn't enough. We had to start spending the night together.

H: Then we had to start the begging to spend the nights together. So then we slept over and man, I don't know what happened but very quickly we were sexual. Real quickly. By the time we were thirteen.

G: I'm sure we were.

H: We were lovers.

G: Seemed like the most natural thing in the world that would happen. For me. It was great.

J: Did you talk about it?

H: I don't remember ever talking about it. Do you remember talking about it?

G: No. No, I don't think we talked about nothing. We just did it.

H: I think the first time we talked about it was when we were seventeen.

J: They hadn't warned you against this in Catholic school?

H: Well, yeah. The nun in eighth grade called me and told me—she called me up after school wanting to talk to me, and she told me that she thought that I should break off my friendship with Gin because she said that she thought that it was unhealthy for me and that someday I would regret it and I was headed for trouble, but I didn't know what she was talking about. Later I figured it out. I just thought she was completely crazy. There was no way I was going to do that shit. Besides, she was jealous of Gin.

G: I was going to ask you about that nun.

H: The eighth-grade nun.

G: The one that I was crushed out on?

H: Yeah, she was crushed out on you, too. The nuns loved Gin, man. All the lesbian nuns, they always were crushed out on Gin. I had to compete with all the motherfucking lesbian nuns. They had God on their side.

G: You think they were crushed out on me?

H: Yeah, they were.

J: How did people relate to your relationship?

H: Well, when we were that young, it was just, like, me and Gin. Gin was my best friend, man. Our friends were just, like, they all felt replaced. My friends felt replaced. Cause I had other best friends, Jane and Paula, and all that shit, and they just felt like they got shoved aside and Gin moved into their place. I think in the early days they didn't realize what was happening. I'm not sure they ever fucking realized what was happening. I guess at some point Paula figured it out but early on they didn't. They just figured Gin took fucking first place position in my life. They just had to get moved down. And, uh, I had a little boyfriend for a while who was a mess—that was a mess.

G: Fucking Bobby? God damn him. Son of a bitch.

H: Little Bobby. Gin and him were—it was really bad. At some point I had this little crush on Little Bobby. In the midst of the same time when we started sleeping together. I was thirteen—it was the same year. It was just adolescent confusion, you know, I think. So I got crushed out on Little Bobby and then he fell in love with me and he's crazy. So for the first year it was exciting for me cause I was doing all this little stuff but after that, that was over for me, but Little Bobby wasn't over. He didn't see it as being over for the next fucking ten years, right? So we had Little Bobby on our hands who was totally street, you know, just out there, but very damaged by his life. So he would do drama, in this real insane, crazy way, right? And then Gin was street, so she could do drama...And I think at that point [the relationship] still hadn't come to the attention of all the other people who had feelings about it later, like our parents and shit.

J: They hadn't figured out what was going on in the bedroom?

H: Well, I don't know. Maybe they did.

G: My parents knew then. My parents knew it, because, I never told them but...

H: Gin's father said I made her into a dyke...He hated me for it.

G: Probably still.

H: Went to his grave hating me for it. For turning you into a dyke. I was a bad influence on her. [Laughter]

G: It was not okay with my parents for me to be gone so much [at Helen's home] but it was too bad because we would go through this little ritual where I would call home and say, 'Ma, can I spend the night at Helen's?' And she would say yes sometimes and there was no problem, or she would say no and then I would like plead and beg and go, 'Ma, oh please, please, please, just this once, please, Ma,' you know. And then if she wouldn't let me, then I'd go off on her. [Laughter]

H: Then she'd say, 'I'm not coming home anyway!'

G: I would go through all this begging and pleading and 'Please' and do everything and then in the end, when she would get real firm and say no, I would be like, 'Well, fuck you I ain't coming home anyway. I'm staying,' you know? And, so they knew, I mean, my parents knew.

J: But nobody ever confronted you about it.

H: My mother did once.

G: Cause she found a letter.

H: She found a letter, a love letter. She had evidence in her hand. And then she got real fucking dramatic. And she just embarrassed the shit out of me and infuriated me. I came home and she was sitting at the kitchen table being a big, fucking martyr, man, being real goddamn dramatic with her hand over her heart and shit and she said, 'We have to talk. I found this letter in your room.' And then she got real nuts, you know, she said, 'I'm going to burn it and we're going to put this behind us,' and she went to the stove and lit it on fire and she had this blazing love letter in her hand. And I was so fucking enraged, man. And she said, she's burning this letter and says, 'Now we can put this behind us.' And I said, 'I'm leaving,' and I took off, I ran away from home. I went to my sister's house. I just walked out the door. I went to [my sister] Irene's house for what, two days or something like that. And she was a wreck and Irene called her and said, 'Helen's really upset about what you did with Gin's letter.' She didn't know what to do.

G: That was a nice letter, man. What the fuck did she do that for, burning it up?

H: And I was, like, you had no fucking business reading that letter. That was my letter. Man, it was personal. I was just enraged.

G: That's real deep, man, ain't it, to think that you were at this point, like you were going off on your ma, saying what were you doing reading my shit anyway?

H: Well, we'd been sleeping together for five motherfucking years, man. It was a little late. You know, to be doing dramatics and burning the letter. I mean, come on. Or four years, or something. Whatever it was. Maybe three years. I don't know. It was too many years, when you're that old, you know? This was old hat, man. She should have done that three motherfucking years earlier. So anyway, she said that, she said that we would never bring it up again. So we didn't, we just kept right on sleeping together. [Laughter] So she made her one little, she made a little stab at trying to kill it, but it didn't work.

G: See, my parents, they knew, because when we would break up, I would like cry and cry and cry, like, right there in front of the whole fucking family, you know. I'd be there on the phone, 'No, no, you can't leave me!' I'd be crying and you know everybody in the whole fucking family is like watching this.

J: One of those phones in the kitchen, where you can't get any privacy.

G: Right, nowhere to go, so you're like sitting there, crying your fucking eyes out, begging your girlfriend, 'No, no, you can't leave me,' and everybody in the family is watching you. I mean, they knew. But nobody ever said anything except for my dad, when he'd get drunk, and then sometimes he'd say something. You know, tell me I was sick, and I was fucked up, and that goddamn Helen. He never did like her, he never was going to like her.

J: Give me some examples of the kind of drama you got into. When you say, 'Do drama,' what kind of shit was going down?

H: Oh, man, whew. We were real street kids. Real fucking street kids. We would do far out shit like, we would scratch ourselves, to see how bad you were, till you could fucking scratch through till you bled and you'd leave these big fucking scars on your hands. Well, that was the kind of stuff. We were doing shit like that. Then we graduated to putting matches on ourselves, burning ourselves.

G: Right. And cigarettes.

H: Self-mutilating types of stuff to show how bad you were.

G: It seems to me there was a lot of drama about me going off and shit. Didn't we get into big fights?

H: Yeah. That was later, though.

G: Was it?

H: Years later. Not those early years. Cause I think none of us knew what we were doing, you know. We didn't know we were dykes.

G: That's for sure, man. I think about that a lot of times and I think, how strange it is that, like, I was just walking around and I'd be holding your hand and we'd be on the bus and I'd put my arm around you and we'd just truck all over like that, and I didn't have a clue.

H: We were fifteen when we started being public. We weren't public till we were fifteen. From thirteen to fifteen we did it real privately, in the bedroom. And we were just seen together all the fucking time. When we turned fifteen, that's when things changed a lot.

G: What grade was that?

H: We were in high school. Sophomores in high school. That's when it really changed. It got really fucking serious. You know? Got really serious.

G: It was before that, wasn't it? I mean even in freshman year? I mean, I remember being out of school, I was out of school already in sophomore year. I was kicked out, like, the first month, the second month or something.

H: The freshman year was when I knocked all those books out of your arms cause I was so fucking mad about something, remember? You were carrying a whole bunch of books, in your freshman year. We were already doing drama by freshman year. Cause she was at school, and I came to the school and her homeroom was down the hall from mine and she was balancing a whole stack of books on her knee. I was really pissed about something already that had happened between us and I walked by her and I knocked the books out and so the entire stack of books that she had been balancing just flew all over the hall. Then she came after me to kick the shit out of me. That already was serious. We were fighting. We weren't playing. I wasn't playing with her, I was really pissed, I knocked the books out. She responded with, she was going to come kick the shit out of me. Remember that time you told me to meet you outside after school? We were going to fight, out in front of the fucking school. And then everybody in school was like, 'Are you going to meet Gin after school? Are you really going to do it?'

J: What did you say?

H: Yeah. I said yeah. And I was determined—I was scared to fucking death that she was going to kill me, but I was determined to face her down. So I went out there and she wasn't there. [Laughter]

G: I wasn't there.

H: Yeah, you didn't want to beat the shit out of me that day. I think that was the day I knocked those books out. I think you said that because I went running up to my homeroom, you were chasing me down the hall, I went into my homeroom, and you said, 'I want to meet you outside after school.'

G: Yeah, of course I was going to say that. Fucking you do that shit in front of people, man, what do you expect me to say? You put me on the spot.

H: So we had drama by that time. That was freshman year. But we probably had drama before then.

J: And this was the girl who didn't speak, two years before?

H: And I hadn't spoken all my life. You know. Real fucking withdrawn.

J: So you really changed?

H: I changed, man. She saved my fucking life. I really changed. Then remember we were on the streets? There was a lot of drama. There was drama early on. Remember we did that shit where we were doing all this far out shit, we were fighting with chains and stuff, in front of the theater? See the bad thing is we'd play around and shit, and then the playing would get too rough and it would turn into a real fight.

G: Man, when was it I started spending all them nights at your house? When was it I started always calling home and begging my mom to let me stay? Your ma, it seemed like she was all right with it. How old were we then?

H: You started spending the night all the time when we were fifteen. When you left Good Counsel [High School] you started sleeping over at my house. You practically moved in.

G: I know, it was really weird.

H: You just ran away from home.

G: It was just like her parents just let me come on in.

H: Yeah. And we were just lovers in the bedroom.

G: It was really strange. It was like, they were just okay with me being over. And my parents were not okay with me being over at her house.

H: But I don't think that it was just like they were okay with you being over. I think it was because my father was drunk every fucking night and it kept me in the bedroom with you being there with the door closed. It made life real easy for my mother because he would just rant and rave and talk all that crazy shit in the living room with the TV on and I was taken care of and out of the way and she didn't have to deal with it. She would have had to deal every night with me being home and this drunk on her hands. This way, you could take care of me and she didn't have to.

G: She had reasons for it, but it was just like sure, sure, I could stay. So I did. I stayed all the fucking time. I was working nights and staying at your house, remember? I mean, living at your ma's.

H: Yeah. When you were like sixteen. When you were seventeen you were out working the night shift. And then you'd come home, my mom and dad would leave for work, I'd go to school and you'd come home and sleep.

G: I was working nights on the South Side. And I'd come and crash. It was a trip.

H: It was funny cause we acted like a little married couple, man. Because you'd sleep all day and you would meet me at the bus stop when I would get off from school, coming home. You'd come walk out and meet me at the bus stop and we would come home together.

G: I'd come home from work every morning, and you would meet me. Then I'd crash and then get up and meet you.

H: But we had gone through a lot of shit together even by then that we didn't even talk about. Gin had already had an illegal abortion where we were doing stuff through Jane [a feminist network that organized illegal abortions in Chicago in the late '60s and early '70s]. You had already been raped, we had to deal with that. And we were always alone. Everything we did we did by ourselves, man, every motherfucking thing we did by ourselves. There was nobody we confided in, there was nobody we could talk to and we did all this shit by ourselves. We had to raise this fucking $250, we were—what?—fifteen or sixteen years old, to get Gin an illegal abortion. The two of us are tramping down to the South Side of Chicago trying to figure out how to find this place where they're doing illegal abortions, you know? I don't even know how we raised that money. Do you remember? I remember really hustling trying to get this money together, I was trying to get money from these kids at school and shit, I was asking women for money to get—for an illegal abortion. And I got a good chunk of money. Maybe it wasn't that much. Maybe it was a hundred dollars.

G: I don't know. It seemed like a lot.

H: You know, I think it was a hundred. If you could come up with a hundred they would do it. How old were you, that first time?

G: Fifteen.

H: It was young, we were young. I remember being really young. Fifteen or sixteen.

G: It wasn't sixteen, because I was nearly sixteen or I was sixteen when they put me in Audi Home [a juvenile detention center], and that happened before I went into Audi Home, because that was one of the things that they had on me.

H: Was that you had an illegal abortion?

G: Right, that I had an abortion. It was in a letter that, you know—probably you wrote me. I mean it was in a letter somewhere my parents found. You know, they went through all my shit and found the letter and so, 'Hah!, this is what we have,' and that was one of the things.

H: You were so fucking scared.

G: Yeah, I was.

H: I thought you might fucking die on me or something and there we were, nobody knew what we were doing, we were out by ourselves out in Hyde Park, didn't even know our way around Hyde Park.

G: It was really weird.

H: And then that night you got raped was hitchhiking home from being with me, wasn't it, cause your mother made you come home that night, and wouldn't let you spend the night? It was real fucking late.

G: Yeah, occasionally I would give in and go home because they would send the police out after me and shit like that. They'd call the cops and say I ran away. You know, just fuck things up so occasionally I'd have to go home. But whenever I would go home I would just stay with Helen until, like, three or four in the morning and then I'd go home. Remember? So I'd fucking be out on the streets taking the subway and then, my parents, by then they'd moved out to Oak Park, I think, so I was going all the way from fucking Helen's house on the North Side, going all the way out to Oak Park on subways and busses and shit at three o'clock in the morning alone. Yeah, I know, and this shit happened with [Gin's lover's daughter, who had been raped a few weeks prior to this interview] and I thought about it—her having a lot of support from the Rape Crisis Center—and, you know, I don't remember, course not to say that stuff wasn't around, but I didn't know about no Rape Crisis. I didn't have anywhere to go or anybody to talk to except to call you, man.

H: Yeah, I didn't know nothing either.

J: It didn't exist then.

H: So, you know, there was a lot of shit there for us to fall in love about, I think. We'd just been through so much stuff together.

G: Uh hunh. I mean, from the time I was fifteen, that's one of the things that got me put in Audi Home is that I just wouldn't fucking go home. You know, I'd just do what I wanted to do and they wanted to make me stay at home and I just kept staying out at Helen's, usually. So they got pissed off and took me to court and said that I was incorrigible. And I guess they had some kind of fucking law that said that they could do that. You know, like you didn't have to get caught doing anything wrong but if your parents just didn't want you and said that you were incorrigible they could lock you up, so they did. For a while, and then they let me out. And after that it was really weird because once I came out of Audi Home my parents just gave up. They just fucking gave up. I'm sure I wasn't over sixteen, anyway. And after that I came home saying, okay, I'd do anything they say because I didn't want to go back there. But that lasted about a week. [Laughs] And then I started to do what I wanted again.

H: Do you remember how long you were in Audi Home? I was tortured.

G: *You* were tortured. Goddamn, man!

H: I hated it. How long were you there?

G: Not long. You know, month and a half, maybe. And then I had a six months probation after that. And my probation officer was really cool, she just thought that my family was fucking nuts. She thought my dad was nuts.

H: Well, he was.

G: Well, yeah, he was, but she kind of was a good thing for me, that somebody...

H: A person in authority.

G: Was saying, yeah, your fucking father's nuts. Because I thought he was nuts but everybody else seemed to think he was A-OK, you know, and like, here was this person saying he was a crazy motherfucker. But after that, you know, after I came out of Audi Home, they just let me go, man. I think they figured if that didn't do it nothing was going to do it, so they might as well just give up. So I really don't know when I got my first apartment, but I know I was never home.

H: But you know that time, from thirteen to sixteen, in the old neighborhood, we were doing all this, like, real neighborhood stuff. You know, outside, on the streets, neighborhood baby dykes, just kind of hanging out, just doing weird shit. Remember, we were, like, sniffing glue, doing all that kind of stuff? I was outside all the time.

J: What did you do in the winter?

H: We stayed inside. That was summertime, when we did the outside stuff. In the wintertime we stayed in my house, with my drunk father and the craziness there. Cause we could be together. Cause I couldn't be in her house, they wouldn't let me. Her parents wouldn't put up with that shit.

G: And my dad was real crazy, I mean, like crazy, and he was real unpredictable.

H: Well, he wasn't even around for a while, before Oak Park. And I still couldn't go over there. Cause your mom didn't want all that. She had too many kids to deal with. She didn't let me go over there.

G: I forget, you were there before he was. Before he came back.

H: Way before. Years before. I was there before him, man. I came into your life before he came back. He didn't count after that. Years before.

I couldn't even figure out like what the fuck he was doing when he showed up on the scene.

J: Who was he?

G: I couldn't figure it out either.

H: Cause there was no man in her life, no dad.

G: Yeah, that was a real trip. He came back like fucking he could just walk in—

H: Years later and just walk in.

G: —and be dad, and I was like, what the...Him and my mom were divorced for eight years, right after my youngest brother was born they got a divorce.

H: So when I met Gin there was no father on the scene.

G: Yeah, you know, I was just hanging out.

H: And then they got together again later. And we were long sleeping together by then.

G: And I was almost grown by then. I mean almost grown, like, fourteen or something, and he came back and starts acting like...

J: Big Daddy.

G: Yeah. And I'm like, who the fuck do you think you are? I mean, I'd been running and doing what I wanted for a long time and suddenly he's going to come in and tell me, like, you be in at nine o'clock, you do this, you do that. I was like, whew, you kiss my ass. So things didn't go well with him.

J: So from thirteen on you were sleeping together. And from fifteen on you were doing drama together. And then when you were seventeen Gin suggested to you that you should go together.

H: Right. We had been going together for four years already. Because I remember very, very consciously, when I was going with Tommy, and you told me I should fucking leave him. And I said, 'Why?' and you said, 'To be with me.' I'll never forget those words cause I thought that was really fucking far out. Now, mind you, we'd been sleeping together for four years and I thought that was really a novel idea. [Laughter] And I broke up with him the next day.

G: You did? Good, man, you should have! I was pissed about that shit.

H: Cause she said that I should be with her, and I thought, I mean, like, an idea—I thought she thought of it. Cause we didn't know no lesbians. We didn't know no lesbian community. We didn't know no dykes, we didn't know nobody, man. I thought she thought of it.

G: What a smart motherfucker, huh? She's a genius, man! [Laughter]

H: Really fucking smart. We should be together. Two women. That's fucking far out.

J: So you never heard of this?

H: No. I don't think so. Not at that point.

J: What happened then?

H: Oh, man, then everything changed again. Then we found other dykes. Everything changed then. She suggested it and I just thought she was brilliant. But we found other dykes then. Yeah, I broke up with my boyfriend who I was supposed to marry...

J: Unofficially or officially?

H: Unofficially, but his mother thought we were going to get married and all that shit, you know.

G: Boy, that's fucked up.

H: I know. Can you believe that?

G: Good thing I said that, huh?

H: It was really funny, too, because I think the thing that struck me about it was that, you know, there was a lot of anger in our relationship. You know, you hated all these guys. There was a lot of anger, with Little Bobby and all that shit. But it was real funny because when she told me that I should break up with Tommy and I asked her why and she said, 'So that you could go with me,' she was real calm and I thought it was a really, really smart idea.

J: Where'd you come up with it?

H: How did you come up with it?

G: I don't know. Why *not* be with me? What the fuck would you want to be with him for? I mean, you liked being with me. We had fun. I couldn't figure out why you kept doing them boys.

H: Then, everything changed. It was really different. Cause then we were really like going together. It was very official. We were—that was when I was still in high school, a junior in high school. I was in my third year of high school. And we were in love. Which was funny, because we fell in love, like, years after we'd been sleeping together. I mean it seems like it happened a couple times, doesn't it? Like we fell in love a few times? But I remember that as being really intense. At seventeen, cause that was like, we got real fucking heavy then. And then we went public. Then we started holding hands publicly—

G: On the bus.

H: Yeah.

G: Everybody knew when I was coming to pick you up.

H: And then shit started happening that was hard for me at school, people were making fun of me and stuff. That was real fucking hard. It was real fucking painful for me.

G: Yeah, and I didn't have to deal with that cause I wasn't in school.

H: You'd kiss me on the corner and I'd hear about it the next day. And I'd be devastated that all the kids were making fun of me.

G: See, me and you had different reactions to that shit, too. I mean, you would be devastated and I would just be pissed.

H: You'd just want to kick someone's ass. It just figures cause I went through all them years of not talking, you know. All those years of terror. And then…I don't know. I probably wanted to be accepted more than you did. Maybe not, I don't know.

G: I think, I know this sounds really crazy, but sometimes I think it was just really naive on some level, in some ways. I mean, I just thought that I was like madly in love with you, that it was the most wonderful thing in the world. For a long time I didn't know that there was anything wrong with it. I mean I really didn't know that there were dykes and lesbians. I didn't know that there were people like that out there really. And so it seemed like, just like a normal thing, you know a real normal, natural thing to do to hold hands or kiss in public or whatever, and when people would say shit it would just piss me off.

H: Well, it's funny, cause I think it's a real unique situation that you were as strong as you were. I think that's real unusual, that you were as strong as you were considering that we didn't know dykes, we didn't know no lesbians, man, we didn't know that even such a fucking thing existed hardly. And your comfort with it was just like, this is what I'm doing.

G: I think it's strange, too. I do just because all the dykes I've talked to, I mean, how many dykes have I talked to, who knows how many I've talked to, and most all the dykes that I've talked to had more trouble than I did. It was just like for some reason I didn't go through a lot of changes about coming out. It was like good! Period. Simple. It was good for me. And for a while, all I did was get pissed off when people would fuck with me about it.

H: It's funny, because it was really hard, at times, for me. It was real torturous, but it never occurred to me not to do it for those reasons either. But then, I think that's cause I was just born a baby dyke anyway. I mean, all that shit that you were pissed off about those boys was never real anyway. Cause I wasn't, really, like into it. I was sexually attracted to you. I couldn't do those boys comfortably. I didn't like it. I never liked it, at all. Not ever. That's why I stuck with you the whole time. [Laughter] Cause I didn't fucking like it, at all. It was really icky. I wasn't going to give up a good thing, man.

J: So then when you were seventeen you decided you were going together and you discovered lesbians.

H: We found a couple other working class dykes. We found Val. Gin did, I didn't. I didn't know no dykes, man. How'd you meet Val, anyway? Oh, the candle factory, at the candle factory.

G: I think we worked together. I knew we had a factory job together. I mean a regular factory job.

H: I think it was the candle factory. That was later, I think. The candle factory was first.

G: Yeah. There was this hippie guy who had this candle factory and I guess he hired both of us. I thought it was real cool to have this job where we were working with a bunch of hippies and making strobe light candles and, you know, it was pretty cool. And I met Val. And she was a dyke.

H: And she [Val] moved out of her mother's house at seventeen and got an apartment. And then we got an apartment to go to, too.

G: And then, that was it, man. We went to town after that. We had apartments, we had another dyke.

H: We were seventeen. We found Val, and there was another apartment. And there were dykes—home was over for both of us. It was over with.

J: So what happened when you met other working class dykes?

H: Well, then, we had somewhere to go, which was really nice. And then greater drama potential got created, that's for sure.

G: Well, you know, then we were getting into a lot of drugs.

H: Yeah, we were all getting high. Everybody was getting high. We were really using. Everybody was getting high.

G: Big party, big party.

H: All the time. Every time we were together we got high. But me and you were already doing acid before we met them for at least a good...we had already been tripping for about a year before then because we were tripping with Carol and all that weird shit in high school. We'd already been doing drugs for a good, good year.

G: Cutting school and going to see 2001 fucked up on acid, you know?

H: So we'd already been doing drugs a good year.

G: So what was the first apartment?

H: Me and you never lived together. The only time we lived together was on Fullerton.

G: Ain't that a bitch? Yeah, that seems fucked up, man, you know?

H: It does to me, too. It seems really weird. I think it was because by the time I got out of high school, you were strung out on heroin. And I was too scared to go live with you, because of that. That was the reason. Cause by the time I got done, you already had a habit. And then I couldn't do it, I was afraid.

J: The level of drama had gone up.

G: Oh, yeah, fucking lots of drama, man. I mean those were the days of nothing but drama, it seems like. Too much drugs, and then you started going out with Val.

H: I was eighteen. A year later.

J: Going out with her? Had you broken up with Gin?

H: No, man. [Laughter] We never broke up.

J: Okay. Just asking. You were just going out with Val, too.

G: Except I wasn't thrilled about it, I can tell you that.

H: You were fucking around with Marcy. I don't even want to hear that shit. I was so motherfucking pissed. Val and Marcy had this apartment together and Gin was crushed out on Marcy. Now, let's get the story straight. I wasn't crushed out on nobody, man, but Gin. Gin was my girlfriend. We were fucking around. What? Don't open your mouth! Who?

G: You weren't crushed out on nobody? You were just crazy about me?

H: Right. From the time we were seventeen on. When I broke up with Tommy it was to be with you. That was it.

G: Yeah. You saying I fucked it up?

H: Well, no, but you got crushed out on Marcy, man. And that just opened the door for all kinds of fucking drama.

J: If Gin was going to go out with Marcy, you were going to go out with Val.

H: Well, no, first we had this big party and I got in bed with this weird fucking guy who Gin almost killed and then instead of almost killing him she went to kill me and we had big drama, man. We had big drama that night. And that was in Val and Marcy's apartment.

G: Right.

H: She was already a sep [lesbian separatist] and didn't know it. She could fuck around with Marcy, but I definitely couldn't fuck around with this guy.

G: Oh, man, it just—I couldn't believe it. I was like, I couldn't believe it. This fucking guy! That was a thing that always would—I mean, not that I was ever thrilled about any of it, but these guys, I mean, fucking around with guys, I couldn't handle it.

H: The thing that was so funny about it is, I always hated it, so I'm not quite sure why I did it. Now with that time I think it could have been just to fucking get even with you for something, maybe cause you were getting high or something. That guy, I didn't like him. It was something to, like, get even with you.

G: I could see that.

H: Cause you were using so much and the drugging was really getting to me.

G: Yeah, well. You got even all right. I was in the front room fucked up and I laid there and I could listen, I could hear them, and I could hear them, and I could hear them, and I knew—

H: I didn't fuck him. We were just...

G: No, but I could hear the covers rustling around and I could hear him moaning and shit and them making noise and I was getting more and more and more and more pissed, and finally I just thought, enough of this shit, man, and I stormed in the room and turned on the light.

H: You had this cup. She had this cup, man, she just kept hitting on the table and it was getting louder and louder. I could hear it in the other room and it was getting louder and louder and louder and she kept knocking this cup on this table and I knew I was in for it, man. We were definitely going to have some drama coming.

G: But that wasn't going to stop her, now. You understand.

H: Next thing I know here comes Gin flying in the room. She flips the light on, yanks the sheets off the bed and there we are.

G: And I picked him up and I threw him across the fucking room—fucking remember that, man? I mean, slammed him into the fucking wall.

H: I don't even remember what happened to him because I—within minutes, you were in the kitchen.

G: I fucking remember. That's all I remember was picking him up, and like throwing him into the wall and his fucking mouth dropped down to the fucking ground, man, because I think he thought I was fucking nuts.

H: There was this big party, fucking big party in the room, all these people getting high, man, and the next thing I know, me and Gin were in the kitchen. She had picked up a coke bottle and was threatening to hit me with the coke bottle and I was so fucking enraged, man, here come my hand from the floor up, slapped her across the face cause she had this bottle over my head and the party literally split in two, man, drug Gin out one door and drug me out another door and split us up from each other. And there we were, out on the streets. Took us apart and— they took us out of there. I mean, they physically split us apart and moved us out.

G: Yeah, it was big drama. I mean, all these fucking people had to come and get us out of there cause—it was getting scary.

H: I was still in high school. I was seventeen.

J: And Gin was working?

G: I don't know, I was probably working, yeah. I guess I probably was working. Getting fucked up all the time. But I was working.

H: I was working, too, part time. From the time I was sixteen on. Working and going to school. But it was really—you know that was the hardships, man. That was the hardships. You know, I think it was real fucking hard for us, because it was so painful, and we didn't know any dykes. I mean, there was no context to put this relationship in, you know. And there was no way to figure anything out because we couldn't even talk about it. We didn't even have words. I don't even think I knew what 'dyke' meant. I don't even think there were words for what we were doing. As far as we knew, anyway.

G: Right. That's for sure.

H: I mean there were in some other world, but we didn't know them. So it was incredibly fucking painful because we were supposed to be straight, and we had no words to put any context to our relationship.

G: Yeah, I'm sure I didn't. It seems like we were together and even when I'd go with other women I still didn't identify myself as a lesbian and it doesn't seem like I knew what the word meant or I'd heard it or something, even.

H: No, we were a lot older before we had heard that word. We didn't know what the word was. We were much, much older.

J: So Helen graduated from high school and moved out of her parents' house. And Gin was using…

H: Yeah. And things were bad between us by then. From seventeen to eighteen we were on honeymoon. By the time I graduated from high school it was really fucking bad. Things had gotten really weird and painful, painful. Gin was really strung out by then. Drugs, fucking drugs did us in. Cause I lived on Fletcher—I got an apartment with Ana and I don't hardly remember you even hardly coming there. Things were really bad. I think at that point we might have actually broke up for the first time that was kind of for real. Sort of. We didn't really break up, break up, but we parted ways for a while there.

G: Yeah, it seems like there was a period of time for a while when we just didn't see each other very much at all and I was just out there on my own, getting fucked up all the time.

H: Yeah, that was the time when I would write in that diary every single night about you. Cause I had this diary, you know—I still have it at home. It's real funny, it's real funny, cause every single entry, every single night, is completely about Gin. And every day I talked about Gin. And what's real funny about it, is like you read weeks and weeks of shit about Gin, and then, suddenly there's this one page you get to and it says, 'I haven't thought about Gin much lately.' [Laughter] I don't know what I was thinking, man, like for the last hour or something, you know? In the writing, it's real torturous stuff about her getting high. You know, 'She's getting high. I don't want to see her.' It goes, 'I don't want to see her, she's getting high. I haven't heard from Gin, I wonder if she's okay. I'm scared that she might be dead, I'm scared that she's dying.' 'Gin called today. I was really glad to hear from her but we had a fight on the phone.' I mean, this is like, how the whole thing goes. It's documentation for her getting high and me being tortured by it. Although the contact seemed real minimal, actually.

G: You showed me that diary, a few years ago, do you remember? It just killed me to read it. I had no idea it was so painful for you. Cause I was just out there fucked up. You know. And it seems like that was a long time to me. I don't know if it was.

H: Well, that year I lived on Fletcher we parted a lot of ways between us. But I was still real obsessive about you, real obsessive. You probably weren't, since you were out partying and getting high. You were much more distant than I was from you, emotionally, I think. Although it was so much harder for me to be with you than it was for you to be with me. I didn't want to be around you because you were so fucked up that I couldn't bear it, I couldn't bear it. But then the next year, was the killer fucking year, man, cause the next year I moved to Fullerton and then I got strung out on speed. And then it was—it was a trip, man. That was really a fucking trip. Cause then we came back together.

J: She was strung out on heroin, you were strung out on speed.

H: And we came back together. We really started seeing each other again, real frequently. We started sleeping together again. Spending a lot of time together. And we had not been sexual during that year before, I don't think. We had really pulled away from each other. That year we got back together again. And it was just like utter, complete, and fucking total chaos and drama every motherfucking day. I think. It sure feels that way looking back at it.

G: On Fullerton? Well, there was a lot of drama. I mean, shit was fucked up. Val was there, she lived there, didn't she?

H: Yeah, me and Val lived together. Me and Val had been going together during this obsessive year where me and Gin weren't seeing each other. But we stayed as roommates. We just broke up and became friends. So we just continued to live together.

J: And you knew other lesbians by this time, too. Or was it just Val?

H: I didn't really know any other dykes, hardly, no. I didn't know any other dykes at that point, no. Gin was starting to hang out with some of the gay boys, then. You found the gay community. I still hadn't. You found the gay community. Cause you were out there getting high and you found the gay community, using.

G: I started hanging out in the bars and you know, it was like, suddenly, there was this one guy, that she hates, this guy, the only guy who I ever liked, in my life, and he was gay. And I started partying and hanging out with him a lot, Robert. And once I started partying and hanging out with him it was like—

H: He was a freak.

G: He—I can't believe you still do that shit, I show you a picture, you throw it fucking down, man.

H: I still hate him.

G: But then the whole world changed for me. It was like, god, there's all kind of dykes out here and there's bars, you know, so then everything opened up to me. But then shit got real fucked up between us cause I was out partying all the fucking time.

H: It was crazy. But our stuff had come together, even more than it was before, the year before. We'd come together again in a real intense way. Because you had got that real fucked up, junky old, broken-out glass-broken apartment in Uptown and you were strung out on heroin, you lived in this completely fucking decrepit apartment on Irving Park, wasn't it? I mean it was a typical junkie's apartment. It was like…

G: A mattress on the floor and that was it.

H: A mattress in the middle of the room cause she didn't want to be near the roaches, the thousands that were crawling up the walls. And I lived in this fucking beautiful apartment on Fullerton and then—

G: A yuppie kind of apartment.

H: A yuppie kind of apartment on Fullerton.

J: Was that with your older sister?

H: Irene lived there too, yeah, and she was going with a junkie, too, so there were two junkies in the house, man, it was really a trip.

G: Yeah, it was nuts. Dangerous.

H: Really nuts. Really violent. I don't know. And then there was poor, poor fucking Val. Val got screwed in that place. Between Butch and you and Little Bobby and me—can you imagine? I'm surprised Val didn't have a nervous breakdown, man. Crazy Little Bobby still survived all these years, too. He was still on the scene, man. Still on the scene even with that apartment.

G: So I lived on Irving Park and you lived on Fullerton at the same time?

H: Yeah, cause I left there to stay with you. We spent Valentine's Day together. I remember that real distinctly. That was Valentine's Day and we stayed in that cold-ass fucking apartment which was freezing cause the windows were broken. And I remember spraying roach spray all around the bed so that the roaches wouldn't get us during the night when we were in bed together. The mattress was in the middle of the room and we put roach spray all the way around, real thick, we sprayed it real thick, and I remember right before I went to bed I wanted to take a bath. So you came in the bathroom with me and opened the bathtub and it was really ugly because the roaches were crawling all around the tub. I hated it, I couldn't stand it, I wanted to get out of that water real fast cause there were so many roaches that they were dropping into the tub. So then, I remember staying with you for a while there, because I wanted to be with you, and I remember that was real intense, that I really wanted to be with you. So I stayed with you in this place. And then, you gave up that place, and you moved in with me on Fullerton for a while. That was the only time we lived together. And shit was really fucking hot and heavy between us. That's when you got the tattoo [Gin has 'Helen' tattooed on her left breast].

G: That's another goddamn thing that didn't please you. 'Look, look, you'll be so excited, wait'll you see what I got!' She said, 'What are you, nuts?'

H: Then Gin went for her second motherfucking illegal abortion that year. It was really interesting, because Gin was really changing a lot at that time and I was getting real fucked up and crazy, real fucking crazy, and she met the [Young Patriots] clinic [a free health clinic run by an organization modeled on the Black Panthers to organize poor whites around revolutionary politics]. That was because of that abortion, probably, wasn't it? Was that how you got hooked into that clinic?

G: I don't know. I don't think so.

H: No? You were already somehow hooked into it?

G: Gee, I don't know. Maybe it was that.

J: They were in Uptown, too.

G: Gee, I don't know cause I was using so much those days are real...you know.

H: We were both getting so high, man, we were using so many drugs. We were fighting, it was really bad. At that time the fighting really escalated. That's when we got a lot more physical. I mean we'd both go into these incredible fucking rage attacks.

G: Well, you were doing a lot of speed.

H: That's why we would both go into rage attacks?

G: Well, I always had. But then you would just go off and get crazy.

J: You were working all during this time?

H: Oh, yeah. We always worked. She was working, too. We were working—we worked a couple of blocks away from each other, as a matter of fact. I was working at M. Born and you were working down the street.

G: At Bausch and Lomb.

H: Bausch and Lomb. We were both working down on Halsted. I had a full-time job at M. Born, it was at Halsted and Adams, and she worked at Bausch and Lomb on Halsted and Washington or some shit like that. We were like three or four blocks from each other. So we could really keep the drama going, all the way to work, you know, and home.

J: What kind of work were you doing?

H: I was working as a bookkeeper for them and you—what were you doing? Working on the glasses?

G: Factory.

H: Making the glasses? Frames, right, you were working on the frames.

G: Yeah. I always did factory work.

H: We were always working. Which is amazing, actually. Because even from early on, from the time we were fifteen or sixteen, I was going to school and working part-time, and it seemed like we never slept, we did all these drugs and we did all this drama, and we still kept fucking working. It was amazing.

G: I was just trying to figure out—that second abortion, you know, is that when I got sick?

H: Yeah, it was really funny cause things really turned then. Because you know what happened after that, what happened after—she met Robert, and she started hanging out with that gay boy, the tables really turned. Cause all that rage that she used to have when I would fuck around with these boys, was exactly the opposite then. I would be fucking livid, man, when she would be dealing with these guys. Just fucking livid.

G: She hated him.

H: I hated him so motherfucking bad. And then fucking Robby, I wanted to kill him.

G: Oh, yeah, about how he dressed me up in lipstick that night...

H: No, not Robert. The other Robby, Robby D. I hated that motherfucker, man.

G: Did you?

H: Yeah. Intensely. I always thought he should die, man. I still think that. [Laughter]

J: What did he do?

H: He fucking got her pregnant.

G: But see, you know what's strange about that, to me now?

H: That you slept with him. [Laughs]

G: Yeah. That's what's strange about it. What's strange about it is when I look back on it I was already to a point—I didn't know nothing, I mean, I hardly knew lesbians, let alone separatists and all that stuff, we didn't know that shit back then—

H: But I was pissed, man.

G: But—

H: That she could fucking sleep with this boy.

G: But I was already to a point where I had—it was probably an unconscious thing already, I mean I had already gotten to a point where I had decided I did not want to fuck with boys.

H: But I didn't sleep with any of them during those years.

G: Shut up, man. [Laughter]

H: Not a one, man.

G: But it was, I was just trying to be friends with Robby, that's all I wanted to do is be friends.

H: Yeah, then you fucking slept with him.

G: Yeah, well, you know how they push, and I hadn't gotten, I wasn't—

J: Besides, you were probably high.

G: Well, yeah, that's a given. Always fucked up. But see Robby did a good thing. You don't think so but he did a good thing. Because what happened out of that was—

H: It cemented it for you.

G: Yeah. It's true. That's what happened out of that. I mean like, I remember arguing with him over and over and over and over again about how I didn't want to fuck him, I wasn't interested in fucking him, I didn't want to fuck boys. I was a dyke, I knew I was a dyke, I loved women, I wanted to be with women, and he kept doing that fucking bullshit, lefty bull, you know. Yeah, yeah, he understood, it's cool, he understood, everything was cool, yeah, it's great, and then he just kept pushing and pushing and pushing. So I slept with him. But then, what happened was I fucking afterwards, I got to a point very soon after that where I just thought, I can't even be friends with them. I don't want to have nothing to do with them. And then I just didn't want to have anything to do with men because it wasn't worth my energy to put up with that kind of shit...all that bullshit trying to be friends with them. So yeah. But I did fuck him and I got pregnant. And then I got an abortion. I got an illegal abortion. And then I almost died. It was a disaster. I got an infection. And then I wouldn't go to the hospital cause I was afraid.

J: Was this with Jane [the underground abortion network]?

H: Yeah, it was Jane.

G: And I was afraid that the police would come and arrest me and shit, you know, like I would get in all kinds of trouble because it was illegal and obviously I didn't know what the fuck could happen. And I wouldn't go and I wouldn't go and I wouldn't go and it was only Sandy that got me to go. I was crazy about her and crushed out on her.

H: She was always crushed out on somebody.

G: I was. That's true.

H: But anyway, she saved your life.

G: She did. She did. Women have saved my life lots of times, come to think about it. But yeah, she saved my life. Because she knew that I was so crushed out on her that she could influence me. And I wouldn't go, I was like, 'No, no, can't do it, can't do it,' and finally she just said, 'You got to go in, something's wrong here.'

H: It's a good thing, because you really were—

G: It was the same thing—it was another woman I was crushed out on, meaning she could get me to do just about anything, that got me into treatment.

H: Yeah, so Gin started branching out in the world and she started making all these new connections with people and getting real political. I was still getting high and then she told me I was strung out. This junkie telling me that I was strung out!

G: She was like, 'You're the fucking dope fiend here. What the fuck are you talking about?'

H: I thought that took a lot of nerve, that shit, man. A dope fiend telling me I was strung out.

G: But you were.

H: I was. I was.

J: And then?

G: Then I got involved with the Young Patriots.

H: We still didn't know any other dykes. She started finding political people. I didn't know those people. She was venturing out. And then Gin moved out and got her own first apartment. Well, no, it wasn't your first apartment. But we lived a couple blocks away from each other again. That time we were like three blocks away from each other. So we were three blocks away from each other, we were both working. Then I got hepatitis and got real fucking sick. She took care of me. She came over and stayed with me.

J: How did you get hepatitis?

H: I don't know. I don't know why I caught it. I think it's likely it was just dirty drugs. Because people that handle drugs tend to pass around these kinds of things. And Gin took care of me. We had already been out doing political stuff, much earlier on. Because we'd go to demonstrations when we were young.

J: What kind of demonstrations?

H: Well, like the Vietnam War. Anti-war stuff. We'd done a lot of political stuff, just the two of us. Going to the shit downtown, demonstrations, the big demonstrations. The Democratic Convention, that all happened when we were teenagers.

G: What year was the Democratic Convention?

J: 1968.

H: She was downtown that day. So we were already active, but we weren't hooked in to anything, you know.

J: What happened then?

H: She found the political people. And then we found more dykes, I think. Because that's when the Fire & Ice time was. [The Fire & Ice was a neighborhood tavern owned by Helen's two older sisters.] We used to hang out there. And then we really got out. These were still working class dykes, though. We hadn't found the lesbian community yet. Right? Had you? I mean, like Kate and Cathy, and all the dykes at the Fire & Ice—bar dykes, bar dykes, that's who we knew. They weren't the lesbian community—they're still not. So we started to know bar dykes then. So we had found people like us. And they were just like us. Except not really. I mean they were and they weren't. They were just like us as far as the way we acted and the way we drank and the way we partied and the way we swore and the drama, but they didn't do politics and we did. And that was a problem for us. We found bar dykes that were just fucking like us, but we weren't just like them. And we'd already been out doing our stuff.

J: Why do you think that was, that you guys were out doing politics and these other women were not?

H: I wonder that a lot. I think there were two different reasons, that Gin was into politics and that I was. I think that Gin got really identified with the hippie culture, and that was political. You identified yourself as a hippie really young. As soon as you saw them you were one of them. You were really fucking young. Eighth grade, you had switched out of your fucking black leather jacket, man, your greaser clothes were off, man, the leather coat, the leather shit, the slicked back hair—you were in bell bottoms and suede and headbands. And this was a political world. Now I got into that, too, a little bit later, but I think that the impetus for me was the home stuff, because my father was always talking about communist, communist, communist. Pro-communist, hated everything about this country. And for whatever reason, racism was not right for me, never was, just wasn't, and I don't even know why that happened for me. It was just something I knew real little. Really, really fucking little. You know, 'Eenie, meenie, minie, mo, Catch a nigger by the toe,'—no, no none of my friends could say that. No, they had to leave. If they did they were not a friend. You couldn't do that, it was wrong. I just know it was really strong, because I was probably like seven or eight years old when I said, 'If you say that you can't be my friend.' I was really little.

G: I just can't figure out how we ended up the way we did.

H: It was partly religion, you know? I went to mass six times a week for nine years. And I believed it. And they said racism was wrong. And I didn't hear that racist language at home. That was American language. My parents didn't speak English. I never heard that kind of stuff. I mean, my father learned all that shit later, not during my formative years. They didn't know all those words. So I didn't hear it for years as a kid. So I didn't have it to begin with, you know. They were so fucking busy just trying to survive and hating everything here that I didn't have patriotism and all that icky stuff that you got. Anyway, as soon as she identified with that whole hippie scene and got swept up into that, that took us to demonstrations and everything, and then I followed behind her and probably, maybe a year later, identified with it, too. But she went first.

J: Why did that happen to you, becoming a hippie?

G: I don't know, really, I try to figure out why, you know. I mean my dad was, like, a Nazi. Hitler was his fucking hero. And he was incredibly racist, and I can't figure out—

J: Seriously? He thought Hitler was cool?

H: Yeah. So did my father. It was probably what we were unified around was our fathers because they both thought Hitler was right.

J: But your father was pro-communist.

H: Yeah. He didn't think there was any contradiction with that at all. He had no problem with it that he could be a communist and still think Hitler was right.

G: My father had libraries full of books and fucking he would listen to speeches, Hitler's speeches, and records…

H: You know, listening to you talk about this, the thing that strikes me about it is that both of our parents verbalized that they were these fascist political people. So it was certainly something that you got to talk about in the home in the sense that politics was talked about.

G: Yeah, he'd be listening to Hitler records and I'd walk in the door after coming back from fucking the Democratic Convention or something and he would like click his heels and 'Heil Hitler' and throw his arm up and expect me to respond like that, you know? And I'd look at him and say, you know, 'You're a fucking idiot. You're nuts.' And we'd get into these huge fights. It was really crazy stuff at home, boy.

J: So then you got more hooked into politics, political people, later. How old were you guys then? Where are we now in time? Eighteen or so?

H: Nineteen is when we started taking ourselves seriously. That's when we got really serious. Then it became a whole different ballgame. Then we moved to new levels. Beyond demonstrations. We were nineteen years old. We lived three blocks away from each other. I was sick and Gin was taking care of me. And for some reason she'd stabilized now at this point. Something had happened here. What happened? Did you stop using heroin?

G: Um-hum. [Nods yes.]

H: Yeah. You'd stopped using heroin. Because you'd found the Movement. Found the Left. Gin always found shit, man. She found the Left. Brought it to my door. She brought the Movement to my door. She'd stopped using, and I'd stopped using. We were both clean, pretty much. We had stopped that heavy drug scene and we both got really serious about politics. And that's when I learned about class consciousness. For the first time both of us could identify who we were and have a name to our experience and to who we were in the world. It was the absolute first time that I had any fucking understanding about our past and about our history. It was like this fucking door opening. It was this incredible fucking awakening to why we had been through all that we had been through and who we were and why it had been so fucking hard and all the pain and all the shit and all the everything. It was this miracle of understanding that took place. It was like the first time, I think, that we had a sense of the bigger picture given to us. I think it was the first time that we probably didn't internalize how fucked up our stuff was. We both had these very powerful internal messages that we were fucked up. I was really fucked up, you know? She was really fucked up. And I think it was the first time that we understood that we were part of a class, that we were part of an exploited group of people and that we couldn't have been any different. That it wasn't our fault that all this shit had happened and the way it happened. That we got to understand the whole power base of the economy of the world and America and all that shit. I mean it was the very first time in my life that I had any inkling that I was who I was not because I just wasn't smart enough or brilliant enough or white enough or whatever the fuck you're supposed to be, that I didn't feel like I was a stupid person, you know. That I actually belonged to a class.

J: Yeah, you were totally convinced that you were stupid up until this time?

H: Right. Oh, yeah. And we were angry, too. Me and Gin had a lot of fucking anger. And it was the first time I think we felt like we had a right to be angry, you know. Cause we weren't supposed to be angry. And we were angry, motherfucking angry. I mean we were really angry. We were both really angry.

G: Sure enough were.

H: We were both fucking angry. And we'd come to a place where our anger was understood and accepted and encouraged to be redirected.

G: Yeah.

H: And that was a big fucking relief, wasn't it?

G: Yeah.

H: Like, it was okay to be that angry and that people really understood why we were that angry.

J: So what happened to your relationship?

H: At that point, we split up. Then we split up. And that was the end. That was when we really, finally split up.

J: Did the level of drama decrease at any point?

H: No, we couldn't even work at the clinic on the same nights. Cause we were too dangerous. We had to work in there on separate days to keep the drama potential down.

J: So even though you had both stopped using, it hadn't decreased the level of drama at all?

H: Well...

J: I mean, not stopped using, but cooled out your drugging.

H: Well, yeah, the drama did cool down a lot. For sure. But we were still drinking and shit.

G: Part of the problem was then I quit doing the other shit but I was drinking a lot.

H: We both started drinking a lot of alcohol. So there was a lot of drinking at that stage. And drinking has a lot of drama potential, too.

G: Much more, for me.

H: So we did this stuff for a while where we both stayed real separate. We couldn't be together. We couldn't be around each other. I don't know what had happened. I don't remember what precipitated that. That we couldn't be in the fucking clinic. I don't know what happened. We couldn't work there on the same days.

J: So you two split, when you got involved with the Movement, and you were doing separate things.

H: Yeah. What had happened was, she had gotten very excited by the Movement, real excited and involved and everything and it brought me into it. And then I got real excited by it and there was this overlapping period of time when she was still in it and I was coming into it. Something happened between us where we couldn't be together. It got real ugly for some reason. There was not a big violent fight at that point. But something happened that was really bad. We could not be together. And—she quit the clinic. And stopped doing political stuff and went with Donna, and I got more active with politics and then we just went in totally different directions.

J: What kind of person was Donna?

G: Well, she was my sister Barbara's friend before she met me.

H: Her sister's best friend from Oak Park, who was this big religious freak. Anyway, Donna wasn't a lesbian, she wasn't a dyke, she was a straight little girl that was best friends with Gin's younger sister. She was very religious.

G: And hot in bed.

H: And hot in bed. Then they became lovers.

J: So you guys had broken up. Were you friends at this point?

H: It was scary. Our contacts were scary. I got very involved with the Movement. She continued to drink and be in this other relationship. And then, during that period of time, within a year or two from there at most, we had that knock-down drag-out fight. We met in the bar, we were drinking together, I was giving her a ride home, and we got into a fight in the car, and we got out of the car and finished the fight in the middle of the street. And the police were called. That was our last physical fight, wasn't it? That was the last fight. That one was really bad. It was the most violent of all of them. We were really fighting.

J: Did either of you get seriously hurt?

H: Not seriously hurt, but we were both hurting physically. She had a black eye, I was sore all over from her slamming me against the car.

J: What was it about?

H: It was—do you remember? I don't want to bring it up. You said something about somebody that I didn't like.

G: Uh hunh. Well, that's not how I see it. [Laughter] You called me a name I didn't like.

H: No, it wasn't.

G: Well, we used to talk about—when we would call somebody a pig, a pig was like, only fucking men could be pigs or cops could be pigs or, you know, pigs were the enemy.

H: I know, but that was because you said something about 'the queen' that—

G: Well, I don't remember that part, but—

H: Well, yeah, that was the whole thing. Anyway. So it escalated from verbal to physical. So I pulled over and told her to get out of the car. She said, 'Fine, I'll get out.' She stepped out and yanked me out and boy, we went to war! That was it, man. It was fucking war. It was really awful. And then, she stayed up all night sitting at her door with a gun. Do you remember that?

G: No. I remember the police came and fucking were going to take me home and I fucking punched him in the face. And he said, 'Fine,' and he left me. 'Fine, bitch, go find your own way home! It's four o'clock in the morning and you're so drunk you can't stand up straight, go ahead and find your own way home.'

H: They let me go. First, they came and they split us up and then they took you in the car, though. They had you in the car for a few minutes, didn't they?

G: I guess, I don't know, I don't remember. All I know is they were going to take me home…

H: And they didn't. I left in my car.

G: The cop put his hand on me is what he did. He touched my shoulder, you know, and I turned around and punched him…so they left me.

H: It was four o'clock in the morning, right?

G: Yeah. I had to call Donna to get a ride.

H: Donna called the next day and said that you had sat up in the chair all night with the gun pointed at the door because you thought I was coming back with a gun to shoot you so you were going to be ready to shoot me. [Laughter] So you were waiting for me all motherfucking night to see who was going to shoot first. So, then Donna tried to make peace between us and it didn't work. So then we didn't speak. And that was the first time in our lives we really didn't speak. The last fight and the first time we didn't speak. Then, everything changed again. But we made up, about six months later. I think that Donna might have even initiated that one. She called. Or did you? You were moving to Madison.

G: I probably called to tell you I was moving.

H: We made up. It was six months later and we made up. We didn't speak for six months. And then Gin—how did you meet Janie? isn't that who you met, Janie? That made this big move in your life?

G: To come here [to Madison]?

H: Um hmm.

G: Well, Janie was Barbara and Janie. I don't know, Barbara knew Janie, met Janie from someplace and then Janie and I got to be drinking buddies, and she was pretty wealthy, her family was pretty wealthy…[pause]

H: Did you and her decide to move up to Madison together?

G: I went with her for the summer to visit her family in Wisconsin...

H: And then she found the lesbian community. That was when the lesbian community got found for us.

J: In Madison.

H: Don't you think? You found it in Madison. And I still didn't. And then I still did bar dykes for a while while she was finishing up Chicago and going to Madison. I was still doing bar dykes and Movement stuff. Then Gin moved to Madison. We resumed our communication but it was minimal. She found the lesbian community, but then I came to visit you, and you lived with Janie in that house, and I remember coming to that house and thinking that was really fucking exciting, you know. Because I knew this was really different than bar dykes, these women I'd been hanging out with. I really immediately sensed that there was something else going on here. Cause there was all these women with this whole other set of politics, now. And then, Gin got more and more involved in the lesbian community and she went to Michigan [the Michigan Womyn's Music Festival]. And then she started hounding me to come to Michigan. And then, well, you know, you're on the scene now, man. You should know the rest of the history!

J: And then we were saved. [Laughter]

H: Then we were saved. Gin saved your life, too.

J: Yeah, she did.

H: Not just mine, but yours too.

J: Sure. It's true. But—all the dykes you had dealt with in Chicago, pretty much, were working class dykes.

H: Every single, solitary one of them.

J: And then you [Gin] moved to Madison, but the lesbian community here is not a working class community, principally.

G: Right.

J: Although there were other working class lesbians who you related to.

G: Here?

J: Yeah. Well, like that woman who you lived with for a while. The one with the kids.

H: Linda.

G: Oh, Linda. Yeah.

H: She was really working class. Poor working class.

J: But the overall community that you got hooked into was middle class.

G: Absolutely.

J: So what was that about? I mean, cause you already had some class consciousness, out of the Movement stuff. So how did you relate to that? How did they relate to you, how did you relate to them?

G: Well, I don't know. I mean, I had problems, because as exciting as it was to move to Madison and meet all these dykes and have this whole new world open up to me it was like I keep running into fucking brick walls on class stuff, because it seems like almost everybody I know—I mean, Linda was an exception and there might have been, you know, I'm sure there must have been other exceptions, but mostly middle class dykes. Like here everybody talks, I mean everybody is in school. It seems like that's all anybody does is go to school. So the first couple years I was here I felt like a real fucking alien because everybody was always talking about, you know, 'So what are you taking in school?', and it was like, fucking I don't go to school, you know? There was just a lot of women who were going to school. And I started to feel real out of place. Like, because I wasn't in school, because I didn't even finish high school, because I didn't know what the fuck they were talking about half the time, and so I decided I should go to school. So I did go to school.

J: What did you go to school for? What did you study?

G: It was just general studies. It was alright, but—I mean it was kind of strange here in Madison because I do feel real out of place, just because the women here don't talk the same way as we talk. And I can tell, I can be in a room with dykes and I can tell that they, like, look at you when I swear or say silly things and I can feel how tense it gets. And if they know me well enough, then they'll just come right out and tell me they don't like the way I talk. And say, you know, stuff about my anger. They seem to think that I'm like real intense and real angry, and that I shouldn't be. So it's kind of weird, you know. And the one thing that's been real exciting, meeting the seps [lesbian separatists], I think it's really exciting to meet these women, but then they make me pissed off all the time, I get pissed off at some point at the bullshit they say about the way I talk.

J: So how is it that when you found this middle class community, you were saved?

H: That's a good question, too. I thought about that earlier, so that's the downside of that—of the class conflict. And that they can talk about this stuff we care about in spite of the class conflict. One time Janet said, 'In spite of the fact that we have a class conflict, we can't leave the lesbian community, because we're getting something out of it that's really helpful.' But I think that the reason for that is because you have this contradiction all the time in middle class anything, anywhere in the world. When you have middle class life, you have academia. In that setting, you have the liberty that you don't have anywhere else to be very challenging with thinking and ideas, and from that there's always generated tremendously liberating ideas. Always. Universally across the world in every culture, in the academic setting you have the generation of challenging, radical ideas that come from every fucking university community across the world and across history. So yeah— valuable shit comes out of that class. But when you put it all together, it's still real messy.

Christian aged 7 or so, helping her sister Helena on with her boots.

Growing Up Upper Class

Christian McEwen

Then this 'niceness': what does it amount to?*

The House and the Gun

One night last summer I dreamt the house was on fire. The nursery chimney-piece had caved in, and the doorway behind was edged with little triangular flames. I ran along the corridor shouting "Fire!" and searching for fire-extinguishers. When I came to the dining-room I found my mother, in her brown mohair dressing-gown. She had my father's shot-gun in her arms. "Here," she said. "Put this away first, before you do anything else."

I took the gun, though very grudgingly. Putting it away was an act of minor tidiness which made no sense to me at all. "But, Mama," I tried to explain. "The house is on fire. We'll all be burnt."

As so often in a dream, there was time to think the words, but not to say them. Mama handed me the gun, and I accepted it. Even if the house were falling down around our ears, the priority was *to put away the gun.*

Houses and guns have literal meaning in our family. The house in the dream, with the nursery and the long corridor, the old-fashioned fire-extinguishers and the big dining-room, is the house where I grew up, a big sandstone house in the Borders of Scotland. The gun is the gun with which, at the age of twenty-two, my brother killed himself.

It was not an accident that the house and the gun should appear in the same dream, nor that it should turn upon a choice between them. That choice had been in existence for as long as I could remember. But it was a false choice to begin with, since *putting away the gun* (the truth, the trouble, the embarrassment, the pain) was in fact an essential part of *preserving the house* (the class, the culture, the expected way of life). That is what I've come to see so clearly, and what, in the dream, I was still struggling to

---

*The Diary of Virginia Woolf, Vol. 2, *ed. Anne Olivier Bell, assisted by Andrew McNeillie (New York and London: Harcourt Brace Jovanovich, 1978), p. 22.*

explain. Neither the house nor the gun should take priority. *What really matter are the human beings.*

Telling

These days I live in London, where I earn my living as a teacher of creative writing and as a reader for a feminist publishing firm. I belong, most obviously, to the fringes of the professional middle class. But as a child in that Scottish nursery, I grew up with a very different sense of my identity. As a child, I grew up upper class.

From across the Atlantic, the British upper classes seem harmless enough. Faded gentry, honorable civil servants, at best they're brilliant figures from the past, there to entertain whenever Brideshead is revisited. But the mass of British people tell a different story. Thatcher-the-milk-snatcher is at the helm, and in their view it is the upper classes who have put her there. Never mind the actual figures: dukes and stockbrokers, old money and new are all jammed together in the same pigeon-hole. Cold, superior and selfish, ideal and irresponsible, these people are blamed for almost everything that is wrong with the country, and for the way in which things are done. If there should ever be a revolution, they'd be the first to go.

As a child and adolescent, I tried to balance my growing knowledge of such stereotypes (and their occasional truth)[1] against the human fact of my family, whom I loved. This wasn't easy. For a long time I thought the stereotypes were actually "right," and took them in, internalizing a tremendous amount of self-hatred and confusion. Then, because I was afraid, I didn't talk about my life at home. The oddities and confusions went unnamed and unconfirmed.

Since then, as a teacher, I've grown used to breaking certain rules, to admitting, "Yes, my father was an alcoholic," to saying, "No, you're not the only one who's tried to kill herself. I've done that too." I have come out as a lesbian in a room of straight (and mainly hostile) London professionals. But I can count on my fingers the number of times I've said, "My father was a baronet." Even now it frightens me to write it down.

If I do write now about my background and my growing up, it is because I think there's information there and that is needed. Despite the flood of upper class memoirs, journals, anecdotes and collected letters, very little has appeared which tries to question such an upbringing from inside, either in its own terms or in relation to the rest of society.[2] Meanwhile, life in Britain continues to be dominated by the class system, to a degree perhaps unimaginable in other countries. People do not talk easily or honestly across class barriers, and the stereotypes remain extremely powerful.

It has taken me two-and-a-half years to finish this, and in that time there have been hundreds of disapproving voices in my head. They range from the imperatives of folk and family wisdom, "Don't betray us. Don't wash our dirty laundry in public—" through the contempt of the working classes, "So what's all the fuss about? It's all right for *you*—," to the well-meant advice of academic feminists, "You don't have the professional training to make sense of this—"

I listen to those voices, but I can't afford to let them shut me down. Guilt and silence are altogether too familiar. In order to change, I need the things I'm trying to explain to myself here, and I believe that other people need them too.

In the piece which follows, I will be using my family history as the basis for some more extended arguments. The people I'm describing here are real. Because I've loved them and been loved by them, they loom too close. It is hard to maintain a consistent perspective, to know when their behavior is peculiar to them, and when it is characteristically upper class. Inevitably there will be warps and failures in my telling. Inevitably too, some of what I write will touch off angry memories in other people. All I can say is that I welcome correspondence. As much as almost anything, I think, we need each other's stories.

Why Have We Not Met?

When I was born, in 1956, my father was working as a barrister[3] at the Inner Temple, London. His father was a politician,[4] and had recently been made a baronet,[5] but Papa, as the second son, was not expected to inherit. He was, at twenty-nine, an upper middle class professional, with a starred First[6] at Cambridge to his credit, and the promise of a fine career ahead.

My mother, twenty-one when I was born, was herself an educated woman, though she had left Oxford after her first year in order to get married. Her parents were a writer[7] and an actress,[8] self-made professional people from Liverpool and County Donegal, and my father, with his connections among the landed gentry, was said to have married beneath him. "Why have we not met her?" asked Princess Margaret when she heard of their engagement.

They had not met because Britain is a highly stratified society, and the different layers don't necessarily mix. As a young bachelor, home from the war in Germany, my father had led a glamorous social life, doing the rounds of the big country houses, staying up dancing till all hours of the

243

morning. Six foot three in his stockinged feet, with his easy jokes, his charm and his enthusiasm, he is remembered as a golden boy whom everybody loved.

Mama, in the meantime, had been living much more quietly. During term time she was still at boarding-school, reading French and Italian, studying for her A' levels.[9] Life in her parents' flat centered round their work. Grandpa Laver was Keeper of Prints and Drawings at the Victoria and Albert Museum; he wrote his books in the evening while my grandmother was at the theater. Mama watched and listened, went to the occasional play. Photographs of the time show a tall shy girl with great hooded eyelids, and the poise and manner of a young Madonna. She already had her quota of admirers, but her social experience was small. There was little chance she would ever have crossed paths with Princess Margaret.

Betterness, But—

Despite their very different backgrounds and experience, one thing my parents had in common was their Catholicism. In the early days of their marriage, my father was a member of a Catholic study group, instructing would-be converts in the tenets of the faith. (His own father had in fact been a convert, with a special devotion to St. Joan of Arc.) My mother wrote a book about the Rhythm Method.[10] As children we were taken to church every Sunday, and made confessions and communions at regular intervals. I remember long mornings playing trains with my rosary along the top of the pew, and pretending to be an early Christian in the catacomb of my closed hands.

Meanwhile, among my parents' friends, Catholicism presented something of an obstacle. It was accepted, I now think, as an endearing quirk, a personal oddity, which, I suppose, is how it manifested itself: a preference for fish on Fridays, some awkwardness of scheduling for Sunday breakfast. But it was never usual, never quite taken for granted, by either of the worlds they moved in then: the literary/intellectual world of Cambridge and the London law-courts, and the closed world (mainly Anglican) of the English country house. Catholics, after all, had not been popular. There were circles in which it was still considered liberal to have a Catholic for a friend. Jokes were made about the Papists and the power of Rome. But behind the jokes lay something else: an embarrassment, an unease, less with Catholicism than with the whole idea of faith. "Must you go on about it?" was the hidden implication. "Surely in the end we're all the same, all human, fallible. Why should you be different?"

Behind these questions (never stated) lurked another two, basis of all mistrust from childhood on. "Don't you think I'm good enough for you? Do you think you're *better* than I am?"

My parents saw themselves as enlightened, open-minded. They would never have agreed that in some final way they believed themselves "better" than other people. Nonetheless, they both devoted a terrific amount of energy to the business of making distinctions: separating themselves off from the rest of the world, and then going on to elaborate why this separation should "naturally" be so. As a child, I learnt that we were "lucky" to be Catholics, because Catholicism was the "One True Faith." Papa had that starred First from Cambridge; he was "cleverer" than other people's fathers. Such things were valuable, not in and of themselves, but because they were better than something, or, all too often, someone else. I took these lessons thoroughly to heart.

Looking back on it now, it is clear that my parents' "betterness" was even then precariously maintained. If my father, in particular, made so much of "betterness," this was perhaps because he couldn't count on it. He had grown up surrounded by all the accoutrements of upper class life, yet as second son he had to make his own way in the world. In addition, he had suffered from bouts of manic depression since his student days. Between 1964 and 1980, he was hospitalized ten times. He took lithium to cope with his mood-swings, but he also drank. By the time I was an adolescent, the doctors had told him plainly he was an alcoholic.

Such language was never used with us, the children, nor, if it could be managed, with the servants and the outside world. Papa was "away in Edinburgh," he was "not very well." He would be "better soon." Mama's first loyalty went to him. If Papa wanted privacy, then he should have it.

We, the children, grew up in the shadow of this privacy, this hypocrisy, this "not-saying." We were extremely well-trained. When Papa collapsed at the dinner-table, we would help him off to bed. When he was driving dangerously, we would start to sing, and he would slow the car to the rhythm of the song. But we almost never mentioned this among ourselves. To complain about Papa, even to give words to what was happening, was somehow against the rules. "Papa's not feeling so well," I told my youngest sister once. "That whiskey—," she tsked, like a grownup woman. She knew the line as well as any of us. Whatever was the matter, it wasn't Papa's fault.

"Alcoholism is a family illness," say the textbooks. "Alcoholism is a disease called denial."[11] In an upper class household, denial is part of the story from the beginning. "You've got to set a good example. What will the servants say?" I remember following my father from sitting-room to library to pantry, trying to get him to surrender the bottle of vodka he had hidden in his pocket. In every room we walked through, we met someone else. The factor,[12] Mr. Weston, was on his way downstairs. Mrs. Mackie, the head gardener's wife, was cleaning. "Good morning, Sir Robert. How do you do, Sir Robert? And how are you, Mary Christian?" We smiled and smiled. In between, I tugged at his elbow. "Let me have that vodka!" "No!" Suddenly he threw off my arm, and made a dash for the nearest bathroom. I followed, but he was already there, had already locked himself in. I ran out to the children's swing and cried. Much later, in the pantry, over a cup of tea, he tried to tell me he was sorry.

Inheritance: Papa

For the first ten years of their marriage, from 1954 to 1964, my parents lived in the south of England. They were originally based in London, where my father worked, but moved to Wiltshire in 1959, a year after my sister Kate was born. James arrived in 1960, followed by another daughter, Helena, in 1961. Meanwhile, Papa commuted every week to London. He continued to practice as a barrister, and did some literary work on the side: writing, not surprisingly, for Catholic and right-wing papers. He wrote a legal column for the *Spectator* with two friends of his, and reviewed books for the *Spectator*, the *Tablet*, and a Jesuit magazine called *The Month*. In 1961, following in the political footsteps of his father, he was appointed Tory candidate for East Edinburgh. But in 1962, his father died.

When Grandpa McEwen died, he left two houses: one on the east coast of Scotland, near Berwick-on-Tweed, and one on the west, not far from Girvan. The one on the east coast was called Marchmont, a large pink sandstone house set in four thousand acres of good arable land, with a river running through, and six or seven farms besides. The other, smaller house was called Bardrochat.

According to Grandpa's will, both Marchmont and Bardrochat went to his eldest son, Jamie, along with a third of the family money. The rest of the money was to be divided equally among the remaining six children. At the time, such a decision would not have been considered in any way unusual or unfair. This, after all, was the law of primogeniture. With Grandpa's death, Jamie had become the baronet. No-one questioned his right to the two properties, or to the funds needed to maintain them.

In writing his will, however, my grandfather had made one important proviso. Should Jamie elect to keep only one of the houses, the other was to be offered in turn to each member of the immediate family. If no-one could afford to run it, the house was to be sold, at which point the proceeds would be divided as before: one-third to Jamie, two-thirds to everybody else.

Jamie had come home to Marchmont after the Second War, wounded and heartsick. The place still had painful memories for him. As soon as he got married, he moved to Bardrochat. It came as no surprise to anyone when he decided to stay on there, and to let Marchmont go.

But if Jamie didn't feel very strongly about Marchmont, the rest of the family certainly did. They had been children there, and they loved every inch of it: the ninety-plus rooms, the long avenue of beeches, the old walled garden with its espaliered apple-trees. Nobody wanted the house to be sold, least of all my father.

In the summer of 1964, two years after Grandpa's death, Papa moved his entire family up to Marchmont. It was, he claimed, a temporary arrangement. He did not have the money to keep up the house, and legally, therefore, no right to live there, which as a lawyer he knew very well. But a couple of years later, he approached Jamie directly, and persuaded him to sign over the estate.

What this meant in terms of family politics, I only know through hearsay. Clearly my aunts and uncles were not pleased. Jamie's wife, my Aunt Clare, was especially incensed. For a while she spoke of taking Papa to court. There were mutters of "asset-stripping," of "taking advantage." My grandmother's skills as intermediary were taxed to the utmost. But in the end, the row blew over. Family attention passed on to something else, and Papa was left to cope with what he'd done.

From the start, there were difficulties with the new arrangement: the most obvious being an acute shortage of cash. The farms were let to tenants for an annual rent, but Grandpa McEwen, benevolently paternalistic, had lowered all the rents after the Second War. Then too, in order to take on the house, Papa had had to give up his career as a barrister. At first he thought he could commute to London as he had done from Wiltshire, combining law with a new career in politics. He was still the Tory candidate for East Edinburgh, and had been writing speeches for the then Prime Minister, Sir Alec Douglas-Home. But when he failed, twice, to get into

Parliament, standing as Conservative candidate for East Edinburgh (October, 1964), and again for Roxburgh, Selkirk and Peebles (March, 1965), his hopes for a career outside the country house began to flag. It was about this time that he had one of his bad bouts of manic depression, and, following it, his first dealings with electroconvulsive therapy or shock treatment (ECT). He still wrote articles and reviews. But he began to drink more and more heavily. And Marchmont, with its interminable responsibilities, absorbed most of the attention he had left.

What Were We Actually Living On?

When my parents first got married, my mother had a larger income than my father. Grandpa Laver gave her £250 a year, while Grandpa McEwen gave Papa only £200. This "only" was the point of the story, which showed the triumph of the literary professionals over the landed gentry, at the same time emphasising that as a young married couple my parents too had had to pinch and scrape. In comparison with their richer friends this certainly was true. But in the larger scale of things they could consider themselves lucky. £450 annual unearned income was a lot of money to most people.

As a child I could make no sense of these discrepancies. All I knew was that from 1964, when we first moved to Marchmont, the so-called "stately home" in the borders of Scotland, there was never what Papa thought of as "enough money." During the years that followed, he had a hundred schemes to "make things work," to "save the family fortunes." An old railway track lay right across the land, and some special grit had been used in its construction. Why shouldn't we dig up the railway line and sell the grit at enormous profit? I remember him standing in front of the library fire-place with a glass in his hand, vigorous, intent, expounding this scheme to the assembled company. Nothing came of it. Other schemes, like selling local game-birds to classy London restaurants (rushing them down on the night train from Berwick) looked promising for a few brief months and then collapsed.

What, my father asked, was he supposed to do? With the house to keep up and six children to educate (John had been born in 1965, and Isabella in 1968), money had to come from somewhere. Papa could have saved several thousand pounds a year by sending us to local schools, but that he never thought of as an option. Instead, he took out covenants with his sister and one of his younger brothers. Along with the interest from his stocks and shares, that provided some sort of basic income. The farms too brought in something, even though most of it had to be ploughed back into their upkeep. "What were the figures though?" I want to ask. "What were we actually living on?" But at this distance it is impossible to know. Papa ran his life and ours on a series of borrowings and overdrafts,[13] tied up with zigzags of red tape by the accountant in Edinburgh. Beyond the rhetoric and the funny stories, what remains clear is the pitch of his anxiety. "You must marry a White Russian," he used to say to Kate and me. "Then we can mend the Adam Bridge."

The Adam Bridge had been built two hundred years earlier, and shook whenever heavy traffic crossed it. Two or three balusters had fallen in the burn, and the sandstone was flaking off the sides. Even as a child, I knew we'd never mend the Adam Bridge. At the same time, I didn't believe that it would ever quite collapse. I accepted its shakiness as I accepted Papa's anxieties: part of the language, part of the atmosphere, like the little jingle that he used to find so witty:

"That money talks, I don't deny:
I heard it once, it said, 'Goodbye.' "

The money "whistling" in my father's pocket (as my aunt once said), never took too long to say goodbye. Yet in its vanishing, it did sometimes transform itself into the most amazing things. There were family holidays in Greece for example, with a villa overlooking the Aegean, and a yacht freighted with champagne. There was a sleek new dark green Daimler. And once there was a racehorse called Bold Daimon, a chestnut gelding with a vicious temperament, bought, Papa told us, as a present for our mother.

There was no way that the stocks and shares could have paid for any of this. The Americans were the source of all these riches.

The Americans

It is difficult to describe the Americans without turning them into one of Papa's stories. "Take five or six millionaires, each with a wife or secretary in tow. Place them in a Scottish country house during the shooting season. Hire a butler from London, along with two matching footmen, and dress them up in ancient livery rescued from the attic. Import cooks and cleaning-women, game-keepers and parlour-maids as appropriate. Require everyone to know their place and keep to it. Swing back the velvet curtains and on with the show!"

A production, a performance, it was always that. Pheasant shooting six days of the week, with breakfast, lunch and tea at three-hour intervals, and in the evening, a full-scale dinner in the dining-room. If it was, as I once said, with childish pomposity, "a purely mercenary venture," at least the Americans got good value for their money. Old friends and neighbors were invited over, and there was always plenty of red wine and conversation. At least once during each visit, the street-sweeper from the local village would dress up in the kilt and full regalia. Starting from the far corner of the house he would walk towards the dining-room playing the bagpipes. As he reached the table, the whine and blast of sound struck conversation dead. Local people knew what they were in for and pretended to enjoy it. That, after all, was part of why they'd been invited. The Americans sat completely still, astonished.

Each "gun," each shooting American, paid my father £1,000 for the privilege. They came back year after year (from 1965 to 1976), and although they never stayed more than two weeks, their presence made a considerable difference to the family finances. It also meant, of course, a great deal of work and planning, especially for my mother. In many ways it was she who set the tone of the occasion, welcoming the guests as they arrived, and looking after the wives while the men were out shooting. As for Papa, he did all that was required of him. He master-minded the shoots, charmed the visitors, and played the laird as best as he knew how. But underneath it all, he wasn't happy. He claimed to prefer "low-ceilinged life," by which he meant, I think, the book-lined Chelsea houses of his friends. He missed those friends very much, and tended to romanticise their busy lives. "The best things in life are *cheap*," he said, citing kipper and scrambled eggs. It was as if, in taking on Marchmont, such modest pleasures had become forever unattainable.

In the Big House

We had moved to Scotland in the summer of 1964, when I was eight. I didn't want to go. I liked Wiltshire: our comfortable yellow-washed house with its solid black thatch, the governess I'd been to for the first few years, and after that the little convent-school in Salisbury. I liked the two-acre field at the side of the house, and the woods behind it, with the view of Stonehenge. Marchmont was different. That house belonged to Grandmama. For me, as the eldest, there was always the sense of treading in someone else's footsteps, trying to copy "the uncles" (my father and his five tall brothers), and somehow doing a very mediocre job of it. For a long time I felt inadequate and small. What I didn't know (and probably it was just as well) was that in social terms my stock was on the rise. In moving from Wiltshire to Scotland my family had gone up in the world. From then on we were landed gentry, established upper class.

That September, as soon as the holidays were over, I was sent to boarding school. This meant another convent, seventeen miles away, just across the border into England. For four years I was driven there every Sunday night by a dour chauffeur called Mr. Corcoran. He had big sad hands and a mutilated ear, and I used to sing to him to cheer us both up. The separations never got any easier. I started off each week tearful and subdued, and by the time I felt settled again, it was the weekend. My brothers and sisters had been at home all week. They were cheerful and belonged, while I was the difficult one, the stranger, fighting for the privilege of sitting between Papa and Mama at the tea-table: "It's my turn now. I'm only here two days."

Perhaps it was in reaction to those perpetual upheavals that I held on so hard to my (fairly idiosyncratic) view of class. I did not understand it as a system, though I remember Papa teaching me the Peerage, from dukes through marquises and earls all the way down to baronets and knights and commoners. My own sense of my class position was simply, "what we were": some idealized version of Papa's place in the world, with a touch of Mama's thrown in to make it "cultured," "sensitive," "exotic." Baffled by the move and by the new girls at school whose fathers were clerks and shop-keepers and farmers, I clung to the family, making of it some kind of sacred unassailable thing, source and fountain-head of our hidden "betterness." Because of Papa's First and Mama's beauty, because we were Catholic and spoke with the "right" accent, we were special, more than special; we were better, we were best.

This version of things sounds like a child's version, a child of five or six perhaps, younger than I was then. Most children defend their families against the rest of the world. But in my case, parental and family betterness was also ratified from outside. I was not the only one who looked up to my mother and did what I was told. The nannies and the servants did that too. Our house was "the Big House" to grownups as well as children.

Out in what we always called "the real world," nothing seemed very different. Papa had friends in London and Washington and New York. His name was in the newspapers and theirs were too. We saw them on the television, heard them on the radio. They all seemed to know each other, and everyone was a success or famous, or at least, "very interesting." Sir

Alec Douglas-Home came over for a shoot. Terence Stamp[14] appeared for the New Year with Jean Shrimpton[15] on his arm. Jim Dine[16] arrived in a Volkswagen bus with a troop of squealing children. One week the exiled King of Uganda came to stay; sometime later it was Princess Margaret.

Nowadays I am perplexed by all of this, as if it had happened to someone else. I know my life will never be quite the same again, and, in retrospect, I miss the glamour and excitement. But as a child, I took it very much for granted. My parents' friends might be interesting and important, but in our house they were simply visitors who didn't know their way from their own bedrooms to the dining-room for breakfast. ("Down the front stairs, through the saloon,[17] and it's straight ahead. Not that door, that's the library.") I soon forgot that we had ever lived anywhere else, in particular the "little house" in Wiltshire. I looked not back, but forwards, far into the future, despising grownups because they were already, irrecoverably, themselves. I would be different: a gardener, an acrobat, a writer, a traveller, a saint. I spent a lot of time constructing different versions, taking as base my parents' hopes and expectations, and building castle upon castle onto that. I would be clever because "we" always were. I'd be the kind of person Gavin was,[18] the kind that didn't have to keep clean all the time. I would be an animal person just like him, someone who lived on an island, someone who broke the rules. I'd have an interesting and exotic and morally irreproachable life. Once I'd cured my jealousy and bad temper, everyone would love me. And I'd be beautiful as well, like Mama.

When I look back, I marvel at my confidence. I really did believe that all those identities were there for the taking. At the same time I had no idea of how to go about acquiring them. I was not prepared for work or for the world. In the end, intellectual freedom was the thing I needed most, the chance to get some distance from my parents' house, and to question the assumptions I'd been taught.

People Like Us

What I know of upper class values, upper class attitudes and assumptions, I mostly learned through my father. Mama did her best to practice them, but Papa spelled them out. Words like "responsibility" and "right" (as in the "right thing to do") I still hear with his particular emphasis. Betterness brought responsibilities in its train, and these we should learn to accept. Grandpa McEwen had been an M.P. for example, not just because he liked the work, but because he had "taken on the responsibility" for the people of Berwick and Haddington. It was a classic case of "noblesse oblige." For the same reasons, Papa accepted a position as local Sheriff,[19] and acted as trustee for the estates of several friends.

He would have done more, certainly thought more should be done, had it not been for his illness, self-disgust. He already found it difficult to maintain a consistent sense of himself. Social competence required more complicated virtues. Manically ebullient, Papa could be dismissive of those beneath him on the social scale, contemptuous of those above, cross and overbearing with his peers. Depressed, he turned to drink, and spoke to almost no-one. At such times, responsibility was not a word he used. The only word was "guilt" and that was endless.

During my childhood and my adolescence, I spent almost all my holidays at home. Once or twice I got a job, and spent the money travelling, but that was seen as selfish, not encouraged. "Papa likes to talk to you," was the family line. "You're an intellectual, just like him."

I was often told that I was like my father, and at the time I took this as a compliment. To me it had the aura of near-genius: passionate, enthusiastic, brilliant. Compared to the stolid men at shooting lunches, with their patched tweed jackets and tiny risqué jokes, Papa was an extraordinary man. "Je n'ai jamais vu un homme aussi éblouissant," remarked one visitor, and at his best, that word was accurate: "warm-hearted, blossoming." Papa knew, as who did not, the values of the drawing-room. But they did not interest him. Bored by small talk, he would do everything he could to get a "real" conversation going, better yet an argument, preferably on some complicated moral issue, preferably unresolvable. There was an endearing innocence in his commitment to this, as if the next thing said might somehow hold the clue, the key he needed to unlock the universe.

As a teenager, I loved all this about him. I saw him as the real thing in a cardboard world, a one-man army battling against the hypocritical inanities of upper-class existence. I knew, of course, that he "wasn't always well," but that could be explained easily enough. He "should have been a writer," he "should have been an artist." He had been to art school after all. There was an oil painting of his on Mama's desk.

Papa himself believed some version of this argument, but it wasn't one he very often mentioned. On the whole his explanations turned on other people: his father, Grandmama, his best friend who'd been killed during the war. He wanted very much to succeed in making sense of things, both of himself and his inheritance, to lay the blame somewhere. "It is difficult," he said, "for people like us to survive."

Listening, I accepted this entirely. At thirteen, I'd been sent to yet another boarding school, this time down in Sussex, where my mother had once gone. I was mocked for my Scottishness ("Do you have running water up there in the Highlands?") and it took me a long time to make friends. "People like us" was a reassuring phrase. Papa and I spent several sets of holidays defining exactly what it should mean. We would be Catholics, we said, but not blindly, foolishly so. We would be upper class, but not in the haw-haw huntin', shootin', fishin' manner. We would be cultured and well-read, but not humorlessly pompous or academic. Above all, we promised, we would stand by each other. We would unite against the enemy.

Choices

By then, I saw this enemy as the upper class itself, personified in most of Papa's friends. On his good days, I knew it didn't matter. Papa triumphed over it. Either he defeated it on its own terms (somehow managing to be more moral, more educated and better bred than anyone else),[20] or he abandoned it altogether (he was the artist, the eccentric). But on bad days the walls of the drawing-room closed in, and I felt him torn apart by contradictory demands, unable to fulfill his "real" self because of the duties he had assumed as a landowner.

"Why did you take the house in the first place? Why don't you let it go?" Those were the obvious questions. But I already knew the answers. Papa was steeped in his parents' values: *duty, honor, loyalty, tradition.* He had taken on the house, he always said, "for the sake of the family." As an angry adolescent, I was up in arms for him. I saw the family as parasites and scroungers, dropping by for shooting parties and excursions, lunches, teas and suppers, while papa was left struggling with the debts.

This view, however, was always too much his to be entirely accurate. Papa was, after all, the second son. No-one had forced him to take on the house. On the contrary. By the early seventies most of the family would have been relieved to sell up. Undoubtedly they would have been grateful for the extra cash. But Papa would not admit that he could ever have done otherwise, or, indeed, that any choices still remained. As far as he was concerned, the house was nothing but a loss, a dead-weight. "The place is going to the dogs," he always said.

What Papa didn't see (and what took me years to realize) was that there were real advantages in the life that he had chosen. As a member of the landed gentry and a baronet (after his brother's death in 1971),[21] he had a definite position in the world. He had an income from the covenants, the farms and stocks and shares and, whether or not he wanted it, he had some place in the community, simply as a result of living where he lived. These things meant power. If Papa had given up the house and land, he would have lost that power. This was a deeply alarming prospect, especially for a man as depressed as he often was.

Thinking about it now, I am tempted to make of that depression the "real" enemy Papa always sought. It is certain that both ECT and drinking (official and unofficial "cures") caused him to forget many things, and likely that they also damaged him in some way, made him less flexible perhaps, more dogmatic and suspicious. In medical terms, the words that come to mind are "grandiosity" and "paranoia." But in upper class circles, grandiosity may be seen as no more than ordinary self-importance; and paranoia can be interpreted as simply "looking out for oneself." Because the labels change depending on the frame of reference, it is impossible to say which set is "right." All I am sure of is that in Papa's case, the systems meshed and overlapped and caused him pain. Whether his depression exacerbated his class position, or vice versa, it is impossible to say. By the time I knew him best, the two were inextricably entwined.

Nannies and Servants

My youngest sister was born in March, 1968, just a month before my twelfth birthday. From then on there were six of us at home, at least during the holidays, six of us in the nursery watching television, hunched on the fireguard and jammed together on the sofa; six of us piling into the back of the Dormobile, all of us dressed the same in Marks and Spencers[22] corduroys (pale brown) and bright red woolen jerseys.

Compared to the intensity of my talks with Papa, nursery life seemed casual and dull. I remember coming home from boarding school and just "hanging around." The nursery itself always seemed to slip into a kind of time-warp. Clothes were airing by the fire, the rocking-horse moved gently in the corner. The cuckoo-clock ticked loud-soft-loud just as it had done in Grandmama's day.

In Grandmama's day, that is, before 1964, when we ourselves moved up to Scotland, there had been a strict line drawn between the nursery and the sitting-room (doubly emphasized by the fact that they were on different floors, and at opposite ends of the house). As little children, we almost never saw our parents. Uniformed nannies got us up in the morning, sent us out into the garden to play, gave us lunch, and took us for long cold walks down the front drive. At five-thirty we were primped and scolded, and hurried downstairs in our "tidy clothes" to "see the grownups" for one hour after tea. Supper followed, and a speedy bed.

By the early seventies, when Isabella was a little girl, many of these things had changed. We still spent most of our time on the nursery floor, but we were free to come and go to our parents' sitting-room. Shirts and socks were still "put out for us," but the nannies no longer wore uniforms, and (except for church and grownup dinners) we were no longer forced into those tidy clothes. Daily life was considerably more relaxed.

Nonetheless, from the nannies' point of view, most of the basic attitudes remained unchanged. My mother talked of "people coming in to help," as if the servants were her friends who had "just happened" to drop by. Nannies, in particular, were supposed to be "part of the family." But the work was the same as it had always been, and the wages (almost never mentioned) were frugal in the extreme. I remember discovering and opening one nanny's paypacket. At that time, about 1969, it was seven pounds a week.

For seven pounds a week apiece, plus board and lodging, the nanny and the nursery-maid took total care of all of us, and all our physical needs. They made the beds and cleaned the rooms and did the laundry; they gave us meals and did the washing-up. They were on call twenty-four hours a day. But despite this vast responsibility, they always remained accountable to my mother. Even now, I remember the atmosphere of the nursery when Mama entered it, the anxious eyes checking round to make sure that everything was in its place, and the "Yes, Lady McEwen," when she gave the orders.

Downstairs in the kitchen and the pantry, another version of this scene would be enacted. Mama would walk in on a tea or coffee break, and everyone would stop laughing and put their mugs back on the table. There'd be jokes about the number of biscuits that had been consumed, and that quiet waiting silence as she spoke. "Yes, Lady McEwen, yes—" when she was finished.

For all the talk about equality, it was clear to me even then that "servants weren't like us," and I capitalized upon it, cruelly, disobeying the nannies and teasing the other servants as I would never have dared to tease my mother's friends. Nor was I the only one. If the nannies did try to control us ("You'll wear that kilt tomorrow, James, because I say so—"), all of us were adept at appealing to our parents. ("I asked Mama and she says I don't have to.") We were proud of this, and thought we managed well, playing the two lots of grownups against each other, and manipulating them to get what we wanted.

As I grew older, things began to change, and I had long serious talks with one particular nanny, who really did become a friend. But this was the exception. In general our parents couldn't be absolutely frank with us because of what we might repeat, and the nannies, naturally, were afraid to lose their jobs if "certain things" got said. For the most part, both sets of grownups found it easier to leave us ignorant, or fob us off with "shoulds" and "oughts" and half-truths: the familiar veneer. The result, for me at least, was a tremendous hunger for what people really thought. Like Papa with his urgent moral questions, I was always trying to chip away at the surface of things, to get at what I believed to be "the truth."

Not Good Enough

In relation to our daily life, that truth was always complicated and ambiguous. On the one hand, there's no doubt that we were privileged. We grew up with space around us, both physical and mental. Arriving home for the holidays, our time was marvellously our own. Everything was done for us: our meals cooked, beds made. We were each supposed to take care of our own pet animals (Katie's rats and ferrets, James' pigs, Helena's fox, my black labrador), but even then there was a back-up person in case we forgot. The house was ours, with its attics and its store-rooms and the long back corridor in which we bicycled up and down on rainy days. In every direction stretched "our" fields and "our" woods, with "our" burn and "our" river running through. We could make whatever use of these we wished: climbing trees and walking half the day, guddling[23] for trout in the burn, and coming home to long hours of dressing-up or "rescue" (our particular version of hide-and-seek). As I grew older, I began to make up little plays which we'd perform, usually one every holiday. I spent an entire summer camping in the attic, reading Dante and Jane Austen, listening to Bach and trying to write a novel, while Katie sang and painted through the wall. There was time for this: time to investigate new things, to make experiments, and encouragement to do so.

The other side of such luxurious self-absorption was a terrifying ignorance and alienation. Despite the comings and goings of those glamorous visitors, our daily life was really very isolated. After we moved to Scotland, there were no streets to play on, no shops just down the road, no ordinary community to which we all belonged. At the time I experienced this as "lack of friends" and complained bitterly to my mother that the little ones were "too little" and I wanted children my own age I could play with. Mama did her best. Our uncles and aunts arrived, bringing with them their various offspring. Some of Papa's friends had children too, and they were asked to stay. But the principle behind this was never mentioned, "You can't play with the local kids. Your friends must be imported. You're better. They're not good enough for you."

Why couldn't we play with the local children? No-one asked. We scarcely knew we might have wanted to. We were afraid of them, just as our parents, I think, were afraid of theirs. Once again, this fear was never stated. On the whole it masqueraded as romanticism (Papa's warmth and admiration for the shepherd, for example), though at other times it showed itself in all its coldness and contempt. Every Sunday we gave a Catholic family a lift to the local church, and I remember Papa noting dryly how they smelt, the girls especially. I winced at this remark (myself fourteen, the age of the chief offender), but I know I didn't really question it. Papa was right. The working classes were dirty, stupid. Above all they weren't interesting, except in a caricatured, rustic sort of way. The ones round us had pretty accents (Scots were immeasurably better than Midlands, for example), and sometimes they said funny things which made you laugh. But they couldn't hold up their end of a conversation, and you had to be polite and not embarrass them. However much you might have wished things otherwise, that was just the way they are.

Blame the Mother

Long before I knew anything about class propaganda, I was not the eldest boy, I was a girl. Boys could be clever and brave and independent and as naughty as they wanted. Girls had fewer choices. Mostly they were very, very good.

In the upper class households that I knew, these stereotypes were exaggerated. Boys wore kilts and sailor-suits, girls wore pretty dresses with satin sashes round their waists. Boys learned to shoot and fish. Girls didn't learn anything much, except perhaps a little flower-arranging. Boys were the important ones, the ones whose choices were taken seriously.

Because Papa and I talked so much, and spent so much time together, it was easy for me to forget that I was "only a girl." Even when he was drunk, and I had to help him into bed, hide the whiskey-bottle, fetch his pills, I thought of myself as a young comrade-at-arms, a friend, rather than a daughter. It was painful to admit that there were gaps between us. And yet, of course, there were. We talked about Papa himself; we discussed the great absolutes like death and immortality. But we never touched on my personal life, or more general "women's issues." We barely mentioned sex or power at all.

At the time I didn't realize this. A "clever girl," I was an honorary boy. I sided with my father against his enemies, upper class hypocrisy, the trivial, the usual, and in this way I learnt to blame my mother.

Mama had not been brought up upper class. Her primary set of values had always been moral rather than social. The women she knew best were dedicated and independent: the nuns at her convent for example, her own mother, with her busy professional life. But marriage to my father brought with it certain obligations. First Mama had to find out what they were. Then she had to pass them on to us.

An upper class woman is expected to be pretty and to get married. If she does some charity work on the side, well and good. She can do anything she pleases: write or paint, play music, take up gardening, so long as it does not interfere with her primary responsibility, her duty to her husband, house and children. I put "house" before "children" because the upper class woman does exactly that. She is a married woman and a hostess first, a mother second.

Until the age of twenty-nine, when we moved up to Scotland, Mama had no particular position to maintain. Thereafter, things were very different. Throughout my childhood and adolescence, Papa worked in his study, read and watched television in the sitting-room. It was Mama who did the rounds of the house every morning, checking the activities of the day with the nanny and nursery-maid, the cook and the cleaning-woman. She was the one who made us (literally) pull up our socks before we went into church, curtsey to the visitors, say "please" and "thank you." Because of this, as we grew older, she was the one who took the brunt of our rejection. "Don't let Mama down," was the line, and we let her down constantly, appearing in the drawing-room ragged and ill-kept, bridling at everything from the crystal chandeliers to the dining-room table laid for twenty-four. It was as if, in taking responsibility for so much, she had become inseparable from it. Quarrelling with the upper classes became quarrelling with her.

While these confrontations were taking place, I failed to understand them. All I knew was that when I looked at Mama, I saw no female future I could want. Kate and I did our best to construct one for ourselves, devouring everything from Simone de Beauvoir's *The Second Sex* to *The Sensuous Woman* by "J." But Mama lived in another world entirely. She seemed to us entirely submerged in those same duties, loyalties and traditions which tormented Papa. When she wasn't at home running the house, she was out on the road, driving to endless Red Cross Coffee Mornings, Benefit Concerts and Catholic Sales of Work. She was forever putting up posters, opening fêtes, and showing people round the house and gardens. Because, unlike Papa, her spirit never seemed to fail her, she was, as she said cheerfully, "always on the go."

I remember standing at the front of the house while Mama was opening a fête. Katie was beside me, and all through Mama's speech we joked and whispered to each other. People stared at us. "Her ladyship is speaking!" But we would not be hushed. That was Mama up there on the platform. This was our front drive. We had to make clear, if only to ourselves, that somehow we refused to be impressed.

Part of what was happening then, I think, was a claiming of the ordinary (our mother) over the saccharine-sweet, public version the loud-speakers were giving us. "I would like to thank Sir Robert and Lady McEwen for their great kindness this afternoon—" As we listened to those speeches we faced our parents' betterness head-on, and therefore our own difference and alienation. It was hard to take. But we talked through Mama's speech for other, more complicated reasons. However ordinary we tried to make her, the truth was she was very often on that platform, "doing her bit," as Papa said, bowing gracefully, accepting flowers. She was Lady McEwen, our father's wife, the lady of the house, and we resented it. *Why didn't she have time to spare for us?*

How Is He, D'you Think?

As a child, I remember Mama rustling across the threshold of the night-nursery, bending over in her scented ballgown to kiss us all goodnight. I remember yearning after her down the corridor. "I didn't really like that social life," she told me years later. "But you couldn't do them both." It was a choice between her husband and her children.

In the myriad ramifications of that choice, Papa always took priority. Almost everything that Mama did, she did for him. She hid his drinking, she placated the servants, she stepped in for him whenever she was needed. Yet the more patient and long-suffering she was, the more critical he became. He was the rebel emperor joining us in our adolescent battles against the status quo; whereas Mama belonged, or so at least he implied, among the ranks of his enemies. Her concerns were dismissed as "boring" and "unimaginative."

Papa must have known that Mama's "boring, unimaginative" concerns weren't hers by nature. That she was so *very* busy was perhaps a choice: her way of protecting herself against the pain of Papa's drinking. But she had taken on the work, at least in part, because she loved him. That was what it meant to her to be his wife. And yet he refused to see this clearly. It was easier to lay the blame outside himself.

For us as children, this had many repercussions. The main one was that although our parents loved us, it was not exactly a united loving, nor was it unconditional. As far as Papa was concerned, we were his little troop of courtiers, a sturdy bodyguard between himself and the outside world. It was important to him that we obey our mother and treat her with respect, but secretly he wanted us to love him best.

Mama did not enter into any kind of competition over this, which in itself was something of a relief. But as Papa grew more difficult to handle, she used to try to turn us into allies. "How *is* he, d'you think?" she'd ask, catching me alone in the garden or in the bathroom while she did her hair. I was never comfortable answering her, partly out of loyalty to Papa, and partly on account of the enormous grudge I carried round with me. *How was Papa, always how was Papa.* Would she never ever ask me about me?

Puzzling over it now, I think I see more clearly how the system worked, and I wish I could have confronted Papa (whom after all I loved), instead of laying so much fury and resentment at my mother's feet. Even if she did see very little of us, this was in fact as much Papa's responsibility as it was hers. It was *his* parents who had placed the nursery at such a distance from the sitting-room, *his* way of life which determined that we should be brought up by nannies and sent away to boarding school. These were the usual practices of the class she'd married into. Mama, on her own, might well have chosen very differently.

Leaving Home

In 1974, when I was seventeen, I had nine months off between school and university. For three of those months I went to Thailand, and worked at a mission for people with leprosy. I put medical cards in order, made physiotherapy drawings, helped out at minor operations, distributed soap and baby-food and vitamins. When I arrived back in England, I had acute culture shock. I felt crazy, suicidal, desperately at odds with my complicated past, and quite unable to make sense of the new world of King's College, Cambridge.

Oxford and Cambridge have always been elitist universities, drawing most of their students from the English public school system,[24] and going on to supply the politicians and civil servants of the capital. The colleges themselves are run like mini-stately homes, each with its own ceremonies and traditions. With Marchmont and my father looming in the background, I might have been expected to fit right in. Instead, I reacted with a long campaign of downward mobility.

During those final years of the hippy era, downward mobility was a fashionable option. For many people it was an aesthetic and moral choice. In my case, it was also a financial one. Other people's parents subsidised their student grants, or gave them free board and lodging while they took a job during the holidays. My parents gave me £40 a quarter, barely enough for food, let alone for bus or train-fare up to Scotland. (Rent was always paid, something I took for granted.) I grew tense and frugal, stealing books on occasion, and buying most of my clothes in the city flea-market. I kept a pet snake during my first year, and I remember there was often a choice between buying a goldfish for the snake (he needed one a week), or a bowl of soup for me.

While I was living in this way, it all seemed real and necessary. It was connected in my mind with the absolute poverty I'd seen in Thailand, the extravagance of Western consumer society, and the sexual games I saw all round me and wanted to reject. What I didn't see was the convenience of such a theory to someone who was, after all, my father's daughter. It gave me an identity separate from his, which, of course, as eldest daughter (and not the heir), I somehow had to find.

Meanwhile I was at Cambridge, which I did not like. I worked hard. I had no idea how to play. As far as possible I passed as middle class, trying to understand what that meant as I went along. But I still believed that somehow round the corner an exotic life was waiting, and I held on tightly to the one strand of my betterness which I still valued. I was a poet, a writer, a misunderstood artist in the top floor garret of my ivory tower. It was perhaps not so surprising then, that I should try to kill myself.

There was certainly an element of melodrama in my suicide attempts: slashed wrists, overdoses, attempted drownings, the time I tried to hang myself with Papa's tie. They were all somehow "good stories." But behind the story, the pre-packaged anecdote, the pain and confusion were real too. "You're just like me," Papa had always said. "You're just like me, so *watch out—*"

The day I went to Cambridge for the first time, Mama and I stopped by to visit Papa. He had had another breakdown, and was being treated at some big mental hospital outside London. I remember opening the door at the end of a long white corridor, and coming upon him from behind, in a big room with a double bed and too many chairs, the grey face of a television. I thought of him knowing the inside of many such rooms, and lying there, and wondering if he would ever get better. Despite my terror that I too was mad, it was not a question that I asked myself.

Now, of course, I realize that I wasn't mad. Nor was I "just like Papa." In fact, it was exactly where we were most dissimilar that my problems arose. If I had been a man, instead of a young woman, my time at Cambridge would have been very different. Among the undergraduates, men outnumbered women nine to one, and though King's itself was an exception, having gone co-ed in 1972, most tutors and professors were still men, as was the bulk of the administration. It was hardly surprising that this should create difficulties for the women students (lack of role models, low self-esteem, competition for the few female tutors that did exist, etc.), and at the same time that it should make for tremendous social and sexual tension.

In my case, the situation was complicated yet again by the attitudes and assumptions I had brought with me from home—the ways in which, for better and worse, I in fact took after *both* my parents. Faced with the baffling cool of the circle round King's bar, I viewed it as yet another version of adult hypocrisy, and fought back as Papa would have done, with the direct argumentative self he had always encouraged. Making love for the first time, I heard my mother's voice inside me, heavy with disappointment and reproach. Catholic guilt sang its way out through a score of Scottish ballads, in all of which the hero loved and kissed and abandoned the poor heroine.

A maid again I ne'er shall be
Since that young farmer lay still with me—
For months I cut myself whenever I made love.

Sorting it Out

It took me years to make sense of this, to add the complexities of class to Papa's illness and alcoholism, and again to student life as it was then. In Cambridge I personalized everything and could get no distance from it. When things were difficult, I blamed myself.

Sometimes this was right: I was to blame. More often, I was only the ground on which the battle was fought out. Way above my head, the upper classes clashed with the middle class intelligentsia, the agnostics with the Catholics, and the women with the men. I was my father's daughter and a clever girl. What was I supposed to do about it?

I had got myself to Cambridge, and I had finished my degree. That in itself was something of an achievement. My mother had left Oxford early in order to get married. My aunt Kisty had not even been allowed to go to university. It was not supposed to be "necessary" for a woman. What good was a B.A. when it came to arranging flowers? Apart from the advantages of being able to keep up "an intelligent conversation" with her husband, the upper class wife had no need for further education.

Throughout my childhood and my growing up, this was the prevailing attitude. My parents were unusual in that they definitely encouraged me to go to university, and were delighted when I got in. All the same, neither of them had the faintest idea of what might be supposed to happen afterwards. Going to Cambridge had become an end in itself. They had no sense of it as the possible preparation for a future career. Papa's First belonged to the masculine world of professional achievement. My own studies were viewed very differently. I was "only a girl," after all. I was going to get married.

When I think about this now, I see how well it blended in with other upper class assumptions. Once again, as so often, energy and ambition were being sapped from below. "Yes indeed, why bother? Why even *try* to aim for anything?" Growing up upper class meant that we already were (owned, had access to) everything that ordinary people worked towards. As children we were constantly reminded just how lucky we were. We had a beautiful house to live in, wonderful parents, and were ourselves "beautiful, talented, intelligent." *In some very basic way this was enough.* Very little emphasis was given to developing our so-called skills and qualities—risking something to further an unknown goal. After all, the only goals that mattered were preservation, conservation, more of the same. Since this "same" was daily criticised (Papa hated the world he lived in, even while he hastened to defend it), the result was that we had next to no initiative. Our sense of what was possible was both stunted and blasé.

Built into my character as a layer of apathy and condescension, this heritage lives on. It is true, painfully and pitifully true, but it is not all of the truth. Even then, as a teenager and a young adult, I did everything I could think of to defend myself against it, coping with what I understood as upper class goals by turning my back on them as much as possible. For a long time I had only the negative versions of choice. "No, I don't want that—" I wanted something else, another life, another set of values. But I had no idea what that entailed. My rage at upper class hypocrisy left me critical and intense. I had very little money ("bourgeois ambition"), nor did I know how to acquire it (upper class ignorance and lack of practical skills). Underneath it all, I was enormously afraid.

Nonetheless, somewhere about this time, an important choice was beginning to be made. It took its impetus from a year I'd spent away from Cambridge, earning money and travelling around the States. On my return I applied for every scholarship within reach. I was lucky enough to win a Fulbright. Soon after, at the age of twenty-three, I moved to Berkeley.

California

Berkeley, California: nobody knew me there. For the first time in my life I was my own person: a student, yes, a foreigner, obviously, but not my father's daughter, my uncle's niece, not part of the family, part of the clan, recognized and placed the minute I opened my mouth.

I rejoiced in that independence and anonymity. I felt strong and well. When my scholarship ran out, I began to earn a living, working as a floor-refinisher, a house-painter, a counselor, a gardener, a kindergarten aide, and a teacher of English. Suddenly I was looking after myself, paying my own way. Living in a communal house with five other people, I learned to cook and clean, to fix the washing-machine when it broke down. To my housemates, these achievements were entirely mundane. To me, they were extraordinary: opportunity for pride and celebration. I could sweep the hallway, I could make a meal. I didn't need a nanny to look after me.

My father died of a heart-attack in May, 1980, towards the end of my first year in Berkeley. I went back to Scotland for the funeral. It was a strained and murky time. Despite everything, Papa had always been the center of the house. Now that he was dead, there was no center. "Papa was, Papa did, Papa used to say—" We had to learn to talk about him in the past tense. It was as if everything he believed in were slowly being dispersed.

I remember the ache and yearning of those days, and how helpless we all were, playing Scrabble, hunched together in the saloon. For a while I wanted passionately to take on Papa's role, somehow adopt his values, if only because I missed him and he wasn't there. Instead I hauled myself back to California to "finish my degree." I had friends there, it is true, but no-one I could really talk to, no-one who understood the complexities of my upbringing, or exactly what I'd lost. In the next couple of years, first in Berkeley, then in New York, I had the time and space to shape a different self: a grownup finally, a lesbian, a beginning writer. All this was good. But

I missed the family consolations, family jokes, support. I grew up in the States, not in England or Scotland, and when I did go back there, I was very much a child.

Inheritance: James

When Papa died, my brother James took on the title of baronet. He was only nineteen, and the responsibilities of the house and land went to my mother until he reached the age of twenty-one. It was her decision to let the big house, and move into a smaller place on the estate, easier to maintain, and much more practical.

Far away in California, I felt only the distant reverberations of this move. Nonetheless, I wasn't happy with it. Marchmont was more than just a house. It was part of my identity. It was as if, at eight years old, moving up from Wiltshire, my head and heart had swollen to accommodate it. I loved the big echoing rooms, the elaborate plaster ceilings, the floor-boards which had been young at the time of William the Conqueror. I'd always thought I loved Marchmont for itself, but now that we were leaving, I found other reasons, harder to admit. The departure in itself was not so difficult, even at that remove; it was *losing possession of the house.*

Grandmama McEwen had six sons, and of these six, five married and had children. In order to distinguish each family of cousins, we were known by our father's name and also by the name of the house we lived in. We, "the Robins," were "the Marchmont ones."

Being the Marchmont ones gave us status, both in the immediate family and beyond it. Papa might be poorer than his brothers. Our clothes might come to us second-hand, in big soft cardboard boxes sent by Mama's friend, Lord Harlech's wife. Out in the big world we might get lost on London Transport, fail exams. But always there was Marchmont to return to. I remember feeling that it couldn't be gainsaid. It was something un-questionably substantial.

If this was true for me, a girl-child, how much more powerfully was it true for James. From the time he was a small boy, James had been brought up to be the baronet, to inherit. There is a photograph of him at eight or nine, standing beside Papa on the lawn in front of the house. Both of them hold shepherd's crooks tilted at identical angles, both have a pleased, proprietorial expression. Now, ten years later, James was standing on that front lawn by himself. Marchmont and the land were his—and yet they weren't. James felt strongly that plans were being made over his head. He wanted to keep the house and one day live in it. He wanted access to the family money. Mama would not listen to him, he said. He felt cheated, disinherited.

James had the makings of a writer in him, and a dazzlingly immediate sense of humor. He would have been a wonderful cartoonist. The difficulty, from Mama's point of view, was that he was not to be relied on. Sent to Eton at thirteen, he left soon after his O' levels.[25] He went from there to a crammer in Edinburgh for his A' levels (which he failed to get), and then to an agricultural college, which he hated. Even before my father died, he had been drinking and had started taking heroin. A couple of stints in various hospitals and clinics cleared him of the drink, but left him vulnerable to massive cravings. He had no job, no settled occupation, and since his writing and his drawing could be dismissed as "hobbies," no sense of his direction in the world. He was a baronet, of course. He was Sir James. But being a baronet was not enough.

In ordinary life you have to earn your identity. In order to *be* someone, you have to *do* something. A fireman is a fireman because he puts out fires. But a baronet? What is a baronet supposed to do? James did what he understood was "right"—joining the Turf Club (at the cost of £130 a year), attending planning meetings with my mother and the farm manager. But beyond that he felt paralyzed. Friends from school were going to art college or university, joining their father's businesses or setting up on their own. James could hardly have imitated them even if he'd wanted to. He had very little formal training, and only the most minimal academic qualifications. Besides, the title held him to the family. Even the more menial jobs he undertook (porter at Christie's,[26] farm helper/laborer on my aunt's estate) were seen as having some kind of bearing on his future position. There was little real chance of starting at the bottom, and furnishing his own way in the world.

In the summer of 1981, he flew out to visit me in California. He seemed very English, very Scottish, lean and white and intense. I feared for him, and wondered how he'd cope. He, more than any of us, had grown up in the shadow of Papa's illness. Sometimes when he spoke I'd hear Papa's voice in his: the same emphasis, the same intonations. He would lean forward across the table, outlining the devastation to come, the fact that there was no future, and there was something horrible in his conviction, as if the spirit of a fifty-year-old man had found its way into the body of a boy. I used to argue with him, to try to separate his life from Papa's dying, and his own future from the future of the world. "You can do things differently," I told him. "And you needn't be a baronet if you don't want to."

James listened to me, nodded, shook his head. It was all very well for me to say that. I was a girl. For James there was rarely any question of doing things differently. Papa had been a baronet. So would he be, and for many of the same reasons. The title promised too much to be refused. It had too much glamour, too much power attached. Sooner or later, he would have to take it on.

In the meantime, he was in the States, where "baronet" meant next to nothing, and things were starting to improve. He did a driveaway to New York with a friend of mine, and found work almost immediately, acting as a driver/houseboy for a picture-dealer and his wife. Back in California for Christmas, he was busy, happy, radiantly in love. By then he had a place to live and money in his pocket. But the love-affair ended sometime in the spring, and so did the job with the picture-dealer. James was (not so metaphorically) back on the street. The family story is that he was "lucky" to be taken in by our cousin's aunt, who had a big apartment way up on Fifth Avenue and 96th Street. Certainly it was a good thing that he had a roof over his head, and Emily was kind to him, and lent him money. But in the long run, such rescues only aggravated his own sense of powerlessness, and led, directly or indirectly, to more drug-taking.

When my lover and I stayed with him that Easter, he showed me his diary, with a list of all the drugs he'd tried since the New Year. The previous weekend he'd gone up to Harlem to score some smack, and in the process lost his bike, his eiderdown, his Walkman and Emily's television set, along with the original ten dollars he'd brought with him. I was thrown by this, and anxious, but James dismissed it as a funny story, one more New York adventure. Really, he insisted, he was doing very well. He had enrolled at Parsons School of Art and Design, and was finally making use of his artistic talents. In fact he had already sold several paintings. In May he pledged himself to one month without drugs or alcohol, and started running regularly. He asked Mama for the money to see an analyst. But by mid-July he had blown it all on heroin, and was back in hospital: an expensive American hospital costing £2,000 a week.

I visited James in that clinic in the August of 1982. I had left Berkeley, and was on my way to London. My lover had just left me for another woman, and after three years our happy communal house had finally broken up. It was strange to shift from such immediate present-day concerns to James' desperate thoughts about the family. "Which of us did Papa love the most? Why were we brought up like that? Who was to blame?"

I brought him books and an inflatable plastic shark, and I tried to answer him as best I could. We went together to visit his psychiatrist, and together we talked about Papa. This was the only time we really faced that past, helped and witnessed by a professional. I no longer remember what we said.

Ten months later, back in Scotland, three years and one month after Papa's death, James took a shotgun into the bedroom next to his, knelt down by the bed, and pulled the trigger.

"Why" was the question everybody asked. "Why did he do it?" Answers became the stuff of consolation, and everybody had a different one. James had been drinking too much, and spending too much money. He had no regular job, no settled place to stay. His friends had lost their patience with him, and he thought he'd lost their love. They were accurate and factual, these answers, but they were really no more than surface descriptions. Underneath them lay the title, house and land, and the immense weight of Papa's despair.

When Grandpa McEwen died, Papa was thirty-five, with the army behind him, art school, Cambridge, and ten or twelve years as a professional lawyer. By the time he moved to Marchmont, he was thirty-eight. He became a baronet at forty-five.

When Papa died, James was not yet twenty. Given the circumstances, it is not surprising that the values he fell back on were Papa's values. They were not useful to him. To solve the dilemma of Marchmont, James would have needed business values, business acumen and skills. He would have needed some sort of professional training. Above all, he would have needed to steer clear of drugs and alcohol. But like father, like son. The aphorism is most grimly apt. Just as Papa had been an alcoholic, adopting as his own the upper class persona of the drunken and eccentric laird, so James, in "sowing his wild oats" as a drinker and a drug addict, chose very much the same path.

If James had not been the eldest son, if he'd refused the title, if he'd somehow found the power to kick the heroin, I believe he'd be alive today. He left behind him a journal, a couple of brilliant short stories, some sketchbooks and several bundles of letters. On the wall of the flat in Scotland, there is a gigantic horse's head he painted. There could have been a life for him in the making of such things. The pity of it is that such a life would never have been thought "appropriate" to his position. The title hung like a curtain across his path, forbidding him his different interests, giving him small chance to follow through. He was not able to refuse his inheritance, nor could he find a way to fulfill himself through what it offered. He saw that clearly, and he took his own way out.

When, less than three months afterwards, my sister Kate was drowned, far away on holiday in Africa, two deaths were pressed together, called a tragedy, as if some evil fortune were responsible for both. But Kate's death was an accident. The current pulled her down. James took the gun and turned it on himself.

Being Nice

"Put the gun away," my mother told me, and in the dream I did what I was told. But hadn't I heard something like that all my life? "Put the gun away, keep still, stop fighting. Please behave yourself!" We hadn't been brought up to fight and to defend ourselves. We had been brought up to deal with "nice" people who kept to certain rules, and to whom we in our turn would be "nice." Being nice meant manners ("please" and "thank you," "ladies first"), and an endless outpouring of hospitality. It meant interest (or the appearance of interest) on the part of the women, laughter and anecdotes on the part of the men. But it did not, perhaps could not, involve saying what you really thought. That, we were told firmly, was called tactlessness.

As a child I was often scolded for this so-called tactlessness. "Why does Roberta have linoleum on her floor when Mama has a carpet?" This was really a social question, "Why are some people richer than others?" But it was interpreted as personal criticism, and thus as an embarrassment. I was snubbed, and told to be quiet. The implication was that I would hurt Roberta's feelings.

It is obvious to me now that both niceness and betterness are maintained on a firm foundation of unasked questions. The pattern of exchange is laid down in childhood, and assiduously reinforced thereafter. People are kept separate from each other, even when they meet and talk and smile. There is small risk, small danger of intimacy. This is bad enough among the upper classes themselves. Across classes, its function becomes altogether more sinister.

Upper class betterness is built on centuries of other people's work. It is built on land and industry maintained by other people, income and profits got at their expense. Most of those involved are well aware of this, and the feelings (understandably) are strong. Guilt and fear and ignorance on the part of those in power, anger and resentment on the part of the workers, threaten to burst through at any minute. Under the circumstances, niceness is a very useful tool. It gives the upper classes some sort of camouflage to operate behind, at the same time as it aims to distract everyone else from what is actually going on. "Lord and Lady Bountiful are so generous, so polite..." If you continue to think along these lines, social privilege soon appears entirely natural.

Growing up as I did, such basic analysis was far beyond me. I did not see that niceness served a purpose. I only knew I did not like or trust it. I thought all nice people must be hypocrites. At the same time I blamed myself for not being able to be as nice as they were. There I was, filled to the brim with moods and jealousies, while they were always calm and self-contained. They might be fakes, I told myself, but I was evil.

This kind of logic left me muddled and unhappy, and blocked my thinking for a long time. Between Mama's composure and Papa's towering self-disgust there seemed no place of rest, no human ordinary.

As I grew older, I fought at least for intellectual clarity. James, I think, did very much the same. It was harder for him because he was a boy, pinned in place by title and inheritance. Intellectual clarity might be a blessing, but it came accompanied by other feelings: guilt, responsibility, the weight of his possessions, some sudden terror that he had *too much*, and that, in consequence, he should be punished. It makes sense to me that when that niceness failed him, the old self-loathing and the pain should both rush in. It makes sense too, given the family drama, that he should pick up a gun, and that, still trying somehow to "behave responsibly," he should have thought it right to shoot.

Behind the violence of that solution lies an extended argument about power. For all of us children, it was difficult to take power without assuming it, to claim it easily, as human beings, rather than asserting it as something due. Living in the States, I went through a long period of refusing power—at least as it might have reached me through the family. I took no money from them and I asked for no advice. I wanted to make my own way in the world.

From my family's point of view, this passionate independence wasn't taken very seriously. Because I was a girl, it hardly mattered how I chose to live. Friends of my parents might scold me for "being irresponsible," and "shirking my social duties," but no-one else seemed to care one way or another. If I wanted to dig gardens and paint houses, that was fine with them.

Looking back on it now, I'm proud and glad to have survived as well as I did. Independence gave me courage and some valuable self-respect, as well as new definitions for old words like "right" and "niceness" and "responsibility." Nonetheless, with all the opportunities that surrounded me, I could definitely have reached further, tried harder, and done more of what I wanted.

I didn't try because I was afraid. I was afraid of lots of things, from being recognized and "placed," according to my background, to taking charge in terms of practical things. But mainly I was afraid of doing too well. I associated success with hurting other people, with the betterness and niceness which had caused so much confusion. Then too, if I came into any sort of prominence, there was no doubt the family would get to hear of it. I saw the family as a long claw reaching out, only too ready to claim me as its own. And that, above everything, I wanted to avoid.

The Endless Conversation

After James died, my brother John, aged seventeen, became the new baronet. Most of the land went to an insurance company, on a sale-and-lease-back basis. Mama moved down the road, to what had been my uncle's house. My father's overdraft was finally paid off.

In the two years which have passed since then, I've done a lot of thinking about what happened, and, necessarily, about the way I was brought up. I used to think I could drop my background, and start again from the beginning, unhampered by old patterns and allegiances. I no longer believe that this can be done. What does seem possible is to name the patterns, claim the allegiances and, with a little luck and kindness, to move on.

When I first came back to Britain for my brother's funeral, I was bombarded with information about class. I doubt, now, that it would strike me quite so forcibly. But returning, easy and anonymous, from the United States, I saw it plain in everyone I met: class, class, and the nervous knowledge of their place on the social scale, where they belonged, or were thought to belong. Accent in particular assumed extraordinary importance. My own, university-educated, upper class, made me immediately acceptable in some circles, while in others it set me on a razor edge of disapproval. It was no longer just a "pretty English accent." It had a power and an identity of its own.

At first I didn't want to acknowledge this fact, even to myself. But then I saw how much we all avoided it. That was the reason for the nerves. Whichever way we turned, an unrelenting scrutiny was being carried out: *accent, occupation, dress-code, taste*: appraisal hovering like dust-motes in the air. "Where've you come from then?" The question wasn't often asked. Class was seen, apologized for, joked about. Very, very rarely was it ever faced head-on.

Because I'd lived and worked outside of Britain, I knew the system I grew up inside was not the only one. I knew that another way of doing things was possible, where social life was seen not in terms of "good/better/best," but of "different and equal," and people asked, "What are you thinking? How do you feel?" instead of requiring silently, "Be nice. Behave yourself." I had friends not just from other classes, but from entirely different cultures: Native American, Chicana, Jewish, Black. I'd heard their stories, begun to read their books.

Despite all this, I might still have kept to the old ways, out of lethargy and fear, if nothing else. But once James and Kate were dead, certain things became very plain to me. If I were going to stick around on this planet, then I wanted to live as richly and completely as I could. I wanted to make sense of things, to tell the truth of what I knew. Talking about class was part of that: an attempt to face the tangles, to draw the pain and awkwardness out into the open. If I was angry and dissatisfied with my family's version of things, surely I was not the only one. And if I wasn't, then perhaps my experiences would be of use to other people. That, in any case, was what I hoped, and what, of course, I've wanted to do here.

For the moment, childhood still hangs around me like a broken cloak, and at times I pull it close to me. I was brought up to be better, and when I am afraid, I run back to the cover of that betterness. Family and class position have come to have no social value in my world, so I replace them with whatever currency (or is it ammunition?) comes to hand. "I'm a cosmopolitan literary dyke. I'm a better dyke than thou." But even as I reach for this, I know what I am doing, and in the knowing, cease to take it seriously.

In the same way, I try to face my cowardice in daily things, legacy of a lifetime of being taken care of. When the roof starts to leak, or the milkbill must be paid, it is easy for me to let things slide. "Someone else will do it." I was twenty-three before I cleaned a bathroom for the first time, twenty-seven before I passed my driving test. Practical responsibilities still frighten me, and money is a part of this. Despite the Big House and the lavish trappings, my father never felt we had "enough." In reaction to this, I am satisfied with security on a very small scale. I have no sense of building for a future.

But even as I write these words, I know they're not quite true. I am building for a future, but it is not a future of bricks and mortar. I cleaned the gun out after James was dead. If the house burns down tonight, it's fine by me. What interests me now is something else, something odd and quirky and unpredictable. It has less to do with conservation than with conversation, of the kind which, at his best, I used to have with Papa.

"What is your story? How were things for you?" In the past few years I've come to ask this more and more. I want to know what it felt like growing up in the suburbs, in the country, or the inner-city. I want to know what it means to be French or Russian, Nigerian or Icelandic or Chinese. What is difficult about it? What is wonderful? In what ways are we different from each other? Where are we the same?

Sometimes, as I write, I see the ruins of an enormous tower. Long ago, in biblical times, it was the Tower of Babel. Now the grass is growing up around the stones, the birds are singing, and the sun and moon shine together out of a cloudless sky. In the courtyard, or what used to be the courtyard, since it too is overgrown with grass, hundreds and thousands of people are massed together. Each one is telling stories in his or her own language, but there are never any problems with translation.

We sit together, and we tell our stories. And in that conversation, everything gets said. It gets said slowly and carefully, and it gets said loudly and extravagantly. It is desperate and angry, it is calm and full of hope. Action is born of it, and fear goes out the window. Everybody talks at once, and everybody listens.

Christian McEwen 1983-85

Author's Note: I started this piece in July, 1983, and worked at it on and off for the next two-and-a-half years. Without the support of the Women's Voices Writing Workshop (Santa Cruz, 1984), the A.A. and Al-Anon Annual Conference (San Francisco, 1984), and the Owning Class Group of the Re-evaluation Co-Counselling Community (London, 1984-85), it would never have been finished. I would also like to thank the following people for their good sense and encouragement: Gloria Anzaldúa, Beth Brant, Chris Edgar, Sharon Franklet, Adam Ganz, Janice Gould, Simon Korner,

Andrea Freud Loewenstein, Ricky Sherover-Marcuse, Maria Margaronis, Samantha McEwen, Nina Crow Newington, Ruthie Petrie, Leonie Rushforth, Elizabeth Tallent, Janey Winter, Anne Witten and Lisa Vice.

It is dedicated to my father, who shared with me so many complications, and it is dedicated to all of the above.

FOOTNOTES

[1] In a country where the top ten percent of the people own more than sixty percent of the wealth, and where that first percentage is still dropping, leaving the rich increasingly rich, and the poor poorer, there is good reason for this. See *The State of the Nation* by Stephen Fothergill and Jill Vincent, for some informative statistics. (Pan Books, 1985).

[2] One notable exception is Ronald Fraser's *In Search of A Past* (Verso, 1984). See also Susanna J. Sturgis' "Class/Act: Beginning a Translation from Privilege" in *Out the Other Side*, edited by Christian McEwen and Sue O'Sullivan (Crossing Press, 1989).

[3] *Barrister*: A student of law, who, having been called to the bar, has the privilege of practising as an advocate in the superior courts of law. The formal title is barrister-at-law; the equivalent designation in Scotland is *advocate*. (*Oxford English Dictionary*); hereafter, *O.E.D.*

[4] Conservative M.P. for Berwick and Haddington, Parliamentary Under Secretary of State for Scotland (1939-40) and Lord Commissioner of the Treasury (1942-44). He was made a baronet in 1953.

[5] *Baronet*: A titled order, the lowest that is hereditary, ranking next in line to baron, having precedence of all orders of knighthood, except that of the garter. A baronet is a commoner, the principle of the order being "to give rank, precedence and title without privilege." (*O.E.D.*)

[6] *First*: the best possible degree.

[7] James Laver: author of more than a hundred books, among them *Nostradamus*, *The Age of Optimism* and *A Concise History of Costume*.

[8] Veronica Turleigh: who worked with such "names" as Paul Schofield, Laurence Olivier and Alec Guinness, for example as Gertrude to Guinness' Hamlet in Guthrie's modern dress production in 1938.

[9] *A' Level*: examination at end of school course demanding an advanced knowledge of a school subject. (*O.E.D.*) Cf. *O' Level*: examination at end of school course requiring ordinary, i.e., less than A' level, knowledge of a school subject. (*O.E.D.*)

[10] *The Rhythm Method*: a natural method of birth control, based on the use of information from past cycles, in combination with observed data (changes in amount and quantity of vaginal discharge and in body temperature).

[11] See *Alcoholism, a Merry-Go-Round Named Denial* by Reverend Joseph L. Kellerhan (© Al-Anon Family Group Headquarters, Inc. 1969), and innumerable other books.

[12] *Factor*: one who has charge of and manages all the affairs of an estate: a bailiff, a land steward. (*O.E.D.*)

[13]*Overdraft*: overdrawing of bank account, amount by which sums drawn exceed credit balance. (*O.E.D.*) Thus, loosely, bank loans.

[14]Terence Stamp: film actor. See, for example, *Billy Budd, The Collector, Far From the Madding Crowd, Meetings With Remarkable Men, The Hit.*

[15]Jean Shrimpton: fashion model.

[16]Jim Dine: American painter.

[17]*Saloon*: this was a kind of hall or second drawing-room at the center of the house; the word is presumably a corruption of "salon."

[18]Gavin Maxwell: author and naturalist, some of whose books my father illustrated. See *Ring of Bright Water, Raven Seek Thy Brother.*

[19]*Sheriff*: the office is now mainly honorary, the specific duties attached to it varying in different towns.

[20]I should say here that Papa had an extraordinarily comparative and hierarchical turn of mind. He was almost unable to praise something in its own terms. "You're very good—but you're not as good as Mozart," he told Jonathan Miller (doctor, stage-director, writer and editor), a remark which astonished Jonathan. He had never supposed he was.

[21]My uncle Jamie died on the 2nd July 1972.

[22]Marks and Spencers is a British department store, roughly equivalent to Macy's.

[23]*Guddle*: to catch fish with the hands, by groping under the stones or banks of a stream. (*O.E.D.*)

[24]What the British call a public school is in American terms exactly the opposite. Eton College, for example, a well-known English public school, is very obviously the equivalent of an American private school.

[25]See endnote 9.

[26]Christie's: a well-known London auction house.

Whenever I Tell You the Language We Use is a Class Issue, You Nod Your Head in Agreement— and Then You Open Your Mouth

Elliott

1. I Never Have Understood Why You Think It's Ok…

Redneck: n. *slang* 1. A member of the white rural laboring class, esp. in the Southern United States.

My father is a redneck, Scottish/Irish by descent, his skin as naturally pale as my own, the back of his neck, between the yellow hard hat and the light blue Big Mac workshirt, is always red, burned through so many Midwestern summers that it barely fades in winter.

My mother is not a redneck, much to my father's family's horror. From a small Portuguese immigrant community in central Illinois, hers is the first generation born entirely in the u. s. Her skin—already suspiciously dark for a real white womon—grows only darker in the sun.

I was born to be redneck—white, rural, working poor.[1] If not for my asthma, my Dyke-hood, my first womonlove who carefully taught me what she called culture and what I now call passing, self-hate, and assimilation, I'd be a redneck now. Instead I've moved from rural working poor to urban working poor; my neck isn't red, and because of this I often pass, especially when I keep my swearing, my snide outsider's humor and my colorful birth language hidden. And even when I'm not passing, most of the wimmin around me are entirely too polite to call me a redneck, at least to my face.

But while my neck isn't red, my eyes often are, from working in front of computer screens under fluorescent lights. Sometimes I wonder if you'd get it if I called myself that—Redeye—or we called ourselves Soreback or Brownlunged or Pesticide-poisoned. Usually I think you wouldn't; we'd still be a "them" and you still wouldn't try to understand us. I can imagine this conversation:

Middle Class, White, Good-Hearted Liberal (or even Radical) Feminist:
  What are we going to do about the women in the pink collar ghetto?
  Those offices are poisoning them, and they're being exploited!

Another of the Same: Why would you worry about them? *They* wouldn't support *you* anyway. Why bother? They're just a bunch of redeyes!

I have a couple questions for you middle and upper class wimmin, especially white wimmin. Do all of you who use *redneck* know that it was invented by the white Southern ruling class? I hope you don't, or my next question will be much harder—why do you think it's ok to identify with that class by using this word as a put-down, often as the ultimate insult?

> 2. "But, but,…(stammer, stammer) I didn't mean to *offend* you! I was just using *redneck* to mean…" or: (whispered) "Did you hear that?! She just admitted that she's a redneck!"

> *Redneck* n. 2. *Offensive Slang* A person who advocates a provincial, conservative, often bigoted sociopolitical attitude considered characteristic of a redneck.

When I was young I often spent weekends at my mother's parents' house. There, on Saturday nights, we'd go to Spatz's, where they made their own ice cream fresh every day. There's a family story about the place—I remember hearing it over and over when I was little, always told by my mom in a proud voice. The story happened in central Illinois in the mid '50s, when civil rights court cases were challenging segregation and in response some businesses were integrating and others were prohibiting Blacks explicitly for the first time.

Yet, as clear as the setting is in my memory, I can't for the life of me remember how the story goes past this. I have two versions of it in my memory and no way to know which is real. The first version goes like this: Spatz's, which had always served Blacks, if less than politely, was ordered to stop doing so by a reactionary town council law. They cunningly got around this attempt to control their business, however, through some trick like having Black customers tell what they wanted to white customers who would then say it to the server, take it from the server, and pass it on. The second version is basically just the opposite: Spatz's, which had never served Blacks, was ordered to do so by the town council. They cunningly got around this attempt to control their business, however, through some trick like only serving people the wait staff would claim to know.

When I think of the story now I would really like to believe the first version—it would make writing this so simple. I could then record it and say, "Look, your stereotypes about rednecks are wrong and here's why." The truth of course is so much more complicated.

Ya see, the pride in my mom's voice, the laughter of whoever was hearing the story, wasn't about defeating or upholding racism. Not that she didn't enjoy perpetuating hate with the openness learned from being herself very poor and not quite white enough—no middle class polite pretensions in her speech. But for her, for my people, the point of the story was that the little family-owned business managed to screw the rich guys using only their wit; no money, no lawyers, no laws, things Spatz's had no reason to trust anyway. The story's lesson is that the system is the enemy, and our heroes were individuals who screwed the system: Spatz's, the workers at the union-busting plant who threw glass into the salad dressing and shut the lines down for weeks, the farmers who took weapons to auctions for foreclosed farms so no one would outbid the family that rightfully owned the place, the womon who found a way to stick it to her cheatin[2] or violent husband.

I learned this lesson, and it's kept me safe many times. My middle and upper class friends constantly surprise me with how they had to *learn* that the system was fucked and with how often they forget this. I'm not surprised that I went from first reading feminist ideas to being a radical feminist/Separatist within a few months; when I first read *Gyn/Ecology* I was appalled but not surprised. I already knew what the medical system had done to my family, and once I got that the individual cheating and violent husbands were actually their own system, I was on my way.

I have this theory, although I can't prove it, that at the beginning of this wave of Women's Liberation it was working class wimmin and working class dykes who insisted that feminist power structures *had* to be different, and that they knew this not so much from a belief in inherently nurturing wimmin and inherently violent men as from deep and clear personal experience with the u. s. caste systems of class and race. Once the middle class white women took over, this knowledge was thrown out, and so, eventually, was the commitment to new ways of organizing. The result is disasters like having Take Back the Night marches run by city governments or the 1990 National Women's Studies Association Conference.[3]

Whether it's true historically or not, I'm now constantly surrounded by middle and upper class feminists who can't or won't understand the lies of their privilege. For their inability or unwillingness to change they often have a long justification which boils down to: "These kinds of systems of power have been abusive because men have been using them but with us wimmin it will be different."[4] I encounter this in all my communities, the magical "us" which is meant to hide class just as surely as it is meant to hide race.

Not that all of us white gals who are rednecks, white trash, working stiffs, factory or office girls have nearly all the answers, either. My heritage was to hate all outsiders—and, as part of that, to fear them. My job now is to take that apart, to interrupt and unlearn the racism and anti-Semitism and to pull from the overpowering hate of the system both knowledge and rage so that I can act as well as feel. And to change the most dangerous lie of my class, that we fight only as individuals and only for ourselves. Marxist and Socialist intellectuals call the breaking of this isolation "class consciousness"—I call it taking my values of sticking up for and sticking by Family and using them for the complex group of communities that sustain me and that I in turn sustain. Without feminist and dyke communities I'd be up shit creek without a paddle—but without us working class girls' outsiders' knowledge[5] and our commitment to staying with our people even when we're fighting, these same communities would be heading for the falls without a paddle either.[6]

3. I *Hate* "Nice"!

Redneck n. as used by most of the wimmin around me. 1. Any person who is racist, violent, uneducated and stupid (as if they are the same thing), womon-hating, gay-bashing, x-tian fundy, etc. 2. Used as a synonym for every type of oppressive belief except classism.[7]

A while back a lover and I were catching a ride to the peace camp with a lesbian couple, in the back of the new mini-van they had purchased just for their summer traveling, and we were talking about working with/ for battered women. One of the lesbians—Muffy, we called her—talked about where she lived in Key West and how blatant the womon-hating was there. Just as I was thinking, "oh, yeah, the privileged on vacation!" Muffy added, "Not that that's surprising, because they're all a bunch of truck-driving rednecks." I instantly wanted to scream (well, actually I wanted to use an icy, cold, calm distancing devastating tone, but knew I'd scream if I opened my mouth at all), "Oh yes, I know exactly what you mean. And how very lucky for Hedda and Lisa that Joel Steinberg was a lawyer and not a truck driver."

But right then I said nothing, because I didn't think Muffy or her lover would get it and because my upper-middle class lover gave me one of her "oh god" looks which I knew meant she recognized that I was upset but didn't understand it as important enough to make a point of. Looking back, I suspect Muffy's lover was passing just as much as I was, but we made no eye contact, no dangerous alliance, and so both sat thoroughly silenced by the combination of intimacy and privilege. Of course, these types of privileged, arrogant, world-owning statements made by lesbians and feminists I'm not close to can silence me as well; this particularly frustrates me among my political "peers," where often the people I disagree with most are the one I'm least able to challenge.[8]

I could go on for pages about such stupid comments and the snide-assed responses I made or wish I had, since I'm surrounded by you who know nothing about my life but constantly reduce it to stereotypes you don't even understand. One example, the thing that has made me most angry this week, is when wimmin who don't even know who Tammy Wynette *is* spit out sentences with these key phrases "…country-western music…stand by your man…redneck." Let me say this now, before I meet you outside of this room and feel like screaming at you. Country music is not simplistic, and it is not a joke. There are plenty of "that broad is mine" songs and "give everything to your man" songs (which are, I'm sure, much more dangerous to wimmin than the way opera, theatre and musicals romanticize rape and battering); there are also wimmin's love songs to their mothers, grandmothers, sisters and daughters which celebrate and teach strength, resistance, self-love and, of course, how to screw the system.[9]

And I could go on and on, selling[10] you country music by downplaying its weaknesses and bragging on its strengths. But my music, even the whole of my culture, isn't the point of this essay. The point is that I shouldn't have this feeling of trying to justify myself, to prove the value of my world. All of you should already get the ties between privilege, ignorance, and stereotypes. Instead, I encounter stuff like my recent informal survey results: every single womon I talked to who claimed that she absolutely hated all country music was middle or upper class. What these wimmin knew about country music could be reduced to the litany of "…stand by your man…redneck…" Surely you all know by now that your class training taught you lies about all people, including us poor white girls. I know that you learned we are dirty and stupid and bigots and sluts and so on. I would like to trust that you know these images are not related at all to our truths about our lives. In fact, I often feel stupid, writing and saying these things, for surely all of you advanced, radical feminists understand the means and ends of the socialization process. But then I hold a conversation with one of you and realize that no matter what anti-classist statements your mouth might utter I can't trust that your brain or critical sensibilities are attached to it.[11] Don't you yet get that you don't know us working class wimmin in all of our many differences, from you and from each other, and that your lack of knowledge is about privilege? And don't you yet get that every time you use a word like *redneck* or *white trash* or *hick* or *midwestern* or *southern* as insulting adjectives you push yourselves further from us, put a barrier between us, make our dreams of lesbian and feminist communities a bit more impossible?

I've stopped working on this and tossed it aside four or five times now. I can't quite convince myself that these things are worth saying, that anyone, even another working class dyke, is going to listen to me defend the word *redneck*.[12] You-all are *so* sure that the word is a synonym for all you claim to hate most (in yourselves?) that I know damn well some of you won't even be able to process what I'm saying and let me tell you, this conviction of yours scares me, cause the way you say stuff makes me believe that your plan for getting rid of lesbian-bashing and womon-hating and racism is to get rid of my kind of people—as if eliminating rednecks would stop, let's say, the rich white men who set Nestlés' third world policy. Now I know you well enough to know that right now your little mind is going, "but that is not what I meant." It is, however, what you say, and where I come from we mean what we say to each other. I wanna rant for about twenty more pages, building my anger and my examples until I fully believe myself and you get this in your gut and not just your theory center. Of course, I know that the way to be taken most seriously by most of my contemporaries is to have long, cool philosophical arguments for my position, and I've done that, but I refuse to pass here; for a change, I want to be taken seriously on my own terms, cussing, metaphors, and original grammatic constructions and all.

A fuller list of these terms would be a whole nother paper. But here's a few so ya get the general idea. First off, if you want to give examples of cultural sexism or some such, use your own damn culture, not mine or anyone else's; the last thing any wimmin need is to have outsiders telling each other about what our lives mean. And don't ever interrupt what I'm saying to correct my pronunciation. That's so fucking condescending and besides, with the linguistic ties between "hillbilly dialects" and early modern english, the way I say it is older, not wrong. Stop blabbing on and on about stuff you don't know, especially when you're around me and what you're mouthing is socialist intellectual theory about *the* urban working class. And any time you think that a working class womon is being rude or impolite, examine what you "know" about manners. Maybe you haven't yet considered that what you learned about manners making social interactions smoother or easier is a crock of bull. Manners are just the way you learned to identify each other and to brand outsiders. If, through your social skills and politeness, you have the ability to make any of us feel comfortable, realize that we know you also have the skills and tools to make us feel *uncomfortable* and that we've seen you use them in this way even if you don't think you ever have. As part of this, just stop being nice or worrying about being nice. I hate nice. I especially hate being silenced by all those nice ways you have of shutting out everything you can't or don't want to recognize. We don't need any more nice, any more social rules. We need theories and communities that are serious about understanding and meeting the needs of lesbians and all wimmin.

I don't think that meeting needs instead of throwing tea socials is a new idea. But as I sit here, wearing used clothes and typing on a used typewriter, I know that my world isn't about new; it's about available, useful, comfortable, and long-lasting. And that's exactly how this redneck dyke wants her families and communities and the theories growing from them— available, useful, comfortable, and long-lasting.

FOOTNOTES

[1] Because my mom was so desperate to pass, and to escape her violent childhood, she raised my brother, my sister and me apart from her own family as much as possible; I grew up with a sense of myself clearly within my redneck relatives.

[2] If you notice, there is neither a "g" nor an apostrophe here. The "g" is absent because this is the way I talk, sometimes dropping final consonants, especially when I'm talkin most like myself and least like the middle-class people I usta model myself after. The apostrophe is absent because it implies that something is missing; it's a grammatical mark used to show dialect or deviance from "standard" english, and although, much to my delight, many things about me *are* deviant, my language is not one of them. I don't know why the middle class white academics around me think that spoken French, which drops many of its written letters, is elegant while looking at me in horror, or treating me as less intelligent, when I drop sounds unnecessary to meaning. If you don't believe me, try holding a conversation with Professionals or Academics while dropping final letters (oh, and swearing a bit, too). You'll soon find them interrupting and ignoring you. Great fun.

Julia Penelope pointed out to me that, in research done on pronunciation of *-ing* among children, girls strive to pronounce a /g/ while boys don't. She has theorized that the looks of horror I (and she) receive are connected to dyke-hating because our talk, to trained, professional, feminine women, sounds "mannish." I think these women are appalled by every way I choose not to pass: my body size, my hair length, the way I talk and what I have to say. Still, class is vital, as I've learned while talking to fat, short-haired, radical, but middle class wimmin.

[3] In Milwaukee, WI, a city office runs the march which is now basically a Sunday afternoon tea protesting violence against people. And my favorite story from the 1990 National Women's Studies Association Conference fiasco, via Lee Evans, is how, during one of the meetings about whether or not their constitution allowed them to have meetings, one Black womon stood up and said that we needed to toss the rules since they obviously weren't working and was silenced by being told she was out of order.

[4] My favorite current example of this is Sonia Johnson, who charges wimmin a lot of money to tell how she got out of the mormon church and how she now wants to set up a feminist community organized around an identical hierarchy.

[5] So, you think it's an accident that some of our best thinking and writing about therapism, the diseasing of our communities, consumerism and such is by working class dykes?

[6]And to take this metaphor a bit further—I've gotten used to wading through shit. What are *you* going to do?

[7]Which I would think all the Mary Daly fans who go on and on about reversals would have noticed and understood before this.

[8]Yet.

[9]When I first wrote this piece, the 2-step craze hadn't yet hit my midwestern dyke communities. Now it is everywhere, and although I am delighted and comforted to hear these familiar words and rhythms at lesbian events, I'm also often appalled and angry to experience the culture I struggle to accept and reject reduced to the newest fad. How long will this last, before wimmin have consumed all they can and go back to "African" drumming or "Native" spirituality or on to something new? Every time a womon yells, "Yee Haw" with a fake Southern accent I want to spit.

[10]As I write this word, I realized that my need to fall into the language of business told me a lot about how I interact with middle, upper-middle and upper class wimmin.

[11]Maybe that's why you have what I regard as the social impairment of not being able to talk and listen at the same time, because your class training never encouraged you, as women, to connect your brain and mouth.

[12]Which is where my culture of resistance comes in handy, cause I just start singing "Coat of Many Colors" or "The Ballad of Hee Haw" or "Take This Job and Shove It'" and then I'm ready for the next round.

Getting Class

Susan J. Wolfe

Forty-seven years old, and only now am I beginning to understand about class.

I'm a college professor in South Dakota. South Dakota has the lowest teacher salaries in the United States, and pays its professors even worse. Still, with my base salary and no children to support, I'm now easily, comfortably middle-class.

A colleague once told me I was *hopelessly* middle-class. She was speaking of values, I suppose. I answered that in the neighborhood where I grew up, being hopelessly middle-class was a goal a lot of people aspired to.

That reply suggests I understood a good deal more about class than I did. At that time, about ten or so years ago, I understood only that I'd been fortunate enough to go to college, to get a job at a university. I saw myself as someone who'd *once* been working-class.

My father was a postal worker. When I was a baby, he had worked for Railway Mail, slinging sacks of mail; later, when Railway Mail was shut down, he sorted mail at the Long Island Terminal in New York. He always worked overtime around Christmas holidays—lots of it, both because there was plenty of mail, and because it was expected of him because he was Jewish. And then, too, we needed the money. For a while, my parents bought beef roasts, corned beef, and pastrami; my mother cooked the meat, and they both made it into sandwiches which he'd sell at work. Like the overtime, the sandwiches brought in extra money.

Then, when I was twelve, my mother went back to work, as a clerk-typist at first, because she hadn't worked outside the home since my birth. The pay wasn't very good, especially when commuting and clothing costs were figured in. I guess that's why she didn't hire a baby-sitter for my brother. Instead, when I got home from school, I was responsible for my kid brother, Larry, five years younger. Until I got home, a neighbor watched him from her walk-out apartment. (She could see him play in the streets from there. Nowadays I guess they'd say he was practically a latch-key child.)

As a kid, I never associated any of this with being working-class. I knew some people had more money to spend than we did, and some had less.

At twelve, I started to attend Hunter Junior High School. One of my classmates, whose father owned a pharmacy in midtown Manhattan, invited me to lunch. They had an apartment on Central Park West. Her mother, on her way out the door, said she hoped I didn't mind if lunch was just "finger food." I didn't know what "finger food" was. It turned out to be hamburgers, carrot curls, and French fries, served by their maid. ("Not a live-in maid," I was told; she was only there to "help out" during the day.)

My neighbors, by contrast, included a cop and his family, one of whose five kids ate supper with us one night. When served some lamb, he asked what it was. "Haven't you ever eaten lamb before?" my mother asked. "No," he said. It turned out Billy had never, to his recollection, eaten meat; we later found that when his mother cooked a small chicken, her husband got the meat, she got a wing, and the kids made do with the gravy on some potatoes.

I slept in a crib until I was five. We lived in a three-room apartment, and, rather than put me in the living room, my parents kept the crib set up in their bedroom. After my brother was born, we got a four-room apartment on the top floor (fifth floor) of the adjoining building, and I had my own bedroom for a while. Some families had several children sharing a room, or two sharing a bed, so I didn't feel bad about sleeping in a crib, but I do remember falling out of bed a few times because I couldn't get used to the lack of siderails.

But the discrepancy between the way my classmate Jane, the pharmacist's daughter, lived, and the way my neighbors' kids lived, was not about *class*. It was about specific people, living under specific conditions. I didn't "get it."

I only started to read about class when I got to college, and I can honestly say that I still didn't get it. We read Paul Goodman's *Growing Up Absurd* (New York: Random House, 1962) in one of my Freshman courses. I didn't quite understand about men with careers *having* to move; my parents had moved from our old neighborhood when our comparative affluence allowed them to—to a garden apartment in Queens, but all the move meant to me (at fourteen) was changing high schools so that I wouldn't have a "two-fare commute" to Hunter High School in midtown Manhattan, and, because my mother *did* have a two-fare commute, would spend more time watching my brother after school.

My parents worried about the gangs in the old neighborhood. I don't know if they'd gotten worse (more visible) as I was growing up. I knew there were "zip guns," made from car antennas, because I'd seen cars missing antennas, and once ours was swiped. I knew that some teenaged boys had switchblades. But I was used to the streets. I'd had my first fistfight at eight, and continued to have them, mostly from having to defend my brother against larger boys. I remember my mother pointing out one of her friend's daughters, who'd been expelled from high school for punching the Vice Principal.

I have a sense my parents only began to worry about gangs after there was money to move away from them. But maybe they were worried my brother would join one.

Whatever my parents thought of the old neighborhood, my brother and I had fun there. There was plenty to do in the city, and what there was didn't cost much. There were two parks on Amsterdam Avenue, within walking distance; everyone called them "the grass park" and "the swing park." At the swing park, you could take out basketballs and wait for your turn to play knock hockey. The littler kids could go in the cement-bottomed wading pool. I remember, when I was about ten or eleven, walking down to the grass park by myself and looking over the four-foot stone wall at the water (the Harlem River), which I loved to watch. When I was in junior high school, I'd take my father's old Army blanket up to the roof sometimes, and lie on my stomach, reading. "Tar beach," we called it.

On the top floor of a brick building in uptown Manhattan, though, summers could sometimes be brutal. The wiring in the building wouldn't tolerate plugging in an air conditioner, even if you could afford one; sometimes we all sat around with damp washcloths on our foreheads. If a Saturday was particularly hot, my mother would sometimes give me seventy-five cents to go to the movies, fifty cents for me and a quarter for my brother. We'd walk the eight blocks to the Empress, a theatre which showed a triple feature plus cartoons. (The Empress had cockroaches, but it was air-conditioned.)

We played in the streets with rubber balls. "Hit the stick" required only a ball, a used popsicle stick (which you could find on the sidewalk), and sidewalk squares. The stick was placed on the crack between two squares, and the two players stood on the end of one square, facing each other. Bouncing the ball and hitting the stick on the first bounce gave you a point. "Points" was played by throwing the ball at the ledge of a brick wall, hitting the ledge, and catching the ball on the fly. A ledge sloping toward you, one at a height of about five feet, was ideal. If you missed the ledge, you had to catch the ball on one bounce or you were out.

But one of my favorite things to do with my brother was to take him on the subway. My fare was fifteen cents; my brother traveled free. Because he was under age, he could legally duck under the turnstile, and get a kick out of doing that before we even got on the train. We'd go on a Sunday and ride North, up to Van Cortlandt Park. By going down the stairs and crossing to the other side of the station, we could ride back and forth on the same fifteen-cent token.

On Sunday, the empty trains became our private playground. We'd run through them, swaying back and forth with the motion, swinging around the posts. My brother, always agile, would grab the metal rings, and walk up the side of the cars; once he turned through his own hands and flipped over, like an Olympic competitor. We'd straddle two cars and watch the tracks move beneath us. To this day, I still love the smell of the subways.

My father died this past March (1993). My brother flew in from Hawaii, and I from South Dakota, to Tamarac, Florida, to the condo my father had shared with my stepmother.

My mother (who died in 1983) and father had been able to move down to Florida in 1977. They had a few thousand dollars, left to her after her father died, and used it to put a down payment on a condo, the first real estate they'd ever owned. Four years ago, when he married my step-mother Raye, she'd owned another condo. When they married, they sold both and bought an upscale condo, with waterfalls marking the entrance, a guard at the gate—well, you get the general idea. Raye made him throw out most of his clothes because "they were polyester" and "no one wears white suits...a white jacket with different-colored slacks, or white slacks with a summer sports jacket...but not white suits."

They'd spent more money redecorating the condo than I'd spent buying my first post-divorce house, spent nearly as much redecorating, in fact, as my mother and father had spent on their condo.

My father had said that "a different class of people" lived in the new condo. At the time, though I may have understood vaguely that he meant these people had more money to spend, I consciously associated the phrase with behavior. "Classy" people had held jobs that impressed my father; they had owned their own car dealerships or contracting firms, or had been professionals or skilled laborers, or, if they worked for the police force, had been detectives, not beat cops. They drove newer cars, wore the right clothes for every occasion.

So I guess our old neighbors in Manhattan weren't working-class poor; they just had "poor form."

During the last few months of his life, when my father came gradually to understand that he was dying, he often told me what "a shame" it was "to go" when he had "this kind of life." He would gesture at the furniture in the condo, at the view outside his window, and refer to the trips he and Raye could still have taken together. (As a retiree from an airline company, she and my father qualified for travel discounts on airline tickets, cruises, hotels, and tours.) Raye echoed these sentiments.

They both seemed to think it would be okay for him to die in poverty, but that he should go on living because, with these material things, life was worth living. At my father's funeral, their friends and neighbors said much the same thing. But unlike my father, they didn't have to repudiate 75% of the lives they'd led to say it.

My brother and I were glad to see each other, and visibly enjoying each other's presence, at the funeral reception. Eventually, someone had asked how often we got to see each other "because you seem so close." I remarked that we hadn't seen much of each other in the past twenty years except on sad occasions, which made me remember how much fun we'd had together as kids. So I told them we'd had fun, and then reminisced a bit about the things we used to do. I don't remember everything I told them, but the highlight of my account was our subway adventures, and, suddenly caught up in nostalgia, I guess I forgot to pay attention to my audience.

When I stopped, I realized the room was completely, awkwardly silent, and the guests were staring at me. No one said anything for a while, and then someone finally said, "Well, you really seem to enjoy each other. That's nice." I stood for a moment, shocked by the realization that I'd *embarrassed* these people. They were sorry for me for having had to play on subway trains, or perhaps surprised that the children of one of their friends did such things, or something. *But they had not heard my story.*

I was talking about what I *did* as a kid, fondly. What they heard was, "Oh, poor *kid!* What a childhood you had!" I was sharing. What I got for my efforts was pity.

Now, I had known, in an offhand kind of way, that my family's lack of money during childhood had affected me. The effects became obvious last year, when my lover Cathy and I decided to remodel our kitchen. The money involved seemed to me like too much to spend, even if we could make the payments. To Cathy, who'd been raised upper-middle-class, spending money was simply something you did; I was frightened of payment books, nervous about writing checks for large amounts, guilty over spending so much on myself when others had less.

What I used to do with my discretionary money was give most of it away. I overtipped, bought people presents too expensive for the occasion, bought tickets to departmental parties for all the graduate students, gave hundreds of dollars at a time to friends and strangers I thought needed it. I could buy Cathy $300 boots, but hesitated over buying myself a pair of fifty-dollar shoes, knowing a similar pair might be on sale at the end of the season.

And I feel guilty even bringing any of this up. I keep thinking, "You're talking about dropping hundreds on presents when other people are living in the streets, starving." (And I don't just mean "politically incorrect"; I mean guilty.)

It took my brother to remind me that my parents were always hovering over payment books, making notes on pads to see if they could make the next payment, to see when they could replace whatever they were paying off. He had to remind me that my mother used to sneak past the grocer's with bags from the A & P, when we still owed the grocer money we couldn't afford to pay yet. He had to remind me that our parents fought over money.

Evidently, I'd suppressed memories of my parents fighting. Odd, given that I remembered being hit or yelled at (that is, physically and verbally abused), but not the fights my parents had. When he reminded me, I realized the battles my parents had had over money must've been more painful to me. ("Don't you remember him packing his suitcase, slamming the door behind him, and staying out all night?" he asked. I hadn't; in fact, to this day I don't really recall my father's staying out all night, after what my brother calls "a money fight.")

Until this year, I never subjected my adult reactions to any sort of class analysis. I wrote of coming out as a Lesbian in a small Midwestern university town, of being Jewish, but I did not write about my working-class origins. As I said, I didn't feel oppressed about "having been" working-class...I felt fortunate to have "gotten as far as I did." Along the way, I may have had brief flashes of awareness—the job interview at a state university in New York, when the department chair said, "Our students here are quite good. Many are first-generation college, of course, but nonetheless, quite good." And I caught myself thinking, in a most un-classy way, "I'm first-generation college, you asshole!"

Now, I'm really starting to understand, at a gut level, where a lot of my conflicts, both internal and external, come from. Sometimes, when I have to give a speech at a conference, or a presentation to a university committee or administrator, I feel like a fraud...as if someone will finally notice I really don't belong here, as if, after years of concealing my worthlessness from everyone, I'll be found out, exposed. And, in my case at least, this "lack of self-esteem" seems to stem not from my identity as a woman, or a Jew, or a Lesbian, but from my occupying a middle-class position I don't feel entitled to.

This summer, I team-taught an institute for primary and secondary teachers. We were reading stories written by Black authors, Chicano authors, Asian-American authors, American Indian authors. Many stories seemed oddly familiar, despite my whiteness. One day, in the middle of class, I suddenly realized that I was able to identify with many stories because they were set in urban poverty, and realized, too, that my inability to identify with characters in my elementary-school readers was due to their setting—middle-class suburbia—where Dad wore a suit and carried a briefcase to work, and Mom stayed home cooking, in a house with a grassed, fenced-in yard.

I'm beginning to sense that class may have been the central, driving force shaping my thinking, my feelings, my relationships. In fact, the influence of class has been at once so pervasive, and so woven into my sensibilities and reactions, that I've never been able to isolate or analyze it before.

At last, I think I'm finally starting to "get" class.

Jamie Lee Evans

What It Means to be the Daughter of My Mother

Jamie Lee Evans

What does it mean to be the daughter of my mother? I who am a woman graduated from the ivory towers of the University of California; a mixed-blood Asian/white claiming my identity as a woman of color; a woman who loves women in the deepest ways, sexual and otherwise, a lesbian; a woman who grew up in the 'hood, and who hates to step a foot into K-Mart, likes shopping at Nordstrom; an owner of a computer, a cd player, a mountain bike, a car, an answering machine; an executive director of a nonprofit organization that raises money for battered women shelters and rape crisis centers; a woman who is shaken from sleep from nightmares of being betrayed, rejected, murdered; a woman still reeling from all the beatings she watched her mother endure, who can remember the exact pattern of her mother's blood painted on the stairs she walked up and down for eight years; a woman who organizes and helps teach women's self-defense to as many women as possible; a woman who puts her life on the line to speak out against racism, sexism and gets it from all angles because of it.

What **does** it mean to be the daughter of my mother? She, who didn't finish high school; she who is a Welsh, Irish, and Native Alaskan woman; whose father was an alcoholic; a woman with varicose veins from all the standing and walking she's done since adolescence as a waitress, bartender, dish washer, deli sandwich-maker; a white woman who still says nigger, chink and wetback; a woman who used to call her daughter "HopSing"; a woman once battered to the point of broken bones: cracked skull, broken jaw, cracked ribs, broken arm, bruised legs, blackened eyes, etc.; a woman who still depends on acceptance/approval from men, who believes that heterosexuality is natural and feels sorry for a daughter who finds warm tenderness in a woman's arms; a woman who raised her children drunk the entire time, spent hours in welfare lines; a woman who gave up her children and then fought again to get them out of a foster home where they were beaten, raped and subjected to ritual abuse from a satanic cult; a woman who now wanders the streets of Oklahoma, homeless, last seen sleeping in her car, drinking herself numb; a woman whose previous batterer sleeps soundly in Nevada with a home and a new wife and no responsibilities to his son and stepdaughter, no remorse or guilt. A woman who hates herself so much she lashes out at the woman who is her child and who tries to help; my mother, the woman who called Anita Hill a nigger, who laughs when I tell her how unforgivable that is; a woman who has felt nothing but agony in twenty years, who waits for her prince charming to save her from the pain, the desperation, the insanity that is women's reality. The woman who gave me life.

Mother, what does it mean to be the daughter of you? I watched you move back and forth between righteously providing for the two children you bore and then giving them up, leaving them for days, weeks at a babysitter's. Mother, what was it like to leave your children behind, knowing that the neighbors called the police, the police called the social workers and the social workers came and took us away? What did you feel when you came to visit us on the weekends, and I would hide from you at first and then cry in the car and beg you not to make me go back to that place called a (foster) home.

I remember your body on the cold pavement, 1970. I was three, and the people all came out to see what had happened to the woman who was lying unconscious in the middle of the street. I remember that you left the apartment and ran after my stepfather, screaming to him that he had to give you some money to buy milk for the babies, and he pushed you away and got into his truck. You decided to hold onto the side while screaming, pleading for milk money for your children and he backed up and you held on and he drove fast, first gear; I heard the engine revving, second gear. I could hear you screaming, third gear and then, directly in front of our apartment building, he slammed on the brakes and you slammed to the ground. I remember being three and looking down onto Vermont Avenue through the kitchen window. My mother, you, were lying there. I remember knowing what it was like to be brave when I saw them put a sheet over your head. The air was an unnatural still. I'm glad I wasn't old enough then to know that they usually only cover a person's head when they are dead. I remember telling the air and no one that that was my mommy. I was too young to get down the two flights of stairs to you. I waited for them to come and take us away.

If we hadn't been dirt-poor then they wouldn't have come and taken us away. Some nanny or something would have cared for us. Some friend of the family would have hired someone to baby-sit for us while you were healing in the hospital. Instead, the state came and took us to a foster home and there we stayed for months. This was our first foster home. Only the first.

I didn't see you for months, I didn't know what was happening. My brother, Tommy, was just a baby and they would let him cry and cry and cry and no one would hold him or anything. We slept in a long room with metal beds. There were about fifteen of us and we slept separate from the family. Separate from the little girl of the foster parents. She had her own room and she had a canopy bed. When Christmas came only she got presents under the tree; all the foster kids got none. Mother, did you buy us presents then? Did you want to?

Did you know that the foster home was only a few blocks from our apartment building and that they would drive by and I would see Dad's truck and I would reach my arms and body out of the car window and I would yell out, "Momma, come get us, come get us!" They would always drag me back in and spank me for being so loud and troublesome. They would tell me I was bad when I started to cry and beg them to take me home to my mommy. I would dream at night of you looking out the window just as we drove by and you would run down the stairs and save me from those mean people. You would run down the steps and give huge mean stares at those awful people and they wouldn't say anything, they would just let us go and you wouldn't have to fight them or anything. You would swoop down magically, no bruises or braces and you would be strong and take me in your arms and you would save me. Save me like mothers are supposed to.

But you never swooped down and eventually we were given back to you but we still lived with my step-father, dad, who had driven his truck fast and stopped and hurt you real bad. You never said a word about it, never, not then and not when we were growing up. No one ever said anything. Tommy was too young and I was too glad to be out of that place where the girl with the canopy bed liked to lock me in closets and tell me there were devils in there. Today I am a woman-loving feminist, but I'd still like to slap that girl for torturing me like she did.

Mother, I never told you about the canopy bed girl or the long lines of cold metal cots and the sad children that slept in them and cried every day. I never told you that, just like I never told you about how mad I was when you left us at a babysitter's house when I was four and she turned us in to the social workers and they took us to *another* foster home. I never told you how they had lots of foster kids and got money every month from the government to take care of us but only fed us one piece of corn bread for dinner. Or how they made us eat tripe with Tabasco sauce. Or how the foster father was white and the foster mother was black and how they made us call them mamma and daddy and how that made me feel like a liar every time I had to say it and how they caged us into rooms and never let us out of their sight. Or how they made us go to church and be Jehovah's Witnesses and how they didn't believe in birthdays and how the white daddy was a racist and hated his wife and the darker children, but liked me because I looked like a hula girl and how his wife hated white children but liked me because I could tan. I never said how she would make me sit in the sun for hours and never get up until I was a dark brown and she told me I could pass for black. I never told you how I found Tommy locked in a garbage can when I came home from kindergarten one day and how I couldn't get him out because I was afraid of what they would do to me if they found out that I had set him free, so I left him there and cried for our lives the rest of the day and night.

I never told you how the foster father and his church friends used to dress up in white robes and lead me down the street and into a tunnel and all of a sudden they weren't Jehovah's Witnesses anymore, but they all of a sudden loved the devil and killed animals and babies for him. I didn't say anything about what they did to me, like burn me and make me take all of my clothes off and stand naked in a circle while the men said things to me, and later did things to me. I never told you, but I did tell the foster mother's son who was a police officer and who told her something and then the foster father didn't come to get me anymore and he didn't make me do things to his thingy and he told me I was bad because I told people about him and now he couldn't kiss me good night and it was all my fault. I never told you that I thought I did something wrong to him and I cried thinking I was a bad girl because he wouldn't kiss me good night anymore.

You got us out of the foster home soon after that, and like before, we never said anything about anything and we went to a new apartment but still lived with dad. Dad who drove the blue truck and who tried to kill you again and again. And you still drank a lot and so did dad and I went to school every day and I would dream of escaping, of a time when I wouldn't have to always be afraid and a place where I could be alone and not have other people hurting me all the time.

I dreamed that you wouldn't cry so much and be so unhappy and drink all of our welfare money away and that you wouldn't ever get hurt. I dreamed that we didn't live in the neighborhood we did, where there was always some woman running from some man and we weren't always having to call the police on all the daddies. I dreamed that the women would all live together and some would get outside jobs and some would have the job of taking care of the kids. I dreamed that no one was afraid and everyone had food and everyone had clothes and there weren't any cockroaches and there was always love for everyone.

I dreamed and I dreamed and that is partially how I am the woman that I am today. Dreams and work. And now I am a woman who is vibrant and alive one day, damaged the next. I am a woman who resisted the negative messages as much as I could and told myself that no matter what, *MY SPIRIT WOULD LIVE*. I now question the truth of that youthfully created conviction. I still question myself. I still question what it means to be the daughter of my mother. How we are so different and then, out of the mirror or in my dreams or in my sighs, and in my sadness, I see you out of the corner of my eye, I feel the mold that hangs in the air and keeps me in front of the television or in bed for hours or makes me mean or keeps me silent. I have the paralyzing moments you had, mother. I have the times when I don't care how or who I offend, just that I will say what I have to say. I still have moments that last like years when depression shadows my accomplishments and I resign my will and forfeit my strength. I give up sometimes; I make promises I don't keep.

Mother, I am not writing this to blame you, though I wish you still didn't say that I was never in a foster home and that I'm a bitch for saying so and that you paid to have us in day care and that's where we were. I wish I didn't have to protect myself from you, the woman who at times worked so hard to keep us fed, who lost us but jumped through government hoops to get us back. The single, unwed mother who didn't want to give her baby up for adoption when abortion was illegal. You, my mother, who inadvertently taught me to be a feminist and never depend on men. Who would come alive like a tiger when her husband tried to hurt her kids. You, my mother who was an abused child, who left home at twelve and was an alcoholic by thirteen selling papers in the cold of Alaska's winter. The girl who stepped into bars to get warm and sell papers to drunks who sometimes offered $10 apiece. The girl who was offered a drink to warm her and who accepted and who found more protection in a liquid than in any family she ever knew.

This is not a blaming, but a meditation.

We work, we love, we make mistakes. We work, we love, we make mistakes. If this world was easier on us, we might just love more and make fewer mistakes. We are women, mothers, daughters, sisters. And yet we are from different tribes. I make this meditation, this offering to you, mother. I hope that you will someday find the voice to offer one to me.

Two of the Murphy girls, Marilyn and Jeanne, in their grandmother's yard.

One of the Murphy Girls

Marilyn Murphy

I knew a lot about class before the summer of 1975, when I went to Sagaris, a feminist "think tank," and learned about class as a concept. When I was growing up, poverty lived with us, quietly wreaking havoc within a family that lacked the emotional strength to survive with cooperation and love. Poverty allows no privacy for disagreements, no time for reasoned debates. Ours was no *Little Women* style of genteel poverty. I knew we were poor, not because of what we lacked, but because poverty was the subject of my parents' frequent, abusive arguments. I knew, from my earliest years, that my mother blamed my father for our poverty, and my father, guilt-ridden over our poverty, tried, unsuccessfully, to blame Mother for her "inability" to make the money "stretch." The motif of their litany of blame was, "If you were a real man, you would be making more money, etc.," and "If you were a good wife, you would know how to economize, etc." They fought constantly, speaking vitriolic, dreadful words, words we children heard and for which we hated them both. They did not swear or use foul language. They did not drink, something we know, now, to be grateful for. They did not hit each other. Often, the fights started at the dinner table with Mother saying, "The children need...," or "Marilyn (or one other of us) needs..." We would feel guilty for causing another fight. My sisters and I didn't talk about our parents, about our feelings, about the physical and emotional abuse we suffered. Our feelings festered, having no outlet. All we could do was to simply stand up for each other, to try to protect each other. We bonded, children against parents, in a poverty-induced war that lasted for years and, in some ways, is still going on. Our father died of poverty when he was forty-four years old. (After years of dental neglect, he had some loose teeth pulled. The infected material caused a blood clot which traveled to his heart. He was dead three hours after leaving the dentist.) Our mother is a healthy, energetic, bitter, eighty-four-year-old woman who continues to abuse us verbally, still tries, unsuccessfully, to cause dissension among us and often wants to beat us up, I'm sure of it.

My father's family was second-generation, lace-curtain Irish. When his father became a captain in the New York City Fire Department, he moved his family from the Hell's Kitchen area, where my father and his three brothers and one sister were born (and five others who didn't survive infancy), to the suburbs and a two-story home of their own. All of the children were expected to work after school and to give their wages to their mother, who returned "spending money" to them. The same rule held when they were working full-time and living at home. A college education was not an option for them. My grandfather died young, like his son, at forty-four. My father and his siblings were expected to support the house and my grandmother and they did, except for Daddy. I remember the arguments my parents had, and my mother's outrage as my father, caught between his wife and mother, tried to give money to his mother that his wife needed for the family.

My parents met when Daddy was still in high school and working as a butcher's boy, delivering orders on his bicycle. Mother was just out of high school, employed as a live-in "mother's helper." As soon as Daddy graduated from high school, in June of 1929, he went to work as a runner on Wall Street, "where the money is," he told Mother. He was unemployed soon after the stock market crashed in late October. That was the beginning of his lifetime of sporadic employment. He was an intelligent person, gregarious, political, a talker, a reader, a dreamer, a lover of ideas and a hard worker. He thought of himself as a common man, a laborer, because that was the work he did. He was an Irish union man, conscious of the oppression of the Irish by the English and of the workers by the bosses. When I was ten, placard in hand, I proudly walked a picket line with him. Whatever the job, Daddy would think of a way to do something more efficiently, would criticize an oppressive work situation, would support a co-worker in conflict with a supervisor, would organize a strike and would get fired over and over again. When he tended bar, his work when he couldn't find work, he refused to serve customers who were drunk. Sometimes he was fired for that, too. Mother was always in a rage over his "irresponsibility." "Won't you ever learn to keep your mouth shut, to mind your own business?" she'd cry. He never did. He was frustrated because he couldn't make enough money to support us, but was not ashamed of the work he did. At the time of his death, he was tending bar at a country club, a job he loved. The members started a trust fund for my youngest sister, then five years old, which helped Mother support her for ten years. The trust fund was a gift Mother was ashamed of, one she would have turned down if her adult daughters hadn't stopped her. A rich man, knowing Daddy had recently purchased his first car, paid for it and sent Mother the pink slip. She was overcome with shame, and went to see him, begging him to let her pay him back in installments. He refused her offer, saying that his gift was his way of showing his affection for my father, and telling her that he grew up poor and never forgot what it was like.

My mother's growing up was a lesson in shame, so it is no wonder that she was ashamed of her poverty, was ashamed of where we lived, was ashamed of the jobs my father worked. She thought of herself as an artist, was enrolled in the art department of New York City's Peter Cooper Union, when she was twenty, but dropped out to get married. She says she never regretted it, but none of her children believe that. She did light factory, sales and office work while my father was alive. After his death, she began selling insurance, making good money "for a woman," and was finally able to buy her own house, which she lost two years later to freeway expansion. She took lessons in painting at night at the local art museum. She retired at sixty-seven, with retirement benefits and a little money in the bank, moved to California where all her daughters lived and enrolled, as an art major, in college. She earned a B.A. in Fine Arts at seventy-seven years of age and was working on a B.A. in English at eighty, when changes in the bus schedule made it too difficult for her to continue. She paints and sculpts, gets a commission now and then. Through her nearby library, she tutors women in the national literacy program. She does yoga and aerobics and walks two miles, three times a week, too. She lives in a pretty condominium complex, government-subsidized housing, and is ashamed of it. She handles her shame for "using taxpayers' money to live on," by voting Republican.

When we were children, Mother told us her mistake was marrying a poor man, that we would get out of poverty by marrying a rich man. "It's as easy to fall in love with a rich man as with a poor one," she told us over and over and over again. One day, when I was eleven, I was sitting on the stoop of our apartment building, reading and thinking, when it occurred to me that I'd have to *know* rich people if I was going to marry one. I was unable to believe that my situation would change enough for me to depend on marrying a rich man. Instead, I decided that I would try to mind my poverty less. I didn't want poverty to do to me what it was doing to my mother. I decided to "rise above" the circumstances of my life and try to need and want less. This was an appropriate solution for a Catholic girl, and one I've never regretted. As a result of this child's decision, I haven't been eaten up by envy or embittered by the losses, disappointments and lack of opportunities caused by my poverty. Also, I've been able to enjoy, to the fullest, whatever material benefits come to me because they feel like a gift, unexpected and surprising. Sometimes I think of her, that serious little girl I used to be. I can see her on that step, meditating on her life, making decisions for me and am overcome with compassion and gratitude.

Of course, it was one thing to decide to train myself not to envy, and another to actually not envy the sole only child on our block, the child who always had a nickel for an ice from the Italian pushcart man, while the rest of us hundred or so children had to be satisfied with a penny ice. That was hard, as, along with the other kids, I punished him for his privilege by calling him "Aloysius," instead of "Al," as he begged us to do.

Learning to rise above envy of my high school classmates was very difficult. I was supposed to go to the free Catholic high school in Manhattan, the school whose student body was composed of the smartest girl and boy from each of the Catholic grammar schools in New York City. Being chosen for that school was an honor, and I was very proud and happy to have earned it. My mother felt differently. She said we were too "proud" to accept "charity," and sent me to a suburban high school to take an entrance exam. I passed and became a student at St. Agnes Academy, a college preparatory school, more than an hour by train and bus from where I lived. The students were predominantly middle class and secure working class girls. (My two best girlfriends were daughters of a fire chief and a pharmacist.) During the two-and-a-half years I attended the school, I was daily wracked with anxiety about having bus and subway fare. Tuition was eight dollars a month and I *almost never* had it on time. Regularly, I had to stand in the hall with the few other "delinquents," where all the girls could see us, waiting for Sister Monitor to call me into her office so I could explain to her why my parents sent me to a school they obviously could not afford. I hated my mother for the unnecessary humiliation I experienced because of her "pride," and my father for his failure to provide. I was lucky the school had uniforms. When my only gabardine jumper was at the cleaners, I simply pretended I was sick and stayed home. I socialized with the girls during lunch break. Fortunately, the school had no cafeteria, so all the girls brought bag lunches. I tried to have a nickel or a dime, stolen from my parents and hidden in my shoe, so I could buy an ice cream cone with the girls when they went to the candy store after lunch. I loved the school, the nuns and my girlfriends but, obviously, I could not participate in after-school activities, nor could I "hang out" with my friends at the soda fountain on the corner where the bus left us to go our separate ways. None of them lived anywhere near me and besides, I was always "needed at home."

My mother began working full-time outside the home when I was eleven. My parents usually worked hours that overlapped in the late afternoon. My after-school responsibilities were to supervise my sisters, buy groceries if necessary, see that the apartment was neat, beds made, clothing put away, the table set and dinner ready when Mother came home from work. After dinner, we children washed, dried and put away the dishes.

Homework and bed followed. We four, and then five, daughters slept in one room. We were seldom allowed to listen to the radio at night. "Children need their sleep," Mother was fond of saying, as we went off to bed at seven-thirty or eight, winter and summer. We children used to sit, huddled against the bedroom door, straining to hear *The Little Theater Off Times Square*, *Suspense*, *The Lux Movie Theater Of The Air*. Most often, I entertained my sisters, whispered stories to them, those I made up and those that were my version of books I had read.

On Saturday, if my parents had the dimes for admission, if we had finished our share of the housework and ironing, if we weren't being punished for something, and if the films were approved for children by the Legion of Decency, we attended the children's matinee. Once in a great while, Jeanne and I were allowed to go to a birthday party in the apartment of a friend. I was allowed to attend one eighth-grade graduation party, but not the big one, the one all my classmates were invited to, because it took place in the projects. "I don't want you associating with riff-raff," was another of Mother's sayings. A few times, when we were in our teens, Jeanne and I were allowed to take the subway into Manhattan with others in the neighborhood and attend a matinee at Radio City Music Hall, the Roxy or other theatres that had a stage show. Because my father worked nights and weekends most of the time, my parents seldom went anywhere. Daddy met and liked only "riff-raff," and Mother didn't want the women at work to know where she lived, and she refused to socialize with the neighbors, so they had no friends to visit or invite in. Once in a while, they went to the movies. We occasionally went on family outings, to the beach, on a day trip up the Hudson River, to visit my father's family. Those couple and family events usually happened when one of them was jobless, so were accompanied by money anxiety that caused angry flare-ups.

When I was thirteen, Mother bought new living room furniture. I can still see the beautiful brocade couch and the mahogany kneehole desk. The purchase was a surprise to my father. Mother was in charge of the money, but he was angry that she made such a huge purchase without discussing it with him. "It's for the girls," she said. "They're growing up and will need a nice place to entertain their boyfriends." I knew she was lying. We were not allowed to let anyone in our apartment. Our friends never came in to play on a rainy day, or came for lunch or dinner. She wasn't about to let boys in! Now, I know that she was unable to say the truth, that she, with her artist's love of beauty, bought something beautiful for herself. However, I wouldn't have cared what she said, anyway. I was furious because she spent the money she made working at a job on unnecessary, expensive living room furniture.

I always wished I didn't have to be so responsible, so depended upon, but, until the furniture came, I didn't resent my situation. I knew that my work at home meant that Mother could work for pay, meant that I was helping to support the family. Not that mother ever mentioned my contribution. Quite the opposite. "Ungrateful brat," she called me when I "talked back" to her, or when I let her see my thoughts on my face. I believed that taking care of children was the responsibility of parents, and didn't think I should be grateful. "I didn't ask to be born!" I'd say, chin jutting out, daring her to hit me—and she would. I never told her, then, that I thought she should be, not grateful to me, since I knew we were all in this together, but *appreciative*. She never was, never said "thank you" for the dinner I cooked, never commiserated with me about a party I was missing or an event I couldn't attend. Rage at her poverty, at the death of her dreams, burned up any empathy she might have felt for the plight of her daughters. Even if I could have told her how betrayed I felt, aware as I was of the price I was paying for "her" furniture, I doubt she would have understood. In our family, parents and children didn't have discussions. We had arguments. So I kept my thoughts to myself and resented her, had contempt for her and for my father whose desire to please her was stronger, in my opinion, than his concern for his children.

We were evicted from our apartment in December of 1945, a few days before a record twenty-six inches of snow fell on New York City. My father was out of work at the time. Just about everything we owned went into storage, while we all found refuge in two tiny rooms in a dark, odoriferous hotel in Manhattan. I remember almost nothing of the time we spent there. I remember the snow and permission for Jeanne and me to go to the movies with two boys from our neighborhood. The rest is a blur of fear and excitement. When we left the hotel, I didn't know where my father was. Mother and our youngest sister stayed with an acquaintance. The rest of the sisters were parceled out to members of my father's family. We had never spent a night away from home, from our parents or each other. We had never even eaten a meal in another person's house. We were frightened and apprehensive. Instead of taking pity on us, our grandmother and aunts and uncles treated us like beggars off the street, barely feeding us and constantly criticizing our parents. I argued with my grandmother and left her house to find refuge in the home of a classmate, Anita Bevelaqua. My sisters were not so fortunate.

Our ordeal lasted three months. I lived with fear, loneliness, humiliation and guilt. I missed my sisters. I worried about my parents. However, the nuns knew of my situation and didn't ask for my tuition, and I was free from supervision, except for the easy-going rules of my classmate's mother.

I was free from responsibility, on my own. I was expected only to make my bed, iron my clothes, which Mrs. Bevelaqua washed for me, and to take my turn washing dishes. I was able to stop at the soda fountain with the girls from school, to stay after school and work on the school paper, to stay up late reading. I was very happy, covered with guilt, but happy nonetheless.

While I was enjoying my freedom, Mother was suffering. She was working, and visited us seldom. We talked on the phone once in a while, awkward conversations, because we had never talked on the phone before, and because I didn't want to hear her misery. My father, in despair, left the city for the Tulsa, Oklahoma, home of a brother. He didn't tell Mother where he was. For weeks, she feared he might have killed himself. She didn't tell us, of course. We learned Daddy was "missing" when Uncle John complained to Jeanne, then thirteen, about how much longer he and Aunt Claire would be stuck with her now that Daddy was missing and maybe dead.

When Daddy found a job in Tulsa, as a short order cook, he wrote Mother with the "good" news. He told her to pack up the kids and come to Tulsa, she would love it there. What she did was pack us up and, with me confidently in charge of my sisters again, shipped us by bus to Oklahoma. We departed on March 29. "I'll see you in August," she said. "I don't want to lose my vacation pay by quitting early."

For me, the bus trip was a great adventure. Those three-and-a-half days on the bus with my sisters was an enchanted time, magic, a fairy tale. We left in the late afternoon and drove through urban areas till dark. I awoke as the dark was lightening, breathlessly curious to see what was out my window. Living always in crowded streets lined with tall buildings, I had never before seen the sun come up. I was ecstatic as I watched it streak color over tree-covered hills, illuminating, in the distance, the city of Pittsburgh with its black canopy of coal dust. What an experience that was. I was three months from my sixteenth birthday and, with my beloved sisters, was seeing the sun rise and set, seeing farmers on tractors, and cows, pigs, sheep and horses, yellow school buses for the first time.

Our arrival in Tulsa was a different experience altogether. Mother had not told my father that we were arriving without her, so he was very upset. When we arrived at the small, filthy home of Uncle Francis, Aunt Alice and their three sons and a daughter, the eldest a boy of twelve, we children were very upset, indeed. There was no celebratory welcome. Daddy went to work, evening shift, as usual, and left us with those sullen relatives we barely knew. Aunt Alice had undergone a mastectomy recently, but no one told me what that meant in relation to her ability to care for her family and house. Mother always said there was no excuse for dirt, so it was obvious to us that these people were the "riff-raff" she was talking about. Jeanne and I, with help from Sally Ann and Carol and our new girl cousin, were to clean house, and do the washing, ironing, cooking, dishes and child care. Daddy did his share when he wasn't working a double shift, or trying to sleep. We refused to pick up after the boys, to do their laundry, wash their dishes. No one could make us do it. Daddy begged us to cooperate until Mother joined us and we got a place of our own. We refused. The little house was a war zone. We begged Daddy to get us to the Catholic high school to register, quick, only to learn that, because of the differences in the school systems, we couldn't start school until September, five long months away. On his small salary, he couldn't save money for first month's rent on a house and still pay our share of Uncle Francis' house and utilities bills and all the rest. I was frantic to get out of the house, so I lied about my age and got a job as a carhop at a restaurant that sold beer and paid a small salary plus tips. Daddy was furious. He called the restaurant and told them I was underage. He got me an evening carhop job at a root beer stand across the street from the cafe where he worked. That meant he could keep an eye on me and take me home at closing. The owner paid no salary, and the tips were meager. I felt like I was working days and nights for free. So, without asking Daddy's permission, I quit the job. He was angry, but I didn't care. I was angry at him for losing me the salaried job and ashamed of him for standing by and letting Alice and Francis oppress his children. I had not a drop of compassion for him. As far as he was concerned, my heart was stone.

Mother's late summer arrival rescued us. She was not about to spend one minute longer than necessary in the house of in-laws she despised. She was furious that Daddy's lazy, good-for-nothing relatives had turned her children into their maids! Within a week, she found a job and a tiny, two-bedroom house with a large front porch, and an enormous, flower- and tree-filled yard, in a "good" neighborhood. Everything we owned was still in storage, so Mother bought some bunk beds and bare necessities, "for the time being," with her vacation pay. I missed the girls from school, but Jeanne and I were accustomed to being each other's best friend, so we managed to adapt. I went to work, part-time, in a flower shop and Jeanne did some neighborhood baby-sitting. We had to give our pay to Mother, who did *not* give some of it back for spending money. Daddy was happy. He loved Tulsa, loved the weather, and the slower pace. He loved the smallness of it. Mother hated it, pined for New York City, fought with Daddy to return. He refused to consider it. We children were on Daddy's side, not that either of them asked our opinion, because of the house and yard.

Jeanne and I finally went back to school. We soon learned that we were two of a handful of poor kids attending the school. The girls wore beautiful clothes. There were no uniforms to hide in. Also, we were expected to buy a plain white blouse, pleated blue skirts and a red scarf to wear at football games as members of the Marquette High School football team Pep Squad. I didn't know what a pep squad was, but I was pretty sure I wasn't going to like it. On the day before the first game of the season, the whole school, about four hundred students, was let out, *during class time*, to snake dance through the halls, down the stairs and around the building, chanting praise for the team and "Kill, Kill, Kill, Holy Family" (the opposing school). I was expected to attend, dressed in my pep squad clothes, cheering and waving a school pennant for the boys. I was aghast, mortified. I was light years older than my classmates, interested in national politics, in the racism and anti-Catholic sentiment I was confronting for the first time. I refused to participate in what I believed to be childish behavior. Instead, I went to the principal and arranged to take the extra classes I would need to do my junior and senior years in one year, possible because New York State had much higher standards for graduation than Oklahoma. I managed to "rise above" the material differences I experienced about clothes with difficulty. Jeanne and I traded clothes, to give the impression that we had more than we did. I sewed, not well and not often, but as much as I could and as much as we could afford. I didn't socialize with my classmates, which significantly reduced my opportunities for envy. My sisters suffered as the school's "poor kids" for their entire high school experience. During the years we lived in that neighborhood, they begged Mother to find a house in Holy Family parish, where the ordinary kids lived, but she always refused. She liked going to Mass with the rich folks, told us we were "inverted snobs," repeated her "It's as easy to love a rich man..." often.

All our problems intensified when Mother became pregnant, with a baby due the end of August, a month past her forty-first birthday. She was distraught. She would never get back to New York now. What would we do for money when she had to quit working? She was too old to raise another baby. Daddy was overjoyed by the news. He would work more, get an extra job. Perhaps she'd get the boy she wanted! Mother didn't care. She didn't want another baby. She wanted to work, to "get ahead." The pregnancy did her in, at least for a while. With no prospects for getting enough money to pay shipping costs, in the foreseeable future, she quit paying the fee for storing our things in New York, bitterly relinquishing the furniture she loved, and with it, her dream of returning to New York City.

Sharon was born on the eighteenth anniversary of my parents' marriage. I was at the hospital with Daddy. She weighed eleven pounds, thirteen ounces and was the most beautiful baby I have ever seen to this day. I was her godmother, and named her. Mother got over not having a boy. She was "used to it," she said. Daddy was wildly enthusiastic about her birth, never wanted boys anyway. He was always carrying her around, showing her off to the neighbors. He even took her to his workplace to show her to his co-workers. Daddy and my sisters and I vied for the joy of holding her, bathing her, taking her for walks in her baby carriage. Mother stayed home, to breast-feed her, for six months. She was angrier than ever.

Mother wasn't the only one to relinquish dreams that year. By the time Sharon was born, I had completed the requirements for a high school diploma, and was working full-time. I was giving my paycheck from my job at the gas company to Mother. I had no one to ask about the ways a poor girl could go to college. I had telephoned the only college in the area, the University of Tulsa, and learned that tuition was thirty-five dollars a unit and that a student had to carry nine units to attend. That was more than three hundred dollars a semester, and didn't include books and other fees. I didn't know enough to ask if the school had scholarships for poor students. The nuns at my high school told me the only scholarships they knew of were athletic scholarships for boys. Besides, Catholic girls married and didn't need an education, or else they became nuns and were educated by their order, they added. I didn't mention my beloved Dominican nuns at St. Agnes, who expected us to go to college. They were in New York and I was here, in a city that had no provisions for educating intelligent poor girls. It never occurred to me that I could return to New York City ON MY OWN and work and go to City College, New York. I never met nor heard of a girl who left home for anything but marriage or the convent, except for girls in books, girls with money. I believed my alternatives were limited. I could stay home and continue to help support my family, clean house, cook, do dishes and laundry, take care of my sisters, AND let my mother continue to hit me when she was angry and to tell me what to do, and when to do it. Instead, I could get married and do all those things in my own house with no one to boss me around. So, when mother started back to work, I told her I wanted to keep half my wage in order to save for my wedding. She was too demoralized by her life, at the moment, to object. Five days after my eighteenth birthday, I paid for my wedding with money I saved from my share of my salary, married my twenty-year-old, machinist boyfriend, and learned, to my dismay, that I had really married my mother.

I married Bob because I knew he would not be like my father. He would be a steady worker, responsible, solid, the sort of worker for whom keeping a roof over the heads of his children, and food on their plates, would be his primary concern. He would not criticize his boss, not jeopardize his job by making unasked-for suggestions. He would "keep his mouth shut and mind his own business." He would not lend money to friends or give it away to strangers on the street. I was right about him. When he was twenty-two, hoping to "better" himself, he went to work for an airline company and stayed with them for thirty-some years, before retiring. He always paid the rent/mortgage and the bills. Because he made the money, he paid the bills, and gave me money for groceries and for other purchases he had previously approved. He thought a clothes dryer and a dishwasher were unnecessary for a woman with four children under six years. Like my mother, he nagged and criticized, yelled and threw things. He did not give me spending money, either. Unlike my mother, he did not hit me.

During the fifteen years I lived with Bob, I learned to despise him. He was mean-spirited and petty. He wanted all my attention, so was jealous of my children, sisters, friends, books, interests, time. He'd come up behind me. "What are you thinking about? Tell me now." I didn't. He took advantage of his Catholic husband, head-of-the-household, and breadwinner privileges to "humble" me. Every time I had to manipulate him, lie, steal money from his billfold, my contempt for him intensified. I was becoming a radical Catholic, but divorce was not part of the radical agenda. Instead, like many other good Catholic wives, I prayed to the Blessed Virgin Mary to let Bob be killed in a one-car accident while he was in the state of grace. Social security and his double indemnity insurance would give me enough money to get by on. I also prayed for a kinder miracle, money to take care of my kids without Bob, but without his death.

Marriage and children did not ease my desire for an education. I made friends with the librarians at my neighborhood library, asking them to guide my book choices. I read footnotes to find other books. Dr. Spock's baby book led me to Freud, who led me to Jung and Adler. Catholicism led me to philosophers and history. I developed a circle of women friends, Catholic housewives with lots of children and no college education. We discussed our reading on the phone and when we brought our children to play at one another's houses. We had occasional "card parties," something "normal" women did. We would deal the cards and lay them on the table, in case a husband came in unexpectedly. Then we discussed books, our latest ideas, world and personal changes till one and two in the A.M. We were educating each other and, we hoped, keeping each other sane. Sadly, the latter proved untrue. By the mid-sixties, all but a few of my friends were victims of psychiatrists and electric shock treatment, efforts to "normalize" them, to help them adjust to their role as wives and mothers. They quit attending our card parties after treatment, at least for a while.

I was luckier than my friends. Unlike theirs, our health insurance did not cover mental health, and the one time I felt desperate enough to suggest going to a psychiatrist, Bob refused to give me the money. "Are you out of your mind, asking for money to pay someone to listen to you talk about me? Call up one of your crazy girlfriends!" That was a close call. When I divorced him, a few years later, I told him I would always be grateful to him for three things, his caring assistance when my father died, his purchase of an air conditioner when I was pregnant with my third child, and his refusal to pay for a psychiatrist.

When I was thirty-three years old, the airline transferred Bob to Southern California. He called, very upset, to tell me the bad news. I caught my breath, and one tear started its journey down my cheek. Then I remembered and said, "I can go to college. It's free in California." He was taken aback. "Well, I guess you could," he said. I did not mention college to him again. The children and I arrived in California during the fourth of July weekend, 1965. On the first weekday after that, when Bob was safely at work, I took the children and went hunting for a college. By the time he returned home, I had all the information I needed and an appointment to take the SAT.* I started college in September, buying my books by working the graveyard shift, weekends, at a local coffee shop. Two years later, shortly after I was nominated for student of the year, Bob demanded I quit school. I suggested divorce, instead. When he realized I was serious, he changed his mind. He would "let" me continue my education. "I'll buy you a clothes dryer and dishwasher," he said with a smile. "I'll let you get that false tooth you want." Instead of killing him, which is what I wanted to do, I divorced him.

While I worked for my Bachelor's and my Master's degrees, I supported myself and my children with a pittance of spousal and child support, student loans and part-time teaching. I liked being in control of money for the first time in my life, and found that I was very good at it. In the summer of 1970, I obtained the first full-time job I'd had since I was eighteen years old. I taught English composition, American literature and social problems at a small (300 students) private, business college in downtown Los Angeles. The pay wasn't good, and it wasn't in academia, but to get any teaching job, in the middle of a (Nixon) recession, was cause for joy. And, OH! I as so happy! I loved my students and they loved me. They were young, multiracial and multicultural. Just about everything I assigned or suggested they

*Scholastic Aptitude Test.—ED.

read and wrote about, and everything we talked about was analyzed for its sexism, racism and classism. The students were wild with enthusiasm. They were the kind of students teachers dream of. And I was *paid money* for teaching them.

On December 12 of that year, the dean of students called me into her office and fired me. The parents were calling for my dismissal. "They send their children to this school in order to keep them away from the radicals," she told me. She, herself, had no problem with my teaching, but money is what matters. I thought our classroom discussions about Vietnam and the antiwar movement were the problem. However, according to the dean, the parents of the girls were doing the most complaining. I had told them about the wage differential between females and males. Many of the students worked part-time at the big, downtown department stores, so they were able to compare their pay. The boys were making fifty cents an hour more than the girls for doing the same work. The girls were outraged. Even the boys were surprised. The girls went to their stores, in groups, and protested the inequality. They received no pay raises, but were proud of themselves for their actions. Then they went home for thanksgiving and told their parents what they'd been up to. Those parents who were employers were asked about their pay policies. It wasn't only my students, either. I learned my students had been talking to the other students, sharing the books they were reading for my classes, discussing the issues raised in my classes and protesting inequality at their workplaces, too. I was flattered and touched that I had made such a positive impression on my students, but was devastated by the dismissal. My students organized a protest, marched to the dean's office with a petition for my re-instatement, signed by two-hundred and eighty-three students—proving to the administration that I was the bad influence the parents said I was.

That was a bad time for me. My kids were great, tried to console me about the loss of my students and my job. I was inconsolable. The specter of eviction haunted me. Looking for a teaching job, especially just before Christmas, was futile, but I tried. Because I'd been working part-time for so long, my unemployment compensation was minuscule. I packed my pride away and headed for the welfare department. I was determined to have a positive attitude about "charity," unlike my mother's "I'd starve before I'd take charity." I found myself in line with dozens of out-of-work aerospace engineers, which made me feel a bit better. However, all my good intentions dissolved when the caseworker asked me to tell her why I was applying for assistance. In an instant, shame poured over me. I burst into tears, covered my face with my hands, laid my head on her desk and sobbed.

For less than a year, my kids and I lived on welfare. There was never enough of anything. We scrimped, did without, made do. I got over the humiliation of going to the bank to have the welfare voucher redeemed. "The food stamp window's been moved to window four!" shouts the teller. I learned to live through the supermarket checkout ordeal. "Sorry," says the clerk, "You can't buy toothpaste with food stamps." The recession deepened, and I could find no work. The man I was seeing, a man who grew up poor, received his education through the WWII GI Bill, and was a successful therapist with a Ph.D., wanted to marry me. "I'll take care of the girls, see they go to college." "I'll buy a house in a good neighborhood, so they can go to a good high school." "I'll support you until you get your Ph.D." I told him I was unable to know if I was considering his offer because I wanted to live with him, or because of the financial advantages I would enjoy by marrying him. He said he didn't care what reasons moved me. He wanted to marry me under any circumstances. So, demoralized and desperate, I married him.

For four years, I enjoyed a middle-class lifestyle. We bought a house in beautiful Corona Del Mar, six blocks from the Pacific Ocean. I was accepted into a Ph.D. program at the University of California-Irvine. I bought pork chops and steak when I wanted to (both my teenaged daughters became vegetarians during this time). I had extensive dental work done. I bought books and gave money (as well as time) to the Women's Liberation Movement, feminist and antiracist work. With Jack, I went on vacations and took some weekend trips. I loved living without the fear and anxiety that accompanies a hand-to-mouth existence. I loved having the time to think and write and study, to participate fully in the excitement of the Women's Liberation Movement. I tried *not* to be a wife and Jack tried *not* to be a husband. Our most serious problem was about the power of money, caused, Jack said, by the "supersensitivity" I had developed during my first marriage.

In the Spring of 1975, I went to Sagaris. For five weeks, with one hundred and fifty other women, I lived, studied, wrote about, cried over and laughed about feminism and how we live it and how we can make it real in the world. It was the happiest, most satisfying time of my life. On my return home, I was shocked to discover that I was a changed person. My political commitment to the work of women's liberation had intensified to a degree that made it impossible for me to live with a man. For several months, I awoke crying. I had recurring nightmares about my teeth crumbling, about being lost and alone. My days were filled with writing my dissertation, worrying about my moneyless, celibate (I was not a Lesbian at the time) future and feeling guilty about Jack. I didn't want to leave my house and swimming pool and easy life. I had long, earnest conversations with my sisters, daughters and friends about my situation. I was unable to convince myself that I could keep my heterosexual privileges and lead an ethical life at the same time. My sisters, daughters and friends agreed, reluctantly, with my conclusion. My mother was furious but, for the second time, she gave me a AAA emergency roadside service contract as a "living on your own" present. By the first of December 1, 1975, I had finished my dissertation (it was rejected), sold my interest in our house to Jack for ten thousand dollars and moved to a tiny, roach-infested, three-room apartment in Los Angeles. My youngest daughter, out of school and on her own, turned down my suggestion that she live with me. "I think it's about time you tried living on your own, don't you?" she said. I was forty-three-years-old at the time.

I am sixty-one at this writing and can say, without reservation, that I never, not once, regretted my decision to leave Jack and my easy life. I found the experience of being responsible *only for myself* exciting in the extreme. I became a Lesbian, an even more exciting experience. I lived alone for a year or so, and then with two and three roommates. I did not live with my lovers. I supported myself with part-time teaching and whatever other part-time work I could find. Money anxiety returned, but I was so happy living a totally female-centered life that I was able to live with the anxiety. When my lover/beloved companion suggested I move into her house, that we live together, I was afraid to risk my independence. Irene was fifty when we met, the only daughter of poor, but educated, Jewish immigrants from Russia/Lithuania. A nurse administrator, she was working at the convalescent hospital of which she was part owner. I knew her, as a friend and then as a lover, for two years before I felt sure enough to move into her house. We lived together easily and had no money issues, at first. Not long after I moved in, Irene took an early retirement and wanted me to quit my job and stay home with her. We would work and play together, living on her retirement check, and whatever we could generate together. We were full-time Lesbian feminist activists and sometimes made some money at it. Now we live in a Lesbian community on the beach in northern Florida, where we continue to be full-time Lesbian feminist activists.

Irene and I have been living and playing together, on Irene's retirement money, for almost sixteen years now. We do not have class clashes. In fact, our money attitudes and behaviors are identical most of the time. We have never disagreed about spending, saving, borrowing or lending any amount over one hundred dollars. Irene has never tried to control me with her financial advantage, or in any other way. However, we did have a few hurtful fights about money. The fights were always the same and almost always involved a small amount of money. I bought, or was about to buy, something. "Are you *sure* you want to spend our money on *that?*" Irene says, with a tone of patronizing disapproval, *in my opinion*. I am instantly offended and angry and Irene responds with angry defensiveness. In the beginning, we wasted time arguing the merits of the purchase, before getting to the crux of the issue, which, *in my opinion*, was Irene's use of the veto power she derives from the fact that the money we argue about is hers. Now, we both acknowledge the dynamics of our situation. Irene tries to remember that I should be able to "throw money away" on frivolities once in a while, just as she does. I try to remember, what I know from years of living with her, that Irene really does *not* think I'm throwing *her* money away, that I add the personal pronoun. When Irene sighs about the telephone bill, I try to remember that I have the right to use my judgment about the time I need to remain close to my long-distance mother, four sisters, children and grandchildren. Keeping alert, being sensitive and understanding in these subtle, potentially volatile situations is sometimes a strain on us both. However, except when we are in the throes of an occasional "money upset," we consider the strain a trifle compared to the happiness we derive from living together.

In this narrative, I have tried to concentrate on the effect my class had on my life. Its effect seems primary, but a narrative concentration on the effects of sexism/heterosexism on my life would be at least as compelling. Catholicism played its part, as well. We don't know the effect race and a healthy body has had on my life, except to know that it must be enormous. My sisters believe my position as the first child in the family gave me an advantage they lacked, the advantage of being born to parents filled with love and hope for themselves and their child. I agree with them. Their narratives are quite different from mine. I have been lucky to have had a second and a third, and even a fourth chance to change my life. I have lived these last twenty years of my life in an atmosphere of love, security, respect, encouragement and freedom. These years have been the most productive and fulfilling years of my life. When I remember that my first book was published when I was fifty-nine, I know I could have had a shelf full, had my life been different—and I feel a pang. Then, the little girl, sitting on the step of the tenement in New York City, reminds me of the joy I have in my first one, and I am content.

WANTED: An Organization for Debutante Dykes Anonymous

Debbie Alicen

Of all the things I'd love not to write about, this tops the list. So why am I even starting it? Because I've been asked, and because I believe it's an important thing to write about. And probably because I've got enough white, middle-class guilt about this being the right thing to do. Certainly I have enough white, middle-class guilt that, right from the git-go, I feel apologetic and defensive. But I neither want to apologize nor defend. Surely there's enough of that floating around already, not that any of it has done anyone of any class any good.

Where to start? Paternal grandfather's father: farmer, physically abusive, didn't believe in education. One night great grandmother gave grandfather a horse and some provisions and told him to hurry and leave before his father woke up. He rode off the farm and made his way to college. His younger sister wasn't so fortunate. She nursed her mother through a long illness and death, then did the same for her father. Taught lower grades while she continued her own education, finally graduating high school in her thirties, finished her BA in her forties. Never married.

Grandfather also became a teacher and school principal after he finished college. Paternal grandmother also college-educated, and a teacher— her father a druggist, her mother a matriarch. Of her siblings, a brother went into business, a sister married a businessman, a brother became a farmer, and a sister married a farmer. My father was an only child.

My maternal grandmother was college-educated, grandfather not. My mother and her three siblings all college-educated—especially the first-born, male twins, both of whom became doctors, one of whom also went through law school before going to medical school. They both married into wealthy tobacco families. Mother's sister was a school teacher, married a cobbler. Mother was a social worker, father a newspaper writer.

Pretty solidly middle-class throughout, mostly white collar with some blue collar middle-class in the mix.

Both of my parents grew up during the Depression, so both knew something of the realities of economic hardship. They married during WWII, didn't start their lives together until he finished two years in Europe and the war was over. He came back to newspaper work and my mother took on motherhood. Times were fairly harsh economically—tales of having only 50 cents for the week and the baby needing milk—but there were family and friends to help—during one rough stretch we (my parents, brother and I) shared a rather small apartment with another family of four. But however difficult those postwar years were, there was always present great hope and expectations for the future, a certainty that the good (middle-class) life was en route.

My brother was born in 1946. I was born in 1949. The first home I remember clearly, beginning at age four, was a five-room ranch, with a carport and storage room and a backyard big enough for neighborhood games of baseball and football. We also had a sandbox and a swing set.

This was during the fifties in Charlotte, North Carolina. A note: my experience of class/classism is inextricable from my experience of race/racism. When writing about my experiences growing up, I will use the language that was common to me then because it's true to my experience and the society I lived in. In describing events in the mid- to late '50s, replacing "colored" with "African American" would, to me, be lying about what was real.

As a young child I wasn't aware of any differences between the lives of colored people and white people until I started kindergarten. That's when my mother got her first job as a social worker, and my parents first hired a maid. Her name was Ruth.

Ruth came in the morning before I went to kindergarten and would leave when my mother got home from work. Usually she rode the bus to and from our house, but sometimes my mother would pick her up or take her home. I remember riding with my mother to pick up Ruth. We got to a part of town that was unfamiliar to me. I was used to seeing colored people, of course, but usually with plenty of whites around too. Here almost everyone was dark-skinned, and the houses were smaller and not in very good condition. I asked my mother where we were and she said "Colored Town." I looked around and the place didn't look very colorful to me, so I asked, "Why is it called Colored Town?" "Because this is where colored people live." With a five-year-old's need to understand, I pursued a series of questions about why they were called "colored," and why didn't *they* call *us* "colored" since we were a different color from them, and if they were called "colored" and we were called "white," was where we lived called "White Town?"

"No," said Mama.

I was very confused.*

My brother and I loved Ruth. When my parents went away overnight and Ruth stayed with us, my brother and I fought as to which of us would get to sleep with her. Then came a weekend when my parents were going to be gone, and my brother and I went to Ruth's house. She lived in an apartment in a long, low row of apartments, with a lot of other long, low buildings just like it—dirty white clapboard. Grass was sparse, bare dirt plentiful, and very few cars. Three other people lived in Ruth's house: her son, her daughter, and her granddaughter. Her son was my brother's age, nine, her daughter was twenty, and her granddaughter was my age, six. I don't remember her son's or daughter's names. Her granddaughter, with whom I played, was named Cookie. All I can remember is that we had a good time, and it became a fairly regular practice in the couple of summers that followed for Ruth to bring her son and Cookie to work with her to play with my brother and me.

The age of five was a momentous year for me. I learned to read at that age, so I saw that some water fountains had a sign over them saying WHITE and others had a sign saying COLORED. Also at that age I went along with my mother when she made home visits to some of her clients. Her job as a social worker was with a county agency called Charity Hospitalization, so all the clients we visited had just gotten out of the hospital. Almost all of them were colored, and I saw for the first time how people lived when they were *poor*.

Five years old was also when I started kindergarten. There weren't any colored children in my kindergarten. (It was a private kindergarten—there was no public kindergarten.) When I got to first grade and there were still no colored children, by then it didn't seem so strange to me. I knew from my brother's and my playing with Ruth's granddaughter and son that they went to a school close to where they lived. I knew colored people lived in different parts of town from us, colored kids went to schools close to where they lived, and colored people were poorer than most white people I saw. But I did see some white people who were poor, and their neighborhoods had dirt yards and run-down houses, too, and schools where the poor white kids went.

What I couldn't understand at age five were the WHITE and COLORED signs over the water fountains in the stores downtown. (No signs

*On another of these rides with my mother, I got another lesson about female class status. My mother and I were talking and I learned that her last name had been different before she married my father. I grilled her as to why, and how did she and my father decide which of them would change names when they married, and why didn't she fight to keep her name the same? I was just as confused by her answers on that occasion, as well.

like that over the water fountains at school—no colored kids at school.) But there also came other experiences, like riding the city buses, with whites riding in the front, coloreds riding in the back; being out in the world where I heard colored people being called "niggers"; and the intensified short course on the occasion of the summertime movie matinee excursion, which happened as follows.

It was late July or sometime in August, which in North Carolina is a horridly hot and humid time. With the breakthrough invention of air-conditioning, movie theaters all over the south were among the first places to install it, to attract business on just such days. For a treat, my parents had given Ruth all the money necessary for her to take me and my brother on the bus downtown and for the three of us to go to a movie and have popcorn.

Ruth wore her maid's uniform and my brother and I were dressed up. (Middle-class children in the fifties did **NOT** go downtown without being dressed up.) On the bus we all sat in the front, which was allowed for Ruth since she was accompanying white children. When we got to the movie theater, though, they would not let Ruth in to sit with us. She would have to sit in the colored balcony. No, white kids couldn't sit with her in the balcony. We left and walked a few blocks to a colored neighborhood and a movie theater there. No go there, either. They didn't have a section for whites—had never had any reason to have a section for whites.

So there were such events and moments regarding class and race during my childhood that were pointed and confusing, but so was much of the world, and the standard answer to anything I couldn't grasp as a child was that I would understand better when I got older. So I went about my life, being a child and waiting to get older.

For the most part my childhood to age twelve was very much like a white middle-class story book—the house in the burbs with the nice yard (we moved to a bigger house in a nicer burb when I was eight), new clothes at the beginning of each school year, dress-up for church and holidays, my own room, a dog, a bicycle and skates and TV.

We had three square meals a day. Mama got up in the mornings ahead of everyone else and made breakfast. Sometimes cereal, sometimes eggs and bacon, and on Sundays maybe pancakes or waffles. There were school lunches during the school years, and during the summer my parents usually came home for lunch, prepared by Ruth, and later Sadie—the maid through my adolescent years. Ruth or Sadie would also cook supper in the afternoon before leaving for home, so we only had to heat up dinner. Mama loved to cook, and was trying out at least one new recipe most weekends.

As a little kid my mornings were given to Captain Kangaroo and Howdy Doody. Two or three years later, when I was becoming more adventurous, my allegiances shifted to Sky King and Captain Midnight. I was hugely disappointed that Captain Midnight went off the air just after I'd sent for my secret decoder ring. The ring came but I never got to decode a single secret message with it. When I matured a bit more I got more into Mr. Wizard. I think I was ten when I got Mr. Wizard's science experiment book, and conducted every experiment in it.

Two things brought about massive changes in the second decade of my life: the civil rights movement and puberty.

The civil rights movement gave me the awareness to understand—in white, liberal, middle-class terms—those things about race/class that had so confused me at a younger age. Puberty thrust me into the mire of upwardly mobile white middle-class femininity, about which my awareness wouldn't start dawning for more than another decade. More on that later.

With the beginnings of the civil rights movement my family's liberalism rose to the top. My grandfather, a few years earlier, had railed at the level of poverty rampant throughout his county—"These kids don't even have shoes to wear to school!" Now he railed against the conditions in the black schools, which hadn't improved along with the white schools. My mother regularly took on neighbors who complained of "welfare cheaters," attesting to the real poverty of the blacks who were clients of her agency. My father wrote scathing pro-civil rights columns for the newspaper, for which he (and we) endured anonymous threats to life and limb.

The high school I went to desegregated (as far as students went—there were no black teachers then in formerly all-white schools) the year before I started there, and racial feeling was still extremely raw when I got there in 1965. I remember my own and my parents' anger when a schoolmate of mine, whose parents were friends of my parents, reported that she had requested a change of seating assignment in English class because she didn't like the color combination of black and purple. She had been sitting next to a black girl wearing a purple dress. And in chemistry class, the teacher held her breath until she saw me pairing with the one black student in the class as my lab partner. She held me after class to say she had been afraid no one would be willing to be partners with the girl.

I was never discouraged from having black friends, of course, but my parents did actively discourage me from having working-class white friends. One of my best friends in high school was my next-door neighbor. Her family was blue collar middle-class, and had moved to our neighborhood from a thoroughly working-class neighborhood. The more I made friends with her friends in her old neighborhood, the less my parents liked it.

I rebelled the more for what I saw as my parents' hypocrisy, especially my father's. When I was in junior high he wrote a series of columns deploring status consciousness among teenagers. Specifically, a kid was hopelessly not "in" if she didn't wear Villager sweaters and blouses and Weejun loafers, for girls, and Gant shirts and Weejuns for boys. Kids went around school turning up each other's shirt and sweater collars to determine who was wearing the real thing and who was wearing the fakes. It was hideous,* and deserved all my father wrote about it, but then where did he get off not liking my having working-class friends?

The pressures of economic class were, I think, felt most acutely by my mother, since there had developed a very clear economic barrier in her family. Her brothers, as I mentioned before, both pursued very lucrative careers and both married into monied families. We had never socialized much with my uncles and their families, and did less so as time went on. In fact, except for my uncles putting in a brief appearance at my mother's funeral twenty-two years ago, I don't think I've seen anyone in their families since I was fourteen or so, when we were given a tour of one uncle's new home. The high point of the tour were the 24-carat gold faucet fixtures in two of the bathrooms. I have five female cousins somewhere in the world, and it's a safe bet that if I showed up on any of their doorsteps, none would throw open welcoming arms to this scruffy-economically struggling-dyke-psychologist relative.

All during my adolescence my family was on the outskirts of wealthier society—what I would now term lower upper class—a position conferred by my father's fame as a newspaper columnist. His credibility and visibility as a public figure bestowed a level of social rank that was several notches beyond my family's economic position. The pay my father received did not put us in an economic class commensurate with the social class status conferred by the job. Dinners out with theatre and movie folk, high-ranking politicians and musicians and writers were not uncommon. For all that we had food and shelter and never really risked not having it, my mother was frequently frantic about money. Growing up in the Depression certainly had something to do with it, but a lot of it was also status-related, involving pressure to achieve congruence between our social status and our economic status, and her feelings about it all being connected to middle-class shame.

It was *shameful* not to dress nicely. It was shameful to be one down to others. It was shameful not to use "proper" English, and it was definitely shameful to cuss. (We weren't even supposed to say "cuss." The proper

---

*When I was in the eighth grade I was walking down a corridor late in the day after most students and teachers had gone home. A ninth-grade boy, one of the really "in" ones, was coming from the opposite direction. He was carrying one large, heavy book, which he raised and then slammed down on my shoulder as he passed, muttering something about the "things your father writes."

pronunciation is "curse," but everyone always said "cuss" anyway.) I was fifteen or sixteen years old before I dared to utter even "hell" or "damn" out loud, and the first time I said "Goddamn," I did it in private, and waited to see if anything terrible would befall me. It didn't, and blue streaks have been easily at hand ever since.

We were WASPs—the "P" part in my case being the methodist church. Each of my parents and my brother and I went through our own rather disjointed tides of religiosity. My parents, but especially my father, pitched a fit when my brother started moving toward fundamentalism because his girlfriend was fundamentalist, and then later my brother and parents, but again most especially my father, pitched a fit when I became enamored of catholicism. (I dropped that particular interest when an older friend who had grown up catholic—and who was the first woman I knew to be lesbian—talked to me rationally about the subject. That's another story.)

Okay, so the part I'm putting off getting to is the puberty part, or rather the puberty-and-what-followed part. As a little kid I was the tomboy, played hard and got dirty, swung on vines across the creek and tore the knee out of every new pair of long pants I ever got the first time I wore them. My first awareness that things were changing came when I was eight, and my mother said I couldn't go around outside with my shirt off any more. I don't remember whether I overheard what followed or if she said it to me directly, but the case was that she had gotten complaints from other mothers in the neighborhood that I was getting too old to go around barechested. Middle-class femininity thus began its dreadful descent to wrap around my existence like a blanket—a heavy, extremely itchy woolen blanket—even though I didn't officially hit puberty until I was eleven.

Oh, the horror of being the first girl in the fifth grade to wear a bra—and have breasts to put in it. Lots of little flat-chested girls were wearing little flat "training bras." Such a hideous term, and none of them knowing just what they were in training for.

It was the same horror repeated when I was the first girl in the sixth grade to get my period. Already lacking in popularity, in large part because of who my father was, but also because my family didn't have as much money as the doctors' and lawyers' kids, I was the recipient of vengeful regard from the other girls who apparently seemed to think they were much more deserving of being "the first" than I could ever be. Perhaps that was because they whispered and giggled and showed each other their training bras, usually stuffed in the bottoms of their pocketbooks, during bathroom breaks, while I was simply in pain (those budding breasts hurt like hell) and enduring the shame of fifth- and sixth-grade boys making comments within my hearing about how "stacked" I was. (I rather doubt that such experiences are limited to middle-class female puberty, but I include it as my middle-class pubertal experience.)

There came too the expectations of dress, and worst of all, expectations of body type. It was much to my parents', but especially my mother's dismay when I hit puberty and not only didn't lose my baby fat, but filled out even more. The assault on my weight began in earnest—not that it hadn't been there before, but before there had always been the hope that I would "slim down" when I matured. That hope dashed, I was finally carted to a "fat doctor" when I was fifteen. She put me on three different amphetamines a day, and valium at night so I'd be able to sleep. Even so I slept only three or four hours a night, but my grades soared, the compliments about my new body poured, and my health went to hell in a handbasket.

I developed truly agonizing migraines—the ones I have now are piddling in comparison. I hallucinated during most of them, but dared not tell anyone because I didn't want them to think, as I did, that I was going crazy. I had horrible kidney infections, and a case of mononucleosis that nearly wiped me out of the whole first semester of tenth grade.

But my closet was full of new, "attractive" clothes, and to my parents' great relief, boys were asking me out. I eventually managed to get around the expectation of dating a lot by waiting for my Peruvian boyfriend to come back from Peru, which he never did and which I really didn't mind. But in the meantime I finished with the doctor, and the weight came back plus more, of course, so other boys weren't asking me out any more.

When the weight started coming back I felt like a failure, and that I had particularly failed my mother. She had, after all, spent all that money on the doctor, but I was getting fat again. (By the way, I now look at pictures of myself then and can't for the life of me see what they thought was wrong, but then it was the era of Twiggy.) My solution to this great failing was to become bulimic. I was, though, at worst, only a half-hearted bulimic. I didn't really like making myself throw up, took no pride in controlling my body, just felt like I should. I gave up my limited bulimia after a year-and-a-half or so. By then I really *hated* throwing up, and figured if the weight came back, I could always get back on drugs.

That's precisely what happened when I was eighteen. Two things played into the perceived (by my mother and to a lesser extent by me) necessity for me to lose weight again. Before I describe the first, let me say that I know for certain this is the real reason Julia asked me to write this—and I'll get you for this, JP—to create new opportunities for me to get razzed about being "Debbie the Debutante Dyke." So, there it is. I was invited to be a debutante. My mother was thrilled. I did it for her. Got the boy next door, who had just come back from Nam, to be my escort.

It was a very middle-class debutante ball. Instead of there being twelve to twenty "cream of society" young women, there were over a hundred of us. Instead of the ball being held in an exclusive country club, it was held in a high school gymnasium. I kept thinking, "This is ridiculous," but my mother was having a good time.

The second reason I "needed" to lose weight again was that I was starting college the next fall. This time, instead of so many amphetamines, I was given hormone injections. Don't know exactly what hormones, just that I got them and the weight came off again. Heaven forbid the first impression those college boys got of me should be fat.

Well, it wasn't, and for the privilege of "looking right" and being able to get a date that first week, my first date attempted to rape me. I got him to stop by telling him I'd get him kicked out of school if he didn't stop. I'm still amazed that my threat worked, and he stopped.

I'll skip over most of the rest of my college life, and return my focus to family, because the overshadowing feature of those years was my mother's alcoholism. I had identified that she was alcoholic when I was sixteen. My father and brother stayed in denial another year or so. Here again, middle-class shame was an impediment to her or my father or brother admitting it and seeking help. I benefited from another older friend, a woman of twenty-five whose mother had died of alcoholism. She impressed upon me the necessity of my getting help to cope, especially because no one else in my family would.

Alcoholism was definitely regarded as a moral failing, and most especially if the alcoholic was a woman. On top of the shame that would attend any middle-class family about it, there was also the factor of my father's fame, and my family having become something of a public role model for what and how families should be, that heaped an additional dose of shame on the situation.

To keep this painful story brief, my mother died between my junior and senior years of college. She had passed out with a cigarette in her hand. She died of asphyxiation.

Throughout my college years my weight had again gone up plus more. I had been out of college and working for a year when I grew very tired of having no social life. So I took myself to Weight Watchers. The process repeated, only this time without drugs. But this time, I got married.

It was the most radicalizing experience of my life. Middle-class wifedom was definitely not how I wanted to live my life. After two-and-a-half years I left my husband and came out as a lesbian. (That story is detailed in "Slow to Learn," *The Original Coming Out Stories* [1989].)

My early years as a lesbian, with my growing feminist consciousness, entailed careful evaluation of heterosexual, white, and middle-class privilege and what I could do about it. I tried making a living in a working-class job, on a production line in a printing plant. I was too slow, and got fired. Besides which, as a lesbian, and the daughter of my father, I felt immensely constricted, as most of my co-workers were either fundamentalist women or good ol' boy roll-around-in-the-hay types. I came to the conclusion that my survival skills are middle-class survival skills, and to survive I'd best use them. At the same time, I resolved to use them as much as possible to benefit those without middle-class privilege.

My economic situation for most of my life as a lesbian has been lower middle class—in debt way over my head, mostly with school loans which financed my master's degree in psychology, and which I'm still taking out to pay for my doctoral program. I've figured that I'll likely be able to get out of debt around retirement age. I'm a psychologist, in one of only two states that still license master's level psychologists. I could make more money if I did as most of my private practice colleagues do and refuse Medicaid clients—and eventually I may have to, to pay back my student loans.*

I still rent, and I rent cheap. Unless Ed McMahon shows up at my door with a check for $10 million, I can't predict being able to buy my own home. I do without health insurance because I can't afford an individual plan and I can't abide the thought of working for a community mental health agency with a regular salary and benefits.

Working for an agency, there are too many things one can't say and do. As it is now, I can challenge whomever, whenever, advocate in court for my clients however, without being afraid my job is on the line. (A favorite recent bumpersticker: Love my job. Love my boss. I'm self-employed!) My middle-class background has given me the skills—e.g., demeanor, style of speech—to challenge and advocate effectively. Middle-class ways of conducting myself are no longer who I am, but things I can do to accomplish the purpose at hand.

Even with all the debt and uncertainty about future money, I like my life very much the way it is, realizing as fully as I can that one reason that may be so is that my life is as it is largely by choice. Unlike many others, I have the option of being better off financially. I have the knowledge and the life history that would permit it.

---

*As I was finishing this writing, the state has dealt with the matter in its own way. As part of a budget-cutting move, Medicaid will no longer pay for psychological services with private practitioners.

Back to the Bare Bones...and the Broken Teeth

Anna Livia

My father's father was a colonel in the British Army. He served in India, helping ensure the smooth running of British Imperialism. He was killed in the Second World War and buried with full military honors.

My father's mother died in 1986 in a home for old women run by the state. She was not allowed to take baths because there was no one to attend her. When she had diarrhea the shit lay on the floor all day covered by sheets of newspaper until someone had time to clean it up. At her funeral the vicar got her name wrong; she was buried under someone else's name.

My mother's father was a stockbroker in Dublin. He had attended the Slade School of Art in London and spent some splendid summers on Capri before the war changed the ambience. His family had been sent to Ireland some three hundred years previously, given land and titles, to quell the native population. His family had been in Ireland for three hundred years, but they never called themselves "Irish."

My mother's mother was also from an aristocratic Anglo-Irish family. From her sixteenth birthday to the day she died, she weighed 112 lbs. This is the only achievement I ever remember her being credited with.

My father went to an English prep school (a high-class boys' boarding school) from the age of seven. He continued at Marlborough, one of the top English public (private) schools and thence to Sandhurst, the officers' training college. He was a captain and a "war major" working in British Intelligence. He was a script writer for the BBC, made documentary films in Africa, went back to Britain to die of cancer sometime in the 1980s...a large event in his own life, no doubt, a rather obscure event in mine.

My mother was taught by nine governesses, avoided her coming-out ball and presentation to the Queen by watching a non-stop film show near Victoria Station. She had six children, published a novel called *Before Summer* about a young Irish woman married to a British homosexual which someone really ought to republish. She worked as a secretary for thirty-five years. Now she lives by herself in a trailer in the West Australian bush. It is a very small trailer. There is no room for a bathroom or toilet; she washes in the shower block shared by the other trailer park dwellers. This is not aristocratic eccentricity. She could not at any time, at the touch of a phone call, reinstate herself in prosperous middle-class life. She lives on a state pension of six hundred dollars a month. She has no savings; there is no family money coming to her. There is no family money coming to me.

One of my sisters has two children, lives on welfare, has no fixed place of abode. The other is married with two children and a husband who is a car mechanic. She earns extra money looking after other people's children. Neither of my sisters graduated from high school. My elder sister died of leukaemia.

My elder brother has a degree in ancient history and archaeology, is a member of the Royal Geographical Society, and works as a welder. My younger brother earns more than anyone else in my family. There is not a lot of competition. He works with computers for the Social Services Department of one of the London Boroughs.

I look back at these simple facts and see, simply and clearly, that the money, the education, the position, the social prestige went to the men. And that the world has changed for my generation; the social fabric which kept the landed gentry in place is no longer there. Class requires money these days; education and accent are insufficient. My English grandmother died in squalor. My Irish grandmother avoided that fate by embracing an emotional suttee and dying a couple of months after my grandfather. My mother is very poor. At sixty she is unable to work; her left wrist is swollen and painful from carpal tunnel syndrome caused by thirty-five years typing men's memos.

I look back at my own life. I am thirty-six. I have a degree in French, an MA in Teaching English as a Second Language and am working on a PhD in French linguistics. I started my first degree at Bristol University. I packed two suitcases, took the tube (subway) to Paddington Station, got on a train, took a bus to the university. Everyone else I met had either been driven down by Mummy, or had been given a car to celebrate their getting into college. I got a full grant because my mother earned so little. When I needed to go to university interviews, my headmistress told me to apply to a special fund for the train fares. I only learned a few years later that she had actually paid out of her own pocket. My school uniform had always come out of the school second-hand cupboard.

I have bunions on both feet and a mouthful of bad teeth. The bunions date from infancy when toes are so pliable they can be bent back in on themselves. The child whose shoes were passed down to me had narrower feet than mine. I smashed my front teeth in Africa diving over a waterfall and my mother asked me,

"How bad is the pain? Can you bear it?"

"How long?" I asked through a mouthful of bloody gums.

"Two years," she said, "Till we go back to London. It'll be free there."

I looked up at her worried face bending over me, her eyes full of that grown-up fear of unpayable bills and I loved her. I nodded. I could bear it. For her, I could bear it. Only the most elementary work was done in Africa, and by London it was too late.

From the time I was fifteen and could legally work, I had a Saturday job. I saved all the money I earned. When I started sleeping with men a year later, I worried a lot about getting pregnant and needing an abortion. I put my money in an account I thought of as "the abortion fund." By the time I was twenty-seven and had been exclusively lesbian for three years, I decided to spend the abortion fund on getting my teeth fixed. I gazed in the mirror at my yellow broken stumps and thought how much I did not want people to know about them. I wanted to pass unnoticed, accepted, rich.

I did not want people to see my mother's face, that sudden wide open fear, so close, so easy for my anxious child's eyes to read. I wanted to protect my mother. It was an impossible choice to make. She should not have passed it on to me. She should not have had to make it. I could not expose her to well-fed Americans with private orthodontists and childhoods full of dental braces who would have found her criminally negligent.

When I told the story of my life I would emphasise my father's family in India—with humorous contempt for British Imperialism, of course, but the message was there all the same: I am from the top drawer, my class position is unassailable. I would dwell on my mother's family, their titles and estates. I lived on a farm in Africa which my father owned. Impressive. This actually said more about the terrible poverty of the Africans as my father did not make much money. He did not own anything any other white person wanted.

I have always lied about money. I have always pretended to have more than I have.

The majority of women I know in the women's liberation movement, or the various lesbian communities I have been part of, is middle class or has assimilated to the middle class. The majority of people I know in academia is upper middle class, or has assimilated to the upper middle class. I too am middle class, by education and aspiration though not by wealth, access to wealth or expectation of inherited wealth. By spending the abortion fund on bought teeth, by speaking only of my family's history and eccentricities, never of their current lives, by hiding my bunions in shoes and socks throughout the Berkeley summer, I too have assimilated.

I suspect all of us of lying to each other. I feel a sense of joyful relief when I realise someone else has poverty to hide, but mostly I find my friends' lies involve pretending to have less money than they really have, not more.

None of the details of broken teeth, bent toes and hand-me-downs are unusual in working-class women's lives, or indeed, in the lives of the African girls with whom I grew up. What is unusual is my family history of colonialism in India and Ireland. That colonial history is shameful: a million small acts of humiliation and tyranny as well as the systematic impoverishment, disenfranchisement and infantilisation of the indigenous population. My teeth, my toes and my second-hand clothes are not shameful. But it is they which make me shame-faced.

My English grandmother gave me a small black box before she died. Inside are a small pair of shoes. Very small. They measure scarcely three inches in length. Who could wear shoes that small?

"Genuine article, you know," said my grandmother.

"Genuine what?"

"Chinese," she said. "Your great-grandfather was there in the eighteen eighties. He brought them back."

I brought the shoes with me when I came to America, though most of my things I sold or gave away. I keep them in that small black box. Who could wear shoes that small?

How could we be so poor that my parents could not afford proper medical and dental treatment for me? Why did we have to get our uniforms from the school second-hand box? While my mother still lived with my father there should have been enough money. We had moved to England when I was fourteen and my father was making television programs about Africa. He must have had a good salary, but he would not spend it on his children. It was, after all, his money.

When my mother left him, she moved to a one-bedroom flat in North London where there was room only to bring my little sister. I moved to my aunt's, where my father was supposed to pay a minimal sum for my upkeep. I got a job working alongside my aunt as a theatrical dresser at a well-known London cabaret. Twenty six-foot "showgirls" would come running off the stage at the same moment, clad in heavy crinolines or cancan skirts, and we would have to strip the clothes off them, rub their sweating backs with a clean white towel, give them a sip of water and hook them into something else. My evenings were full of G-strings and red lace bodices, a scurrying up and down of stairs to get things from the wardrobe mistress because I was the youngest. The changing room was full of mirrors and the dancers were always peering at themselves, at each other, and at us watching them.

Over the summer I went to stay in my mother's new flat, sharing the bedroom with my little sister till the light green plants growing on the wall began to turn black and fill the room with a smell of decay. Then we shared my mother's bed in the living room. We slept under an enormous patchwork quilt she had made, not being able to afford blankets. My best friend's father was the manager of a local shoeshop and his wife had given my mother all the old orange and blue curtains they had used in a display. My mother used the material as a thick backing, and sewed our old shirts and dresses in patches on top. I liked to see those little flashcards of our lives lying on us as we lay down, as though all the things we'd done and seen would protect us in this new strange place.

I told one of my lovers once about that quilt. She was a working class American, dirt poor from South Carolina. Her face closed over as though to say,

"I don't believe you. You have such a plummy accent, you know about opera, hell, your family owned a box at the Royal Albert Hall. How could you be so poor that three of you slept under a shoeshop window display?"

But one day, when I was out, she had searched the cupboards, the bathroom and the boxes under the sofa. When I came home she had pulled the quilt out from the inaccessible back drawer under the bed. She sat with it on her knee, running her finger round the faded pattern of my little sister's summer frock.

"You must keep this, Anna," she said, looking straight into my eyes. "Don't ever throw it away."

By then it was falling to pieces. It was sixteen years old. When I packed to come to America I kept the new down comforter I had just bought and gave my mother's quilt to the Salvation Army. No one wants to import poverty, there is quite enough already in the United States.

The trappings of poverty. My mother's flat had no bath. We heated water on the stove and poured it into a tin tub which hung on the back of the door. There we bathed my little sister while my mother and I showered at the college where she worked and I was a student. This is as true, as vivid and as significant as the summers we spent back in Ireland swimming in my grandparents' private pool, playing tennis on their courts, while the gardener picked the best of the raspberries and brought them to us in a little basket.

It is not hard for me to know both these things, to be the person of whom both these things are true. What is hard is representing myself to the world which likes its truths to be simple, single-celled creatures. Questions about where I am from, how many brothers and sisters I have, what my parents do, take on unexpected complexity and I tend to simplify toward the mean. I am from London, I have two brothers and two sisters, my father made films in Africa. It is not true, of course, at least not the whole truth. But the whole truth is invariably not required.

And what effect does all this have on my daily life, my relationships with my lovers and others, my colleagues and fellow students at UC Berkeley? At Berkeley my English accent gets there first and imposes the interpretation: English therefore wealthy and well-read. Each time I say anything in public, at lesbian or gay conferences, readings, linguistics conferences, someone will obligatorily make a speech against intellectualism. It never matters what I have said; the point is that I said it in an English accent and that is against all the downwardly-mobile ethics of the radical community. At a writers' conference, for example, I once tried to point out that the term *lesbian* is often used to describe a literary genre and that it means "realist, domestic and somewhat squalid and, more recently, sexually explicit." This did not seem to me a frighteningly highbrow observation to make, especially since everyone there was a lesbian and a writer. A feminist publisher immediately declared that she personally would be incapable of observing the literary trends in lesbian fiction, she just knows what sells. Clearly, she knows what sells because she is an acute observer of literary trends. But her point was to dissociate herself from the last speaker, viz: me, and condemn any hint of an intellectual approach. This is, actually, perfectly fair since the radical Brits hate Americans just as much as radical Americans hate Brits. Whereas radical Britain views Americans as arrogant warmongers whose greatest dream is to own, radical America seems to find Britons arrogant intellectuals whose joy is to scorn.

Friends who do manage to hear beyond my accent nevertheless make the same association of Englishness with wealth, despite the fact that as soon as an American leaves the States they are inevitably travelling in a poorer country. They make assumptions about inherited wealth and access to wealth and I usually don't bother to correct them. It is my experience that people who are assumed to have money are treated with more interest, consideration and respect than those who are known to have none. One learns these things, one never mentions them, but one acts on them just the same. Whereas in Britain there seems still to be strong working class solidarity, in the States communities are more likely to form on the basis of ethnic identity than class ties. Getting rich in the States involves no break from a sense of class belonging, thus there is nothing to lose but poverty.

My family's class history affects me more tangentially. Phrases will suddenly form in my mind unbidden. "Net curtains, how vulgar!" "People like us do not use tea strainers." "Buying antiques? Good gracious me. One does not buy antiques, one inherits them." It enables me to pass as moneyed even though I am not. Mostly these attitudes are a rather ludicrous throwback, inadequate and irrelevant in a technological world, though occasionally one of my lovers will stumble across one and wonder why I am so contemptuous of cane furniture, which is so innocent and so versatile.

One time my accent and attitude, borrowed from a generation ago, did smooth away all obstacles. I was living in Paris for a year as part of my French degree. The rules were changed that year for British passport holders and all English students were advised to go to the British Consulate to get "Holder has the right of abode in the United Kingdom" stamped in our passports. It was considered a formality. The other students got the stamp swiftly and automatically while I, with my Irish birth certificate, was called into a separate room.

"How did you get hold of this passport?"

"What makes you think you are British?"

"We will have to hold your passport until you show due proof that you were given it legally."

They seized my passport and I had to travel to London the following week to be a witness in a trial against union activists. The French let me out of France with the grim words,

"We will let you go, but the British will not let you in."

I took the night ferry from Calais to Dover and stood in line at immigration control like the others.

"Hello," I said, to the man checking passports. "I'm afraid I don't have my passport on me right now."

"Oh?" he said.

"Mmm," I said. "Rather silly." He looked over at me, smiled and said,

"Well, of course you're British, just show them this card at the other end." And he waved me through.

I do not know what would have happened if I had had a working class accent, or been Black British. I imagine I would have been turned back and possibly arrested. What's more, I do not know whether I would even have tried to get in without a passport if I hadn't been white and middle class.

I look back at that statement, "One time my accent and attitude did smooth away all obstacles..." One time? I ask myself. Only once? What a wealth of class privilege rests in that simple statement. What I mean is there was one time when I had to notice where my privilege got me.

Crossing country borders without a passport is such a big screen event one cannot fail to notice when one has achieved it. How many of my achievements have I imputed to my own intelligence, wit or charm which would more honestly be explained by my class position? Did my headmistress pay my train fares because she liked me and valued my intelligence or because it seemed wrong that a nice middle class girl like me should be down on her luck? How many equally nice, equally intelligent working-class girls have not been helped to university interviews?

There is so much written about class; class alliances; class conflict; where women fit into men's class divisions; if we do; how class and race and gender interact. It seems to me often to have little relevance to my life, or the lives of women I know. The divisions are so clearcut, unchanging. I have not attempted an analysis of the incidents presented here. I have tried to relate only the things I remember happening, a return to the bare bones of raw experience, to outline some of the contradictions and conflicts which are my daily life.

Funeral Food

Elliott

I didn't necessarily want to be a writer. I wanted to be an artist, but in a way that counts, like being in a bluegrass or string band, or having the best garden, or sewing everything I needed, including quilts, or keeping a truck running after it has rolled 100,000 four or five times. But I never learned to play a banjo or dobro or fiddle, much less a *mean* one, and I don't sing or sew or garden or fix stuff. Instead, words pour through me; I'm a writer, from a world that judges you by what you do, not what you say. How the hell am I supposed to write out of my experience and values when writing itself was not part of them? At home our lives didn't have to be reflected in print to have value to us and so it never occurred to me to want writing by working class and poor wimmin until college prep and college english, when I was suddenly alone. I still have a hard time valuing my ability with words; this is neither a false modesty nor a problem with my self-esteem.

I really swear that one of these days, after I've said something about being working class and some womon comes up to me and starts talking about how she really understands what it's like being poor now that she herself is broke or about how hard it's been for her to understand and confront her class privilege, and she doesn't even know me, that I'm going to turn to her and say, "Look, bitch,"—which will prove to her, depending on who exactly she is, that 1) I am hostile, 2) I am not really a Separatist, 3) Separatists are hostile, or 4) working class wimmin are hostile and not really feminist—but anyway, I'll say, "Look, bitch, unless you are going to pay me either as much as you pay for tuition or as much as you pay your therapist, I don't wanna hear you whine." Later, I might feel a little bad about how I treated her, but only if it doesn't happen again that same day.

How much control do you have over whether or not you make rent, bills and food next month? How refined are your money management skills?

Egg Noodles
1 lb frozen egg noodles
2 cans Campbell's Cream of Mushroom Soup
Salt and Pepper
Milk

To Cook
Mix soup with milk in large pan until smooth. Add salt and pepper.
Add package of noodles. Cook over low heat until noodles are tender.

To Deliver
Put mixture in large glass noodle bowl. Cover with two layers of plastic
wrap. Set on a plate and cover the bowl and plate with tin foil. Take along
a serving spoon with your initials on masking tape on the handle.

To Reheat
Cut some of the noodles away with a fork. Place in a bowl with a pat
of butter in the bottom. Salt. Microwave until hot.

———————————

It seems to me that my middle and upper-middle class friends spent
their entire childhoods being trained to leave home—summer camps, reli-
gious/cultural camps, sports camps, music camps, prep schools, trips abroad,
trips alone to see grandparents or divorced parents, and so on—to get
them ready for their adult lives of going away to college and away to follow their, or their husbands', professional careers. Somehow, once they
were grown up, physical and emotional and economic independence were
to be interchangeable for them (all polite lies, of course, that cover what
class privilege actually does for you).

The only leaving I ever witnessed was about death or violence, including the economic violence of losing a farm or a job. I grew up six
blocks from where my dad was born, a mile from my grandparents, a half-
block from my aunt and cousins. When I did go somewhere I borrowed a
suitcase, since I'd always be coming back.

Now I've left home, to join the ranks of dykes who have chosen to be
"orphans." But I, too, left because of violence, not by choice, and I didn't
get out with my heart whole. Sometimes I wonder if there will ever be
enough dykes in my world to fill the emptiness of leaving home. I know
there will never be enough family—dykes who will be there when I'm in
trouble, even if they don't much like me, just because that's what we have
to do to survive.

———————————

About food and myself and my two lovers. Mari is lower-middle class,
grew up one generation away from farming in a Midwest city, went to state

universities, is culturally x-tian. Otter is upper-middle class, grew up in a ritzy suburb of a big east coast city, went to private colleges, is Jewish. The amount of money our families had for food and where it was spent was completely different. But Mari and I share a background of good, commonsense Midwestern food and a tradition of "supper on the table when Dad comes through the door," while Otter and I have a similarly twisted mess of cultures in which food is love and comfort and family ritual, and, as fat girls and wimmin, the control and denial of food as "love." Any of our mothers could be a tv commercial of a self-hating, self-starving Everywoman, although my mom wouldn't be dressed right. From this knowledge I make inferences about all of the intersections of gender, culture, identity, and class.

I'm on my way to being a bitter womon. I write because I can, because I enjoy it. But I always write knowing that what I say might never be taken seriously by the communities I perceive myself as part of. My words won't get into academic journals and be a hot topic; women's festivals won't pay me to lead workshops and lesbians with their notebooks and checkbooks ready won't flock to ones I participate in; I won't be getting big name, big bucks grants (check the biographical notes in any feminist/lesbian/gay anthology if you don't already know what I mean). What does it mean to be creating theory and stories that won't be read, or understood and valued even if they do get into print?

It's so easy to just stop writing, to be angry and to refuse to give any more of myself. Times when I need all of me just to get by, this is not a self-defeating attitude. I've had strength and integrity when I've been joyful and included; I've also been strong and honest when I am bitter and cynical and removed. What I do best at any one time is whatever I need to do to survive; calling this self-centered implies that I have a choice.

I could live a long time without having some middle class lesbian tell me how much "our" community *needs* my words.

Greenbeans

Dump a couple quart jars of greenbeans in a large pot. Add a quart or so of water, a hambone, some chunks of bacon, and salt. Cook over low heat for about an hour. Pour the beans, the juice and the bacon into a deep bowl; serve with a slotted spoon.

In the fall of 1988 I was at a Society of Women in Philosophy conference in Minnesota. During one session when they were all talking about confronting oppression and owning their privileges, I fled outside to be appalled and snide with my girlfriend, who is middle class but willing to think about it. I started the "Middle Class Academics' Theme" which I've been working on ever since. Here's what I have so far. It's sort of bluesy, set vaguely to the tune of "Cause I'm a Woman":

> I don't want to own my classism (ba da da dat)
> I want to sell it for a profit (ba da da da dat)
> You might work for your money (ooooooo)
> But my money works for me (let me tell you baby)

and so on. To be sung only when appropriate, of course.

I was 27 and in grad school before it clearly dawned on me that where I grew up is what is called "rural." After all, I was clearly a townie in the city kid/country kid split in school, and Waverly is the second largest town in Morgan county, with more than 1,500 people. I don't find my shock of realization charming or quaint.

At a Young Separatist/Young Radical Feminist Lesbian conference in 1990, we went around the room introducing ourselves. One of the first dykes talked about where she was in college and what she was doing there and everyone after her did the same. Part way around one dyke spoke out about how identifying ourselves by our education was really elitist and made her uncomfortable and sad. Most of us agreed but we kept doing it, and I was part of that we. I've thought a lot about that ever since. When I'm in a group of mainly middle and upper class wimmin, I don't want to talk about college because it pisses me off that, of all the things I've done, school is the only one all of them will value. In a group of all working class and poor dykes I don't want to talk about school because in college I was trying hard to pass for middle class and I'm still furious at myself for my complicity. But I also want to talk about college with these dykes cause they get it, they don't treat it as a given, they understand what it meant for me to be there. So I'm most comfortable with other working class and poor dykes who also went to college, in a world where we are always balancing between home and strangeness. It seems to me that we are always tired.

Ham Sandwich

Take leftover ham, mayonnaise, lettuce, tomatoes, cheese, butter and pickles from the fridge. Get bread or hamburger buns form the breadbox. Spread mayonnaise on one slice and butter on the other. Cut some ham, salt it, and put it on. Unwrap a slice or two of cheese and add it. Put on some lime pickles, some lettuce, and some salted tomato slices. Serve it with a coke and potato chips.

Since I came out I've written about all kinds of wonderful and horrible things, but almost nothing about my birth culture and even less about the moments of shock, confusion, embarrassment and shame that too often surround me in my now mainly middle class world. The stories I have to tell don't fit on a page because the language isn't right, forced into Standard spelling and constructions or mangled by the apostrophes and quotation marks that scream, "Warning! Substandard dialect ahead!" and if I leave these little marks of deviance out, some well-meaning editor—lover, friend or stranger—is bound to put them in, assuming, I spose, that I don't know what I meant to do, and even if this doesn't happen the written form is still only an approximation of real talk, anyhow. And my story lines and logic don't seem to work, cause if I don't put explanations in someone will say, "I don't get it, what does this mean?" and if I do put them in then it's no longer the story I'm tryin to tell but a story about the story I'm tryin to tell, and that makes me a translator when what I want to be is a writer.

Whenever a dyke asks me why I think there hasn't been a really good anthology about class and classism (the kind of dyke I'm thinking about would probably use the word "definitive"), I want to turn to her and not say a thing and see if she gets it.

If you were reading this because you have an investment in the lesbian community, do you feel that it has been worth your time?

In order for any oppressed group to get through life with their hearts whole, their culture must be able to replace what the world strips from them every day. I don't know how much lesbian cultures do this. Are we, as Dykes, willing to sustain each other? And I mean *really* sustain, not just entertain, challenge, instruct, appease, or even please and delight each other. Stopping class oppression isn't about needing a better philosophical understanding of privileges. It's not about being anti-oppressive or being a more effective ally, because class isn't about theory. Class is about survival, about which of us will and won't make it.

In order for any oppressed group to get through life with their hearts whole, their culture must be able to replace what the world strips from them every day. So that is why funeral food is salty.

Pam McMichael, taken at 1993 rally, We Will Remain.

Toothpaste, Socks and Contradictions

Pam McMichael

On a camping trip last fall, a good friend picked up my toothpaste in the shower house, squeezed it onto her brush, started brushing and quickly blurted out "Yuk! What kind of toothpaste is this?"

I told her it's Arm & Hammer baking soda toothpaste and that I like it because when I was little and we ran out of toothpaste we used salt and baking soda to brush our teeth. It's comforting to me.

I'm house/farm sitting for this same good friend now several months later, grabbing some desperately needed retreat and rest, and one of the things I love about her and her home is that this place is always full. By that I mean you don't run out of things. There is always toilet paper, coffee filters, the right medicines or herbs in the cabinet. I forgot shampoo and it's here. I forgot honey for my cereal and it's here. I want to make guacamole and she has lemon, nutritional yeast, and chili powder.

Brushing my teeth in her bathroom with Arm & Hammer I was having these appreciative thoughts and reflecting back to our exchange in the campground shower house, and a new realization took my knees out from under me a bit. My family ran out of toothpaste, not because we lived on a small farm and couldn't get to the store. We ran out of toothpaste and used salt and baking soda because we couldn't afford to buy more toothpaste until the next payday.

While I am no stranger to my own poor/working class roots and their shaping of me and my politics, and while I am motivated in a core way by the inequality between the "have's" and the "have not's," this info about the toothpaste was a new and significant understanding for me.

I have often told people that I grew up poor but not hungry. That means I grew up poor but didn't really know how poor until I was older and able to see things with adult eyes and activist understanding. Or, more true, it was the understanding that led to the activism.

I grew up on a farm in rural central Kentucky. At first my parents farmed full time—a tobacco crop, a few cows and a big garden. By the time I came along as the youngest of three daughters, both parents also worked in factories to make ends meet. We killed a beef every year and lived on it during the winter. In fact, my reluctance in finally becoming a vegetarian is because meat was so connected to my working class family survival.

My Mom is very talented and very bright. A needle and thread sang in her hands. Whether it was new Easter outfits for her girls, a suit for my Dad, or a lone star quilt, people marveled at her talent and creativity. For a long time we had no bought clothes and wore entirely what she had made us.

For the last seven years, she has done breathing treatments four times a day, can barely get around, and now needs oxygen all the time. Hot lava and alcohol fumes on the assembly line have left her lungs damaged and beyond healing.

Class means Mom lost her health sooner than she should have. Class means I lost my Mom sooner than I should have.

My Dad also worked for a while in the factory, then drove a wholesale grocery truck. In the summer before my eighth grade, we left the farm and "moved to town" so both parents could be closer to their jobs. Soon after we moved my Dad became a police officer, serving the 5,000 people of Lawrenceburg, Kentucky until he retired.

In my family, class meant confronting sexism early on.

"If I'm going to the fields with you every day," Mom told Dad, "then you're going to help me in the house when we come in." He agreed it was only fair, and I was born into a household where the man also took responsibility for cooking, laundry and cleaning.

Class also meant confronting racism. My Mom worked night shift at the factory. At work she met an African American woman who lived in the town through which Mom passed on her way to work. They developed a friendship and started riding together. Our families were in each other's homes. Mom and Wanda were some of the first to cross the color line in 1963 Anderson County.

Class meant being forced out of stereotypes and roles. I admit it doesn't always work that way.

I never bought in to the American myth about working hard and making it. I knew no one could work any harder than my parents, and making it meant survival. There are others who work hard and don't survive. My Mom has health insurance. Many do not.

I have some rich friends. Sometimes I am furious at them for being rich. Sometimes I think I'm a shit for feeling that way. Other times I think it's perfectly understandable to have strong feelings of rage and resentment when that kind of discrepancy is right in your face.

For example, a friend's parents gave her $20,000 for her birthday. Three weeks later my parents gave me $20. How do you balance love and letting go with that kind of range?

One of my closest friends is independently wealthy. She is a committed, passionate full-time activist, using her time and money for social change. Based on who she is, her values and politics, I am happy that kind of money is in her hands. I respect what she does. Still, I sometimes resent her control of her time and freedom. I cannot imagine the ability to choose exactly what she wants to do with her day, every day. I can't fathom "not having to work." I would love to know how it feels.

It's hard to write these feelings. I have certainly benefited from this friend's money. Repaired transmissions. Deposit money so I could move. Even a vacation. Not just timely needed loans, but generous gifts. Still, sometimes I am jealous.

I grew up southern Baptist. While I have totally rejected "He is the way, the truth and the light," there is one Bible story which I loved at the time and still appreciate—the widow's mite.

A poor woman gives a small donation to the church and rich people are chastising her for her "pitiful" contribution. Jesus says, "No, she gave more than anybody because she gave more of what she had."

Too often I have seen comparisons which make me uneasy. The thousand dollar contributions to a campaign or cause get more applause than someone's five or ten, when actually that five or ten may have been more generous a donation in terms of what someone had to give.

Or also someone's time. People who have financial situations which allow them more time to work on an issue are often heralded as "giving more" when others are doing their work on top of full-time jobs.

In 1986 I went to Nicaragua as part of Somos Hermanas, a national multi-racial delegation of lesbian and straight women. One day in response to my fundraising letter, I received these two donations in the mail. The first was a check for $75.00 from a woman I didn't know very well. I was elated that she had given so generously. The next envelope contained a one dollar bill from a student I barely knew at all. With her dollar, she had written a note I still have. "I don't have much money these days but I hope this will help. It is indeed an important event in the solidarity of women as well as in the solidarity for human rights."

I loved the contradiction of those two gifts and I left the note by my bed for a long time.

I don't have pride about people with more money giving some of it to me. I did once. An out-of-town friend was flying me to meet her at her grandparent's on the Georgia coast. This friend definitely had the money. I did not. I was struggling with her offer. An older friend and co-worker flipped my arm with the back of her hand. "Don't you give what you have?" she asked. I got the point.

During a Marxism class, a friend and I argued whether my parents were part of the bourgeoisie because we owned a farm. I maintained that we really didn't own the farm (the bank did) and that farming didn't support the family anyway. Also others around me who didn't own their own farms but worked even in different factory jobs had higher standards of living than we did. We did not take vacations, own a boat, etc. It gets complex.

As a thirty-eight-year-old woman who consistently made decisions, including professional ones, based on class values, I find myself now thinking about financial goals, something foreign to me. It's also scary.

I want to own my own home.

Class means I never really thought it possible on my own.

Also as I near forty, and despite my desire to feel differently, class has found its way into being a yardstick of self-esteem and accomplishment. Several months ago I was in what I called a crisis of self-esteem and part of the way this crisis manifested itself included laments like "I'm thirty-eight years old and I've never owned a washer and dryer. I'm thirty-eight years old and I'm still renting." (I now have a washer, charged on my Sears card, as part of getting over this crisis. I am, however, still renting.)

At this point in my life I am disappointed by the lack of collective ownership and helping each other both on the left and in the lesbian community. I admit I also have not helped make this happen.

Several of us have sat around this same farm, dreaming, envisioning and planning how we would build cooperatives and collectives. For instance, I might take a year off and write. Then I would work and help some other sister pursue her interest. What happened to us? Were these ministrations of a naive group of women without commitment? Absolutely not. While there have been changes, we are still passionately in each other's lives, and have been for years.

Maybe one of the things that happened was twelve years of Republican administrations that have taken their toll on working people. Taking a year off is scarier now when you know it will be hard to find a job when it's your turn. Also, the hits people have taken meant they had to be more focused on individual survival than building collectives. If you're barely making it, then what's left toward a friend's special project?

I know one collectively owned household in Louisville. A good heterosexual friend, her husband and daughter live in a collectively owned house with separate units or apartments for different people or families. I find myself thinking more and more about doing this with women, both for the financial help it would give each of us as well as the safety for women in this society.

I was thrilled when a Tennessee friend sent me the call for papers for this anthology. As I said, the struggle between the "have's" and the "have not's" is at my core, just as much as my lesbianism and my being woman. But I have also been nervous trying to write honestly about my feelings about women and class, from a personal standpoint. It meant bringing up some painful feelings concerning people close to me and holding up some of those truths to a scrutinous light. And it meant bringing people out. How could I write about women and class on a personal level and not talk about some of my friendships in which we are delicately, passionately and some days better than others working out these divisions and differences?

Would I be using this essay to rub it in? How to present my feelings and thoughts honestly without it sounding like that?

I mentioned wanting to own my own home. But there is a huge tension because I also want to work less hours and have more time to write and do activist work. Every person I know in my life who works part-time in order to pursue other interests is helped by a partner, and by that I mean sexual partner. Sharing financial resources seems more obvious, I guess, if you're doing it with someone.

This is perplexing to me. Why are sexual partnerships automatic access to each other's money when other forms of relating are not?

I'm not saying making a financial commitment to someone is an easy or light matter. It takes trust and is a huge commitment. Still, in my life, it is friends, more than lovers, who have been there for the long haul. I have seven-, ten-, twelve-year friendships full of love, caring, trust, commitment, passion and being there for each other. Lovers, however, have come and gone. What is a single woman to do?

I have been blessed and helped, tremendously and generously, by friends more financially well off than me and by friends with less resources than me. And I have generously helped other friends. But I know of few examples where another person who is not a sexual partner is empowered financially to do what they want or to pursue an interest or dream. And I have to wonder why.

I tell an older friend that when I win the lottery the first thing I'm doing is buying her a house, and the second year I'll get one for me. This is a nice notion, but overwhelming odds are even more against her since I rarely, if ever, play the lottery. I have a couple of friends who tell me they will help me write if they win the lottery. This is more exciting because they actually play it.

I don't play the lottery because I feel so ripped off when I don't win. I feel like such a chump to fantasize what altruistic and wonderful things I could do with the money and then face the reality that most of us will never know that kind of money.

In Louisville we have been in an intense campaign to get antidiscrimination legislation for lesbian/gay and bisexual people. I am on the coordinating committee of the campaign, coordinating the lobbying effort in the early stage of the campaign and now on the negotiating team which meets with the elected officials. There are numerous things to say about our experience here but one pertinent to a personal narrative on women and class is my surprise sometimes that I am doing this. Sometimes I do feel like the kid from the farm or have a sensation of disbelief that I'm doing this. People have rolled their eyes when I try to explain this and have also challenged me in a positive way to move past the feeling. But in my body sometimes, the feeling is still there. And it comes from class.

During the campaign, the *Courier Journal* ran an article on "Being Gay in Louisville." Six of us, three lesbians and three gay men, told our stories on the front page of the feature section of the Sunday edition of a 325,000-circulation newspaper. Full-body color photos. A subsequent letter to the editor criticized that "only preppies were featured in the story." I was irritated by his assumption. Because of finances, none of the lesbians own our own homes and one of the gay men did not. And the green silk shirt I was wearing is the only silk I have ever had, a present from my boss and friend.

I have focused much of this narrative on my experiences as they relate to people who have more than I do. But there is also much to say about the contradictions the other way, both professionally and personally.

I work as an assistant director in a University-based social service employment and training program for low-income women. For ten years, daily, I have been face-to-face with women—AFDC* recipients, displaced homemakers, single parents, older women, ex-offenders (most women's crimes are economic crimes), refugees, immigrants—whose lives according to class are certainly a different struggle than mine.

I must seem the bourgeoise with my car that runs, my dress-up clothes (when I have to), and my health insurance.

The lives and the stories to which I can bear witness have for ten years touched me, angered me, humbled me, and above all, politicized me.

A single parent with three children and a bad back gets a $4.25/hr job sewing buttons in the top of baseball caps, and I have awakened at night with the horror on my mind.

Quality of life needs are one thing. Survival is another.

When I'm sitting around wondering what it would be like to "not have to work," I come smack up against the despair and reality for millions

* *Aid to Families with Dependent Children (what is usually called "welfare").* —ED.

of women and poor men whose opportunities for meaningful work at livable wages is a myth and a farce.

My work has been about women and class, and race and class, and the intersection of gender and race and class. And after a decade of doing this, even with providing essential services and opportunities for thousands of women, needs are deeper than ever, resources fewer, and hope diminished, including my own.

And what is most difficult about my experience with class is the number of people, including women, who assume that the way class plays out in the U. S. is okay.

Or who assume that sisterhood will bring us all together as women, ignoring our race and class differences.

A few years ago the local NOW chapter met at the office of the Kentucky Foundation for Women. During a monthly meeting which was running late, an African American award-winning lesbian writer on staff at the Foundation poked her head in the meeting and asked if they were about finished. She was staying late that night so the chapter could meet. A woman answered her question, "Oh, do you need to clean?"

A 59-year-old African American friend called me one night to take her to the emergency room. Her nose was bleeding and it would not stop. With head tilted back in the examining room chair, my friend joked, "I think that nurse has a crush on you. I'm getting a lot better service than when I was here last week." (Her daughter and son-in-law had brought her then.) But we both knew the reason behind "better service." I had no money in the bank, but in that situation my white skin still had bought my friend better care.

This same friend and I have helped each other out many times, juggling paydays, floating bread, milk or toilet paper, literally feeding each other. One night she says to me, "You know neither one of us is ever going to have anything." And the sad thing is, she's probably right. And the contradiction is, she and I have also sat by the river catching summer relief in a late night breeze, and talked of no regrets and how blessed our lives have been.

In 1991 I received a grant from the Kentucky Foundation for Women for a series of short stories about four generations of rural Kentucky women in my family. I resigned the percentage of my job the grant would cover, crowded the remaining hours into a four-day work week, and set out with this heavenly day off to write.

It still was not enough time. Pulls from work, organizing, phone calls, cleaning my apartment so I could be settled in to write.

I was complaining to a friend about how precious little time this was, and she said, "Okay, let's look at how you can maximize it."

There were some obvious things. "Don't answer the phone. Let go of some of the political work. Put boundaries on what kind of job calls you'll take on your writing day." And then the suggestion, "What if you came to your writing day with your apartment all clean? What if you hired someone to clean your space?"

This was an intense suggestion, and one to which I felt immediately resistant and yet drawn. It seemed ridiculous in some ways to pay someone to clean my apartment. After all, it is not that big. Plus the class feel of the whole thing.

But I sat with the suggestion, my feelings about it, and ran the numbers. I really could afford a couple of hours every other week. (If I was going to do this, I definitely wanted to pay well.) And here was a lesbian friend who makes her living cleaning homes and needing to pick up a job.

While it took some time to give myself permission for this, I have to admit I loved it, and valued coming home to a clean space and the time it freed up for me. Still, I was acutely aware of the differences in our situations. I have health insurance. She does not. I take a day off work and it is a paid vacation or sick day. If she doesn't work, she gets no money.

This same friend represented our grassroots interracial women's organization for a special project to bring a Guatemalan Indian woman to Louisville. After the event, she told our group she never wanted to work in that same coalition again. The class impact has been too difficult. And some of it was basic—like where to have the event so it is accessible to people without cars.

I mentioned earlier my friend paying for the flight to Georgia to visit her at her grandparents'. During that trip a significant thing happened. Our first morning we had grapefruit. I sat down at the table and picked up my spoon, then realized the pulp was already neatly sectioned and ready for me to enjoy. I was slightly stunned. Yes, I had eaten grapefruit before that someone had sectioned for me—my mother, for instance, or someone else who loves me. But this was the first time hired help had sectioned my grapefruit. I was uncomfortable and felt out of place there.

It was class similarity, however, that broke down the barrier with a former lover's very homophobic parents. The first time I met them, we sat in their living room. Her Dad was a mechanic who now owned his garage. The parents totally ignored me and my lover did as well. This went on for over an hour and then my girlfriend said, "That's a nice shirt, Dad."

Her father answered, "Yea, when I wear this people think I'm rich." I laughed immediately and three sets of eyes turned on me, this stranger in their living room. Then all four of us were laughing and the rest of the visit I even received some eye contact.

In my experience I have noticed two basic reactions when someone grows up with limited means. One watches parents and grandparents struggling to make ends meet and says, "I'm never going to live like that." The other watches the same struggle for survival and says, "I don't want to live that way, and I don't want anyone else to have to, either."

A generous friend of eleven years is a welder and now full-time union organizer. If you're at this friend's house and need, say, a pair of socks, she will tell you to go get a pair out of her top drawer. Any pair you choose would be fine. I have been in this situation where other friends hand me a pair, ones they don't like or that have holes in them even.

Now there are some people making money, maybe even getting rich, by calling this kind of thing co-dependent. But I call it a generosity that comes from class survival, a giving that knows what it's like to be without, and doesn't want anyone else to be there.

Marilynn, age 6, and her father, 1953.

mixed-class confusion

zana

i've wanted to write about my class background for years, but have always been stopped by the fear that i'll just sound defensive: "i may seem middle class, but there are other reasons i do such-and-such."

and, in fact, there *are* other reasons. and, in fact, there are reasons that boil down to privilege anyway, even if they didn't start out that way. for instance, some of the values i get from being half jewish help me get along in the middle class even though my jewish father grew up in the ghetto, poor.

class is hard to talk about partly because it *is* complex. many people's backgrounds are mixed—their parents were from different classes, and they (or their parents) have moved up or down on the class ladder. this fragmentedness describes my background, but only partially; there were other factors that added to the confusion. for years i've tried to make order out of something that doesn't want to be orderly. instead, now, it occurs to me that there can be value in just talking out the details.

i guess my first big jolt of class confusion came in sixth grade. my father confided in me that we had $33,000 in the bank. i'm not sure why he chose to honor (and burden) my young ears with this information. it does go along with the way in which i was raised: included in much of the adult business. also, my father likes to show off his financial acumen. he takes pride in the hard work, hard saving, and intelligence that allowed him to escape poverty.

whether he specifically said so or not, i got the idea that i shouldn't tell my friends about the money. certainly, they never would have guessed. we lived frugally, to say the least. i used to feel that in our house the depression had never ended. i first saw a piece of moldy food at the age of 11 in someone else's house. food waste in our house was more than a crime— it was unthinkable. we saved string, bags, rags, rubber bands, gift wrap, you name it. to this day i have rarely bought any of those things which are gotten for free. back then i felt like a freak when i found that other kids didn't save those things. still today i feel that way when one of my dyke land-sisters opens my sewing basket and exclaims, "wow, look at all those safety pins!" yeah, and a lot of them are over 34 years old: the little brass ones that came on doll clothes i shoplifted. i've had the basket that long, too. you don't buy new things when the old suffice.

thirty years ago, $33,000 was an even more impressive sum than today. my 12-year-old mind was torn between what it meant to "have" such an astronomical amount, and the fact that in daily life, we didn't. yes, it was good to know it existed. once we went to peer at $30,000 houses (we owned a $10,000 house) and i shared my father's pride that he could have bought one outright. i knew from adult talk that most people didn't pay cash for big things. they bought them on credit, and that's how the rich got rich and the poor got poorer. we bought cars and houses outright and paid no interest. how my father managed to save so much, to get that far ahead while supporting a wife and four kids, is a mystery only he knows, cause when i was born he was scooping ice cream for a living. (that is, i know nothing of investments, wheeling and dealing, illegalities, veteran's benefits, etc. the part i know all too well is the scrimping and saving. and i know my father rarely had "free time"—working probably 12-14 hours a day as a fuller brush man.)

the second great confusion for me, when i became aware of class divisions, was about "culture." my family took great interest in the arts. at nine, i had two favorite records—one from a walt disney cartoon movie, and one by tchaikowsky. there are opera arias i still hum automatically because daddy sang them all the years i was growing up. in the bathroom there would be a book with two markers in it—both parents were reading it and discussing it. i did not, like my friends, go ga-ga over elvis. one of my biggest thrills ever was getting to hear lily pons live in concert—a special concert with all seats a dollar, so we got to sit on the main floor instead of the second balcony.

i was greatly encouraged in artistic pursuits. mom bought me a small set of oil paints; my aunt raved over my drawings and said i got my talent from grandpa siegel, a russian-jewish immigrant who, working in a factory, still found time and energy to paint, copying scenes from postcards.

we lived in a neighborhood that was working class/lower middle, and that's where most of my friends came from. they mostly weren't interested in books, plays, classical music. i learned not to talk about these things or i would be thought of as weird. it may be that these kids were rejecting their parents' values more than i was. it may be that if i had dared talk about things as they really were in my home, i would have eventually found i wasn't the only one. but i didn't, and so i did feel like the only one. and i related that both to being jewish in an anglo environment, and to class. somehow i felt of a different class than my neighborhood friends. yet when i made friends outside the neighborhood—middle class friends—there was so much in their homes, their assumptions, and their nicey-nice conformity that made me uncomfortable.

when i moved to lesbian land in 1980, class soon became a bigger issue than ever before in my life. i suppose because we all wanted utopia and were so angry when we couldn't make that happen. in those years, in that place, there was only one angry womon of color and one angry disabled womon (me), but there were groups of angry mothers, jewish wimin, and working class/poor wimin. those were hard, bewildering times. having grown up watching supposedly "middle class" people on tv—people who lived with much more affluence than my family—and not identifying with them much at all, i was alarmed to suddenly be called middle class. alarmed, offended, defensive. didn't middle class mean conforming, and buying into the status quo? besides having worked for years at low wages, i had never felt at home in mainstream american culture.

it was painful to be told that wimin didn't trust me because i spoke in a precise way, with school-perfect grammar. or because i'd had the privilege of artistic encouragement and thus felt comfortable identifying as an artist and writer. i'm sure many people had felt those ways about me in the past, but only in the relative honesty of lesbian community was anyone saying them out loud. with all the pain i felt, i still was relieved to have the truth come out. better than playing guessing games!

maybe i could say "i can't help it" about those kinds of privilege, but then there was money. it was mind-blowing to suddenly be perceived as "high income" because of getting a regular (disability) check—but there you have it. among dykes on land, a monthly check of nearly any amount beats trying to live off of odd jobs, craft sales, savings, etc. my disability settlement of $5,000 plus another $5,000 i was able to get from my father by asking him to give it to me now instead of in his will, was money i immediately put into our purchase of the land we lived on. i also paid one of the highest monthly portions of the land payment. yet for some of my poor/working class land-sisters, this was not enough. i was pressured to do more money-sharing. at this point class and disability issues began to collide for me. my monthly check bought me goods and services i needed as a disabled womon—as well as some comforts that helped compensate for my limitations. if i gave up more of that money, would the group ensure that my needs were met?

it has taken me years to get any kind of perspective on that situation—one that ended hurtfully for all concerned. i'm living on a different lesbian land now. for many reasons, which i hope include my own growth, class has rarely been an issue for me here. having a close friend from a poor background enables me to learn more about class in an environment that doesn't feel hostile.

i assess who i am now, in my mid-40s. less denying of the label "middle class." (i define myself as lower middle class.) less defensive about it. if someone is put off by how i use the english language, so be it. i've been turned off by others' mannerisms, and sometimes that's just how it is. i don't, any more, seek to deny that it's a class privilege. my working class mother was the one who did the hard work of learning how "educated" people spoke and passing it on to us kids. slowly i've come to understand just how much that particular gift benefits me, for survival in a hierarchical society...in subtle ways, like how i'm treated by store clerks, as well as the more obvious advantages like having been able to breeze through english classes without even studying.

disability and class is still a tough one. one of the hardest realizations for me has been that many wimin from poor or working class backgrounds push beyond pain and fatigue in ways i don't. i grew up getting medical care for physical problems. (that's one thing the savings were for.) wimin from lower class backgrounds than mine often appear (to me) to be more able-bodied than i am, and then i may want help from them that taxes their own bodies. they may not think to refuse, being unused to making a big deal of their own body limitations. in several situations, wimin have ended up annoyed or angry at me when they realized they were sacrificing their well-being for mine. only through time, trust, communication and friendship does it seem possible to stop these dynamics. i hope we come away from such interactions with a better understanding of ourselves and each other. those are the tools that will help us act differently in the future.

money-sharing...is something i want to do with wimin i care about. i don't want to end up resentful, though. to avoid that, i've found it necessary to go slowly and carefully into this dangerous territory. what's my motive, my intent? do i expect something back? if so, i need to let the other woman know about that expectation!

i've shared money most often by paying a larger amount of land payment or rent than wimin with less income. i've shared by giving money in emergencies and by paying for necessities or a fun evening out when friends didn't have much money coming in. i recognize the point at which i still hold power and control: *i choose* which wimin i will be generous with and in what situations; i decide how much of my income i can spare. even when i've had an ongoing monthly commitment with someone, that can end at *my* discretion. i'm on the other end of this often enough—sometimes around money but usually around disability—so i know it injects something unpleasant into friendships. there's the constant knowledge that if you displease the other womon, her aid may end.

another aspect of class privilege is those resources we have hidden access to. i have had to come to terms with the fact that even though i don't *want* to take money from my father (let alone ask for it), i do have that option. he's not rich, but he could help out in crisis. i also expect i'll inherit *some* money from my family—maybe not a lot, but some. and i know wimin who have no family alive, or whose families have no money or assets to leave them.

as i learn to take more responsibility for my privilege, i want others to do so as well. if i pay the middle of a sliding scale admission, it makes me mad to find someone with hidden resources paying the bottom because she's "broke" this week. to me, "broke" means you have no money anywhere—no trust funds, CDs, savings—nada. i don't want to hear friends saying they "can't afford" things when what they really mean is they don't choose to spend their money that way.

it seems to me that the first step in combating classism is being honest about the facts of our lives. it's hard to talk about money. hard to admit to privilege. hard to open oneself to criticism. this article has been hard to write. it's the product of years of thought. it comes out of being pushed up against the wall about class issues—and also from having poor and working class sisters be gentle and loving and patient with my process. i know i'm still near the beginning of this journey—the learning of how to share privilege, the understanding of how class has shaped me and what it continues to mean in how i live my life.

Juana Maria Gonzalez Paz, Fayetteville, Arkansas, 1983.

From Battered Wife to Community Volunteer: Testimony of a Welfare Mother

Juana Maria Gonzalez Paz

In 1976 my husband began beating me with a frequency and inten-sity that caused me to fear for my life and that of my nine-month-old baby, Mary Ann. We lived in a small cottage on the Florida coast and I supported all three of us with my veteran's benefit that enabled me to go to college for the first time.

In June of that year, Brion admitted some startling things—that he'd made sure he slept with me every day until I got pregnant and that he'd manipulated me during the entire relationship through an elaborate sys-tem of lies and deceptions. He laughed and said it was easy, that I had a moral code that I lived by and he could always anticipate how I'd react to any situation. He also said he wasn't letting me go alive. I threatened to leave and he threatened to kill all of us, including the baby and the dog.

The night he dragged me around the house closing windows with one hand, to muffle the noise, and covered my mouth with the other, I knew he was serious. I held the baby with one arm and with the other I tried to loosen his grip on my mouth so I could breathe. I broke free long enough to scream bloody murder and the police arrived within minutes, checked me for external injuries and tried to get me to make a statement but the inside of my mouth was cut and I couldn't talk. They assured me that my neighbors were looking out for me and urged me to yell if I needed help. They said someone in the neighborhood would hear me and call them.

They left and Brion apologized. Actually, he wanted to have sex. I refused and he waited until the next day to rape me. Things went from bad to worse and I made plans to leave town. I was all packed and waiting for a ride to the bus station when he came home drunk and carrying a loaded gun. He held me hostage for four hours and slapped me and knocked me down so many times that I can't remember them all.

He wanted to kill me but I think he was afraid to live without me. He raped me until he couldn't get an erection anymore. Mary Ann cried at first but I closed the door so she couldn't watch and she sat down in her crib to play her red piano.

Brion decided I should cook one more dinner before he killed me and I ran away from him on the way to the grocery store, despite his promise to shoot me in the back if I made any false moves. He disappeared when I started screaming and I got to a phone and called the police. Since I looked like a victim from a horror movie by then and I'd called many times before, they had no trouble believing my story but they did think I might change my mind later and refuse to press charges. I explained that the only way for me to get out of town alive was for them to keep him in jail overnight. The bus to Los Angeles left once a day and I had already missed it.

I dropped out of school when Brion sabotaged the car. The campus was several miles away and public transportation inadequate so that was the end of my steady income. (I'm a Vietnam-era Navy veteran and I was going to school under my GI Bill.) Brion had quit his job so he could watch me every minute and I didn't trust him to stay home with the baby while I went out to work. I tried to get welfare but I wasn't eligible while Brion lived with me and he refused to leave. I had to get out of town to save my life and I had to get to a major city with emergency social services. I chose Los Angeles because it was far away and on the west coast. I knew how to survive on my own in a big city but I didn't want to go back to New York.

I arrived in L.A. after three days on the bus and I didn't know a soul there. I got on welfare quickly and again, no one had trouble believing my story. My bruises were starting to get large and purple and yellow and my face was sore and swollen, too. There I was, a young woman walking around a strange city with a baby, a suitcase, and signs of a recent beating. I guess it was pretty obvious. "I know, I've been there," women on buses and street corners seemed to say to me with eyes. Wherever I went people seemed to know I was on the run.

I spent nine months staying home, taking care of the baby, healing, forgetting, remembering and letting go. Some days I was too upset to leave the house. When I did, I often returned to my roach-infested apartment near MacArthur Park to face a dreaded image of my husband standing in the shadows, red-faced with beer and violence, holding a gun and sneering, "Hello, honey...get undressed."

"That it could come to this," I thought as I calmed down and assured myself that it was just my old fear welling up inside me and making it seem so real. Surely he could never find us. After all, the police had arrested him. After the better part of a year I was ready to face the world again. I went to a welfare conference and plunged headlong into welfare rights work. I gave and gave and gave, trying to change a system that basically never budged, though minor concessions were made, and I, personally, could have become a token minority at a low-paying social service agency job.

I stayed on welfare and learned how to cope with people's assumptions about me, mostly that I'm not working and that I am more dependent on "the system" than they are. People seemed to expect me to feel ashamed of being on welfare and they thought I would want to keep it as secret as possible. Like when I was a battered wife, I wanted *everybody* to know and I wanted them to know how I got there. I made a conscious choice to stay on welfare, especially as I became more employable. Aside from people's attitudes about my supposed inferiority, shame and dependence, the life is not that bad. I had my time to myself, and I had already learned the "ins and outs" of the welfare department so I knew I was eligible and how to stay that way. The money wasn't much but I'd been buying all our clothes and household supplies at thrift shops for years anyway, so it didn't really involve a major change in shopping or lifestyle. Also, I was already pretty much a vegetarian and by eliminating expensive meat and dairy products from our diet and cooking from scratch a lot, I could feed both of us on my food stamp allotment.

I basically like living alone and don't miss having a mate. I never wanted to marry again, although I did despair at the beginning of ever resuming "normal relations" with men. Then I decided I didn't know what that was and didn't care. I was not afraid to face the world alone and never thought I needed another person to co-parent my child, although a lot of my plans were postponed for years while she was little.

When welfare rights became a never-ending cycle of infighting and meetings that went nowhere, I went on to other things—women's land, school again, feminism, writing, lesbianism, and to tie it all together, I began writing regularly for lesbian/feminist publications. I still have to contend with people's judgment and hostility, their resentment that I'm getting "easy money" or that I'm getting paid to "sit home and be creative" because I had a baby, while they have to go out and work for a living. I make a clear choice to forego the social status and higher income of regular employment in favor of the income maintenance and freedom of movement that I now enjoy.

Most people who hate me for being on welfare would not want to live the way I do. Until recently, at my daughter's insistence, I had never bought furniture, appliances, or any kind of entertainment equipment such as TV, radio, tape recorders, etc. It was fine with me to live without these things, but at seven years old and in public school my daughter feels a tremendous pressure to be "normal." In fact, I've done such a good job of living within my income that she doesn't seem to know that we're poor people and she regularly tells people that we "have a lot of money."

I have to watch that because most of the people who get prosecuted for welfare fraud get turned in by a friend or neighbor. People continually ask me how I manage to stay on welfare and if I really lie about my income. They always seem disappointed when I assure them that I am completely legal and I report everything. My book business is well-documented in my AFDC* case and it doesn't generate enough income to affect the amount of my monthly check. I am careful about not telling people in the community "my business" because even though my continued eligibility remains unchanged, any investigation into my case could keep me busy for a long time and basically make my life miserable while I clear myself of all accusations.

The hostility and put-downs are constant and subtle and all of a sudden I'm not so sure of what I want anymore. I think all my early volunteerism was a way of proving myself to be a capable and worthwhile person and to give something back to the taxpayers who support me.

In addition to the women's movement, where I wrote for free, I have also been a volunteer at a mental health association, community radio and TV station, a food cooperative, and I put in hours at a Feminist Women's Health Center until they decided volunteerism was oppressive to women and sent me a check for my work. I'm not sure how much appeasing my own sense of guilt and inadequacy for not being a wage-earner has actually helped, either myself or the world around me, since pandering to people's hostility about welfare never changes their minds. If anything, the resentment increases both inside and outside the feminist movement, as I become more successful and happy and learn to use my welfare income to promote my career as a writer and media personality.

I have accomplished enough now that I do not have to keep proving myself again and again and I want to be more clear and focused in my goals and activities instead of just keeping busy for the sake of being active. I still want to work to make the world a better place but now I want my own goals to be a priority and I think it's okay if there's something in it for me, too, when I give my time and energy.

One of the biggest obstacles to achieving my full potential is people's continued presumption that I am not working and my time is available, or that I should work for them for free or just generally let them waste my time. I should make it clear that these responses and presumptions are just as strong and hateful within the New Age "counter culture" and the women's movement as in what can be called the mainstream United States culture.

I have enough plans and ambitions to last a lifetime if I don't let other people's attitudes undermine my enthusiasm and will to achieve, but it's a constant struggle. Usually, it's easier not to discuss welfare with anyone,

*Aid to Families with Dependent Children.—ED.

especially white people who hate me for so many things anyway. It's alarming sometimes to think about how many minority groups I belong to and what that means, that it takes enormous energy and inner strength to overcome both the external obstacles and my own fears. I spend a lot of time just working on myself, coming down from the last episode and preparing for the next idea or goal, and I think I have come farther in order to be where I am than people who don't carry the following labels: I'm a woman, Puerto Rican, I have no college degrees, I'm a veteran, a single parent, a lesbian, on welfare, a vegetarian and kind of a counter culture progressive type. I've eaten organic food for years and I make and wear my own flowing matriarchal costumes. Also, I'm more downwardly mobile in terms of lifestyle and upwardly mobile in terms of accomplishments and work.

Some days it's just too much and I don't want to face the outside world. That's why it's important for me to live alone, with just Mary Ann, so I don't have to. When I can't take it anymore I just go home and lock the door. With no phone I'm pretty inaccessible and I discourage visits from all but the best of friends, those people who don't put any pressure on me.

As far as the broad assumption that I am more dependent on the system than someone with a job, I can only contend that I feel freer now than I did when I was being controlled by a boss, a husband, a university and even the feminist movement. Keeping the welfare trip together gives me a lot of leverage in dealing with the rest of the world. If my books don't sell I don't have to worry about how to pay the rent and if the people I work with on a volunteer basis don't like my performance, they can't withhold the paycheck. I would never want to be financially dependent on a husband or a lover again.

In a way, being on welfare has given me the freedom to be a totally independent artist and also to stay celibate as long as I want. I acknowledge the fact that white lovers, male or female, usually represent an opportunity to increase my access to money or privilege and in that way, I always depend on the relationship to make my life easier, whether that capability is realized or not. I've opted out of the whole lover game by concentrating on myself and my own process and progress.

I no longer ask for those things that are mine by right—respect, freedom of choice, privacy, tolerance, and understanding. I'm not sure I believe in mass reeducation anymore. I think misjudgment and ignorance are deliberate excuses that people use to get what they want at other people's expense. The people who value my work and myself seem capable of doing that without long involved explanations so I have stopped qualifying my life as well as my statements and I am less likely to let myself get put on the defensive by someone else's accusation or desire to monopolize my time.

Although more opportunities exist for me in the feminist movement than anywhere else, I'm not sure it has all the answers, either, since mistrust and malevolence continue to divide women and keep us from realizing the full extent of our power together. As people take their freedom, in all walks of life, I believe the answer for all of us lies in the ability to increase our own and each other's choices. I don't think the energy expended hating people like me with my $116 per month welfare check is helping anybody and that kind of jealousy/anger/resentment is something that women continue to undermine each other with. It is time we started applauding each other's freedom, choices and movement in many—different—directions.

My daughter and I stayed on welfare in Arkansas till 1988, when we moved to Florida with a former partner of mine for a year during which I was on welfare but had a higher standard of living; there were three incomes in the home: mine, my partner's, and her mom's. When my partner and I broke up, my daughter, then thirteen, and I moved to Puerto Rico, where my parents were born. There we received food assistance, about a hundred dollars a month, in cash, not food stamps.

Since 1990, we've been at Twin Oaks, a large commune in Virginia. The commune provides food, shelter, clothing and a small cash allowance of $50 per month. Mary Ann, now 18, starts college in the fall of 1993. She'll major in theater. In future, I'm interested in building a simple shelter on lesbian land and being as independent of the cash economy as possible.

Thank you to author and healer Billie Potts. This article arose out of topics first addressed in our correspondence. We still exchange letters on a variety of lesbian community issues.

This essay was a prizewinner in the 1983 Gay and Lesbian Latino/an Essay Contest sponsored by Gay and Lesbian Latinos Unidos de Los Angeles. Juana Maria Gonzalez Paz, Twin Oaks Commune, Rt. 4-Box 169, Louisa, VA 23093. 703-894-5787.—ED.

Why Women Are a (Set of) Class(es)*

Fox

This paper explores what it means to say that *women are a class.* (While the assertion focuses on the class difference between women and men, I do not intend by it to deny the reality that there are class differences between groups of women as well.) The first section discusses the economic significance of reproduction. The central section then presents a marxist-type class analysis of men's exploitation and oppression of women in present-day industrial society. Although I have found marxist class analysis useful in this case, I am not in any other sense a marxist. Actually the paper began 20 years ago, when I knew a number of academic socialist feminists. I thought if I could put down on paper the obvious conclusions to which their own theory led, they would put their own and other women's oppression first. (I was wrong.) The final section extrapolates the discussion to the future, and to the future of lesbians in particular.

Reproduction

The key to making such a class analysis is understanding the economic and social significance of reproduction, i.e., of conception, pregnancy, childbirth, and nursing. When it deals with the topic, feminist theory generally sees reproduction as a debilitating factor which either has directly prevented women's having social and economic power equal to men's or has weakened women and allowed men to seize power over us. (See for example, Firestone, 1970, and Atkinson, 1970.) I argue, however, that childbearing is not an impediment but a source of great economic and social power, and that women's herstory is in large measure the herstory of the struggle with men for the control of this power. The current emer-

---

*The first version of this paper ("The Housewife and Marxist Class Analysis") was self-published in 1975. A second version ("Why Men Oppress Women"), including a new look at the literature, was (self) published in the first issue of Lesbian Ethics in 1984. For this third version, I have revised some of my argument, but have not done another survey of the literature.

gence of the lesbian movement signals a major shift in this struggle. Lesbians are, I believe, the future of women. We are what women are becoming. To see reproduction clearly, we need to see that reproduction is a socially constructed rather than a biologically determined activity. The issues I'm going to raise here are seldom discussed in sufficient depth, because of the assumption, fostered by male propagandists and widely held in current society despite the evidence to the contrary, that there is a high, biologically given rate of intercourse leading to conception. This assumption has prevented full consideration of the sexes' struggle for the control of reproduction. Even Elizabeth Gould Davis (1971) and Helen Diner (1973), strong matriarchists, assume that women naturally seek frequent intercourse. From most people the question, "Why do women have babies?" produces snickers, not analysis. Discussions are of "society's" "technological" struggle with biology. If "society" needs to reduce its population, the task is to find the birth control technology that will "separate sex from reproduction." If "society" needs to increase its population, the tasks are to improve health care and food supplies and to limit access to the just mentioned birth control technologies.

As lesbians know, separating sex from reproduction is, physically, a simple thing to do. While developing the means for separating intercourse from reproduction, means such as the diaphragm and abortion, may be a difficult technological task; separating sex from intercourse is not. There are several kinds of satisfying sex besides intercourse and several kinds of people to do them with. Theory needs to explain why women and men in any particular society at any particular time practice some kinds of sexual and reproductive activities and not others. As Ti-Grace Atkinson (1968) argues, intercourse and conception are social, and I would specify economic, institutions. It is not just the variations in family and other social structures surrounding intercourse and conception, it is the *existence* of intercourse and conception that must be explained.

Imagine an egalitarian society in which men did not oppress women. Imagine this is how women and men started out, thousands of years ago. What would the egalitarian control of reproduction look like in this society? Both women and men would have complete control of their bodies. Women would decide whether or not we wished to conceive, carry the baby to term, or breast-feed. Men whether or not they wished to impregnate. Neither sex would be coerced physically, economically or socially into reproduction or into any kind of sexual activity. Such a situation would give women considerable power, from at least two sources. The first source is the emotional and religious allegiance to women as childbearers. The second source is the control of the birth rate and population size. The first has been with people since we were capable of allegiance, emotion, and awe. The second becomes significant whenever population size is significant to the socioeconomy, as, for example, in war-making societies and in agricultural and industrial economies that appropriate the labor of many for the benefit of a few.

Looking at the first source, we can find several reasons to believe that the tie between women and children would be stronger than the tie between men and children, and women would thus have the power which comes from the allegiance of the next generation. Breast-feeding, necessary in most times and places, would build the tie between nurse and child, particularly if it were accompanied by other forms of child care. All misogynist societies have developed means of wresting children, particularly boy children, from the influence of their mothers. There is also the social and psychological power women would derive from the salience of biological motherhood relative to biological fatherhood. The existence of the individual and the species is created and nurtured in the bodies of women. The awe in which motherhood was formerly held and the male struggles to build a counteracting ritual and ideology have been documented in many places, e.g., Davis (1971), Diner (1973), Hays (1964), Stannard (1970). When Marge Piercy, in her future society in *Woman on the Edge of Time* (1980), used non-womb reproduction, gave children three parents, and had men breast-feed babies, she was reducing the power advantage which childbearing gives mothers and thereby reducing the possibility of male backlash.

As for the second source of power, since women would not only share control of conception with men but would also have sole control over abortion and breast-feeding, women would have more control than men over the birth rate and population growth and thus more of the power that comes from that control. Matriarchy would be an apt name for such a system. Women's power would be considerable. The birth rate affects the size of the labor force, the size of the army, the standard of living, and the relative power of the classes within the system and of the system with its neighbors.

Control over the birth rate is the power to make the rate go up or down. However, conflict between women and men would most likely occur around increasing the birth rate. Since pregnancy is a risk to life and health, and physically painful as well, women have a stronger motive than men to limit reproduction and to reproduce only when the benefits to ourselves are high. For example, among recent gatherer-hunter peoples studied by women anthropologists (Goodale, 1971; Kaberry, 1939), the primary reason the women gave for attempted abortion was avoiding the pain of childbirth. Infanticide was common, from 15% to as high as 50% of births; reasons, in addition to the healthiness of the infant, were the burdens of carrying and caring for the child.

A matriarchal system would not be inherently oppressive to men. Men would find matriarchy noxious ONLY if they WANTED to do things that require a high birth rate, things like war and slavery and appropriation of the labor of others, and ONLY if they were willing to subjugate their own mothers, sisters and daughters and confine them to lives of physical and emotional deprivation.

Obviously, thoughts such as these lead me to take seriously the evidence for matriarchies and amazons. Even if matriarchies and amazons are myths, these myths are still evidence of the dynamic which creates male supremacy. (See, for example, Bamberger, 1974.) Evidence of women's and men's awareness that reproduction gives women potential power and that women's inferiority is itself a myth.

It is men's urge to violence and destruction which has caused the devastation of our planet and the misery in which our species lives. This devastation is founded on the oppression of women, specifically on the confining of women to absurdly high rates of childbirth. These birth rates make war, slavery and exploitation possible, while the overpopulation itself directly depletes the planet. History is the story of men's struggles with each other, fought on the ground of women's oppression, fought with the children extracted from our bodies against our will.

Is It Testosterone Poisoning?

How did things get this way? Male violence and cruelty cannot be explained as results of learning and conditioning. The argument for conditioning leads to an infinite regress. That is, at some point there would have to have been teachers and conditioners, men whose violence was an innate part of their biological maleness.

There is, however, some evidence that at least initially some strains of males may have been more virulent than others. The earliest people, gatherer-hunters, lived off the land, either as nomads or settled in caves and small villages. Archaeological evidence and observation of present-day gatherer-hunters tell us that their lives were good. Gathering and hunting provide an excellent diet with a low investment of labor even in apparently sparse environments. Population size was small and relatively steady. Currently or recently existing gatherer-hunter societies show a wide range of relations between the sexes. Men in some societies are intensely misogynist, oppressive to women, and war-making; men in other societies are less so. Some societies are egalitarian and peaceful. There are no recorded cases of societies in which women are cruel and oppressive to males.

Perhaps, then, there was originally some biological variation in males. The more violent conquered first their own sisters and then their more peaceful neighbors. The more peaceful, whether so by learning or genetic inheritance, always face The Pacifist's Problem. Gentleness, by its nature, has no defense against the warlike. Through rape and murder, the conquering males would have greatly reduced the frequency of the more peaceful male strains in the population. That some genetic variation in males may still exist is suggested by the fact that methods for propagating and reinforcing violence—methods such as army training and multigenerational sadistic cults—still exist.

Elizabeth Fisher (1979) describes how the transition to maleocracy took place in one area of the world, Mesopotamia, and convincingly links the change to the development of farming. Farming actually represented a decline in the quality of life, especially for women. Compared to the previous gathering and hunting economy, farming provides a poor diet, is very hard work, and *requires a high birth rate*. Wherever in *history* we find an agricultural society, i.e., large-scale farming, domesticated animals, surpluses and cities, we also find male dominance, i.e, cruelty to women and children and animals, war, slavery and exploitation. In a system dependent on agriculture, private property becomes not only possible but important; stored grains are hedges against natural disasters and famines; farm animals, women (as producers of children) and children are essential productive property.

Fisher describes how the Sumerian farming villages of Mesopotamia evolved in several stages from a collective, tribal, and communal structure to a hierarchical, bureaucratic, male state, in which warring and raids on neighbors were major occupations and in which the few acquired private property from the overworked majority. The male authoritarian state and the male authoritarian family evolved together, "...but there is today more evidence for the authoritarian state preceding the power of the fathers—patriarchy—than vice versa" (299). At the beginning of Sumer, 5000 years ago, both women and men could have several spouses and could divorce freely. At the end of the Sumerian period some 1700 years later, a man could divorce a wife freely without any further financial responsibility, while a woman was to be stoned to death for taking a second husband. A woman who attempted abortion was to be impaled on a stake and left unburied, and a husband could split his wife's ears for going out with her head uncovered.[1]

The Class Analysis

In order to present my analysis of the sex classes under industrialization, I need to take you through a short course on marxist class analysis.

A premise of marxism is that economic forces are primary, i.e., that economic factors have a stronger determining effect on social forces such as politics, law, religion, education, science, art and personal psychology than any or all of these do on economics. Part of the mystifying screen the maleocracy[2] (pronounced male-ocracy) weaves around sexism is that "women's problems" are personal, psychological, emotional, private and noneconomic. Even those of us who know better can fall into the trap of arguing that noneconomic factors are important as a way of arguing that women's issues are important. We can sometimes even fall into the trap of agreeing that women's issues are not important. For example, in the April 1984 *WomaNews* I found the headline, "Salvadoran Women Battle Dire Poverty, Sexism a Secondary Concern." When the Women's Liberation Movement said, "the personal is political," we meant that what the maleocracy *calls* personal is *in fact* a **political** *system*. This meaning is seldom understood now, the phrase usually being interpreted to mean that even if we are focused on what is *in fact* personal we can still *call* ourselves political. This turnaround is evidence of the power of the lie the phrase was intended originally to confront. The personal is political. The personal is also economic. Women are outside an analysis of the economy, but we are inside the economy. On the bottom.

In order to determine one's economic class, marxist class analysis cuts through the verbiage to ask, simply: What deals do you make in order to eat? Or, in more formal marxist terms, What exchange relations do you enter into in order to get the means of subsistence? All the people who take the same part in the same exchange relation (also called one's "relation to the means of production") belong to the same class. If the exchange is unequal, there is exploitation. That is, if you give out more than you get back you are exploited. If you are exploited, you can also expect to be oppressed in a whole range of noneconomic areas such as law, politics, education, religion, science and the "arts." That is, the economic (exploitation) causes the social (oppression). Exploitive exchange relations cause class conflict and eventually revolution. The marxist concept of "class" is different from and a lot more precise than our everyday use of the term to convey differences in income, education, and occupation. The definition is a structural one: A description of the classes is also a description of the structure of the economic system. Different economic systems, through history or around the world, are distinguished by their different class structures.

The exchange relation between the industrial worker and the capitalist is the only relation marxism analyzes in depth. A few people, the capitalist class, own the raw materials, the factories, and the goods produced in the factories. The great majority of men own only their own labor power. Most of these workers, the proletariat, rent their labor power to the capitalist in return for wages. With these wages they buy the means of subsistence, products of their own labor, from the capitalist. These commodities are used to reproduce their labor power daily and to raise the next generation of workers. (Think we're skipping over something there?) The capitalist combines the rented labor power with the raw materials and machinery to produce commodities. With money from the sale of these commodities they buy their own means of subsistence, luxury items and services, more materials and machines, and more labor power. The relationship between the proletariat and the capitalist is an exploitive one. The capitalist insures that the workers add more value to the product than they receive back in wages. It is exploited labor, materialized as profits, which maintains the capitalist's high standard of living and which is invested into expanded means of production. The workers are forced into the most vicious and destructive of positions: With their own labor they reproduce their own exploitation. This self-regeneration of exploitive exchange relations is one of their essential and most important features.

Of course, to realize a profit, the capitalist still has to sell the products. Since it is the wages of the workers which buy the products and the total wages are less than the total value of the products, the capitalists cannot as an aggregate realize a profit. But some individual capitalists can at the expense of others. This is why capitalists "compete" with each other. It is also why capitalism is inherently wasteful, because all the products cannot be purchased. But whether or not they are purchased, the workers are still exploited in producing them.

There are some difficulties and confusion surrounding the marxist concept of exploitation. In earlier, more existentialist versions of the concept, the exchange relation between the proletariat and the capitalist was seen as inherently exploitive because the workers had put themselves into the product and therefore rightfully owned it. When the capitalists took ownership of the product, they were appropriating the workers' labor and stealing from the workers. This concept of exploitation was never fully abandoned, and still resonates for many today, but marx later shifted his focus to the more "scientific" "labor theory of value." This theory posits that the market value of a product is determined by the labor hours used to produce it. Labor is the only component of the manufacturing process which is exploitable and which can therefore produce a surplus over the long term. However many labor hours it took to make a machine or obtain raw materials, the machine and materials over their useful life will add only this much value to the resulting products. People, however, can work more hours than it costs to (re)produce them, and it is these extra hours, not compensated for by wages, which produce the surplus. It is doubtful that the labor theory of value holds up as a description of how the market operates. And my analysis below finds it descriptive only of some parts of the industrial economy only under some conditions.

Whatever theoretical terms we use to explain exploitation, the workers are motivated by it to revolution, to "seizing the means of production," in order to take back what is theirs. This revolution is possible because capitalism itself has grouped them together in factories, where they can organize themselves. When people on the left fight to be labeled the most exploited, or the most importantly exploited, it is because marxism says that that exploitation qualifies them to be leaders of the revolution.

The middle class and the poor are not significant in marxist analysis and are both seen as essentially part of the proletariat. The "Bourgeoisie" are the capitalists, not the present-day middle class. (When monarchies and nobility were still powerful, at the beginning of capitalism, capitalists *were* the middle class.) Both the middle class and the poor operate to keep the industrial workers in line, in different ways. The middle class work for the capitalists and are exploited as well, but they are given less boring and less physically dangerous and demanding work (and sometimes but not always better pay). They manage the industrial workers and serve as a buffer between them and the owning class. The existence of the poor keeps industrial workers in fear for their jobs; the workers are also able to dump their angers and frustrations on the poor, rather than direct them at the capitalists.

Sexism is Classism

As you have probably noticed, the above analysis does not describe much about the lives of women under capitalism. Two feminist marxists, Margaret Benston and Mariarosa Dalla Costa, made important contributions in this direction. Benston (1969) was one of the first to turn our attention to housework. She emphasized that women do essential and important labor and that we do it without pay. She goes even further; she says women "…as a group do have a definite relation to the means of production and…this is different from that of men." I was excited when I read that sentence, because it is only a teeny step from there to the statement that *women and men are classes in the marxist sense.* Benston, however, does not take this step and, thus, leaves two major flaws in her argument. First, although she asserts that housewives are exploited, she does not define their exchange relations and thus cannot demonstrate that they are exploited. The best she can offer is that housewives are disrespected because they are not paid money (only goods) for their work. But housewives suffer more concrete oppressions than what others think of them. Second, as are most definitions of economic classes, her description of the housewife is sex-neutral. That is, there is nothing in her description of housework—cooking and cleaning, etc.—that requires the worker to be a woman. As there is nothing in the definition of the proletariat or the capitalist that requires the class members to be male. Why **are** housewives women, anyway?

Dalla Costa (1973), in a wonderfully fiery paper, shows us the direction of the answer, although she too refuses to go all the way. Dalla Costa draws our attention to the parts of the capitalist production cycle that we sensed were skipped over in the above analysis of the industrial worker and the capitalist. To persist, any production cycle must reproduce itself, from day to day and from generation to generation. It is women who are the reproducers. Women reproduce the labor force, from day to day through housework, and from generation to generation through childbearing and child care. Women's bodies are means of (re)production. Labor is labor. There is a glaring gap in marxism where the analysis of reproduction should be. Men may find themselves in industrialized production, but as theorists they must be able to see beyond factory walls and follow their analysis to its logical conclusions. That requires that they see into their own homes, where their own dinner does not materialize itself upon the table.

Dalla Costa, then, has solved part of the sex-neutral problem. Only women can be in a class of childbearers. We have now only to understand why the childbearers also do housework. Dalla Costa, however, does not see that she is defining a new class; she insists that housewives really work for the capitalist and are part of the proletariat. It just won't wash: The housewife does not work for the capitalist, who pays her nothing, but for the husband and children, who own the product of her labor, their own labor power. If in fact housewives were members of the proletariat, they would be equally exploited with men, and Dalla Costa would have failed to explain sexism, to explain why women are *more* oppressed than men.[3] Why **do** men oppress women, anyway?

The step that Benston and Dalla Costa do not take, and indeed the step that would surely cause their expulsion from the society of marxists, is to state that women and men are in a class conflict with each other. I do not see how we can avoid this step, even if we would want to. By saying that women are a class in relation to men, I do not mean to say that all women are in the same class with each other. There are class differences among women as there are among men. I would expect male control of reproduction to be the major factor in the exploitation and oppression of all women. However, the dimensions along which women differ, and the exchange relations between classes of women, remain to be defined. (In fact, the notion that women can relate to each other economically at all is a revolutionary one.) The economic class system is multidimensional. It is way past time to surrender the simplistic "working, middle, upper" litany. A major area this paper works out for future theoretical work is the development of this long overdue multidimensional class analysis.

The woman we call a "working-class woman" and the man we call a "working-class man" do not in fact belong to the same class. Our use of these terms continually reinforces the assumption, which most of us would recognize as an error if we thought about it, that women and men can have the same class position. **The** working class does not exist, neither does **the** middle class. We need to find new terms for women and men; every time we use the old terms we erase awareness of male supremacy.

Sexism is **classism**. Women are always poorer, always earn less, always work harder, eat less, starve sooner than men. These are qualitative not quantitative differences, these are class differences. At the base of all this, I am saying, is pregnancy, is childbearing, nursing, and child care. At the bottom are women's bodies, manufacturing labor power.

The Evolution of Housework under Industrialization

To understand how reproduction has ensnared women in our present complex economic situation, it works best to look first at how women's work—wage labor and housework—has evolved under industrialization.

Industrialization developed in England from the 1400s through the 1700s. The first textile factories appeared in the early 1800s. Over the preceding seven centuries (700 to 1400) England had gone through a process not unlike that described above for Sumer. A tribal society had been replaced by a male authoritarian state and the accompanying male dominant family system (Hartmann, 1976). Male farmers and artisans, as heads of families, possessed their wives and children and all the products of their labor, including any wages they earned. What happened to the wives of wealthier men makes it clear why we need a multidimensional class analysis. They were not needed to do physical labor, but were often condemned to perpetual labor in childbirth. The job of nursing their infants was given to poorer women (nursing inhibits conception of a new pregnancy), and the wives of the elite became more purely breeders.

In England, Ann Fanshawe bore twenty-one children in the twenty-three years and twenty-nine days which her marriage lasted. Her childbearing career was brought to a close only by the death of her husband in 1666... The composer Pleyel...was one of forty-some children of his father... Enrico Caruso was the fifteenth child of his mother, the first to survive. (Fisher, 1979, p. 389)

These examples of continual pregnancy also illustrate that once men had seized control of reproduction, they could use reproduction itself, specifically pregnancy, as a *means* to oppress women, by draining our energy and constricting our lives. In a very different time and place, the u. s. today, teenage pregnancy is constricting the lives of young women barely into their teens, destroying their chances for getting an education or a decent job.

Industrialization required overturning the older agricultural socioeconomic order. The first workers in the factories were women and children.[4] Men, who had more powerful and central positions in the old order, were able to maintain themselves outside the factories for a longer time. Eventually, as small farms were taken over and accumulated into large land holdings and as industry took over the manufacture of commodities, capitalism eroded men's power base outside the factories so extensively that men had to enter the industrial labor force in larger numbers. This same pattern was repeated in the u. s., where men of color were also among the earliest industrial workers. The union movement was the male struggle to push women and children, and, in the u. s., men of color out of industrial jobs. The male protectionist nature of the union movement has been well documented by Hartmann (1976) and Falk (1973). Exclusion of women from unions, and from the wage labor force if possible, was often an explicit goal of male unions. "Protective" labor legislation limiting women's and children's working hours was part of this strategy, and the feminists who opposed it (only a few did) were essentially correct. The right thing to do, of course, would have been to legislate decent working hours and conditions for all adults and to include all adult workers in the unions. As it was, women's alleged protection became another pretense for not hiring women and for paying women lower wages than men. And union membership became a far better protection for wage-earning men than protective laws could ever have been. The sanctimonious "working people's struggle" mantle around the union movement is a lie. We should pull the covers at every opportunity.

What the privileged male worker won through the union movement, by the early 1900s, was the family wage. That is, he won from the capitalists a wage sufficient to support not only himself but a wife and children. This man does own something which fits the marxist definition of labor power, because the wage he receives for it pays for all the commodities and labor necessary to reproduce it. He is paid enough to obtain a housewife, or to eat out and send his clothes to the cleaners. These men do not do the labor of reproducing themselves so they can go back to work the next day, nor the labor of raising the next generation of male workers. In these terms **women do not own labor power**. We earn 64 cents for every dollar a man earns.[5] Women's jobs, such as secretary, pay less than do men's jobs, such as groundskeeper or garage attendant, which require less education and skill. Women, with few exceptions, do not make enough money to hire maids or eat out. Women, as women on welfare and/or as housewives and/or as wage laborers, do the labor involved in the daily replenishing of ourselves and in raising our next generation.

The least advantage a privileged male worker gets out of the family wage is more free time than women. If he has a housewife, however, he can extract even more surplus. She is on call and working for him 24 hours a day. In addition, a housewife's labor can substitute for commodities, if she grows vegetables or cans food, for instance. The more housework she does, the more of his wage the man keeps. The man can use his surplus time and money for leisure and hobbies. He also can and does use the surplus in the variety of ways which maintain men's control of the money economy. He uses it to increase the value of his labor power through education and training (called putting hubby through school), he uses it to work long hours "to get ahead," he "capitalizes" it by starting his own business, he uses it to do the union and political work which protects men's interests. During the last century, while these men were meeting in bars to form unions, women (excluded from bars, interestingly enough) were working 12-14 hours in the factory and then going home to do the cooking and sewing.

What I am saying is that the well-known sex differences in the economy are structural. They are due to a classic exploitive exchange relation between women and men. Men and not women own labor power. To own labor power is to be paid enough to obtain a housewife whom one can then exploit. With the surplus from this exploitation, men control women's access to money and thus force us to continue doing housework.[6] When women's wages are only enough for the material necessities, we do not have the time and money men have to invest in labor power. When there are fewer jobs for women than men, women have even less time, because many, wage earners or not, are coerced into the "security" of marriage and are doing men's housework as well as their own. With that housework, women reproduce men's control over the money economy.

This exploitive exchange relation is seen most clearly among women and men above the poverty level. The situation of the poor, more often women and men of color, shows both similarities and differences. The extent to which poor men own labor power, for example, is an important question for a multidimensional class analysis.[7]

There are two remaining questions about the exploitive housework system itself. The first one is: Why did the capitalists accede to the family wage? Marxists are fond of saying that sexism and housework are in the interests of capitalism. They take as given that capitalism is the main source of evil, so assume that other evils must be caused by capitalism. The theorist's task becomes nothing more than constructing the best argument that leads to the known conclusion. A more objective look reveals ways in which the family wage, housework, and sexism are not in the capitalists' interests at all. If women had an equal position with men in the wage labor force and if far fewer women were doing housework for men, competition for jobs would be greater, wages would be lower and more "rationally" related to the skills required, male workers would have fewer resources with which to extract higher wages from industry and great new business opportunities would be opening in the area of industrialized housework services. Why have the capitalists given all this up?[8]

The privileged male worker's ownership of labor power is the only part of the wage economy which conforms to the labor theory of value. And this conformity does not appear to have occurred because of some general market law determining value, but because these men used force and intimidation to reassert their control over women. Basically, men own labor power because they stole it from women; just as the capitalists own the means of production because they stole them from men. Capitalists continually try to undermine the family wage, and lately with much success. They have moved their plants to "third world countries" where, guess what, the workers in the factories are women and children. In this country the number of families where the woman and the man both have to work for wages is increasing rapidly. And newspaper stories are appearing about single men who have to go home and live with Mom, in order to keep some of the disposable income they've been used to.

The second question is: How does childbearing fit into the picture? I've said that housewives are women because housework includes childbearing, yet my description of the current exchange relations between women and men has said nothing about children. The answer to these two questions is going to tie everything together.

Reproduction under Industrialization

Reproduction has been in a conflicted state since the beginning of industrialization. In the preindustrial system, children, and therefore mothers, were a considerable economic resource for the average man. Both were productive property, owned by him and supported by him when necessary. Upon separation of the parents, custody of the children was always given to the father. In the industrial system a wide network of family ties is still an economic resource for the ruling elite and the poor, for different reasons. For the people of moderate means, however, the bearing and raising of children is an economic responsibility without any apparent economic benefits to the man or the woman. Thus, in the u. s. since the middle of the last century, custody has been given in almost all cases to the mother, increasing even further the real income disparity between women and men. Child support is inadequate, rarely paid, and nonpayment rarely prosecuted. The more centralized the economy and the state become, the more the benefits of controlling reproduction pass from individual men to the male ruling elite; yet the actual control has passed only partially to the male elite. The family as a unit of reproduction looks like an outmoded institution, out of kilter with the mode of production.

Control of reproduction is important to the rulers of the industrial economy. It is commonplace to hear that one country or another, in order to increase or decrease the size of its labor force (or army), is restricting or easing access to birth control or abortion, is encouraging late or early marriages, is giving financial awards to mothers or tax incentives to single people, and so forth. These reports come as often from socialist as capitalist countries. The three groups we have been discussing are women, the more privileged male wage laborers, and the ruling elite of the male authoritarian industrialized state. The reproductive issues confronting these three groups are essentially the same in all industrialized countries.

For example, this was the situation in then communist Romania (*WomaNews*, June 1984):

> According to...*The Observer*, the Romanian government is intending to force women industrial workers to have a monthly blood test to check whether or not they are pregnant. Those women who are shown to be pregnant one month and not the next will have to explain why.

Abortion is illegal in Romania...However, the Communist Party discovered recently that out of 743,000 registered pregnancies, only 40% resulted in live births.

Here the state's problem was a too low birth rate. The state's real interest is in controlling the birth rate, up or down depending on its needs. Usually, however, women will be coerced to have more children, for two reasons. First, as I said at the beginning of this paper, women have strong motives for limiting reproduction and, when given real alternatives in their lives, do not become frequently pregnant. Second, industry and the army still need a large labor force.

The ruling elite's difficulty at present is technological. The system has not developed the organization and technology necessary to a centralized control of reproduction and child care; the Romanian method, for example, is crude. The male state is channeling resources into researching reproduction, however. Advances are being made in male laboratories towards sex determination, genetic engineering and fetal surgery, implanted fetuses, cloning, parthenogenesis, and artificial wombs. To date industrialization has evolved through three stages, extending itself first to capital goods (machines and materials), then consumer goods, and most recently to services. I suggest that we are now in the early part of the fourth stage, the industrialization of reproduction and more generally of biology.

Because the control methods for the present remain primitive, the male state is still forced to rely on the old method, indirect control of childbearing through control of individual women by individual men. The price more privileged men have extracted from the ruling male class in return for controlling reproduction and child care is precisely the family wage, the ownership of labor power, and the current housework system. This deal between two male classes is why industrialists agreed to the family wage, and why housewives are women.[9]

The forces behind the situation of poor women, who because of racism are disproportionately women of color, now become clearer. Poor men, those who don't belong to the class of privileged male wage earners, do not have the economic power to individually control the reproduction of individual women. Poor women are "out of control." That is, they have to be controlled by the male state, the public maleocracy, on top of suffering abuse from the men around them. The pittance they are given for welfare reflects what portion of the family wage is for childrearing. The state's cruel and floundering attempts are contradictory: Forced sterilization, birth control experiments, welfare cutbacks on the one hand; the elimination of funding for abortion, birth control and health services on the other. The crazy-making demands—stop breeding on the one hand, stop using abortion and birth control on the other—reveal a basic contradiction in the system. The male state does not want to pay for the birthing and raising of children, but it also fears the existence of a large set of independent women who control and limit their own reproduction.[10]

The treatment of poor men and gay men also contains contradictions. Men distrust any man who does not for whatever reason do his fair share of controlling women; such men are potential traitors. At the same time, fear of competition and of lowered wages causes the more privileged wage-earning men to oppose poorer men's access to the employment that would allow poorer men to control "their" women. Gay men are hated by other men because, not individually controlling individual women, gay men are traitors to their class. The hate can be particularly intense because many gay men, unlike poorer men, are paid the family wage and thus have the economic resources to control individual women but choose not to. (Thus it can be important for gay men to demonstrate that they control lesbians, that the gay movement includes lesbians and the gay men run it.) However, because gay sexuality is the logical extension of the woman-hating and male solidarity inherent in maleocracy, the hatred of gay men cannot be unconflicted. Thus, members of the male ruling class can and do take stands against the oppression of gay men. In the early '80s, for example, Ronald Reagan spoke out against an antigay initiative on the California ballot, and the initiative failed.

Because poor men and gay men are oppressed within maleocracy, women can feel more in common with these men than with more privileged men. The more politically inclined can also experience a sense of identification with revolutionary struggles led by such men. These sympathies are a dangerous mistake. These men are as much constrained by the need to control reproduction as are all other men. Inevitably their struggle for power, when successful, includes the seizure of the means of reproduction (that's us) as well as the means of production. What women must get clear is that all three classes of men—ruling class, privileged wage-earning males, and poor males—are our enemies; none of them are working in our interests. Hopefully, we are learning to use them against each other.

The Future

We are in a period of extraordinary turmoil in the economic-reproductive areas I have been discussing. In many ways the economic picture I've described above seems to be fading into the past.

The family wage is under attack and probably will not survive. Only 15% of u. s. workers are currently union members. In more and more families, the man's salary alone cannot support the family. The number of mother-child families is increasing much faster than the number of two-parent families, and women and children are becoming a greater and greater percentage of the poor. Single-motherhood is threatening to destroy the lives of overwhelming numbers of teenage women, some as young as 12. At the same time, women continue to fight for the right to abortion, with some success.

Child custody is being debated in a number of arenas. Parents are fighting with the state over control of school systems. The courts are taking more control over the conditions under which children live with their parents or are reared by those deemed more acceptable. Children are suing for release from their parents. While most fathers are continuing to refuse to pay child support, some fathers are suing for custody of their children. The number of father-child families has recently been increasing rapidly. Lesbian mothers are asking for custody of their children and defending against suits that they are unfit mothers. Women are selecting men as biological fathers and then deserting them; lesbians are practicing artificial insemination.

And beyond all this is what I believe is the most significant portent of the future: Lesbians are a far larger politically organized force than we have been at any other (known) time.

What all this ferment—including the present-day lesbian and gay movements—represents, I believe, is a society which senses itself moving toward a future in which social relations between women and men will not be necessary for reproduction. This sense in turn, I suggest, is based on two factors: The growing need for a significant lowering of the birthrate, and the industrialization of reproduction.

The forces currently working towards a lower birth rate are the automation of manufacturing and weaponry, which greatly reduces the size of the needed labor force and army, and the overpopulation of the planet, which has reached emergency proportions. The development that might reverse this need for fewer births is space travel. If men decide to try to colonize the universe, they will want women to produce a lot of colonizers. We'll be in for a long struggle.

While a low birth rate is always in women's interest, it does present at least one possible problem of its own. If the economy needs only a low birth rate, it would be feasible to specialize some women to be pregnant and produce children. We already have surrogate mothers and implanted fetuses. The breeders would almost certainly be women of color and women from other oppressed groups. Even an all-women's society, if it relied on pregnancy to produce children, could go in this direction.

The development of a breeder class would be consistent with some of the directions males are taking in their attempts to gain industrial control over reproductive biology. The portents of genetic engineering for women are ominous. Different gene materials could be combined outside the womb and then implanted in the wombs of the breeder class, who would be forced to bear vile experiments. Various kinds of fetal surgery and interventions could also be done in utero. Janet Gallagher (1984) describes how doctors and the courts are already asserting their right to decide what happens inside the uterus. Doctors have asked for and in some cases judges have granted them the right, against a woman's will, to confine her in a hospital or give her a Caesarian, in order to increase the fetus' chances of survival. The male state is extending its colonization of women to the physical occupation of the womb itself.

The real issue in the abortion struggle is bodily integrity, not "choice." The issue is not whether or not the fetus is a person. That is irrelevant. The issue is whether or not the woman is a person. Not even a fully developed adult is given the rights over another person's body that the fetus, fronting for the maleocracy, already has been given over a woman's body. Gallagher (1984) cites the case of a man who was dying of cancer and who went to court to compel his cousin to donate some bone marrow to him. The court refused. I recall reading of a similar case in Texas where a boy needed a kidney transplant and the only possible donor was his older, 13-year-old sister. The court assigned her an attorney to protect her from being coerced into donating the kidney (although of course we are skeptical of the attorney's will or ability to do this!). Both these cases illustrate the strong legal precedent that a person has complete right to control their body, even when another person needs part of that body to stay alive. What these examples make clear is that men and the male state treat women as less than persons, as machines for producing persons (and future machines).[11]

Male scientists and other men have been talking about "egg farming" for some time now. (The phrase refers to the extraction of ova for experimental use from a woman's ovaries.) The model for the future breeder class is in fact the farm, where the overwhelming number of animals are female. Even if future babies were grown in artificial wombs, women would still need to be "farmed" for our eggs, until men could figure out how to create those too. Men's horrific genetic engineering is creating chickens with huge breasts and no feet. I bet they can think of things even more horrible for women breeders and for their "organ farms" more generally.

In a system where reproduction was not done through marriage and similar oppressive relationships between women and men, gay men would cease to be traitors to their class. The gay sexuality which has always been present underneath male solidarity would be openly expressed. The men in this future would almost certainly not be less misogynist but they would necessarily be misogynist in different ways than now. The lesbian represents the more hopeful future, one in which women, free of the reproductive tie to men, can create our own world. Even if we have to fight men to gain the world and space we need, we can fight them as a people, just as other oppressed peoples have to fight their oppressors. Mary Daly (1984) refers to women as a race. We are not yet a race, because we cannot yet reproduce ourselves, but potentially, yes, we are.

The Lesbian Future

What do we lesbians think of artificial wombs? How do we want our lesbian society to be reproduced? Up to now we have relied primarily on women attached to men to produce future lesbians, and those young lesbians have had to fight their way through years of abusive training and torture to find us. If we want to live without men—either because there aren't any, or because we take and defend our own territory—and especially if we want to become our own species, then we have to take responsibility for running our entire society and reproducing it. We have to take responsibility for and decide how to birth and care for girl children, lesbian children.

Is the sperm essential to the healthy development of the ovum? Is the mixing of genes essential to a healthy species? Can any of the reproductive technologies being developed in male laboratories be useful to us? Do we believe being nurtured in a lesbian's womb for nine months, rather than an artificial womb, is essential for a healthy and happy life for a young lesbian? If it is essential, then we will face some of the problems that occur in non-lesbian societies. We will have to be sure that certain women are not oppressed in order to force them to bear children. What kinds of settings and nurturing are best for the young growing lesbian? If we don't know the answers to these questions, how can we find out? These are questions for today, so that we'll have the answers tomorrow when we need them.

I am a lesbian who has never wanted to bear or raise a child. I feared the physical pain. I didn't want my body torn apart. I wondered if I was a coward. When I was young and pregnant, I knew immediately that society had no right to the sacrifices it was demanding of me in order to reproduce itself. I have never felt guilty about the abortions. We are not means of production, we are not life support systems for other persons. I have never wanted to raise a child. I hate being interrupted when I am concentrating on something. I hate spending a lot of time around people who don't understand me. We are not servants. We are not food for the growth of others.[12]

I am glad to see other feminists and other lesbians expressing similar ideas (see Allen, 1983; Giminez, 1983; Breeze, 1984). Nor do I think it is an accident that we are coming to a new view of "mothering" during this time when reproductive technology is developing. It is only possible to really think about a thing on the ground of its alternatives.

I have wanted lesbians to be a whole world unto ourselves. I want lesbian universities, restaurants, lesbian cities, countries, lesbian space travel. I want to be free of the necessity to adapt to this reality of childbearing, to this world where childbearing has to be done in this brutal way. I do not want to have to fight to change this ugly system. I want to grapple with the problems we will create between us when we do not have to contend with breeding. I want to be fully who I am. I want the future.

And yet, writing this, I have also become aware of my identity as intersticed with pregnancy and motherhood. I am surprised to find how much I am still to myself not-man and not-wife. It is to not these nots that Monique Wittig (1981) says she is not a woman and not a lesbian. If lesbians are the future of women, who then are the future of lesbians? If there is no pregnancy, what then are breasts, what is a vagina, a clitoris, what is a womb? What is sex between lesbians? What is orgasm? I truly don't know. But I want to find out. I'm bored with this world conditioned by reproduction. Let's go somewhere else now.

REFERENCES

Jeffner Allen, Motherhood: The Annihilation of Women. In *Mothering: Essays in Feminist Theory*, ed. Trebilcot (Totowa, NJ: Rowman & Allanheld, 1983), 315-330.

Ti-Grace Atkinson, The Institution of Sexual Intercourse. *N.Y. Free Press* (December 13, 1968). Reprinted in *Notes from the Second Year*, eds. Firestone and Koedt (1970).

Ti-Grace Atkinson, Radical Feminism. In *Notes from the Second Year*, eds. Firestone and Koedt (1970), and in Atkinson, *Amazon Odyssey* (New York: Link, 1974).

Joan Bamberger, The Myth of Matriarchy: Why Men Rule in Primitive Society. In *Women, Culture and Society*, eds. Rosaldo and Lamphere (Stanford U. Press, 1974), 263-280.

Margaret Benston, The Political Economy of Women's Liberation. *Monthly Review* 21 (September 1969), 13-27.

Nancy Breeze, Who's Going to Rock the Petri Dish? *Trivia* #4 (Spring 1984).

Mariarosa Dalla Costa, Women and the Subversion of the Community. In *Power of Women and the Subversion of the Community*, 2nd ed., Dalla Costa and James (Briston, England: Falling Wall Press, 1973).

Mary Daly, *Pure Lust* (Boston: Beacon, 1984).

Elizabeth Gould Davis, *The First Sex* (New York: Putnam, 1971).

Helen Diner, *Mothers and Amazons* (Garden City, NY: Doubleday, 1973), written in German in the 1930s.

Gail Falk, Women and Unions: A Historical View. *Women's Rights Law Reporter* 1, #4 (Spring 1973), 54-65.

Shulamith Firestone, *The Dialectic of Sex* (New York: Morrow, 1970).

Elizabeth Fisher, *Woman's Creation* (New York: Anchor/Doubleday, 1979).

Janet Gallagher, The Fetus and the Law—Whose Life Is It Anyway? *Ms.* (September 1984), 62 ff.

Martha Giminez, Feminism, Pronatalism, and Motherhood. In *Mothering: Essays in Feminist Theory*, ed. Trebilcot (Totowa, NJ: Rowman & Allanheld, 1983), 287-314.

Jane Goodale, *Tiwi Wives: A Study of the Women of Melville Island, North Australia* (Seattle: U of Washington Press, 1971).

Heidi Hartmann, *The Unhappy Marriage of Marxism and Feminism: Towards a More Progressive Union*. In *Women and Revolution*, ed. Sargent (Boston: South End Press, 1981).

Heidi Hartmann, *Capitalism, Patriarchy and Job Segregation by Sex. Signs* 1, #3 pt. 2 (Spring 1976), 137-170.

H. R. Hays, *The Dangerous Sex* (New York: Putnam, 1964).

Phyllis Kaberry, *Aboriginal Women: Sacred and Profane* (London: Routledge, 1939).

Marge Piercy, *Woman on the Edge of Time* (New York: Knopf, 1981).

Una Stannard, The Male Maternal Instinct. *Transaction* (Nov.-Dec. 1970).

Monique Wittig, One Is Not Born a Woman. *Feminist Issues* 1, #2 (Winter, 1981).

FOOTNOTES
[1]Some readers may note a similarity between this analysis of the role of agriculture in intensifying misogyny with Engels' theory that men's oppression of women began when the farming economy produced surplus and private property. [Friedrich Engels, *The Origin of Family, Private Property and the State* (New York: International Publ., 1972)]. However, in Engels' analysis male supremacy is essentially an accident. It "just happened" that the sex division of labor gave to men those farming activities which produced a surplus, and so men "just happened" to become the first owners. Since men then "naturally" wanted to pass property on to their children, they suppressed women and established the male authoritarian nuclear family. Engels does not address or explain forced increases in childbearing. In my analysis, on the other hand, forced childbearing and men's willingness to exploit women and each other are necessary for the development of agriculture.

[2]I do not use the term *patriarchy*, because it lets younger men off the hook. For similar reasons I do not refer to women or men as *heterosexual* or *homosexual*, since this usage implies that women and lesbians share some quality, socioeconomic position, or experience with

men and gay men.

[3]Because marxism does not pay much attention to women's work and focuses on the exploited workers in the factory, it is quite common for (male) marxists to argue that women are less exploited and oppressed than men, because their work is less alienating and more meaningful (!). In doing so, of course, they are refusing to acknowledge their own cruelty to women. I suspect that Dalla Costa, in arguing that women are part of the proletariat, was trying to convince her marxist colleagues that women are *as* exploited and thus *as* important as men. But theory needs to go much farther than this.

[4]Any rebellion against the established order mobilizes the people with the least investment in that order. Since these days the old order will always be male dominant, any rebellion, whether from the "left" or the "right," will mobilize women and children. But if the revolution is successful, women's gains are always gradually dismantled. Likewise new religions are often started by women or quickly find women adherents.

[5]I do bookkeeping for a business owned by a man who hired his wife as a secretary and paid her $12,000 a year; when she left he hired a male for the same job and paid him $25,000. The male-controlled economy also has means for stealing portions of even women's measly 64%. Taxation, for example, is a method for stealing the wages of women and the poor and redistributing them to (white) males.

[6]Even lesbians do more housework than men. And often we do it for men. See, for example, R.A.E.'s description of cleaning houses for gay men, "The Sexual Politics of Household Help: My Life as a "Cleaning Girl,'" *Lesbian Ethics* 4:2 (1991), 87-91.

[7]Poor men's jobs still pay better than poor women's jobs or welfare. One possibility that occurs to me is that poor men do own labor power and that their poverty is maintained through unemployment, where poor women are kept poor through lower wages and low welfare payments.

[8]The sacrifice is substantial; housework has been estimated to be worth as much as 60% of the GNP. Heidi Hartmann (1981) discusses well the conflicting interests of capital and maleocracy, but describes these as two separate systems, one having classes and the other apparently having none. Thus women and men are within "the" working class. She also refers to the "partnership" of maleocracy and capital, and in my view underestimates the conflict between them.

[9]This rather dry description does not convey the extraordinary brutality, the physical and sexual torture by men of women and girls, that often is the means of oppression in families. The family is the most effective means of exploitation and oppression ever devised. By keeping women isolated from each other, the male-dominant family prevents them from organizing together to overturn maleocracy; and by keeping women in minute-by-minute intimate connection to their exploiters and abusers, the family creates in women an intense internalized oppression. That the lesbian movement and the women's liberation movement have occurred at all is testimony to women's extraordinary strength.

[10]Aurora Levins Morales recently reported on her extensive research into the Spanish colonization of her home, Puerto Rico. "What strikes me repeatedly. . .is how terrified the Spanish administration was of [native] women in charge of their own reproductive ability. From the earliest days an astonishing proportion of the laws, decrees and government correspondence coming out of Spain concern women's sexuality and reproduction, and their movements from one place to another" (*Women's Review of Books* [July 1992], p. 9)

[11]"On the other hand, there is the recent case where a mother had another child so that that child could donate an organ to a fatally ill child. The newborn seems to have been given no legal protection. I find this vile. Does it signal an important and ominous change in legal precedent?

[12]There is a sense in which pregnancy is inherently exploitive. The woman risks her life, goes through great pain, and uses her body to create life for another person, and yet she cannot rightfully have any ownership of the product, this other person. In a just society, women to whom pregnancy was an increased physical risk would be left free from pregnancy. How could the women who birth the children society needs be justly rewarded?

Nett Hart

The NEW! IMPROVED! Classless Society

Nett Hart

In the first place it would be accurate to say amerikans never have understood class, even in the clarity of the Great Depression. In my family of farmers the land was lost to the bank and the most able took jobs for which they had skills: carpentry, slaughter, and mechanics. Unions gave a measure of security and mobility unknown on the farm and for this we were deeply loyal. I could find a union label before I could read. Even when the GI bill sent my daddy to school so he could become an industrial arts teacher, an entry level position to middle classness, our affiliations were union. To this day I cannot imagine crossing a picket line.

Class solidarity, however, is elusive. At the same time the labor movement organizes workers into a body with power, the possibility of social mobility is accepted as the greatness of the American Dream. This leaves many of us confused about class, which class we are, when it changes, which of our attitudes and attributes are a product of class, what class we identify with at what times. It might be oversimplified, but reasonable, to say that organized labor plays into this fantasy of class mobility as it increases the wages and benefits of workers so that individually we can become more effective consumers which in amerika *is* social mobility, lacking lineal nobility as we do. Both the actuality and the fantasy of class mobility undermine the strength of worker identity.

Amerika is a class-based society, even though the basis of the class stratification is more flexible than the remnants of the feudal systems with which europeans and asians contend. The great social movements of this century have flirted with socialism enough to give a vocabulary of class consciousness without the reality. Such social programs as the New Deal and Great Society have intervened in the process of lower class conscientization and quelled the social unrest such consciousness leads to. Just enough become tokens of escape from the lower classes to lie about opportunity, the amerikan lottery of success. The presence of a large middle class or class of people who think they are "middle" because of the consumerability they enjoy continually aligns the majority of working people with our cultural nobility—the rich and famous. This alignment is based on *appearances* of social class privilege and access. The pursuit of appearances is counterproductive to self-worth, self-assessment, and class identity. Having the right accessories promotes passing. No wonder amerikans can't think about class.

Because class was a vogue discussion at the time of feminism's rebirth, class became a discussion *within* the movement not *intrinsic* to sexism, so we have a list of oppressive "isms" that includes classism as a recognition that inside the movement working class women are oppressed by the attitudes and behaviors of women of middle and upper classes and poverty class women are oppressed by all of the above. Because the examination of class takes place as an oppression within, though not caused by, the movement, the discussion goes only so far as to analyze and check attitudes and behaviors of individuals with respect to their would-be peers, which is to say feminism takes on class as an identity politic but does not take on class.

To say class is an identity politic is to personalize the political strata, to reduce the issues of classism to a series of personal slights and inadequacies rather than attend to the structures of domination and subordination that create and hold in place a class differentiation. You may hurt my feelings when you criticize my speech, or make disparaging remarks about other people of my background. You may remedy this through apology and sensitivity. But that is not the same as expecting that the woman who cleans your house or tends your children should be paid less than you are paid or less than you pay your lawyer or accountant. That underpaid expendable labor supports the income base and growth of the middle and upper classes is a feminist issue not only with respect to women and men but within the women's movement between women. To take on class within the women's movement would be to develop an analysis of how class defines and shapes expectations and opportunities and then level the playing field.

Within the Women's Liberation Movement of the '70s many women emulated the "independence" of working class women. Downward social mobility is only fashionable for those who can go down. That middle and upper class women flaunt their rebellion from class expectations by wearing the work clothes of less class-privileged women and in some cases taking the employment available to poverty and working class women does not eliminate class differences. In some ways "downward" mobility exaggerates them.

When class analysis takes place only inside of an identity politic, it cannot address justice. At best it questions some assumptions about what is available to "everyone" and creates some remedies such as sliding-fee scales, child care, and travel assistance to be offered occasionally. But at worst it causes dishonesty and incomplete information about one's true resources and ability to be supportive of women's institutions and other women. When this is added to the general lack of awareness of class in amerika we have the words to hurt and pacify one another but not the political action to undermine class stratification within our community. Truly, as a whole, women earn 59¢ to a man's dollar, but that 59¢ is an average, not a leveler of resources nor a source of solidarity.

So is it any surprise that after this incomplete analysis of class the gains of feminism have most notably allowed some women a degree of independent social mobility, that is, the opportunity to become better consumers while the real costs are still borne by lower class women? Women can now independently stratify ourselves by class without reference to the males in our lives to whose class status we previously were annexed. Curiously, the number of women who have "transcended" their class of origin is about the same, in my observation, as would happen by tokenization anyhow in this system. Revolution, my ass!

The agendas of feminism flow from the class from which they come as differently as if they were not of a single movement. Some women cannot understand how homelessness, welfare travesties, police brutality, "open shops," and treaty rights are feminist issues, just as some women will never develop sympathy for the glass ceiling.

Because middle and upper class values (buying and owning classes) dominate the media and mainstream consciousness, the goals of class mobility have replaced those of classlessness. Even within the movement some women of class privilege speak of being held back by the multidimensional issues of lower class women. The concerns of poverty and working class women are just too costly to the "success" of climbing women and receive the same gratuitous liberal "concern" as guilt has always produced. As new opportunities open for women there is increased pressure for women to succeed—economically, for what else really matters or is substantially different from the kinds of undervalued success that have always been women's? Within the women's community the achievements of women are celebrated who accede to, and succeed in, this new frontier which not too subtly replicates within the pressures from outside. The Women's Liberation Movement is becoming the Women's Consumer Market as women's economic successes mean more and more products, advertising, and media focus on women. This all keeps us inside the same system fighting for the crumbs. We may create better work places, own our own businesses, and endure all the stresses of career compounded by unrelieved female expectations. We've come a long way.

Within the movement we are also a market. The development of women's culture has been done entrepreneurially, which makes sense inside a capitalist system in which every other activity is remunerated. But what that means in our own communities is that participation in women's culture comes from a cash outlay, giving us a culture in which we consume each other and leave some women totally outside because they lack disposable income, not politics.

Throughout this process our consciousness about oppression pushes us to include and be sensitive to women who are more oppressed than we are. Inclusion and sensitivity, however, still come from status quo-maintaining values, insuring that awareness produces no substantial systemic changes. Because some can buy in, women's success depends now more than twenty years ago on the maintenance of the system as it is. To effect change, the movement of women cannot move without a clear examination of class.

Any vision of classlessness must begin in new territory instead of obedience to marx and his brothers. Not only do individuals' class identities change, but in a changing economy, class itself changes and changes meaning. Because class is an artificial construction of difference we must take apart what is false to our experience of one another and find the core of connectedness from which to build an equal and just society. This cannot be accomplished by a gloss on difference or sensitivity to one another's issues, that is, neither equal rights nor identity politics will create justice. But by beginning in a willingness to acknowledge that there are differences, and that these differences create injustice, we can open the dialogue.

None of us escapes oppression by class, although I am not arguing that we are all equally oppressed by class. There is a vast difference between being oppressed by not having choices, not having enough, not having a sense of entitlement that allows any expectation of having your needs met and being oppressed by class because you are of a class that is owned by its capital, that makes life choices valuing the maintenance and development of one's possessions over self-development. Stratification by class in amerika alienates all of us not only from our labor but from the notion of right livelihood, the ability to conform the work we do to the values we hold, and to value our work. Our time at work should buy us more than the ability to consume, both processes that alienate us from ourselves as well as one another. If in spending the largest part of our waking hours in situations that compromise us and in which we compromise the integrity of others we develop a stance of defensiveness rather than resistance, we actively perpetuate our own oppression. We are left with little time or energy for an alternative system. This insures that the values any of us are permitted to enact are either wholly consistent with the dominant culture or culturally insignificant.

It is time to make an honest critique of class in amerika and mobilize new organizations to challenge the injustice. It is intolerable that in a democracy a segment of the population should be consigned to generations of poverty. Too many people, especially too many women, are so disenfranchised in amerika that they are outside the concern and protection of organized labor. As a result, the social justice the unions were meant to address has been subverted. Any radical analysis of class must take into account unrepresented and unemployed workers as well as the second and third shifts women also pull at home. This critique should flow from a feminist analysis of oppression and should focus on the intersections of oppressions. That sexism has not been addressed in class discussions, except again as an identity politic, means any previous analysis is incomplete and flawed.

In the long haul we may need to completely remove ourselves from this present system and learn the means of home production and self-sufficiency in order to reconnect our labor to meaning before we can come together in communities where the labor of all is valued and where no one is valued for her labor, but for who she is. If we stop owning things, allow each thing to have a meaning independent of us and our use of it, we will begin to see ourselves in relationship to everything else. Only when persons and animals and land and tools and plants have a value in and of themselves in our world can we begin to approach the justice of which we are capable.

It is the task of feminism to take on class, not to give us a more class culturally aware women's consumer society, but to understand how class holds in place its hierarchy even while "allowing" at different times various outside groups to have a place. The goals of feminism, to end domination and subordination and create a world in which the lives of women are honored and possible, cannot be accomplished without undoing the class system, the capital system, the consumer society. To do otherwise places the gains of feminism in the arbitrary control of the controlling interests, substituting blamelessness for justice. As a movement our long-term social change depends upon building alternative structures to those we intend to dismantle.

Bonnie J. Morris

Class Beyond Classroom

Bonnie J. Morris

In April of 1992 I was mistaken for a homeless woman and asked to leave a fashionable storefront in Harvard Square. This incident, more than any other, has led me to reexamine my assumptions about class privilege based on appearance. As a lesbian, I position myself on the margins of class dialogue in the U. S., for I deliberately eschew and dishonor the standard "achievements" which accord women privilege: marriage, motherhood, association with powerful men. But I move through very privileged academic environments in my work as a university professor, despite the scholarly sexism which calls smart women aberrant. I am well aware of the irony with which I compose text critical of Harvard on this computer made available to me at Harvard.

The daughter of middle-class, politically conscious parents—whose controversial Jewish-Protestant intermarriage in the late 1950s provoked considerable scandal—I grew up atheist, feminist, anti-establishment, but firmly imbued with the Jewish cultural beliefs which place education above all other achievements. My parents' moderate income did not enable me to attend an expensive university; nor did our middle-class standard of living warrant the scholarships which might have made up the difference. Therefore, I put myself through graduate school at a "public Ivy," the State University of New York at Binghamton, and attained a Ph.D. in U. S. women's history just after my twenty-eighth birthday. Within a year of completing my graduate work, I not only won a visiting fellowship to a humanities research think tank at Dartmouth, but also received a one-year faculty appointment to Harvard Divinity School as a visiting scholar in Jewish women's history. My parents' delight that their radical daughter had finally made it into the Ivy League ballpark was exceeded only by my own admixture of delirium and apprehension. As a professional historian, I naturally coveted the libraries, resources, and educational opportunities awaiting me at Harvard. As a Jewish lesbian, I had no idea how I might be received at Harvard Divinity School, and I was pleasantly surprised by the friendliness and altruism of that particular student body. During my year as visiting scholar, I made many a faux pas at the cumbersome fêtes hosted by

Harvard auspices. The youngest visiting scholar ever appointed, I could seldom discern whether I had committed an error of manners as a woman, as a lesbian, as a Jew, as a youngster on the faculty, or as a result of growing up in a very informal, beatnik household. Sitting in an armchair at a faculty dinner while hired students served wine and played string quartets, I knew I was glimpsing and participating in a privileged world my immigrant ancestors never experienced. Daily, I struggled with the choice between graciously accepting the very temporary climate of privilege and condemning outright the absurd loftiness of Harvard ambiance.

At twenty-nine, a Harvard professor; at thirty, unemployed. Despite the stature of my one-year appointment, my publications, and my diligent application to history positions all over the United States, I received no offers for work for academic year 1991-92. With a nationwide recession, mounting antipathy toward women's history as a credible field, budget cuts in higher education, and universities' resistance to implementing affirmative action hiring, I understood that my own efforts were not to blame for my unemployment. I found part-time work at another university in the Boston area and resigned myself to living off the meager savings I'd accumulated. What I was *not* prepared for was how quickly the Harvard community closed to me, despite my status the previous year. Without a Harvard I.D. card, I was merely one more unaffiliated writer attempting to hang out in Radcliffe Yard. Although many of Harvard's facilities are generously open to the public, my preferred haunts of the previous year were closed to me now—and I suffered many a public humiliation when security guards who had once waved me in with a smile chased after me, commanding, "YOU'RE NOT ALLOWED IN THERE!"

Now my comparative youth, my young appearance, began to work against me, as I was either mistaken for a student and shut out of faculty events or spoken to with the dismissive tone some faculty and staff reserve for students. I no longer lived in Harvard housing but in a cramped one-room apartment where I was robbed. I rarely heard from the Divinity School, although I still lived nearby and would have happily participated in its events. With my pockets empty, I had to utter an embarrassed "No, thank you" when former students of mine from Harvard invited me to dine out. Perhaps the most symbolic event in this transitional year occurred when I tripped and fell down the immense steps at Harvard's Widener Library, spraining my ankle. Alone in my room, telephoning pharmacies, I found none would have crutches delivered at a price I could afford—and I was not comfortable telephoning my former Harvard friends and ex-lovers for assistance.

Despite these challenges to my ego, I chose to remain in the Harvard neighborhood because it still offered the best free show in town: a continual roster of cutting-edge speakers and activists presented lectures every night of the week, open to the public and free. Whatever one might say about the endemic racism and sexism of Harvard as an institution, its enormous budget comfortably fit in visiting speakers who represented a range of exciting theories. My intellectual hunger, at least, was well-fed as I listened to speeches by Angela Davis, Lillian Faderman, Joan Scott, Patricia Williams, Susan Faludi, the Guerilla Girls, Mary Daly, Gloria Steinem, Juliet Mitchell, Patricia Ireland, Winona LaDuke, Joan Nestle, and scores of other remarkable women. I found, eventually, that I enjoyed very much working independently on my own articles by day and attending others' lectures by night. My standard of living had changed dramatically, but my learning continued. Like the [male] Talmud scholars of my ancestors' Jewish villages in Russia, I was no longer a professor but a wandering *yeshiva* girl of sorts, fed by friends in the community, studying for the sake of [in my case, a lesbian-feminist] heaven.

So it was that in April of 1992 I pulled on a sweatshirt and went for a happy bike ride along the Charles River, content with my writing work, optimistic that I would find a job for the next year. It was a beautiful spring day and crowds of people filled Harvard Square, listening to street musicians play. I, too, wanted to hear the free music, and I settled onto a bit of sidewalk with my back against the corner of a building. I had written several pages in my journal about the happy crowds, the interesting contrasts of people, when suddenly a saleswoman emerged from the store I had leaned against. "EXCUSE ME," she said in an exasperated tone, "but I'm going to have to ask you to move on. This is our property." Startled, I answered "I'm sorry. I wanted to watch the musicians perform." "Well, they're done now," she said, "so you just move along." She slammed the door in my face.

It took me several minutes to grasp what had just happened. Of course...I was seated on the ground, wearing an old sweatshirt and jeans. Another dyke would have known I was dressed as a dyke; but through other eyes, my scruffy clothes under a face a bit too old to be an undergraduate suggested not hip downward mobility, but actual poverty—a threat. Many doorways in Harvard Square were filled with homeless people, watching and sleeping, asking for help from passersby. I had unfortunately elected to lean against a posh new store. And I had been mistaken for a beggar.

I must say that it was extremely difficult to go back into that store, but I forced myself to confront the self-righteous clerk, who appeared to be precisely my age. I explained that there had been a misunderstanding;

that I was not attempting to homestead on the store's pavement or intimidate passersby; that I was, in fact, a university lecturer who had merely paused to take notes on the pleasant weekend scene. The saleswoman declared that perhaps I was, in fact, an upstanding citizen [note: as opposed to one who lies down, for whatever reason], but that her manager had a strict policy of keeping folks off the property. I suggested that this policy would be sorely tested in the coming warm-weather months, when a continual roster of street performers would be delighting crowds on the very pavement defined as store property. I asked to see the manager, but she was not present. Instead I took her business card [printed on recycled paper, it said] and went home to write a blistering two-page document demanding an apology. I never received a response.

In that instant I felt the shame, the public embarrassment, the unnecessary harassment experienced hourly by the genuinely homeless women and men of any city. My scruffy appearance made me a threat to the "nice" clientele of the store, a store which, not incidentally, sold expensive "natural" beauty products to women. As a university lecturer, I was, in fact, exactly the sort of person the store hoped to attract, and had I been more nattily attired I would no doubt have been welcomed inside. Patricia Williams, in her text *The Alchemy of Race and Rights*, chronicles the agonizing experience—not atypical for people of color—of being denied entrance to fashionable city stores. White privilege had hitherto permitted me free entry to most institutions. Now, the ambiguity of my class standing had resulted in public mistreatment. Were I an older male taking notes in an academic pad, would the saleswoman have spoken to me so contemptuously in front of my peers and passersby? Is not the lesbian by definition a rebel and therefore dangerous, forsaking the class symbolism of feminine clothes for androgynous comfort, thereby associating herself with a working-class male stance?

In Boston, where race and class lines are carefully drawn, I had encountered another disturbing situation in the very lesbian community I thought of as safe harbor. When I first moved to Boston to begin my Harvard appointment I naturally inquired about lesbian groups and establishments. My interest was in joining the Daughters of Bilitis, the oldest lesbian association in the United States, whose herstory I had studied for years. DOB retained a friendly and open meeting with a mix of working-class and middle-class members. Another group, newly formed, called Boston Quality Women, solicited my membership. This latter group promoted an image of upwardly mobile, successful professional women, and I went to one of their events hoping to encounter a few university professors. Instead I met a woman who called Jews "pushy broads," and I never returned. However, I did end up at a BQW Valentine's Day event by accident, where I learned another lesson about class.

It so happened that BQW rented space for their dance in the very church also used by the Daughters of Bilitis. I was returning books to the DOB library when I heard music and party sounds downstairs. Curious, I wandered right into the BQW Valentine bash, and decided to buy a drink from the cash bar and chat with a few members. Abruptly a woman sang to me, "Do you have bedroom eyes?"

"Oh, I do," said the woman next to me, and handed a coupon to the first speaker. It then emerged that BQW's dance was carefully planned to encourage romantic mingling, and at the door each new arrival received a packet of amusing puzzle pieces to match with other guests. When I explained that I did not receive any Valentine coupons, I found out I had entered the dance through the wrong door and had therefore not paid a certain admission fee, which included coupons.

Immediately, one of the women I had been talking to informed me that she was one of the organizers of the dance and I would have to re-enter and pay, or leave. I apologized for the confusion and explained that I would leave as soon as I had finished my drink, as I did not have sufficient cash on me to cover the cost of the dance. I saw, in that moment, the change come over several women's eyes, the transmitted question flying between them: who IS she? Did she just wander in here off the STREET? If she can't afford our dance fee, she must not be a Quality Woman: why won't she just leave at once? In my black leather jacket I suddenly transmogrified into Street Girl, to whom no class standing could be accurately ascribed; therefore I was a threat, a risk, a potential low-life detraction. Two women literally stood guard over me and waited right in my face as I finished my screwdriver, then escorted me to the door. In my pocket, at that time, was my Harvard I.D. card, identifying me as a visiting scholar, again, precisely the sort of person BQW wished to claim as clientele. I made no mention of my "quality" status, as I was grotesquely fascinated by the visceral responses to my outward appearance. Femme since childhood, or assumed so because of my thick blond hair and Norwegian-influenced features, I had never created much of a quake on the dyke richter scale when among other dykes. But in a class-conscious atmosphere like that of the BQW dance, my youth, my anonymity, and my empty pockets created an "outsider" formula that hardly suggested Harvard professionalism. I left the dance feeling both irritated and amused. Was I really so scary?

I write of these events to make plain the *signals* of class, the cues and clues, used against women *by women* in the name of protecting "genteel" women's space. Why does a store catering to politically conscious women take pains to advertise its recycled and rainforest-safe products, yet casually harass women outside the door? Why does a lesbian organization call itself *quality* women, implying that there exists a lesbian spectrum with low-quality women at the other end? Both postures suggest an interest in protecting like-minded women from exposure to other economic classes, during certain hours and in certain places. With my Harvard faculty I.D. I might flock, welcomed, to such cordoned-off memberships. Remove the I.D., though, and I become Everythreat, a creature whose conversation and life experiences could not possibly be mindful of the polite mannerisms called for.

This is what class is all about, to me: as a gifted child, literate at an early age and endlessly ahead of my peers in most situations between the ages of two and graduate school, I learned through books and observation to engage in conversation several steps "above" my family's social class. I arrived at Harvard knowing how to do Harvard, but no more so than I knew how to "do" the California surfing scene, the women's music festival scene, the Jewish radical scene, the various genres of U. S. subculture which carry a specific vocabulary and insider's tongue. My father taught me well how to blend into each cultural scenario where appropriate, how to absorb and retain behavioral cues. But woe betide the chameleon whose different identities tumble out at the wrong place! Using surfer slang at Harvard branded me as less than to the manor bred. Using academic theory at a beach party might be equally out of place, a bit of unnecessary elitism, branding me as other. Class, then, is more than economic status; it is also about the social boundaries we keep. In Boston, at thirty, unable to lean against a store without censure, I learned that my Ph.D. could not protect me from my country's escalating fears of poor people, and that even in the lesbian community the lines tighten anew to define who might be "quality" dyke material. For one year of unemployment I saw and learned how little one needs to survive: only that greatest of intangible luxuries, human dignity.

Personal Revelations Concerning Class

Jackie Anderson

I have been resistant in writing this paper because I am confused. It is not clear to me that my confusion is real, or really denial. I do understand that it is not acceptable to me to write in the first person and that that is part of my resistance to writing this paper. I also understand that I am considerably less articulate when writing in this style. However, that may be only an excuse for not wanting to be vulnerable, and it is concerning vulnerability that I have touched my relationship to class.

I am African American. My experiences as a person have been more conditioned by that than by any other life experience. But I realize that my background and familial training have allowed me to ignore class as a factor in my life and my relations with others. There have been times in my life when others have commented on my differences or similarities to them, but I have ignored those comments—until now. I recently read *Lesbian Ethics*, the special issue on class (4:2), and found myself thinking that I might be guilty, though I was not certain of what. I mentioned this to my lover who assured me that I was guilty and that she had spent some time attempting to make sense of our relationship because of this issue.

I was shocked!! However, I was forced to confront myself and my denial. Since my mother's death almost ten years ago, I have spent some time looking back on what might have framed me. I now see that I was raised to ignore class. I was raised to ignore all differences between myself and other African Americans, except those who paid attention to class. In fact, I was raised to avoid and dislike African Americans who paid attention to class. My family is what was referred to in the old days as a "race" family. I was taught that we were a people and that there was "them" and "us" and that "they" made no distinctions, so we should not make distinctions. I was also taught that those of us who could had a responsibility to those of us who could not, and that the only "bad" Negroes were those who did not understand their responsibility to the "less fortunate."

I must pause here and say that I was raised by a strong matriarch. I did not realize that until her death. I grew up in a context of wimmin, some stronger than others. But my mother was acknowledged to be the strongest of all. She had a strong and uncompromising set of values and lived in an ordered universe, but I was her life. For her, the enemy was the white world, not individual whites. Her ethic was that each individual deserved respect for their integrity, but with white people reciprocity could not be expected. So I was not allowed to hate, but was cautioned to always be careful.

I was taught pride as an African American, so those aspects of my life that may have separated me from others were never mentioned. When I entered college, the African American students, as we talked of ourselves, made much of the fact that I was second-generation northern born and fourth-generation college-educated. I was again unnerved by this observation which had never been brought to my attention in my family. So, I learned not to talk about that part of myself and, frankly, it did not bother me not to share that with other African Americans. I was taught that class divisions were betrayals. Even though I grew up with some upper-class Negroes, I did not know that until I was an adult. I was never allowed to use family contacts to my advantage; I did not even know that they existed until I was out of college. Pride was something to use to establish to white folks that we were equal, and possibly better.

I attended public schools until college. Until the seventh grade, I lived in an African American context and attended a public school that was entirely African American, except, of course, for the faculty. My mother worked for most of my life and I was what is now referred to as a "latch-key" kid. We lived in apartments which were large and spacious and I always had my own room. My mother remarried when I was about seven years old and though it was not a happy marriage, it provided the financial security and family stability that she wanted for me. I remember knowing that when I was quite young and it affecting my attitudes concerning wimmin and children. I also remember my mother impressing upon me that birthing more than one child was a very bad idea, though one could be a source of great joy.

I always knew that I was more fortunate than many of my friends, but I saw that as a function of material wealth and not social class. In our family discussions, differences in economic class were attributed to the effects of racism. Some of us were simply luckier than others for reasons more related to our economic and social positions after slavery, but **all** subject to the same arbitrary victimization at the hands of white people. Thus, it was considered ludicrous that some Negroes could conceive of themselves as "better" than others for any reason.

I knew more than most of my friends about our history and present conditions, but I attributed that to the fact that my family talked much about those things; my uncle is a historian, and I have always lived with books.

One reason that it was possible to ignore class was that most African Americans of my generation were raised with what might be characterized as middle-class values. We were not allowed to speak other than standard english at home; our table manners had to be "right"; and education was understood to be of unquestioned importance. We lived very much under the gaze of white eyes ready to judge us as unworthy at any moment. There could be no opportunity for "them" to confirm any of their stereotypes of "us" through any behaviors of ours.

To say now that I have been able to ignore class is something that I recognize as an expression of privilege, similar to white people saying that they can ignore race when people of color cannot. But that is new knowledge—a link that has just recently come to my attention. When I entered high school, I watched with great dismay and anger classism practiced with a vengeance by African American students and rather vicious color prejudice. There were after-school clubs in which membership was based on being very very fair-skinned. In others, the requirements for membership were being from a well-known family and/or being very well-dressed. These also formed the bases for school friendships. Students who did not fit either profile were ignored and isolated by both groups. However, the members of these clubs interacted with each other and with like-minded students from other schools.

It was my first experience with color prejudice and something for which I was quite unprepared. It seemed rather bizarre and counter-productive to me since the school was predominantly white and many of the teachers, in varying degrees, racist.

The interesting aspect of the color-prejudice was that it seemed only to be practiced between wimmin. The male students were not required to be light complexioned to be in the inner circle. Being a star athlete, having access to a late-model car, dressing well, being smart, being from a well-known family, or being the boy-friend of an acceptable girl were the male criteria for acceptance. During school hours, another qualification for acceptance was having white friends.

My family moved to a changing neighborhood when I was in seventh grade and I was thrust into a completely foreign environment. I was transferred from an entirely Black school to an almost entirely white school. I was one of two Black students in my class. It was there that I first learned of anti-Semitism since the school had a large population of Jews. Until then, I thought that white people hated only Negroes. I believe that I received most of my education concerning the pervasiveness of bigotry in white culture during my tenure at that school. None of the white students knew why they hated the groups that they hated, they simply knew the language and attitudes of bigotry.

When I entered high school (ninth grade), I entered knowing very few Black students and many white students, since we were graduated from the same grammar school. The overwhelming majority of Black students entering were having their first contact with white people. So, I was immediately popular and had the privilege of snubbing the snubbers. I supposed that I felt superior to them because I did not value relations with white students and was much more sensitive to subtle racism that was present in the personalities of my white classmates. I had learned them earlier in my relations with them. But I was also protected from personal experiences of classism and color-prejudice because I was a middle-class kid too.

I had no desire for membership in any of the after-school clubs and, as a dark-complexioned African American, I certainly did not qualify for those based on color. My distaste for color prejudice and the fact that it was not practiced by my family of many colors made me contemptuous of those to whom color was important.

Luckily, the '60s were approaching and the Black students became inclined to bond with each other by our senior year. That was facilitated by some other factors, such as the presence of a few Black teachers for the first time, and the support of many white students. I left high school without enduring friendships and deliberately chose a super-liberal college in the city that none of my classmates would be attending. Those who were college-bound went away. I was quickly recruited by the socialists, entered the civil rights movement and forgot all about class, except in the theoretical Marxist sense.

During the various nationalist movements that occurred subsequent to the civil rights period, class was discussed with great frequency and African Americans who could be identified as middle-class were spoken of as the enemy of the people. The advantage of knowing that some of those shouting the loudest were pursuing Ph.D.s at major universities allowed me not to take seriously much of the shouting. I was also troubled by the hostility and degradation directed to wimmin that was so much a part of the nationalists' movement. So, I spent my time counseling African American men subject to the draft and other antiwar activities.

Class entered my life again with Feminism, but still as a conceptual/moral issue. It was of great concern to me that the white lesbian contexts in which I moved seemed to have greater class variety than those of my African American lesbian community. There is virtually no interaction between more privileged African American lesbians and those less privileged, and the more privileged seem to prefer it that way. Young African American lesbians (under thirty-five) are also avoided by those who are older. I recently had a disturbing conversation with an African American lesbian introduced to me by a friend. She had space that she was willing to make available to African American lesbians for group meetings. However, she also made clear that she was interested only in those who were professional and over thirty-five. While her attitude in its extremity is not typical, I do find that dressing fashionably and acting "correctly" are highly valued.

The class lines are not as rigid as those I encountered in school, probably because as lesbians we cannot be so absolute. However, there are similarities in attitude and self-perception.

There never seemed, however, to be any class issues in my relationships. At least, not until recently. My mate has pointed out to me that it would not have been an issue because my lovers and I were not very different from each other with respect to politics and life-style values.

It is impossible for me to imagine not being engaged in some way in efforts for social justice. My life-mate, also an African American Lesbian, has said to me, sometimes impatiently, that the ability to construct and act upon political commitments represents privilege. When I question what appears to me to be a lack of planning concerning childbirth of African American wimmin of her generation (I am fourteen years her senior), she responds that I assume an amount of control and decisiveness in the lives of these wimmin that I had in mine. When I am depressed and frustrated at the number of African American wimmin her age who are now struggling to educate themselves while raising multiple children as single parents, she points out that I am speaking from a position of class privilege.

My assumption, as a member of the generation that did not have access to legal abortion as young wimmin, was that this, along with the use of contraception, would result in younger wimmin exercising reproductive decision-making. However, it has been pointed out to me that this view supposed that a young woman would see her life as within her control.

It is not entirely clear to me that my insensitivity is not only a function of class, but also generational. When I talk with other African American wimmin of my generation, we are perplexed by the same issues and ask the same questions. Many of us raised children as single parents while pursuing advanced degrees and working. We believed that our daughters would see the difficulties presented by our circumstances and not follow our example. The questions we ask do not concern poor wimmin, but rather those who, it seems, could have chosen differently—"should have known better."

The question that I have not asked and that most represents my heretofore unacknowledged class bias concerns exactly what it is that they "should have known better." I, and I believe many African American wimmin of my generation, believed that achievements were valuable in themselves; that reproduction should be subsequent to completing the requirements for an independent life, and that our daughters would recognize that they had the possibility of futures more fulfilling than ours and should want that for themselves.

These values sound prescriptive and presumptuous to my mate, especially when framed as questions concerning the life of a particular womon. They do not feel prescriptive to me, but rather self-evident. My mate argues that they feel self-evident to me because of my background and training, because I assume that everyone was trained to hold them, and because I always believed that I had some control over my life. I view these values as life-preserving—that is how I learned them. I learned them, however, not as preserving a class status, but rather as preserving myself as an African American womon. So, it remains difficult for me to discontinue asking the questions that sound like judgments.

Class-ification by Intelligence: Some Questions

Pat Dean

1) How is women's intelligence related to the economic class in which we grow up?

2) By whose standards has women's intelligence been assessed?

3) How does schooling affect women's intelligence?

4) What expectations are placed on girls and women who are perceived by other people to be highly intelligent?

5) Are women's minds different than men's? Whose research can we trust?

6) Does intelligence confer empowerment of any kind?

   a) Are powerful women intelligent?
   b) Are intelligent women powerful?

7) Is the value of intelligence tied to accomplishments resulting from 'its' use?

8) Do 'good' thinkers deserve material subsidies to pursue their thinking in the same way that 'gifted' artists are subsidized to 'devote' themselves to art?

9) Is there any way to conceive of using our minds in ways unrelated to:

   a) competing within a meritocracy?
   b) 'earning' a living?
   c) strategizing to stay alive?

10) Who is the agent in the statement "A mind is a terrible thing to waste?"*

11) Is there any safe place to think creatively, experimentally, or 'differently' and share the results:

   a) in academia?
   b) through publicly distributed media?

12) Are any of these questions important outside the heteropatriarchy?

---

*For a discussion of some of the English sentence structures that allow us to suppress the agent of actions, such as the infinitive to waste, see Speaking Freely: Unlearning the Lies of the Fathers' Tongues by Julia Penelope (New York: Pergamon Press, 1990; Teachers College Press, 1992).

Viola, Linnea, and Erik Johnson in the mid 1950's.

"Just Who Do You Think You Are?"

A SOCKDOLAGER ON SOCIAL CLASS VIS À VIS WOMEN, in Catechetics, Poem, Story, and Cha Cha Cha, and featuring The Lettermen, me and my mom and dad, John Wayne as Elvis, and Spam

Linnea Johnson

> *"It is only through a misunderstanding that I am in the midst of this whirlpool of world history, whereas in reality I was born to look after the geese in the fields."** *

These days, the conversations on social class I've been having with other women, as well as the ones I've been having with myself, go something like this:

What is social class?

A construct. A construction. An entity thinged; built, put together, composed from parts—like Spam—formed, interpreted, construed, informed by arrangement: an arrangement, as of sense into sense into thought into word into sense-tence/sentence. "Construct state," in Hebrew and in other Semitic languages, is the situation of a noun relating to, being near enough to fall over onto, another noun, which in Aryan languages would be in the genitive case (genitive indicating origin, kind, or class to which a thing is said—by whom?—to belong), as in "House of God" and "House of Cards," "house" in those phrases being in the construct state. From the Latin, "construĕre, -structum-con, struĕre: to build, to pile together." A pile. A ranked pile in this case; a ranked pile of society, community. Society piled, and spammed.

What is society and who constructs it?

Honey, society always constructs, forms itself: it's community, folks getting together for their own reasons, like fishing, farming, friendship. There are a number of ways of looking at and talking about folks getting together. One way is to describe, another way is to prescribe: how things are, how things should be.

Describers, oh, watch birds. Describers plant seeds when the weather is right. Describers tell stories about the way things are; they know magic

---

*Rosa Luxemburg to Luise Kautsky as quoted in Solomon's Marxism and Art (1979), p. 144.

when they see it, know it as magic and are amazed. There's the usual range of human looneytunes and bizarre-o-s in this crowd but, generally, you might say that if one of them wants, for instance, someone to jump off a cliff, one of their own will do the jumping.

Prescribers don't believe in magic, they believe in rules they have made up—science, government, and religion. In science, if a phenomenon cannot be replicated, it not only didn't happen, it can't happen. Government is the rule of those held responsible by those who hold themselves exempt. Religion is male wish-making gone hyperbolic and genital, a pathetic and self-serving hashing of what of the infinite men can comprehend, and that, then, is all dolled up in gossamer jock strap and halo, sutured to science, and resembling government: worship replaces wonder and all things seen and unseen are male-quantified, delineated, and cudgeled off into heavy bats of Lesson and Should. Prescribers don't jump off cliffs: they have governmentlings, religionites, and scientists prescribe rule/roll others off their priest-scribed cliffs while hierarchs in their arks approve, and live to rule again another day.

Now there are prescribers and there are prescribers. There was my nightcapped old prescriber of a grandfather, for instance, forever finger-waggling about how things should be. Him we'd fry up a pork chop for and, soon, he'd amble off to bed to mumble and pray himself to sleep: we'd all been polite, my mommy and daddy and me, and nothing else, in this instance, was required of us. Not that he wouldn't have loved to be able to enforce his prescriptions of How Things Should Be, but he wore that nightcap, remember, instead of, say, a mitre or crown, and carried the weight in his fist of neither orb nor sceptre, test tube nor paycheck, and he had no standing army to speak of.

The problem, we see, occurs when prescribers powerize themselves and rule. The power to prescribe, to rule, comes with and in enforcement: enforcement comes about not only by being able to convince others of the rectitude of one's wishes, whims, and beliefs, but by being willing and able to otherize, trivialize, cul de sac, or/and quell the force of others. The problem occurs when an understanding of community originates not from those who *describe* who gets together how and why and when, but when *the* understanding of community originates from those who *prescribe* who gets together how and why and when. In totalitarian states, the prescribers are evident in the form of official censors and so on, but in so-called "democratic" states the prescribers are not usually either evident or immediately recognizable. Noam Chomsky, in *Language and Responsibility* (1979), says, "No doubt a propaganda system is more effective when its doctrines are insinuated rather than asserted, when it sets the bounds for possible thought rather than simply imposing a clear and easily identifiable doctrine that one must parrot—or suffer the consequences" (p. 12).

Prescribers with power have jostled the matrix of community, of society, into their own vertical construction of society, scribing their classifications into rule and definition, and establishing by their enforced say-so the ordering of and ordered thinking about society.

"Social class," if not an irrelevancy for women, is at the very least one of those subjects women are forced to discuss because we live in a capitalist patriarchy, but it is not our subject: "subject," as you'll remember from anatomy class, is "a dead body for dissection." Society, the association of individuals for reasons particular to those individuals, is a woman's topic: "topic" meaning "place" in all imagined ideas of place, intellectual, physical, and otherwise. Certainly, the destruction of class, of patriarchy, and of capitalism is our topic. Our reasons for associating with those with whom we associate is our topic. An infinitude of topics are women's topics. Why and how women are pulled away from discovering and talking about women's topics is certainly a topic for women's consideration—disassembling the subject of "social class" is our topic, but "social class" as how and where men fit or don't fit women into this, that, or another male pigeonhole, ghetto, kitchen, and/or category, well, that's similar twaddle to women speaking about dick length in the way men speak about it—if not an irrelevant subject for women, it is certainly no place in which women dwell.

There's more, isn't there?

Yes. Have a cookie, then let's change places. You know this stuff, too: tell me what you're thinking.

I'm thinking that sons place themselves as sun to all minerals, mammals, seasons, and thought, and that male constructs always follow two straight lines: 1) down and up—the plane on which their dicks occasionally operate; ergo, hierarchy and most light switches; and 2) back and forth—ditto; ergo, The Continuum, ducks in shooting galleries, and those really head-banging arguments. Male (and isn't that "evil" in Latin: "male"?) society is an extrapolation of two lines at which intersection is the male behavior (and consequent hyperbolic construct) of fucking. "To fuck," as we all know all too well, is used as a synonym for "lovemaking," as well as shorthand (so to speak) for wishing someone ill, as in the phrases "wanna fuck?" and "fuck you!" In male society "fuck" pretty well sums up the sense of both hierarchy and continuum, those two straight (yes, *straight!*) lines, "fucking" being the (old rugged) seminal (double) crux of male/Western behavior/thought. Fucking is something men want to (be able to) do all the time and they have, therefore (because they can't really fuck all the time), made the(ir) language their prosthetic device, a way of extending that activity by metaphor: men can actually fuck only during rare moments in which they are in a state of full bloodbag erection. By extending the actual into metaphor, men extend the sense of fucking; men can, therefore, in one way or another—up and down, back and forth, positively and negatively—fuck everything all the time.

This prescriptive power, especially in the light of being able and eager to fuck things (up) all the time, is hegemonic; this is the power to define and rule and, ultimately, to fuzzy up the distinctions between things, to, indeed, not only name and change meaning but also to subvert and invert meaning; for instance, all things round or not, dimensional or not are male-thought of, male-spoken of, and male-scribbled/bibled about as though all things belong to or along one or two lines. So powerful have these prescripters become that they regularly construct words which invert/contra-state the obvious and inherent meaning of whatever phenomenon they supposedly name. Men/prescripters have devised a word which is to mean "straight across"; it is "horizontal"; the phenomenon of the "horizon" is, of course, innately curved: these prescripters would have us forget, or re-make and remember *that*, even the shape of the world. We are to see, according to prescripters, bubbles, bellies, faces, heads, all known planets, cycles, and society as stratification and line, as up and down across a line of back and forth.

So, we're saying that women must disassemble male subjects/patriarchal constructs such as "social class"—and caste?—and women as, what?, outcast(e)s—and to, instead move beyond patriarchal thought (such as it is—simpleminded, if epidemic) and begin (again and again) to assemble (and assemble again and again) women's topics. Instead of talking about, for instance, women and social class, women will perchance talk about women, of women, by women, and for women; women associating for women's reasons—how, why, when, where, and whatever, yes? Run through some more reasoning on that with me.

I feel a poem coming on:

men
are
like
a
po-
em
in
mo-
no-
me-

ter;
ev-
er-
y
one
else
is
in
the
mar-
gin.

Patriarchal constructs like "social class" breed concepts like "women's equality." Gerda Lerner, in *The Creation of Patriarchy*, says that "Class is not a separate construct from gender; rather, class is expressed in generic terms" and that,

> class for men was and is based on their relationship to the means of production..... For women, class is mediated through their sexual ties to a man. It is through the man that women have access to or are denied access to the means of production and to resources.... Women who withhold heterosexual services...are declassed. (p. 9)

When women see society (and social constructs like, for instance, "social class") in the manner prescribed by prescribers, by male society, women believe in male-promulgated promised ideas like ideals (a-fraud not!). Ideals like those said to be within law; ideals such as my personal favorite and the state mock-o/motto of at least one: "Equality under the law"[1]: and what would that *BE* in an hierarchy, not to mention, for women, in a patriarchal hierarchy, in a capitalist patriarchy? Lying down sitting up? Women's equality under male law: oxymoron—even conceptually, this can't happen. Equality can't be dealt out by an authority to those the authority has stratified. Equality is to patriarchy as round is to flat, as circle is to straight line, as pantisocrasy[2] is to capitalist patriarchy.

But frankly (eleanorly?) I can imagine men Oz-imbuing women with "equality," writing it into their laws—it's the perfect malemindfuck, the perfect inversion of how things are and ever will be for women within capitalist patriarchy: "pay no attention to that man behind the curtain": it sounds so good. Maybe this time they'll mean it. Maybe this time we can work together in the world. Right.

When subjects like "social class" keep women busy, scams like the dangle of (round) female equality within (vertical) male hierarchy could keep women busy and bamboozled for almost ever, that is, if women keep tending male subjects, attending to male debate/bait, ideals/deals. Perhaps if women's lives were some PBS documentary maybe then women could recognize the joke like yolk on their faces, yokes on our necks. Maybe a quiz at the end of the documentary would be useful. With the answers. Something like this.

> Question: Why, in the face of all law, custom, tradition, practice, and belief to the contrary, do women of fin de siècle 20th-21st century continue to refuse to fire randomly into groups of men, particularly into groups of men wearing flag pins, robes or other insignia and/or uniforms of the patriarchy?
>
> Answer Choices:
> A. Neither Avon nor Nike make assault rifles.
> B. Some women feel that (legal) marches, political (political!) reading and NOWcha-cha-cha groups, potlucks, legislationeducation (I think I can, I think I can), lesbian coupling, singing in Michigan, or some combination of those things will, without lifting a trigger finger, eventually accomplish the same ends. Why, often rulers educate themselves then legislate their cattle and chattel into equality, freedom: serf's up! Don't they! Don't they! Besides, many women coalition-build and/or gene pool with men: give 'em time—men—the benefit of the doubt; don't pout and do put on your biggest say cheeseschrist dicklicker smile.
> C. Some women hope to be, and indeed (Hill)are(y) invited onto the Noah's Patry-Arky, Ink. Wham, bam, flimflam man. Bite. Don't bite. Hope you can swim.
> D. Women write books, not right wrongs.

Here's your pencil. Take your time. Ding. The correct answer is "E". "E"?

Patriarchal constructs like "social class" are like the Busy Box a beleaguered parent straps to the bars of a curious-fidgety child's crib—it's all levers and flaps, mirrors, wheels, and buttons designed solely to buy time for the parent by keeping the kid's hand occupied—like questions and answers on a test; like keeping women busy thinking that there is an answer, that there is a correct answer, and that women's choices are among what is presented to women, within the "known," and "given," the "A" to "D." Unoccupied with the Busy Box, the child might learn to operate the drop mechanism for the crib's side.

Of course me being me and you being you, we knew that my test was simulation and sport. But I could learn better than I have, could learn to mimic male stuff more effectively: many women have so learned and we all know lots of them. Then, of course, there's male society and the test(ee)s we get there.

Patriarchal constructs like "social class" are also like the insidious Federal Emergency Management Agency (FEMA) *Shelter Management Handbook,* a manual written for use by bomb shelter, fallout shelter captains after a nuclear war (WHERE? WHO? WHEN?) and oh, goodie, available now for pre-holocaust reading: this is a tome full of rules of order pertaining to everything including, for instance, sleeping arrangements within the shelter—sardine style: head to toe in rows of single men, single women, heterosexual couples, and children. The manual gives us a diagram for this. There are tips on what to do with urine and vomit and a whole paragraph on body-stacking advice (away from the living and under cover "for hygienic reasons," I remember it stating: out of sight, out of mind and black plastic garbage bags obviate even the headiest perfume of stacked-like-cord-wood rotting family members and friends, I guess the reasoning goes here). To whom and how to dispense tranquilizers is discussed, and the manual gives us tips on counseling those who may (MAY!!!!!) be mourning. The manual further suggests that the collecting of water (water?) outside the shelter should be conducted by the older shelter residents, those who will likely not outlive the effects of the extra radiation they, early out, will encounter.

So effective is the focusing of the fingers and questions and answers of our attention on the infinitesimal flat and bizzybox detail of the manual, that the assumed premise and true message of the words is (to be) missed, that message being that nuclear war is survivable, which it is not, and that YOU will survive, which you will not. Captains? What captains? Survivors? What survivors? Just where (oops!) are all those boxed and ready survival crackers (older now than some of us) of the 1950s; where, for that matter, are the "shelters"? Shelter? From what would those shelters, if they still existed, shelter us? From surface wind and rain in Toto-land, maybe, but thermonuclear blasts make big, deep, fiery craters well into the earth vaporizing ev-er-y-thing around *a* (not *the*) blast, incinerating rock and cracker alike around that, and generally melting, or at the very least, tying up traffic thereabouts—what with all the weeping, wailing, gnashing of teeth, and the generalized aggravation associated with absolute oblivion.

The male-assumption behind the busyfingerthink of such propaganda, the "don't worry," and also, deeper, the "do not think (for yourself)," and the foundational "patriarchal rule and order will outlast the end of the world" persists, even while it does not seem to hold up to surface-scratching analysis; the larger system of capitalist patriarchy holds it in place. The prescribers behave like the naked emperor—what is said to be so is so; the emperor is clothed, they say, even as he is truly and really naked.

And when one little kid of us screams "naked" and a couple of others realize nakedness for the nakedness it is, the emperor has but to change/modify his "clothes"/story and the folks believe again—so strong is the system which the emperor-prescriber has built. Just when the 1950s fallout shelter became the laughably and demonstrably naked concept and reality it truly and really always had been, up pops Nixon-Raygun-AmBush propagandists who produced a non-tangible (and therefore not as visibly subjected to crumbling as those 1950s physically real shelters and crackers) version of the same thin(k)g: SDI, the Strategic Defense Initiative, that non-visible, nonsensical floating in the sky (like pie) weapons system which was patterned, apparently, after an Ipana toothpaste t.v. commercial of the 1950s which promised an "invisible protective shield," too—against tooth decay. The sex appeal of an Ipana smile too arcane a referent? Fine, the prescribers hooked into "Star Wars," the wildly popular space cowboy fantasy movie trilogy of the 1970s.

SDI is a concept so "naked" even the military are said to laugh and point, but the system is described and prescribed by powerful prescribers—why, there are representative prescribers everywhere: there are men, men, men, men, men, men, men everywhere clogging up home and office, propping up church and state and science alike and women are to embroil ourselves (broiler chicks!) in a(nother) male constructed and (surprise! surprise!) headed ("head," as in the pus-filled portion of a pimple) system of kinship, the Family: tote that charge, lift that male. If only we could visualize every family head as a duplicate Charlie Manson we might more clearly see the paradigm of "family" for what it is—no matter which form it takes, be it actual men-children family or social institution-as-family.

Why don't women notice that within patriarchal social organization women are to rely not on rights—those things men deem necessary as air, water, women, and fire for men's own survival and well-being, those items which men deem entirely *un*inalienable for women—but women are to rely on privilege as men offer it to (certain) women (at certain times); privilege, the "fetch-bits" ("fetch, bitch") of patriarchal social organization. And remember, the more intermittent the reward, the better is attention held. The family is, of course, the microcosm of patriarchal social structure.

Patriarchal constructs like social class tell women that women belong to/in male society: honey, keep on keeping on with/as male subjects. Women (are to) intellectualize ourselves as There, apparent (a parent), on the page—oh, in the margins, maybe, but There. Patriarchal constructs like social class keep women busy with patriarchal finger exercises, questions, answers, and assumptions; women are trained to see what is not there, trained to interpret along intersecting straight lines—like learning to draw by using only a pencil and the side of a ruler (there's the word/concept again, "ruler"). Women are trained to see ourselves on the page, if only implicitly, to keep male laws, for instance, although women are not so much as included as persons in men's founding/foundering document, the Constitution. Women are to read ourselves as (even!) included in the "generic *he*"; that is, when reading *he*, women are supposed to read/see/sense/sentence ourselves as included. "Quick! Define *horizon*"! Women are trained to see women as written by men (who write women wrong) as ourselves, women written, usually, in a lemon juice invisible ink; women written, usually, by men as either an exercise in (predictable fuck-or-kill) male fantasy, or as an instruction to women. But women are not where or who or why or when men say women are no matter what men say.

Patriarchal constructs like social class have women asking the wrong questions—like "my goodness, into which social class do I fall, lodge, wedge, cower?" Nor do women constitute a social caste, no matter that there is a certain appeal to caste—at least we fit somewhere—even if it's "out" (cast(e)) that we're "in". And, certainly there are a couple of caste markers like, oh, forever hearing and knowing that women still earn some pathetic, antebellum, and biblical percentage of what men earn. White men, yes, ruling class men, yes, too; The Lettermen, of course, but and indeed (as well as in thought and in word) most men of whichever hue, rank, education level, or dick length, most all men in this Trumped up, crosshatched society almost always outearn most women, although for several hundred years women have been subjected to the male do-wop hymn thang about men only trying to help (HELP!): you know—the On Our Side Boys. You know The Gang—one more trying guy or gal The Gang's a-gonna screw or plug into the malecongress, malegislature, male-governor's socket. Why do women keep believing this old shell game is CHANGE, the sort of change that could transform women's lives? This sort of change is like changing a bulb on a string of lights and believing that at some point one will get sunlight; light bulbs keep getting screwed in and out—some are brighter, some a different color, but it's still a string of light bulbs, gals, not sunlight. Honey, women are not There in patriarchal society except women's relationship with men; unless women relate to men.

Right about here John Waynebob Elvis Bush has just about had enough of me (Oh, no, well before now—you're a burger at a Moscow McDonald's pages ago, sweetie), goes for his six-shooter or legislative blue pencil, misses, and, instead, grabs the universal referent for every male metaphor—yes, his own—and I couldn't have sung it better than Chuck Berry myownself—ding-a-ling, saying something manly about me being a bitchy impatient sort of ungrateful bitch. And, because, for once, this is my movie, I get away, I get to say, "Men trying to help women is like Flo Kennedy's fish trying to ride a bicycle and I don't need your trying un-help; and just like that ding-a-ling—keep it to/for yourself."

Something else which looks ever so much like a caste marker is violence—who does it to whom, for whom is it allowed (and allowed by whom), and for whom it is yea, verily, a right? This pecker/pecking order is like, oh, a thermometer of patriarchy: sometimes, for some men against men, violence is allowed; it is sometimes situational, contextual. Men allow men the bar fights and men allow the petit-bougie boss the occasional murder. Women in this society are not allowed to be violent, even (or maybe most especially) against men who beat women, who murder women, who attempt regularly to murder women; women are not allowed anger or the force of heated opinion. The male standard for women in this society is silence. Unless the patriarchs are hanging out one of their own to dry, or to buy off or throw off women's proto-anger towards men, not only is male violence at, on, against, over, and towards women hardly an arrestable offense, rarely a convictable offense, scarcely an offense at all, but male violence against women is, indeed, not only acceptable (to men in other men for themselves) but it is a right, a given, a god-given right. Neither male law nor men protect women; it and they are like the phony custom of men opening doors for women, a male behavior opposite to reality: in no real way do men "open doors" for women in male society. In male society men beat and kill women in every way. All the time. In no way does male society protect women; it was not and never male-designed to do so, and it does not. But, again, the reasoning women are to adopt is one of counter-reality: in a region of rabid dogs, pal up with a rabid dog for protection.

Women are neither social class nor social caste; women are women and it might do us well to identify as such and maybe fiercely organize ourselves around our common-as-a-loaf-of-Judy-Grahn-bread issues, needs, ideas, plans, wants, hopes, and dreams. And here's the part where women take over the world. I am convinced that patriarchal capitalism is a system women cannot revise any more than we can "reform" water so that we might breathe it. As long as the law is male, women must be outlaws. The system of patriarchal imperialism is inimical to women; it always has been and it always will be. We live by the tolerance or privilege or oversight of the patriarchs. Law is patriarchal say-so; nothing grander, certainly nothing nobler. The rights of women are unacknowledged and structurally, fundamentally incompatible with patriarchy: women are treason and heresy. I think that women should embrace that we are treason and heresy: I think women should consider it kernel, nucleus, and core to being women.

Say-so regarding abortion is part of the power patriarchy holds over women. Abortion is an issue of hegemony and imperialism, women being the virgin territory into which flags, for instance, can be rammed for the purpose of claiming same, renaming same, gaining same. It is no wonder to me that abortion law does not reflect women's needs, rights, and thoughts—why would it? How could it? Which laws do?

Adrienne Rich, in *Of Woman Born* (1976), states:

> The woman's body is the terrain on which patriarchy is erected....The repossession by women of our bodies will bring far more essential change to human society than the seizing of the means of production by workers. (p. 55; 285)

Women must demedicalize abortion and begin again to do abortions ourselves. Bring back safe and illegal abortions done by women, for women, and because of women. I was a part of a group of women (JANE) who did safe and illegal abortions. I was proud of those abortions being safe; I am proud now of those abortions being safe *and illegal*. The medicalization of health and the colonization of women's bodies has obfuscated what women can, have, and must again do. What women must not do is to continue to go back again and again (or ever again) to the patriarchs whose right/rite it is to rape women, beat women, and to force impregnation and childbirth of/on women. If women continue to have sex, willed or unwilled, with men, women must take away from men and take for women the say-so and performing of abortion. Women need to practice this and other forms of disobedience (civil, if you like) to male (this is redundant) law. Women must not obey laws which women did not write and which are written at women's expense and which keep us asking, begging, and even marching for permission. For me, fighting for women is not a matter of asking patriarchs pretty please, or even of educating patriarchs or their bag boys: certainly they *know* what they are doing and, indeed, they educate one another to continue doing it. It is women who must learn (about) the capitalist patriarchy in place and that it works and works well for those who designed, maintain, and benefit from it—prescribers/patriarchs/hierarchs/men. Capitalist patriarchy makes a show of being democratic while what actually happens is that the patriarchy grants itself rights, extends privilege to whom it chooses, and institutes oppression for the rest of us.

The illegal abortion work I did with JANE in Chicago between 1970-72 was, besides my writing, the work of me as an outlaw: abortions and writing are the best work I have ever done, are the best work I do—that and my work teaching writing, literature, and Women's Studies, a job a few of patriarchy's bag boys are currently trying to end for me. Like Rosa Luxemburg, I was born to look after the geese in the field; actually, I was born to less than that, my birthmother circumstantially required to consign me to strangers. But had I not been born to the looking-after of geese in the field, or less, I was certainly raised to something like that, reared as I was to the tune of my mother's hymns and my father's incantation, "Who do you think you are?!" a chant that herded me and bit at my heels as though I were a wayward sheep and it, a tenacious and yipping collie. My father wanted "better" (read: "up") for me than he had; he wanted me to be able to get "a job a mule doesn't do," which is how he characterized his job as a steelworker, but neither my father nor my mother wanted me to be beaten down from aspirations higher than their social assignation. Better than anyone, smarter, stronger, and more hard-working; bested by no one and still, what was more important than anything about my father once he was in this country was that he was an outsider, an immigrant, and was, therefore, "entitled" to what the native-born working class didn't want—to wit, those jobs mules and strong backs could do. My father saw me as worse situated even than he was—I was a girl with a brain, a sense I could do anything, and a nature and mouth which questioned everything and everyone all the time, any one of which qualities could be fatal in and of itself. Compounding the infamy, I was naive and rapacious and willful; I did not listen to my mother's advice about submitting myself to first, the will of one's father and/or husband, and, not for long, anyway, did I adhere to her advice about submitting myself to the will of god, as expressed, apparently and ubiquitously, by any tom or hairydick who set himself up as father, husband, minister, boss, or other supposed earthly embodiment of godswill/god swill.

I am not now nor have I ever been, except as defined by men, a member of a social class or caste. I withhold heterosexual sexual service to men, and withhold every other sort of heterosexual/gendered service I can manage. As it is now, I was a daughter to parents who are dead; I am a mother to a daughter and a son who are grown. I love teaching and I am being forced to learn one more way how I, as a woman, have a right to nothing including a job I do well: it is a demonstration of subservience and not of job competence which might have ingratiated me to the men who will or won't grant me (as conditional privilege) continued employment.

It might be useful if women begin to see ourselves as OutLaws vis-à-vis male society: that is, while women organize women's society while we are all still within male society, perhaps knowing ourselves as OutLaws might be a useful moat between women and the often kittenish-looking wild tiger over there on the zoo island—who is only trying to help (him-self—to us), and who oh, so earnestly, wants to be On Our Side (of the moat—yum for him). Women as Out Front OutLaws would know immediately that women would have no divided loyalties—while making women's society, women OutLaws would be obeying no male law: we would not forget to see men as the clan/Klan they are and to see male law as the sheet fabric it is (but, hey, when else do men both "bond" AND care about the linens?). Soon, women's homeland and home would be fully women's society, and women could see ourselves not as outlaws, not as class, classed, classified, caste or cast out, but as women.

FOOTNOTES

[1] "Equality Under The Law" is the state mock-o/motto of (at least) Nebraska.

[2] "Pantisocrasy": "A utopian community in which all are of equal rank or social position," Chambers's *Twentieth Century Dictionary*.

WORKS CITED

Chambers's *Twentieth Century Dictionary*. Toronto: The Musson Book Company, 1910.

Chomsky, Noam. *Language and Responsibility*. New York: Pantheon Press, 1979.

Federal Emergency Management Shelter Handbook. United States Government Printing Office, n.d.

Lerner, Gerda. *The Creation of Patriarchy*. New York: Oxford University Press, 1986.

Rich, Adrienne. *Of Woman Born*. New York: Norton, 1976.

Solomon, Maynard, ed. *Marxism and Art*. Detroit: Wayne State University Press, 1979.

Chrystos

Headaches & Ruminations

Chrystos

Author's Note: Throughout this piece, I refer to under & over class, because middle class has become such a broad term in the u. s. as to be useless. We under class people always know who we are, although our experiences of poverty are often very different depending on whether we are rural/urban/reservation; of Color or pink; immigrant/ assimilated; whether our families drank & abused us or whether they valued education/ upward mobility. It is my belief that poverty, in and of itself, is not the cause of our lack of self-esteem but, rather, how we were valued by our families. If they believed that they were "no good" because of poverty, then we internalized that. However, some families escaped this pervasive myth. I dislike the division of middle & working class because it implies that middle class people don't work and further obscures the fact that many blue collar workers earn higher salaries than white collar workers—particularly teachers.

I further define class as a war between the really rich (often called ruling, which is a misnomer, as corporations are the rulers of our planet) and the poor. In this war, the broad working classes are used as the shield/battering ram to protect the rich from ever having to talk to or cope with the poor. This group as a whole pays the highest percentage of taxes & consists of both blue & white collar workers, and, very rarely, pink collar workers. They also serve as the "police force" in various capacities to oppress the poor in service of the rich. Most Lesbians in my observation fall into the white or blue collar group, because pink collar work (which is how my work as a maid is defined) is not enough to support a household. I define myself as poor, although for two brief years when I received grants, I was "middle class"—that is, I could afford to buy a used car, pay insurance on it, have repairs made to it, go to doctors, and travel. I don't know any single mothers who are not poor, nor are any of my friends with disabilities free from the constant exhausting struggle with money, as government medical "care" does not begin to cover their needs. Recently, when I broke my foot and could not work as a maid, I had to borrow considerable sums of money from friends & lovers to pay my rent & utilities and received my food from the local food bank. I have no health insurance, no vacation pay, no sick leave, and I live from paycheck to paycheck, constantly juggling & bouncing checks. There has now come to be another class in the u. s., which is the homeless, which I am not a member of at the moment. I've observed hostility between the various classes all of my life. The confusion in the u. s. about class place is a deliberate political condition which fosters the consumerism which fuels corporations. It is a part

419

of the "melting pot" myth, which has stripped everyone of their cultural heritage & ancestors. These are deliberate acts in order to create an artificial emptiness inside of people, so that they will buy more things.

Class is a weapon of the money system under which we live at this time. It is usually difficult for us to see how we wound one another with it, when we need to be working around it. This is due to the fact that "money" is considered a dirty subject by all groups, & each group has very distinct values surrounding "money." It is very interesting to me that sex is also considered a dirty subject. When we try to speak to one another about money (this is also true of the word "love"), we are literally speaking different languages, depending on how we were raised. It is my experience that those with the least are always the most generous, unless someone with more has worked specifically to understand their place in society. Thus, I give money when I can to beggars & the food banks, while my wealthy clients primarily donate to the opera, ballet, and other amusements which are their entertainment. The tax laws are written to foster their charity but not mine. The fact that they are "donating" to something for their own benefit is, of course, never addressed. I come to a discussion of class with a great deal of apprehension & confusion. I carry the usual scars of an under class child: fear that I'm not smart enough to write this; that I won't "talk right" & thus, be judged negatively; that nothing I have to say will mean anything to anyone or is important in a general sense. This is despite the fact that I am better read than many college professors I meet. Immediately, I realize that the "correct" phrase is "more well read." The very structures of language have a class system and I am acutely aware that I use "big words" to cover the inadequacy I feel because I do not have a good education. This is not how I spoke as a child, as a teenager, or as a young woman. In becoming an intellectual, in order to be taken seriously as a writer, I feel I have betrayed my originating class, as well as my ethnic group of First Nations people, who also do not speak in this way. Writing is a constant class struggle of translation. This lack of self-esteem and confidence to "take space" is the most clear division I sense in my relationships with over class Lesbians, even though I am seen as a very confident woman. It is still a mask to me, not an authentic presentation of my self. A shy over class Lesbian will often be angry because she feels I take up too much space (as loud & opinionated) and will often resent me (thus being able to dismiss my scars because I don't act like I am suffering). I feel this resentment (which is not expressed for women who dominate in a more middle class style), in fact, I expect it before I start, so I become louder, angrier, and more articulate. I become the "bad guy" in a vicious circle, in which none of us gets our needs for acceptance met (because most Lesbians have very little to give one another—it is all we can do to survive the hatred we are daily bombarded with, make ends meet & keep our lovers & friends happy). I have often noticed that the most assimilated/accepted under class Lesbians (& Lesbians of Color) are the ones who rarely speak in a mixed situation or who act as "fixers," even though in a non-mixed group they might be very critical of those whom they seem to "get along with." This is a dynamic of under class & ethnically oppressed groups which is deeply ingrained for our survival. Therefore, a pink over class Lesbian could think she was friendly with someone who actually hates her guts. My more honest approach is feared by all classes or groups. I don't know how to use those observations to make our relationships with each other easier. I'm lousy at shutting up.

In the u. s., class has none of the clear boundaries of accent & historical control that it has in europe. Traditionally, the phrase "middle class" referred to owning class people who were not aristocratic and did not engage in commerce. They had a leisure which is unimaginable to us today. The u. s. has only been an entity for a very short time period, so all our systems of class have none of the entrenched power of european versions. The class systems of Indigenous Peoples around the world have been destroyed by colonizer contact. Therefore—what IS my class background? I can respond by naming the work my parents did (secretary & ship steward) and be called working class. However, my family had drinking problems, my father often gambled away his paycheck or didn't send it because he was angry with my mother; there were four children and my mother (also angry) often refused to do care of the household. So I grew up with panics about not having enough food, responsibility for my younger siblings, fending off bill collectors, stealing food, lying to social workers & many of the problems associated with a "lower" class.

Because almost everyone I've known in my life, including those with far more money & privilege, have had to work at jobs they don't like—I think the term "working class" is appropriately given to anyone who has to work to live. The Marxist analysis of class does not function in the u. s. because we are not the racially homogeneous population he discussed in his theories (I also like to point out that he had servants)—in the u. s., race is a far more pervasive & deadly weapon of control than class has ever been. My racial heritage has had a deep impact on my life, more so than whatever my class background could be named. This class background was further diluted by experiences of family violence, incest with my uncle, and the hatred my mother feels for me.

In working with other First Nations people (which is my primary political focus), my class is not an issue. Of far more importance is the fact that I was not raised on a reservation. Class is not our divider—but rather, degrees of assimilation to colonizer culture & the acceptance or rejection of that assimilation as a goal are intense points of conflict. In working with Indian people, I've been somewhat isolated from the feminist Lesbian gang, which still does not grant Land/Treaty Rights equal status as a political issue, with, say, abortion. I can't resist adding that this is despite the fact that there are far more Native Lesbians than there are Lesbians who seek abortions.

Class rears its smelly head every time I'm in a group of pink-dominated Lesbians. But then, I'm never sure—IS it class or is it race or is it my age or is it my feminine appearance (I came out in the pre-feminist bar Dyke world) or is it my verbal skills or my intelligence or my humor or my "fatness"? I make a lot of women very uncomfortable and they are almost always over class & usually pink. But I'm not easy to get along with unless you like me & I far more readily trust a Lesbian of Color or under class pink Lesbian or any old-time bar Dyke (fem or butch) than I do a middle-class identified Lesbian. Not that this is always a wise choice. I have been most often betrayed though, in all kinds of painful ways, by Lesbians who identify as over class. This is partly due to the difference in values. This means that if I run into you at the store, I'll ask you home for dinner or lend you money if I have it or treat you if I know you are broke or spend $200 on food for a party or talk to you long distance for nine hours when your mother dies, etc.—these are all sources of arguments I've had with women who value privacy, nuclear family interactions (i.e., just the two of us) and money used for personal benefit rather than for sharing. Some of these value conflicts may be due to the different way that First Nations people view money (i.e., not very seriously—we spend it instead of saving it). These generalizations are uncomfortable but seem inevitable (unless I write a novel delineating all the fights). I also think these betrayals are due to the disposable economy of over class life, which assumes that you can always get a new one & throw the old out. I do understand that class is one of the reasons I work as a maid (on & off since I was twelve, when I earned 50¢ for washing kitchen floors), didn't get the college education that I still crave & worry every month about whether I'll be able to pay my bills and am a frequent, embarrassed visitor to the food bank.

All of my long-term relationships have been with pink women of significantly higher class backgrounds than myself. The irony of this (especially that they had maids as children) has not escaped me. In living alone for the last year, I've finally had time to understand that what I sought from them was primarily protection. I wanted to be safe & thought they were the source of it. I've finally understood, though, that their safety was an illusion, because the lack of communication between us was more dangerous than any struggle for money. In unconsciously desiring to be "saved" from poverty, I set up dynamics which encouraged abuse.

In political situations, the Lesbians who blow up at me are always pink, over class & college-educated. I'm not sure what to make of this, although, as typical of under class people, I have spent a lot of time trying to figure it out & also blaming myself. Most of these Lesbians have never bothered to clarify or apologize later. This is definitely class privilege. The pink Lesbians I feel more comfortable with are generally working class-identified, probably because they have had relationships with People of Color previously, as they rarely grew up in white suburban ghettoes. This is occasionally not true when a Lesbian has experienced incest, incarceration, medical invasion as a child, violence, or has a long-term deep relationship with another Lesbian of Color or is disabled. This brings me to my original confusion—class is not the most useful category for me, although I clearly recognize & resent the obnoxious attitudes, ignorance & complacency that the over class often represents.

A Lesbian's originating class background is not as important to me as her political ability, or lack of it, to comprehend what I term "real life"— consisting of the struggles of all Indigenous Nations (every single one of which is fighting for survival), the millions of homeless, all of those living in inner city ghettoes & fighting drugs, those with disabilities (physical & mental)—in short, anyone who'd probably spit in my face if I said, "Let's have coffee & talk of class differences." This real life is a place where suffering & struggle are constant. Anyone who has to fight to get to the grocery store or can't go because their food stamps are late is a part of real life and this is our biggest population despite the lies of politicomorons. The "american dream" is a bitter farce to us. The purpose of keeping real life divided from the over class is to keep us ignorant of & afraid of one another. As long as we see each other as the enemy, we can be seduced or manipulated by the corporations. Once we deny our need for a BMW, we can begin to define ourselves. One way in which we're kept separate is through the different kinds of education we get. For example, under class people are denied information about how to stockpile & manage money (do you know what the futures market is?) & that is usually the primary focus of all over class education (in addition to the preservation of "western culture"—i.e., white heterosexually-presumed male culture). I can hear the screams of outrage from over class Lesbians, but I'm discussing MY experience, not The Truth. In breakups with over class women, money has always been the most bitter struggle & I've given in to ridiculous demands & in fact, bought a house for the last one with my NEA* money & have not been reimbursed. She claims that she has a broken heart & I've ruined her life. However, one of her ex-friends says that she always planned to get a house out of me. How much of that is bitterness about a failed friendship and how much is the truth? I can't tell you the number of women I've helped by paying their bills or by not asking for rent money for a year, because of my value of sharing what I have within my family & friends. It is only recently that I've come out of my daze enough to realize that each of these women continues to have a much higher income than myself (all work in computers) & feels no responsibility to me. Although I'm angry about being ripped off, I am more deeply angry that my generosity has been undercut with bitterness.

This bitterness about money & arguments I've had with lovers over things shames me deeply. The things which I had brought into the relationships (curiously, I have more things than most middle class-identified Lesbians who don't own houses, probably because I never part with anything—another under class value) are used furniture, old love letters, sets and sets of dishes, etc. Although I could take my last lover to court over the house, I have resisted because of my deep distrust of the injustice system. No one in the community has been willing to pressure her into behaving ethically, although I have received much sympathy "under the table" at parties & in conversations. These are the raw nerves under our distrust of one another. One of my ex-lovers has an uncle who "owns" a bank & she can rely on him in emergencies for cash on her signature. None of my relatives works in a bank & when my mother was still speaking to me she might have been willing to lend me $20. When I try to fight with over class lovers I've already lost & I know it. I CAN'T be casual, although I envy those who can. Talking about the lost house is considered "putting my business in the street" and "low class." The phrase "low class" bears much resemblance to another one I hate, "indian giver."

One of the more painful political messes I've been involved with concerned a Lesbian conference, in which I was orally promised that a speaker for Land & Treaty Rights would be given a forum. I gave a list of names of possible speakers and spoke on the important issues that I'm aware of over the phone. When the plenary speakers were lined up, I was puzzled because the Indian speaker was a Lesbian who has been most identified as an s/m or leather speaker. She proceeded to talk about s/m, unaware of the other agenda. There was quite a protest, much misunderstanding & general problems. The over class (she is an heiress) Lesbian to whom I spoke

---

National Endowment for the Arts.—Ed.

has never taken responsibility for this mess—she treats me as a trouble-some fanatic & I treat her as an insensitive jerk. The Native woman was being used to function as a double token, to shut up two groups that are only superficially allowed territory in Lesbian land. The heiress & I, more than four years later, have no relationship at all & there has still been no Lesbian forum on Land & Treaty Rights though that was another verbal promise during the mess which ensued. In fact, the only time I have been asked to speak on that specific issue was by the Dynamics of Color Con-ference, which was organized by Lesbians of Color. No one in the Lesbian gang is concerned by the fact that this woman & I hate one another. This mess is replicated millions of times across this continent. This is an ancient dynamic in any culture where money disparity is the criterion of relation-ship. I say she was irresponsible and ignorant. Relationship is central to my life. I do not mean this in a do-or-die love obsession sense. I mean: my belief is that we are all powerfully connected to each other, to air, to stones, to the sea and earth. It is our individual & collective responsibility to heal each other, ourselves, and to be profoundly respectful of our mother, as she manifests herself in her myriad ways. Class is always disrespectful of all persons because it proposes that material goods are more important than our relationships to one another and to ourselves. People who cannot feel good about themselves unless they can acquire status "things" (BMWs, go on Olivia cruises, have expensive commitment ceremonies, etc.) are cer-tainly not free. So the question remains—what to do with ignorance—which I must presume is deliberate, as in this media-blitzed era it is not possible to be truly ignorant after age twelve.

Obviously, I have no glib answers to the class war which continues inside Lesbianism (a rare & wonderful herstorical book on this issue is *Boots of Leather, Slippers of Gold**). I can't solve my own messes. It would give me profound relief to go into the dynamics more thoroughly. But it isn't useful because it wouldn't be dialogue. Under class Lesbians might be glad to see the troubles in print—because this is a constant between us—but over class Lesbians would not hear me any more easily in print than in person. I'm not supposed to talk about how they oppress others because then they would have to change, which is unpleasant, difficult & offers no rewards—you can't get a raise or win a new car because you change your behavior. It is much easier to wallow in being a victim of men or the patriarchy. Noth-ing in most over class lives has prepared one for struggle or despair. This discussion is very similar to attempting to get a heterosexual pink male to understand sexism. No matter how sincere his attempt, he is still INSIDE his privilege so deeply that it IS the way the world is. He may be sad or

**Elizabeth Lapovsky Kennedy and Madeline D. Davis (New York: Routledge, 1993).*

angry or empathetic with women but every moment of his existence is colored by how much his privilege has shaped his very way of thinking; his existence is formed by centuries of sexism and everywhere he goes, his complete experience is different from mine.

To move outside of privilege is an act of great courage for which there is no bonus. It *is* possible, just as it is possible to not be White—i.e., there are white people, then there are the WHITE white people & then the really dangerous WHITE WHITE WHITE people (& they mean it). While I want over class Lesbians to move over, to educate themselves about value differences, to be more respectful of those of us with less opportunity, I'm personally more focused on encouraging other under class Lesbians to speak up in groups (where we're often silent but always take out the garbage), to work to make our lives sane & comfortable WITHOUT giving up our identities or "passing," to encourage each other to develop self-esteem and reach for "impossible" goals, to pay close attention to how money controls us and work to undo that, to go ahead & BE angry & act "low class" (shout when excited, laugh loudly, etc.) & to be acutely aware of how racism, sexism, ableism & ageism continue to impoverish our lives. Miz Ann may not change but we can focus on caring for each other & doing what needs to be done—the work we've always done so well. As long as we allow money to be our criterion of our worth as people—they're winning.

Comparing Class Notes

Donna Allegra

I grew up in a family which had middle-class values and two working parents at the start. My mother is light-skinned. That put her up in the ranks of what meant class to Black people. My father is very dark-skinned. He got points for marrying her.

We Jamaicans felt that we were better than African-Americans. My Jamaican father would sometimes jest, "Don't mutilate the King's English," and I would hear family members refer to the Queen.

In my adolescent years, we were the only West Indians on the block in an African-American neighborhood. As little as thirty years ago, the influx of West Indians with the acceptance and eventual dominance of that culture which one sees today in Brooklyn did not exist. My Crown Heights address was not yet on the map of familiarity. I always had to explain to non-New Yorkers, "I live near Bedford Stuyvesant," in order to get some geographic recognition.

What is class anyway? I experience it as a caste system based on whatever translates into who has money and gets to make lots of it; what people get social recognition, respect; and which ones are accorded privileges. They have "class" just because of where they come from—the suburbs is a good starting point; what they look like—white and healthy is the ideal; and whatever other factors are important, e.g., one's manner of speech, styles of dress, body image, specifics of education.

Money is usually the most important determinant in the U. S., but there are preliminaries of race and sex and looks that allow for whether one can acquire more money than one was born to by class. Image and sex appeal are also parts of the package that translate into class status.

How does class add up in my book of numbers? First, you've got to factor in race. Racism gives some people an outlet to play out their assumptions of superior and inferior. I see these attitudes as connected to the presumptions of belonging to a superior sex or class. The attitudes extend to body type, physical beauty, artistic worth and accomplishment. The same dynamic is at work. The products we buy and identify with—car, clothes, health foods—also support the "My dog's better than yours" stance which our class-conscious culture promotes. Patriarchy seems particularly fond of making clubs that exclude people.

In America everyone wants to be what they are not. Advertisers engender self-doubt, promote the notion that what we are is not good enough and sell "classiness." The idea is that if you buy the image that the product advertised represents, you can change the person. We buy goods and services to signal a certain class identity.

This belief in hierarchy serves both as a distraction to keep people busy and America in business so that the rich stay rich and the poor hope to escape their class, rather than change the whole ball game and its rules. Because we deny there is a class system even as we speak of "high class" and "low class," we also deny that there is enormous wealth and poverty. The main, but not only, factor to class is wealth.

Education is very tied up with class. More education led to better jobs for the poor and middle class. Skills and training directly translated to greater ability to make and maintain money and advance up the ranks.

Intelligence is universally admired in and of itself. We somehow believe that intelligence is an attribute of the upper classes, "our betters." Certainly this amorphous quality leads to better economic opportunities if one goes the conventionally accepted routes of schools and job-training. Street smarts are also praised and admired by the lower and middle classes. The person who knows how to hustle on the street and make a buck can do better than the one who won't apply herself to the task of getting over in that realm.

The intelligence that one needs to hustle is a technique that transfers to the boardroom and executive suite, though the upper class likes to pretend to be too genteel to lie, steal, manipulate, bully and kill. But it is intelligence as communicated by language skills, facility with current events and hard knowledge of mainstream values that advance a person on the class scale. This mode of information is a given to those of the upper classes, simply as a matter of course. The middle class claim it as a right and a possession. The lower class is systematically and effectively denied the opportunity to acquire the full range and fine points of these social skills. To top it off, they are looked down upon and blamed for being "stupid," "ignorant," and "low-life." The poor person who can acquire the mainstream fashions of knowledge and demonstrate intelligence in a manner that the privileged can recognize as their own has an advantage over those who use "bad grammar" and "nonstandard" English, i.e., the manner of the ruling class being the standard.

African-Americans rank in the lower echelons on the American scale when it comes to who merits respect. Americans fiercely weigh and measure. Hierarchy is the name of the game. The ones on top get to exercise unquestioned power and have access to make money in a big way.

In my elementary school social studies classes, I was taught that America is a classless society. This was learned in the same breath as my ABCs and arithmetic—basic concepts never challenged. That early orientation has been ingrained in most people's consciousness as well. But of course it is not true that America is a country without class distinctions. It is no more true than the notion that this is the land of the free, home of the brave; that America welcomes "tired masses yearning to be free."

No one says it directly, but one learns to think in terms of "better than" and "less than" and how people are ranked. Those with more points for approval and privilege are more desired as friends and associates at all ages after adolescence—that time of life when one becomes socially self-conscious. The very words "upper class" and "lower class" promote the values this hierarchy fosters. The idea of different and equal is not one easily held in the palm of one hand in our culture.

For example, most people in the north looked down on southern accents. The dialects represented low-class ignorance. Of course, most of the American-born Blacks in my neighborhood had immediate family down south, though they themselves spoke like northerners. Their background roots were in Virginia, Georgia, the Carolinas. This was never formulated as a direct thought of superiority, just ideas in the back of my mind that can be traced to their full implication of a scale of "better than" as I examine them now.

When I was growing up, the -isms and awareness of institutional oppression and cultural imperialism were not common parlance. No identification of our class systems and subcultures came up in anyone's conversation; in fact, there was much denial about it. Yet everyone in America wants to be better than someone else. I think that this is part of the attraction to British culture—to identify with the upper classes, if you're poor, and with the lower classes if you are wealthy. We abhor the East Indian caste system, but get off on the Brits.

And speaking of denial, there's a word fraught with it: *comfortable*. It means upper class and financially secure.

I expected to be an American-dream success. I was smart, i.e., I got good grades in school and I was well-behaved. In my family, we took pride in our intelligence. We saw this as something that made us better than the rest of the class. Points *up* on the scale.

My brother and I went to sleep-away summer camp. Some form of scholarship to the poor and culturally deprived was involved. That, to my way of thinking, put me above the kids on the block back home. But at these camps, we were two of only a handful of other Black kids at camp, and decidedly lower-class in ranking.

I never felt poor or realized that we weren't financially middle-class until I went to college and read some sociology. This was a good thing. Self-esteem came with feeling middle-class. Poor meant "bad" and "low" morals. I never heard my parents worry aloud or complain with any ferocity about money. It was a given, somehow by osmosis, that we children should not ask for too much. In addition, my brother and I were kids; money was adult business which our parents kept from us.

The unspoken indoctrination to the class hierarchy comes early. I can now admit that I consciously wanted to be in a higher class than I lived. I aspired to be able to claim superiority on the basis of my intelligence, by being smarter than other people.

Recognizing the race component to the upper echelons of class, I used skin-lightening cream because I am not a light-skinned Black person. This cosmetic was a lesser version of the whitening process Michael Jackson succeeded in doing. I bragged about the fact that my mother's side of the family once had servants when they lived in St. John, The Virgin Islands, and came to this country and had to become other people's servants. I repeated my mother's tones of sad bitterness, a pseudo-acceptance. I was, in truth, fascinated; I wanted that heritage.

Being "smart" gave me status. Intelligence, education—these were to be my passport on the road to the good jobs, money, security, respectability and middle-class-ness. In my family, it was a given that both my brother and I would go on to college. Because I was smart, I'd naturally be a doctor/lawyer/engineer. I never questioned or protested or felt at all uncomfortable with that assumption. I too wanted to "better myself." And that is in keeping with my class background. We were on the low end of the scale, which is determined largely, but not entirely, by money. We wanted to, "move on up," as the African-Americans say in church. We identified with the higher classes, perhaps as a way of getting there. Today one might call it positive visualization—or wanna-be-ness.

Our class status was in our state of mind, our values and attitudes. Financially, we were a working-class people on my block. I heard adults speaking admiringly and with approval of city jobs. Children were encouraged towards these, and young adults congratulated for winning that prize—a job with the government. A job at the post office was a boon. My light-skinned great uncle on my mother's side was one of the early Blacks in Harlem to be able to boast of a post office job.

We read *Jet* and *Ebony* magazines to get news of success trailblazed by other Black people. They were sources of pride and self-esteem. The outlaw, the rude boy, the gangster image were not admired nor role models to be sought after for Black people, in the days of my youth. These marked the underclass who embarrassed us, whom we wanted to get away from and dis-identify with.

Only with the Blaxploitation films like *Superfly*, *The Mack*, *Troubleman* and *Shaft* did pimps, numbers runners, hustlers, drug dealers and the street life become admired, cool in the eyes of a great many African- and Caribbean-Americans. Until then, these images were disdained, somewhat tolerated, but looked down upon as lower-class and not at all to be desired.

The people I come from were proud to be able to say, "So and so was the first in the family to finish high school, went on to college and got the diploma." We wanted to show off at those school graduation ceremonies.

In my circle of friends today, yuppies, buppies, luppies and/or guppies are sneered at. We profess to look with disdain at the upwardly mobile, yet that is the very thing I was raised to reach for, and, in fact, still want in many ways. To be fair, or more complete, political consciousness and social awareness also make for not buying into the American dream, which I now recognize as a nightmare. The American mainstream offers a toxic pie and getting a piece of it is at best a questionable enterprise.

On the other hand, Americans like to boast about having had to work for their money, deride, even as we envy, the rich and monied. I think the phrase, "I had to work for every penny I ever got," is in part a denial and a defense. Heaven forbid anyone think the speaker "has money" or "got it easy." Americans of a lower class, or who come from less money—aren't they one and the same?—and now have more money, are, most often, defensive about it.

Still, I know full well that I do not want to be poor, financially vulnerable, without resources. That's death to a Black person. It means lesser health care, lesser life expectancy, greater stress, greater exposure to crime, increased disrespect from everyone around you, etc. That's the down side to being of African heritage which people who find "class" in the "hip" and "coolness" of African-American culture don't fully appreciate.

It is because of this perpetual second-class status that my parents raised their children to be so well-groomed, not to have ashy arms and legs, to straighten our hair, to dress neatly and be clean. This would distinguish us from lower class, i.e., POOR Blacks. We were good Negroes and our elders hoped that this neatness, these good manners, and that well-behavedness would keep the police from needlessly bopping us upside the head, tossing us in jail and our lives in the trash heap. The strategy didn't always work, but that was the theory of how children were raised in my family, in my neighborhood. We wanted to look like the "good" Negro, not the "bad" one.

I can't tell which is the chicken, which the egg: classism or racism/sexism. Where did the mechanism of hierarchies for human beings begin? Is racism/sexism a subset of classism or the other way around? I think they both stem from patriarchal values.

It is easy to see class differences among racial and ethnic groups of the same type and to see race differences amongst people of the same class background. It seems to be that the hierarchy of race forces people of color ever into a lower class. An example: I may make the same money as a married co-worker, have more education and have more of my money to spend because I am single, without kids. But he is accorded more credibility, status, and respect because he is white and male. Another: I make a larger hourly wage as a construction worker than my brother, who is a copier repair technician. But he has more class because he has an engineering degree to get him his job position and he is named a "technician."

Other determinants of class status, like good English, gave one points, as did light skin. Let's not forget about language as a marker in the hierarchy. Don't have no Spanish accents in this town. French is delightful to Americans, as is a British accent charming. German is fine too; Dutch, Scandinavian, oh so sexy. Americans will be very tolerant of a European's broken English in our homeland. African accents, however, are highly suspect and questionable. We start to wonder if these Africans and the Latins can understand and be intelligent. They get no points for being able to speak two and often more languages. A southern accent? Well, then we think you're probably stupid...well, ignorant. Spanish is definitely unacceptable here where all men (hee hee) are created equal and entitled to pursue life, liberty and happiness. Just stay in your place and don't get too uppity, OK?

My father came to the U. S. from Jamaica. He got rid of his accent soon after coming to Harlem in the 1940s. Native-born Blacks teased him mercilessly for his accent and he spoke of having to fight his way home from school on account of it.

A motif from my childhood was to hear people say, "You don't sound like you're from New York. Where are you from?" I can now understand that such remarks came from the assumption that I don't "sound" Black, i.e., how the speaker perceives the speech of Black people, as "stupid," "loud," "ignorant," like Blacks from the south or from the islands. The real question was, "How come you speak so nicely and sound white?"

Nor was I offended by such questions at the time of my growing up. I agreed. It was better to sound white. My dialect raised me a notch on the class rating scale. Consider the fact that I had no trouble identifying with Stephen Gordon when I read Radclyffe Hall's *The Well of Loneliness*. Stephen was an upper-class, rich, British lesbian noblewoman. She fit my inner image just fine. In my mind, that is what I aspired to.

I chose to go to Bennington College as much from that inner identity as from figuring that there'd be more lesbians at that school than at the other women's colleges I could choose from, given my good grades in school. Radcliffe and Smith were also on my list, but Barnard and Sarah Lawrence were too close to my New York City home.

At sixteen, I went away to school and came face to face with the reality of upper-class white Americans. I realized something at a deeper level than I had previously: They thought I was a nigger; a poor, welfare, probably hoodlum type, at Bennington on a needy, charity scholarship— and not, as I knew, a merit scholarship candidate—on account of the fact that I was so smart and superior and in the upper ranks of the social class hierarchy that is based on one's intelligence. Didn't these people know that I was spiritually an upper-class British noblewoman who could fence, ride a horse and play tennis?

Why did they expect, even want, me to be a street-smart hustler, a Black panther radical, someone angry and filled with rage?

And why did they act like they didn't have money?

The students I went to school with could casually disdain getting Bennington's designer-name college degree and leave school without the worries I certainly had. I knew I could not cop that attitude. It would spell disaster for my life; I'd be just another nigger on the street. I needed to be able to say I graduated with this pedigree: Bennington College.

No one talked (to me) about their context of coming from wealth, so that they could afford to adventure with family support to fall back on, or even fund the expedition; of trust funds to live on after graduation (or non-graduation), so that they could make different choices about what to study, what major to go for or not bother to complete. And perhaps they didn't realize the extent of their wealth, as it appeared to me.

I don't know what my peers knew, or didn't realize and took for granted. I can tell you that I had a bad acid trip at school and a subsequent nervous breakdown.

My friends today say, "Die yuppie swine" and "Eat the rich," and I agree, but I also have a track which wants financial security, wealth, and not to be hated for having it.

There's not much language for recognizing class issues because we're taught that America is a class-less society with equal opportunity, and that anyone can make it rich. While most of us are fluent about racism, sexism, homophobia and able-bodied-ism, money and the classes it creates are not spoken of or easily identified with any openness or sophistication.

The poor are blamed and despised by the middle and upper classes. The rich are envied and hated by the middle and lower classes. We recognize that something isn't fair in wealth's distribution and poverty's none-too-distant threat, yet we've also been brainwashed to believe that we all have a fair shot at achieving riches, if we just work hard enough. Well, that's not true.

What truth there is in the American possibility that any kid can grow up to be president—RICH is really the dream's proper name—is largely qualified and tempered by class factors that include one's race, sex, looks, etc. I think heterosexual women can buy into the fantasy of marrying a man and a white picket fence and living happily ever after, more so than lesbians.

As Maua, an elder in the African-American lesbian community has pointed out, the middle class serves as a buffer zone for the rich. Those "poverty programs" and "trickle-down" plans are designed to protect the rich. These give the mass of lower classes the illusory hope that they can get a spot in the system and a few crumbs of the pie. Those hopes are meant to keep them from tearing the whole thing apart.

I see class, like race, as a tool in the arsenal of the divide-and-conquer technique that the rulers in the upper class use so well. The false idea of a class-less society, as an advertiser might phrase it, "Keeps America great."

Just the Facts, Ma'm

(notes from a conversation with Chrystos)

Bǫ   (rita d. brown)

Because no one has studied Lesbians in prison extensively, the information that follows is from the general female prison population figures—approximately 10%-25% or more are Lesbians.

- Nonviolent first offenders make up about 70% of female prisoners

- 70%-80% come from impoverished backgrounds

- 1984 statistics estimate about 51% of female prisoners are Women of Color; in 1985 46% were Black (although the percentage of Black women ARRESTED for crimes is much lower than whites—revealing the racist nature of the injustice system)

- A high percentage have not finished high school

- About 75% had no job for six months prior to arrest and less than $50 at the time of booking

- Women who can't make bail are far more likely to do hard time (a direct correlation of poverty with imprisonment)

- *Time* magazine refers to women behind bars as the fastest-growing group of women in the u. s.

- What was formerly named misdemeanor substance abuse is now called felony drug charges—which accounts for much of the population increase in women's prisons

- Although Women's Liberation has been blamed for the rise in the female prison population, the rate of violent crime has remained about the same for women throughout u. s. history

- Many prisoners experienced violent homes and sexual abuse as children, with no access to ways of healing

- 90% have serious drug and/or alcohol problems, which are not necessarily addressed

- Overcrowding (200% or more) means that women held for misdemeanors are often in maximum security units for lack of other facilities

- Women's prisons have fewer medical, educational, and vocational facilities than men's

- Most guards in women's prisons are men and sexual abuse of prisoners is common

- Illegal transfers to mental prisons are used as an implied and real threat to control women

- Psychological counselors offer no confidentiality. In a cell search, all personal writing may be confiscated at the discretion of the guards, which makes keeping a journal (one of the prime cheap ways to heal from abuse) an impossibility. All incoming and outgoing mail is read—there is no privacy

- Homophobia is exemplified by rules which prohibit any type of physical contact (even a friendly hug in hard times) between prisoners

- The general prohibition against physical affection is enforced more against known Lesbians, who usually endure extra surveillance or are treated "like men"

- In control units, women are on camera at all times, with no doors to bathroom stalls or shower curtains, most often observed by male guards

- Of the over 200 political prisoners and prisoners of war in the u. s. (using conventional definitions), more than 25% are women—of these, we know of five out Lesbians: Judy Clark, Laura Whitehorn, Linda Evans, Susan Rosenberg, and Norma Jean Croy

- The u. s. imprisons more people per capita and for longer sentences than any other country in the world (the former soviet union is second and south africa is third)

- The most common crimes for women are forgery, bad checks, stolen property, fraud, drugs, and prostitution (economic crimes) and retaliation for sexual abuse or battering

- The 1991 *Prison Discipline Study*[1] reveals that severe physical and psychological abuse in the maximum security prisons nears the internationally accepted definition of torture. The most commonly abused are jailhouse lawyers,* Black prisoners, and the mentally disabled

*A "jailhouse lawyer" is a prisoner who has taught herself law while serving time and (often) gives legal advice to other prisoners.—ED.

- Because of overcrowding, almost no rehabilitation programs now exist in women's prisons

- Lesbian prisoners are singled out for particularly severe sentences, constant harassment, including sexual threats and assaults, strip and cavity searches by male guards (including putting a whole fist in a woman's vagina), punitive transfers away from friends, censorship of reading material/mail and denial of medical care

- An increasing number of prisoners are no longer allowed to make collect calls, which means that women with no money in their commissary funds cannot talk to anyone outside of prison, including their children

- Commissary prices are sometimes higher than street prices, while prison wages average from 1¢ to $1 an hour—making the u. s. the largest employer of slave labor in the world (prisons make an average of 400% profit on their various industries—making chairs, etc.)

- If a prisoner doesn't work in the factories (because of ill health, for instance), her "allowance" is about $10 a month (which does not cover a carton of cigarettes, for instance)

Women's prisons have been used historically, and in the present time, as instruments of social control, particularly to enforce and reinforce women's traditional roles, to foster dependence and passivity. These behaviors are rewarded in prison, which is part of why there is such a high rate of return. (Additionally, if a woman is an ex-con, it's hard for her to get a job that pays a livable wage, and, of course, no one can live on welfare.) Wardens have control of the rules in each individual prison—there is no one standard of conduct. Therefore, recently, in Pleasanton federal prison in California, women were sent to the hole for not tucking their T-shirts in at the dinner meal. Rules are often arbitrary and almost always not uniformly enforced.

Lesbian prisoners are more likely to resist being treated like little girls and the more butch prisoners suffer increased discrimination from the guards. Social groups in prison often form around a butch and her wife. These extended families are a key factor in survival—they watch each other's back, help obtain food and cigarettes and spread the news about who is in the hole, up for parole, etc. This support is crucial because of the violence which women are subjected to in prison from guards. Butch women are sought after by both other Lesbians and straight women because of the protection they offer. While sex is difficult to accomplish in the prison system, it flourishes.

My political work at this time is with the Out of Control Lesbian Committee to Support Women Political Prisoners and with a group called Revolting Lesbians. I am a working class Dyke, white, a former political prisoner who spent eight-and-a-half years in federal prisons around the country because of my actions as a member of the George Jackson Brigades.[2] In those years, I was moved from prison to prison, almost as soon as I developed support systems. During that time, I spent almost a year in a control unit at Davis Hall in Alderson, Virginia. Sister Assata Shakur[3] and I were held there along with reactionary and Nazi prisoners. I was kept for extra long periods in isolation and threatened and harassed specifically because I am a butch Lesbian. The control unit is based on total physical and sensory deprivation, constant surveillance, and is usually built underground so that no daylight ever reaches you. More and more women are being placed in these because of their political beliefs. Political prisoners receive some of the longest sentences in the world—in many cases, equal to life imprisonment—while KKK members and abortion clinic bombers do next to no time. Women routinely do two to three times longer than men for the same crimes. Women of Color and working class Dykes often do even longer times.

Here are some of the Lesbians in the prison systems:

Judy Clark: Arrested in October of 1981 for attempted appropriation of a Brinks truck, acting with the Revolutionary Armed Task Force (please note that she has done more time than Dan White, who murdered Mayor Moscone and city supervisor Harvey Milk of San Francisco). Her activism began as a teenager with the civil rights movement in New York City. She was a member of Students for a Democratic Society (SDS)[4] and an activist against the war in Viet Nam. She was a plaintiff in a law suit against the f.b.i. and the u. s. government for harassment and disruption of the New Left through its COINTELPRO[5] program.

Susan Rosenberg: Arrested in 1984 and convicted of possessing weapons, explosives, and false ID. In May of 1988 (while in prison), she, along with six other political prisoners (also in prison), was indicted for actions in resistance to u. s. war crimes. She has been an activist all of her adult life. While in high school, she worked with and was greatly influenced by the Young Lords[6] and the Black Panthers.[7] She was active in the antiwar and women's liberation movements. She is a doctor of acupuncture and Chinese medicine.

Laura Whitehorn: Arrested in May, 1985, for harboring a fugitive and other charges. She was held for over three years without a conviction. She is now serving a 23-year sentence for "conspiracy to oppose, protest, and change the policies and practices of the u. s. in domestic and international matters by violence and illegal means." This included the bombing of the capitol after the u. s. invaded Grenada and shelled Beirut (called the Resistance Conspiracy Case). She has fought the KKK and organized white supremacy, supported Puerto Rican independence, and sought the liberation of Lesbians and gay men. She was recently transferred from Lexington to Mariana (control prison) (federal prisons in Kentucky and Florida) after she participated in the first women's prison uprising in twenty years.

Linda Evans: Arrested in May, 1985, for harboring a fugitive, false statement to acquire guns and ammunition, and is part of the Resistance Conspiracy Case. She was an SDS regional organizer, opposed the war in Viet Nam and supports Black Liberation. She belonged to a guerrilla theatre troupe, an all-women's band, and a women's printing collective in Texas. She was very active in the Lesbian community. She has recently been organizing AIDS education inside prison, which the prisons have failed in the past to do.

Norma Jean Croy: Arrested in 1978 for murder, although she did not use a weapon and was shot in the back by the police. Her brother Hooty did thirteen years (eight on death row) for the same incident, before he was released on a "cultural" self-defense plea, which the parole board refuses to acknowledge as new evidence. Norma Jean was again denied parole in July of 1993. Her case has recently been accepted in the federal court system and will be heard early in 1994. (It is important to point out that forty-nine percent of u. s. death row prisoners are people of color: 40% African American, 7% Latino, 1.76% Native American, 1% Asian. In California, 36.6% of those on death row are Black even though they comprise only 3.5% of the state's population. A disproportionate number of women on death row are Dykes. A 1990 University of Iowa study found that people convicted of killing white people were more than four times as likely to be sentenced to death as those who killed people of color.)

To find out additional information on Lesbians in prison, please contact:

Out of Control Lesbian Committee
3543 18th St., Box 30
San Francisco, CA 94110

Norma Jean Croy Defense Fund
473 Jackson Street, 3rd Floor
San Francisco, CA 94111

FOOTNOTES

[1] For copies of this document or more information write: Box 1019, Sacramento, CA 95812.

[2] A multiracial, working class underground group that provided armed support for various Native American, labor, and prisoner struggles in the Pacific Northwest in the mid-seventies.

[3] Part of the leadership of the Black Panthers in New York and accused member of the Black Liberation Army (BLA) during the late sixties/early seventies. She was framed by COINTELPRO for a life prison term. Assata escaped after seven years of torturous imprisonment and was granted political asylum in Cuba.

[4] An antiimperialist group of mostly white college students involved in organizing on campuses across the u. s. Perhaps most known for their activism during the 1968 Democratic convention in Chicago.

[5] An infamous government unit responsible for the murder or imprisonment of a whole generation of Black, Latino, and Native American political leadership and for terrorizing their supporters.

[6] A Puerto Rican gang that transformed itself into the Young Lords Party, bringing together for the first time pro-Puerto Rican independence work with community programs to feed, educate, and organize in the Puerto Rican communities in the eastern u. s.

(Un)Common Justice[1]

Joanna Kadi

Introduction

My family knew that capitalism is bad, that the owners of general motors exploited us, and that we could not expect justice. But no one believed the situation could change. "Life isn't fair," my mother said frequently, giving voice to a belief system by which we lived.

In this essay I want to use common justice—which I define as fair treatment in daily living—as a vehicle to explore issues of internalized oppression among working-class people. I believe a crucial task of lesbian theory is to identify and analyze aspects of structural oppression involving racism, sexism, classism, heterosexism, and/or other oppressions. I also believe the theory we write must emerge from our racial and class identities, and must grapple with what those identities mean in terms of power. Usually that doesn't happen. Instead, from my vantage point as a working-class lesbian of color, I've observed this: Lesbian/feminist theory has been and is being shaped, defined and written predominantly by middle-class women mimicking mainstream beliefs that working-class and poor people cannot theorize because we are too stupid to think clearly and are only good for menial labor jobs. One hope I have in writing this essay is contradicting that idea.

Let me begin by stating three key assumptions. First, capitalism is a violent system that routinely causes personal and institutional tragedies. Personal tragedies include lost dignity, crushed spirits and obscurity for brilliant artists and thinkers. Institutional tragedies include land theft, hunger, "accidents" that lead to thousands of deaths, poverty, illiteracy.[2]

Second, framing my arguments in practical, concrete terms is important because discussions of class are often obscured and weakened by abstract language and theories. As Maxine N. Tynes indicates in a story about African-Canadian domestic workers, it is crucial to speak plainly about "knees sore from years on hardwood floors...(and) always going to and coming from the back door."[3]

441

Third, the term *internalized oppression* does not adequately describe the depth and horror of working-class oppression, and so I have created my own two-part phrase: *the conquered self/the conquest of the self.*[4]

The conquered self accepts oppressive acts; she does not recognize them as oppressive but as the normal course of life, and/or comes to believe she deserves them. The word *conquered* implies an act of successful domination requiring forethought and intent by the oppressor. The word *self* indicates the person's mind, body and spirit is affected. The grammatically passive structure of this phrase echoes the passivity of many working-class people too beaten down to resist. The conquered self is revealed in heavy shoulders and downcast eyes, self-deprecating remarks, silence, slumped body, creeping steps, refusing to fight, the ever-present belief (founded upon hard reality) that life is over at an early age,[5] accepting abuse.

The phrase "the conquered self" has a partner phrase, a hopeful corollary with an active grammatical formation that points to spirited resistance. "The conquest of the self" describes the successful process of a vigorous, determined struggle to win back what was taken—in this case, our personhood. It holds out the hope that we can leave oppression behind and move toward liberation. I have identified several elements necessary in order for the conquest of the self to occur.[6] In this essay I want to focus on one element, and that is recognizing and then transforming belief systems left behind by the oppressors.

Belief systems are negative or positive core ideas that shape our daily life. They are sometimes hidden deep within the self, and are sometimes spoken in daily conversation. A positive belief system that enables a person to act creatively or confidently might be "I am worthy of love and affection." A negative belief system is illustrated in Cy-Thea Sand's first lesson of life in the working-class neighborhood of Verdun, Québec: "You are nothing in this world without money."[7] Negative belief systems provide internalized justifications for constant oppressive experiences; they are mind-sets developed to rationalize day-to-day abuse. Negative belief systems are signposts of oppression and defeat that explain where we stand in relation to oppression. The word *belief* indicates a conviction, doctrine, or principle that shapes a person's world-view and actions. The word *system* implies oppression is organized in the self and it implies a connection between external and internal oppression; belief systems can be traced to social institutions.

I now want to examine the issue of justice in relation to my conquered self, the belief system that developed around it, and my conquest of the self. One hope I have is that my process might provide a model for others ready to grapple with issues of class.

The Conquered Self

The experiences of class-related injustice that defeated me are myriad. I constantly observed the powerlessness of the adult members of my family in the larger world. My great-grandmother spent the last days of her life in poverty in a shabby apartment. My Aunt Rose worked a lifetime at meaningless jobs until she retired at age 65 and then died of cancer. One grandmother couldn't survive financially on her own after decades of employment; the other (whom I have met through a black and white photograph in which she looks 75) died at 57, after decades of 18-hour work days on an isolated prairie farm. My mother cried the day my father got a speeding ticket because the $7.00 represented a large sum of money. The sporadic layoffs my father experienced only made things worse.[8]

These experiences were intensified by our belief we could not change anything. Continual injustice is one way the ruling class defeated my family and extinguished our fighting spirits. We did manage one victory: we put the responsibility for our condition squarely on the shoulders of the owners of general motors, whom we called "fat cats."[9] That our political analysis got to that depth is a great example of working-class resistance, especially since many working-class people blame themselves for their class location.[10] But this could not and did not prevent our subjugation.

Belief System

A belief system, often spoken aloud by my mother, supported our experiences of injustice, in a grim voice, hardened by decades of oppression and despair, she repeated "Life isn't fair."

"Life isn't fair" is a belief system. It is also a creed for victims rooted in the hard reality of unfair lives. Other people had power and things and an easy life, and we did not. This belief system is not unique to my family. Carolyn Steedman, a working-class woman who wrote *Landscape for a Good Woman*,[11] continually heard about life's terrible unfairness from her mother[12] and Steedman wrote about it:

> My mother's sense of unfairness, her belief that she had been refused entry to her rightful place in the world, was the dominant feature of her psychology and the history she told: her life itself became a demonstration of the unfairness.[13]

Steedman believes the issues of justice and fairness are central to class analysis.[14] I now want to discuss the belief system "Life isn't fair" in terms of what lies behind it, what it did to me, who benefits from it, who imposed it, and whether it is true.

The underlying message of this belief system rationalizes constant injustice and offers a political theory about capitalism's inevitability. "Life isn't fair" is a given that describes the way things are; it is not a debatable point. Because so many unjust experiences are connected to our economic system, capitalism itself comes to be seen as inevitable, as part of the unchanging nature of the world. I believe this acceptance of capitalism as natural is widespread among working-class people, and that it is not accidental. The ruling class wants us to believe this system of social domination is inevitable, logical, and natural,[15] and goes to much trouble to make people believe this; other powerful social institutions such as the christian church and the media support and maintain it.

I can attest to my family's belief in the inevitability of capitalism not only through its "Life isn't fair" manifesto but through our attitude toward two progressive forces in our lives, my father's union and the New Democratic Party (N.D.P.).[16] We supported both, and in particular regarded the union with high esteem because of the differences it made in our daily lives with benefits such as dental care and eyeglasses. However, we understood these organizations as buffers that quelled the worst ravages of the system, not as forces that could dismantle it.

Starting from a young age, I linked this "natural" economic system to the common injustice in our lives. I did not perceive capitalism as a human construct established by a group of rich white people who wanted to become more rich and powerful, and neither did anyone in my family. That piece of the truth had to be kept from us because capitalism can only succeed if working-class people perceive it as inescapable (or at least highly preferable to the "horrors" of communism). We saw this economic system as fixed in stone and that's one major reason we became acquiescent victims instead of active fighters. How can anyone fight against something "natural"? These perceptions allow me to understand how well members of the ruling class are served by the belief system "Life isn't fair." Instead of being confronted by rebellious hordes, they have acquiescent victims accepting the inevitability of a nonsensical system.

That understanding tells me the ruling class is responsible for this belief system. I first asked whether we imposed it on ourselves as a result of lived experience, or whether it had been drilled into us by the system from an early age. Then I realized both questions point to the ruling class. We formed a belief system from our daily experiences. These experiences happened because of the power of the ruling class. This belief system was and is of great benefit to the power brokers and so they maintain it, generation after generation, by forcing people to experience unfair treatment on a daily basis.

Finally, is there truth in the bitterness of one of my mother's favorite sayings, "Life isn't fair"? Yes, it is true. My family is not a group of deluded paranoids who invented weird conspiracy theories. And yet it is not the whole truth.

The Conquest of the Self

All my life I acted in a way that presupposed the truth of the belief system "Life isn't fair." My conquered self reacted to experiences of oppression with resignation, with acceptance, with a shrug of "Well, what else is new?" But the time came when I no longer wanted to live that way.

I needed to become aware/take action. First, psychologically and politically, I reflected on and analyzed the principles by which I lived and acted in the world. I uncovered the belief system "Life isn't fair." Then I had to place that idea into a political framework so I could truly understand it.

Of course, awareness is not enough. Major change of any kind involves hard work, action, movement, time, a dedicated heart, a committed spirit. I needed all of those as I tried to change the "Life isn't fair" belief system through political/theoretical action, historical evaluation, and community-building.[17]

First, in terms of political action, I began to work for social justice because I finally understood that all of us, myself included, deserve fair treatment in daily living. After being exposed to radical activist nuns, I joined groups working for justice for the people of Central America. I had to start caring for other people before I could care enough about myself to demand personal fair treatment. That came with time, as I worked on a variety of issues ranging from the Nestlé boycott to self-determination for Palestine to ending violence against women. I began to peel back the lies and lay bare the system of global imperialism, oppression and domination that affected me and billions of others. Among other things, I realized capitalism is not a natural system nor is it ordained by any cosmic force: it is a human construct designed to serve the rich white people who created it. These people took great pains to ensure that working-class experiences will lead us to believe life is not fair and never will be, a perfect creed for the victims who will do the work to produce their wealth. I thought of these truths as I carried out various actions (attending demonstrations, organizing, writing pamphlets, spraypainting, marching) and as I felt my heart's desire for social justice grow stronger and more passionate.

My initial forms of political action centered around grassroots organizing and direct action. Theory I left for others; after all, I didn't have the brains for that. However, as I empowered myself, I recognized my desire to theorize and began doing it. I also became painfully aware of the politics of theory as I have experienced them.

From a young age, I knew that fit occupations for me, my family, and all the people in our neighborhood involved working with our hands but not our minds. We couldn't think, and we certainly couldn't analyze our experiences (or anyone else's) in any kind of conceptual framework.[18] Theory was the prerogative of a specific group within the middle class, the intellectuals.

As a lesbian-feminist activist, student, and writer, I rarely saw other lesbians challenge that perception of the dominant culture. Other working-class dykes did theorize, but I saw no evidence that they received encouragement from middle- and upper-class lesbians. I know that I did not. I was encouraged, by lesbian feminists and heterosexual feminists, to share my "interesting and colorful" family stories, so that they could transform my raw data into their theory. Several times I've been told to stick to writing/telling anecdotes and leave theory alone.[19]

It is oppressive for a privileged group to control theory and to use poor and working-class experiences as raw material. It is also oppressive to silence working-class/poor women who somehow reach the point of believing we have something to say. I believe my attempts to theorize hit a raw nerve, and I'm thankful I had the political analysis to realize what was happening. I did not revert to handing over my personal stories (brawn) and letting the experts (brain) analyze and theorize about them.[20]

Second, I examined history critically. Thanks to political activism and an unorthodox university education that actually taught me how to think, I learned to ask and figure out who wrote the history books and why they wrote what they did, and where to find the common people's history. A key tenet of class struggle is understanding and labelling the past.[21] As all working-class people do, I learned we contributed nothing to history. But understanding that the ruling class has controlled the writing and telling of history made me question that. The fact that history books say little or nothing about working-class life and/or resistance doesn't mean we don't exist and resist. It means the history books lie. In actual fact, a critical examination of history informs us of a long tradition of working-class resistance involving, among other things, the formation of unions, the writing of theory, and grassroots activism. A key example of this is the Luddites, a radical working-class group active in Britain in the late 1700s and early 1800s. Portrayed in many history books as stupid men foolish enough to

446

try to ruin new machinery designed to "help" workers, other sources present the Luddites as radical activists with a sophisticated political analysis around technology, class oppression, and how new machinery would mean lost jobs for workers.[22] This sense of belonging to a group of fighters is a great source of inspiration to me.

Neither my critique of history nor my political activism can be done alone. Community is essential for that work and for the work of changing a belief system. It is, quite simply, impossible to do it any other way. A supportive community with which I can discuss ideas, have fun, engage in political work, and receive emotional support is critical to transforming a long-held belief system about the injustice of life for the working class. Further, my community, made up of people from a mixture of racial/ethnic groups, classes, and sexual orientations, models the possibility that people from disparate class backgrounds can be respectful of class differences and can do the work involved in building a just community. Understanding our social locations, and the points at which our privileges and oppression connect and diverge, is essential for deep friendships (and for forging workable alliances among political movements). While I am hopeful about what is happening in my personal network, I need to say that this is not widespread among lesbian communities. I and other working-class/poor lesbians have repeatedly experienced an unwillingness among middle- and upper-class lesbians to confront this oppression even at its most basic level.

Conclusion

I can still hear my mother's voice, bitter and grim, making its pronouncement about one of her deepest learnings, "Life isn't fair." Some days I hear that bitterness in my own voice. But mostly I say "Life should be fair." It's a new belief system, one with an active grammatical structure that demands change, one that perceives capitalism not as innate but as a rather ridiculous human construct that we must overturn.

Writing essays like this allows me to use my ability to think clearly and to link that with my spirit's passion for social justice. Writing essays like this helps me remember that deep, far-reaching, and radical change is possible not only for individuals but for communities. If a working-class Arab girl from a factory town, destined for the assembly line and nothing else, can take herself seriously as a theorist, then there is indeed hope for change.

FOOTNOTES

[1] I am grateful to Janet Binder for all the help she gave me in the formulation of the ideas concerning justice. Thanks to her, Lisa Albrecht, Elizabeth Clare, and Elliott for their help in editing this manuscript.

447

[2] See, for example, Frantz Fanon. 1966. *The Wretched of the Earth*. New York: Grove Press, p. 79.

[3] Maxine N. Tynes. "In Service," *Fireweed: A Feminist Quarterly*, 26 (Winter/Spring 1988), p. 10.

[4] Dr. Katie Cannon, associate professor of ethics, Episcopal Divinity School, encouraged me to create such a concept during her time as my advisor at that school, September 1988-May 1990. I would like to express my gratitude for all of the support and affirmation she has given me.

[5] Richard Sennett and Jonathan Cobb. 1973. *The Hidden Injuries of Class*. New York: Vintage, p. 49

[6] These elements are described in detail in my master's thesis, *Searching for Words, Searching for Knowledge* (Cambridge, MA: Episcopal Divinity School, 1990). They include: remembering and reclaiming individual and collective history; formulating and acting on political analysis; finding community; allowing repressed feelings to surface. This article is a shortened version of one thesis chapter.

[7] Cy-Thea Sand. "A Question of Belonging," *Class is the Issue, Fireweed: A Feminist Quarterly*, 25 (Fall 1987), pp. 55, 57.

[8] Thanks to the union, my father received part of his salary during layoffs.

[9] I applaud any working-class person attempting to critique the ruling class. However, I must note that this term, like so many other negative descriptions of people, is an example of speciesism. Human beings continually project unappealing qualities onto other species, who rarely if ever fit the description. Also, the term "fat cat" assumes there is something wrong or bad in being fat.

[10] Sennett and Cobb, p. 95.

[11] Carolyn Steedman. 1986. *Landscape for a Good Woman*. London: Virago.

[12] Steedman, p. 8.

[13] Steedman, p. 112.

[14] Steedman, p. 8.

[15] Dr. Katie Cannon made this point in a lecture entitled "Class and Ideological Struggles," March 7, 1990 in Ethics 180, The Genealogy of Race, Sex and Class Oppression, Episcopal Divinity School, Cambridge, MA.

[16] The New Democratic Party is a socialist party; it is one of three major political parties in Canada, and routinely wins one-quarter of the votes during federal elections. The work of the N.D.P. has led to a national medicare plan for Canadians, as well as other progressive social programs.

[17] I will discuss political/theoretical action at greater length than history and community.

[18] It's worth noting that this article was rejected by an academic feminist journal. My rejection letter concluded with the statement: "As it stands, the article contributes little or nothing to lesbian theory and praxis."

[19] The clearest example of this occurred at my presentation on working-class oppression at a private high school in Boston. Afterwards, the head of the women's studies department, a white, middle-class, heterosexual feminist, said, "The stories about your family are wonderful. You should have let them stand on their own."

[20] In offering this critique I am not saying middle-class and upper-class lesbians don't need to theorize about class. On the contrary, I believe there is a tremendous need for those groups to begin writing theories about how class privilege is passed to each new generation, how to break the cycle, and how to be in solidarity with working-class and poor people. I have not seen evidence that this is happening.

[21] Lecture by Dr. Katie Cannon referred to in endnote #15.

[22] That the Luddites were taken seriously by the ruling class is evident in a 1769 law passed by the British Parliament stating that anyone ruining machinery at a place of employment could be put to death.

Felice Yeskel

Coming Out About Money:
Cost Sharing Across Class Lines

Felice Yeskel

The first time I participated in cost sharing was eleven years ago. I was participating in a two week training program for social change activists sponsored by Movement for a New Society (MNS). We were putting the theory into practice, so why did I feel sick to my stomach? After years of hiding, of pretending, of silence, of passing, I was going to have to come clean. I could no longer stay vague or conveniently forget, and the prospect was absolutely terrifying. I was going to share what I had never shared before with nineteen virtual strangers. The intensity of feelings I had to push through to disclose my financial situation and decide what was my "fair" share of paying for the training program were testament to the power of class and classism. I was also pushed up against the realities of anti-Semitism (both internalized and otherwise), as I feared talking about money issues with a predominantly non-Jewish group. I feared being misunderstood and my particular money patterns being associated with the fact that I am Jewish. Once on the other side of the cost sharing process I felt a tremendous sense of relief.

During the cost sharing process I learned that there was such a thing as a trust fund, that people inherited money before their parents died, and that I was sitting in a room with some people who didn't have to work to survive. I also heard first hand accounts of the indignities of the welfare system, and about the resourcefulness of people living below the poverty line. After hearing about the financial realities and backgrounds of the nineteen other activists, my world grew in depth and texture. It was as if before I had seen a flat world and all of a sudden it had become three-dimensional. Through participating in cost sharing I realized that I wasn't raised middle class. But it wasn't until some months later, when Fai, a working-class Jewish woman, suggested that I had come from a working-class background, that all the pieces fell into place.

In my experience of doing workshops on diversity issues, I have found that in the United States class consciousness is so low that many people cannot identify their class background or their present class status. This is the result partly of class mobility (which is greater in the U. S. than in

451

most places), but largely it is due to the myth that "we are all middle class." This myth equates the "middle class" with the status quo. Prevailing cultural beliefs as well as institutional structures, policies, and practices (such as how we pay for things) keep this myth securely in place. Most institutions base fees for events, services, or programs on the belief that everyone should pay an equal share of the costs. That's fair! That's democratic! Organizers and planners make the assumption, often hidden and unchallenged, that everyone has the same resources. Because of this assumption, they act as if an equal share is synonymous with an identical share.

Individuals, groups, and institutions which acknowledge that not everyone has equal assets may make various accommodations. Often feminists have acknowledged class differences and tried different methods of dealing with this in planning events, gatherings, or conferences. Typically, they establish a fixed, standard fee based on the middle-class norm. They may set aside a certain amount for "scholarships," for "underprivileged," "low-income," or "needy" women. This manner of dealing with our class differences makes the middle-class the standard, and those that can't afford the "regular" share the exception.

Some groups offer the option of a "work exchange" for those who cannot afford the standard, "normal" cost. In this scenario, some of the folks who cannot afford the "real" fee pay a reduced fee *and* do a specified number of hours of work. Sharing the work of a gathering or conference is an effective way of reducing overall costs and can be a group-building activity; however when organizers link doing the work with not having enough money they penalize the people with less resources. The practice of work exchange may hide another class myth—"those who don't have money don't work hard enough." In my experience, almost the exact opposite is true; the folks who have the least resources are already working incredibly hard.

Using a sliding scale is another means to meet costs that takes into account people's class differences. Because sliding scales include a range of legitimate fees, I think they are better than the "one standard fee for most people and scholarships or work exchange for the exceptions" methods. Sometimes sliding scales are fixed (*under $10,000 pay a; $10,000-20,000 pay b; $20,000-30,000 pay c; over $30,000 pay d*), and sometimes they are open (*pay $90-$150*). Sometimes fee scales vary with the number of dependents. However, sliding scales are typically based on a middle-class standard, with a fairly narrow range of options below the norm and a few options above it. Unfortunately this reinforces the "we are all middle class" myth. Many times folks on the lower end of the class spectrum cannot afford the bottom of the sliding scale and folks on the upper end of the spectrum could well afford much higher than the top end.

All of the above methods of attempting to address our class differences only take into account people's current financial situation, and usually only people's yearly income. For people on the upper end of the class spectrum, owned assets, not income, account for the bulk of their wealth. These methods also do not take into account the relationship between the choices we make ("I feel like working only part-time," "I work two jobs, live with other people, and save most of what I earn so I have a pretty decent income and savings") or lack of choices available ("I'm a single parent without a H.S. diploma and my minimum wage job pays no health benefits") and income levels. Additionally, these methods do not incorporate class attitudes and values.

Cost sharing is an alternative way to pay for events. It was developed in 1978 within the context of a two-week training program for social change activists sponsored by Movement for a New Society. Refining the process over time, members of MNS came to use the cost sharing process to pay for national gatherings, training programs, and conferences.

Two years ago I had the opportunity to experience the cost sharing process in a Jewish context. Betsy Wright and I (both MNS members and members of a Jewish feminist community), suggested we use the method of cost sharing to pay for our yearly gathering. The Jewish feminist spiritual community meets once a year for four days. Growing out of discussions of community and commitment, our suggestion was met with both excitement and trepidation by the women of the community, but we decided to give it a try. After trying cost sharing once, we decided to use this process to meet the costs of our annual retreats.

Session I

The process we used at our annual meeting involved three sessions. Embarking on cost sharing was scary; there were rumors a few women had not come to the retreat this year because they didn't want to have to do cost sharing. These women came from a variety of places on the class spectrum. Disclosing and negotiating about money often brings up feelings of fear, anger, shame, and guilt. And since these may differ depending on someone's actual financial situation, it was important that we develop a solid foundation for doing the work of cost sharing during the first session.

Step 1—Laying the Foundation

The facilitators (Betsy and I) set the process of cost sharing within the larger framework of the class system in the U. S. and the dynamics of classism. Betsy and I explained the steps of the cost sharing process, and suggested some basic ground rules. All disclosures, emotional sharing and financial pledges are *voluntary;* we will keep each other's stories *confidential;* we'll *speak from our own experience and not speak for others; any question or feeling is o.k.,* we'll speak up if confused or uncomfortable; when we challenge each other we'll question the behavior and not the person; if we have a question about someone's pledge we'll talk with them directly; we'll make *space for each person* to tell her story and be deeply listened to; and we'll go through this process and not judge it until it is over. We asked participants if they had other suggestions or if there was something they didn't like. There were no changes suggested so we all agreed to abide by these ground rules. Everyone chose a buddy with whom she felt comfortable, to check in about feelings that had come up. We discussed why it was hard to discuss and disclose about money, and what it was like to do this in a Jewish women's group.

Step 2—Forming Class Identity Groups

We then formed class identity groups of four women with whom we would disclose our financial situations and make initial pledges. The goal was to find other women with whom we would have some shared experience. Women chose to group around various identities. For some this was around class background, for others around current financial situations, while others wanted to group around common work. There were groups of single mothers, working-class women, artists, women with inherited wealth, students, etc.

Step 3—Disclosure of Background and Current Financial Situations

Using the "Guidelines for Disclosing our Class and Money Stories," we shared our situations. Cost sharing is even more effective when it is preceded by a workshop on class and classism so that the complexities of class standing, which are reflective of wealth, power, and status, become clearer. Since we had such little time together we skipped over this step and provided the very simplified "Cheat Sheet on Class Backgrounds" and "Class Background Indicators" sheet.

Guidelines for Disclosing our Class and Money Stories

Background

- What was your class background?

- What was good about growing up as you did? What positive things did you learn?

- What was hard about growing up as you did? What negative messages did you learn?

- As an adult, what struggles and personal growth have you gone through related to your class and money background?

Financial situation

- What is your current money situation? (See "Achyot Or Pledge Form") Income? dependents? income-sharing? assets? debts? expenses?

- Are there ways you benefit from others' **privilege** (e.g., male partner, expenses paid by wealthy parents, network of "richer" friends)?

- What are your habits of earning, spending, and saving?

- What choices have you made that have limited or increased your income, assets, debts, or earning capacity? Are you earning the most you could? If not, why not?

- What are your future prospects? Do you expect to inherit money? Do you expect to support parents or others in old age? Do you have disability insurance? What is your current age/stage of life? What are your prospects for old age?

- Do any of these **other factors** affect your current or future financial situation?

    —Disability or health problems (including emotional health)
    —Age
    —Physical or sexual abuse
    —Going back to school
    —Living in Israel or elsewhere
    —Relationship situations
    —Alcohol or drug abuse
    —Planning to have children

Session II

Step 4—Sharing Information About the Amount To Be Raised

Session II began with a quick review of the session's agenda, and a presentation of the expenses for our gathering by the planners. The costs included things like site costs, food, child care, materials, printing, postage, phone, and start-up for next year. Following this presentation there was time for clarifying questions. The average cost, the total cost divided by the total number of women, came to $250 per woman.

Step 5—Making an Initial Pledge

When everyone understood the total costs for the gathering, women returned to their identity groups to fill out the Pledge Form. After discussion with identity group members, including support and challenge, each woman decided on an initial amount that was her pledge.

> I found the process of coming up with a pledge painless, and while I certainly had compassion for those who were struggling over issues relating directly to money, my biggest discomfort was over the confrontational nature of the challenge part of the process. (middle class woman)

> Over the two years I got more comfortable admitting to myself and to others what my actual status is (poor). It became easier. We as a group/community had decided to look at class and money consciously and to understand our assumptions. This decision gave me an opening to look at this issue. I wasn't fighting a closed system that was uninterested in what I was seeing.

> My underlying feeling was—I grew up with advantages so it is irresponsible for me to go on a five-day retreat and not be able to pull my own weight. It was pretty liberating to talk about it and get a reality check, to hear what other people's situations are. Other women without kids, living alone, were making almost 2/3 of what my husband and I were making together. Hearing about it gave me reason not to beat myself up about our financial situation.

Step 6—Grouping by Amount Pledged

The cost sharing facilitators (Betsy and I) collected all the pledges and arranged groupings by amount pledged. Next new groups were formed. Women who pledged between $0–100 met together, women who pledged $100–175 met together, $175–250, $250–350, $350–450, and over $450. In these pledge groups women shared an abbreviated version of their situations and why they chose the amount they chose. Women noted similarities and differences with the other women who had pledged the same amount.

> I was really surprised when people with less money than me pledged the same amount. I always assumed we all felt the same way about money: my sense of security depends on having some in the bank. Not having parents and being single means I have no one to rely on to take care of me. It wasn't until the "fishbowl" the first year that I realized that it was money, not other human beings, that gave me a sense of security—somewhat of a frightening thought. Some folks with no money in the bank had a greater sense of security than I did. (middle class woman)

> It was uncomfortable for me when people challenged me to up my pledge. First of all, good for them to have the nerve to do it, I've never done it and don't foresee it in the future. Who am I to challenge someone else's decision? I'd like to learn how others do it. But when folks challenge me, I get defensive, how could they know how I feel. On the other hand I think maybe they're right about me, it feeds into my assuming everyone else is right. (middle class woman)

> The cost sharing process created intimacy, it was sometimes liberating and sometimes scary. It elicited different emotions to talk with women with different situations, notably the desire to get women with more money to pay up, some excitement about access and our ability to pay for the retreat. When I ended up in the wealthiest group (highest pledges), some fear about being isolated from friends and potential friends with difference access. I sometimes felt the weight of the responsibility of having more. Overall it was a positive experience. (raised working class, now has upper middle class resources)

Step 7—Return to Class Identity Groups to Check-in and Adjust Initial Pledge

After more support and challenge from this new group, women returned to their identity groups to share their experience in their "groups by amount pledged" and to possibly adjust their initial pledge. At this point women turned in their Pledge Form. They had the option of placing it in an open file or a confidential file to which only the cost sharing facilitators had access. Everyone paired up with her buddy and did a brief feelings check-in. Session II ended with an evaluation.

Step 8—Reading Pledge Forms & Support/Challenge

After Session II, women were free to read each other's forms (those in the open file) and challenge anyone to increase or decrease their pledge. One middle-class woman remarked,

> When reading the forms it felt like I was butting into someone's private business, breaking all the boundaries that patriarchy sets up.

Another woman raised working class who now has upper-middle-class resources realized,

> I felt positive enough and responsible enough in my own choices to challenge others.

It was a learning experience for another middle-class woman,

> I got some perspective on my own situation. At times I feel I don't make enough money, but compared with others I'm doing well. There are others who don't save at all. It was so eye-opening, seeing others with similar salaries who don't save.

Meanwhile the cost sharing facilitators added up all the pledges, compared the total amount raised with the total amount needed and determined if there was a deficit or surplus.

Session III

Step 9—Learning the Total Amount Pledged

Session III began with a presentation of the total amount pledged and the range of pledges made Our pledges ranged from $75 to $600, far more reflective of the reality of our class differences than most sliding fee scales would allow.

Step 10—Revising Pledges in Class Identity Groups

We raised more than we needed, so women met with their identity groups and discussed whether to revise their pledges. Although some pledges were again revised, we still had more than we needed so we decided to give the surplus to tzedakah.*

---

*tzedakah: Hebrew, righteousness, acts of giving.

Step 11—Processing the Cost Sharing Experience

We next formed fishbowls, a process where a small group of women (the fish) sit in the center of the larger circle and talk while the rest of the women (the bowl) sit on the outside and listen. We listened to one group who had been challenged to lower their pledges and another group who had been challenged to raise their pledges. A middle-class woman remarked, "The first year was very hard for me, three people challenged me to up my pledge so I talked about how that felt." Another woman, from a poor background, shared,

> Everyone assumed it was easier to ask someone to lower their pledge than to raise it, but it was damn hard to lower my pledge. We didn't talk much about how difficult that was to do. It raised questions about whether I was contributing enough to make it OK to pledge less. The second year it felt easier for me to pledge closer to my actual financial situation (poor) because I had worked on the planning committee and I had made a significant contribution.

The second year the fishbowls allowed women from different class backgrounds to talk about that experience. There were three fishbowls, one for women raised poor or working-class, one for middle-class women, and one for women from upper-middle class or owning class backgrounds. For some it was the first time they publicly claimed a particular class background identity. A woman raised working class who currently has upper-middle-class resources shared the following,

> I carry around my parents' working class/poor background in a deep place in my psyche. Through choices that they have made, I have made, and as luck would have it, I have become very middle class. I have some deep sense of loss and alienation that comes from being separated by geography and experience, from my parents' families and my extended family. This is very connected for me with being working class. Joining the working class fishbowl was a liberating emotional and tearful experience for me, a "coming home." Although I still feel some embarrassment about it, that I'm not legitimate or I don't belong.

Class Background Indicators

Ancestry

- From what part of the world? How long in the U. S.?
- Grandparents, great-grandparents: Education, work, income, language, neighborhood

Parents (or guardians)

- Source of income; kind of work
- Education
- Status in community
- Upward or downward mobility during your life
- Assets

Growing Up

- Material comfort—not enough? enough? luxuries?
- How many kids in family?
- Did your family own or rent? How often did you move? Why?
- What kind of neighborhood(s) did you live in? Rural or urban?
- What were the expectations for your education?
- How much education did you get? If college/grad school, how was it paid for?
- Summer/leisure activities?
- Was anyone paid to work in your home?
- When did you first work and why?
- Who were you taught to look down on? to look up at?

Other factors pushing class status up or down

Did any of these affect your family?:

—Divorced, or unmarried or lesbian/gay parents

—Older parents/younger parents

—War

—Health problems

—Alcohol or drug abuse

—Political choices, such as Communism or voluntary poverty

—Abuse

—The Great Depression

—The Holocaust

—Immigration

—Emigration

An upper-middle class woman described her feelings,

I grew up middle class when very young and then upper middle class. In between my childhood and current life (during my 20's and 30's) I experienced a very marginal existence—poverty, lack of resources, no security. This was a result of choices I made, political actions that led to being underground and later in jail. This experience took the "glamour" out of poverty and made me very scared of ever being that poor again. I realize it's all tangled up with being a fugitive, but I think a lot of richer middle-class people either romanticize or vilify poor or marginal people. Poverty is not a crime or someone's "fault" but neither does it make people noble. My experiences bring into focus in a very visceral way the fear I have that blocks me from wanting to give up my current privilege. The fear is that there is no safety net, and I need this huge amount of money or property (on a deep, irrational level, nothing is enough) just in case tragedy strikes. If we lived in a culture where everybody got their basic needs met—food, shelter, decent health care and safety—this wouldn't be such a source of terror.

A raised poor woman described the sense of solidarity she felt,

I have a sense that those of us who grew up poor or working class have a kind of language between us now. A certain cohesiveness grew among working-class women through the cost sharing process. A number of women realized they grew up working class.

An owning-class woman shared,

It's a double-edged sword, I feel close with people and connected to them, because we are talking about the intimate subject of money and class—and yet because of my class situation, I also feel less connected to people.

Another owning-class woman said,

Talking about money was scary at first, then liberating. It was scariest to talk with women with different access to money—my fears of jealousy, accusation, feeling that I don't deserve to have the amount of resources that I do compared to other women here, much less the rest of the world.

Many of the more privileged women experienced confusion and contradictions as their class consciousness was raised. A woman with upper-middle-class resources captured the contradiction succinctly,

It is uncomfortable (to say the least) to recognize privilege that is unfair but that on some levels I do not want to be without.

Learnings from Cost Sharing

Cost sharing had paid for our annual meeting, and increased our sense of intimacy, but more importantly it was a powerful learning experience about an often hidden and unexamined topic. What's more, the effects carried over into women's lives during the year. I asked women to tell me about their reactions to the cost sharing process. Their responses can be grouped into the following categories:

Taking More Control Over Finances

Women realized they didn't really know about their financial situations. Some grew determined to change this and become more empowered about their financial lives. A currently middle=class woman who was raised upper middle class shared,

> *Many women were embarrassed because they didn't know their real financial situations. I didn't know how much my father was paying for my health insurance. Women with partners didn't know their situations, it was embarrassing. My father and brother are CPA's. I didn't take full responsibility or have total information. After the cost sharing process I went and found out all the information. Cost sharing has made me seek out more financial info. Five years ago I had inherited some stock, but I had no idea how much it was worth. Because I knew I'd have to list it on my cost sharing form, I went and found out. I don't think without cost sharing I would even now know.*

Dealing More With Class Issues in Relationships

Women became more aware of and better understood class issues and dynamics in relationships. Previously confusing issues with partners, roommates, siblings, and parents began to make more sense. Many women initiated conversations about class and money issues in various relationships.

> *The cost sharing process revealed that so much of our feelings about money are tied to security and self-worth. Cost sharing made me realize that lots of conflicts with my partner about money, were not really about money but about what money symbolized for each of us. When I came back from our meeting the first time, Steven (my partner) and I talked about a budget. After cost sharing the second time we talked about what it means to spend money, to save money, to deal with our*

parents about money, and how the differences in how our families dealt with money come into play when we have conflicts. Both of us came from middle class families, but their approaches were different.

Class issues in groups and organizations were also an arena for struggle and learning.

Since having had my consciousness sufficiently raised, I've had a lot of fights with family members, friends, and community members over the issue of economic justice. I've alienated some people, and have failed to make much of an impact on the various communities in which I am involved. I don't think I've developed adequate skills with which to implement this process in my daily life. It's disappointing and frustrating, but I'm still learning. (middle class woman)

Cheat Sheet On Class Backgrounds
(A very oversimplified spectrum)

Raised poor
Unmet basic needs;
One or more of these: move a lot, disrupted family, chronic unemployment, subsistence farming, public assistance, erratic work, dropping out of school, homelessness

Working class
Parents had no college; rented home (or able to buy only because of skilled trade or union job); worked for an hourly wage; basic needs met

Middle class
Owned home; college; summer camp; "white-collar" skilled work; worked for a salary; comfort but not luxury

Upper-middle-class
Second home; elite colleges; professional jobs; expensive vacations; some luxuries

Owning class
Assets could support family, no one *has* to work to survive; travel, luxury; exclusive clubs

Ruling class
Positions of great power in business, politics, media

Mixed class
Parents come from very different classes; OR Dramatic upward or downward mobility while you were growing up OR High status/low pay (teachers) or low status/high pay

---

Class Issues for Jews

Cost sharing also highlighted some of the unique class issues for Jews. Internalized anti-Semitism is often tied up with issues of money and class. Dealing with class often was a step forward in claiming pride in being Jewish.

> Talking about money in a Jewish context was liberating for me because of my fears of anti-Semitism. It also provided a safer environment to deal with internalized anti-Semitism, the stereotypes we all have of Jews and class and money. It made greater honesty possible. There was some commonality in our experiences, an immigrant inheritance of poverty, foreignness, nonacceptance, and assimilation. The generation before us wanted to be "normal" Americans, that equals middle class, educated, English-speaking, having good manners. We've attained it, but it's not enough. We're uncomfortable with the preoccupation with money and upward mobility. Since the stereotype of all Jews being rich is portrayed everywhere and assumed by many, it is only through listening to individuals' stories that we learn reality. (middle class woman)

Jewish terror, due to oppression, often impacts on attitudes and behaviors about money. The sense of security symbolized by money is often a more intense concern for Jews.

> I come from an upper-middle class background, private college, a nice home, vacations, Europe when I was 11. I never verbalized it or talked about it. I never thought about what criteria would make me a certain class. Currently I'm middle class, a rabbi. I'm doing quite well compared to others. In rabbinical school we had a seminar on money, but we never talked so personally, never disclosed our own situations. I have psychological security, even if I was to go bankrupt tomorrow, because of my parents and potential access. I'm upper middle class, but being the daughter of Holocaust survivors means there was always the feeling of gloom and doom, there was no extravagance. There was a mixture of having plenty, but being very frugal with resources.

Some Jewish values, such as the emphasis on education, are similar to middle-class values. This can make things quite confusing for poor and working-class Jews who may share values with middle-class folks, while having vastly different access. Talking about class in a Jewish context helped clarify the specifically Jewish class dynamics.

> Because of the Jewish emphasis on education, class becomes cloudy. I grew up thinking I was middle class. Although I grew up on a chicken farm and when the farm failed my father worked in a factory, I still thought I was middle class. I thought that was the only way for a Jew to be. It was a revelation to me to discover I was poor.

Cost sharing also made it very clear that in order to truly build community, we have to deal with class issues and class differences. For those women involved in the Jewish community this became imperative.

> It's really critical for Jews involved in Jewish communal structures to deal with class issues. If you want to talk about Jewish community, you need to talk about money. (middle-class woman who works in a Jewish organization)

Tzedakah! Giving Money Away
For women with resources, participating in cost sharing caused them to think more deeply about how they share money during the rest of the year. For some this translated into giving more money away, while for others the impact was on where and how they gave.

> I've always given tzedakah, but I give more now. (a middle class woman)

> Cost sharing was a window to thinking about myself and others on an important level...it helped my partner and I begin to change our behavior some in terms of priorities, giving tzedakah in a different way. It helped me to clarify some of my thinking and feeling about social justice issues. (raised working class, currently has upper-middle-class resources)

> On an individual level, cost sharing has been helpful to me in thinking about money, class, philanthropy, etc. It has certainly helped me to confront issues with my family about my ability to give to philanthropy in my name with the wealth that is in my name. (owning-class woman)

Greater Understanding of Class Structure/System
Because of the silence and invisibility surrounding class, cost sharing helped a number of women gain a greater understanding of the realities of the class structure in the U. S. Through hearing different women's stories, the issues of women and poverty became more than statistics. Some women were motivated to go out and learn more about economic issues.

This past year I learned how many women really make very little money. We don't have great economic strength. Cost sharing concretized the issues of women at the bottom end of the class spectrum. Other than very close friends, I don't know other folks' situations. (middle-class woman)

Another woman was motivated to go out and teach.

The class structure wasn't new to me, I'd known it all along. But I was shocked at how little more privileged women knew about the realities of class. Once they became aware, they were willing to do something. It made me want to help raise class consciousness. (working-class woman)

Greater Understanding of Own Class Background and Feelings About Class

Finally, cost sharing helped women clarify their own class backgrounds and the impact of their backgrounds on their feelings, attitudes, values and choices. For some, greater understanding led to feeling more empowered.

I'm currently financially poor, although my brother makes a lot of money so I have access to some help. Cost sharing clarified my actual situation. I was finally able to admit to myself the reality of my financial situation.

I've thought about this stuff a lot and I've been sensitive to people with less and resentful of people with more, but I never had as much clarity about my own situation. Money and class were dirty, evil, nasty parts of the world and I felt powerless about them. I didn't understand how or why they affect people. Cost sharing was empowering. (lower-middle-class woman)

A lot of us are 2nd, 3rd, or 4th generation, and we have the experience of living in one class with the memories of another class close at hand, and the aspirations of a third class. I resonated with the working-class women because of my history, and with the upper-middle-class women because of people I went to school with. As a middle-class woman, i have to work hard to have some identity in terms of class. We're a mix of what's up and down, it's harder to grasp. Cost sharing helped make the experience of being middle class more visible.

Pledge Form

Name_____

Income

- Your individual income may come from various sources:
    - Employment/wages
    - Income from inherited assets
    - Income from personal investments (stocks, bonds, etc.)
    - Public assistance
    - Pensions
    - Direct gifts from family or friends
    - Income from property
    - Loans (currently providing income)
    - Scholarships
    - Social Security
    - Unemployment benefits
    - Other (explain)
- Yearly Total Individual Income: $_____
- Do you share your income with other adults? How many?
- Total family/group income: $_____
- Do you support dependents?   How many?

Assets

- These may be some of your assets:
    - Property
    - Savings (in a bank account)
    - Car
    - Stocks or bonds
    - Life insurance
    - IRA
    - Other (explain)
- What is the total monetary value of your assets? $_____

Debts:

- **These may be some of your debts:**
  —School loans
  —Mortgage payments
  —Owe money to individuals
  —Credit card bills
  —Car loans
  —Other loans (explain)
  —Medical costs

- What is the total amount of your debts? $_____
- Monthly payments? $_____

Expenses

Approximate monthly expenses (rent, childcare, tuition fees, car, food, utilities, phone, clothes, medical, therapy, philanthropic contributions, etc.)

- Do you have any unusual expenses?
- Total Monthly Expenses? $_____

What is your class background?

Financial Backup
- If you lost your major sources of income, do you have reliable financial backup?

Future Financial Outlook
- Does your financial outlook for the coming year(s) vary greatly from your current situation?

What were your transportation costs to get here? $_____

Did you lose income from taking days off work to come to this meeting? How much? $_____

Are there other factors affecting your pledge?

_____

PLEDGE

first pledge _____
revised pledge _____
final pledge _____

Cautions About Cost Sharing

Although cost sharing compares favorably to other means of paying for events, it has some obvious drawbacks. It is time-consuming, since it must be done collectively rather than individually. Depending on the situation, the full cost sharing process may not be feasible. Cost sharing depends upon a reasonable level of trust. Higher trust can usually be found in groups with clear boundaries—it's clear who's in and who's not, and folks are not coming and going constantly. The benefits of cost sharing are multiplied when an intact group uses this process over the course of years. This happened in a group I belonged to and the cost sharing process became a vehicle for people to take more control in the financial part of their lives. Those with surplus resources were challenged to take greater responsibility for sharing their privileges while those who had been living on the edge got support to take more control over their situations. The deeply ingrained patterns of entitlement vs. inadequacy were shaken up as guilt gave way to activity and shame to anger and action.

Cost sharing also makes more sense if there is a reasonable level of commitment to the group and its members. To take the risks involved and devote the time necessary, a group needs to embrace progressive values and support the longer term educational benefits derived from cost sharing. While only 36 women participated in the Jewish feminist retreat's cost sharing process, I have done cost sharing with as many as 125 people. However, at some point the process would become unwieldy.

The experience of cost sharing is largely determined by the situations of the participants. Obviously, the greater the diversity the greater the learning. Because vulnerability is required, participants in a unique situation are placed in an uncomfortable position. In general the Jewish feminist group was weighted toward the privileged end of the spectrum. Did women at the lower end of the class spectrum feel alienated? We raised more than we needed, but what if most of the group had been poor or working class? I have used cost sharing as the means of payment for a week-long training program for low-income women activists, where most of the participants were welfare mothers. We did not raise the necessary money to cover the costs, so the group undertook a collective fund-raising project to make up the deficit.

Another limitation of cost sharing is that it only addresses how to divide up the costs, which it takes as a given. It does not attend to how the costs were generated. Who makes decisions about the things that will result in costs—where the event will take place, food, etc.? What standard, or perhaps whose standard, is chosen is a class issue? One way to keep events accessible to the greatest number of people is to keep costs down. When we plan events who is the fantasy participant we have in mind? Is she usually middle class? Can she afford to stay in a hotel, or will she be marginalized by staying in "community housing"? But, because cost sharing opens the whole can of worms, questions like these arise.

Conclusion

We ended the whole process of cost sharing by discussing what we had learned, and how the cost sharing process related to Judaism, feminism and spirituality. Some women felt that cost sharing, while wonderful, "took up too much of our precious time together." They felt that the annual meeting was intended as a spiritual retreat, that we were there for spiritual purposes and that money was clearly secular. But I think of cost sharing as a spiritual process. Many of the practices of Judaism are intended to sanctify daily life. Cost sharing is a process that allows us to bring integrity and connection to dealing with money issues. In so doing it is a practice that helps us to sanctify the money part of life.

It is difficult to truly redress the class inequities among a group of women without changing the larger class system that creates these inequities. Sometimes even when we attempt to deal with class differences, we simply perpetuate them through the hidden assumptions in our approach. From the personal perspective (if there is no fixed scale I often have a difficult time deciding what to pay) to that of an organization (which system do we use), the problems seem so complex and overwhelming we often want to give up.

I am often plagued with questions about class issues. I have wondered for a long time about what is my "fair share." These days when I raise such questions with my friends and acquaintances I feel like I'm breaking a taboo. It seems no one wants to think about these questions too carefully; they might raise feelings of anger, guilt, shame—and necessitate changes. Back in the '70s, those of us active in feminism seemed to endlessly challenge (often without much understanding or compassion) each other on our choices. After all, if the personal is political then how much I make, how I make it, and how I spend it are all political issues, and as such worthy of collective debate. But I think many of us grew tired of having every decision scrutinized and the '80s seemed to swing towards a "there's no one right way, so do your own thing" type of isolated individualism.

The questions that I have about class, about money, about resource use, and about work choices are not things I believe I can or should figure out alone. Class is a relative thing, who we compare ourselves with often determines how we feel. Except for the people at either end of the class spectrum who may only look one way, either up or down, the rest of us can have the experience of turning our heads either way and encountering different realities. When I think about someone further down the class spectrum, I realize I have a lot and I feel guilty, not deserving, lucky, or privileged. When I look the other way, I have little compared to someone else, and I feel angry, resentful, or deprived. Because the feelings I experience can be so changeable, I need a community of others from a range of class positions with whom to think, question, argue, and be mutually accountable. How often have I heard people excuse themselves from any class accountability by saying something like, "I don't have all that much, even if I gave all my savings away there would still be hungry people in the world, so why should I sacrifice what I want?"

In learning about class and classism, in naming our class identity, and in understanding the reality of class structure, we can develop a greater class consciousness. This awareness improves our ability to interpret what happens to us and in the world from a class dynamics perspective, which can in turn lead to working to eliminate classism on personal, institutional, and cultural levels. Cost sharing provided the opportunity for tackling the confusing, personal questions of class and money in a collective context, where both support and challenge were real. Each of us made the decision about our share, but not in isolation. There was collective accountability as well as safety. The glimpse of the possibilities that cost sharing provided was empowering for many. I look forward to hearing of the many ways women weave their deepened understandings and sense of empowerment into fighting classism in their lives.

I would like to thank the many wonderful women of the Jewish feminist retreat who shared their experiences with me. I would also like to acknowledge the M.N.S.ers who developed and refined the cost sharing process over the years including: Jerry Koch-Gonzalez, Joan Nikelsky, Betsy Rausch-Gilman, and Betsy Wright. I am also deeply indebted to many friends and comrades who spent many hours talking through the clouds of class and classism, especially Jerry Koch-Gonzalez (with whom I've talked the longest), Julie Greenberg, Marta Mangan, Grace Ross, Amy Waldman, Betsy Wright, Vicky Pillard, Christopher Mogil, Marion McNaughton (a powerful working-class mentor for me, who lives in England and offered the clarity of an outsider's view), and Fai Coffin (a Jewish working-class woman, a pioneer in the class arena, who helped me claim an identity I had been taught to despise).

If you would like to further explore issues of money, class, and classism, please be aware of the following resources:

For more information about cost sharing or information about workshops, mediation and consultation on class and money issues, you may contact me at Diversity Works, Inc., POB 2335, Amherst, MA 01004, (413) 256-1868.

Contributors' Notes

DEBBIE ALICEN is graying at the temples, still fat, still loves lifting weights, and has the privilege of sharing life in Vermont with AnnaBel, the most magnificent creature on the face of the Earth, who just happens to be a great fly-catcher, to boot!

DONNA ALLEGRA writes poetry, fiction, and essays. A 1992 co-winner of the Pat Parker Memorial Poetry Prize, she has been published in *Sinister Wisdom, Heresies, Conditions, Lesbian Ethics, Common Lives/Lesbian Lives,* and *Aché.* Her work has been anthologized in *Finding the Lesbians* (Penelope and Valentine, eds.), *Lesbian Love Stories,* vol. 2, and *Quickies* (Irene Zahava, ed.), *The Original Coming Out Stories* (Penelope and Wolfe, eds.), *The Persistent Desire: A Femme-Butch Reader* (Joan Nestle, ed.), *Home Girls: A Black Feminist Anthology* (Barbara Smith, ed.), *Sister/Stranger: Lesbians Loving Across the Lines* (Jan Hardy, ed.), *Woman in the Window* (Pamela Pratt, ed.), and *Lesbian Culture: An Anthology* (Penelope and Wolfe, eds.). Her cultural journalism has appeared in *Sojourner, Gay Community News, WomaNews, Sappho's Isle,* and *Colorlife!.*

JACKIE ANDERSON: I teach philosophy and world literature in a two-year college in Chicago. Sometimes I teach akido to wimmin. I am on the Lesbian Community Cancer Project Board, the editorial board of *Hypatia,* and the steering committee of "Yahimba," an African American Lesbian organization in Chicago. I love Lesbians, cats, and all of my friends.

BQ (rita d. brown): i was born in the northwest and currently live in San Francisco. i've been out of prison now almost as long as i was in, continuing to do work with Lesbian and women prisoners. My primary politico-work group is Out of Control, Lesbian Committee to Support Women Political Prisoners and POWs. i've just finished a video about Norma Jean Croy, a Native Lesbian prisoner. i'm working class, a Libra born in 1947. i am a former member of the George Jackson Brigade, a multiracial liberation force, active in the 1970s and named after a revolutionary Black man killed in prison.

KAREN CHANEY lives and works in San Francisco. She hopes an anthology of this nature will provide deeper understanding of the subject for its readers and prompt further dialogue among feminist women on the effects of socioeconomic class upon our lives and communities.

CHRYSTOS: I was born off-reservation, in San Francisco, on November 7, 1946. Birthday cards are welcome. My mother and father met in night school, working toward high school diplomas. My mother worked throughout her life as a secretary. My father worked as a steward on government ships after he met my mother (prior to that time he was a hobo for seven years). When he retired, he continued to work for the Equal Opportunities Commission, as a representative for claimants and for his union, which occupations are ongoing. My mother retired at age 65. I have worked variously as a hooker, drug dealer, store clerk, waitress, maid, computer programmer, marketing researcher and performance poet. I continue to do readings, but they are not enough to support me, so I also work as a maid. I am in the process of figuring out how to return to college, so that I can teach writing and do art therapy with sexually abused children and adults. I am a very good maid and am not ashamed of that occupation. My body is simply wearing out, so I have to get a "desk job." Most of what I have understood about class I've figured out by watching the difference between the homeless and the old money clients I work for. In rereading and working on this piece, I've been aware of how my language shifts back and forth between under and over class constructs. This language assimilation is one of the ways in which the over class dominates our thinking.

PAT DEAN will be 45 in 1994. She is white. She grew up in the Chicago suburb of Oak Park, which was all white when she was growing up. She has never married. She raised a daughter who is attending college but she is not 'sending' her daughter to college (or anywhere, for that matter). She hasn't a clue how to assign a 'class' to her life experience; she has been comfortable sometimes, and very poor in a money sense for a long stretch of years as well. She has attended a number of different institutions of 'higher learning' without attaining, or obtaining, a degree. She has written poetry which has been self-published with other women and published in anthologies and periodicals created by and for women. She has worked for the benefit of women in Jane, the abortion collective; in rape/spouse abuse service; in publishing a local feminist newspaper; in workshops and affinity groups offering her various skills and insights to other women and learning from them. Once she opened a women's bookstore in partnership with some women but the partnership did not work and the bookstore closed. She is currently caring for her disabled mother in her home and would enjoy corresponding with women about the relationship of class and intelligence TO OUR LIVES AS RADICAL FEMINISTS. She enjoys thinking more than anything else. Her address is: 1805 "B" Street, Lincoln, NE 68502.

TERRI DE LA PEÑA recently completed a residency at Cottages at Hedgebrook where she worked on *Latin Satins*, her second novel. She is the author of *Margins*, which has been included as supplementary reading in Chicano Studies and Women's Studies courses throughout California.

ELLIOTT: I think that class in the U. S. is really complex, but that we can learn to be absolutely honest about it. I grew up solidly working-class, especially after my dad got a union job. My mom, who grew up really poor, taught me that being poor was about being dirty and lazy but that what kept me from being poor was Luck. Unravel that.

These days I live on SSI, which, in Official-Speak, makes me poor, but crazy instead of lazy. Radical Feminism, especially Dyke Separatism, made a space for me to survive and continues to encourage the best of my thinking, and for all of my community's classism I'm gonna stay and make everyone deal.

My poems, essays, book reviews, articles and cartoons have appeared in *Common Lives/Lesbian Lives, Sinister Wisdom, Sojourner, Lesbian Ethics, off our backs,* and several anthologies. I'm currently an editor, writer and general flunky for *Labyrinth*, the Philadelphia Women's Paper.

There are two photos I'd like to have here. One is me, at age four, in 1967, with my family's first TV set. The TV and I are in the living room of our five-room house, with the worn sofa and the furnace showing (almost everyone I knew had the kind of gas furnace that sat right in the middle of the living room, where there was always the possibility of kids getting burned or something catching fire). The other is the outside of that house, with the tilting garage in the background and my Dad and Uncle's stock car on a trailer in the driveway. The car is totaled, having just flipped end-over-end three times in a race at the county fairgrounds.

But I don't have these photos, cause the last time I left home I didn't know I'd never be back. Julia's request for a photo reminded me of how much I lost by leaving home; writing this bio note reminds me of how much I've gained.

LEE EVANS is a Dyke Separatist living in Cleveland, Ohio. Her writing has appeared in *Lesbian Ethics* and *Sinister Wisdom*. She co-organized The Radical Thought Conference for Women in 1987, and is founder of Headstring Pro-Dyketions, an ongoing speaker's series of radical lesbian thinkers and writers. She believes that surrounding herself with good friends and bad cats has not only helped her to survive, but to thrive.

JAMIE LEE EVANS, a mixed-blood lesbian cultural feminist of color and activist, makes her living teaching mainstream women about the politics of misogyny and peddles books for the Aunt Lute Foundation in San Francisco. She has nightmares of theft when she acquires anything worth more than $25 and is looking for better words than "poverty class" and "poor" to describe her class background. Passion, justice and expression help keep her alive.

FOX: I'm the current and founding editor and publisher of the journal *Lesbian Ethics*, which first appeared in 1984. I'm 53 and find getting older is intriguing. I'm a separatist and I believe in magic.

PAULA GERBER has been writing and publishing most of her life; despite this, the issue of poverty remains most difficult to share. Because of the economic abuse of lesbians, and because she is an educator, she has chosen to use a pen name.

NETT HART is a Lesbian centrist feminist who lives in rural northern Minnesota where she entertains radical dykes and ideas. She works as an artist and writes, publishes, and produces conferences for the Lesbian community. Her book, *Spirited Lesbians*, is available from Word Weavers.

LINNEA JOHNSON is the first winner of the Beatrice Hawley Prize in Poetry and has published, with Alice James Books, *The Chicago Home*. In addition to poems, she publishes stories, essays, and photographs, and has compiled a biography of Anne Lee (1947-1981), a founder of *Common Lives/ Lesbian Lives;* she is completing her first novel. She loves teaching and loves making gold flax paper. She has a daughter and a son.

JOANNA KADI is a writer and activist. Recent articles appeared in *Working-Class Women in the Academy: Laborers in the Knowledge Factory* (University of Massachusetts Press) and *Piece of My Heart: A Lesbian of Colour Anthology* (Sister Vision Press). Her first book, an anthology of writings by Arab-American and Arab-Canadian feminists, will be published by South End Press in late 1994.

HELEN ELAINE LEE is a fiction writer who grew up in Detroit, Michigan. She lives in Washington, D.C., where she supports herself with law-related and social policy work. Her short stories have been published in *Callaloo, SAGE,* and other journals. Her first novel, *The Serpent's Gift*, was published by Atheneum Publishing Company in April, 1993.

ANNA LIVIA is the author of four novels and two collections of short stories, the latest of which are *Minimax* and *Incidents Involving Mirth*. She is also the editor and translator of a collection of the work of Natalie Clifford Barney entitled *A Perilous Advantage*, published by New Victoria Publishers.

CHRISTIAN McEWEN teaches poetry and story-writing in the New York public schools, and works as a writer with Roots & Branches (an intergenerational theater group). She has also taught at Eugene Lang and Parsons, written reviews for the *Nation* and the *Village Voice*, and edited *Naming the Waves: Contemporary Lesbian Poetry*, and, with Sue O'Sullivan, *Out the Other Side: Contemporary Lesbian Writing*, both published in this country by Crossing Press. She is currently working on her first novel, to be published by Virago Press in England.

PAM McMICHAEL is a writer and activist in Louisville, Kentucky. Her poetry has been published in *The Poetry of Sex: Lesbians Write the Erotic*, *These Dark Woods I Cross*, and *Feminary*. She has spoken as part of an inter-racial team at state, regional, and national conferences on building a diverse movement and organizing across lines of difference.

BONNIE J. MORRIS: I am 32, a Jewish Lesbian writer and professor of women's history—and a festival worker and performer. My present interests include traveling the U. S. with my one-woman plays, *Passing* and *Revenge of the Women's Studies Professor*, and documenting the enormous contributions of the women's music festivals to lesbian culture in the late twentieth century. I work as a staff writer for *Hot Wire*, and my lesbian essays and diatribes have appeared in over fourteen books.

MARILYN MURPHY: I hope readers who thought my essay was interesting will look for my book at their local bookstore or public library, or order it from the publisher: Clothespin Fever Press, 1039 Spur Court, La Mesa, CA 90042; (619) 224-2656. *Are You Girls Traveling Alone? Adventures in Lesbianic Logic* is a collection of the best of my column, "Lesbianic Logic," from the first eight years of its publication in the Los Angeles *Lesbian News*. At present, I am working on my second book, tentatively titled *My Life is an Open Book*. Irene and I are now living in a small women's community on the Atlantic Ocean. Residents own their cottages, and we share our good fortune by administering and taking care of a five-bedroom, wheelchair-accessible guest house with a swimming pool, and a small theater, for women only. For information please write the Pagoda, 2854 Coastal Highway, St. Augustine, FL 32095; (904) 824-2970.

MERRIL MUSHROOM has published extensively in Crossing Press anthologies. She lives in rural Tennessee and has been losing her teeth since 1982.

ALIEN NATION: I'm a poor white disabled Gemini with pink hair. I eat Cheetos that I buy with food stamps and watch TV with my teenaged daughter, Myra. I spend my time rescuing myself from patriarchy by acting out my fantasies, going to therapy and support groups, and by telling the secrets of my soul to anyone who'll listen. If anyone wants information about Sister Homelands on Earth Land Trust or Saguaro Sisterland land community, they can contact me c/o SHE, POB 5285, Tucson, AZ 85703.

CATHERINE ODETTE: I own, pridefully, a whole slew of labels, which inform my life and my politics. I am a disabled Jewish daughter of Holocaust Survivors, a lifelong Lesbian Separatist man-hater, an anti-psychiatry survivor of much of its abuses, a shit-kickin'-raised poor dyke who thinks pain is painful and love is lovely. I have the perfect partner, Sara Karon, and together we work hard to make the world a better place. I am the publisher-member of a group who put out the only lesbian-only radical disability rag, called *Dykes, Disability & Stuff*, located at POB 8773, Madison, WI 53708-8773. Recently, I have completed a collection of works by Jewish Lesbian Daughters of Holocaust Survivors called *The Chosen of the Chosen*, which is still looking for a publisher. And, just for the record. . .I still like potato skins, but I think they're *way* overpriced at restaurants.

JUANA MARIA GONZALEZ PAZ is a New York-born Puerto Rican writer, waitress, and former welfare mother and welfare rights activist. She's the author of a book on lesbian of color land and numerous articles on lesbian community issues. Presently living at a large Virginia commune, her present focus is on lesbian community-building, lesbian land movements, community-based education, and her daughter's college. Happy 18th birthday, Mary Ann (August 23, 1993). No one could be happier than I am in having you for a daughter!

J.P., b. 1955 in Bronx, New York, now makes her home in Brooklyn, New York. She is a lawyer who works in the field of personal injury and negligence defense. This is the first piece she has ever written for publication. She hopes that she will be able to share more of her thoughts in the future with sister/reader/travelers.

JESSICA ROBBINS has written for and worked on women's newspapers, including *WomaNews* and *Labyrinth*, since 1984. She is an active member of Sisterspace of Philadelphia, a lesbian community organization. She has worked in copy shops for a living for the past ten years.

JOAN SCHUMAN: This essay took a year to write, a year to submit and a year to publish. Things have changed and stayed the same. I am now recently exiled (chosen) in Santa Cruz, California, and am still an audio artist and writer.

SUSAN J. WOLFE: I was born in Washington Heights, New York City, and raised first as working class and then, with the income added when my mother returned to work, lower middle class. I identify myself as a Jewish Lesbian, but everyone in my parents' and my generation except me intermarried with Roman Catholics; my father's mother was an Irish Catholic, in fact. I spent nine years married to a middle-class Jewish man, but accepted my place in the family pattern when I moved in with my lapsed-Catholic lover, Cathy Flum, with whom I've spent the last sixteen years, in South Dakota. There, I am an English professor who currently chairs the department. I've published articles in journals and books on language; most of these are on language change, or on sexism in language and within the discipline of linguistics. The books I coedited with Julia Penelope (*The Coming Out Stories*, *The Original Coming Out Stories*, *Sexual Practice/Textual Theory: Lesbian Cultural Criticism*, and *Lesbian Culture*), on the other hand, all express Lesbian life experiences and perspectives. I am also a Cancer with a Capricorn moon, born in the Chinese year of the Dog; perhaps these facts explain as much about me as anything.

FELICE YESKEL is a white, Jewish (from an Ashkenazi background) lesbian who grew up working class in New York City. She has been an activist for over twenty years and has worked on many social justice concerns including: feminism, lesbian and gay liberation, antiintervention, peace, and disarmament. She currently works at the University of Massachusetts at Amherst as an adjunct faculty member of the Social Justice Education Program, where she teaches both graduate and undergraduate courses on oppression, classism, racism, sexism, heterosexism, anti-Semitism, and ableism. Additionally, she is the Founder and Director of the UMass Program for Gay, Lesbian, and Bisexual Concerns. Felice is also a member of Diversity Works, Inc., a collective of social justice educators. In this capacity, she has the opportunity to travel across the U. S. speaking and doing workshops on a wide range of social justice concerns, including issues of classism. Felice also writes on these social justice themes. Other articles by Felice have appeared in *Twice Blessed: On Being Lesbian, Gay, and Jewish* (eds. Christie Balka and Andy Rose), *Bridges*, and *The Women's Review of Books*.

zana: going through menopause, with such profound changes i can't really say *who* i am right now. staying close to the ground—growing my food and experimenting with solar cooking. being silent reconsidering everything.